APOLLOS OLD TESTAMENT
COMMENTARY

25

HAGGAI, ZECHARIAH & MALACHI

TITLES IN THIS SERIES:

LEVITICUS, Nobuyoshi Kiuchi
DEUTERONOMY, J. G. McConville
JOSHUA, Pekka M. A. Pitkänen
1 & 2 SAMUEL, David G. Firth
1 & 2 KINGS, Lissa M. Wray Beal
ECCLESIASTES & THE SONG OF SONGS, Daniel C. Fredericks & Daniel J. Estes
DANIEL, Ernest C. Lucas
HAGGAI, ZECHARIAH & MALACHI, Anthony R. Petterson

APOLLOS OLD TESTAMENT
COMMENTARY

25

HAGGAI, ZECHARIAH & MALACHI

Series Editors
David W. Baker and Gordon J. Wenham

ANTHONY R. PETTERSON

Apollos
London, England

InterVarsity Press, USA
P.O. Box 1400
Downers Grove, IL 60515-1426, USA
www.ivpress.com
email@ivpress.com

APOLLOS (an imprint of Inter-Varsity Press, England) SPCK Group,
Studio 101, The Record Hall, 16–16A Baldwin's Gardens, London
EC1N 7RJ, England
www.ivpbooks.com
ivp@ivpbooks.com

InterVarsity Press®, USA, is the book-publishing division of InterVarsity Christian Fellowship/USA® and a member movement of the International Fellowship of Evangelical Students. Website: intervarsity.org.

Inter-Varsity Press, England, is closely linked with the Universities and Colleges Christian Fellowship, a student movement connecting Christian Unions throughout Great Britain, and a member movement of the International Fellowship of Evangelical Students. Website: uccf.org.uk.

First published 2015

USA ISBN 978-0-8308-2524-0
UK ISBN 978-1-78359-211-1

Set in Sabon 10/12pt

Typeset in Great Britain by CRB Associates, Potterhanworth, Lincolnshire

Printed and bound by CPI Group (UK) Ltd, Croydon, CR0 4YY

green press INITIATIVE *As a member of the Green Press Initiative, InterVarsity Press is committed to protecting the environment and to the responsible use of natural resources. To learn more, visit greenpressinitiative.org.*

Library of Congress Cataloging-in-Publication Data
A catalog record for this book is available from the Library of Congress.

British Library Cataloguing in Publication Data
A catalogue record for this book is available from the British Library.

P *21 20 19 18 17 16 15 14 13 12 11 10 9 8 7 6 5 4 3*
Y *33 32 31 30 29 28 27 26*

To my twins:
Luke & Emma,
Sophie & Hugh

CONTENTS

EDITORS' PREFACE

The Apollos Old Testament Commentary takes its name from the Alexandrian Jewish Christian who was able to impart his great learning fervently and powerfully through his teaching (Acts 18:24–25). He ably applied his understanding of past events to his contemporary society. This series seeks to do the same, keeping one foot firmly planted in the universe of the original text and the other in that of the target audience, which is preachers, teachers and students of the Bible. The series editors have selected scholars who are adept in both areas, exhibiting scholarly excellence along with practical insight for application.

Translators need to be at home with the linguistic practices and semantic nuances of both the original and target languages in order to be able to transfer the full impact of the one into the other. Commentators, however, serve as interpreters of the text rather than simply its translators. They also need to adopt a dual stance, though theirs needs to be even more solid and diversely anchored than that of translators. While they also must have the linguistic competence to produce their own excellent translations, they must moreover be fully conversant with the literary conventions, sociological and cultural practices, historical background and understanding, and theological perspectives of those who produced the text as well as those whom it concerned. On the other side, they must also understand their own times and culture, able to see where relevance for the original audience is transferable to that of current readers. For this to be accomplished, it is not only necessary to interpret the text, but one must also interpret the audience.

Traditionally, commentators have been content to highlight and expound the ancient text. More recently, the need for an anchor in the present day has also become more evident, and this series self-consciously adopts this approach, combining both. Each author analyses the original text through a new translation, textual notes, a discussion of the literary form, structure and background of the passage, as well as commenting on elements of its exegesis. A study of the passage's interpretational development in Scripture and the church concludes each section, serving to bring the passage home to the modern reader. What we intend, therefore, is to provide not only tools of excellence for the academy, but also tools of function for the pulpit.

David W. Baker
Gordon J. Wenham

AUTHOR'S PREFACE

It has been God's kindness to me to have had some wonderful teachers of the Old Testament, including Graeme Goldsworthy, John Woodhouse and Barry Webb, who, as all great teachers do, inspired further study of their field. After pastoring the Baptist church in Hornsby Heights, Sydney, for several years, I had the 'grand' opportunity to do PhD studies on Zechariah under Desi Alexander at the Queens University, Belfast – a delightful experience. After I published my thesis, Desi made the approach to the editors of this series for me to write this commentary and I consider it an immense privilege to make this contribution. Any strengths of this work are all a result of God's many blessings to me, especially through my teachers.

Commentary writing is largely a solitary task. Yet as far as possible I have tried to make the process collaborative. I have taught courses on the post-exilic prophets at Morling College in Sydney and each class has given feedback on earlier forms of this commentary (special thanks to Aidan Luke and Ross Carruthers who took a special interest in this). Long-time friend Martin Pakula read each chapter as I completed it and gave invaluable feedback, particularly on my translation. Michael Stead has been an astute conversation partner, not only through his published work on Zechariah, but many times via email and in person. I also had the privilege of contributing the study notes on Haggai and Zechariah to a new edition of the NIV Study Bible and the editors provided detailed comments on my 'summaries' of this work. Several recent PhD graduates have also kindly provided me with their dissertations on significant aspects of these books and these have proven very timely – thanks to Chris Thomson and Jonny Gibson (both Cambridge) and Matthew Patton (Wheaton). Greg Goswell also generously sent me several of his journal articles in advance of their publication. The editors of this series and Philip Duce at Inter-Varsity Press have been a real pleasure to work with and I owe them a great debt of gratitude. The keen eyes of my copy editor, Eldo Barkhuizen, have also been of terrific service. While I have sought and received feedback on many fronts, all the deficiencies in this commentary remain my own.

My prayer in writing this commentary has been that it proves to be a valuable resource (particularly for pastors, teachers and students) for preaching and teaching these often unjustly ignored prophets, for the growth and strengthening of the church for the glory of God. While they are certainly not the easiest books of the Bible to understand, my experience is that the effort to study them is richly repaid. Their message is as pertinent now as ever.

Thanks must also go to the board and principal of Morling College who provided two sabbaticals over which substantial progress on this commentary was made. Board member Bill Peirson went beyond the call of duty and read much of this work and provided feedback and encouragement. Funding from Morling and the Australian College of Theology also enabled me to attend and present material at several Society of Biblical Literature meetings on the Book of the Twelve, and conversations and relationships formed there have been very stimulating and have opened up further avenues of research.

I would also like to thank my colleagues at Morling College who have encouraged me in the task and have taken a special interest in my progress, especially Andrew Sloane, David Starling and Ian O'Harae. The same goes for our research students Caroline Batchelder and Geoff Harper. The library staff, particularly Jenny Holmes, Lynette Todd and Gabrielle Fury, have proven invaluable – ordering books and tracking down obscure journals. Steve Sherriff has also helped to keep me sane in many ways – not least by cycling a few thousand kilometres with me over this time.

Finally, I wish publicly to acknowledge my family. I am thankful to my parents, who always encouraged me in my studies. My wife, Megan, is my greatest supporter and ally, whom I cannot thank enough. My children have kept me grounded while writing this commentary. Having four teenagers in the home (ages nineteen and sixteen at the time of writing) is a humbling experience – they constantly remind me of my inadequacies! I dedicate this commentary to them in the hope that they will one day appreciate their dad's work.

Soli Deo gloria.

Anthony R. Petterson

ABBREVIATIONS

TEXTUAL

4Q76–4Q82	Qumran texts of the Twelve Minor Prophets
4Q174	*Florilegium*
4Q253a	*Commentary on Malachi*
b. B. Bat.	*Babylonian Talmud Baba Batra*
HB	Hebrew Bible
Hebr.	Hebrew
Ḥev	Greek Minor Prophets scroll from Naḥal Ḥever
Jub.	*Jubilees*
K	Kethibh (the written Hebrew text)
LXX	Septuagint
MS(S)	Manuscript(s)
MT	Masoretic Text
MT^{A}	Masoretic Text, Aleppo Codex
MT^{C}	Masoretic Text, Cairo Codex of the Prophets
MT^{L}	Masoretic Text, Leningrad Codex
Mur	Murabba'ât 88
Q	Qere (the Hebrew text to be read out)
Syr	Syriac Peshitta
Tg	Targum
Tg. Zech.	*Targum Zechariah*
Vg	Latin Vulgate

HEBREW GRAMMAR

abs.	absolute
acc.	accusative
act.	active
adj.	adjective, adjectival
adv.	adverb, adverbial
article	art.
attrib.	attributive
cohort.	cohortative
conj.	conjunction
cons.	consecutive

const.	construct
dat.	dative
def. art.	definite article
demon.	demonstrative
distrib.	distributive, distributively
f.	feminine
gen.	genitival
hiph.	hiphil
hish.	hishtaphel
hith.	hithpael
hithpo.	hithpo'el
hoph.	hophal
imp.	imperative
impf.	imperfect
inf.	infinitive, infinitival
interr.	interrogative
juss.	jussive
m.	masculine
ni.	niphal
pass.	passive
pf.	perfect
pi.	piel
pl.	plural
plupf.	pluperfect
pr.	pronominal, pronoun
prep.	preposition
ptc.	participle, participial
reflex.	reflexive
rel.	relative
sg.	singular
subst.	substantive, substantivally
suff.	suffix

MISCELLANEOUS

ANE	ancient Near East(ern)
aka	also known as
AV	Authorized (King James) Version
ch(s).	chapter(s)
diss.	dissertation
ESV	English Standard Version
ft	foot/feet
gal	(UK) gallon(s)
JPS	Jewish Publication Society

kg	kilogram(s)
km	kilometre(s)
l	litre(s)
lb	pound(s)
lit.	literally
m	metre(s)
mi.	mile(s)
NASB	New American Standard Bible
NEB	New English Bible
NIV	New International Version (2011)
NKJV	New King James Version
NLT	New Living Translation
NRSV	New Revised Standard Version
NT	New Testament
OT	Old Testament
pt	pint(s)
v(v).	verse(s)

JOURNALS, REFERENCE WORKS, SERIES

AB	Anchor Bible
ABD	D. N. Freedman (ed.), *Anchor Bible Dictionary*, 6 vols., New York: Doubleday, 1992
AcBib	Academia biblica
ACCS	Ancient Christian Commentary on Scripture
ANESSS	Ancient Near Eastern Studies Supplement Series
AOTC	Apollos Old Testament Commentary
ArBib	The Aramaic Bible
ATD	Die Alte Testament Deutsch
AUSS	*Andrews University Seminar Series*
BBR	*Bulletin for Biblical Research*
BCOT	Biblical Commentary on the Old Testament
BDB	F. Brown, S. R. Driver and C. A. Briggs, *The Brown-Driver-Briggs Hebrew and English Lexicon*, Boston: Houghton, Mifflin, 1906; repr. Peabody: Hendrickson, 2012
BHQ	A. Gelston, *The Twelve Minor Prophets*, *Biblia Hebraica Quinta*, Stuttgart: Deutsche Bibelgesellschaft, 2010
BHS	K. Elliger and W. Rudolph (eds.), *Biblia Hebraica Stuttgartensia*, 2nd ed., Stuttgart: Deutsche Bibelstiftung, 1977
BibInt	*Biblical Interpretation*
BN	*Biblische Notizen*

BQ	B. Ego, A. Lange, H. Lichtenberger and K. De Troyer (eds.), *Biblia Qumranica: Minor Prophets*, BQ 3B, Leiden: Brill, 2005
BST	The Bible Speaks Today
BT	*Bible Translator*
BZAW	Beihefte zur Zeitschrift für die alttestamentliche Wissenschaft
CBC	Cambridge Bible Commentary
CBET	Contributions to Biblical Exegesis and Theology
CBQ	*Catholic Biblical Quarterly*
CNTUOT	G. K. Beale and D. A. Carson (eds.), *Commentary on the New Testament Use of the Old Testament*, Grand Rapids: Baker Academic, 2007
ConBOT	Coniectanea biblica: Old Testament Series
CTR	*Criswell Theological Review*
DCH	D. J. A. Clines (ed.), *Dictionary of Classical Hebrew*, 6 vols., Sheffield: Sheffield Phoenix, 1993–2008
Did	*Didaskalia*
EBC	Tremper Longman III and David E. Garland (eds.), *The Expositor's Bible Commentary*, rev. ed., 13 vols., Grand Rapids: Zondervan, 2006–12
ÉBib	Études bibliques
ET	*Evangelische Theologie*
ETL	*Ephemerides theologicae lovanienses*
FOB	Focus on the Bible
FOTL	Forms of the Old Testament Literature
GKC	E. Kautzsch (ed.), A. E. Cowley (ed., rev. and tr.), *Gesenius' Hebrew Grammar*, Oxford: Clarendon, 1910
GTJ	*Grace Theological Journal*
HACL	History, Archaeology, and Culture of the Levant
HAR	*Hebrew Annual Review*
HBM	Hebrew Bible Monographs
HS	*Hebrew Studies*
HTS	*Hervormde Teologiese Studies*
IDB	*Interpreter's Dictionary of the Bible*, G. A. Buttrick, T. S. Kepler, J. Knox, H. G. May, S. Terrien and E. S. Bucke (eds.), 4 vols., New York: Abingdon, 1962
IECOT	International Exegetical Commentary on the Old Testament
ISBE	G. W. Bromiley et al. (eds.), *The International Standard Bible Encyclopedia*, 4 vols., Grand Rapids: Eerdmans, 1979–86
JBL	*Journal of Biblical Literature*
JBPR	*Journal of Biblical and Pneumatological Research*

JBQ	*Jewish Bible Quarterly*
JETS	*Journal of the Evangelical Theological Society*
JHS	*Journal of Hebrew Scriptures*
JNSL	*Journal of Northwest Semitic Languages*
JSNTSup	Journal for the Study of the New Testament, Supplement Series
JSOT	*Journal for the Study of the Old Testament*
JSOTSup	Journal for the Study of the Old Testament, Supplement Series
JTS	*Journal of Theological Studies*
KZAT	Kommentar zum Alten Testament
LHBOTS	Library of Hebrew Bible / Old Testament Studies
LNTS	Library of New Testament Studies
LSTS	Library of Second Temple Studies
MSJ	*Masters Seminary Journal*
NAC	New American Commentary
NBD	J. D. Douglas, N. Hillyer, F. F. Bruce, D. Guthrie, A. R. Millard, J. I. Packer and D. J. Wiseman (eds.), *New Bible Dictionary*, Leicester: Inter-Varsity Press, 1982
NCBC	New Century Bible Commentary
NDBT	B. S. Rosner, T. D. Alexander, G. Goldsworthy and D. A. Carson (eds.), *New Dictionary of Biblical Theology: Exploring the Unity and Diversity of Scripture*, Downers Grove: InterVarsity Press; Leicester: Inter-Varsity Press, 2000
NIB	New Interpreter's Bible
NICNT	New International Commentary on the New Testament
NICOT	New International Commentary on the Old Testament
NIDOTTE	W. A. VanGemeren (ed.), *New International Dictionary of Old Testament Theology and Exegesis*, 5 vols., Grand Rapids: Zondervan, 1997
NIVAC	The New International Version Application Commentary
NSBT	New Studies in Biblical Theology
OTE	*Old Testament Essays*
OTG	Old Testament Guides
OTL	Old Testament Library
PEQ	*Palestine Exploration Quarterly*
PFES	Publications of the Finnish Exegetical Society
PNTC	Pillar New Testament Commentary
Presb	*Presbyterion*
PTR	*Princeton Theological Review*
RB	*Revue biblique*
RevExp	*Revue and Expositor*
RTR	*Reformed Theological Review*

SBL	Society of Biblical Literature
SBLDS	Society of Biblical Literature Dissertation Series
SBLMS	Society of Biblical Literature Monograph Series
SBLSS	SBL Semeia Studies
SCJ	*Stone-Campbell Journal*
ScrHier	Scripta hierosolymitana
SHBC	Smith & Helwys Bible Commentary
SHS	Scripture and Hermeneutics Series
SJOT	*Scandinavian Journal of the Old Testament*
SJT	*Scottish Journal of Theology*
SSN	Studia semitica neerlandica
STDJ	Studies on the Texts of the Desert of Judah
TDOT	G. J. Botterweck, H. Ringgren and H.-J. Fabry (eds.), *Theological Dictionary of the Old Testament*, 15 vols., Grand Rapids: Eerdmans, 1974–2006
TOTC	Tyndale Old Testament Commentaries
TTS	Trierer theologische Studien
TWOT	R. L. Harris, G. L. Archer Jr. and B. K. Waltke (eds.), *Theological Wordbook of the Old Testament*, 2 vols., Chicago: Moody, 1980; repr. as one vol. 2003
TynB	*Tyndale Bulletin*
UBS	United Bible Societies
VT	*Vetus Testamentum*
VTSup	Supplements to Vetus Testamentum
WBC	Word Biblical Commentary
WTJ	*Westminster Theological Journal*
YNER	Yale Near Eastern Researches
ZAW	*Zeitschrift für die alttestamentliche Wissenschaft*

GENERAL INTRODUCTION

1. THE 'POST-EXILIC PROPHETS'

The trend of the last century or so has been to study the prophets according to their historical period (e.g. 'Eighth Century Prophets', 'Exilic Prophets', etc.). The books of Haggai, Zechariah and Malachi are commonly called the 'Post-exilic Prophets' since they are set in the period after many had returned from exile in Babylon to rebuild Jerusalem and their community life. Sadly, this period was often portrayed as a 'dark age' in Israel's history with the prophets reverting to formalism and legalism. Nothing could be further from the truth. The reality is that these books present a vital and living faith to God's people. They are a challenge to covenant faithfulness in view of God's reality in the world and his coming kingdom.

The historical context is only one of several contexts that must be taken into account in order to appreciate fully the message of these books. In more recent years, the importance of the canonical and literary contexts of the prophetic books has come to the fore, particularly with the recognition that the books of the twelve 'Minor Prophets' were from a very early stage collected and ordered into a 'Book of the Twelve'. The acknowledgment that there is an intelligent design in the ordering and compilation of the books raises the questions of what the final three books contribute to the message of the collection as a whole, and then what the Book of the Twelve contributes to the message of the HB.

For Christian readers, the books of Haggai, Zechariah and Malachi are set in an even larger context, with the NT showing how the HB finds its fulfilment in the life, death and resurrection of Jesus the Messiah. Since Christians consider the Old and New Testaments to be divine revelation that discloses the unfolding purpose of God, this further presents a biblical-theological context for these books. Each of these prophetic books is quoted or alluded to in significant ways in the NT. Indeed, Zechariah is the most quoted prophet in the passion narratives of the Gospels.

This 'General introduction' begins with a brief account of each of these contexts and an exploration of their importance for understanding and appropriating the message of the books of Haggai, Zechariah and Malachi for Christian readers. In the commentary on these books that follows, I will seek to explain these books against the background of these contexts and explore their contribution to Christian thought and life in the 'Explanation' section of each chapter. In this 'General introduction' I also offer a survey and critique of methodological approaches to the prophets and outline my own approach. Each book also has its own introduction.

2. HISTORICAL CONTEXT

2.1. Cyrus and the rise of the Persian Empire

The books of Haggai, Zechariah and Malachi are set in the Persian period. Cyrus the Great was the founder of the Persian Empire and is referred to directly twenty-four times in the HB (as *kôreš*) (2 Chr. 36:22 [twice], 23; Ezra 1:1 [twice], 2, 7, 8; 3:7; 4:3, 5; 5:13 [twice], 14, 17; 6:3 [twice], 14, 29; Isa. 44:28; 45:1; Dan. 1:21; 6:28[29]; 10:1). Sometime around 550 BC Cyrus succeeded in gaining control over the Medes, thereby creating a powerful fighting force. His army achieved victories in Asia Minor and India before turning towards Babylonia, which had been the dominant power in the ANE. Cyrus incorporated Babylon into his empire in 539 BC with very limited resistance (where possible, dates in this commentary follow the chronology of De Vries 1962, 1: 580–599). Babylon had been weakened by the ineffective leadership of Nabonidus, who went to dwell in the desert oasis of Tayma and left control of government in the hands of his son Belshazzar for ten years (cf. Dan. 5, 7 – 8). Nabonidus had alienated the priests of the Babylonian god Marduk by elevating the status of his own god to be supreme god of the empire, the moon god Sîn. This meant that when Nabonidus was away, the priests and people readily accepted Cyrus, who came to Babylon in Marduk's name and reinstated worship of Marduk.

Babylon's reception of Cyrus is recounted in the Cyrus Cylinder, a clay cylinder inscribed in Babylonian cuneiform, discovered in 1879 in Babylon, and now located in the British Museum. Written from Cyrus' perspective (and a wonderful example of propaganda), it presents Cyrus as Marduk's agent who liberated the people from Nabonidus' tyranny (lines 2–19) and restored worship of Marduk in Babylon. Indeed, Cyrus is called the legitimate 'king of Babylon' (line 20). Cyrus' reception is also recounted in the Verse Account of Nabonidus, thought to have been composed shortly after 539 BC, but known only from a single later copy (Beaulieu 2007: 137).

Having incorporated Babylon into his empire, Cyrus issued an edict allowing the peoples whom the Babylonians had earlier exiled to Babylon to return to their countries and rebuild their temples, and this included the Jewish people (Ezra 1:1–4). This was in marked contrast to the policy of repression that had characterized the Babylonian Empire, and the Assyrian Empire before it. Evidence outside the OT for Cyrus' repatriation policy is also found on the Cyrus Cylinder (lines 26–36), though it does not directly name the Jewish people. All this happened some twenty years before the prophetic ministries of Haggai and Zechariah.

2.2. Return from exile

Why did Cyrus allow the Jewish people (and others) to return to their homelands? Jon Berquist (1995: 25) notes that many scholars explain this as Persian sympathy to monotheistic religions, or that Cyrus was enlightened and more open to religious freedom. Yet both of these explanations are problematic as there is no indication Cyrus was monotheistic, or that he was more sensitive to human rights and freedoms than his predecessors. Berquist argues it is more likely that the Persians operated with their own interests at heart. Whereas the Babylonian Empire moved populations to the centre of their empire so as to farm land that was otherwise underutilized, the Persians moved people away from the centre and towards the peripheries of their empire for two main reasons. The first was national security. If the Persians had strong supportive populations at the edges of their empire, it made it more difficult for invading forces. It also provided support for Persian travelling armies with bases on the outskirts of the empire from which to extend the empire. The second reason was taxation. The Persians believed that the various populations would be more productive in their homelands than they were in Persia. Working from home, they were more able to pay tribute to Persia, and greater amounts. In these ways, Cyrus believed that allowing the Jewish people (and others) to return to their homeland would assist his policies of empire expansion.

Of course, the ultimate reason that Cyrus allowed the Jewish people to return to the land was because it was Yahweh's appointed purpose. While from a human point of view Cyrus had good reasons to send the Jews back to Jerusalem, the OT shows clearly that Cyrus was an instrument in

Yahweh's hand and that he stirred up the spirit of Cyrus so that his word might be fulfilled (Ezra 1:1).

The book of Ezra recounts how a first group of exiles (cf. 2:64–65), led by the Persian-appointed Judean governor Sheshbazzar, returned to Jerusalem (in 538 BC). This first group of returnees gave offerings to rebuild the temple (2:68), built the altar (3:3), reinstituted the sacrifices and festivals (3:4–6), and laid the foundation of the temple (3:10). However, they soon faced many difficulties. A major factor in the political situation in Yehud (Judah/Judea; see below) was the hostility of the province of Samaria, probably inhabited by descendants of the former northern kingdom and those who were settled there by the Assyrians (J. Kessler 2006: 94). It is reasonable to assume that prior to the return of the exiles those living in the region of Judah were also under the control of the governor of Samaria. The arrival of the exiles to Jerusalem threatened to reduce the power and influence of the Samaritans (and neighbouring provinces). The Samaritans responded by seeking to exert influence and involvement in the emerging political, economic and religious centre in Jerusalem. When they were denied this, they sought to frustrate the building of the temple (Ezra 4) and later the city walls (Ezra 4:7–23; Neh. 2 – 4, 6). Other difficulties the returnees faced included famine (e.g. Hag. 1:9–11; 2:15–19) and internal opposition (Zech. 8:10), which may have been between those who remained in the land and those who returned. These factors and particularly the hostility of the Samaritans meant that the initial work of rebuilding the temple soon came to a standstill (Ezra 4:24), and did not progress for some twenty years until Haggai and Zechariah began to prophesy.

2.3. From Cyrus to Darius

Cyrus ruled until 530 BC, when he died in battle and was succeeded by his son Cambyses, who in 525 BC invaded Egypt and brought it into the Persian Empire. In January 522 BC, while Cambyses was in Egypt, one of the leaders in the court, Guamata, falsely claimed to be Cambyses' brother and led a revolt in Persia by taking the throne. Cambyses set out to return to Mesopotamia, but on the way accidentally stabbed himself in the thigh with his sword and died in April 522 BC. One of Cambyses' military commanders, Darius, raced back and assassinated Gaumata in September 522 BC with the help of a group of six leading nobles. With the death of Guamata, the Babylonian rival king Nidintu-Bel (Nebuchadnezzar IV), thought to be a son of Nabonidus, reasserted imperial authority over Babylonia in December 522 BC. That same month, he was defeated by Darius with the aid of elite Persian troops. A new revolt broke out in August 521 BC, led by the Armenian Arakha (Nebuchadnezzar V). He was finally deposed by Darius' commander in November 521 BC (Berquist 1995: 51–53; Albertz 2003: 112–119).

A very significant historical source for this period is the Behistun Inscription (a translation is offered by Diana Edelman [2005: 353–361]). This is a record of Darius' rise to power carved as a monument on a sheer cliff about 230 ft (70 m) above the ground near the city of Kermanshah in western Iran. The carving is thought to have been made between 520 and 518 BC and depicts Darius accompanied by a spear bearer and a bow bearer treading on Gaumata and leading nine bound captives as prisoners. Surrounding the picture are inscriptions in three languages – one in Babylonian, two in Elamite (one a copy of the other) and one in Old Persian. It reveals a fair degree of turmoil in Persia in the period just before the time that the books of Haggai and Zechariah are set (the second and fourth years of Darius; cf. Hag. 1:1; Zech. 1:1; 7:1). For instance §52.4: 'Says Darius the king: This is what I did by the favor of Ahuramazda in one and the same year after that I became king. [19] battles I fought; by the favor of Ahuramazda I smote them and took prisoner [9] kings' (Edelman 2005: 359). Much of the history of this period is also recounted by Herodotus.

Once Darius had asserted his rule, he settled into a relatively long and stable reign until 486 BC. His legacy includes the publication of laws throughout the empire (Berquist 1995: 51), organization of the Persian administrative structure, reform of the tax system (Albertz 2003: 118–119) and the introduction of imperial coinage, a postal system and expansion of the network of royal roads that connected the Persian Empire (Leith 1998: 389).

2.4. The political situation in post-exilic Yehud

Herodotus (3.89) explains that the Persian Empire was organized by Darius into twenty satrapies. These were administered by satraps who were appointed by and accountable to the Persian Emperor. The 'Beyond the River' satrapy was made up of Syria, Phoenicia, Cyprus and Palestine and was subdivided into some fourteen provinces. A significant feature is that the territory of pre-exilic Israel west of the Jordan River was divided into no fewer than seven small provinces. Judah was a tiny (sub-) province of 'Beyond the River' called 'Yehud' (the Aramaic name for Yehudah or Judah), covering an area of approximately 40 by 30 mi. (60 by 45 km). God's people were therefore a very small part of a massive empire stretching from Greece to India. Yehud was a distinct political unit but, with neither king nor army, had no military or political power. Their lack of power meant their total dependence on the goodwill of Persia (see Ezra 4:6–23; 5:1–17; Neh. 1 – 2).

During this time, Yehud was ruled by a Persian-appointed 'governor' (*paḥat*). The three recorded in the post-exilic biblical literature (Sheshbazzar, Zerubbabel and Nehemiah) were all Jews. The names of other governors are not recorded in the Bible, but archaeological evidence has revealed some of their names, all apparently Jewish (Fried 2004: 184–187). It seems that the Jewish people had a measure of autonomy in religious affairs, though the extent to which they exercised self-governance in other matters remains a matter of debate (Fried 2004: 1–5; Jigoulov 2009: 147).

Some twenty years after the first exiles returned, in the time of Darius, the prophets Haggai and Zechariah were instrumental in getting the construction of the temple back on track (cf. Ezra 6:14). Reasons scholars give for Darius' support for the rebuilding of the Jerusalem temple include shoring up his support in Yehud so that he might have a source of supplies and rest for his army as it passed on its way to Egypt (Berquist 1995: 63), or so that the temple might serve as a centre for gathering taxes (Schaper 1995). Ezra 6:15 indicates that the temple was completed on the third day of the month of Adar, in the sixth year of the reign of Darius (usually considered 12 Mar. 515 BC).

Outside Yehud, after bringing Egypt into the Persian Empire, Darius' attention was focused on Greece, which proved far more resistant. In 498 BC, an Athenian-led force revolted against Persia and burned Sardis, the satrapic capital. In 490 BC, the Greeks famously defeated the Persians at Marathon (Yamauchi 1990: 164–172). While Darius was preparing for an assault against Greece and raising taxes to that end, Egypt revolted, which raised a threat to the unity of the Persian Empire. Before Darius could address this, he died in 486 BC. This is all significant since many argue that the reference to Greece in Zech. 9:13 reflects the time of Alexander the Great and a much later time of composition for Zech. 9 – 14. Yet Greece posed a real threat to the Persian Empire during Darius' reign and the time of the prophet Zechariah (see 'Introduction' to Zechariah).

After Darius (522–486 BC), the Persian emperors were Xerxes (486–465 BC) and Artaxerxes I (465–424 BC). There is little biblical or extrabiblical literature that provides direct information on events in Yehud from the completion of the temple in 515 BC to the work of Ezra and Nehemiah after 458 BC. Ezra 4 reports an accusation against the Jews in the reign of Xerxes (4:6) and a report of a successful attempt to stop the reconstruction of Jerusalem in the time of Artaxerxes (4:7–23). It is thought that this period was one of relative stability in Yehud. Yet there is archaeological evidence that sites in Yehud were less prosperous than elsewhere (Kelle 2012: 416–417). While Malachi is undated, it is well suited to a date in the fifth century since it assumes a functioning temple and attests drought and lack of resources (e.g. Mal. 3:10–11). (See 'Introduction' to Malachi.)

Subsequent biblical history focuses on Ezra (458 BC) and Nehemiah (445 BC). Persian rule came to an end *c.*332 BC when Alexander the Great (336–323 BC) took over the Persian Empire and the region of Judea came under his control.

3. CANONICAL CONTEXT

3.1. The Hebrew Bible and the Old Testament

The HB orders the books differently to the OT of the English Protestant Bible, though the contents of the books are the same (apart from different numbering of some verses and chapters). It was not until the second and third centuries AD that the 'codex' (book) form forced decisions about book order. Prior to this, the individual books were written on separate scrolls and 'order' was generally not fixed, though there is evidence from the Dead Sea Scrolls that the shorter prophetic books were combined on one scroll, comprising the 'Book of the Twelve' (see below).

The LXX (Greek translation of the HB from third to second centuries BC) was the basis for various codices (books). These include Codex Sinaiticus and Codex Vaticanus (fourth century AD) and Codex Alexandrinus (fifth century AD). These have the books in different orders and there is evidence of competing orders among the church fathers (Bruce 1988: 68–82). From AD 390 to 405 Jerome produced a Latin translation based on the LXX, but revised it in the direction of the Hebr. text of his day. This translation is called the Latin Vulgate and was adopted as the official Bible of the Roman Catholic Church at the council of Trent in 1546. Since the Bible was first translated into English from the Vulgate (by John Wycliffe in about 1384), it seems that the order of the OT books in the Vulgate became the basis for the order in the English Protestant Bible. This explains why the order of the Twelve Minor Prophets is the same in the HB and English Protestant Bible, but differs in the LXX. This can be seen in the table below.

MT	*LXX*	*English*
Hosea	Hosea	Hosea
Joel	Amos	Joel
Amos	Micah	Amos
Obadiah	Joel	Obadiah
Jonah	Obadiah	Jonah
Micah	Jonah	Micah
Nahum	Nahum	Nahum
Habakkuk	Habakkuk	Habakkuk
Zephaniah	Zephaniah	Zephaniah
Haggai	Haggai	Haggai
Zechariah	Zechariah	Zechariah
Malachi	Malachi	Malachi

The earliest extant complete HB is the Leningrad Codex (AD 1008). This reflects the MT because it is the product of the Masoretes who preserved and unified the Hebr. text from AD 135 to 1000. The Leningrad Codex is reproduced in *Biblia Hebraica Stuttgartensia*, the Hebrew Bible of the Bible Society (the only variation in order compared to the MT is that Chronicles begins the writings in the Leningrad Codex, and comes at the end of the writings in *BHS*). The Bible Society, in a new edition called the *Biblia Hebraica Quinta*, is currently updating the textual apparatus, particularly to take into account the Qumran texts. The volume on *The Twelve Minor Prophets* was released in 2010 and is the Hebr. text on which this commentary is based.

3.2. The 'Book of the Twelve'

There is substantial evidence that from an early stage the twelve books of the Minor Prophets were referred to as one book: 'the Twelve' (*tĕrê ʻāśār* in Aramaic), a scroll approximately as long as the book of Isaiah. The *Wisdom of Sirach* (175 BC) refers to 'Isaiah' (49.1), 'Jeremiah' (49.7), 'Ezekiel' (49.8) and 'the twelve prophets' (49.10). While this probably refers to the prophets rather than their books in the first instance, it suggests that the books also circulated together (Schart 2012: 807). The oldest extant Hebr. texts from Qumran (dating from the mid-second century BC to the first century AD), although very fragmentary, also give evidence that the books were considered as a collection since they do not begin at the top of a new column, but are separated by only three empty lines. All Qumran manuscripts in which the order of the books can be determined confirm the order of the MT, except for one, 4Q76, where Malachi seems to be followed by Jonah (Schart 2012: 808). Josephus (late first century AD) counts the Twelve as one book when he numbers the books 'justly believed to be divine' as twenty-two (*Against Apion* 1.8). *4 Ezra* 14.45 numbers the books as twenty-four, indicating that the Twelve were counted as one book. The Babylonian Talmud (*c.* AD 500) refers to 'the twelve' (*b. B. Bat.* 14b). It also stipulates that only three lines separate the individual books, whereas normally four lines separated books (*b. B. Bat.* 13b). The Vulgate introduces 'the Twelve Prophets' with the statement 'one book to be the twelve prophets' (*unum librum esse duodecim Prophetarum*). A final note after the last verse of Malachi in MT^{L} contains the term 'the Twelve', totals the verses of the collection and notes that the middle verse of the book is Mic. 3:12. MT^{A} (AD 930) presents only the total number of verses in the Twelve at the end of Malachi. It seems that the term 'Minor Prophets' was coined in Latin (*prophetae minores*) by Augustine in *City of God* (Sweeney 2012b: 788). It refers to the small size of the prophetic books, rather than their significance!

While it is generally agreed that the books of the Minor Prophets circulated from an early stage as a 'Book of the Twelve', the nature and extent of 'editorial' activity in its compilation continues to be debated among scholars. See Ben Zvi et al. 2009. My own view is that the books were composed separately before they were brought together, probably in stages with minimal 'editing', to contribute to an overarching storyline. The different order of Amos, Micah and Joel in LXX suggests any editing was minimal. In terms of the MT order of the books, those dated in their introductions with reference to the kings of Judah, Israel and Persia are ordered chronologically. These are Hosea, Amos, Micah, Zephaniah, Haggai and Zechariah. See Petterson 2010: 238–239. Other books seem to have been placed with thematic concerns. For instance, Joel is undated; but, as just noted, it gives content to the 'day of the LORD', a major theme of the collection and is therefore placed early. Obadiah follows Amos with its mention of Edom (Amos 9:12; Obad. 1). The first six prophets also alternate between those who minister in Israel and Judah: Hosea (Israel), Joel (Judah), Amos (Israel), Obadiah (Judah), Jonah (Israel) and Micah (Judah) (Van Leeuwen 1993: 34).

In any case, the value of reading the Twelve as a book is in tracing the plot and the development of themes through the collection, rather than simply proposing a grand theory about production and redaction. Reading the individual books in the light of their wider context in the Book of the Twelve is like looking at a picture in a frame. The picture (the individual book) is the same regardless of the frame, but the frame (the book's place in the Book of the Twelve) can impact to a remarkable extent the way the picture is viewed. This is particularly the case when themes are traced through the collection, with earlier books informing themes of later books. For instance, a key theme of the book of Joel is the 'day of the LORD', portrayed as a day of destruction and judgment, but also a day when God will be victorious. When this theme appears in the next book (Amos 5:18), Joel has already informed the reader and hearer of the Twelve about its character, and Amos seems best read in this frame of reference. In this way, while each book contributes its own distinct voice, the whole is greater than the sum of its parts.

3.3. The books of Haggai, Zechariah and Malachi in the Book of the Twelve

Space does not allow more than an introductory sketch of the themes and plot of the Twelve. Further detail can be found in the following studies: House 1990; Sweeney 2000a; Seitz 2007; LeCureux 2012; Sweeney 2012b. Where possible, these themes will be traced in this commentary.

Hosea begins the Book of the Twelve by explaining the breach between Yahweh and his people. It also affirms up front the covenant love of God, who persists with a faithless people. It anticipates God's judgment as punishment of his people, but also salvation and restoration on the other side of that judgment, including a reunion of the northern and southern kingdoms under a future Davidic king. All these themes are played out in the Twelve. In terms of the unfaithfulness-in-marriage theme, this is paralleled at the end of the Twelve in Mal. 2:10–16.

After Hosea, Joel develops the picture of the coming 'day of the LORD', an important theme in the Twelve. Joel also expands God's judgment of sin to include the nations (Joel 3:1–8), and this lays the foundation for the indictment of the nations in Amos 1 – 2. The book of Joel warns what happens when the prophetic message is ignored. It also speaks of a future restoration accompanied by the pouring out of God's Spirit, with Yahweh again dwelling in Zion (Joel 3:21; cf. Amos 1:2).

Amos begins, 'The LORD roars from Zion' (1:2; cf. Joel 3:16). The judgment on the nations is a foil for the coming judgment on Judah and Israel. The book ends with the hope that the house of David will be restored and inherit the remnant of Edom. This change from judgment to hope is expected, given the wider pattern of the Twelve (Goswell 2008: 682).

The very next book, Obadiah, concerns Edom (cf. Amos 9:12). Seitz (2007: 139) argues that Edom in Obadiah is an example of what lies ahead for the pagan world on account of their sins: 'The judgment over Edom belongs within a much larger tableau, extending through the length of the Twelve (as well as the Major Prophets), regarding the nations as a total reality in opposition to God.' It also anticipates the restoration of Jacob and Mount Zion.

There is a great variety of interpretations of the book of Jonah. When read in the context of the Twelve, several themes come to the fore. Jonah underlines the fact that repentance may avert disaster (LeCureux 2012: 143). If God averts his judgment with the repentance a people as awful as the Ninevites, how much more will he do this for his covenant people? Israel failed to learn this lesson and suffered the consequences. Seitz (2007: 146) notes that the theme of the gracious and compassionate Yahweh, pivotal in the plot of Jonah, is a consistent one in the Twelve. The question 'Who knows?' (Jon. 3:9) has previously been seen in Joel 2:13–14. In Jonah, it is on the lips of a pagan king (cf. Jon. 1:6). What the nations hoped for about God, Yahweh had already revealed to his people at Sinai (Exod. 32; 34:6–7; cf. Num. 14:18–19). The book also continues to offer hope that the nations may share in Yahweh's mercy, a theme of Zechariah.

Micah speaks about Jerusalem's downfall and looks towards the Babylonian exile. However, it does so from the perspective of the Assyrian period. McConville (2002b: 204) observes that Micah is 'the first of the Twelve to turn the spotlight of prophetic criticism directly on Judah and Jerusalem. Micah's realization that even the Jerusalem temple was not immune to divine punishment (3:12) is the primary canonical example of this'. Micah also offers the hope for a future restoration under a Davidic king (Mic. 4:8; 5:2–5).

Nahum opens with the same character creed that has been identified in Joel, Jonah and Micah ('The LORD is slow to anger'; cf. Nah. 1:2–3).

This time Assyria is in for judgment rather than mercy (as in Jonah) on account of its sin: 'for who has not felt your endless cruelty?' (3:19). Nahum shows that Jonah's prophecy of judgment was only postponed, not annulled.

Habakkuk points towards Yahweh's raising up the Babylonians to bring justice to his people and foreshadows the destruction of Jerusalem (1:5–11). Yahweh's people are called to faith in view of his sovereignty: he will bring the eventual downfall of the nations. In the final chapter, Habakkuk exemplifies the faith required by God's people in his prayer.

Zephaniah announces, 'The great day of the Lord is near – near and coming quickly' (1:14). The book reveals the coming devastation of Jerusalem at the hands of the Babylonians. Yet the book ends with a vision of Jerusalem cleansed by judgment. The exiles are gathered home with joy and their fortunes restored, while the nations who had served as agents of Yahweh's judgment are destroyed.

Like the book of Isaiah, the Book of the Twelve passes over any description of the destruction of Jerusalem and exile. Jeremiah and Ezekiel have filled out those details (along with 2 Kings). There is a temporal gap with the books jumping from the time of King Josiah (Zeph. 1:1) to the second year of Darius (Hag. 1:1).

In terms of themes, the last three books in the Twelve concern the restoration of Jerusalem. Haggai and Zechariah focus on the restoration of temple and kingship. Zechariah and Malachi focus on the cleansing of the people and the land. All see the national covenant with Israel at Sinai continuing to be operative. While Jerusalem is certainly not the cosmic centre that earlier prophets hoped for (e.g. Isa. 2:1–4), the coming day of Yahweh will set this right and the treasures of the nations will come (Hag. 2:7–8; Zech. 14:14), along with peoples of the nations recognizing Yahweh as king (Zech. 8:20–23; 14:16–19).

House (1990: 161) contends that the plot of the Twelve matches the Aristotelian definition of a comedy, where there is eventual triumph over adversity and enemies are included in the hero's victory. However, the content is more complex than this. While the focus, particularly of Haggai and Zechariah, is restoration, it is very evident that sin remains an enduring problem (Boda 2009: 349). The judgment of Jerusalem has not changed the hearts of the people. Each of these three books continues the call for repentance (e.g. Hag. 2:17; Zech. 1:3–4; Mal. 3:7) and understand that the day of Yahweh still lies in the future. Like Moses' speech at the end of the Pentateuch (Deut. 28:15–68), Malachi finishes the collection on a note of disappointment and pessimism about human ability to remain faithful to God. At the same time, as in Moses' speech (Deut. 30:5–10), Malachi looks towards God's coming to act both in judgment and salvation. God will send his messenger Elijah to change the hearts of his people. In the meantime, the people are called to fear Yahweh and honour his name.

4. BIBLICAL-THEOLOGICAL CONTEXT

4.1. Defining 'biblical theology'

'Biblical theology' is not just theology that is biblical; it is an approach to the Bible that seeks to understand the various parts in the light of the whole. It seeks to map out the key landmarks in the Bible's story and orient the reader of any part of Scripture by means of these landmarks. The central landmark is the life, death and resurrection of Jesus Christ, which is the fulfilment of the OT hopes for Israel and the nations and the beginning of 'the end' or the 'day of the LORD'. The concern to read the books of Haggai, Zechariah and Malachi in their biblical-theological context bears some degree of overlap with the concerns to read them as part of the Book of the Twelve. However, biblical theology is concerned to connect the themes of these books with those of the wider canon of the Old and New Testaments.

The viability of biblical theology flows out of a number of presuppositions about the nature of the Bible, which are derived from the Bible itself (the hermeneutical spiral). For instance, the Bible claims a dual authorship – it was written by human authors who were inspired by God (e.g. 2 Tim. 3:16). The divine and human nature of the Bible (like the divinity and humanity of Jesus) explains why in all the diversity of human authors, time periods, cultures and literary forms there is unity and coherence of message. Paul House (2002: 270) rightly points out that 'a biblical theologian must be committed to interpreting the Bible as a coherent whole because it is the word of an inherently coherent God'.

Many today are reluctant to speak of a unifying theme of the OT (sometimes called the 'centre' of OT theology). Some do this because they reject the divine inspiration of the Bible and therefore see no grounds for a unity of its parts. Others, who believe that the Bible is inspired by God, are hesitant to find a unifying theme because of the seemingly subjective nature of the task and since there is no scholarly consensus on what this 'centre' might be. For instance, Tremper Longman and Ray Dillard (2006: 36) contend that the vast amount of OT data should not be squeezed into one central concept. However, I believe it is a useful exercise to attempt to identify an organizing theme of the OT – human minds generally crave organization and structure. Moreover, because the Bible is God's revelation of himself and his purposes for the world, it seems reasonable to expect that one can summarize the nature of these purposes as he has revealed them. The task is by nature reductionist, but this need not be a pejorative thing, especially if the limitations of the task are recognized.

An important question is, 'How do we go about such a task?' There are two legitimate ways. The first is to piece together inductively (by reading and rereading the OT itself) the ideas and themes that seem to be of key importance and to determine how these relate to each other. From the web of interconnecting themes, what lies at the centre? The second is to look at the way Jesus and the apostles understood the message of the 'Old Testament'. What do they see as being central? This method is deductive. Both of these methods should yield the same result if they are correctly undertaken and presuppositions about unity in the diversity of Scripture are correct.

A growing number of scholars argue that the central theme of the OT is the establishment of the kingdom of God (Goldsworthy 1981; Bartholomew and Goheen 2004; Waltke 2007; Gentry and Wellum 2012; Schreiner 2013). Graeme Goldsworthy (2000: 618) explains the kingdom of God as 'the idea of the rule of God over creation, over all creatures, over kingdoms of the world, and in a unique and special way, over his chosen and redeemed people'. While the phrase 'kingdom of God' does not occur until late in the OT, Goldsworthy contends that the concept is there from the beginning of Genesis. It is also encapsulated in the Lord's prayer as a summary of God's purposes: 'hallowed be your name, your kingdom come' (Luke 11:2). While others have suggested that the OT be organized under the themes of 'covenant' (Eichrodt 1961; 1967), 'promise' (Kaiser 1978) or 'creation/salvation' (Westermann 1982), these are better understood as the structures in which God's kingdom is worked out. House (1998: 56) argues that 'God' is the centre of the OT. While God is undeniably central, this does not really explain the unfolding storyline.

There is a forward movement throughout the OT as the nature of God's kingdom is revealed and as it is progressively established (and at points undone). This reflects the historical character of God's revelation. Goldsworthy speaks of God's kingdom being worked out in different 'stages' or 'epochs' of Israel's history. Put very succinctly, Eden establishes the kingdom pattern – God, his people and the place all exist in perfect relationship. This kingdom is dislocated and confused by humanity's sin. The rest of the Bible is about the restoration of a people to be the willing subjects of God who rules perfectly. The kingdom is promised to Abraham where God's people (Israel) will dwell in God's place (land), under God's rule. The great redemptive event that saves God's people from captivity is the exodus, yet sin is ever-present. The covenant with Israel at Sinai sets out what it means to be the people of God – to reflect God's character to the world. Israel enters the land under Joshua and the kingdom is eventually foreshadowed under the monarchy, particularly that of David and then of Solomon. The wisdom literature flowers during this period (and afterwards) as the various contours of God's kingdom are explored and mapped.

However, the kingdom is lost again on account of sin, particularly the idolatry of the people and their kings. After Solomon, Israel divides into the northern kingdom of Israel and the southern kingdom of Judah. The northern kingdom is judged by God through the Assyrians in 722 BC. Judah fails to learn the lesson and is judged by God through the Babylonians in 586 BC – Jerusalem and the temple are destroyed, the Davidic king is removed from the throne and many Judeans are sent into exile. During this period the prophets call on the people to repent, and announce God's judgment. Yet they also restate the kingdom promises for a new exodus, a new covenant, a new people and a new creation once the punishment has been served. In Jesus' life, death and resurrection the kingdom is at hand. Where Adam and Israel failed, Jesus carried out God's purposes perfectly and establishes God's people under his rule in a new covenant relationship. The kingdom will be consummated at Jesus' return.

4.2. The books of Haggai, Zechariah and Malachi in biblical-theological context

Most introductions to the plotline of the Bible (including my sketch above) give minimal treatment to the post-exilic prophets. An exception is Schreiner (2013: 397–419). Yet the books of Haggai, Zechariah and Malachi have a crucial contribution to the Bible's storyline, particularly coming as they do at the end of the prophets.

As noted, the prophets of the exile promise that the kingdom which was lost when Israel and Judah were exiled will be restored. For instance, Jeremiah promises that after seventy years of Babylonian service (25:11; 29:10), God 'will bring my people Israel and Judah back from captivity and restore them to the land I gave to their ancestors to possess' (30:3; cf. 16:15; 23:8; 27:22; 29:10–14). The people will return with great joy and again experience God's blessing (31:12–13). Jerusalem will be rebuilt (30:18) and God will raise up a righteous Davidic king (23:5–6; 33:14–22) and restore the priesthood (33:18–22). Key to the restoration of God's people is a new covenant where God will

> put my law in their minds
>   and write it on their hearts.
> I will be their God,
>   and they will be my people.
> (31:33; 32:37–41)

In this, God promises to deal with the enduring problem of sin.

The post-exilic prophets are one instance of restoration. Many of the people return from Babylon and rebuild the city of Jerusalem and the temple. The priesthood and sacrificial system are reinstituted in line with the hopes of the earlier prophets. The fulfilment of these promises underlines the reliability of God's word. Yet, despite the return to the land, the post-exilic prophets all testify to the fact that the exile has not finally dealt with the underlying problem that led to it, namely the nation's sin. Each of the books in various ways speaks of the failure of God's people to live out the requirements of the Mosaic covenant. While there are optimistic moments when people respond to the messages of the prophets in repentance (e.g. Hag. 1:12–15; Zech. 1:6; Mal. 3:16), the books all indicate that the exilic experience has not finally dealt with the sinful human heart. In Haggai, the people are defiled (Hag. 2:14). In Zechariah, the high priest is clothed in foul garments (3:4), and theft, false-swearing, iniquity, wickedness, idolatry and false prophecy persist in the community (5:1–11; 8:16–17; 13:2–6). In Malachi, the people have forgotten their calling to mediate the knowledge of Yahweh to the nations and have assimilated with the nations and their gods (e.g. Mal. 2:11; 3:5). They are repeating the sins of the past. Yet the books ultimately are not pessimistic, but optimistic about the future, for they each look to a work of Yahweh when he will come and establish his kingdom in all its glory. God's work in their present circumstances to keep his promises is seen as the basis of hope for a future act of God (e.g. Hag. 2:4–9, 20–23; Zech. 3:8–10; 6:9–15; Mal. 4:5–6[3:23–24]).

N. T. Wright (1992: 268–272) argues that while Israel in Jesus' day had returned from exile, most Jewish people would say that they were still in exile. Yet I think the post-exilic prophets would put it differently. They would say that even though Israel had returned from exile and the restoration was underway (albeit as a 'day of small things'), there was another exile-like experience that the nation would have to go through before Yahweh's kingdom would finally arrive. Even though the people had returned to the land and some of the promises were being realized (such as the temple being rebuilt), there was still a further refining purification of Jerusalem that was needed before God's kingdom would come in all its glory. Zechariah in chs. 9–14 particularly connects this future exilic experience with a coming Davidic king. The outcome is cleansing and a new covenant relationship with God in which the nations will share. It is this future exile-like experience which the post-exilic prophets speak of that Jesus undergoes for his people in his death on the cross to finally establish God's kingdom.

In many ways the situation of the people in the post-exilic period mirrors that of Christians. Both live between the partial coming of God's kingdom and a future more glorious realization. Like the people in the post-exilic period, Jesus has called his people to build his temple (the church), and this is a task both charged with hope and laced with disappointment. As in the post-exilic period, God is doing wonderful things, yet living the Christian life is often accompanied by painful circumstances that can lead to despondency. Like the people in the post-exilic period, Christians are to look at how God has kept his promises in the past and how he is keeping them in the present as a basis of hope for the full realization of his promises in the future. These books also remind God's people that their future hope has radical ethical implications in the present (e.g. Zech. 7:8–10; 8:16–17; Mal. 1:6–8, 13–14; 2:11–16; 3:5, 8). In these ways and more, the post-exilic prophets continue to have a vital message for the church today.

5. METHODOLOGICAL APPROACHES TO THE PROPHETS

5.1. Historical-critical approaches

Historical-critical approaches (such as source criticism, earlier form criticism and redaction criticism) seek to reconstruct the historical process that lies behind the composition of a prophetic text. They are also called 'diachronic' approaches since they seek to trace the development of the text through time. Source criticism seeks to recover the earlier sources of a text. It looks for what seems to be inconsistencies in the final form of the text that are taken as indicators of earlier written sources. Earlier form criticism (in distinction to the 'new form criticism') looks for the different conventions of speech that lie behind the units that source criticism has isolated and seeks to reconstruct the social setting (*Sitz im Leben*) in which a particular passage may have arisen. For instance, in Zech. 1 – 6, form critics seek to isolate the oracles from the visions and see them as coming from different stages and social settings in the compositional history of the text. Redaction criticism seeks to identify the later hand that edited the material together. For example, Julius Wellhausen (1903: 5392) believed that Zechariah originally claimed that Zerubbabel was Shoot (the hoped-for king of Jer. 23:5; 33:15). When this failed to take place, a later editor tried to rehabilitate Zechariah's prophecy by substituting Joshua's name for Zerubbabel's in 6:11. Another example of this approach is seen in the NEB, which cuts out Zech. 13:7–9 from its present location and inserts it at the end of ch. 11, because the translators think it was all originally one unit talking about the same shepherd, and a redactor split it later on in the process of editing.

While many of the assumptions of the historical-critical approach are reasonable, such as a prior history of the text and different hands contributing to its final form, a major issue for those who adopt this approach is that it is inherently subjective and any results must remain hypothetical. There is simply no external evidence of earlier stages of the books of Haggai, Zechariah or Malachi circulating in any other form. Another problem with this approach is that it tends to operate in binary terms and fails to allow for complex thought. For example, strands of biblical material may be categorized as anti-monarchy or pro-monarchy and used to justify different authors or groups within ancient Israel who held these different views. The methodology does not allow for the possibility that the same author could both be critical of historical kingship and at the same time express hope for a future ideal king, a possibility that seems entirely reasonable.

A recent example of the diachronic approach is by Martin Hallaschka (2011; 2012), who argues that Haggai and Zech. 1 – 8 were originally two separate works but were combined into one with a complex arrangement of dating formulae. He discerns five redactional layers in Haggai and at least nine in Zech. 1 – 8. Hallaschka arrives at very different conclusions to Heinz-Günther Schöttler (1987), who adopts the same diachronic analysis. Jakob Wöhrle (2006), although again adopting the same approach, provides a different proposal. In a review of Hallaschka, Al Wolters (2012b: 350) rightly concludes that this approach is

> a highly speculative affair that lacks methodological controls. The fact that competent scholars come up with entirely different results shows that there is very little *wissenschaftliche* [scientific] rigor in this kind of exercise. Consequently, the degree of plausibility that can be assigned to these results is very low.

The same phenomenon is seen with Malachi where scholars who adopt this approach also reach very different conclusions (Bosshard and Kratz 1990; Redditt 1994; Wöhrle 2008). James Nogalski (2011: 999), who is favourably disposed to this approach, shows the lack of consensus on fundamental issues when he comments, 'Some of the tensions noted by Bosshard, Kratz, Wöhrle and others are real, but they could be explained as editorial adaptations of source material in the service of the compilation just as easily as indicators of redactional layers.'

In addition to this process being very speculative, Ehud Ben Zvi (2005: 5–6) makes the following valid point:

> There is no indication that the intended readership of the [prophetic] book was asked to divide it into potential sources, read each of them separately and then reconstruct the possible redactional processes that led to the book in its present form. There is no reason to assume that any historical (ancient) community read the book in such a manner.

Furthermore, the results of these approaches do not readily yield exegetical or theological insights. Commenting on this approach, Dempster (2006: 315) says, 'The result in general in prophetic studies was a trend toward atomization and fragmentation and lost in it all was the concept that the prophet had a word from God!'

5.2. Literary and canonical approaches

Robert Gordon (1995) documents a shift in the study of the prophets during the 1970s and 1980s, where rather than looking behind the text to reconstruct the history of Israel and its social institutions, or to recover the 'historical' prophet and the pre-literary origins of prophetic texts, there was a shift to apply approaches from the wider study of literature to the final form of the biblical books in the canon. The work of Brevard Childs (1979) was enormously significant in this shift in directing attention to the text as it appears in its final canonical form, called the 'canonical approach'.

A literary approach seeks to explain how the books as a whole work as literature. It analyses literary structure, rhetorical devices, poetic elements, figures of speech, and so on. It is said to be 'synchronic' since the final form of the book represents a distinct point in time, though this point in time is often a matter of debate among scholars. A vital aspect of the literary approach is the study of how later writers used earlier biblical texts, particularly relevant since Haggai, Zechariah and Malachi are late writings. This is commonly called 'intertextuality' or 'inner-biblical exegesis' or 'inner-biblical interpretation' (these terms are variously defined in the scholarly literature and there is no consensus at present). Michael Stead (2012: 357) defines a spectrum of usage of earlier texts: trace, echo, allusion, quotation, citation. Locating the use of earlier texts can throw light on the meaning of a later passage since earlier ideas may not be present explicitly in the later text. A key figure in this enterprise was Michael Fishbane (1985).

Those who adopt a 'new form-critical approach' seek to reconstruct the social location in which the prophetic books were written to discover the intention of the author and what they wanted to achieve among readers and hearers of their book (Toffelmire 2012). This focus shares a key feature of rhetorical criticism and contrasts with some approaches to the prophets that seem to assume that the books are doing little more than recording the prophets' words for posterity. Marvin Sweeney (1996: 12) rightly says:

> the prophetic message was not read exclusively as an archival chronicle of past prophetic speeches delivered to an earlier Israelite or Judean community. Rather, the prophetic literature was preserved, transmitted, supplemented and reformulated because later writers and communities believed that it addressed them and their situations respectively.

Some who adopt a literary approach set history aside. For instance, Edgar Conrad (1999: 7) in the preface of his commentary on Zechariah says, 'I am not concerned with reading Zechariah as providing information about a world external to it.' Yet this attempt to cut the text loose from any historical context is problematic. Indeed, V. Philips Long (1999: 162) concludes that literary studies may provide 'an opportunity to hear more clearly what the texts have to say, including what they may have to say about the historical past'.

The shift towards literary and canonical approaches is a valuable one as it seeks to understand the prophetic books not simply as an amalgam of different sources, but as intentionally crafted literary works that display coherence and unity. A potential weakness of the literary and canonical approaches is that the historical and theological claims of the text may still be neglected.

5.3. A confessional critical approach

Wolters (2000) has set out what he calls a 'confessional critical approach' that reflects my approach in this commentary. By 'confessional' Wolters means 'rooted in the classical Christian confession of Scripture as the Word of God'. 'Criticism' simply means 'scholarly analysis' – reclaiming the meaning this term had in biblical studies before the Kantian split between 'knowledge' and 'belief'. Wolters (2000: 108) identifies nine dimensions of biblical interpretation and orders them as follows:

9. Confessional discernment
8. Redemptive-historical analysis / 7. Ideological criticism
6. Historical analysis / 5. Synchronic literary analysis
4. Diachronic literary analysis
3. Syntax
2. Lexicography
1. Textual criticism

This approach begins at the bottom and moves up. The first step is to establish the text to be interpreted, comparing the MT with its variants (textual criticism). In step 2, lexicography determines the meaning of the words and these are then put in syntactical relationship with each other (step 3). Diachronic analyses may then be considered, but there is often little consensus here (as noted above in 'Historical-critical approaches'), and results are so uncertain that I have mostly disregarded this level in this commentary, though I certainly interact with those who adopt this approach on other matters as appropriate. The next level of synchronic literary analysis considers the insights of structuralism, the new form criticism and rhetorical criticism. Among other things, these approaches recognize that the audience of the prophet is not the same as the audience of the prophet's book. A prophetic speech may have a different intent when it is incorporated into the final form of the book than it did when the prophet first gave it. Also very significant here is the use of earlier biblical texts ('inner-biblical exegesis' or 'intertextuality') and to this extent this level is also diachronic since earlier texts are located in time. Step 6 considers how knowledge of the ANE background might illuminate aspects of the text, yet a measure of caution is called for here that these insights are not forced on to the text. There is also some overlap here with steps 1–3 since these earlier levels also rely on comparative language usage in the ANE. The seventh step, ideological criticism, considers how an author's 'social location' is significant in interpreting his or her work, and the insights of the new form criticism are often helpful here. In many instances, the interpreter's own ideology is a major consideration at this level and this is even more pronounced as one progresses up the levels from here. The eighth step looks at the passage within the grand narrative of the Christian canon, which includes an analysis of any use of the passage in the NT, but is broader than this as well. While Wolters calls this 'redemptive-historical analysis', I call this 'biblical theology' and consider it so important that I have devoted a section to explain it above. Wolters (2000: 102) rightly says:

> That grand narrative climaxes in Jesus Christ as portrayed in the New Testament, that is, as the long-awaited Messiah through whom the God of the Jews offers salvation to all nations – in fact, promises the ultimate restoration of all things. A redemptive-historical reading within this perspective means tracing the connections of any subordinate part of the biblical metanarrative with this center. Those connections may be direct or indirect, explicit or implicit, but they are never completely absent.

Finally, confessional criticism focuses on hearing what God has to say to his people through the text, the most important level of interpretation. While there is an unfolding story of redemption, Wolters (2000: 103) makes the important point that 'the past and present meaning of the text are intimately conjoined: the Word of God to the post-exilic Jewish community is simultaneously the Word of God to the community of faith today'. In this commentary there is an 'Explanation' at the end of each section where, after summarizing the meaning of the passage and tracing its themes into the NT, my concerns are chiefly theological and ethical: What does this passage teach us about God? What does God say to us through his Word about living fruitfully in his world? One of the benefits of reading the books of the OT in their biblical-theological context and in relationship to their fulfilment in Jesus Christ is that these help to avoid the twin dangers in application of allegorizing the OT without any control, and moralizing the message and thereby gutting it of grace. See further, Edmund Clowney 2003: 32–34. Biblical theology helps to ground any application in the gospel.

While interpretation first involves moving up the various levels, Wolters notes that each interpretative judgment at a lower level also hangs on decisions made at a higher level. That is, higher-level commitments inform lower-level decisions, yet reading from the bottom up must also confirm, challenge or change higher-level commitments. This reciprocity is often called the 'hermeneutical circle' (or 'spiral') and requires reading and rereading the biblical text. In all steps epistemic humility is required, along with prayerful dependence on the power of God's Spirit to illuminate his powerful Word.

HAGGAI

INTRODUCTION

1. SETTING

The decades following the first return of exiles from Babylon to Jerusalem proved to be a time of pronounced hardship for God's people. They experienced agricultural and economic adversity (e.g. Hag. 1:6, 10–11), opposition from neighbouring peoples (e.g. Ezra 4:4–5), and internal division (e.g. Zech. 8:10). Earlier prophets had promised a glorious restoration after exile (e.g. Zeph. 3:20). For those who had returned to Jerusalem, the reality fell far short of this hope.

A narrative account of this period is found in Ezra 1 – 6. It records that the first returnees under the governor Sheshbazzar began the difficult task of rebuilding, but vigorous opposition from the neighbouring Samaritans soon brought the work to a standstill (see 'General introduction', 'Return from exile'). The prophet Haggai understood that the temple was central to God's restoration purposes. Earlier prophets had promised a key role for the temple in the restoration of God's people (see e.g. Isa. 2:2–3; 44:28; Ezek. 40 – 48; Joel 3:18; Mic. 4:1–2). Hence when the people returned to the land, rebuilding the temple was to be their priority. Yet the opposition that they faced contributed to their losing sight of God's priorities.

Haggai's prophetic ministry began in 520 BC, almost twenty years after the first exiles returned. Haggai spoke God's word of rebuke, challenge and comfort to get the temple construction back on track. He also spoke of a future work of God to 'shake the heavens and the earth' (2:6, 21) and establish his kingdom, moving from disappointment to hope.

While the book of Jeremiah contains more dates, the book of Haggai contains the highest frequency of dates of any of the prophetic books, all in the second year of the Persian king Darius (520 BC). As well as locating the book's historical context, the dates function to structure the book and also to identify key moments in the temple reconstruction, as presented in the table below. Regarding the equivalent contemporary dates (column 2) Baldwin (1972: 29) comments, 'It has proved possible with the help of evidence from well over a hundred Babylonian texts, and from new-moon tables calculated from astronomical data, to synchronize the old lunar calendar with the Julian calendar. The results are accurate to within one day.'

Reference	*date*	*Significance*	*Addressee(s)*
1:1	1st day of 6th month (29 Aug.)	The date of the 1st prophecy	Zerubbabel, Joshua (1:1), the people (implied in 1:12–14)
1:15	24th day of 6th month (21 Sept.)	Beginning of the work on the temple	
2:1	21st day of 7th month (17 Oct.)	The date of the 2nd prophecy	Zerubbabel, Joshua, the remnant of the people (2:2)
2:10	24th day of 9th month (18 Dec.)	The date of the 3rd prophecy	The priests (presumably including Joshua) (2:11)
2:18	24th day of 9th month (18 Dec.)	Foundation of the temple laid	
2:20	24th day of 9th month (18 Dec.)	The date of the 4th prophecy	Zerubbabel (2:21)

2. AUTHOR AND DATE

The prophet Haggai is remembered outside his book for the vital role he played, along with Zechariah, in rallying the Jewish community to rebuild the temple after its destruction by the Babylonians almost seventy years earlier (Ezra 5:1; 6:14; Zech. 8:9). In Hebr., Haggai means 'festal', but this does not seem particularly significant for the meaning of the book.

Traditionally, the prophet Haggai is understood to be the author of the book. However, the trend of the last century or so is to trace different redactional layers in the text. For instance, Beuken (1967: 27–48, 80–83) contends that an editorial framework was added in a 'Chronistic milieu' since it reflects affinities with the community of the chronicler. In contrast,

Tollington (1993: 23, 180) argues that Zechariah (or one of his close followers) was responsible for compiling Haggai's oracles and placing them in a narrative framework before the completion of the temple. Since Haggai shares similar dating formulae to Zech. 1 – 8, many scholars contend that they were originally combined as a composite work and used in the rededication of the temple (Meyers and Meyers 1987: xliv).

While it is certainly possible that a later hand compiled Haggai's oracles into a book and that this may have taken place in a number of stages, any theory about how this occurred or who was responsible is inherently subjective since there are simply no earlier extant sources. Floyd (1995: 473) rightly contends with respect to the book of Haggai:

> The kind of analysis that seeks to distinguish redactional material from source material, and to differentiate the originally separate prophetic speeches from one another, should therefore be abandoned, along with the kind of historical speculation that has often been based on this practice.

There are good reasons for viewing the book as substantially coming from shortly after the final date (twenty-fourth day of the ninth month in the second year of Darius). First, the book does not record the completion of the temple, which occurred in 515 BC. This would be expected given it is so much a focus of the book. Secondly, Zech. 8 (dated two years after Haggai's last oracles) contains many echoes of Haggai, so the oracles of Haggai most likely circulated in some written form before this time for them to be accessible to Zechariah. Thirdly, J. Kessler (2002: 41–51) argues that the dates in Haggai reflect earlier dating practices, rather than later ones and it is unlikely that Haggai's oracles were preserved but not dated for a lengthy period.

3. GENRE AND STRUCTURE

The book of Haggai reports four prophetic speeches (or oracles) of Haggai in a narrative framework – it speaks about Haggai in the third person and how the word of Yahweh comes to him and is then mediated through him to the community of Yahweh's people. Each speech is introduced by a date formula (1:1; 2:1; 2:10; 2:20). While there are common elements, there is also variety in the content and presentation of each of the speeches. The first three prophetic speeches report a problem (1:2; 2:2–3, 14), and the first two include a direct call to rebuild the temple (1:7–8; 2:4). The people's response to the first prophetic speech is reported in 1:12–15, which includes a promise of God: 'I am with you' (1:13). The other three prophetic speeches also include promises of God (2:4–9, 19, 21–23). A feature of the first and third speeches is an account of adverse circumstances (1:6, 9–11;

2:15–19) and a call to 'consider your ways' (1:5, 7) or 'consider carefully' (2:15, 18). Haggai also uses questions to raise key issues (e.g. 1:4, 9; 2:3, 12–13, 19).

The structure of the book has an A/B/A'/B' pattern (J. Kessler 2012: 302). The first and the third oracles concern immediate circumstances of the community in Jerusalem. The prophet admonishes the people, but also offers hope. The second and fourth oracles shift from the immediate circumstances of the community to the future, when God 'will shake the heavens and the earth' (2:6, 21). These oracles give consolation and promise (Assis 2006: 536).

Another pattern is that the first and second prophetic speeches are addressed to the leaders Joshua and Zerubbabel (1:1; 2:2). The second speech also includes 'the remnant of the people' (2:2). The third speech is addressed to the priests (2:11), which presumably includes the high priest Joshua. A fourth speech is given on the same day as the third, which is addressed to Zerubbabel (2:20). There is symmetry with both leaders being addressed in three of the four oracles, and both are addressed on the same days.

4. OUTLINE

First prophecy: an exhortation to build the house of the Lord	1:1–11
Response: obedience, assurance from God and action	1:12–15
Second prophecy: the greater glory of God's house	2:1–9
Third prophecy: a defiled people will become blessed	2:10–19
Fourth prophecy: God's promise to establish his kingdom and send his king	2:20–23

5. TEXT

This commentary is based on the Hebr. text of *Biblia Hebraica Quinta*, prepared by Anthony Gelston (2010). This reproduces the MT of the Leningrad Codex and collates it with the Aleppo and Cairo codices, noting differences in the apparatus.

Only a few pre-Masoretic texts of Haggai survive. The Minor Prophets scroll from Wadi Murabba'ât (Mur) contains Haggai, though it becomes increasingly fragmentary. Qumran texts that include parts of Haggai are 4Q77 (small portions of 1:1–2; 2:2–4) and 4Q80 (small portions of 2:18–21). These are well set out in *Biblia Qumranica*, edited by Ego et al. (2005: 158–167).

BHQ also notes variant readings in the LXX, Tg Jonathan, Syr and Vg. In almost all instances, divergences from MT can be explained as a misreading, translational adaptation or stylistic variation (Gelston 2010: 7*–9*). These are noted where relevant in the commentary under 'Notes on the text' for each passage.

6. KEY THEMES

6.1. Covenant

The book of Haggai must be read against the background of the national covenant with Israel at Sinai; otherwise there is a real danger of distorting its message into one that seeks to manipulate God by human-centred religion (i.e. 'build the temple to win God's blessing'). This is a distortion that denies God's grace and runs the risk of twisting the message into a 'prosperity gospel'. In Exodus, God saved his people by grace and gave them the law to show them how to live as his saved people. This is formalized in a covenant where the people commit themselves to obey in the light of all that God has done in initiating the relationship and saving them (Exod. 24).

At the end of Leviticus and Deuteronomy, Moses spells out the blessings that will continue if God's people obey, but also the curses that will come should his people disobey, the ultimate curse being exile from the Promised Land (see e.g. Deut. 28:63–68). Even then, God promises restoration and blessing when they repent ('return') and obey (Deut. 30:1–3). In Deuteronomy, this repentance is ultimately brought about by a work of God (30:6), highlighting his grace.

Haggai does not say, 'Give to the temple and God will make you rich.' Rather, he calls the people back to covenant obedience and promises the blessings of the covenant. Furthermore, when the people heed the call to obey, Haggai explains this as God's working in their midst by his Spirit through his powerful word (1:12–14; 2:4–5). This response in Haggai's day anticipates the new covenant (cf. Jer. 24:7; 31:33; Ezek. 11:19–20; 2 Cor. 3:3; Heb. 8:10).

6.2. Temple

The temple is a central theme in Haggai and one that traverses the Bible. God's intention since creation was to dwell in the midst of his people. Indeed, Eden is portrayed as a garden sanctuary (Wenham 1994) and Adam and Eve as priest-kings who serve therein (Alexander 2012: 119–133). Yet Adam and Eve are cast out of the garden sanctuary on account of their sin.

After the exodus, God established the tabernacle as the visible representation of his presence and rule (Exod. 25 – 31; 35 – 40). In Moses' song, the goal of the Israelites' journey from Egypt, the Promised Land where they will live, is called God's 'sanctuary' (Exod. 15:17). After king David built his house of cedar in Jerusalem, he desired to build a permanent house for God (2 Sam. 7:2). This temple was built by David's son Solomon (1 Kgs 5 – 8). When God later judged his people by the Babylonians in 586 BC, the temple was destroyed and the people were cast out of the land (2 Kgs 25:8–17).

The prophets promise a key role for the temple in the restoration of God's people (see Isa. 2:2–3; 44:28; Ezek. 40 – 48; Joel 3:18; Mic. 4:1–2). Gordon McConville (2002b: 235) captures well its significance: 'The temple is, therefore, first of all, a sign of Yahweh's faithfulness to his promises, of his presence with his people, and of his determination to bless them.' Hence when the people returned to the land, rebuilding the temple was to be their priority and Haggai reminds them of this.

God's ultimate purposes for the temple find their fulfilment in Jesus (e.g. John 2:19–21), the people of the church (e.g. Eph. 2:21; 1 Peter 2:4–5) and the new creation (e.g. Rev. 21 – 22). This is explained further in the commentary.

6.3. Future hope

While much of the book concerns events in Haggai's day, the book also looks to a future day when God will shake the heavens and the earth and establish his kingdom. The second and fourth prophecies shift to focus on this eschatological dimension. In 2:6–9, God promises he will shake all nations and the treasure of the nations will fill the temple with great glory. In 2:21–23, God promises that he will overthrow foreign kings and their armies and establish Zerubbabel as his signet ring.

Many scholars argue that the prophet Haggai had a realized eschatology: that Haggai believed the kingdom had arrived and Zerubbabel was the expected Messiah. See Finitsis 2011: 121. Yet it is clear in hindsight that Zerubbabel was not the Messiah and the kingdom did not arrive in his time. For Finitsis (2011: 121–122), 'The fact that the temple got built but Zerubbabel never came to the throne proves the prophet's failure. . . . it is typical of the biblical text to allow loose ends to stand.' Yet this argument poses significant difficulties. If this were the case, how was Haggai's prophecy ever received as prophetic scripture, especially since it flies in the face of popular expectations of a prophet? See Floyd 2006: 269.

This is a difficult issue to resolve, but it seems there is a 'now' and a 'not yet' dimension to Haggai's eschatology. With the construction of the temple and the return of Zerubbabel to Jerusalem (Zerubbabel is a descendant of king David; cf. 1 Chr. 3:17), there is a sense in which God is presently shaking the nations. Yet the book holds out hope for a greater shaking (cf. Heb. 12:26–28) when the promise for a Messiah who will subdue the nations and establish God's kingdom will ultimately be realized. Indeed, the book does not directly say that Zerubbabel is the Messiah (Petterson 2009: 63–65). Rather, against the backdrop of Jer. 22 all that is being promised is that Zerubbabel will re-establish the Davidic line in Jerusalem, from whom the Messiah will come.

The book of Haggai therefore confirms that God's purposes for the temple, along with his covenant with David (cf. 2 Sam. 7) and the concomitant hope for a future king (Messiah) still stand. Rather than being a failure as Finitsis contends (also Carroll 1979: 157–158), it is more likely that Haggai's prophecy continued to be treasured among later generations of God's people precisely because of the hope it holds out for a glorious future.

TEXT AND COMMENTARY

HAGGAI 1:1–15

Translation

1:1 In the second year of Darius the king, in the sixth month, on the first day of the
month, the word of the LORD came through Haggai the prophet to Zerubbabel
son of Shealtiel, the governor of Judah, and to Joshua son of Jehozadak, the high
priest: 2 So says the LORD of hosts, 'This people says, "The time has not come, the
time for the house of the LORD to be built."'
3 And the word of the LORD came through Haggai the prophet, 4 "Is it time for
you yourselves to dwell in your panelled houses, while this house is desolate?' 5 And
now, so says the LORD of hosts, 'Consider your ways. 6 You have sown much and
brought in little; [you] eat but there is no fullness; [you] drink but there is no
merriment; [you] put on a garment but no one is warm. And the one who earns
wages is earning wages [only to put them] into a pierced purse.'
7 So says the LORD of hosts, 'Consider your ways. 8 Go up the mountain and
bring timber and build the house, so that I will delight in it and I will be glorified,'
says the LORD.
9 'You expected much; but look, [there is] very little. And you brought [it in]
the house and I blew it away. Why?' declares the LORD of hosts. 'On account of
my house – since it is desolate, and you are running, each to his [own] house.'
10 Therefore, the heavens above you have withheld dew and the earth has withheld
its produce. 11 And I called for a desolation upon the earth, and upon the mountains,

and upon the grain, and upon the new wine, and upon the new oil, and upon that which the ground brings forth, and upon humanity, and upon beast, and upon all the toil of [your] hands.

12And Zerubbabel son of Shealtiel, Joshua son of Jehozadak, the high priest, and all the remnant of the people obeyed the voice of the LORD their God, that is, [they obeyed] in accordance with the words of Haggai the prophet, because the LORD their God had sent him. And the people feared the LORD.

13And Haggai, the messenger of the LORD with a message of the LORD, said to the people, 'I am with you, declares the LORD.'

14And the LORD stirred up the spirit of Zerubbabel son of Shealtiel, the governor of Judah, and the spirit of Joshua son of Jehozadak, the high priest, and the spirit of all the remnant of the people, and they came and they did work in
the house of the LORD of hosts their God. 15On the twenty-fourth day of the sixth
month, in the second year of Darius the king.

Notes on the text

1:1. 'through': *bĕyad*. Lit. 'by the hand of' (cf. 1:3; 2:1; see 'Comment').

LXX adds *legōn eipon*: 'Haggai the prophet *saying, say* to Zerubbabel . . .' Some LXX codices add *legōn eipon dē*: 'Haggai the prophet *saying, say now* to Zerubbabel . . .'.

'governor': *paḥat* (also 1:14; 2:2, 21). See 'Comment'.

lē'mōr introduces direct speech and is not translated.

2. 'The time has not come': *lō' 'et-bō'*. My translation takes *'et* as the subject of the verb *bō'* (an inf. abs.). Alternatively: 'It is not a time for coming', where *bō'* is taken to be an inf. const. with an implicit subject (the people) (J. Kessler 2002: 104).

LXX and Syr omit one of the references to 'the time' (as do most English translations) and translate, 'the time has not come to build the LORD's house'.

3. 'through': *bĕyad*. Lit. 'by the hand of' (cf. 1:1; 2:1).

4. 'you yourselves': *lākem 'attem*. The personal pr. in apposition with a prefixed pr. is emphatic (Waltke and O'Connor 1990: 299).

'your panelled houses': *bĕbāttêkem sĕpûnîm*. See 'Comment'. Some LXX codices, Tg and Vg do not have the pr. 'your'.

5. 'Consider': *śîmû lĕbabkem 'al*. Lit. 'set your heart upon' (cf. Hag. 1:7; 2:15, 18).

6. There is a string of infinitives here: 'eat', 'drink', 'put on a garment'. Waltke and O'Connor (1990: 595) note that the inf. abs. without waw may be used to make 'emphatic expressions and indignant questions'. Person and aspect must be supplied from the context.

'merriment': *lĕšokrâ* usually means 'drunkenness' (e.g. 1 Sam. 1:13), but the negative moral connotations do not seem appropriate here (unless it is ironic). Rather, it is simply drinking for 'merriment' or 'enjoyment' (e.g. Gen. 43:34; Song 5:1).

'no one is warm': *lô* translates, 'no one' – a prep. with an indefinite pr. points to 'someone or other' (Wolff 1988: 30).

Two MSS have *yśtkr* (he will earn wages) for *miśtakkēr* (is earning wages).

7. 'Consider': lit. 'set your heart upon' (cf. Hag. 1:5; 2:15, 18).

8. 'and bring': *wahăbē'tem* is a weqatal in a coordinate relationship with the imp. 'go up' and is translated as an imp.

'so that': *wĕ*. The two weyiqtol verbs ('I will delight . . . I will be glorified') are in coordinate relationship with the three imperatives ('go up . . . bring . . . build') and express purpose or result.

K: 'I will be glorified' (*'ekkābdâ*) is probably the 1 sg. ni. weyiqtol (unpointed). In MT it is pointed as a defective cohort. (without a final he), which is restored in Q: 'I will be glorified'. As a cohort. it expresses God's desire and emphasizes his personal interest in it (Arnold and Choi 2003: 65).

9. 'you expected': *pānōh* is an inf. abs. (lit. 'expecting') and is used in place of a finite verb for emphasis (Waltke and O'Connor 1990: 595). Person and aspect are determined from the context.

'but look': *wĕhinnēh*. LXX, Syr, Tg translate it, 'and it became'. Whether this is an intentional change or within the bounds of an idiomatic rendering of the wider phrase is debated. See further, Cathcart and Gordon 1989: 178.

'very little': *lim'āṭ* has an emphatic lamed (Waltke and O'Connor 1990: 211).

'blew it away': *wĕnāpaḥtî bô*. Lit. 'I blew against it'.

'declares the LORD': *nĕ'um yhwh* is strictly a noun phrase ('oracle . . .' or 'utterance of the LORD'). Cf. 1:13; 2:4 (three times), 8, 9, 14, 17, 23 (three times).

'since': *'ăšer* seems to function to emphasize the cause (cf. Zech. 11:2, 5; 13:6) (R. J. Williams 2007: 166).

10. 'above you': *'ălêkem* (e.g. NRSV, ESV) is unusual in terms of word order. It is absent from LXX. Alternatively, it emphasizes the reason: 'because of you' (NIV).

'the heavens' is indefinite in the MT. Some MSS have inserted he to make it definite and agree with 'the land' in the second part of the verse. The same phenomenon occurs in Zech. 12:1. See further, Meyers and Meyers 1987: 31–32.

'dew': *mittāl* is difficult. Motyer (1998: 978) suggests it is a partitive *min* (some dew), hence 'they were not living in drought conditions'. However, the idea seems to be that there is a store of dew in the heavens and none *from* this dew has been bestowed on the earth (cf. Gen. 27:28; Deut. 33:13).

11. 'a desolation': *ḥōreb*. The adj. form ('desolate') is used to describe the temple in vv. 4, 9 and this translation makes this connection clear. While it is often translated 'a drought' (e.g. NIV, ESV), the context seems to demand a broader idea (e.g. how is there a 'drought' 'upon all the toil of [your] hands'?). LXX and Syr have mistakenly translated *ḥōreb* as 'sword' (*ḥereb*).

Many MSS add 'all' to the phrase 'upon [all] that which the ground brings forth'.

'humanity . . . beast' are both definite (and sg.) in Hebr., but designate class.

'all the labour of your hands': *kol-yĕgîaʿ kappāyim*. Lit. 'all labour of hands'.

12. 'And . . . obeyed': *wayyišmaʿ* has the form for a sg. subject, but 'if a subject consisting of more than one word follows the predicate, the predicate can be congruent with the first word of the compound subject' (Miller-Naudé et al. 1999: 250).

'Shealtiel': *šaltîʾēl* (also 1:14 and 2:2) is a shortened form of the name used in v. 1.

'that is': waw is explicative (Wolff 1988: 31).

'in accordance with': *ʿal* indicates action according to a standard (Arnold and Choi 2003: 122).

'their God': *ʾĕlōhêhem*. LXX renders as 'to them' (*ʾălêhem*). Other LXX codices, Syr, Tg, Vg, read 'their God to them'. 'The LORD' does not appear without a modifier elsewhere in Haggai and so MT is followed.

'the people feared the LORD': lit. 'the people were afraid from the face of the LORD'.

14. 'Shealtiel': see note on v. 12.

Form and structure

Hag. 1 contains the first of four dated prophetic speeches or oracles in the book. Each is presented as part of an overarching narrative that runs through the book. This narrative is an account of the word of Yahweh through the prophet Haggai, the impact of the word on the post-exilic community, and the hope that it holds out for the future. Dates mark the beginning of each of the speeches (1:1; 2:1, 10, 20) and also record key moments in the temple reconstruction (1:15; 2:18). The unique feature of the first prophetic speech in the book is that it also reports the people's response (vv. 12–15), which includes a promise of God (v. 13).

Meadowcroft (2006: 108–110, 135–137) argues that vv. 3 and 13 introduce second and third speeches (oracles) without date formulae, resulting in six oracles in the book. However, the lack of date formulae to introduce these is a significant obstacle to accepting his proposal. Furthermore, v. 13 begins with a waw cons., and I argue that it links thematically with v. 12 (see 'Comment'). Floyd (2000: 269) also disagrees with the usual division of the chapter, arguing that v. 13 is a second report of prophetic speech and that the first response of the people in v. 12 is inadequate. He believes that after the second speech in v. 13, the people take proper action (v. 14).

However, again one would expect another date introducing v. 13 if this were the case, and the exegetical and theological grounds for Floyd's decision are unconvincing (see 'Comment'). A majority of commentators consider 1:1–11 to be the first oracle with a response in 1:12–15, with both sections closely linked (Meyers and Meyers 1987: xlviii; Verhoef 1987: 43; J. Kessler 2002: 113–114; Taylor 2004: 100; Willi-Plein 2007: 20–21). I concur and consider the final date in v. 15 as more concerned to mark the beginning of the temple reconstruction, rather than simply functioning to close the oracle.

One of the characteristic features of Haggai (and Zech. 1 – 8 and Malachi) is the questions the prophet asks, which function to draw in the audience (Pierce 1984b; Craig 1996; Boda 2000). The first question in the book in v. 4 is rhetorical, expecting the answer 'no', and highlights the people's indifference to rebuilding the temple, earlier identified in v. 2. A second question in v. 9 serves to advance the plot. Interestingly, there is also a link between these questions since they repeat the words/phrase 'house', 'desolate', 'you' and 'Yahweh of hosts', which concludes the clause in vv. 4–5 and begins it in v. 9 (Craig 1996: 233). These questions also highlight key issues addressed in the first prophetic speech and help to define the genre more closely as 'prophetic disputation'. In this genre the prophet summarizes the popular attitude and then takes issue with it by employing oracular speech of Yahweh (Floyd 2000: 273, 638). Assis (2006: 536) categorizes the genre as 'an oracle of admonition', which captures its general tone.

The first prophetic speech (1:1–11) and response (1:12–15) have the following structure: MT has paragraph markers at the end of vv. 2, 6, 11 and 14, which indicate how Jewish rabbis of the Talmudic period (AD 35–500) understood the division of the text (Brotzman 1994: 47).

1:1	**Date of the first prophetic speech and messenger formula**
1:2	**The popular saying 'The time has not come'**
1:3–11	**Reasons to build the temple and a command**
1:3–4	Yahweh challenges the popular saying
1:5–6	Consider your adversity since not building
1:7–8	Consider again and build for God's delight and glory
1:9–11	Further evidence of adversity for failing to build
1:12–15	**Obedience and fear, assurance and action**
1:12	The leaders and the people obey and fear
1:13	A word of assurance: 'I am with you'
1:14	God's work and the people's work
1:15	The date the work on the temple commenced

Comment

1:1. Each of Haggai's prophetic speeches begins with a date in the second year of Darius. Darius was the Persian king who succeeded Cambyses (see

'General introduction' for further details on the historical background). Around 538 BC, Cyrus decreed that the Judean exiles in Babylonia could return to Jerusalem and rebuild the temple (cf. Ezra 1:1–4). An initial attempt to rebuild the temple came to a standstill (cf. Ezra 4:24). The date in this verse is some twenty years later (520 BC) and 'the sixth month, on the first day of the month' is considered to be 29 August, two months before Zechariah commenced his prophetic ministry (cf. Zech. 1:1). (See 'Setting'.)

Earlier prophets are dated with reference to the kings of Israel and Judah (see e.g. Isa. 1:1; Hos. 1:1) and reference to a 'king' creates a measure of continuity with the past (J. Kessler 2008: 10–11). However, in the destruction of Jerusalem by the Babylonians, the Davidic king was removed from the throne (cf. 2 Kgs 25; Ps. 89:39). Referring to 'Darius the king' reminds the reader and hearer of Haggai that this was a time when the people remained under the shadow of exile, with no Davidic king in office, but a foreign king instead.

The dating formula also locates Haggai (and Zechariah) in relation to the seventy years of desolation for Judah that Jeremiah had prophesied (Jer. 25:11–12) (Curtis 2006: 94–113). This is more explicit in Zechariah than Haggai (cf. Zech. 1:12), but the significance of this time period in relation to the temple may lie behind the people's reported comment about the timing of its reconstruction in Hag. 1:2. If the destruction of the temple is dated to 586 BC, then 520 BC is some sixty-six years later, near the end of the seventy years.

Into this context, 'the word of the LORD came through Haggai the prophet'. The translation 'through' is literally 'by the hand of' (*bĕyad*), and is also found in 1:3 and 2:1. This expression is used in relation to the prophets generally (e.g. Ezek. 38:17; Dan. 9:10; Zech. 7:7, 12), once of Isaiah and Malachi (Isa. 20:2; Mal. 1:1), and twice of Jeremiah (Jer. 37:2; 50:1). It indicates that they are agents of God and mediate his word. It is used almost thirty times of Moses' words (e.g. Exod. 9:35; Lev. 8:36; Josh. 14:2; 1 Kgs 8:53; Neh. 8:14) and if this allusion is picked up by the reader and hearer, it suggests Haggai's prophetic authority is like that of Moses.

Yahweh's word addresses the two leaders of the community of Judah: Zerubbabel and Joshua. The name 'Zerubbabel' is Babylonian and means 'seed of Babylon'. In Ezra and Nehemiah, Zerubbabel is listed among the returnees from Babylon who rebuilt the altar and relaid the foundation of the temple (Ezra 2:2; 3:2, 8; Neh. 12:1). In Zech. 4, he is told that he will build the temple by the power of God's Spirit (vv. 6–10). As the 'son of Shealtiel', he is in the line of David, which is an important qualification to rebuild the temple (2 Sam. 7:12–13; cf. 1 Chr. 3:17). Haggai refers to him as the 'governor [*paḥat*] of Judah' (cf. 1:14; 2:2, 21). While it is difficult to know exactly what this role entailed, and it may have varied from place to place across the empire, it seems that Zerubbabel had administrative oversight of the returned exiles and was appointed by and accountable to the Persian authorities (Meyers and Meyers 1987: 13–16). The term is also used of Tattenai, 'governor' of the province 'Beyond the River' in Ezra 5:3 (ESV).

Joshua is called 'the high priest' or literally 'the great priest' (*hakkōhēn haggādôl*) (cf. 1:12, 14; 2:2, 4; Zech. 3:1, 8; 6:11; 2 Chr. 34:9; Neh. 3:1, 20; 13:28). While the usage of this title in the pre-exilic period is debated (Josh. 20:6; 2 Kgs 22:4, 8; 23:4; 34:9), the role is clearly established from the relevant passages as referring to the head of the priestly family (Duguid 1994: 59–61). The Pentateuch shows that the high priest was responsible for ensuring the purity of the community through the sacrificial system, so removing the threat of Yahweh's judgment that fellowship may continue (e.g. Exod. 28:38; Lev. 16:1–17; 23:26–32). As the 'son of Jehozadak', Joshua stands in the priestly line of Levi (cf. 1 Chr. 6:15).

The word of God is explicitly addressed to these two leaders of the community of Judah, yet it is apparent that the wider community also heard Haggai's words since they too respond in obedience in vv. 12 and 14. The second prophetic speech is addressed to Zerubbabel, Joshua and the remnant of the people (2:2).

2. God is described as 'the LORD of hosts' (or 'Yahweh of armies': *yhwh ṣĕbā'ôt*). This title occurs 14 times in Haggai (cf. 53 times in Zechariah and 24 times in Malachi). Tollington (1993: 70) notes that it is a title for God that became prominent in the early monarchy period and was associated with the theology of the Jerusalem temple and the dwelling of God among his people (e.g. 2 Sam. 7:8, 26–27). The 'hosts' are literally 'armies' and may be the armies of heaven ('angels'), armies of earth (military might) or encompass all multitudes in heaven and on earth. Since the post-exilic community had no army, its immediate reference seems to be to the armies of heaven (Stead 2009: 209). Alternatively, the term *ṣĕbā'ôt* may be an intensive pl. abstract and be rendered with the phrase 'Yahweh, the Mighty' or 'Yahweh, the Almighty' (Van der Woude 1997: 1045). In any case, it is a phrase that speaks of the might of Yahweh as king and in this context underlines a reason for listening to his word.

Haggai addresses the leaders about 'this people', namely the community in Jerusalem, presumably comprising those who had remained in the land and those who had returned from exile in the previous two decades (see 'Comment' on 1:12). Calling them 'this people' is probably pejorative and indicates relational distance between them and Yahweh (J. Kessler 2008: 13). Ideally, Yahweh would address his people as 'my people' (cf. Jer. 30:22). The people's sin has distanced them from Yahweh (cf. Exod. 32:7; Hos. 1:9). This is made clear in the third prophetic speech (2:10–19).

The reason for Yahweh's displeasure is their failure to rebuild the temple, reflected in their reported statement 'The time has not come, the time for the house of the LORD to be built.' The emphasis of the Hebr. (reflected in my translation) is 'the time'. They did not deny that it needed to be rebuilt or even its importance, but questioned when. Perhaps they were making excuses, saying the end of Jeremiah's seventy years had not yet come (cf. Jer. 25:11–12; 29:10; Zech. 1:12; 7:5), or that they were waiting for a Davidic king to rebuild the temple as Ezekiel prophesied (Ezek. 37:24–28). Perhaps they thought God had not yet returned to them and they needed to wait for this first (Assis 2007a: 3; Patrick 2008: 46). In any case, this is the problem Yahweh addresses through Haggai. While some see a pious reluctance of the people here, J. Kessler (2008: 14–15) seems closer to the mark when he argues that the wider context of 1:2–11 portrays 'the people as lazy, self-centered, and recalcitrant'.

3–4. V. 3 uses the same expression as v. 1 ('the word of the LORD came through') and reinforces Haggai's agency of the word of Yahweh and therefore his authority as a prophet. Picking up the 'time' element in the people's saying of v. 2, Haggai asks a rhetorical question expecting the answer 'no'.

It is not entirely clear what a 'panelled' house is. The root *sāpan* seems to have the broader meaning 'to cover'. In 1 Kgs 6:9, it refers to covering Solomon's temple with beams and planks of cedar, probably 'roofing'. In 1 Kgs 7:3, 7 and Jer. 22:14, it refers to lining a palace with cedar, so 'panelling'. Commentators also debate whether panelling was a normal feature of homes (J. Kessler 2002: 128), or an extravagant feature of the well-to-do (Nogalski 2011: 775). Unlike elsewhere, Haggai does not mention the type of timber used (such as cedar), which suggests that the emphasis is not on the wealth in these houses so much as the people's wrong priorities, evident in the fact that they had finished their own houses while the temple remained 'desolate'. Extravagant personal wealth also seems inconsistent with the hardships described in vv. 5–11.

The temple is described as 'desolate' (*ḥārēb*), often translated 'a ruin'. The same description is repeated in v. 9. There is also a wordplay in v. 11, which I have tried to capture in my translation: because Yahweh's people have left the temple 'desolate', Yahweh has called for a 'desolation' (*ḥōreb*) upon the land in order to get their attention.

Meadowcroft (2006: 106, 112) notes an ironic reversal of the situation in David's day. When David was in his cedar house and wanted to build the temple, the prophet Nathan told him to delay (2 Sam. 7). Now the people are in their panelled houses, they want to delay, but the prophet Haggai tells them it is time to build the temple.

5–6. The adv. expression 'And now' (*wĕʿattâ*) continues the theme of the time to build the temple but signals a shift in perspective. Yahweh calls on the people to 'consider your ways', which is literally 'set your heart upon your ways'. In Hebr. thought, the 'heart' is the seat of the will, rather than emotions, and corresponds to Western notions of the mind, hence I have translated it 'consider'. This is the first of five calls to 'consider' in the book (also 1:7; 2:15, 18 [twice]). Here the people are to consider the outcome of the way they have lived their lives, an outcome spelled out in

v. 6. The implication is that failing to rebuild the temple has adversely impacted their lives.

It is crucial to understand the adversity of v. 6 (and vv. 9–11 and 2:16–17) against the background of the covenant with Israel at Sinai and the curses stipulated for disobedience (see 'Explanation'). For instance, Moses warned that turning from Yahweh and failing to obey his commands and decrees would bring drought and famine (Lev. 26:26; Deut. 28:16, 18, 38–40), lack of wine (Deut. 28:39), and general want (Deut. 28:19, 23–24, 44). This is reflected in the conditions experienced in v. 6. It is not that there is abject poverty, for the people still reap, eat, drink, put on clothes and earn wages, but there is a general experience of inadequacy across each of these endeavours – the harvests are small, food does not bring satiety, there is not enough drink for 'merriment' (see 'Notes on the text'), clothes do not bring warmth, and wages just seem to disappear as if they have been put into a 'pierced purse'. At this time, wages were often carried in a small pouch or 'purse' attached to a waist cord (Meyers and Meyers 1987: 26). The phrase indicates that since resources are scarce prices are high. These experiences clearly demonstrate that the people are not enjoying the abundant blessing of Yahweh. Hence while many have returned from exile, they are still suffering the curses of the national covenant for their disobedience. In failing to rebuild the temple, they demonstrate that they have not returned to Yahweh to love and obey him with all their heart and soul (cf. Deut. 30:1–6).

7–8. The link between the people's present adverse circumstances and their failure to rebuild the temple is only implicit to this point, but the invitation to 'Consider your ways' invites them (and readers and hearers of the book of Haggai) to make the connection for themselves.

Yahweh charges the people to 'Go up the mountain and bring timber and build the house'. My translation differs from most of the English versions, but follows the Hebr. more closely. I have adopted the suggestion of Sweeney (2000b: 538) that 'the mountain' (*hāhār*) that they are to go up is the temple mountain (cf. Isa. 2:2–3; Zech. 8:3). This interpretation is more likely since timber in the surrounding mountains was not suitable for temple construction (cf. Neh. 8:15). Indeed, provision was made earlier to acquire timber from Lebanon (Ezra 3:7), just as with Solomon's temple (1 Kgs 5:6–11). While speculative, perhaps it was some of this imported timber that had been used in their own houses (v. 4). Instead, it was to be taken up the mountain to build the temple. The stones from Solomon's temple were probably still located at the site. Although not mentioned here, they are in Hag. 2:15.

A reason is given to build the temple, which amounts to a promise: 'so that I will delight in it and I will be glorified'. The verb 'delight' (*rāṣâ*) is used elsewhere of Yahweh's acceptance of a sacrifice (e.g. Lev. 1:4; 23:22–27; Mic. 6:7), his favourable acceptance of people (e.g. 2 Sam. 24:23; 1 Chr. 28:4; Job 33:26; Ps. 44:3[4]; Isa. 42:1; Ezek. 20:40–41) and his pleasure in their uprightness (1 Chr. 29:17). Given the use of 'delight' elsewhere, it seems that Yahweh will delight in the temple because of what it demonstrates about the attitude of his people. There is debate about how 'I will be glorified' should be translated and understood (see 'Notes on the text'). Many give the ni. form of the verb 'glorify' (*kābēd*) a reflex. sense and translate it 'I will glorify myself' or 'I will show my glory' and understand it to refer to Yahweh's presence in the temple (Verhoef 1987: 68). This is how it was translated in the Targums: 'I shall be pleased *to make my Shekinah dwell* in it *in honour*' (Cathcart and Gordon 1989: 177; italics original). Alternatively, the ni. can be understood with a pass. sense and translated 'I will be glorified', referring to Yahweh's being given praise and gaining prestige (Petersen 1985: 51). Given all the other uses of the ni. of this verb have the second sense, this is how it is best taken in this context. Yet 'glory' (*kābôd*) is a loaded term, and at the very least the use of the verb hints at the return of Yahweh's glory to the temple (cf. Ezek. 43:1–4). This theme is more fully developed in Zechariah (e.g. Zech. 2:5[9]). Boda (2004: 92) makes the important observation that ultimately the people are to build the temple not for relief from covenant curses, but for the pleasure and glory of God.

9. Further adversity is mentioned, but there is no object supplied for 'it'. The reference to Yahweh's blowing 'it away' suggests 'it' is their agricultural produce. Earlier prophets held out a glorious hope of agricultural abundance after the people returned from exile (e.g. Jer. 31:11–14; Amos 9:13–15), hence they had grounds to expect much. Yet the people's experience is nothing like this. What they bring to 'the house' (their homes, not the temple since it is not yet built) is literally 'blown against' by Yahweh.

For the first time, Yahweh makes the connection between the people's adverse circumstances and their failure to build the temple explicit when he answers 'Why?' This question serves to advance the plot of the narrative and draws together ideas already expressed (Craig 1996: 232–233). 'Why?' is literally 'On account of what?', with 'on account of' (*ya'an*) repeated to introduce the answer. Like v. 4, the contrast is between the way the people have been treating their own houses and the way they have been treating the temple (now more personalized as 'my house'). The expression 'running, each to his [own] house' appears colloquial, but seems to express the idea of being busy constructing their homes. It reveals that 'the people have time, energy, and the inclination to build, but their energy is misdirected' (Craig 1996: 233). Their priorities are skewed towards themselves rather than towards Yahweh and they experience his punishment. Understood against the backdrop of the covenant with Israel at Sinai, the purpose of the punishment (or 'discipline') is that the people might return to Yahweh (e.g. Lev. 26:18, 21, 23, 27, etc.).

10–11. God gives further evidence of the ways he has sought to gain his people's attention. Implicit is the belief that Yahweh governs 'the heavens . . . and the earth' (v. 10). The heavens have 'withheld dew', important for crops from May to October when there was no rain (Redditt 1995: 22). The earth (*hā'āreṣ*) has withheld its produce (v. 10) and this is further elaborated upon in v. 11, where God calls for a desolation 'upon the earth' (*'āl-hā'āreṣ*). As noted in v. 4, the noun 'desolation' (*ḥōreb*) is from the same root as the adj. 'desolate' (*ḥārēb*), used to describe the temple in vv. 4 and 9, indicating a connection between the state of the temple and the state of the land. While it is often translated 'drought', it should be understood more broadly since it refers also to the effects on various agricultural and economic activities (J. Kessler 2002: 140). The curses of the national covenant are again echoed here (cf. Lev. 26:19–20; Deut. 28:23–24, 30, 38–40, 48). Assis (2007a: 12–13) notes a close connection between vv. 10–11 and the words of Deut. 11:14–15, 17. There are also echoes of Gen. 1 – 3 with reference to the 'heavens and the earth' and the curse on 'the ground' (*hā'ădāmâ*) that results from disobedience (Gen. 3:17). The people's failure to rebuild the temple has resulted in Yahweh's punishment, which has negatively impacted not just them, but all creation. Again, implicit in all this is Yahweh's using these circumstances to call his people to repentance (cf. 2:17).

12. The obedience of the people to the first speech of Haggai is reported in vv. 12–15a. Floyd (2000: 269) proposes a two-stage response, where the people first 'hear' (rather than 'obey') and are 'afraid' (v. 12), before Yahweh announces he is with them (v. 13), which then results in true obedience (v. 13). A similar two-staged response is proposed by Assis (2007b: 522–527), where the response of v. 12 proves to be inadequate until Yahweh's intervention in v. 14. Yet it is better to consider vv. 12–15a as a unit, with the people's response first reported from the human perspective (v. 12) and then from God's perspective (v. 14) (Boda 2004: 106). The logic reflects the theology of Zechariah, where Yahweh says 'return to me . . . and I will return to you' (Zech. 1:3). V. 12 reports the people's turning back to Yahweh, and v. 13 gives the people the assurance that God has turned to them with the promise 'I am with you'. With the relationship restored, v. 14 reports God's working in his people to recommence the building of the temple.

The leaders Zerubbabel and Joshua are reported as obeying (see 'Notes on the text'), along with 'all the remnant of the people' (v. 12). Zerubbabel and Joshua are the addressees of the prophetic speech (v. 1), but the people seem to be in view from v. 3. The word translated 'obeyed' (*šāma'*) can simply mean 'to hear', but the echoes of Deut. 4:30 and 30:2, which envisage a time after exile when the people return to Yahweh and 'obey' (*šāma'*), suggest this idea is uppermost. There is possibly also an echo of Jeremiah, whose hearers refused to obey (e.g. Jer. 43:4) (J. Kessler 2008: 20). The leaders and people all respond in obedience to 'the voice of Yahweh their God, that is, [they obeyed] in accordance with the words of Haggai the prophet'. The 'voice of Yahweh' and 'the words of Haggai' are one and the same and indicate the divine and human nature of the prophetic word, which here powerfully works obedience among God's people. Like Moses and other prophets, Haggai is 'sent' by Yahweh as the mediator of his word (e.g. Exod. 3:10–15; Zech. 7:12). Yahweh's sending Haggai also indicates his initiative to restore the relationship.

The people are called the 'remnant' (*šĕ'ērît*), which in the earlier prophets describes those who will survive the exile and emerge as a purified and faithful people (e.g. Isa. 10:20–22; 37:4). Some argue that the 'remnant' refers to the returning exiles as opposed to those who had remained in the land (Wolff 1988: 51–52); however, this proposal has largely been rejected and the terms 'remnant' (cf. 1:14; 2:2), 'people' (cf. 1:13; 2:14) and 'people of the land' (2:4) are best understood as synonymous. Whereas they were 'this people' in v. 2, expressing relational distance (see 'Comment' on v. 2), now that they have obeyed they show themselves to be the 'remnant of the people' and Yahweh is 'their God' (twice) (cf. Exod. 6:7; Lev. 26:12; Deut. 26:17; Zech. 8:8). Having encountered Yahweh in his word, and returning in obedience, relationship is restored.

In addition, 'the people feared the LORD'. This fear of Yahweh could simply be another way of speaking about the obedience of covenant faithfulness (e.g. Deut. 6:13; Ps. 128:1). However, the syntax here suggests a closer parallel with Exod. 9:30, Eccl. 3:14 and Ps. 33:8, where 'fear' refers to the subjective feeling of terror towards Yahweh once his power is truly recognized (J. Kessler 2002: 147). These meanings overlap to some extent. However, Yahweh's response in v. 13 suggests the latter idea is uppermost.

13. Yahweh responds to the people's fear with a message through Haggai: 'I am with you.' This assurance is often given to an individual in the face of fear, particularly accompanying a theophany or when being commissioned for a daunting task (e.g. Gen. 28:15; Exod. 3:12; Josh. 1:5; 2 Sam. 7:3; Jer. 1:8). It is also a promise, given to God's people in the face of fear, that he will save or uphold them (cf. Ps. 46:7, 11; Isa. 8:10; 41:10; 43:5; Jer. 30:10–11; 42:11). The same promise is repeated in 2:4–5 where Assis (2008a: 590) notes that these words reaffirm that Yahweh's covenant with the people at Sinai remains operative.

Haggai is described as Yahweh's 'messenger', which can be a human or angelic designation. Clearly, it is human here (cf. Mal. 1:1; 2:7; 3:1). Taylor (2004: 142) observes a wordplay where Yahweh's 'messenger' (*mal'ak*) has Yahweh's 'message' (*mal'ăkût*), so that in v. 14 the people may 'work' (*mĕlā'kâ*) in the house of Yahweh.

14. The people have responded in obedience in v. 12, but now a different perspective is given (rather than a subsequent action) that reveals that Yahweh is at work in his people. In Hebr. thought, the 'spirit' (*rûaḥ*) of a person is 'the impulse that governs a person's life and controls his or her behaviour' (Routledge 2008: 144). In other words, it is a person's 'will' or 'disposition'. Yahweh moves the wills of the leaders and the people by his powerful word and they come and work in the temple (cf. Ezra 1:1, 5).

This experience of Yahweh's sovereign power should give further confidence to his people, that they might continue to trust and obey.

15. As well as dating the prophetic speeches, the book dates significant points in the temple reconstruction (cf. 2:18). The 'twenty-fourth day of the sixth month' corresponds to 21 September 520 BC and marks the beginning of the work, some twenty-three days after Haggai's first prophecy (cf. 1:1). It is likely that the people used the intervening time to 'consider their ways' (vv. 5, 7), to complete the harvests and to assemble the required building materials.

In some English translations, the final phrase 'in the second year of Darius the king' is separated from the end of v. 15 and added to the beginning of the next chapter (e.g. NIV). However, the regnal year notice rounds out the unit (cf. 1:1). It serves a double duty by also informing the date in 2:1 (Meyers and Meyers 1987: 37). There is no need to duplicate it in translation or relocate it to the beginning of 2:1.

Explanation

The first speech of Haggai is in the genre of a prophetic disputation. The people say that it is not yet time to rebuild the temple (v. 2). Indirectly and directly, Haggai challenges this view. Indirectly, he asks them to acknowledge that they are still suffering the curses of the covenant with Israel at Sinai for their wrong priorities (vv. 6, 9–11). They have put time and energy into their own houses, but not Yahweh's house (vv. 4, 9). Haggai directly charges them to build the temple for Yahweh's pleasure and glory (v. 8).

Somewhat remarkably (given the history of God's people refusing the prophets and hardening their hearts), the people obey Yahweh's word and commence the work to rebuild the temple (vv. 12, 14). While there is fear (v. 13), Yahweh promises, 'I am with you' (v. 13; cf. v. 4). Yahweh is at work in his people to obey (v. 14).

It is vital to read the book of Haggai against the backdrop of the national covenant with Israel at Sinai; otherwise, there is a danger of distorting its message into one that seeks to manipulate God by human-centred religion. Haggai can easily be twisted into a 'self-help gospel' or a 'prosperity gospel' when it is heard to be saying 'build the temple to win God's blessing' or 'give to the temple and God will make you rich'. Religion treats God like a slot machine – put in the coin of good works, pull the handle and hope for the jackpot! It is the antithesis to the gospel of grace and makes out that God is there only to serve our whims. In Exodus, Yahweh saved his people by his grace. The law was then given to show the Israelites how to live as his saved people so as to continue to enjoy his blessing. Moses warned the Israelites that if they turned from Yahweh and disobeyed, he would remove his blessing and they would come under his curses (e.g. Lev. 26; Deut. 28). Yahweh's purpose in this was that his people might turn back to him; but if they did not, he would exile them from the land (e.g. Deut. 28:63–68). Even then, Yahweh promises restoration and a return to blessing when the people repent and obey (e.g. Deut. 30:1–3). Moses understands that this repentance will ultimately be a work of Yahweh's grace (Deut. 30:6). In this context, Haggai is effectively saying that the people are suffering the curses of the covenant because of their failure to love Yahweh with all their heart and soul, evidenced by their failure to build the temple. Haggai calls the people back to covenant obedience so that they may enjoy the blessings of the covenant. It is important to note that the ultimate motivation to rebuild the temple is not the people's well-being, but the delight and glory of God (v. 8; cf. 1 Cor. 10:31; Rev. 4:11). Furthermore, as if to highlight Yahweh's grace, the book explains that when the people obey, it is because Yahweh is working in them by his Spirit through his powerful word (1:14; 2:4–5). This response in Haggai's day anticipates the new covenant, where Yahweh will change the hearts of his people (cf. Jer. 24:7; 31:33; Ezek. 11:19–20; 2 Cor. 3:3; Heb. 8:10).

Some reject the idea that God sends adversity as a warning to repent. J. J. Collins (2012: 50) argues that 'Haggai's attempt to give a theological explanation of natural conditions must be considered dubious.' While it is true that elsewhere the Bible teaches that the rain falls on the righteous and the unrighteous (Matt. 5:45), and not all suffering and adversity are a direct result of a particular sin (e.g. Job; John 9:1–3), sometimes even today adversity is God's punishment or 'discipline' as a warning to repent (e.g. Luke 13:1–5; 1 Cor. 11:30; Heb. 12:4–13; Jas 5:14–15; Rev. 2:22). To believe otherwise may reflect a deistic view of God, where God set the world up but now stands outside its day-to-day operations, but this is not the God of the Bible.

The significance of the temple can also be misunderstood. Wellhausen believed that the post-exilic prophets had lost the ethical dimension of the earlier prophets and had reverted to what he saw as 'a sad decline into the bricks-and-mortar Temple mentality', where there was an unhealthy concern regarding what he understood as the more primitive religion of temple and sacrifice (Ackroyd 1991: 245). Yet this does not reflect the concern of Haggai (or Zechariah). The temple is a much richer theme, and one that traverses the Bible (see 'Key themes', 'Temple'). The earlier prophets promised a central role for the temple in the restoration of God's people (e.g. Isa. 2:2–3; 44:28; Ezek. 40 – 48; Joel 3:18; Mic. 4:1–2). Against the background of earlier prophetic expectation it is easy to see why, when the people returned to the land, rebuilding the temple was to be their priority. Yahweh's dwelling once again among his people to bless them was central to his purposes. The temple will be for his delight and glory (v. 8). God reminds the people of this through Haggai and calls them to get on and build it. See further, Assis 2008b.

God's ultimate purposes for the temple find their fulfilment in Jesus (e.g. John 2:19–21), the people of the church (e.g. Eph. 2:21; 1 Peter 2:4–5), and the new creation (e.g. Rev. 21 – 22). Hence, the Christian's priorities in this life are not about a building in Jerusalem, but Jesus (Matt. 6:33) and building his church (Matt. 16:18; 28:19–20), in view of his return. Given the way that the NT understands the hopes for the temple being fulfilled, the message of Haggai is not about giving money to the church building fund (in the first instance, anyway)! Church is not a building but the people, and Jesus' church is built by giving oneself first and foremost to the work of the Lord in evangelism and edification (cf. Eph. 4:11–16). This is often difficult work, but like the people in Haggai's day, Christians are strengthened with the promise 'I am with you' (cf. Matt. 28:20).

HAGGAI 2:1–9

Translation

2:1 In the seventh [month] on the twenty-first [day] of the month, the word of the
LORD came through Haggai the prophet, 2 'Say now to Zerubbabel son of Shealtiel,
the governor of Judah, and to Joshua son of Jehozadak, the high priest, and
to the remnant of the people, 3 "Who remains among you who saw this house in
its former glory? And how are you seeing it now? Does it not seem as nothing
in your eyes? 4 And now be strong Zerubbabel, declares the LORD; and be strong
Joshua son of Jehozadak, the high priest, and be strong all the people of the
land, declares the LORD, and build, for I am with you, declares the LORD of hosts.
5 This is the promise that I made with you when you came out from Egypt, and
my Spirit is standing in your midst. Do not fear." '

6 For so says the LORD of hosts, 'Once again, it will be soon, and I will shake the
heavens and the earth and the sea and the dry ground. 7 And I will shake all
the nations and the desire of all the nations will come, and I will fill this house
with glory,' says the LORD of hosts.

8 'The silver is mine and the gold is mine!' says the LORD of hosts.

9 'The latter glory of this house will be greater than the former,' says the LORD
of hosts. 'And in this place I will grant peace,' declares the LORD of hosts.

Notes on the text

2:1. The words for 'month' and 'day' are absent (cf. 2:10) and must be understood by analogy with 1:1, 15.

'through': *bĕyad*. Lit. 'by the hand of' (cf. 1:1, 3; see 'Comment'). Mur has 'to' (*'el*), but MT is followed by LXX, Syr, Vg and Tg, which suggests it is original.

2. 'Shealtiel': *šaltî'ēl* is a shortened form of the name used in 1:1 (*šĕ'altî'ēl*), but the same form as 1:12, 14.

'and to the remnant': *wĕ'el-šĕ'ērît*. LXX and Syr have 'and to all the remnant', probably to assimilate to 1:12, 14. Mur, Vg and Tg support MT as original.

3. 'Does it not seem as nothing': lit. 'is it not like it, like nothing', where the construction *kĕ . . . kĕ* forms a comparison (Arnold and Choi 2003: 109). The comparison is between the temple ('it') and 'nothing'.

4. 'and build': *wa'ăśû* usually means 'and make' or 'and do', but in view of the temple 'and build' seems appropriate. While often translated 'work' as in 1:14 (e.g. NIV, NRSV, ESV), this is a different Hebr. word (*mĕlā'kâ*).

5. 'This is': *'et* is unusual. Mishnaic Hebr. uses *'et* as a demons. (Waltke and O'Connor 1990: 178) and this seems to be the case here also (cf. Zech. 7:7).

'the promise that I made with you': lit. 'the word/thing that I cut with you' (see 'Comment').

The first part of the verse to 'from Egypt' is absent from LXX, but present in Syr, Tg and partially in Mur.

6. 'it will be soon': *mĕ'aṭ hî'*. Lit. 'it is a little'. This phrase is absent from LXX and Syr, perhaps to reduce the sense of imminence when translated at a later time (Taylor 2004: 159).

'will shake': *mar'îš* is a hiph. ptc., which can announce imminent action, or action already in progress; cf. 2:21 (Arnold and Choi 2003: 81). It does not always imply imminent future (e.g. 2 Kgs 21:12; Isa. 13:13; Jer. 30:10; 31:8; 32:37; 33:6; 46:27; 50:18; Zeph. 3:19) (C. J. Thomson 2013: 56).

7. 'will come': *ûbā'û* is pl., but the subject ('the desire of all the nations') is to be understood with a collective sense (their wealth). The verb is sg. in LXX, Syr and Tg. See 'Comment'.

'with glory': *kābôd*. The prep. 'with' is understood from the verb 'fill'.

9. LXX adds, 'and peace of soul as a possession for all who build to erect this temple', probably to spiritualize a more material promise (Petersen 1985: 70).

Form and structure

Hag. 2:1–9 is the second of four prophetic speeches in the book. These speeches form a narrative account of the word of Yahweh, through the prophet Haggai, addressing the post-exilic community. The first speech was addressed to the leaders Zerubbabel and Joshua (1:1), with the people implicitly addressed (cf. 1:12, 14). In the second speech, the people are included as addressees from the beginning (2:2). The second prophetic speech has similar elements to the first: after a date (2:1), a problem is reported (2:2–3; cf. 1:2), to which comes a challenge to build the temple (2:4; cf. 1:8). The promise of God's presence is repeated (2:4–5; cf. 1:13). Unlike the first prophetic speech, the response of the people is not reported.

Furthermore, this speech looks to Yahweh's acting dramatically on the world stage to bring glory to his temple and establish peace (vv. 6–9). This future action of Yahweh is also a feature of the fourth speech (2:21–23), which sets the shaking of the heavens and the earth in an eschatological time frame (cf. 'on that day' in v. 23). MT has paragraph markers at the end of vv. 5 and 9 that reflect this shift.

While some see the genre of 'prophetic disputation' continuing from ch. 1 (Wolff 1988: 72), in this speech Haggai does not disagree with the popular sentiment. Instead, although he agrees with it (v. 3), at the same time he urges a different stance towards it – action rather than despondency. Floyd (2000: 283) categorizes the genre as a 'commission to prophesy', where Yahweh instructs Haggai what to say and whom to say it to. Assis (2006: 536) categorizes the genre as 'an oracle of consolation', which captures its tone.

Haggai engages the post-exilic community with three sequential questions in v. 3, heightening the rhetorical effect of his speech and capturing the attention of his audience (Craig 1996: 230). Reading between the lines, there seems to be a sense of discouragement in the community, and the intention of the prophetic speech is to encourage the people to continue the work of rebuilding the temple, first reminding them of Yahweh's enabling presence (2:4; cf. 1:13). Haggai then raises the expectation of Yahweh's intervening in world history to establish the temple at the centre of his restoration plans for the world (vv. 6–9).

Comment

2:1–2. The second prophetic speech is introduced with another dating formula: 'In the seventh [month] on the twenty-first [day] of the month'. This corresponds to 17 October, some twenty-seven days after they began the work on the temple (cf. 1:15). The year notice that finishes 1:15 carries over and is applicable to this verse too, hence 'in the second year of Darius the king' or 520 BC.

In the Jewish calendar, the seventh month included several festivals (cf. Lev. 23:23–43). This day corresponds to the seventh day of the Feast of Tabernacles, 'Sukkoth', a festival of joy and thanksgiving for the harvest and God's goodness. 'Sukkoth' can also be translated 'booths' and refers to the tents the Israelites lived in when they came out of Egypt (cf. Exod. 23:14–17; Lev. 23:33–43; Deut. 16:13–15; 31:9–13; Hag. 2:5). This feast was closely associated with the temple. For instance, Solomon's temple was dedicated at Sukkoth (1 Kgs 8:2, 41–43, 65), and in Ezra 3:1–4 the people celebrated Sukkoth after Joshua and Zerubbabel had set up the altar at the old temple site. It was also a festival that included the foreigner (e.g. Deut. 16:13–15), a theme that is relevant later in the prophetic speech with the inclusion of the nations (v. 7).

Like Haggai 1:1, 3, the word of Yahweh came 'through' (*bĕyad*) Haggai. This time he is instructed to speak to the leaders Zerubbabel and Joshua and to the 'remnant of the people' (see 'Comment' on 1:1, 12).

3. Haggai poses three sequential questions to the post-exilic community that draw in his audience (Craig 1996: 230). Each 'you' is a second-person pl. in the Hebr., indicating all the people are being addressed. The 'glory' (*kābôd*) of the temple is a key idea through these questions. The first question asks, 'Who remains among you who saw this house in its former glory?' Solomon's temple had been glorious both in its splendour and by virtue of the presence of Yahweh's own 'glory' (cf. 1 Kgs 8:11). Solomon's temple was destroyed in 586 BC, some sixty-six years earlier, so those who remained were likely to be few. Yet all would have known of its 'glory'. The second question draws a comparison and creates a stark contrast: 'And how are you seeing it now?' Significantly, there are not two temples in view, but one temple before and after its destruction (cf. v. 9). The third question affirms the contrast: 'Does it not seem as nothing in your eyes?' The Hebr. syntax of 'Does it not' (*hălô'*) suggests an affirmative answer. The present state of the temple cannot be compared with its pre-exilic state. There seems to be a similar experience in Ezra 3:12–13. When the first exiles returned and laid the foundation for the temple, those who remembered the former temple wept aloud. Hence, while it is not stated explicitly, there seems to be a sense of despondency among the community that Haggai is responding to. Perhaps the realization of the immensity of the task was dawning on them and they were discouraged, or perhaps the project seemed to be of a much smaller scale than Solomon's temple.

4. The adv. expression 'And now' (*wĕʿattâ*) continues to address the theme of the disappointing state of the temple, but signals a shift in perspective (cf. 1:5). The addressees of the prophetic speech (cf. v. 2) are all identified again and each is urged to 'be strong' – the effect is emphatic. The phrase 'the people of the land' is used in parallel with 'the remnant of the people', which suggests they are synonymous (see 'Comment' on 1:12). The same exhortation to 'be strong' is given to an earlier Joshua in view of the daunting task of taking the Promised Land (cf. Josh. 1:6–7, 9, 18). It is a call to trust Yahweh's word of promise: that he will deliver on what he says he will. Given the present state of the temple and the people's implicit state of discouragement, trust in Yahweh is required so that they may 'build' it to its former glory. The charge to 'build' is the primary rhetorical goal of the passage (Sweeney 2000b: 546). Christensen (1992: 455) contends that vv. 4–5 are the structural centre of the book.

The word 'build' (*ʿāśâ*) is more usually translated 'do' or 'make' (see 'Notes on the text'). Meyers and Meyers (1987: 51) move it into v. 5 and translate it, 'Do the Word which I covenanted with you', but there is little textual warrant for such a radical change and the meaning of this phrase is even less clear. Elsewhere the verb *ʿāśâ* is used with reference to constructing various projects, such as Noah's ark (Gen. 8:6), or of Yahweh's work of creation (e.g. Gen. 1:7, 16, 25; Neh. 9:6; Job 9:9; Ps. 100:3). Translating it 'build' (with reference to the temple) seems appropriate in this context.

Like in the first speech, Yahweh promises, 'I am with you' (cf. 1:13). As noted there, this assurance of Yahweh's presence is given in the light of the people's fear, a factor recognized again in 2:5. Fear can hinder trust in God and obedience to his word (see e.g. Ahaz in Isa. 7:2, 4, 9, 14; cf. 41:10). Yahweh's promise is a reassurance that he will support the people in their building efforts. The same encouragement is given by David to Solomon when he built the temple (1 Chr. 22:16, 18; 28:10, 20). Assis (2008a: 590) notes that these words are also a reaffirmation of Yahweh's covenant with the people at Sinai (cf. v. 5).

5. The Hebr. at the beginning of this verse is unusual, but explicable (see 'Notes on the text'): 'This is the promise that I made with you'. The word 'promise' (*dābār*) is more usually translated 'word' or 'thing', but since it most naturally refers back to Yahweh's promise in v. 4 ('I am with you'), it is translated this way. In addition, the verb 'made' (*kārat*) is normally used with reference to a covenant, not a 'word'. But since covenants entail promises, this is a further reason for translating *dābār* as 'promise'. Yahweh's presence among his people was a central promise of the covenant with Israel at Sinai (Exod. 25:8; 29:45–46). The rhetorical 'you' clearly views the community in Haggai's day as standing in direct continuity with the people of the exodus (J. Kessler 2008: 26).

A further encouragement to the people is the assurance that 'my Spirit is standing in your midst', where 'standing in' has the sense of 'present'. The Spirit of Yahweh had empowered his people in the past in many ways. He had been at work in the exodus and given the Israelites rest (Isa. 63:11–14). He had been at work among those who built the tabernacle (Exod. 31:2–3; 35:30–31). He had empowered the judges for battle (e.g. Judg. 6:34). He had empowered kings for service (e.g. 1 Sam. 16:13). He was powerfully at work through the words of the prophets (e.g. Mic. 3:8; Zech. 7:12). Here Haggai promises that Yahweh's Spirit is present to empower them to build the temple (cf. Zechariah's promise to Zerubbabel in Zech. 4:6 that he will build the temple in the power of the Spirit). Haggai repeats the most frequent command of the Bible, 'Do not fear'. Fear can hinder obedience to God (cf. 2:4), but looking to his past actions and recalling his promises gives no grounds for fear.

6–7. Like the fourth prophetic speech (2:20–23), this speech shifts to look towards a time when Yahweh will act dramatically and directly to reorder the world, subduing the nations and establishing his kingdom of peace (vv. 6–9). Central to this programme is Yahweh's establishing a greater glory for the temple than even Solomon's temple had. This glorious temple is envisaged as the centre of a new world order. These hopes are not new: Haggai reasserts standard elements of earlier hopes for Zion and its temple with little modification (J. Kessler 2008: 27). This would naturally act as further encouragement for the people to build it. For the first readers and hearers of the book of Haggai, for whom the temple had been built or was nearing completion, this prophecy would engender hope for the temple to be transformed in this way.

'Once again' indicates that Yahweh has acted this way in the past. Given the reference to the exodus in v. 5, the event in the past is most likely Yahweh's appearance at Sinai when the mountain 'trembled violently' (Exod. 19:18). Yahweh will again shake the cosmos ('the heavens and the earth'), the world ('the sea and the dry ground') and 'all the nations' (v. 7). This speaks of Yahweh's sovereign power over all creation that will be evident when he establishes his kingdom. Haggai expects that this shaking 'will be soon' (J. A. Kessler 1987: 165) (see also 'Notes on the text' and 'Explanation').

There is a long tradition going back to the patristic period that interprets 'the desire of all the nations' (v. 7) to refer to the Messiah. While there is arguably a strong hope expressed in the prophets for a future Davidic king (cf. 2:20–23), the Hebr. syntax does not support this interpretation here. The verb 'will come' is pl., but the sg. verb would be expected if 'the desire of all the nations' is an individual (see 'Notes on the text'). Furthermore, the immediate context suggests it refers to the wealth of all the nations that will be collected when Yahweh shakes them (v. 6). In this case it is what the nations desire (wealth) that 'will come' and 'fill this house with glory'. Other prophets also express the hope for the wealth and riches of the nations to be given to God's people (cf. Isa. 60:5, 11; 61:6; 66:12, 20; Zech. 14:14). It echoes the plundering of the Egyptians in the exodus (e.g. Exod. 11:2–3; 12:35–36), and the wealth of the nations pouring into Solomon's kingdom (e.g. 1 Kgs 10). To some extent this was realized when Darius decreed to provide from the royal treasury (Ezra 6:8), and some sixty years later when silver and gold were given to Ezra for the temple by the Persian king Artaxerxes and the surrounding nations (Ezra 7:15–23).

While the 'glory' Yahweh will fill the temple with is primarily wealth, there is also a strong implication that his own presence will fill the temple once again since the same expression elsewhere refers to his 'glory' filling the tabernacle and temple (Exod. 40:34–35; 1 Kgs 8:10–11; Ezek. 43:5; 44:4) (Assis 2008a: 592).

8. Yahweh is entitled to claim the wealth of the nations for the glory of his house (cf. v. 7), because he owns it. Similar statements, where God's ownership of everything is grounded in creation, are seen in Exod. 19:5; Deut. 10:14; 1 Chr. 29:11–12; Job 41:11; Pss 24:1; 50:12; 89:11.

9. Yahweh promises that after he has shaken the universe and the nations, 'The latter glory of this house will be greater than the former.' This links back directly to address the people's perceptions of the current state of the temple, identified in v. 3. Like the earlier prophets, Haggai promises a future temple that will surpass even Solomon's temple for its glory (e.g. Isa. 2:2–3; 44:28; Ezek. 40 – 48; Joel 3:18; Mic. 4:1–2). Just as there is continuity between Solomon's temple and the present building (cf. v. 3), so it seems that Haggai envisages continuity between the present and future temple. Hence the prophetic speech functions as an encouragement for the people to build it in view of Yahweh's promise to transform it dramatically (cf. v. 4).

Along with the promised transformation of the temple is the 'peace' (*šālôm*) that will accompany it. The idea of 'peace' is wholeness, well-being, prosperity and right relationships. While 'this place' probably refers to the temple, or more broadly to the city of Jerusalem (the 'city of peace'), it is from here that peace will spread to the world (cf. Zech. 9:9–10).

Explanation

Some twenty-seven days after the people began the work on the temple, the word of Yahweh came to Haggai a second time with a prophetic message for the leaders and people. The three initial questions to the community in v. 3 indicate that the state of the temple is nothing compared to Solomon's. This strongly implies that a sense of discouragement has set in among the community and Yahweh addresses this, through his prophet Haggai.

Haggai encourages the people to continue the work of rebuilding the temple, first reminding them of Yahweh's enabling presence (2:4; cf. 1:13), and then raising the expectation of Yahweh's intervening in world history to establish the temple at the centre of his restoration plans for the world (vv. 6–9). The date of the speech, corresponding to the seventh day of the Feast of Tabernacles (Sukkoth), further underscores the importance of rebuilding since it was a festival closely associated with the temple. It also draws a link between their past and present circumstances since the 'tabernacles' reminded the people of the tents the Israelites lived in when they came out of Egypt in the exodus. In the midst of discouraging circumstances, Haggai reminds the people of Yahweh's great provision for his people in the past, particularly in the exodus (v. 5), and that he is with them and at work in the present – there are no grounds for fear.

What is the temple that Christians are to build? Many Christian Zionists believe that the temple must be rebuilt in Jerusalem for OT prophecies to be fulfilled. However, this belief effectively ignores the teaching of Jesus and the apostles. See further, Sizer 2004. John's prologue introduces Jesus as the word made flesh who 'tabernacled' among his people and as the presence of God's glory among his people (John 1:14). In John 2, Jesus clears the temple, but also has some important words about the way he fulfils all that the temple represents:

> 'Destroy this temple, and I will raise it again in three days.'
> They replied, 'It has taken forty-six years to build this temple, and you are going to raise it in three days?' But the temple he had spoken of was his body. (John 2:19–21)

Jesus' interaction with the Samaritan woman in John 4 reveals the way he fulfils and reshapes all the temple stood for. For historical reasons, the Samaritans repudiated Jerusalem and had their own worship focused on Mount Gerizim, and this lies behind the woman's question to Jesus about whether Jerusalem or Mount Gerizim is the true place of worship (v. 20). Jesus responds by saying that the time will come, and has now come (in Jesus), when they will worship neither on Mount Gerizim nor Jerusalem (v. 21), but 'in the Spirit and in truth' (v. 23). 'The Spirit' and 'truth' are closely connected to Jesus in John's Gospel. The Spirit reveals the kingdom (John 3:1–8), but Jesus is the one who makes the Spirit available (7:37–39). Jesus is the truth (John 14:6), who brings people true knowledge of the Father (17:3). Jesus says that now that he has come, worship is not confined to the Jerusalem temple (or any other place). True worship is 'located' in Jesus. In this way, the OT prophecies about the temple find their fulfilment in him. As noted at the end of the 'Explanation' of 1:1–15, now that Jesus has come, the NT also uses the temple imagery to refer to the church, which Christ is building by his Spirit.

For Christian readers, this passage in Haggai is a wonderful model of motivating God's people. There is every temptation today to become discouraged in building God's temple, the church. In the West, secularism is making inroads into society and challenging many Christian beliefs and behaviours. Often Christians can be tempted to look to the 'glory days' of the past, doubt that God is at work in the present and give in to discouragement. Just as Haggai gave hope in the present by recounting Yahweh's promises and recalling how he has acted in the past towards his people, so Christian hope is grounded in the promises and past actions of God, revealed all the more fully in the gospel of Jesus Christ. Ultimately, it is God himself, through his powerful word, who motivates his people to remain faithful in adversity and to commit themselves to the task of building his church by proclaiming this word. Motyer (1998: 987) is worth quoting:

> The Lord's rejoinder to his people's despondency is to turn their minds from what they think to be true of themselves (we cannot match the past, we cannot achieve in the present) to what is true about him. They say 'we,' the Lord says 'I . . . my Spirit' they are speaking and he is speaking . . . To which word will they listen? The key to tackling despondency is found here: stop listening to ourselves and start listening to him and his word of promise.

For the early readers and hearers of the book of Haggai after the temple had been rebuilt, the promises of vv. 6–9 awaited their fulfilment and would have engendered hope. They were probably one of the reasons that the book of Haggai was treasured and preserved. For Christian readers, these wonderful promises about a restored universe have begun to be fulfilled in the first coming of Jesus Christ and will be fully realized at his return. The book of Hebrews quotes v. 6 in its climactic warning to heed God's voice and not presume upon the grace of God (P. T. O'Brien 2010: 492). It speaks of a time when the shaking of the earth and the heavens will result in a kingdom that cannot be shaken (Heb. 12:26–28), and this is connected with a vision of the heavenly Jerusalem (vv. 22–24). For the writer of Hebrews, this kingdom is something that Christians begin to participate in when they receive the gospel, and will be fulfilled when God visits judgment on the universe at the end of the age.

The Gospels claim that Jesus' glory surpasses the temple and that the coming of his kingdom (at his first and second comings) shakes the heavens (cf. Matt. 24:1–2, 29–30; Mark 13:1–2, 25–26; Luke 21:5–6, 26–27). Rev. 21:22–27 also develops the themes of this passage in relation to Jesus. He is the one who replaces the temple in the heavenly city of Jerusalem by his own presence as the Lamb, along with the Lord God Almighty. The 'glory' of God and the lamp of the Lamb will give light to the city (v. 23), and into it the glory and honour of the nations will be brought (v. 26). This is the Christian hope.

HAGGAI 2:10–19

Translation

[2:10]On the twenty fourth [day] of the ninth [month], in the second year of Darius, the word of the LORD came to Haggai the prophet, [11]'So says the LORD of hosts: Ask the priests [for] a ruling: [12]If a man carries consecrated meat in the fold of his garment, and with its fold touches some bread, or some stew, or some wine, or some oil, or any other food, will it become consecrated?' And the priests answered, 'No.' [13]Then Haggai said, 'If a defiled person touches any of these, will it become defiled?' And the priests answered, 'It will become defiled.' [14]And Haggai answered, 'So is this people and so is this nation before me,' declares the LORD, 'and so is every work of their hands, and what they offer there – it is defiled.

[15]'And now consider carefully, from this day on, before you placed stone to stone in the temple of the LORD [16](so that they would not be going to a heap of twenty and there were ten; [and] going to the wine vat to draw fifty measures and there were twenty), [17]I struck you with blight and with mildew and with hail; [I struck] all the work of your hands. But you did not [return] to me,' declares the LORD. [18]'Consider carefully, from this day on, from the twenty-fourth day of the ninth [month], namely from the day when the temple of the LORD was founded – consider! [19]Is the seed still in the grain pit? It [the seed] has not yielded even as much as a vine or a fig tree or a pomegranate or an olive tree. From this day I will bless.'

Notes on the text

2:10. The words for 'day' and 'month' are absent (cf. 2:1) and must be understood by analogy with 1:1, 15.

11. '[for] a ruling': *tôrâ*. See 'Comment'.

12. 'If': *hēn* is unusual, but based on its use in Aramaic, it is best understood as introducing a condition (R. J. Williams 2007: 182). Cf. *'im* in v. 13.

'some': *'el-ha*. The prep. *'el* indicates the indirect object and is not translated (i.e. 'touches [it] to ['*el*]'). The def. art. on each noun designates a class (Miller-Naudé et al. 1999: 191) and is translated 'some'.

'stew': occurs also in Gen. 25:29 and 2 Kgs 4:38. The contexts suggest a vegetable stew.

'the priests answered': lit. 'the priests answered and they said' (also v. 13).

13. 'any of these': *běkol-'ēlleh*. Like *min* in v. 12, *bě* is partitive of 'these' (i.e. the items in v. 12) (R. J. Williams 2007: 100).

14. LXX adds, 'Because of their early profits, they shall be pained because of their toil, and you have hated those who reprove at the gates' (Petersen 1985: 71). LXX seems to be a gloss based on Amos 5:10 to explain that uncleanness is due to moral failure (Ackroyd 1968: 169–170).

15. 'Consider carefully': *śîmû-nā' lěbabkem*. Lit. 'set your heart' (cf. 1:5, 7). The addition of *nā'* is emphatic, so 'carefully' is added (also 2:18).

'on': *wāmā'lā* (cf. v. 18). J. Kessler (2002: 207) notes this expression is used elsewhere of 'moving onward' in space and time (e.g. 1 Sam. 16:13; 30:25).

'before': *miṭṭerem*. The *min* is not translated (J. Kessler 2002: 198).

'you placed': *śûm* is an inf. const. with person and aspect determined from the context (cf. 'you expected' in 1:9).

16. 'so that they would not be': *mihyôtām*. MT is difficult to translate and may be an idiomatic expression (Motyer 1998: 997). Gelston (2010: 132) is representative of many who believe MT is in error and should be emended, following LXX, to *mî hěyîtem* ('How did you fare?'; cf. NRSV), where *mî* is the interr. adv. 'How?' I have followed Rogland (2013: 70–73), who preserves the MT, arguing it is a periphrastic ptc. construction introducing a parenthetical comment subordinate to v. 15b. The verse division is also difficult, as the ideas are closely associated with v. 15. Indeed, NIV transfers this phrase to v. 15 ('how things were'), which captures the overall sense.

'measures': *pûrâ* occurs only here and in Isa. 63:3. The use in Isa. 63:3 suggests it is a winepress, but the context in Haggai suggests it is a measure for wine, perhaps what results from a single pressing. There is insufficient evidence to be certain. For a survey of options see Taylor 2004: 184. Note also that nouns can be in the sg. with numerals greater than one (Miller-Naudé et al. 1999: 268).

'and there were': *wěhāytâ*. Lit. 'and it was' (twice).

17. 'But you did not [return] to me': *wĕ'ên-'etkem 'ēlay* . The word 'return' (*šûb*) is not present in MT. Yet it is translated in LXX, Syr, Vg and Tg. The context seems to demand that it be supplied in order to make sense of the verse. The parallel with Amos 4:9 also supports this. See further, Hildebrand 1989: 157–159; LeCureux 2012: 166–171.

18. 'Consider carefully': *śîmû-nā' lĕbabkem*. Lit. 'set your heart'; cf. 'consider' in 1:5, 7. The addition of *nâ* is emphatic, so 'carefully' is added (also 2:15).

'on': *wāmā'lă* (cf. v. 15).

'namely from': *lĕmin*, where *lĕ* is used to specify more closely.

'consider': *śîmû lĕbabkem* lacks the emphatic *nā'* (cf. 2:15, 18).

19. The syntax of this verse is difficult and debated, particularly the use of *wĕ'ād*. Rogland (2013: 74–76) argues *wĕ'ād* is a temporal prep., and the subject of the main verb (*nāśā'*) is the 'seed' of the previous clause. In this case, each of the nouns has a generic art. that is not translated. Alternatively, *wĕ'ād* can have an adv. sense (e.g. NRSV): 'Do the vine, the fig tree, the pomegranate, and the olive tree still yield nothing?'

Form and structure

Hag. 2:10–19 is the third prophetic speech in the book. It is addressed to the priests (v. 11), which presumably includes Joshua the high priest, who was an addressee of the first two speeches (1:1; 2:2). On the same day, a fourth speech is later addressed to Zerubbabel (2:20–23), which provides a measure of symmetry to the book, with both leaders being addressed in three of the four speeches, and all on the same days. Like the first two speeches, the third prophetic speech is introduced by a date (v. 10), a problem is reported (v. 14) and there is a promise of God (v. 19). Like the first prophetic speech, another date is included that marks a significant moment in the temple reconstruction (v. 18; cf. 1:15). This date marks the founding of the temple, a point at which curse will turn to blessing (v. 19). Unique to this speech is the report of Haggai's dialogue with the priests (vv. 11–13).

Floyd (2000: 294, 639) classifies the genre as 'prophetic history', where the writer discerns how God's involvement in past situations sheds light on his involvement in the writer's contemporary situation. He further classifies it as a 'report of a prophetic symbolic action', yet I am not convinced of this description as there is no specific prophetic action involved, apart from speaking to the priests. Assis (2006: 536) categorizes this oracle as a further 'oracle of admonition', like 1:1–15.

Like the earlier prophetic speeches, this one also contains questions. There are questions directed towards the priests in vv. 12–13, whose answers form the basis for Haggai's explanation for why the people are suffering adversity (v. 14). A final two questions in v. 19 mark an abrupt turn (Craig 1996: 242) from curse to blessing. The passage functions to explain further why the returned exiles are suffering adversity and challenges them (and later readers) to return to Yahweh in obedience in view of his promised blessing.

A number of scholars have suggested that 2:10–19 was originally placed at the end of 1:15a (Chary 1969; Elliger 1982; Amsler 1988). Wolf (1988: 57–60) relocates only 2:15–19. However, these views have largely fallen out of favour. Clark and Hatton (2002: 42) rightly contend, 'There is no textual support for changing the traditional order of the verses either in Hebr. manuscripts or ancient translations; and furthermore, there is no support from discourse analysis for any such change.'

Comment

2:10. The third prophetic speech is introduced by a dating formula with the order of day, month and year reversed from 1:1, but the same order as 1:15, perhaps playing down the significance of Darius at this point (Darius is not mentioned at all in the introduction to the fourth speech in 2:20). In addition, the description of Darius as 'the king' is not present (cf. 1:1, 15). This suits the wider thematic movement of the book, which shifts from judgment (represented by a foreign king; see 'Comment' on 1:1) to blessing and hope, including the hope for a future Davidic king in the final prophetic speech (2:20–23).

The date corresponds to 18 December, exactly three months after 'they came and they did work in the house of the LORD of hosts their God' (Hag. 1:14–15). The same date is repeated in 2:18 as the date 'when the temple of the Lord was founded' and 2:20 as the date of the fourth speech to Zerubbabel. There is no known significance of this date for any festival in Haggai's day, but it later came to mark the beginning of the festival of Hanukkah, which commemorates the rededication of the temple after its destruction by Antiochus Epiphanes in the second century BC.

11. Haggai is instructed by Yahweh to 'ask the priests [for] a ruling'. The word translated 'a ruling' is *tôrâ*. Meyers (1983: 71) argues that this is a new idiom (similar to Mal. 2:7), where the priests are asked to render a decision on a matter of ritual purity on the basis of the legal texts of the Pentateuch. The Pentateuch indicates that the priests are interpreters of the law (*tôrâ*) and the ones who were to distinguish between the holy and the common, between the clean and unclean (Lev. 10:8–11; Deut. 17:8–13; 33:10). That they functioned (or failed to function) this way is evident in the prophets (e.g. Hos. 4:6; Jer. 18:18; Ezek. 7:26; 22:26; Zeph. 7:4). There is a similar situation in Zechariah, where a delegation is sent from Bethel to the priests of the temple (and the prophets) with a question about fasting (Zech. 7:2–3).

12–13. The first question concerns the transfer of holiness (v. 12). 'Consecrated meat' is meat made holy through sacrifice. It is most likely from a 'fellowship offering' since it could be carried and eaten by the one who offered it (cf. Lev. 7:15–16). Other offerings were either burned completely by the fire of the altar (e.g. Lev. 6:23, 30) or given to the priests (e.g. Lev. 2:10; 5:13; 7:10). In Haggai's day, people wore long robes they could fold up to carry goods in. The first question is: If the fold touches some other food, will that food become consecrated? In the holiness system, the answer is clearly 'no'. Consecrated meat made the garment holy (see Lev. 6:27), but the garment could not then pass on the holiness to another object. The situation described here is transfer 'at a second remove' (Milgrom 1991: 444–445).

A second question shows the opposite movement: 'If a defiled person touches any of these [the foods listed in v. 12], will it [the food] become defiled?' A 'defiled person' (*ṭĕmē'-nepeš*) is someone who is unclean. The term 'person' (*nepeš*) is often understood to be an abbreviation of 'dead body' (*nepeš mēt*) on the basis of comparison with Lev. 21:11 and Num. 6:6, and the full expression is substituted in translation (e.g. 'a person defiled by contact with a dead body' NIV; cf. ESV). However, the translation is awkward and a subject not present in the Hebr. has to be inserted ('a person' or 'someone'). While this gives a specific reason for the defilement (contact with a corpse), it is not necessary for the question to work. People who are defiled for whatever reason are to be isolated from the community until they have been cleansed by washing and/or sacrifice because they risk defiling others (see e.g. Lev. 13:45–46; 15:1–15; 21:11; 22:4). Priests who are defiled are also unable to enter God's presence. The affirmative answer by the priests shows defilement does transfer to objects (and persons) that are touched. Indeed, defilement transmits much more easily than holiness. This has important ramifications.

14. The questions to the priests in vv. 12–13 probably had the effect of drawing in the audience (Hill 2012a: 87). Haggai then starkly applies the lesson on consecration and defilement to the people of Judah. The expressions 'this people' and 'this nation' again imply relational distance between them and Yahweh (cf. 1:2, 12). While they had been saved and called to be a 'holy nation' (cf. Exod. 19:6), now they are defiled and it contaminates 'every work of their hands' (probably particularly their agricultural labours; cf. v. 17) and all that 'they offer there' (sacrifices offered at the altar on the temple site; cf. Ezra 3:1–3). Like the second question (v. 13), their defilement is transferred.

Petersen (1985: 82) reverses the movement to say that the people are not unclean but their work is, because the altar has not yet been purified, which then makes them unclean. Yet this goes against the natural flow of vv. 13–14. Haggai does not state the reason that the people have become defiled, but the wider context suggests it is their earlier sin of neglecting to build the temple (cf. 1:9–12). See further, Boda 2011: 21. Meyers and Meyers (1987: 58) capture the sense well: 'Failure to act in accordance with God's will in one area constitutes disobedience, or defilement, which contaminates all other activities in which the people engage.' The implication of Haggai's lesson is that the people must return to Yahweh to experience his cleansing forgiveness, and this return will be demonstrated in their building the temple (cf. vv. 15, 18). This will change the nature of their relationship with Yahweh and curse will turn to blessing (vv. 15–19).

15. Haggai urges the people to 'consider carefully, from this day'. The same expression introduces vv. 18–19. The expression 'consider carefully' (lit. 'set your heart'; cf. v. 18 [twice]) is an abbreviated form of 'consider your ways', found in 1:5, 7. As noted there, in Hebr. thought the 'heart' is the seat of the will rather than emotions, and corresponds to Western notions of the mind. The people are to consider 'from this day on', which suggests they are to consider their future (see 'Notes on the text'), yet they are to consider this in relation to their experience, which is sketched again in vv. 16–17. More specifically, the 'day' that marks the turning point is 'before you placed stone to stone in the temple of the LORD'. Placing 'stone to stone' appears to be an idiomatic expression for rebuilding the stonework of the temple. Given the description of the same day in v. 18 as 'the day when the temple of the LORD was founded', 'this day' (v. 15) most likely refers to the twenty-fourth day of the ninth month, rather than the beginning of the work on the twenty-fourth day of the sixth month (cf. 1:14–15). The beginning of the work (in 1:14) probably involved transporting supplies, clearing the site, and the like, before the stonework commenced and the temple was founded exactly three months later. Meadowcroft (2006: 190) observes a wordplay that is not present in my translation, but the same verb (*śîm*) is used in the expression 'set your heart' and 'set stone to stone', which reinforces 'the link between the state of the people's heart and the state of the temple'.

16–17. There are several difficult translation issues in v. 16, but the general sense is clear (see 'Notes on the text'). Like 1:6, 9–11, the curses of the national covenant with Israel are again in view. In v. 16, agricultural expectations are halved or less. The type of produce is not specified in the first instance, but a 'heap' (*'ărēmâ*) usually refers to some kind of grain (e.g. Ruth 3:7; Neh. 13:15), though it may refer to produce more generally (e.g. 2 Chr. 31:6, 8–9). In addition, the yield of wine was only 40% of expectation. A lack of grain and wine is earlier mentioned in 1:6, 11.

V. 17 offers an explanation for the low crop yields in v. 16. In Deut. 28:22, Yahweh threatens the curse of 'blight and mildew' on his people if they should forsake him. This curse is also found in Amos 4:9, before the exile, as a warning so that Yahweh's people might return to him. Blight is the browning of plant leaves caused by dry heat. Mildew is a fungal infection prevalent when there is excessive moisture. Both of these would destroy crops, as would hail, which was one of the plagues on the Egyptians (cf. Exod. 9:13–32). Like 1:11, these curses come by the hand of Yahweh ('I struck'). Yahweh also struck 'all the work of your hands' (cf. v. 14), which in the context suggests all their agricultural labours, rather than any prior work on the temple. Yahweh's purpose is that his people might 'return' or 'repent', a word that must be supplied since it is strangely absent from the MT (see 'Notes on the text'). In recalling the past, Haggai is calling on the people to repent at this time (Hildebrand 1989: 165–166).

18. The charge to 'consider carefully' is repeated (cf. v. 15) and then slightly less emphatically at the end of the verse (see 'Notes on the text'). The date is specially marked for attention and is the same date as 2:10, 20. This date is a turning point and seems to have great significance. For this reason, many commentators follow the hypothesis of Petersen (1974: 366–372), based on the work of Ellis (1968), that this refers to a special ceremony of rededication. Petersen's suggestion is built on the discovery that Mesopotamian cultures attest what is called a *kalû* ceremony at the rededication of a temple. When an earlier temple had been destroyed, a stone or brick was taken from the previous structure and then ceremonially laid as the foundation of the new temple. The purpose appears to be to establish continuity between the former and later temples and ritually purify the site. See also Halpern 1978. However, a measure of caution is called for in accepting the hypothesis that an Israelite version of the *kalû* ceremony occurred in Haggai's day, especially when Israel is called on many times not to assimilate the cultural practices of other nations (cf. Ezra 4:1–5; 9:1–15). The text of Haggai does not directly refer to such a ceremony. Yet this passage does highlight the date 'when the temple of the LORD was founded' (v. 18) and when they 'placed stone to stone' (v. 15). The fact that exactly two months later the governor Zerubbabel is said to be responsible for it (Zech. 4:9; cf. 1:7; 8:9) also indicates that it was an important event. In addition, Ezra 3:10–13 refers to the foundation of the temple being laid with praise, singing and shouting, some seventeen years earlier in 538 BC. If the event in Haggai's day was merely an act of construction, then why was it needed twice? This all suggests that the founding of the temple was some kind of ceremony, but its details are lost.

19. A 'grain pit' (*mĕgûrâ*) is a hole dug in the ground for storing grain, rather than a 'barn' (Nogalski 2011: 791). The 'vine', 'fig', 'pomegranate' and 'olive tree' are all domestic trees and shrubs in Israel (Koops 2012: xiv). Their fruit is associated with peace, prosperity and blessing (see e.g. Num. 13:23; 1 Kgs 4:25).

Commentators are fairly evenly divided about whether the rhetorical question 'Is the seed still in the grain pit?' should be answered 'yes' or 'no', and whether the second phrase is a further question (to be answered 'yes' or 'no', or a positive or negative statement; see 'Notes on the text'). Floyd (2000: 293) is representative of those who read this verse positively. He says, 'the people's support of the rebuilding project has indeed led to increased prosperity in only a very short time . . . Yahweh's promise of socioeconomic blessings is already being fulfilled, thus engendering confidence in his intentions to bless the project in other ways as well.' On the other side, Boda (2004: 149–150) argues the first two phrases are negative, based on the date of the prophecy and the agricultural cycle:

> the completion of seeding in mid-December leaves the people little on which to survive until the next harvest . . . grapes, figs, pomegranates . . . were harvested in the early fall (August/September), while olive trees bore fruit in the later fall (September–December). Now from the vantage point of mid-December, the prophet reminds them that the harvest is over and there is no fruit.

On balance, the phrase 'from this day' (v. 19), which is repeated through the passage (vv. 15, 18), indicates that blessing lies in the future rather than the present and so the rhetorical question should be answered 'no', and the second phrase be understood negatively. This is the sense of ESV, NIV and NASB. However, the promise 'From this day I will bless' raises the expectation in this third prophetic speech that since the people have turned to Yahweh and founded the temple, curse will soon be replaced by blessing.

Explanation

Haggai's third prophetic speech is given a little over two months after his previous one and exactly three months after work began on the temple (1:14–15). The date marks the day when the temple was founded, a significant event that marks a turning point in Yahweh's relationship with his people. Their progress on the temple demonstrates that they have turned back to Yahweh in obedience and he now promises that curse will soon turn to blessing.

Haggai highlights the significance of Yahweh's change of stance towards his people by first engaging the priests in a dialogue about the transfer of holiness and defilement. While strange to most people today, the ancient Israelite viewed the world through the lens of what was clean and unclean, what was holy and what was defiled or profane. This 'holiness system' is articulated in Leviticus with the purpose of understanding God's holiness and what it means for Israel to be his holy people (Wenham 1979: 18–29). Sin and death made people unclean and defiled, and various rituals such as isolating, washing and sacrifice were needed to cleanse and make holy. In Lev. 10:10, Aaron and the priests were charged with the responsibility to 'distinguish between the holy and the common, between the unclean and the clean'. Haggai engages with the priests of his day in a discussion on this topic to demonstrate that because the people are defiled, so is all that they do and all that they offer to Yahweh (v. 14). The remarkable thing is that one would expect their sacrifices to bring cleansing, but Yahweh says that what the people offer is defiled. This is consistent with other places in the OT which teach that obedience is more important than sacrifice (e.g. 1 Sam. 15:22; Ps. 40:6–8; Isa. 1:10–20; Jer. 7:22–23; Hos. 6:6; Mic. 6:6–8). In his third prophetic speech, Haggai implies that now the people have rallied to rebuild the temple in obedience to Yahweh's word (cf. Hag. 1:12–14), they demonstrate that they have finally returned to Yahweh (cf. v. 17) and he will restore the blessings of the covenant (v. 19).

Haggai does not explain exactly how Yahweh will cleanse the people from their defilement, and many see the building of the temple itself as having a key role in this. For instance, Sweeney (2000b: 551) says, 'The people have not been properly purified by the presence of the Temple, and all that they touch must therefore be considered impure or unfit for sacred use on the altar until the people are properly sanctified.' But this cannot be the whole solution since the people had a temple in the past and were defiled. Haggai's contemporary Zechariah has a lot more to say about how the people will be cleansed, and, among other things, links cleansing with the work of a future Davidic king who will also serve as a priest (Zech. 6:12–13). Through this king's death a fountain will be opened to cleanse the inhabitants of Jerusalem from sin and impurity (Zech. 12:10 – 13:1). Jesus is the one who ultimately fulfils these hopes. He is the one who cleanses the unclean with a touch (e.g. Mark 1:40–42). The writer to the Hebrews explains how Jesus' sacrifice in the 'more perfect tabernacle that is not made with human hands' (9:11) is God's ultimate act of cleansing and forgiveness for sin. Having been cleansed, Christians are to persevere in hope (10:23), hold on to faith (10:39) and spur one another on towards love and good deeds (10:24). Indeed, Hebrews speaks of the sacrifices Christians are to make, which include praise ('the fruit of lips that openly profess his name'), doing good and sharing with others (13:15–16).

Returning to Yahweh ('repentance') is a major theme through the Book of the Twelve, most prominent at the beginning (Hosea, Joel) and end (Zechariah, Malachi). The curses the people have experienced as God's judgment (vv. 16–17, 19) are also an expression of his holiness and love since he desires repentance in his people and restored relationship. The book of Haggai stands as a testimony to God's grace to those who repent and obey.

This passage comes to a climax with the promise of blessing (v. 19). Blessing is a theme that traverses the Bible. God's purpose since creation was to dwell among his people and bless them (Gen. 1:28). Sin alienates people from God and brings his curse (Gen. 3:14, 17), but Yahweh commits himself to bring blessing to the world through his covenant with Abraham and his descendants (cf. Gen. 12:2–3). Similarly, Yahweh's covenant with Israel entailed enjoying his many blessings in the Promised Land (e.g. Deut. 28:1–14), but should Israel turn from God, they would experience his curses (Deut. 28:15–68). As I have noted, this is the backdrop for understanding Haggai's situation – the people were experiencing the curses of the Mosaic covenant on account of disobedience for not building the temple, but, because they have repented, God now promises blessing. The books of Zechariah and Malachi at the end of the Twelve Minor Prophets give evidence that this repentance was only ever short-lived and the nation awaited the full experience of God's blessing on a future 'day', a day that has come and will come in Jesus Christ (e.g. Eph. 1:1–10). This 'day' is also anticipated in the final speech of Haggai (2:23).

HAGGAI 2:20–23

Translation

[2:20]And the word of the LORD came a second time to Haggai on the twenty-fourth [day] of the month, [21]'Say to Zerubbabel, the governor of Judah, "I will shake the heavens and the earth. [22]I will overturn the throne[s] of kingdoms and I will exterminate the power of the kingdoms of the nations, and I will overturn chariot[s] and their riders, and horses and their riders will fall – each by the sword of his brother. [23]On that day, declares the LORD of hosts, I will take you, Zerubbabel son of Shealtiel, my servant, declares the LORD, and I will set you as the signet ring, for I have chosen you, declares the LORD of hosts."'

Notes on the text

2:20. The word for 'day' is not present (cf. 2:1, 10) and must be understood by analogy with 1:1, 15.

21. LXX has 'Zerubbabel, son of Shealtiel' (cf. 1:1, 14; 2:2). It also adds at the end of the verse, 'and the sea and the dry land', probably to conform with 2:6.

'will shake': *marʿîš* is a hiph. ptc. This can indicate imminent action or action that is already in progress (cf. 2:6) (Arnold and Choi 2003: 81), but this is not always the case (see 'Notes on the text' for 2:6).

22. 'chariot[s] and their riders': lit. 'a chariot and its riders'.

After 'their riders' LXX adds, 'and I will overthrow all of their power, and bring down their borders, and strengthen my chosen ones'.

Form and structure

A fourth and final prophetic speech is given on the same day as the third (cf. 2:10). This speech is directed towards Zerubbabel, who is also an addressee of the first two speeches (cf. 1:1; 2:2). Since the third speech to the priests presumably included Joshua, this fourth speech to Zerubbabel provides a balance to the book as the leaders are addressed in three of the four speeches and all are addressed in speeches on the same days. Like the first three speeches, this speech begins with a date (v. 20). The dominant feature is a promise of God (vv. 21–23). Like the second speech, it looks towards a time when God 'will shake the heavens and the earth' (cf. 2:6) and looks to Yahweh's acting dramatically on the world stage.

With the restoration of Yahweh's house under way, Yahweh reaffirms the earlier promises to David concerning his house (i.e. his dynasty). Motyer (1998: 1000) observes how the book of Haggai captures the sequence of 2 Sam. 7, where David who wanted to build a house for Yahweh learns that Yahweh has plans to build a house for him (cf. Ps. 78:68–72). The link between the two houses is strengthened by the fact that the prophecy comes on the same day as the temple is founded (cf. vv. 10, 18, 20).

Floyd (2000: 300, 640) classifies the genre as 'prophetic promise', where Yahweh states his commitment, in the first person, to act in a certain way or bring about a specific situation. Assis (2006: 536) categorizes it as a further 'oracle of consolation', like 2:1–9. Motyer (1998: 1000) colourfully likens Haggai in this passage to 'the literary equivalent of an impressionist painter – he gives the general tone and effect without elaborate detail . . . every stroke is designed to lead the eye to what is central'. In doing this, the speech draws on many images and ideas from other parts of the OT, and it is important to identify these in order to understand exactly what is promised to Zerubbabel.

Comment

2:20. The fourth speech continues and concludes the book's narrative concerning the word of Yahweh and its work. The word comes 'a second time to Haggai' on the same day as the third speech (v. 10) and the same day that the temple is founded (cf. vv. 15, 18). In this instance, there is no reference to Darius in the dating formula (see 'Comment' on v. 10), possibly because this speech focuses on the hope for a future Davidic king.

21. The speech is twice directed towards Zerubbabel (see 'Comment' on 1:1). In the first instance (v. 21), Zerubbabel is called 'governor of Judah' (cf. 1:1, 14; 2:2), and in the second (v. 23), he is 'son of Shealtiel' (cf. 1:1, 12, 14; 2:2). This is possibly because the first part of the speech in vv. 21–22 focuses on the power of the nations, and the title 'governor of Judah' is a reminder that Judah is a small minion of a large empire. The speech promises that this situation will be overturned. The second part of the speech in v. 23 concerns the future of the house of David, and so Zerubbabel's descent from Shealtiel and hence his Davidic lineage is underscored (cf. 1 Chr. 3:17).

This speech repeats a clause from the second speech, 'I will shake the heavens and the earth' (2:6). It looks to a time when Yahweh will act dramatically on the world stage (see 'Notes on the text' and 'Explanation').

22. The images in this verse resonate with many OT passages. Haggai paints a picture of the future in terms of the nation's past. The verb 'overturn' (*hāpak*) is used often to describe Yahweh's judgment of Sodom and Gomorrah (Gen. 19:25, 29; Deut. 29:23[22]; Amos 4:11). The 'throne[s] of kingdoms' refers to the kings of the foreign nations who will be overturned. It is akin to what Yahweh will do to foreign kings and their nations in the royal Pss 2 and 110 if they do not acknowledge Yahweh and his anointed king. Similarly, Yahweh will also 'exterminate the power of the kingdoms of the nations', a power that was particularly exerted by Persia in Haggai's day. 'I will overturn [*hāpak*] chariot[s] and their riders' brings to mind the song of Moses in Exod. 15, which celebrates Yahweh's conquest of the Egyptians in the exodus (cf. 14:26–28; Jer. 51:21). The verb 'overturn' (*hāpak*) is also used in Exod. 15:5. There are also similarities to Isaiah's victory song in Isa. 43:16–17. The image of an army falling 'by the sword of his brother' echoes Gideon's defeat of the Midianites in Judg. 7:22 (cf. Ezek. 38:21; Zech. 14:13). In drawing together all these images, Haggai indicates that there is continuity between what Yahweh has done in the past for his people and what he will do in the future (Petersen 1985: 105).

23. Yahweh's action is set in an eschatological context: 'on that day'. This is the only instance of this phrase in Haggai, but the idea of a future 'day' appears some twenty-five times across the book of Zechariah and eight times in the final chapters of Malachi (from 3:2). The phrase is also used by earlier prophets to refer to the time when Yahweh will establish his kingdom on earth in glory (e.g. Hos. 1:5; 2:18; Joel 1:15; 4:18; Amos 9:11). Petersen (1992a: 579) summarizes the features of the prophetic expectation 'on that day': the coming of Yahweh (often pictured in military terms); Yahweh's enemies receiving their just deserts; those who fear Yahweh (including the nations) being incorporated into his kingdom; his kingdom bringing a time of paradise in the land; the mediation of Yahweh's rule through a righteous Davidic king; and a new covenant. Several of these elements are present in this brief final passage of Haggai, but the focus is Yahweh's covenant with David: 'Your house and your kingdom will endure for ever before me; your throne will be established for ever' (2 Sam. 7:16). Here the overthrow of foreign powers (v. 22) sets the stage for the renewal of the Davidic throne (Patrick 2008: 44).

A mosaic of terms with Davidic associations is pasted together in this final verse. As Yahweh 'took' (*lāqaḥ*) David from tending the flock and appointed him ruler (2 Sam. 7:8; Ps. 78:70), so he will 'take' (*lāqaḥ*) Zerubbabel. The term 'my servant' is used with Davidic overtones in the prophets, not least because the designation 'my servant' is used thirty-one times of David, including twice in 2 Sam. 7 (vv. 5, 8; cf. Pss 78:70; 89:3;

132:10; Isa. 42:1; 52:13; Ezek. 34:23; 37:24) (Dempster 2007). The designation 'son of Shealtiel' sets Zerubbabel in the Davidic line, as noted above (cf. 1 Chr. 3:17). In addition, David was 'chosen' by Yahweh (1 Sam. 16:8–12; 2 Sam. 6:21; Ps. 78:70; Isa. 42:1), and now Yahweh says he has chosen Zerubbabel. But what is he chosen for?

The key term that helps to explain what Zerubbabel is chosen for is the term 'signet ring' (*ḥôtām*). A 'signet ring' or 'seal' was a symbol of authority for a king and used to authenticate royal documents and legal pronouncements (e.g. Gen. 28:18; 1 Kgs 21:8). The 'signet ring' is a reference to Jer. 22, where the Davidic king Jehoiachin (aka Coniah) is judged on account of his predecessors forsaking justice and righteousness. Yahweh pronounces the following punishment: '"As surely as I live," declares the LORD, "even if you, Jehoiachin son of Jehoiakim king of Judah, were a signet ring on my right hand, I would still pull you off"' (Jer. 22:24). As the Davidic king, Jehoiachin is the earthly representation of Yahweh's authority (like a signet ring), yet Jehoiachin will be pulled off Yahweh's right hand in judgment (Patton 2013).

This is exactly what happened when the Babylonian king Nebuchadnezzar removed Jehoiachin from the throne and took him into exile in Babylon just before Jerusalem fell in 586 BC (2 Kgs 24:8–17). Yahweh did indeed cast off his signet ring and disown his anointed (cf. Ps. 89:38–45). As part of this judgment oracle, Jeremiah says:

> Record this man as if childless,
>   a man who will not prosper in his lifetime,
> for none of his offspring will prosper,
>   none will sit on the throne of David
>   or rule any more in Judah.
> (Jer. 22:30)

At the same time, in the very next chapter, Jeremiah promises:

> The days are coming . . .
>   when I will raise up for David a righteous Branch,
> a King who will reign wisely
>   and do what is just and right in the land.
> In his days Judah will be saved
>   and Israel will live in safety.
> This is the name by which he will be called:
>   The LORD Our Righteous Saviour.
> (Jer. 23:5–6; cf. 33:15–16)

Hence Jeremiah did not envisage that the judgment against Jehoiachin would ultimately negate the Davidic covenant; rather, the removal of the Davidic king was only for a time (cf. 2 Sam. 7:14; Ps. 89).

This is the essential background to understand what is promised to Zerubbabel here. Haggai is not saying that Zerubbabel is the Messiah (contra Clines 1994: 77). Clearly, he was not, and, if Haggai is saying this, it is difficult to account for the preservation of his book since he got it so wrong. The suggestion of Kashow (2013) that Haggai's promise is to be understood as conditional is unlikely as it is too important a point to be only implicit (cf. Zech. 4:9; 6:15). Instead, now that the people have returned and the building of Yahweh's house is underway, this final prophecy that Yahweh will set Zerubbabel 'as a signet ring' amounts to a statement that Zerubbabel will re-establish the Davidic line in Jerusalem. This is an effective guarantee of Yahweh's promise to David concerning his house, that at a time in the future he will raise up a righteous Davidic king, the Branch or Shoot, a promise reiterated by Zechariah (cf. Zech. 3:8; 6:12). Indeed, the book of Zechariah offers the best elucidation of these promises to Zerubbabel.

Explanation

With the restoration of Yahweh's house (the temple) under way, and Yahweh promising future blessing (v. 19), this final prophetic speech reaffirms the earlier promises to David concerning his house (dynasty). A number of scholars dispute this and argue there is nothing royal here (Dumbrell 1978: 39; Rose 2000: 215–218, 239; Goswell 2010: 77–90). Yet the link between the two houses is seen not only in the vocabulary, but also the structure of the book and the wider theology of the OT. The prophetic speech is given on the same day as the temple is founded (cf. vv. 10, 18, 20), which links the two. Furthermore, in the OT kingship and temple are intertwined from creation, with Adam and Eve created to serve as priest-kings in the garden sanctuary, representing Yahweh's rule to the world (Gen. 1:26–28; 2:15). This role later devolved to the nation of Israel, who were to be priestly kings (Exod. 19:6) in the sanctuary of the Promised Land (Exod. 15:17), representing Yahweh's rule to the nations. Within Israel's history, the roles of priest and king were separated, but the institutions of kingship and temple were still central, seen especially in the covenant and promises in 2 Sam. 7 (cf. Jer. 33:17–22). With the exile, the temple was destroyed and the king removed from the throne, but the prophets consistently held out hope for the restoration of both of these institutions. I have noted the hope of the earlier prophets for a new temple in the 'Explanation' of 1:1–15. The hope of the earlier prophets for a future Davidic king or 'Messiah' is extensive and seen in passages such as Isa. 9:6–7; 11:1–10; 16:4–5; Jer. 22:4; 23:5–6; 30:9; 33:15–26; Ezek. 21:26–27; 34:23–24; 37:21–25; Hos. 3:5; Mic. 4:8 – 5:5[4:8 – 5:6]; Amos 9:11–15. See further, Block 2003, Boda 2007, Petterson 2010 and Rydelnik 2010. While much of Haggai has focused on the restoration of the temple, this final prophetic speech looks to the restoration of the Davidic throne.

The exact timing envisaged by Haggai for the coming of this king poses some difficulties. If, as I have argued, this passage promises Zerubbabel that he will re-establish the Davidic line in Jerusalem in anticipation of a future Davidic king, the difficulty is that this all seems to be set 'on that day' (v. 23) when Yahweh will 'shake the heavens and the earth' (v. 21). The solution seems to be to see that to some degree the 'day' has arrived in the events taking place with the construction of the temple and the return of Zerubbabel the son of Shealtiel to Jerusalem. To some extent Yahweh is presently shaking the nations and the Hebr. may suggest this (see 'Notes on the text'). Yahweh has worked in the heart of the mighty king Cyrus who decreed that God's people could return to Jerusalem and rebuild the temple (e.g. Ezra 1:1–4), and more recently in Darius, who also decreed that the work on the temple was to continue (Ezra 6:1–12). These were world-shaking events if the language of physical upheaval is symbolic of political upheaval (Clines 1994: 65). Yet in each instance, the restoration of the temple and the Davidic dynasty in Jerusalem is only a small taste of something much bigger that Yahweh will accomplish when the physical creation is also shaken (cf. Heb. 12:26–28). In 2:6, Yahweh promises to intervene in human history to bring a greater glory to the temple than even Solomon's temple had. Similarly, even though Zerubbabel has re-established the Davidic line in Jerusalem, there is a greater hope beyond this that God will completely overturn the power of nations and their kings, and send a king even greater than David. While the earlier prophetic promises were to some degree being fulfilled in the time of Haggai, the book of Haggai looks to a future time when these hopes will be realized on a much grander scale. After Zerubbabel died, Haggai's prophecy was not thought to have failed (it would not have been preserved in that case). Indeed, one of the reasons the book of Haggai was treasured and incorporated into the canon must have been that those who read it still looked for the complete fulfilment of these promises.

This same 'now and not yet' timescale is seen in the fulfilment of these promises in the Messiah Jesus, descendant of Zerubbabel (Matt 1:12; Luke 3:27). Jesus realizes the hopes for the temple and Messiah in his life, death and resurrection, yet his ultimate triumph over the nations who oppose God and his people will be seen at his return (1 Cor. 15:20–28). Like the people in Haggai's day, Christians are to look back to what God has done in the past as assurance for what he has promised to do in the future. Christians wait in faith for the one who has come and is to come. Faith in God's promises is never wishful thinking: it is perfectly rational and grounded in the history of God's dealings with the world, and supremely in his Messiah Jesus.

ZECHARIAH

INTRODUCTION

1. SETTING

Like Haggai, Zechariah's prophetic ministry began in 520 BC, some twenty years after the first Jews returned from exile in Babylon. Earlier prophets had promised a glorious restoration, highlighted in the Book of the Twelve, with the last book before the exile, Zephaniah, promising the return and restoration of Israel's fortunes after exile (Zeph. 3:20). For the exiles who had returned to Jerusalem in Zechariah's day, the reality fell far short of these expectations (see 'General introduction'). It was a time of disappointment, disillusionment, despondency and guilt. Into this situation, Zechariah calls the people to trust and obey God's word. Zechariah deals in the first instance with the rebuilding of the city of Jerusalem and the temple. The high priest Joshua and the governor Zerubbabel have important roles to play in this project, along with the prophets. The book also looks beyond this reconstruction to the return of God, so that a cleansed Jerusalem will become the centre of worship for all nations. Central to this latter project is a future Davidic king. In proclaiming this message, Zechariah maintains that the restoration hopes of the earlier prophets still stand and he calls God's people to live in the light of God's promises.

The book of Zechariah is not easy to understand, but is richly rewarding to study. After the book of Psalms, it is the most quoted part of the OT in the passion narratives of the Gospels. It seems the book of Zechariah was part of the script Jesus followed as he went to Jerusalem. For instance, he rode a donkey into Jerusalem (cf. 9:9), and quoted the saying 'strike the shepherd, and the sheep will be scattered' (13:7) on the way to the cross. Jesus' teaching on prayer with the Mount of Olives being thrown into the sea resonates with ch. 14, along with his driving out the merchants in the temple (14:21). In addition, Jesus' betrayal by Judas for thirty pieces of silver echoes 11:12–13 (cf. Matt. 26:15; 27:3, 9), and the piercing of Jesus' side by the soldier fulfils 12:10 (cf. John 19:37). Among other things, Zechariah wonderfully enhances an understanding of the work of Jesus.

2. AUTHOR AND DATE

The prophet Zechariah is known outside his book for the key role he played, along with Haggai, in rebuilding the temple (Ezra 5:1; 6:14). His genealogy places him in a priestly family (Zech. 1:1, 7; Neh. 12:4, 16). If he is the 'Zechariah son of Berekiah' of Matt. 23:35, then he was later 'murdered between the temple and the altar'.

There are three dates in the book (1:1, 7; 7:1) that correspond to the years 520, 519 and 518 BC. Since the seventeenth century, some scholars have challenged the traditional view of Zecharian authorship of the book. While the scholarly consensus is that much of chs. 1–8 come from the prophet and were written in the period closely preceding or not long after the completion of the temple (Boda 2004: 29–30), the different literary style of chs. 9–14 and some of the historical references (such as 'Greece' in 9:13) are taken to indicate that another author wrote chs. 9–14 (some propose even further authors for different parts). My own view is that the book is essentially the product of the prophet Zechariah, with chs. 1–8 containing prophecies from before the temple's completion and 9–14 containing prophecies from after this event (the book's authorship is addressed in more detail in the next section). The book as a whole is shaped to address an audience after the completion of the temple.

3. UNITY AND AUTHORSHIP

One of the first to cast doubts on the unity of Zechariah was Joseph Mede in 1653. Mede was concerned by the attribution of the quote of 11:12–13 in Matt. 27:9–10 to the prophet Jeremiah. His solution was to posit that chs. 9–11 were not the work of Zechariah, but of Jeremiah before the exile, and that Matthew was correcting the previous attribution to Zechariah. Other scholars then considered this issue and in 1684, Richard Kidder not only agreed with Mede but argued further that chs. 12–14 were also from Jeremiah (Otzen 1964: 14).

The view that the authorship of chs. 9–14 was pre-exilic was further developed by Newcome (1785: 194–195), who argued that chs. 9–11 were written much earlier than Jeremiah, with chs. 12–14 being a separate prophecy probably also written before the exile. At the same time, Flugge published an anonymous work that divided chs. 9–14 into nine different prophecies and postulated various dates on the basis of internal evidence (Smith 1984: 243).

Reaction against a pre-exilic dating of chs. 9–14 came from Corrodi in 1792. He believed that chs. 9–14 were written sometime after the prophet Zechariah, arguing that ch. 9 was written in the time of Alexander the Great, and ch. 14 in the time of Antiochus Epiphanes (H. G. Mitchell 1912: 250). This view was supported by Eichhorn in 1824, who argued that chs. 9–14 were written much later than this. He maintained that he had found historical parallels for the events described in these chapters: 9:1 – 10:12 described the invasion of Alexander the Great in 332 BC; 13:7 – 14:21 was a song composed after the death of Judas Maccabaeus in 161 BC; and 11:1 – 13:6 came from the intervening time. Eichhorn found some support. However, defenders of the pre-exilic view became more numerous, and from 1840 onwards scholars were more or less divided between those who argued for the unity of the entire prophecy and those who argued for a pre-exilic date for chs. 9–14.

This was to change with the work of Bernhard Stade (1881). He revived the view that chs. 9–14 were written later, positing a date soon after the death of Alexander the Great during the period of the Diadochi (306–278 BC). He based this on the reference to Greece in 9:13, by reading the references to the Assyrians and Egyptians as a cryptic cipher for the Seleucid and Ptolemaic kingdoms, and on seeing references to the invasion of Alexander the Great in ch. 9. Stade also maintained that chs. 9–14 were essentially one literary unit. His hypothesis of a late date was to replace the pre-exilic view and become the dominant scholarly position throughout the twentieth century.

Recent studies in the make-up of the Book of the Twelve (see 'General introduction', 'The "Book of the Twelve"') also place chs. 9–14 at a later time by a different author. However, at present there is no consensus on when and how they were incorporated into the larger collection. For instance, James Nogalski (1993a: 53–56) contends that Malachi originally followed Zech. 1 – 8, and 9 – 14 was inserted later (after 332 BC). Aaron Schart (2000: 42) holds that Malachi was added after Zech. 9 – 14 had been added to 1 – 8. At the same time, several commentators since the 1990s have argued that chs. 9–14 should be dated to the mid-fifth century BC (Meyers and Meyers 1993; Petersen 1995; Sweeney 2000b; J. M. O'Brien 2004), and some earlier (post 515 BC) (Boda 2004). Others go further and argue for Zecharian authorship (Webb 2003; Curtis 2006; Klein 2008; Wenzel 2011; Hill 2012a). Wolters (2012c: 898) writes, 'there is currently little distance between the mainstream scholarly consensus and the traditional conservative view that the entire book of Zechariah goes back in all essentials to the prophet Zechariah himself, perhaps to different stages of his life'.

Strictly, the issue of the unity of the book of Zechariah is different from the issue of authorship. Multiple authors may write a unified work and a single author may write something incoherent. However, the issues are closely related. If one can demonstrate that the book of Zechariah is a coherent whole, then this lends support to Zecharian authorship since 'incoherence' is one of the main grounds for positing multiple authorship in the first place. Having said this, simply not enough is known about the composition of prophetic books to be certain about the process whereby prophetic speech became a written 'book' (scroll).

In arguing for Zecharian authorship, I do not mean that it had to be the prophet himself who 'put pen to paper' or 'quill to scroll', so to speak. It could have been a disciple(s) or scribe(s) who heard and recorded his preaching. Nor does Zecharian authorship necessarily exclude some kind of editing of an earlier form of the book to its 'final form'. What I mean by 'Zecharian authorship' is that the book is essentially the transmission in written form of the various prophecies and actions of the prophet Zechariah since this is how the book presents itself, and that this brings a unity to the work, especially since this process is also superintended by the Holy Spirit. While this view is consistent with my evangelical presuppositions about the nature of Scripture, I believe that history and the literature itself also support this.

In terms of history, the final editors of the book of Zechariah and those who were responsible for its incorporation into the Hebr. canon clearly considered it to be a coherent prophetic book and they attributed all fourteen chapters to the prophet Zechariah. As Michael Floyd (1999) notes, this is a historical phenomenon that those who argue for multiple authorship often fail to give adequate weight to. In the earliest extant documents from Qumran, Zechariah is a single work (even though it is quite fragmentary). There is no external evidence that the book of Zechariah ever circulated in parts. Therefore, common sense dictates that the burden of proof lies with those who would argue for disunity and multiple authorship. Furthermore, in the absence of external evidence for disunity, the evidence must come from the text of the book itself. However, I believe that the internal evidence used to support disunity and multiple authorship can be alternatively explained.

The main arguments for multiple authorship are the different literary styles of the book and the supposed different historical and theological outlooks. However, these arguments are not as strong as they may first appear. While the different literary styles of chs. 1–8 and 9–14 are undisputed, it is reasonable to account for this as the different literary genre that the prophet adopts for a different purpose (Baldwin 1972: 66–70; Webb 2003: 43–46). Furthermore, the absence of the prophet's name in chs. 9–14 can also be explained in terms of style. The often unstated assumption that Zechariah was able to write in only one literary genre is deeply flawed. It is not only refuted by comparison with other prophetic books, but from human experience.

Some have argued that the similarities of chs. 9–14 to apocalyptic mean that they must be dated later, since it is believed that apocalyptic did not arise as the literature of the persecuted until the Maccabean period. The same issue arises with the 'mini Apocalypse' of Isa. 24 – 27. While it is generally conceded that Isa. 1 – 39 comes from the prophet Isaiah, those who argue that apocalyptic is late argue that this was a later insertion into Isaiah. The reasoning is circular and raises the question 'Why could prophecy and apocalyptic not have grown up together?'

Some scholars have sought to resolve the issues of unity and authorship through computer-aided linguistic studies of the book, but these have yielded conflicting results. For instance Stephen Portnoy and David Petersen (1984), critiquing and building on the work of Yehuda Radday and Dieter Wickmann (1975), conclude that there are three distinct sections in Zechariah with different settings. In contrast, Andrew Hill (1982) concludes that chs. 10–14 are linguistically similar to chs. 1–8, and dates these chapters in the period 515–475 BC, the time of Zechariah. Again, if it is conceded that the same author is able to write in different genres, then the studies that show linguistic differences between the parts of the book cannot prove different authorship.

Others have sought to date chs. 9–14 by identifying historical events and people within the prophecy. However, this has proven rather elusive. The conquest mentioned in 9:1–8 does not reflect any known conquest, and the reference to Greece in 9:13 could be contemporary with Darius. Greece is mentioned in Isaiah, Ezekiel and Daniel (Isa. 66:19; Ezek. 27:13; Dan. 8:21; 10:20; 11:2). The identity of the shepherds in ch. 11 has yielded no consensus. See the penetrating critique of this approach by Paul Redditt (1995: 97–100).

On the other hand, several scholars note literary features of the book that indicate a unity to the book and hence support Zecharian authorship. Ronald Pierce (1984a: 281–282) finds a unity across the book in the use of the earlier prophets, the theme of salvation and the call to covenant fidelity. James Hartle (1992) notes unusual and repeated expressions that are found across the book. These include the expressions (as Hartle translates) 'from one passing through and from one returning' (7:14; 9:8; elsewhere only in Exod. 32:27 and Ezek. 35:7); 'LORD of hosts' (occurs 53 times in Zechariah, evenly throughout the book); 'says the LORD' (occurs evenly throughout the book); 'in that day' (occurs 3 times in chs. 1–8, and 19 times in chs. 9–14). While chs. 1–8 are clearly of a different literary style to chs. 9–14, Hartle notes that both parts of the book contain sign actions (6:9–15; 11:4–17), and both contain oracles. In addition, specialized theological words occur throughout the book. These include 'return' (1:3–4, 6, 16; 4:1; 5:1; 6:1; 7:14; 8:3, 15; 9:8, 12; 10:6, 9–10; 13:7); 'Spirit' (2:10[14];

4:6; 5:9; 6:5, 8; 7:12; 12:1, 10; 13:2); and 'save/deliver' (8:7, 13; 9:9, 16; 10:6; 12:7).

Brevard Childs (1979: 482–483) notes themes that run across the book, such as the security of Jerusalem (2:5; 9:8; 14:11); the judgment and conversion of the nations (1:18; 8:20; 14:6, 16); paradisal fertility (8:12; 14:6, 8); the gathering of the exiles (8:7; 10:9); cleansing and the outpouring of the Spirit (4:6; 5:4; 12:10; 13:3); and a messianic figure (3:8; 4:6 [6:12]; 9:9–10). Yohan Im and Pieter Venter (2013: 8) observe the consistent eschatological focus throughout the book, with the phrases 'on that day' (2:11[15]; 3:10; 9:16; 12:3–4, 6, 8–9, 11; 13:1–2, 4; 14:4, 6, 8–9, 13, 20–21) and 'in those days' (8:23). This continuity of themes and theology supports the unity of the book and provides a good reason for seeing chs. 9–14 arising from a later period in the prophet's ministry, after the completion of the temple (9:8).

Mike Butterworth (1992: 296) concludes that the themes of the centrality of Zion, God's deliverance and protection and his presence within, the divine provision of leadership of a sign of the new age, the cleansing of the community, and the note of universalism demonstrate a strong continuity between Zech. 1 – 8 and 9 – 14. For Butterworth, the greatest difference is the tendency towards 'collectivization' or 'democratization' of the leadership that Yahweh will provide in chs. 9–14. Yet elsewhere I have argued that this reading of the Davidic hope in 9–14 is flawed (Petterson 2009). Indeed, the hope for a future king from the house of David developed across the book is another theme that demonstrates its unity.

4. GENRE AND STRUCTURE

Most scholars divide the book into two main sections (chs. 1–8 and chs. 9–14). Some see a further division at the end of ch. 11. More recently, Edgar Conrad (1999), Marvin Sweeney (2000b), Barry Webb (2003) and Serge Frolov (2005) divide the book into two parts (1:7 – 6:15 and 7:1 – 14:21) along with an introduction to the book (1:1–6), on the basis of the dating formulae that head each section (1:1, 7; 7:1). However, the change in genre at the beginning of ch. 9 is marked. In addition, chs. 9 and 12 are introduced as 'An oracle' (*maśśā'*). For literary and thematic reasons, I consider 7:1 – 8:23 as a separate section (cf. Boda 2003a; Wolters 2012c), and divide the book into three main sections: 1:1 – 6:15; 7:1 – 8:23; 9:1 – 14:21, with a further subdivision of 9:1 – 14:21 into 9:1 – 11:17 and 12:1 – 14:21.

Chs. 1–6 contain an introduction (1:1–6), eight night visions of Zechariah (1:7 – 6:8) and a sign action (6:9–15). This section is dated to the second year of Darius (520 BC; cf. 1:1, 7), some twenty years after the initial return of exiles from Babylon. The introduction (1:1–6) issues a call to repent and a challenge to learn from the example of the earlier generations. The visions (1:7 – 6:8) largely concern the rebuilding of the community in Jerusalem with the reconstruction of the temple under Zerubbabel and the re-establishment of the sacrificial system under the high priest Joshua. Hope is held out that with evil removed, sin atoned for and Yahweh present once more among his people, Jerusalem will experience his blessing and this will flow over to the nations. There is a thematic pattern to the visions, observed by Webb (2003: 106). In visions 1–4, God returns to his people, bringing forgiveness, cleansing and prosperity. The opposite movement occurs in visions 5–8, where sin departs and all that is opposed to God is driven from the land. In each vision the prophet is shown a scene, and in most an angel interprets its key features. The sign action (6:9–15) draws on the themes of the night visions (such as temple-building). It looks towards the coming Davidic king and issues a further call to obedience. Sign actions were visible representations of the prophet's message. It is important to read the visions and the sign action against the backdrop of the earlier OT writings, as they provide keys to interpretation.

Chs. 7–8 are dated in the fourth year of Darius (518 BC; cf. 7:1). Boda (2003a) rightly argues that this section functions as a bridge or segue between chs. 1–6 and chs. 9–14. However, I disagree with his characterization of chs. 1–6 as a vision of 'realized' restoration in the present, and chs. 9–14 as 'frustrated' and directed towards the future. Both address the present and future, and there is a measure of realization and future anticipation in both (see Im and Venter 2013). This middle section of the book is framed around a question about the continued relevance of fasting, begun after the destruction of Jerusalem some seventy years earlier (7:5). This question is posed, presumably because the completion of the temple is imminent. However, it is not directly answered. Instead, it provides an occasion for Zechariah to reapply pertinent covenant requirements to the community and to call them to set their sights on the consummation of Yahweh's kingdom, when fasting will become feasting and the nations will come to Jerusalem to share in this blessing. These chapters transition the two main parts of the book.

Chs. 9–14 dramatically portray Yahweh's returning to his people and establishing his kingdom. They are clearly a different style of prophetic literature to chs. 1–8. These chapters are undated and lack any direct reference to readily identifiable persons, including the prophet himself (though the prophet plays a role in ch. 11). Structurally this section can be further divided into chs. 9–11 and chs. 12–14 on the basis of the 'oracle' (*maśśāʾ*) introductions (9:1; 12:1). While much of this section is oracular prose, 11:4–17 contains two sign actions of the prophet, with the first rehearsing Israel's history.

Many of the themes of chs. 1–8 continue through chs. 9–14, though one of the new features of this third section is warfare imagery. While some see in this section a sequence of battles that will usher in Yahweh's kingdom, this section is better read as looking at the same end-time battle from different perspectives, each focusing on the implications for different groups of people. While this is similar to the genre of apocalypse (cf. Ezek. 38 – 39; the book of Revelation), which also reflects a radical eschatology, Zech. 9 – 14 also lacks many of the defining features of apocalypse, such as pseudonymity, angelic mediation or otherworldly journey. Julia O'Brien (2004: 282) rightly comments that Zechariah frustrates modern scholarly attempts to classify it, and that the book demonstrates that in the Persian period 'prophecy' was understood in a much broader way than in contemporary scholarship. Thematically, chs. 9–14 look towards Yahweh's return to his people along with a Davidic king, the overthrow of oppressive leadership, the cleansing of his people from sin, the transformation of the created order with the nations sharing in the worship of Yahweh.

5. OUTLINE

Part 1: 'Return to me and I will return to you'	1:1 – 6:15
I. Introduction: a call to return to Yahweh	1:1–6
II. Eight night visions of Zechariah	1:7 – 6:8
A. Riders on horses	1:7–17
B. Four horns and four craftsmen	1:18–21
C. Measuring Jerusalem	2:1–13
D. Joshua cleansed, clothed and commissioned	3:1–10
E. A gold menorah and two olive trees	4:1–14
F. A flying scroll	5:1–4
G. A woman in an ephah	5:5–11
H. Four chariots	6:1–8
III. Crowning Joshua and the coming of Shoot	6:9–15
Part 2: From fasting to feasting	7:1 – 8:23
I. Justice and mercy, not fasting	7:1–14
II. Yahweh promises to bless Jerusalem	8:1–23
Part 3: Two oracles	9:1 – 14:21
I. First oracle	9:1 – 11:17
A. Yahweh's return to Jerusalem	9:1–17
1. Judgment on Israel's enemies	9:1–8
2. The coming of Zion's king	9:9–13
3. Yahweh will appear	9:14–17
B. Yahweh will care for Judah	10:1 – 11:3
C. Two shepherd sign actions	11:4–17
II. Second oracle	12:1 – 14:21
A. Jerusalem's enemies destroyed	12:1–9
B. Mourning for the One they pierced	12:10–14
C. Cleansing from sin	13:1–6
D. The shepherd struck, the sheep scattered	13:7–9
E. Yahweh comes and reigns	14:1–21

6. TEXT

This commentary is based on the Hebr. text of *Biblia Hebraica Quinta*, prepared by Anthony Gelston (2010). This reproduces the MT of the Leningrad Codex and collates it with the Aleppo and Cairo codices, noting differences in the apparatus.

Only a few pre-Masoretic texts of Zechariah survive. The Minor Prophets scroll from Wadi Murabba'ât (Mur) contains only Zech. 1:1–4 and there are no variants here. Qumran texts that include parts of Zechariah are 4Q76 (a part of 14:18), 4Q80 (small portions of 1:4–6, 9–10, 13–14; 2:10–14; 3:2 – 4:4; 5:8 – 6:5; 8:2–4, 6–7; 12:7–12) and 4Q82 (small portions of 10:11 – 11:2; 12:1–3). These are well set out in *Biblia Qumranica*, edited by Ego et al. (2005: 170–187).

BHQ also notes variant readings in the LXX; the Greek Minor Prophets scroll from Naḥal Ḥever (*Ḥev*), which is an early revision of the LXX to conform to a Hebr. text close to MT containing Zech. 1:1 – 9:5, Tg Jonathan, Syr and Vg. In most instances, divergences from MT can be explained as a misreading, translational adaptation or stylistic variation (Gelston 2010: 7*–9*). There are only a few instances when I have not followed the MT, and the reasons are noted in the commentary under 'Notes on the text' for each passage.

7. KEY THEMES

7.1. Yahweh's return

A key theme of Zechariah is Yahweh's return to his people after the judgment of exile. Ezekiel depicts the glory of Yahweh departing from the temple and Jerusalem on account of sin (Ezek. 8 – 11). This was a death sentence for Jerusalem, and destruction came by the Babylonians shortly after. Yet Ezekiel also anticipates Yahweh's return to a new temple after the exile (Ezek. 43:1–5). The presence of Yahweh among his people will be accompanied by covenant restoration and blessing.

Almost seventy years after the destruction of Jerusalem and some twenty years after the first group of Jewish people returned from Babylon to Jerusalem, Zechariah says that Yahweh has now turned from judgment to mercy (1:16; 8:3). The punishment that the nation has experienced in exile has been served and God offers mercy to his people. Furthermore, Zechariah reiterates Ezekiel's promise that Yahweh will return to dwell among his people (1:3, 16; 2:5, 10–22[2:9, 14–15]; 4:9–10; 8:3; 9:8, 14; 14:4, 9, 16–17). In view of God's promise to return, his people are to build the temple and obey his covenant requirements.

7.2. Yahweh's sovereignty

The book of Zechariah consistently calls God 'the LORD of hosts'. This phrase speaks of God's might as king (see 'Comment' on 1:3). At a time when Judah was a very small player in contrast to the might of the Persian Empire, Zechariah reminds the people who is really in control. Yahweh is the true king over all the earth (14:9). The nations are agents of his will. Yahweh will judge enemy nations (1:21; 2:9[13]; 6:8; 9 – 14), save his people (Jerusalem/Zion), and those from the nations who seek him (2:11; 8:20; 9:7; 14:16).

While Yahweh's people have an important role to play in the restoration, it is ultimately God's work (e.g. 4:6; 9:16; 12:7–10). The restoration of covenant relationship with all of its ensuing blessings also underlies much of Zechariah's hope (e.g. 8:8; 13:7).

7.3. Future hope

Zech. 1 – 6 is often said to have a realized eschatology, with Zechariah believing that Joshua and Zerubbabel were the ones who would usher in the glory of Yahweh's kingdom with the full hope of the earlier prophets being realized, but this hope was later disappointed and Zech. 9 – 14 projects the kingdom into the future. Yet a closer reading of the relevant material shows that while Joshua and Zerubbabel had a pivotal role in rebuilding the temple and re-establishing the Jewish community in Jerusalem, chs. 1–6 and the book as a whole look beyond them to a future time when God's kingdom will come (Im and Venter 2013: 7–9; Petterson 2014b).

There are several strands to Zechariah's hope. The return of Yahweh to Jerusalem to fill it with glory is central (see above, 'Yahweh's return'). Yahweh will gather his people from among the nations (2:7[11]; 6:15; 8:7; 10:6, 8–10), remove their sin (3:9; 5:1–11; 13:1–6, 9), reunite the northern and southern kingdoms (9:1, 10, 13; 10:6), and establish a new covenant relationship with them (2:11[15]; 8:8; 9:16; 13:9). The city itself will overflow with people and animals and there will be agricultural abundance (1:17; 2:4–5[2:8–9]; 3:10; 9:11, 16–17). Similar to Isaiah, Zechariah looks to the judgment of the nations (1:18–21[2:1–4]; 2:9[14]; 6:8; 9:1–8; 10:11; 11:1–3; 12:1–9; 14:2–5, 12–15, 17–19), but also expects that some from the nations will come to worship Yahweh along with his people (2:11[15]; 8:20–23; 14:16).

Zechariah also continues to hold out the hope of the earlier prophets for a future Davidic king who is central to Yahweh's restoration purposes. In chs. 1–6, this figure is called Shoot (Zech. 3:8; 6:12), picking up on the terminology of Jeremiah (Jer. 23:5; 33:15) and the imagery of Isaiah and Ezekiel (Isa. 11:1; Ezek. 17). This king will serve as a priest (6:13) by cleansing sin and reversing its consequences (3:9; cf. 13:1). Importantly, neither of these passages identifies Zerubbabel as Shoot. Instead, Shoot is a Davidic king beyond Zerubbabel and beyond Zechariah's day. I concur with Wolter Rose (2000: 141) that Zechariah's oracles concerning Shoot 'do not announce, encourage or instigate a restoration of the monarchy in the person of Zerubbabel'. See further, Petterson 2009: 87–128.

Zech. 9 portrays Yahweh's coming to re-establish a kingdom like David's (9:1–8) with a coming king who is the linchpin of a restored land and people (9:9–17). Zech. 10 – 14 then 'telescopes' different aspects of this battle to focus on different themes. Zech. 10:4–5 speaks of a new leadership Yahweh will raise up for his people who will overcome the enemies of his people. Identifying the one who is pierced (12:10) and the shepherd who is struck (13:7) has proven elusive to many. If these passages are treated in isolation from the wider context of Zechariah, then identifying these figures is uncertain. However, if these passages are read as an integral part of the book of Zechariah, then the only coherent identification within the book is that they refer to the coming Davidic king, who is killed in the coming battle by Yahweh's intent. The result is a restored covenant relationship between Yahweh and his people (13:9; cf. 11:10). Zech. 14 pictures the fruit of the coming king's work, establishing the untrammelled reign of Yahweh.

The NT identifies this king as Jesus, who fulfils the hopes for God's return (e.g. John 1:14). After the Psalms, Zechariah is the most quoted part of the OT in the passion narratives of the Gospels (see the table below). Zechariah understood, like Isaiah before him, that God's kingdom would come only with the atoning death of God's Messiah (12:10; 13:7; cf. Luke 24:25–27). The book of Revelation richly mines Zechariah's treasures and relates them to the work of Jesus. See Jauhiainen 2003. These connections will be traced in the 'Explanation' sections, when they arise. See the table below for quotations of Zechariah in the Gospels.

Zechariah passage	*Summary of content*	*New Testament passages*
9:9	The king comes to Jerusalem riding on a donkey	Matt. 21:5; John 12:15
11:12–13	God insultingly paid off for thirty pieces of silver	Matt. 27:9–10
12:10	Mourning for the One they pierced	John 19:37
13:7	The shepherd struck, the sheep scattered	Matt. 26:31; Mark 14:27

TEXT AND COMMENTARY

ZECHARIAH 1:1–6

Translation

[1:1]In the eighth month, in the second year of Darius, the word of the LORD came to Zechariah, son of Berekiah son of Iddo, the prophet, [2]'The LORD was very angry with your fathers. [3]And you will say to them, "So says the LORD of hosts, return to me, declares the LORD of hosts, and I will return to you, says the LORD of hosts. [4]Do not be like your fathers to whom the earlier prophets cried out, 'So says the LORD of hosts, turn now from your evil ways and your evil deeds.' But they did not listen and they did not give attention to me, declares the LORD. [5]Your fathers – where are they? And the prophets – do they live for ever? [6]But my words and my statutes which I commanded my servants the prophets, did they not overtake your fathers?"'

And they turned and they said, 'Just as the LORD of hosts has planned to do to us, according to our ways and to our deeds, so he has done with us.'

Notes on the text

1:1. Syr adds, 'on the first day of the month'.

'of Darius': *lĕdārĕyāweš* is a gen. use of the prep. (Arnold and Choi 2003: 113).

2. 'very angry': *qāṣap . . . qāṣep* uses a cognate object to strengthen the verbal idea (J. C. L. Gibson 1994: 114–115). A similar construction is used in 1:15.

3. 'declares the Lord': *nĕ'um yhwh* is strictly a noun phrase ('oracle' or 'utterance of the Lord'). Cf. 1:4, 16; 2:14; 3:9–10; 5:4; 8:6, 11, 17; 10:12; 11:6; 12:1, 4; 13:2, 7–8.

'declares the Lord of hosts' is not present in LXX. Neither is the third mention of 'of hosts'. The threefold repetition of the phrase 'the Lord of hosts' in MT is striking and has been retained in translation.

4. 'your evil deeds' follows K (*ûma'ălylêkem*), rather than Q reading of MT^L (*ûma'ălĕlêkem*) or MT^C (*ûma'ālĕlêkem*). Gelston (2010: 133*) argues that the noun underlying K (*m'lyl*) is most likely a genuine byform of *m'll* and is to be preferred as the *lectio difficilior* (more difficult reading). *BHQ* also suggests that both K and Q readings omit a preceding 'from' (*min*) by haplography, which is required for the sense attested by LXX and Syr ('from your evil deeds'). While possible, LXX and Syr could also have derived this sense from MT.

Form and structure

The dating formula (1:1) is a structural marker for the book (see 'Genre and structure'), and a second dating formula in v. 7 marks vv. 1–6 as a unit. This introductory section is 'a very tightly structured whole' (Butterworth 1992: 89). There are a number of words such as 'fathers' (vv. 2, 4–6), 'return/turn' (vv. 3 [twice], 4, 6), 'prophet(s)' (vv. 1, 4–6), 'ways' and 'deeds' (vv. 4, 6) that recur and connect the ideas in vv. 1–6. There is a clear logic: in the second year of Darius (v. 1), the word of God comes to the prophet Zechariah, informing him of Yahweh's anger with the fathers (v. 2). Yahweh charges Zechariah to call his contemporaries to return to him, with the promise that he will return to his people (v. 3). This charge and promise is the central idea of the introduction. The importance of rightly responding to this charge to return is then underlined in vv. 4–6. The fathers failed to heed the prophets of their day (v. 4) and were judged (v. 5–6a). The word of God has its effect – the repentance of Zechariah's contemporaries is reported (v. 6b).

The return of Yahweh to his people is a key theme of the book and thematically structures the night visions. Similarly, the call to return to Yahweh is unpacked in the eight night visions – it is given content that largely concerns the reconstruction of Jerusalem and the temple. The disobedient will be judged and driven from Yahweh's presence. The other frame to the night visions, 6:9–15, finishes on the same note as the introduction, by underlining Zechariah's prophetic status and by calling the people to obedience (v. 15). The content of this obedience is further developed in chs. 7–8.

Comment

1:1. The book of Zechariah begins by orienting its readers and hearers to its historical and theological contexts, and does this in the first instance through a dating formula (cf. 1:7; 7:1). Darius was the Persian king who succeeded Cambyses (reigned 530–522 BC) and Cyrus (reigned 559–530 BC). In 539 BC, Cyrus decreed that the Judean exiles in Babylonia could return to Jerusalem and rebuild the temple (cf. Ezra 1:1–4). However, an initial attempt to rebuild the temple came to a standstill (cf. Ezra 4:24). The date in this verse is some twenty years later (520 BC) and 'the eighth month' is late October or early November, two months after temple-building had recommenced (cf. Hag. 1:14–15).

Unlike the other dating formulae in Zechariah (and Haggai), this one lacks a day. There are various explanations for this. Sweeney (2000b: 568) suggests that the addition of 'on the first day of the month' in the Syr may indicate that the first day of the month was understood. Meyers and Meyers (1987: 90) argue that it is an editorial attempt to show that Zechariah 1 – 8 interlocks with the book of Haggai. However, as was noted in the 'Comment' on Hag. 1:1, the dating formula is doing more than simply locating Zechariah in the geopolitics of the Persian Period or in relation to his contemporary, Haggai. Curtis (2006: 94–113) demonstrates that the dating formula locates Zechariah in relation to the seventy years of desolation for Judah that Jeremiah had prophesied (Jer. 25:11–12).

Jeremiah uses a number of variations of the dating formula throughout his book (Curtis 2006: 96). Significantly, Jeremiah begins with a year and month formula (no day) that locates his ministry in relation to the kings of Judah and the captivity of Jerusalem in the eleventh year of Zedekiah, in the fifth month (Jer. 1:3). Furthermore, Jer. 39:1 uses the dating formula of year plus month (no day) with reference to the pagan king Nebuchadnezzar to introduce the description of the fall of Jerusalem to Babylon. That this period of seventy years is in mind is clear in Zech. 1:12, and its further significance will be discussed at that point.

It is therefore highly significant that the book finds its historical location with reference to the reign of Darius. Darius was no Judean king, but the king of Persia (see 'General introduction'). At this point in history, the people of God reckoned their national life with reference to a foreign king who ruled over them. The shadow of exile still hung over them.

Into this context, 'the word of the LORD came to Zechariah'. This phrase is a standard message-reception formula that indicates Zechariah's status as a prophet of Yahweh. 'Zechariah' means 'Yah[weh] has remembered', which is an entirely fitting name for a prophet concerned with the return of God to his people and the fulfilment of his covenant purposes (cf. Exod. 2:24), though the book itself does not make anything of his name. Zechariah is identified as 'the prophet' (*hannābî*). This title places him in the company of those whom Yahweh called to serve as his messengers with the role of guiding, warning, foretelling and interpreting history, as well as interceding for the people (M. J. Williams 2003). Zechariah functions in each of these prophetic roles as he speaks the word of God.

Zechariah is also identified by his family lineage: 'son of Berekiah son of Iddo'. The book of Nehemiah indicates that Iddo was one of the leaders of the priests in the days of Joshua the high priest (Neh. 12:4–7, 16), which probably meant that Zechariah was a young man. While Ezra 5:1 and 6:14 call Zechariah the 'son of Iddo' (omitting 'son of Berekiah'), the word 'son' is broad enough to mean also 'descendant' or 'grandson'. This places Zechariah in a priestly family and explains something of the book's focus on the temple and cleansing from sin (cf. the prophets Jeremiah and Ezekiel). If he is the 'Zechariah son of Berekiah' of Matt. 23:35 and Luke 11:51, then he was later 'murdered between the temple and the altar'.

2. The word that comes to Zechariah is that 'The LORD was very angry with your fathers' (cf. 1:15). In context, the 'your' (2 m. pl.) refers to Zechariah's contemporaries. The 'fathers' were those on whom the judgment of exile fell. The phrase 'your fathers' (*'ăbôtêkem*) appears twenty-two times in Jeremiah and eight times in Ezekiel, and this makes a connection with the warnings these earlier prophets gave (Stead 2009: 78). This verse indicates that the exile was an outworking of God's great anger (see 'Explanation').

3. In view of God's great anger, Zechariah is to warn his contemporaries by speaking the word of 'the LORD of hosts'. This description of God occurs three times in this verse and fifty-three times throughout the book of Zechariah. Tollington (1993: 70) notes that it is a title for God that became prominent in the early monarchy period and was associated with the theology of the Jerusalem temple and the dwelling of God among his people (e.g. 2 Sam. 7:8, 26–27). The 'hosts' are literally 'armies', and may be the armies of heaven ('angels'), armies of earth (military might) or encompass all multitudes in heaven and on earth. Since the post-exilic community had no army, its immediate reference seems to be to the armies of heaven (Stead 2009: 209). The heavenly 'hosts' of the final vision (6:1–8) makes this almost certain. Alternatively, the term *ṣĕbā'ôt* may be an intensive pl. abstract and be rendered with the phrase 'Yahweh, the Mighty' or 'Yahweh, the Almighty' (Van der Woude 1997: 1045). In any case, it is a phrase that speaks of the might of Yahweh as king and in this context in Zechariah its threefold repetition underlines the reason for listening to his word.

Zechariah is to call the people to 'return to me'. 'Return' or 'turn' (*šûb*) is a word that occurs five times in ch. 1 and four times in this section (1:3 [twice]; 4, 6, 16). Holladay (1988: 362) notes that while this word generally means 'motion to point of departure', in the context of a covenant relationship, the prophets use it to mean 'change of loyalty', 'return [to God]' or 'turn back [from evil]'. With the accompanying prepositional phrase 'to me', in this context God's call is to return to covenant obedience. The call to return is a key thematic thread through the Book of the Twelve, particularly in the opening writings (Hosea–Joel [cf. Hos. 6:1; 14:1[2]; Joel 2:12–13]) and the end (Zechariah–Malachi) (LeCureux 2012).

The resulting promise from Yahweh is, 'I will return to you' (cf. Mal. 3:7). While this also speaks of the restoration of covenant relationship after the judgment of the exilic experience, the wider context of Zechariah suggests that there is more going on here. The return of Yahweh to his people is a key motif in Zechariah (cf. 1:16; 8:3, 15; 9:8–9; 14:16–21). There is a close connection between the return of God to Jerusalem, the reconstruction of the temple, the coming of a future Davidic king, and the restoration of covenant relationship with all its ensuing blessings. These ideas are also closely connected in Ezekiel, where the staged departure of the glory of Yahweh from the temple in Jerusalem is his judgment on his people (Ezek. 10:3; 10:18–19; 11:23). Ezek. 37:26–27 envisions a reversal of the departure, with Yahweh's sanctuary and his dwelling being among his people once again. This is also pictured in Ezek. 43. Just as in Ezekiel, God departed from Jerusalem in stages, and Zechariah envisions his return in stages (see 'Explanation').

4–5. Zechariah challenges his contemporaries not to be like their fathers who rejected the word of God sent through his prophets. The 'earlier prophets' or 'former prophets' most likely refers to prophets such as Jeremiah, Ezekiel and Isaiah (Stead 2009: 55–68). Sweeney (2012a: 171) believes the designation of the books of Joshua to 2 Kings as 'Former Prophets' derives from its use here in Zechariah, where the 'former prophets' called Israel to repent and avoid the divine judgment of the Babylonian exile. The call to 'turn now from your evil ways and your evil deeds' is found at a number of places in Jeremiah (e.g. 18:11; 25:5; 35:15), but Zechariah's reference should not be limited simply to the occurrence of this phrase. There were a number of 'evil ways' and 'evil deeds' of the fathers that the earlier prophets called God's people to turn from, such as idolatry, religious hypocrisy and social injustice. Interestingly, Zechariah does not mention any of these here (though he will in ch. 7). Zechariah highlights the ultimate reason for the exile, which was not any of these individual 'evils', but the sin of rejecting the word of God that called them to repentance – 'they did not listen and they did not give attention to me'. Zechariah claims that rejecting the word of God is rejecting God himself. The rhetorical effect of this is to heighten the importance of responding appropriately to God's words through the prophet Zechariah.

Three rhetorical questions are used in vv. 5–6a, which are designed to cause Zechariah's contemporaries to reflect on the consequences of rejecting the word of God. They have the same effect on the readers and hearers of the book. The first question 'Your fathers – where are they?' is designed to make the point that the fathers are no more, as is made explicit in v. 6a.

'And the prophets – do they live for ever?' is an interr. expecting the answer 'no'. Some scholars argue that the prophets here are false prophets (there is no term 'false prophet' in the OT and the nature of the prophet must be determined from context). For instance, Beuken (1967: 100) believes that the pairing of 'the prophets' with 'your fathers' in v. 5 means that the prophets are false. The prominence of false prophets in Jeremiah (such as Hananiah), who are simply called 'prophets', also supports this. In this view, Zechariah is saying that judgment came upon the false prophets as well as the fathers. However, the prominence of true prophets in the immediate context of 1:1–6 and the expectation that false prophets would be referred to as 'your prophets' or 'their prophets' to make the contrast clear (cf. Jer. 37:19) means that on balance they are better understood as true prophets (cf. 13:2–6). The implication is that God's patience eventually ran out and the (true) prophets themselves were caught up in the judgment that fell on God's people, and they died. Hence Zechariah's audience should heed him while there is still time.

6. A final rhetorical question is set in contrast to the first two, a contrast indicated by 'but' (*'ak*). It calls on Zechariah's contemporaries to recognize that the exile was a result of God's word. The interr. 'did not' (*hălô'*) in most instances expects the answer 'yes' (Waltke and O'Connor 1990: 684, n. 48).

'My words and my statutes' is the language of Deuteronomy used to refer to the stipulations of the covenant and the covenant itself (e.g. Deut. 28:15, 45; 29:1[28:69]). 'Which I commanded my servants the prophets' underlines again the divine status of the prophetic message and that the prophets were God's servants. At the core of their task, the prophets called Israel back to the Sinai covenant and the words of God through the great prophet Moses. Meyers and Meyers (1987: 101) note that this allusion to Deuteronomy serves to remind Zechariah's hearers that the exile was the enactment of the curses of the national covenant for disobedience (e.g. Deut. 28:36–37).

'Overtake' is used throughout the OT, mostly with negative associations, of being overcome by an army or some other disaster (e.g. 2 Sam. 15:14; Jer. 39:5). The language of 'overtake' is also found in Deut. 28:15 to speak of the curses that would come upon the people for disobedience, particularly the judgment of exile (cf. Deut. 28:2, 45).

This opening section of Zechariah finishes by stating that 'they turned' and acknowledged that God had acted in accordance with his word by judging as their ways and deeds deserved. In this context, 'turned' indicates repentance. The question that divides scholars is who 'they' are who turned. Was it the fathers, or Zechariah's contemporaries, who repented? In favour of the fathers, it must be noted that the most immediate referent of 'they' is 'your fathers', and if the 'fathers' are conceived broadly as those who lived between the exile and the return (some twenty years earlier than Zechariah's address), then not only was it true that the fathers who refused to return from their evil ways and evil deeds were overcome with the judgment of exile, but also that there were those among the exilic fathers who came to recognize and confess their sin afterwards (e.g. Lam. 1:18; 5:19–22). Furthermore, Moses' programme for restoration in Deut. 30:1–5 envisages repentance before there is a return to the land (a sequence also seen in Zech. 10:9). It could be argued that this sequence is followed only if 'they' refers to the fathers, since the return to the land has already taken place.

However, against this interpretation is the rhetoric of the section, which makes the point that judgment has overtaken the fathers (v. 6) and that they are no more (v. 5). They are certainly not in a position to repent and acknowledge the rightness of God's ways (v. 6). Hence, from a rhetorical point of view, it must refer to Zechariah's contemporaries, whose repentance in response to Zechariah's preaching is reported. Boda (2003a: 61–69) argues that this repentance is rooted in penitential prayer, where the unresolved anger of Yahweh towards the earlier generation is put to rest through the repentance of a later one. This same response of repentance and obedience by the post-exilic community is reported two months earlier by Haggai (see Hag. 1:12–14). While the passages from Lamentations indicate that some of the fathers repented, and this is consistent with Moses' programme, this repentance of the fathers is less likely to be what Zechariah has in view.

Wenzel (2011: 54) argues that the repentance is that of the fathers since subsequent texts in Zechariah indicate that the people in Zechariah's generation and their leaders had not changed their hearts (including 2:6–13[2:10–17]; 4:10; 7:4–14; 8:6, 9–19; 10:1–2; 13:2–6). However, rather than showing that Zechariah's contemporaries did not repent, these passages simply demonstrate the need for ongoing repentance among God's people.

Explanation

Zechariah opens with a charge to repent in view of God's anger exhibited in the exile and the certainty of his word's achieving its purposes. The fathers are held up as an example of those who refused to repent and found themselves under God's judgment. The challenge to Zechariah's contemporaries, to the first readers and hearers of the book, and to later readers and hearers is to learn from the example of the fathers who failed to listen to the word of the prophets, and to repent by returning to Yahweh to listen and give attention to him.

Theologically, repentance is more than simply feeling sorry. Repentance is not 'doing penance' or punishing yourself for your sin. Repentance is not itself a work by which a restored relationship with God can be earned. Repentance is turning from 'evil ways and evil deeds' back to God and to obedience to his word. The call to repent issues from God's grace, as does restored relationship (see 'Comment' and 'Explanation' of 1:16). As will become clear in Zechariah, repentance is no one-time act since the prophet continues to call the people back to God. As Luther later put it, the entire life of the believer is to be one of repentance.

This opening of Zechariah shows us that 'evil' is ultimately rebellion against God. It is understood relationally as a refusal to obey and listen to his word. While the language of 'evil', rather than 'sin', is used here, it is the same nonetheless. God's response to this evil is great anger. Because of who God is, sin must be dealt with. It was the false prophets who spoke peace, when in reality God's anger had been aroused and his judgment would fall.

In the background of this passage, as the dating formula implies and as the first vision will make explicit (1:12), is God's promise to restore his people after seventy years of exile. The promise of God that 'I will return to you' introduces a key theme of the book, namely the presence of Yahweh among his people. Historically, the presence of Yahweh in the life of the nation was seen in two main institutions: the temple where God dwelt, and the king who was the agent of his rule. Indeed, this pattern is seen in the opening of the Bible, where Adam and Eve were created to rule and serve in the garden sanctuary. Just as the first human couple were exiled from the presence of God in the garden for disobedience, so Israel was exiled from the land for disobedience in the events of 586 BC with the destruction of the temple and removal of the king. The restoration of these two institutions is a key aspect of Zechariah's message. Ultimately, they come together in the Lord Jesus. He is the perfect king (Mark 8) and the one who realizes the OT hopes for God's presence in the temple in his own body (John 2:19–21). Through his perfect obedience Jesus brings God's presence and restored relationship to those who repent and put their trust in him.

The opening of Zechariah demonstrates also that God's word achieves its purposes (cf. Isa. 55:11). A contrast is made between the impermanence of the fathers and the prophets on the one hand, and the permanence and effectiveness of God's word. As secure and important as the fathers thought they were, and as seemingly impervious to the word of God as they appeared, history demonstrated a great reversal: God's word won out.

ZECHARIAH 1:7–17

Translation

1:7 On the twenty-fourth day of the eleventh month (that is, the month of Shevat), in the second year of Darius, the word of the LORD came to Zechariah, son of Berekiah son of Iddo, the prophet, 8 'I saw in the night, and look! A man riding upon a chestnut horse and he was standing between the myrtles which were by the deep, and behind him – horses: chestnut, sorrel and white.' [9]And I said, 'What are these my lord?' And the angel who was speaking with me said to me, 'I will show you what these are.' [10]And the man who was standing between the myrtles answered and said, 'These are the ones whom the LORD sent to patrol throughout the earth.' [11]They answered the angel of the LORD who was standing between the myrtles and they said, 'We have patrolled throughout the earth. And look, all the earth sits [at peace] and is quiet.'

[12]The angel of the LORD answered and said, 'LORD of hosts, how long will you not be compassionate towards Jerusalem and the cities of Judah with which you have been angry these seventy years?' [13]The LORD answered the angel who was speaking with me with good and comforting words. [14]The angel who was speaking with me said to me, 'Proclaim: So says the LORD of hosts, I am jealous for Jerusalem and Zion with a great jealousy. [15]And with great anger I am angry with the nations at ease with whom I was a little angry but they helped to [the point of] evil. [16]Therefore, so says the LORD, I have turned to Jerusalem with mercy. My house shall be built in it, declares the LORD of hosts, and a measuring line shall be stretched out over Jerusalem. [17]Again, proclaim: So says the LORD of hosts, again my cities shall overflow because of prosperity, and the LORD will again comfort Zion, and again choose Jerusalem.'

Notes on the text

1:7. 'that is': *hû'* introduces a verbless clause of identification (Waltke and O'Connor 1990: 130–131).

8. 'in the night': *hallaylâ* is an adv. acc., locating the action in time (Arnold and Choi 2003: 19). Tg adds the prep. *bě*, which makes this clear (Cathcart and Gordon 1989: 186).

'chestnut': *'ādōm* is a basic colour lexeme that represents colours ranging from 'orange' to 'brown' to 'red' and 'bright red' (Hartley 2010: 34, 119). As well as referring to horses, it can refer to human hair, the male complexion, wine, soup, dyed animal skins, and shields. When it refers to horses, it is 'chestnut' or 'bay'.

'the myrtles which were by the deep' is translated in LXX as 'in the midst of the two overshadowing mountains' (*meson tōn dyo oreōn tōn kataskiōn*), probably to harmonize it with the final vision in 6:1–8, which contains mountains and horses. Syr renders it, 'among the myrtle trees which gave shade'. See 'Comment'.

'sorrel': *śārōq* is a colour lexeme with restricted use. It focuses on a 'bright, glowing light color', which may have a 'yellowish, golden, or reddish tint' (Hartley 2010: 37, 174). As a breed of horse, it is 'sorrel', 'bay' or possibly 'greyish'. It also identifies a vine that bears grapes of this colour (Isa. 16:8), which suggests it is not 'greyish'.

'white': *lābān* is an achromatic colour lexeme and references light colours from 'light grey' to 'light yellow' (Hartley 2010: 33). It modifies 'teeth' (Gen. 49:12) and 'snow' (Isa. 1:18; Ps. 51:9), which confirms that 'white' is the focal colour.

Some LXX manuscripts add an additional group of horses after the chestnut ones ('and speckled': *kai psaroi*), which seems to be an attempt to harmonize with the horses in 6:2–3.

12. 'these seventy years' is lit. 'this [*zeh*] seventy years' (cf. 7:5).

13. 'who was speaking': *haddōbēr* is an attrib. or adj. ptc.

'with good and comforting words' translates *dĕbārîm ṭôbîm dĕbārîm niḥumîm*. The descriptions are in parallel; 'with' is understood.

14–15. 'I am jealous . . . with a great jealousy' and 'with great anger I am angry' both use a cognate object to express a concrete instance of the verbal action (J. C. L. Gibson 1994: 115).

16. Syr has 'LORD of hosts' in the first instance of 'LORD'.

17. 'because of prosperity': *miṭṭôb* is best understood as a causal use of *min* (Arnold and Choi 2003: 117).

LXX has 'will have mercy' (*eleēsei*) on Zion rather than 'will comfort' Zion. This change is understandable in the context of vv. 12 and 16, hence MT is followed as original.

'choose Jerusalem': the object of the verb 'choose' (*bāḥar*) takes the prep. *bĕ* (cf. 2:12[16]; 3:2).

Form and structure

Zech. 1:7 – 6:8 contains eight visions of the prophet Zechariah. While the language of 'vision' (*ḥāzôn*) is not used, they are to be understood as visions rather than dreams, since they report what Zechariah 'saw', and in 4:1 he is 'awoken' by an angel to be shown the menorah, about which he then asks questions. Some scholars want to make a clear distinction between the 'visions' and 'oracles' in these chapters, but these are not always possible to demarcate. Sometimes Zechariah speaks within the visions (e.g. 2:4[8]; 3:5). Stead (2014) demonstrates that vision and oracle must be read together as a literary unit.

One of the functions of the visions is to give content to the initial call to repent in 1:1–6. Repentance will involve returning from exile (2:6–8), rebuilding the city (1:17; 2:4), rebuilding the temple (1:16; 4:7–10), singing and rejoicing (2:10), along with covenant obedience (3:7; 5:4, 8). Yet this first vision along with the introduction (1:1–6) demonstrate that the mercy of God is logically prior to these actions.

While not strictly apocalypse, the visions of Zechariah share many of the features of this genre, and it is helpful to interpret them in this light. For instance, sometimes in apocalyptic imagery some features of the vision simply contribute to the overall picture rather than having specific significance, like the 'myrtles which were by the deep' and the colours of the horses. Similarly, some aspects of the vision are elusive; for instance, do the horses speak in v. 11, or are there unmentioned riders who speak? We must not be too troubled by these things but leave them in the background and focus on the elements highlighted and explained in the text.

In terms of structure, 1:7 functions as a heading for the section that runs to the end of chapter 6. This section not only contains eight visions, but finishes with a sign action that Zechariah is to perform (6:9–15). In 1:8–17, Zechariah is shown a vision (v. 8) for which he asks for an explanation (v. 9a). A dialogue between Zechariah, an interpreting angel and various persons in the vision results (vv. 9b–11). The angel of the Lord then asks a question (v. 12). This then results in an extended reply from Yahweh (vv. 13–17), which ties into the vision and some of the themes of the introduction.

Butterworth (1992: 91–92) observes that 'mercy', 'good' and 'comfort' in vv. 12–13 are taken up again in vv. 16–17, and 'Jerusalem' and 'LORD of hosts' recur throughout (vv. 12, 14, 16–17).

Comment

1:7. The introduction to the first night vision is given with another dating formula, this time with a day. The first word from God to Zechariah, calling the people to repent, came in the eighth month (1:1–6). This word comes towards the end of the eleventh month, hence around three months later. The eleventh month is identified as 'Shevat'. Baldwin (1972: 94) notes this is the Babylonian name adopted by the Jewish people after the exile (cf. Chislev in 7:1). Like dating to the reign of the pagan king Darius, this speaks of a situation that should not be – God's people are reckoning their history with the language of the nations.

Since this verse is so similar to 1:1, many of the comments regarding that verse are relevant here, such as the relationship to Jeremiah's seventy years of desolation, a theme that becomes explicit in v. 12. The date is best understood as the date on which all the visions were received, rather than the date when Zechariah spoke. It must be assumed that Zechariah's proclamation came shortly afterwards.

8. The word of God initially comes to Zechariah as something that he 'saw' (*rāʾāh*), hence a vision (see 'Form and structure'). There is a long tradition of prophets 'seeing' the message that they then proclaim (e.g. Num. 12:6–8; 1 Sam. 9:9; Amos 7:1). While we may be curious about how the message impinged itself on the consciousness of Zechariah, this information is not given. What is clear is that Zechariah was in no doubt that he had been given a message from Yahweh.

The phrase 'in the night' (*hallāylâ*) is an adv. acc. of time (Arnold and Choi 2003: 19), and this accounts for the lack of prep. in the Hebr. (cf. Gen. 20:3; 31:24; 1 Kgs 3:5; 2 Kgs 25:4; Neh. 4:22[16]). There are a couple of indications that all the visions were given during this night. First, each of the subsequent visions begins with a waw cons., which serves to join them all (Sweeney 2000b: 575–576). Secondly, 4:1 says that Zechariah is awoken by an angel who returned after speaking with him. This suggests that Zechariah had momentarily fallen asleep and the visions then continue throughout this night.

The phrase 'and look' (*wĕhinnēh*) points to a newsworthy or unexpected entity (Miller-Naudé and van der Merwe 2011: 61). It also 'forcibly imposes a character's point of view on the narrator/reader' (Walsh 2009: 49). See also v. 11, and throughout Zechariah (1:18; 2:1, 3[2:1, 5, 7]; 4:2; 5:1, 7, 9 [twice]; 6:1; 9:4, 9; 11:6). The phrase 'for look' (*kî hinnēh*) may indicate the irreversibility of the accompanying promise, or its imminence (Miller-Naudé and van der Merwe 2011: 65). It occurs in 2:9, 10[13–14]; 3:8; 3:9 [twice]; 'look' (*hinnēh*) occurs in 6:12; 9:4, 9; 11:16; 12:2; 14:1.

Zechariah sees 'a man riding upon a chestnut horse'. In her captivating study on horses, Cantrell (2011: 59) argues that 'the horse was the most powerful and noble domestic animal, providing speed and invoking awe in the ancient imagination'. They were used primarily for military, royal or diplomatic purposes. The function of this chestnut horse is explained in v. 10.

The horse and its rider are 'standing between the myrtles which were by the deep'. Zohary (1982: 119) notes that myrtles are evergreen shrubs that grow to approximately 6.5 ft (2 m). They are native to the eastern Mediterranean region and are found on damp plains such as the banks of the Jordan River. The phrase 'by the deep' (*bammĕṣulâ*) has troubled many scholars (and the LXX translators; see 'Notes on the text'). This form of the word (with a qibbûṣ rather than a šûreq) appears only here. BDB 847 believes it is a 'dubious word' and suggests it may be derived from *ṣll*, which means 'to grow dark', hence referring to a dark or shadowy place such as a 'glen' or 'ravine' (ESV, NIV). However, the usual meaning of the closely related word 'deep' (*mĕṣûlâ*) (cf. 'depths'; pl. *mĕṣôlôt*, *mĕṣōlôt*, *mĕṣûlôt*, *mĕṣulôt*) makes sense here, especially given the preference of myrtles to be located near to water. In addition, the pl. form (*mĕṣûlôt*) is used in Zech. 10:11 to mean 'depths [of the Nile]'. Kline (2001: 6) notes that the prep. 'by' (*bĕ*) is often used in connection with a body of water (e.g. 1 Sam. 29:1; Ezek. 10:15, 20).

Behind the rider on the chestnut horse are other horses – 'chestnut, sorrel and white' (see 'Notes on the text'). There is a general tendency to harmonize the number and colours of these horses with those of Zech. 6:2–7, but this is unnecessary. Each of these colours is in pl. form, which suggests a herd of coloured horses, rather than only three horses. In addition, these 'horses' answer the angel of the Lord in v. 11, which implies they too have riders. This host of horses and riders who do the bidding of God connects nicely with the description 'LORD of hosts' (Zech. 1:3, 4, 6, 12, 14, 16–17). While they are not arrayed for battle here, they do represent his sovereignty over the world.

There are many suggestions for the significance of the colours. Kline (2001: 5) suggests they represent the component colours of fire. Sweeney (2000b: 577) believes they are the colours of the myrtle flowers. Similarly, Meyers and Meyers (1987: 113) think they are the colours that would be most prevalent in nature at the time of Shevat (v. 7), and hence the horses would be well camouflaged. These must remain hypothetical. We are on safer ground if we concern ourselves with how the vision is interpreted by the book of Zechariah itself. Significantly, it is not the location, colour or number of horses that Zechariah picks up on, but what they are doing (v. 10).

9. 'my lord' (*'ădōnî*) refers to 'the angel' or 'the messenger' (*hammal'āk*) who talks to Zechariah and explains many of the features of what he sees: 'I will show you what these are'. His access to God and his insights into Zechariah's visions support the translation 'angel' rather than 'messenger'. He is often referred to as 'the interpreting angel' because he interprets the key aspects of the visions (though much is left uninterpreted). This angel features in seven of the next eight visions (1:9, 13–14, 19; 2:3[7]; 4:1, 4, 11; 5:2–3, 10; 6:4). Hanson (1979: 250) notes that this angel is a feature of apocalyptic literature. There is a similarity to the 'man' of Ezek. 8:2 and 40:3 who is associated with Ezekiel's visions.

10. The 'man who was standing between the myrtles' refers to the rider on the horse who was described similarly in v. 8. Interestingly, he is the one, rather than the interpreting angel, who explains the function of the horses as 'the ones whom the LORD sent to patrol throughout the earth'. The word for 'patrol' (*lĕhithallēk* – a hith. inf. const. of *hālak*) indicates a repeated sense of 'walking back and forth', hence 'patrol' (cf. Gen. 3:8; 13:17; Job 1:7; 2 – 3; Ezek. 28:14; Zech. 6:7). The Persian Empire employed riders on horses as a form of surveillance and security. The riders of Zechariah's vision provide surveillance for Yahweh and are an expression of his sovereign rule.

The 'earth' (*'ereṣ*) or 'land' occurs forty-two times in Zechariah and has several possible meanings. The meaning must be determined from context, and in several instances is ambiguous. It can mean the 'earth', as in the whole world (e.g. 4:14; 6:5), the 'land' of Israel's inheritance (e.g. 3:9; 7:5; 11:6), the 'land' of the nations (e.g. 5:11; 6:6; 10:10), the 'earth' as opposed to heaven (5:9) or the stuff from which plants grow (e.g. 8:12). In the context here where there is a report that concerns the nations (v. 15) it has been translated 'earth', indicating the known world including the land of the nations (there is a similar 'patrol' in 6:6–7 that explicitly extends beyond the borders of Israel).

11. The ones who patrolled answer the angel. Presumably, 'they' refers to previously unmentioned riders on the groups of horses (cf. v. 8), rather than the horses themselves. Their response is given to 'the angel of the LORD'. Since he also 'was standing between the myrtles', this is best understood as a further description of the man riding the chestnut horse (vv. 8, 10).

The 'angel of the LORD' appears only in this vision and the fourth (3:1, 5–6). Elsewhere in the OT he is a somewhat mysterious figure (e.g. Gen. 22:15–16; Exod. 3:2–5). Sometimes he speaks and acts for God in a way that gives the impression that he is God in human form (cf. 3:1–2, 5–6, where he speaks as Yahweh). At other times, he is distinguished from God (as here, where he speaks to God). Some have suggested that he is an appearance of the preincarnate Christ; for example, Phillips (2007: 25). However, the NT never makes this link and so caution is called for.

The response of the riders to the angel of the Lord from the result of their patrolling mission is to report that 'all the earth sits [at peace] and is quiet'. This may initially be thought to be a good report, but the response of the angel in v. 12 indicates that this is a lamentable situation. Why is this?

The verb 'sits' (*yāšab*) can also be translated 'dwells' and is also found in 7:7, where it refers to the prosperity of Jerusalem and the cities of Judah before the judgment of exile. Here the association with 'quiet' indicates they dwell or sit at peace. The 'quiet' (*šōqāṭet*) is the relief from war such as was experienced after the conquest (Josh. 11:23; 14:15), intermittently during the time of the judges (Judg. 3:11, 30; 5:31; 8:28) and after times of conflict during the monarchy (e.g. 2 Chr. 14:1[13:23]; 14:6[5]; 20:30; 23:21). However, the Behistun Inscription records that during the first few years of Darius' reign great political turmoil threatened the Persian Empire (see 'General introduction'). How could this be described as 'quiet'? Wolters (2008: 141) argues that these were largely battles that Darius won against a Neo-Babylonian resurgence. His victories could be seen as continuing the defeat of the great foe Babylon, some twenty years earlier, hence establishing 'quiet'. Importantly, Wolters and Stead (2009: 91–92) note how the earlier prophets use 'quiet' (*šōqāṭet*) to describe the situation that will accompany restoration after the exile (Isa. 14:7; 32:17; Jer. 30:10; 46:27; Ezek. 38:11–12). Therefore the riders' report is lamentable because the prophetic expectation was that after the judgment of exile, the nations would be overthrown and God's people would inhabit the land and be quiet. Now the nations are experiencing the habitation and quiet promised to God's people, while his people remain under foreign rule.

12. The angel of the Lord responds in the form of a lament (cf. Isa. 6:11; Pss 6:4; 74:10; 80:5; 90:13; 94:3). There is a parallel with Ps. 80:5, a psalm that cries for restoration after the destruction of exile (Stead 2009: 93). Lam. 2 may also be in the background, with reference to Yahweh's 'anger' with the exilic generation (Lam. 2:6) and to his showing no 'mercy' (Lam. 2:2, 17, 21). The verb 'angry' (*zāʿam*) can also be translated 'cursed' (cf. Mal. 1:4). Clearly, this verse in Zechariah portrays the exile as an expression of God's judgment, and continues the themes of the introduction (1:1–6). On 'LORD of hosts', see 'Comment' on 1:3.

Like the introduction (vv. 1–6), this verse looks forward to the end of the judgment of exile. While Jeremiah's seventy years was implicit in the dating formula of 1:1, 7, now it is explicit. What is debated is how the seventy years should be reckoned. Is it a literal seventy years, or symbolic, representing a lifespan? In Jer. 25:11–12, the seventy years is the length of time that the people of the land will serve the king of Babylon (see Jer. 29:10). This could be understood as an approximate seventy-year period from the rise of Nebuchadnezzar in 605 BC until 539 BC, when the Persian king Cyrus came to power and decreed that the exiles could return home. Winkle (1987: 299) argues for an exact seventy years from Nabopolassar's overthrow of Assyria in 609 BC to Cyrus in 539 BC. Curtis (2006: 131) argues that for Zechariah, the seventy years are not years of exile, but years of temple desolation. This must be the case since almost two decades have passed since the first exiles returned and they still anticipate the end of the seventy years. Interestingly, the temple was destroyed in 586 BC, and Ezra 6:15 claims the temple was completed in 515 BC, which is very close to seventy years. Perhaps there was some debate among the exiles in Zechariah's day too on how the seventy years were to be calculated (this seems to be the case in Dan. 9:2). On any score, the end of the seventy years looked for the end of judgment and the restoration of God's blessing, and for Zechariah this is closely connected with the return of Yahweh and the building of the temple.

13–14. Yahweh responds to the lament with 'good and comforting words'. Stead (2009: 95–96) notes the 'striking thematic parallels' with the message of Isa. 40 – 66, where Isaiah announces the message of 'comfort' that the exile is over and God is coming to save his people (Isa. 49:13; 51:3, 12; 52:9; 61:2; 66:13; cf. Jer. 31:13). The end of the seventy years is near.

Like Isaiah, Zechariah is told to 'proclaim' (cf. Isa. 40:6). Presumably the content of the message is what is contained in vv. 14–17, and is described as 'good and comforting words' (cf. v. 17, where 'comfort' is repeated). It begins by announcing that God is 'jealous for Jerusalem and Zion with a great jealousy'. Jealousy often has negative connotations today. However, in the OT God's jealousy describes his concern for what is rightly his and his willingness to overthrow all opposition to defend it (e.g. Exod. 20:5; 34:14; Deut. 5:9). Baldwin (1972: 102) comments, 'God's jealousy is a measure of the intensity of His love towards those with whom He has entered into covenant.' Here God's jealousy is about to be expressed towards the city he has chosen (v. 17; cf. Zech. 8:2).

'Jerusalem' and 'Zion' are essentially synonymous, though Meyers and Meyers (1987: 120) believe that if there is a distinction, 'Zion' refers to the mountain of Yahweh's temple and 'Jerusalem' has a more political nuance to it, as the city of David. Together they capture the religious and political significance of the city.

15. The response that correlates with God's 'great jealousy' for Jerusalem (v. 14) is his 'great anger' with the nations. Back in 1:2, Yahweh's anger was directed towards the fathers and this anger resulted in the judgment of exile. Now that the seventy years are ending, his anger is shifting from his own people to the nations who are 'at ease' (*haššaʾănannîm*). This expression ('at ease') is used in a couple of different ways by the earlier prophets, both being relevant here. It is used to speak of those women who are condemned for their complacency about the covenant unfaithfulness of God's people, while enjoying their own prosperity (e.g. Isa. 32:9, 11; Amos 6:1). Just as God's judgment fell on his own people for their smugness, now it would fall on the nations. Secondly, 'at ease' is used to describe future blessing for God's people and Zion (e.g. Isa. 32:18; 33:20). In this use it is expressing the same motif as the report in v. 11 that 'all the earth is inhabited and at rest'. It anticipates God's coming to act on his promises through the 'former prophets' to reverse this situation, so that his people rather than the nations will experience his blessing.

The idea that Yahweh 'was a little angry but they helped to [the point of] evil' is that he used the nations as agents for the punishment of his people, but the nations overstepped the just punishment. In addition, in their pride they committed evil themselves. These ideas are present in Isaiah's critique of Assyria (Isa. 10:5–15) and Babylon (Isa. 47:6; 54:7–8) (Stead 2009: 99). Zechariah does not identify the 'nations'. While Babylon comes into focus in the next two visions, the reference at this stage is general and should probably not be limited to it.

16. 'I have turned to Jerusalem' translates the qatal (*šabtî*) with a past tense, which is usual, but not required. Many understand it as a 'rhetorical' or 'prophetic perfect', in which case it is translated with a future sense: 'I will return' (Arnold and Choi 2003: 55–56). Another option is to give it a present continuous sense: 'I am returning'. In context, v. 16 goes on to speak about the temple being built (a yiqtol with a future sense). Similarly, 8:3 uses the qatal 'I have turned to Zion' along with a weqatal, 'I will dwell in the midst of Jerusalem'. The key for deciding on the tense in my view is how the return of God is to be conceived. If the return of the presence and dwelling of God is entirely dependent on the rebuilt temple, then it must be translated as a future ('I will return'). Alternatively, if the 'return' of Yahweh speaks of God's turning from judgment to mercy with the end of the exile (suggested by 'I have turned . . . with mercy' or 'I am returning. . . with mercy') with an intensified presence of God still a future hope when the glory returns to the reconstructed temple ('my house will be built' and 'I will dwell'), then the normal translation of the qatal can stand. There are several reasons for preferring this latter interpretation (Petterson 2014b: 124). First, since this statement comes in response to the lament of the angel of the Lord in v. 12, the statement that Yahweh has turned with mercy better suits the rhetoric of the section (i.e. offering comfort). Secondly, in 1:3 the yiqtol is used to indicate the future return of Yahweh. It is unusual that if it is a future return, it is not spoken of here in the same way (or in 8:3). Thirdly, the use of the 'rhetorical perfect' would be exceptional in chs. 1–8. The only other possible instances are in 2:8[12] and 5:4, though these are unlikely (it is more common in chs. 9–14).

Fourthly, in ch. 4 God is said to be already present and at work by his Spirit to see that the temple is built. Fifthly, if the 'return' is entirely connected with the temple, one would expect the phrases to be in reverse (i.e. 'my temple will be built and I will return'). Sixthly, the same form of the Hebr. is found in 8:15, where it is almost universally translated 'again', but in context has the same sense as here. Seventhly, Hag. 1:13 declares that Yahweh is with his people, even before the temple is rebuilt, and I would argue this is the case here too.

Accompanying the turn of Yahweh towards Jerusalem with mercy is the promise that his house (the temple) will be built along with his city ('a measuring line shall be stretched out over Jerusalem'). This twin hope of restoration of city and temple is expressed in Isa. 44:28.

17. Zechariah is given a further word to proclaim. 'Again' (*'ôd*) is used four times in this verse to underline the hope of restoration: 'again my cities shall overflow because of prosperity'. While 'overflow' (*pûṣ*) is commonly used in the OT with a negative sense of Israel's being 'scattered' among the nations in the exile, here it speaks of a city overflowing on account of good things (*miṭṭôb*) that have come on account of Yahweh's return (see Gen. 45:23 for a similar use of *miṭṭôb*). It is another image of the exile being reversed. Similar imagery of an overflowing city is used in 2:4[8].

Yahweh 'will again comfort Zion' repeats the message of 'comfort' announced in v. 13. There the close parallels with the message of Isa. 40 – 66 were noted, where Isaiah's 'comfort' was the end of exile and God's salvation of his people. Zechariah promises this salvation.

Finally, Yahweh will 'again choose Jerusalem' (cf. 2:12[16]; 3:2). He will choose Jerusalem 'again' because he rejected it in the Babylonian destruction (cf. 2 Kgs 23:27). Yahweh's choice of Jerusalem is found in Deuteronomy as an expression of his sovereignty in choosing the place where he will put his name (e.g. Deut. 12:5; cf. Ps. 78:68–70). In Deuteronomy it is associated with the temple, and, as Meyers and Meyers (1987: 124) remark, this phrase therefore provides a fitting recapitulation of the themes of v. 16: Yahweh's return to Jerusalem, the rebuilding of the temple and the city.

Explanation

Zechariah's first vision is of horses that have patrolled the earth for Yahweh (modelled on Persian surveillance, like Sauron's Ringwraiths in *The Lord of the Rings*). They report that the habitation and rest promised for God's people is being experienced by the nations. The angel of the Lord laments this situation. Yahweh replies that he is about to reverse this state of affairs. His anger, experienced in the exile, is about to turn towards the nations. Jeremiah's 'seventy years' of judgment are at their end, and the nations whom God has used as an instrument of his judgment will themselves be judged. Yahweh is jealous for his city and has returned to his people in mercy. The temple and the city of Jerusalem shall be rebuilt and blessing and salvation shall come to God's people.

There are a number of rich theological themes in this passage: God's sovereignty, his anger at sin in his own people and the nations (see 'Explanation' of 1:1–6), his presence to empower, save and bless his people. Underlying all of this is God's covenant relationship with his people. This covenant is the context in which his jealousy is to be understood. The exile was his judgment for sin; yet on account of his covenant, God has not turned his back on his people for ever. He is jealous for them.

If the correct translation of v. 16 is, 'I have turned towards Jerusalem with mercy' (as I have argued above), this has an important theological implication. It makes the mercy of God prior to the call to obedience (cf. Exod. 20:2, which precedes the Decalogue). While building the temple is dependent on the people's obedience (e.g. 6:15; cf. 4:9), in the first instance God has initiated the restored relationship by his mercy. Religion says 'do' in order to earn God's favour. In contrast, Zechariah emphasizes God's mercy from which obedience is to flow.

In thinking about how Zechariah's message applies today, Zechariah's context must first be appreciated. The people in Zechariah's day had been restored to Jerusalem, but still anticipated the greater restoration promised by the earlier prophets. God had turned from his anger to compassion, and yet there was the promise of a greater realization of his presence in the future. As I hope to demonstrate more fully later in this commentary, the NT writers see the realization of this greater hope in the first instance with the coming of the Lord Jesus Christ – Immanuel (God with us). It is in Jesus that God's mercy is experienced (e.g. Rom. 12:1).

Now that Jesus has come, God's people find themselves in a similar situation to the people in Zechariah's day. Living between the two comings of Jesus, Jesus is present by his Word and his Spirit, yet there is a greater presence that Christians look forward to at his return. Like Zechariah's day, many in this age seem to be 'at rest' and 'at ease', while God is not acknowledged for who he is. Like the angel of the Lord, the souls of the martyrs in Rev. 6:10 now cry, 'How long?' Christians long for the day when God will punish the persecutors and vindicate the oppressed, when Jesus will return and put things right and God's kingdom will be seen in all its glory.

Like Zechariah in v. 14, God's people have a message to proclaim – the gospel that announces Jesus' sovereign rule (and the Messiah's death for cleansing from sin, as Zechariah will reveal). Like Zechariah's message, the gospel is 'good and comforting words' for God's people, but a message of God's anger and judgment on his enemies – it is both good and bad news! Like God's people in Zechariah's day, Christians can get seduced into living for this world as if it is all there is (cf. 1:1–6). Christians can likewise look for 'rest' and 'ease' in this world, rather than in Jesus' kingdom. Or else despair that it is all too hard, and give up.

Zechariah's first vision is a call to live in the light of God's sovereign rule. The riders on horses (cf. Rev. 6) are a reminder that God knows what is happening in his world. Even though the nations may appear to have the upper hand over God's people, his purposes are firmly in hand (Jauhiainen 2009: 160–161). He is the God of the nations – they are not to be feared but are merely instruments in his hands. God has turned with mercy, and will come to save and judge.

ZECHARIAH 1:18–21[HB 2:1–4]

Translation

[1:18[2:1]]And I lifted my eyes, and look! Four horns. [19[2:2]]And I said to the angel who was speaking with me, 'What are these?' And he said to me, 'These are the horns that scattered Judah, Israel and Jerusalem.' [20[2:3]]And the Lord showed me four craftsmen. [21[2:4]]And I said, 'What are these coming to do?' And he said, 'These are the horns that scattered Judah so that a man could not lift up his head. And these have come to terrify them – to throw down the horns of the nations who lifted up a horn against the land of Judah in order to scatter it.'

Notes on the text

1:18[2:1]. 'and look!' translates, 'and I saw and look!' (cf. 2:1[5]; 5:1, 9; 6:1).

19[2:2]. LXX and Syr have 'What are these, Lord?', where 'Lord' is most likely an addition to conform to usage elsewhere (e.g. 1:9; 4:4).

'Israel' is absent from some LXX manuscripts, and 'Jerusalem' from others. This is perhaps because of the unusual ordering of the names. MT is followed as original (and more difficult). See 'Comment'.

21[2:4]. 'so that': *kĕpî*. BDB 805 gives the meaning here as 'in such proportion that'.

'to terrify' is a hiph. inf. of *ḥārad*, which is 'to cause to tremble or shudder'.

'to throw down': *lĕyaddôt* is the only instance of this pi. inf. in the OT. *yādâ* occurs one other time as a pi. (imperf.) in Lam. 3:53, where it refers to throwing stones into a pit.

Form and structure

Zech. 1:18–21[2:1–4] forms the shortest of the eight night vision reports. It can be divided into two parts (vv. 18–19 and 20–21), each with something

Zechariah sees ('four horns' and 'four craftsmen') along with a question by Zechariah ('What are these?') and an explanation. In the second section, most of the first explanation is repeated and elaborated upon to explain the relationship between the objects Zechariah sees.

The HB begins a new chapter at 1:18. Perhaps those making the chapter divisions (a late development) saw a closer link between the second and third visions, as both begin in the same way ('And I lifted my eyes') and concern more extensively the judgment of the nations.

Comment

1:18–19[2:1–2]. 'And I lifted my eyes, and look!' is a phrase that also introduces visions 3, 6 and 8 (2:1[5]; 5:1; 6:1). It provides a transition into the next scene and underlines the visionary character of the word of the Lord that came to Zechariah. On the function of 'and look' (*wĕhinnēh*), see 'comment' on 1:8.

Zechariah sees 'four horns'. There are various proposals for the type of horns, including animal horns, musical instruments, the horns of the temple altar (e.g. Amos 3:14) or an iron fighting implement (1 Kgs 22:11; 2 Chr. 18:10; Ps. 18:2). If it is animal horns, scholars debate whether they are to be envisaged as being attached to wild animals, or to some kind of headpiece worn by warriors in the ancient world. The type of horn is not further identified in the vision, but what the horns represent is explained to Zechariah in vv. 19 and 21, and this helps to clarify the nature of the horns.

First, the horns are those 'that scattered Judah, Israel and Jerusalem' (v. 19). This phrase refers to the exiles of the northern and southern kingdoms in 722 BC and 586 BC respectively. The exile as a 'scattering' or 'winnowing' (*zārâ*) is an agricultural image, where grain husks are scattered by the wind (cf. 2:6[10]). It is one of the curses for disobedience listed in the Torah (Lev. 26:33), and is found elsewhere in the prophets (e.g. Jer. 15:7; 50:17–18; Ezek. 5:2, 10, 12; 6:6; Joel 3:1–2[4:1–2]). The reference to 'Judah, Israel and Jerusalem' indicates an interest in the northern and southern kingdoms, consistent with other parts of Zechariah (e.g. 8:13; 10:6–7). Stead (2009: 105) believes that Joel 3:1–2[4:1–2], which speaks of the nations scattering 'Israel' and God restoring the fortunes of 'Judah and Jerusalem', has influenced Zechariah here. The conflation of ideas supports this and explains the unusual combination of place names that is altered in LXX (see 'Notes on the text'). This description of the horns is repeated (minus the mention of Israel and Jerusalem) in v. 21, along with the statement 'so that a man could not lift up his head'. Butterworth (1992: 96) notes the threefold use of 'lift up' (*nāśā'*) in this passage (vv. 18, 21 [twice]), and suggests that this phrase could mean either that no one among the nations gave any help or no one in Israel offered any resistance.

BDB 805 explains that the conj. 'so that' (*kĕpî*) means, 'in such proportion that', which favours the second explanation and is consistent with the oppression of exile – they were bowed in oppression and subjection to the extent that they could not lift up their faces.

Secondly, the four craftsmen are said to 'terrify' and 'throw down' the horns (v. 21). The exact nature of this will be discussed further below, but these descriptions aid an identification of the horns. While it is right to see the temple associations in this second vision of Zechariah, it is difficult to see how the four horns of the altar could possibly have scattered Judah, Israel and Jerusalem. The suggestion of a musical horn seems to derive only from the conclusion that the 'craftsmen' of v. 20 are 'blacksmiths' who work with metal, but this limited understanding of the 'craftsmen' is unlikely for reasons that will be outlined below. In addition, it is difficult to conceive how the horns of an altar or a musical instrument could be 'terrified'.

Alternatively, the horn of an animal is a common metaphor for military and political power (e.g. Deut. 33:17; 1 Sam. 2:1, 10; Ps. 132:17; Ezek. 34:21). Animal horns represent kingdoms opposed to God and his people in Dan. 7 – 8 (cf. Jer. 48:25). Identifying the horns as those of an animal is consistent with the horns later being 'terrified' and 'cast down' (v. 21). Significantly, Mic. 4:13 also combines the metaphors of threshing and horns, where the daughter of Zion is given a horn of iron and hoofs of bronze to thresh the nations. This is the reverse situation to Zechariah.

While it was chiefly the nations of Assyria and then Babylon who were responsible for the exiles of the northern and southern kingdoms respectively, other nations are also indicted (e.g. Ammon in Jer. 49:2, Philistia in Joel 3 and Edom in Obadiah). However, the number 'four' probably does not refer to four nations (if so, there is no agreement about which nations they are). Rather, the number 'four' is more likely being used symbolically to refer to all nations of the earth that scattered God's people. The number 'four' symbolizes north, south, east and west (cf. 2:6[10]; 6:1, 5).

20–21[2:3–4]. After being told about the horns by the angel, Yahweh shows Zechariah four craftsmen coming to do something. This mention of the 'LORD' has the effect of emphasizing again the divine origin of the vision and the certainty of what is to come to pass. Presumably, it is the angel who then replies to Zechariah in v. 21, picking up where he left off in v. 19, after the additional revelation.

The number 'four' here corresponds to the number of horns. The word for 'craftsman' (*ḥārāš*) is a broad term that encompasses those who work with various media ('smith' or 'blacksmith' is too narrow as a translation). It is used in a number of different contexts in the OT. While it refers to one who fashions idols (e.g. Deut. 27:15; Isa. 40:19–20; Hos. 13:2) and one who makes weapons of war (e.g. 1 Sam. 13:19), the greatest frequency of the term 'craftsman' is in connection with those who constructed the tabernacle (Exod. 35:35; 38:23) and temple (1 Kgs 7:14; 1 Chr. 22:15; 29:5), and who were responsible for its repair later under Jehoash (2 Kgs 12:11; 2 Chr. 24:12) and Josiah (2 Kgs 22:6; 2 Chr. 34:11). Ezra 3:7 refers to 'carpenters' (NIV) or 'craftsmen' (*ḥārāšîm*) responsible for rebuilding the temple under Zerubbabel.

Zechariah observes that these four craftsmen have come to do something. This is explained, 'these have come to terrify them – to throw down the horns of the nations' (see 'Notes on the text'). 'Terrify' (*ḥārad*) seems to be a wordplay with 'craftsmen' (*ḥārāš*). The immediate context suggests that 'throw down' (*lĕyaddôt*) refers to the power of the nations being brought down after they have 'lifted up a horn'. While horns usually terrify and throw down, here the craftsmen do to the horns what the horns usually do to others. Whether or not the 'horns of the nations' are destroyed is uncertain. However, a similar idea is found in Ezek. 21:31, where 'craftsmen of destruction' destroy the Ammonites.

Who are these four craftsmen? Many scholars believe they refer to the Persians whom God will use to judge the vestiges of the Babylonian Empire. For example, Curtis (2006: 133) states, 'The second night vision of the prophet Zechariah thus portrays the Persian Empire (550–331 BC) as a benevolent, protective force raised up by Yahweh to assist his ancient people in their exilic plight.' This interpretation depends upon seeing the Babylonians in some way still awaiting judgment by the Persians. Yet there is nothing in the text that would suggest that the Persians should not also be understood as 'horns of the nations' (cf. Hag. 2:22). If the associations of the 'craftsmen' with temple workmen elsewhere in the OT is taken seriously, a different interpretation more in keeping with the overall thrust of the night visions ensues. Rather than looking to Persia for deliverance, this vision functions to demonstrate the significance of temple-building. The book of Haggai notes that temple-building began in earnest some five months earlier (Hag. 1:14–15). Zechariah's vision demonstrates the important role the craftsmen have in rebuilding the temple. The nations who have oppressed God's people will be terrified and thrown down when the temple is rebuilt (cf. Hag. 2:20–23). While the craftsmen may seem too passive for these activities, this misses the point. The craftsmen end up doing to the horns what horns normally do to others, but, ironically, this destruction does not come through their own power, but through God's return to the rebuilt temple. The subsequent vision explains how this works, namely as the glory returns to Jerusalem (2:5[9]) and the nations are plundered (2:9[13]) and God dwells in the midst of his chosen people (2:11[15]).

Explanation

The first vision finished by proclaiming God's anger with the nations who 'helped to [the point of] evil' (1:15) and that God's house would be built in Jerusalem (1:16). The second vision develops this by portraying the nations as four horns that will be terrified and cast down by four craftsmen. The number of craftsmen matches the number of horns, yet ultimately the horns are no match for the craftsmen. The vision portrays a great reversal where the foreign nations that had been responsible for the scattering of God's people in the exiles of the northern and southern kingdoms will themselves be terrified and thrown down. It underscores the importance of rebuilding the temple in God's restoration purposes, a theme developed in the subsequent visions.

It is common to see the craftsmen as powerful figures. McComiskey (1998: 1048) states, 'we imagine heavy hammers in their strong grasps. Perhaps they are smiths.' Yet if the power to overcome the nations comes from God's dwelling in the rebuilt temple, then it is not necessary to see the craftsmen as powerful in themselves at all. Webb (2003: 76), who believes the craftsmen are temple workers, argues they are figures of weakness, and so in this vision there is a strange conjunction of power and weakness, with the weak overcoming the strong (to return to Tolkien, perhaps they are like the dwarves in *The Lord of the Rings*). Indeed, this aspect is consistent with other aspects of Zechariah's prophecy, particularly 4:6, where the temple is said to be built not by Zerubbabel's might and power, but by the Spirit of God (cf. also 9:9; 10:5). It is also consistent with the NT theme of God's choosing 'the weak things of the world to shame the strong' (1 Cor. 1:27; cf. 2 Cor. 4:7).

This theme is a great rebuke, encouragement and comfort to God's people today in the building project he has given – the building of Christ's church. It is not by great power that the forces ranged against God's people will be overcome, but by God himself. God's people are simply called to be faithful in the building tasks he has given (I will say more about these tasks in relation to ch. 4).

ZECHARIAH 2:1–13[HB 5–17]

Translation

2:1[5]And I lifted my eyes, and look! A man with a measuring line in his hand. 2[6]And
I said, 'Where are you going?' And he said to me, 'To measure Jerusalem, to see
how wide it is and how long it is.' 3[7]And look, the angel who was speaking with
me was going out, and another angel was going out to meet him. 4[8]And he said to
him, 'Run, say to that young man, "Jerusalem shall dwell as a city without walls
because of many people and animals in its midst. 5[9]And I myself will be for it",
declares the LORD, "a wall of fire all around, and for glory I will be in its midst."'

6[10]'Listen! Listen! Flee from the land of the north,' declares the LORD, 'for like
the four winds of the heavens I scattered you,' declares the LORD. 7[11]'Listen, Zion.
Escape! (The one dwelling [in] the daughter of Babylon.)' 8[12]For so says the LORD
of hosts, 'After glory sent me to the nations who have plundered you, surely

whoever touches you touches the pupil of my eye. [9[13]]For look, I am waving my hand against them and they will become plunder for their servants.' And you will know that the LORD of hosts has sent me.

[10[14]]'Sing and rejoice, daughter of Zion! For look, I am coming and I will dwell in your midst,' says the LORD. [11[15]]'And many nations shall join themselves to the LORD on that day, and they will become my people and I will dwell in your midst and you will know that the LORD of hosts sent me to you. [12[16]]And the LORD will possess Judah as his portion upon the holy land, and will again choose Jerusalem.

[13[17]] 'Be silent, all flesh, before the LORD, for he has roused himself from his holy dwelling.'

Notes on the text

2:1[**5**]. 'and look!' translates, 'and I saw and look!' (cf. 1:18[2:1]; 5:1, 9; 6:1).

'A man with a measuring line in his hand': J. C. L. Gibson (1994: 168) notes that there are anomalies in word order when something other than the subject comes after waw. Here it is lit. 'And in his hand a line of measuring'; 'with' is supplied in translation.

2[**6**]. 'And I said': LXX and Syr add 'to him'.

'Where': *'ānâ*. Meyers and Meyers (1987: 150) note the he of direction attached to the interr. *'ān* indicates direction (lit. 'to where?').

3[**7**]. 'was going out': *yōṣē'*. LXX translates as 'stood' (*eistekei*).

'who was speaking': *haddōbēr* translates a rel. ptc. (the art. agreeing with the noun), describing the interpreting angel of the earlier visions. See Waltke and O'Connor 1990: 621.

4[**8**]. 'that': *hallāz* is a rare demons. pr.

'as a city without walls': *pĕrāzôt*. See 'Comment'.

'because of many': *mērōb*.

6[**10**]. 'Listen! Listen!': *hôy hôy*. See 'Comment'.

'for like the four winds of the heavens I scattered you': LXX translates this as 'from the four winds of heaven I will gather you'. This is the opposite idea to MT, which expresses past judgment, but still fits the context as a promise of restoration. MT is followed as original.

7[**11**]. LXX has 'to Zion' (*eis Siōn*). The vocative of MT has been followed.

8[**12**]. 'After glory': *'aḥar kābôd*. See 'Comment'.

'my eye': MT has 'his eye' (*'ênô*). Rabbinical tradition holds that the original was 'my eye', and that this was changed out of respect for God. *BHS* calls this one of the 'tiqqune sopherim' (scribal corrections). 'my eye' is found in one LXX manuscript, Tertullian and Vg. Gelston (2010: 136*) argues the context suggests 'my eye' is original and this is followed in translation here.

'surely': *kî*. See 'Comment'.

11[**15**]. 'they will become my people': lit. 'they will be for me for a people'. LXX and Syr have 'for him for a people' to make it clear that it is a reference to the Lord.

Form and structure

This section can be divided as a third vision (vv. 1–5) followed by an oracle (vv. 6–13). While Yahweh's speech ('so says the LORD') is contained in both v. 5 and v. 6, and some have seen vv. 4–6 as 'oracular', in vv. 4–5 speech is directed towards the characters in the vision, and in v. 6 the direction of Yahweh's speech shifts to Zechariah's hearers, which continues to the end of v. 13.

Butterworth (1992: 65–66) notes the difficulties involved in further dividing vv. 6–13. MT divides it at the end of vv. 7, 9 and 13. Structurally, the imperatives of vv. 6, 7 and 10 stand out. Thematically, vv. 6–9 form a section charging exiles to return in view of God's coming judgment on the nations, vv. 10–12 form a section anticipating Yahweh's return to Jerusalem with the incorporation of the nations, and v. 13 rounds out the unit.

Commentators note the connections between the oracle and earlier visions (particularly the punishment of the nations in vision 2 and the return of Yahweh in vision 1). While these observations are correct, the message of the oracle must not be separated from the immediately preceding vision (Stead 2014: 161–163). The vision of an uncontainable, God-protected and glory-filled Jerusalem provides the basis for the imper. applications to Zechariah's hearers. The applications (flee, escape, sing and rejoice) all flow from the glorious picture of the new Jerusalem. The visions give content to the call for repentance in 1:1–6, and this vision shows repentance involves returning to Jerusalem from the land of exile, for the nations are about to experience the judgment and salvation of God.

Comment

2:1–2[5–6]. 'And I lifted my eyes, and look!' (see 'Comment' on 1:18). In the third vision, Zechariah sees a man with a measuring line (*ḥebel middâ*) in his hand (v. 1). Zechariah speaks directly into the vision (without angelic mediation), asking the man where he is going, to be told that he is going to measure Jerusalem (v. 2). This raises questions about the nature of his measuring and the identity of the man, which will be dealt with in turn. 1:16 declared that 'a measuring line shall be stretched out over Jerusalem', and while it uses different vocabulary for the 'measuring line' (*qāweh*), it must be understood in context as referring to the same task, namely surveying Jerusalem as part of its rebuilding. Jer. 31:39, which uses the same measuring imagery, indicates that such measuring is to determine the city's boundaries.

In 1:16, measuring Jerusalem is closely connected to rebuilding the temple. While the rebuilding of the temple is taken up directly in the fifth vision (ch. 4), city and temple are intimately connected. This is also the case in Ezek. 40, where Ezekiel is given a vision of buildings that looked like a city (40:2); but the vision then focuses on a man who measures the temple with a measuring rod (*qĕnēh hammiddâ*) in his hand (40:5). It seems that Ezekiel's vision is very much in the background of Zechariah (Boda 2008: 185). Interestingly, the vocabulary of 'measuring' (*middâ*) is used twenty-five times in Ezek. 40 – 48. Elsewhere in the OT, *middâ* is used in connection with the building of the tabernacle (e.g. Exod. 26:2, 8), Solomon's temple (e.g. 1 Kgs 7:9, 11), the restored temple (Jer. 31:39), and later, the walls of Jerusalem (e.g. Neh. 3:11–30). Similarly, the combined terminology of 'width' and 'length' occurs most prominently in connection with the tabernacle in Exodus, Solomon's temple in 1 Kings and 2 Chronicles, and the new temple in Ezek. 40 – 48. In Zechariah's vision there seems to be a merging of temple and city, with God's glory filling it (v. 5). This is later reflected in 14:20–21.

The man has been variously understood as the angel of the Lord, an angelic interpreter or a man who symbolizes the exiles. Since the man is later corrected (v. 4), he seems unlikely to be an angelic figure, whom one would expect to be doing the will of God from the beginning. He may be a representative of the exiles, but since no identification is made explicit, his identity must remain hidden while the elements explained in the passage are concentrated on.

3–5[7–9]. When Zechariah questioned the man in the vision directly (v. 2), the interpreting angel was curiously absent. Here we are told this angel was 'going out' (*yōṣēʾ*), a phrase used when the angel is directly involved with the vision (cf. 5:5). Another angel goes out to meet the angel with a message for 'the young man' (*hannaʿar*). While some have suggested that the 'young man' is Zechariah, the context seems to direct the message to the man who was 'going' to measure Jerusalem (v. 2), presumably because he had now gone. Meyers and Meyers (1987: 154) argue that 'young man' is a technical term for an official of the royal court and translate it as 'official'. In either case, Zechariah (over)hears the message.

The second angel has an urgent message, indicated by the call to 'run'. Jerusalem shall dwell as a 'city without walls'. This expression translates *pĕrāzôt*, a pl. form difficult to define precisely. Elsewhere this word occurs only in Esth. 9:19 and Ezek. 38:11 (a variant occurs in Judg. 5:7). Petersen (1985: 170) notes another noun with the same root in 1 Sam. 6:18, where the fortified city is contrasted with the unwalled village. From these references and the immediate context in Zechariah, which goes on to speak about Yahweh's being a wall of fire around the city, 'city without walls' is the best inference. Furthermore, the reason there is to be no wall is 'because of many people and animals in its midst'. Stead (2009: 111) notes the language here echoes Gen. 8:17 and 9:1, where the multiplication of animals and humanity is a sign of God's blessing, a contrast to the curse of exile (Jer. 33:10–11). The image is therefore of a city unable to be contained by walls because of its overflowing animal and human population.

A wall functions to fortify a city, and Nehemiah later takes the initiative to rebuild Jerusalem's wall for this reason (cf. Neh. 2:17–20). The angel's message of a city without walls would raise the question of its security. God allays these fears: '"I myself will be for it", declares the LORD, "a wall of fire all around"'. 'I' (*'ehyeh*) is emphatic and may be an allusion to Exod. 3:14. Fire is a common means of protection in the OT (Gen. 3:24; Exod. 14:19–20, 24; Deut. 5:23–24; 2 Kgs 6:17; Pss 46; 48). Rather than walls of stone, Yahweh himself will protect Jerusalem, presumably in a way that allows for expansion. Furthermore, 'for glory I will be in its midst'. The key significance in Zechariah of the theme of Yahweh's return to Jerusalem has already been noted (1:3, 16). While God has returned 'with mercy' in the sense that there is restored relationship after the exilic experience, Zechariah holds out hope for a future intensified presence of God. Whereas the location of this presence elsewhere is in the temple (1:16; 4:1–14), here it is the city itself – temple and city are merged. The background for the concept of glory (*kābôd*) returning to Jerusalem is again Ezekiel. The movement of the glory of Yahweh from the defiled temple (Ezek. 10 – 11) to the exiles by the Kebar River in Babylon (Ezek. 1) and then back to the temple (Ezek. 43:1–5) is one of the structuring motifs of Ezekiel. Zechariah's vision poses no challenge to Ezekiel's programme, pace J. M. O'Brien (2004: 183), as Zechariah too awaits the return of the glory of Yahweh.

This vision shows that the young man's conception of the restored Jerusalem is too small and serves to challenge readers and hearers of the book about their own conceptions. Achtemeier (1986: 116) puts it well:

> This man has believed the prophet's message that Jerusalem will be rebuilt, but he expects the new Jerusalem to be no different from the old; and he would therefore conform its measurements to those it had before its fall. The man has no vision of a greater city 'whose builder and maker is God'.

6–7[10–11]. 'Listen!' (*hôy*) is usually used in a context of lamentation and translated 'woe'. Here (twice in v. 6 and once in v. 7) it serves to introduce charges to escape judgment (cf. Isa. 55:1). The first charge is given as an imper. from God: 'Flee from the land of the north.' The imper. 'flee' is elsewhere found only in Jeremiah (Jer. 48:6; 49:8, 30; 51:6), with the 'land of the north' being a typical Jeremianic expression for Babylon (Jer. 3:18; 16:15; 23:8; 31:8). While Babylon strictly lay to the east of the land of Israel, the geography is such that the route to Babylon was to the north (and then east).

The phrase 'I scattered you' recalls the fact that the exiles found themselves in a foreign land by God's will, as judgment on their sin. This has already been highlighted in 1:2–6, 12. 'Scattering' is a common metaphor for exile (e.g. Lev. 26:33; Deut. 28:64). Here the idea is not so much that they were scattered 'to' the four winds, but 'like' or 'as' the four winds since the prep. *kĕ* has no spatial use, but shows comparison or correspondence relationships (Arnold and Choi 2003: 109). Like the winds of a storm that blow in all directions, the Babylonian exile scattered God's people in all directions. Indeed, Jer. 44:1 reports Jews living in Egypt. This storm had been God's judgment on his people, but now the punishment was over. Yahweh had returned to his people with mercy (1:16) and his glory was returning to the city. The nations who had been instruments of his judgment were now to be judged (1:15; 1:18–21[2:1–4]). Hence the call to 'flee'.

The second imper., 'escape', heightens the notion of coming judgment on the nations (v. 7). While LXX translates 'Zion' as an acc. of direction (i.e. 'escape to Zion'), it is more likely a vocative that addresses the exiles as Zion (on 'Zion', see 'Comment' on 1:14). Either way, the remaining exiles are to escape from Babylon and return to Jerusalem in view of Babylon's demise.

'daughter of' is an expression that occurs four times in Zechariah (2:7[11], 10[14]; 9:9 [twice]). It is a poetic personification of the inhabitants of a land or city (i.e. Babylon, Zion, Jerusalem). Carson (2012) has demonstrated that the expression 'son of' (or 'daughter of') often indicates identity and function, rather than biology. Hence the expression also questions people's allegiance as either a 'daughter of Babylon' or a 'daughter of Zion' (v. 10).

Boda (2005) suggests the reference is to Babylon rather than Persia since the promised judgment of Babylon is yet to take place. Stead (2009: 125) argues that it is deliberately cryptic in order to conceal the message from Judah's Persian overlords. Alternatively, Babylon simply refers to the region in terms that bring to mind the exilic experience.

8–9[12–13]. The interpretation of v. 8 poses many challenges. Who is speaking? Who is being sent and where? What does the 'glory' refer to? The syntax and vocabulary are not well understood, and each of the many attempts to resolve these issues raises further difficulties. Many commentators understand the speech to be that of Zechariah, who was sent either to the nations (there is no indication elsewhere that this happened) or to preach against the nations. On this interpretation, 'glory' refers either to God (the glory), who sent Zechariah, or the (glorious) vision that sent him. Alternatively, Tiemeyer (2004: 352–372) suggests that the verse is a metaphorical expression describing how God is sent by (his) honour to proclaim punishment for the nations. In terms of syntax, she argues that 'for so says the LORD of hosts' introduces the direct speech of God, and hence 'my eye' should be understood as original, referring to God's first-person speech. She proposes that 'glory' is to be understood as an abstract quality, referring to God's glory or honour, and 'after' (*'aḥar*) is an adv. of time. She offers the translation (2004: 371–372) 'Afterwards, honour will send me against the nations who are spoiling you, because whoever touches you touches the pupil of my eye.' The difficulties with her interpretation are the unusual (but not impossible) translation of *'el* as 'against' rather than 'to [the nations]' and the translation of 'send' as a prophetic perfect (unusual in chs. 1–8).

Against the background of Ezekiel (the prophet of glory), I propose another interpretation that also understands the phrase as God's direct speech. Zech. 2:5 has already mentioned the glory returning to Jerusalem. Why did God depart in the first place? Ezekiel makes it clear that Jerusalem had become defiled. The temple was filled with idols. God's glory or honour is what drove him or 'sent him' to the nations (Ezek. 8:6; 9:3). God's own character compelled him to depart from his defiled temple and sinful people, and his glory took up residence with his people among the nations – by the Chebar River (Ezek. 1:3).

There had always been a tension in God's relationship with his people between his covenant mercy on the one hand and his judgment of sin on the other. In the golden calf incident at Sinai, God's burning anger wanted to destroy the nation, yet Moses interceded and pleaded on the basis of God's character and his promises to relent (Exod. 32:14), which he did. This tension is captured in Exodus in terms of God's 'glory', namely his character as the merciful and gracious God . . . who will not clear the guilty (Exod. 33:18; cf. 34:6–7). Both of these aspects of God's character are pivotal in future visions (Zech. 3; 5:3).

In the Babylonian exile, God's glory meant he was sent from Jerusalem in judgment on the city. It also meant that among the nations he could call his people 'the pupil of my eye'. The 'pupil' is a hapax legomenon, and is best understood to be analogous to 'apple of his eye' in Deut. 32:10 and Prov. 7:2 (Stead 2009: 116–117). The nations have struck something precious to God. It is not that Israel was precious in itself, but it was precious to God on account of the covenant promises he had made. In the exile, this tension in the character of God was felt acutely. God's own reputation (glory) was on the line – he had judged, but would he save? On this interpretation, 'surely' (*kî*) functions as an asseverative (Arnold and Choi 2003: 153) to place emphasis on the surety of a fact. It is on account of God's glory that he promises to save his people from the nations.

Meyers and Meyers (1987: 167) believe that the expression 'I am waving my hand against' can express God's initiating military activity by waving his hand as a signal to his forces. Alternatively, it may express his direct action (cf. Isa. 11:15; 19:16). The reference to the 'hosts' (armies) in the immediate context supports the former idea, and that God is about to act. In either case, God's judgment of the nations is a theme that has already been encountered in the first and second visions. Here again God promises to reverse the present situation of his people. Redditt (1995: 60) notes Exodus overtones, with the Egyptians being plundered by their slaves (Exod. 3:21–22; 11:2–3; 12:35–36).

The phrase 'For look' at the beginning of v. 9 occurs also in 2:10[14] and 3:8 (as *kî hinnî*) and 3:9 and 11:16 (as *kî hinnēh*). Petersen (1985: 205) believes it adds emphasis. More recently, Miller-Naudé and van der Merwe (2011: 65–66) argue that it can indicate either the imminence of the accompanying promise or its irreversibility. The latter use suits the context here, especially when tied with the sentence 'And you will know that the LORD of hosts has sent me.' This is to be understood as Zechariah's underlining his own authority as prophet of Yahweh. There are similar phrases in 2:11[15], 4:9 and 6:15. Significantly, only the promise attached to 4:9 had come to pass by the time the book of Zechariah was incorporated into the HB. For this reason, in the context of the book this phrase must be understood as a rhetorical device claiming divine authority for his words and giving the expectation for their fulfilment, rather than giving direct evidence for such authority.

10[14]. Two further imperatives call on the inhabitants of Zion (on 'daughter of Zion' see v. 7) to 'Sing and rejoice'. The reason for this is Yahweh's promise to come and dwell in their midst. Stead (2009: 117–119) argues that there is a combination of elements from the earlier prophets here. The singing and rejoicing reflects Isa. 12:6 and Zeph. 3:14–15. However, in these passages the presence of God is a present reality, whereas in Zechariah it is a future hope (cf. Joel 2:23, 27). The language of 'dwelling' is usually associated with Yahweh's presence in the tabernacle or the temple (e.g. Exod. 25:8; 29:44–45; Lev. 26:11; 1 Kgs 6:12–13), and is picked up again in Ezek. 37:26–27 and 43:7 to refer to a future dwelling. Again, Ezekiel seems to be prominent in the background. The promise here reflects v. 5, with Yahweh's returning in glory. There is a similar imperative to rejoice in Zech. 9:9 when the future Davidic king comes to Zion. On the phrase 'For look', see the 'Comment' on 2:9[13].

11[15]. This verse contains the first instance of the phrase 'on that day', a phrase that occurs around twenty times across the book of Zechariah. It is used by earlier prophets to refer to the time when Yahweh's kingdom will come (e.g. Hos. 2:18; Joel 4:18; Amos 9:11; Hag. 2:23). Petersen (1992: 579) summarizes the features of this prophetic expectation: the coming of Yahweh (often pictured in military terms); Yahweh's enemies receiving their just deserts; those who fear Yahweh (including the nations) being incorporated into his kingdom; his kingdom bringing a time of paradise in the land; the mediation of Yahweh's rule through a righteous Davidic king; and a new covenant. Each of these elements is present here apart from the Davidic king and paradise, but they will be mentioned in 3:8–10.

The idea that 'many nations shall join themselves to the LORD' is found also in Isaiah (14:1; 56:3, 6), where it refers to the nations turning to Yahweh, the God of Israel. In Isa. 2:1–4, this idea is pictured as the nations flowing to the temple in Jerusalem, which connects well with the third vision of a rebuilt and glorified Jerusalem/temple. In addition, the phrase associated with the new covenant in Jer. 31:33 and 32:38 ('they will be my people' NIV) is now extended to the nations. The incorporation of the nations will be seen elsewhere in Zechariah (8:22–23; 14:16).

The statement of prophetic authority is repeated (cf. v. 9). Stead (2009: 122) suggests this reflects the twofold message of Zechariah – Yahweh's anger at the nations (1:13; cf. 2:13[17]) and his return to Jerusalem (1:17; cf. 2:10[14]). The repetition of the prophetic 'validation formula' serves to underline each aspect of his message.

12[16]. After the universal tone of v. 11, this verse rounds off the section with a statement of the place of Judah and Jerusalem within this future. There are echoes here of the language of Deuteronomy. Whereas the land was the inheritance of the tribes, Deut. 32:9 says that

> The LORD's portion [*ḥēleq*] is his people,
> Jacob is his allotted inheritance [*naḥălâ*].

In Zechariah, God is said to 'possess' or 'inherit' (*nāḥal*) the tribe of Judah as his portion (*ḥēleq*) in the holy land. There may also be an allusion to the language that portrays the special place of the Levites. They had no portion in the land since Yahweh was their inheritance (Deut. 10:9). Inverting this idea, Judah is Yahweh's inheritance and portion in the holy land. Either way, this phrase speaks of the privileged position of Judah (cf. Zech. 12:7). The holiness of the land comes from Yahweh's presence (cf. 2:13; 14:21). On Yahweh's choice of Jerusalem again, see 'Comment' on 1:17.

Hence the return of Yahweh and incorporation of the nations as the people of God will not diminish the significance of Judah and Jerusalem. Judah is the tribe of David from which the future Davidic king will come (3:8; 6:12; 9:9), and Jerusalem is the city of David and the location of the temple (4:7–10). This verse anticipates the themes of the next two visions – the coming Davidic king (ch. 3) and the building of the temple (ch. 4).

13[17]. 'Be silent' (*has*) is a particle that is onomatopoeic and functions in a similar way to 'hush' or 'sh' in English. The phrase 'all flesh' in context refers to all of humanity (Israel and the nations) and also conveys a sense of weakness or transience in contrast to Yahweh (cf. Isa. 40:6). The reason people are to be silent is because Yahweh has roused himself from his 'holy dwelling'. Elsewhere, when Yahweh is 'roused' (*'āwar*), it is to save his people and bring judgment on his enemies (e.g. Pss 44:23[24]; 59:5; 73:20). There is a similar passage in Hab. 2:20, where the nations are called to be silent in view of Yahweh's renewed presence in the temple. In the context of Habakkuk, it anticipates the judgment of Babylon (Boda 2008: 186).

In the immediate context, which views Yahweh as returning to Jerusalem and the temple, the 'holy dwelling' could be the nations, to which Yahweh had departed in the exile (v. 8), though this dwelling is 'holy' only by virtue of God's dwelling there. More likely, however, it is Yahweh's heavenly abode (cf. Deut. 26:2, 14). While implicit, this verse also serves to heighten the sense of Yahweh's imminent return to dwell with his people in

Jerusalem, a return that will be complete when the temple is rebuilt (Stead 2009: 127).

Explanation

The third night vision of Zechariah functions to expand the readers' appreciation of the glorious scope of the new Jerusalem. Rather than being constrained by walls, the new Jerusalem will be uncontainable from the renewed human and animal population within, and protected all around by God himself, who will also fill it with his glory. The vision of this glorious Jerusalem (vv. 1–5) serves as the basis for a number of imper. applications.

First, the charge to those who had not yet returned from the scattering of exile is to flee and escape from the land of Babylon and, by implication, to return to Jerusalem (vv. 6–7). This charge is intensified by a repetition of the message of the first two visions, namely judgment coming on the nations with a great reversal of destiny for God's people (vv. 8–9). Secondly, the inhabitants of Jerusalem are to sing and rejoice at the prospect of Yahweh's return (v. 10). On the day God establishes his kingdom, not only will his enemies be vanquished, but those from the nations who join themselves to him will be incorporated into his new covenant people (v. 11). Furthermore, Judah and Jerusalem have a key role in this future (v. 12), anticipating themes of the next two visions. The unit finishes with a call to be silent in anticipation of God's return (v. 13).

The theme of God's glory is a rich biblical-theological theme. God's glory is connected in Exodus with both his visible presence (e.g. Exod. 24:16; 33:22; 40:34) and his character (e.g. Exod. 33:19). His glory is also said to fill Solomon's temple (1 Kgs 8:11). The book of Ezekiel records the departure of the glory from the temple, its residence among the exiles in Babylon, and promises its return to the new temple in Jerusalem (Ezek. 43:1–5). This return of the glory is anticipated in Zechariah's vision. Furthermore, God's glory as his character has been exhibited in the way he has judged his people and will save them.

While the book of Zechariah anticipates the return of the glory to the rebuilt Jerusalem, there is no indication in the post-exilic writings that the glory ever returned to the temple. Yet the book of Zechariah preserved this hope. It is against this background that the words of John 'we have seen his glory' (John 1:14) take on a great richness. God has returned to his people in the Word become flesh, the one who 'tabernacled' among his people, the one in whom God's grace and truth came together, the one who made God known (John 1:17–18). Jesus was the one who was glorified in his death and resurrection (Mark 13:26). Similarly, Paul says that in Christ we behold the glory of the Lord (2 Cor. 3:18). In this way, Jesus fulfils Zechariah's hope for God's return to his people.

Zechariah's vision of an uncontainable Jerusalem finds its fulfilment in Jesus. In him the structures of Israel's faith are greatly expanded. The gathering is no longer to a plot of real estate in the Middle East, but to the new temple, which in the first instance is Jesus (e.g. Mark 14:58; 15:29; John 1:14; 2:19–21; 4:20–24), then the church, of which he is the keystone. Jerusalem comes to represent heaven itself (Gal. 4:26–27; Heb. 12:22). Rev. 21 draws on Ezekiel and Zechariah in its portrayal of a figure who measures the 'length and width' of the new Jerusalem with a measuring rod. The glory of God resides in this holy city (21:1–2, 4–5, 19–21, 24–26; 22:5). Indeed, temple, city and land are merged into one picture that conveys the reality of God's presence with his people (cf. Rev. 21:22, which states there is no temple in the new Jerusalem, for the Lord God Almighty and the Lamb are the temple).

Christians live in the now-and-not-yet period between the two comings of Jesus, and Zechariah's imperatives are readily applicable today. First, Christians are to flee from Babylon. In Rev. 18, Babylon is a prostitute who deceives the nations. Babylon represents an anti-God world that seduces people to live for themselves rather than for God. Babylon is attractive. Many exiles had become wealthy and comfortable in Babylon and did not want to return. The call is the same today:

> 'Come out of her, my people,'
>   so that you will not share in her sins.
> (Rev. 18:4)

This theme will be traced further in the 'Explanation' of the seventh vision in chapter 5.

Secondly, singing and rejoicing is an appropriate response now that God has come in Christ as God's people give voice to the joy of knowing him (e.g. Eph. 5:19; Col. 3:15; Heb. 2:12; Jas 5:13; Rev. 5:9). Christians have every reason to sing (cf. Acts 16:25). Furthermore, now is the time when those from the nations are joining themselves to the Lord. Jesus envisaged this in Mark 13:27, as he promised to send out his messengers to gather his elect from the four winds. This gathering will conclude at Jesus' return (2 Thess. 2:1). There is an exclusiveness as well as an inclusiveness to this, and the basis of inclusion is whether people are joined to the Lord Jesus Christ by grace through faith (cf. Acts 15:14).

ZECHARIAH 3:1–10

Translation

[3:1]And he showed me Joshua the high priest standing before the angel of the LORD and Satan standing at his right hand to accuse him. [2]And the LORD said to Satan,

'May the LORD rebuke you, Satan! May the LORD, who has chosen Jerusalem, rebuke you! Is not this [man] a brand plucked from a fire?' 3Now Joshua was clothed in foul garments and was standing before the angel.

4He said to the ones standing before him, 'Remove the foul garments from him.' And he said to him, 'See, I have taken your iniquity from you, and I will clothe you with clean garments.' 5And I said, 'Let them put a clean turban on his head.' So they put the clean turban on his head and they clothed him in garments. And the angel of the LORD was standing by.

6And the angel of the LORD charged Joshua, 7'So says the LORD of hosts: If you will walk in my ways and if you will keep my requirement, then you shall rule my house and then you shall guard my courts, and I will give to you admittance among these who are standing [here].

8'Hear now, Joshua the high priest, you and your associates who are sitting before you; indeed, they are men of a sign. For look, I will bring my servant – Shoot. 9For look, the stone that I have placed before Joshua. Upon one stone are seven facets. Look, I am engraving its inscription, declares the LORD of hosts, and I will remove the iniquity of that land in a single day. 10On that day, declares the LORD of hosts, each of you shall invite your friend to come under your vine and fig tree.'

Notes on the text

3:1. 'Satan' follows the major translations (NIV, ESV, NASB). The Hebr. is *haśśāṭān* ('the accuser'; also v. 2), where the art. gives prominence to an individual of the class (J. C. L. Gibson 1994: 27). LXX has *ho diabolos*, which also seems to be the translation in the Greek Minor Prophets scroll, though it is fragmentary. See 'Comment'.

2. Syr reads, 'And the angel of the LORD said', seemingly to smooth the apparent awkwardness of the Lord's then speaking of himself in the third person.

'chosen Jerusalem': the prep. *bĕ* often accompanies the verb 'chosen' (*bāḥar*) to indicate its object – see BDB 103. It is not translated.

'Is not this [man]': *hălô' zeh*. The object ('man'; i.e. Joshua) is supplied in translation.

4. 'He said': translates 'And he answered, and he said . . . saying' (cf. 4:4, 6). Syr clarifies this is the angel speaking.

'and I will clothe you' translates the inf. abs. (*wĕhalbēš*), taking its time/aspect feature from the context (Arnold and Choi 2003: 73). Since the clothing happens in v. 5, it must have a future sense. LXX translates it as a command, 'and you clothe him', which alters the subject and object. *BHS* suggests following the LXX 'and you [2 m. pl.] clothe [hiph. imp.] him' or preferably 'and they [3 m. pl.] clothed him'. However, this *BHS* preferred option also involves deleting the phrase about clothing in v. 5. I have followed MT (also Syr).

'clean garments': *maḥălāṣôt*. Winton Thomas (1932: 279–280) argues that the context calls for *maḥălāṣôt* to be translated as 'clean' or 'pure' garments, rather than 'festal' garments (e.g. NRSV). LXX has 'with a robe to the feet' (*podērē*). Tg translates as 'righteous deeds' (Cathcart and Gordon 1989: 191).

5. 'And I said, "Let them put"' follows MT and takes *yāśîmû* as a juss. LXX simply has the imper. 'put'. Syr, Tg and Vg translate it, 'And he said, "Put".'

7. There is debate about where the protasis ends and the apodosis begins. In terms of syntax, the two 'if' clauses are introduced by *'im* and *wĕ'im*, and the two 'then' clauses are both introduced by *wĕgam* (so Syr and Vg). There are several instances, including 8:6, where *gam* introduces the apodosis (cf. Gen. 13:16; Jer. 31:36–37; 33:21, 26) – see BDB 169. There is no *gam* before the final phrase and this can be explained on the basis that it is redundant since the apodosis has already been introduced.

'admittance': *mahlĕkîm*. Follows Gelston (2010: 137*) in preferring the Masoretic vocalization as an abstract noun. See 'Comment'.

8. 'indeed': an asseverative use of *kî* (Arnold and Choi 2003: 153).

'they are men of a sign' in MT is 2 pl. in Syr ('you are'). MT may or may not include Joshua in the group, whereas Syr does.

'For look': *kî-hinnî* (cf. 2:9[13], 10[14]; 3:8). See 'Comment' on 2:10.

'I will bring': *mēbî'*. Following 'For look', the ptc. usually expresses future action (cf. 11:2). It does not necessarily imply imminent future (e.g. 2 Kgs 21:12; Isa. 13:13; Jer. 30:10; 31:8; 32:37; 33:6; 46:27; 50:18; Zeph. 3:19) (C. J. Thomson 2013: 56).

'Shoot': *ṣemaḥ* is often translated 'Branch'. See 'Comment' for a defence of this translation.

9. 'facets': *'ênāyim* (or 'eyes') uses a dual form, but has a pl. meaning (C. J. Thomson 2012). While *'ayin* predominantly means 'eye', it can denote a reflective surface like the surface of an eye (e.g. Exod. 10:15; possibly Ezek. 1:18; 10:12), so in relation to a stone (particularly a gemstone) *'ênāyim* refers to its reflective 'facets' or 'surfaces'.

BHS suggests that Joshua's name is a later addition and the original was 'before you' or 'before him'. There is no textual support for this.

'and I will remove': *ûmaštî*. Barker (2008: 759) believes the root *mûš* probably derives from the Akkadian *mêšu*, 'to forgive, disregard sins'. 4Q80 reads *wmsyty*, which elsewhere in the OT means 'draw out', but this seems inappropriate here.

10. Lit. 'you shall invite, a man to his friend, to under vine and to under fig tree'.

Form and structure

The fourth prophetic vision report pictures a heavenly court scene, similar to the one found in the prologue of the book of Job. The participants are

Joshua the high priest as the accused, the angel of the Lord as his spokesperson, Satan as the prosecuting attorney, Yahweh as judge, the prophet Zechariah looking on and contributing at one point (v. 5), and Joshua's associates.

Many scholars divide the chapter into two parts: a visionary section (vv. 1–5) and oracular material (vv. 6–10) (e.g. Petersen 1985: 187, 202). However, the division is not this tidy, since figures in the vision are spoken to in vv. 1–5, and features of the vision are developed in vv. 6–10 (unlike ch. 2, which moves from vision to an oracle addressed to those outside the vision). Butterworth (1992: 113–114) believes the primary division is vv. 1–7 and 8–10. He also notes that the ptc. 'standing' appears six times in vv. 1–7 to form inclusios that divide it into two sections: 'Verses 1–3 describe the scene and Yahweh's intention; vv. 4–7 describe the symbolic vindication of Joshua (and therefore Jerusalem).' A more thematic structure is as follows:

3:1–3 Joshua accused and defended
3:4–7 Joshua cleansed and commissioned
3:8–10 Signs of the coming Shoot

Comment

3:1. The subject of 'he showed me' is not explicit and could refer either to the angel, who not only explains various aspects of the vision to Zechariah, but also 'shows' him other things (cf. 1:9, 14), or else it could refer to Yahweh, who also 'shows' (cf. 1:20[2:3]). Since there is no dialogue with the angel in this vision as there is in the others, it seems most likely to refer to Yahweh and serves to underline the divine origin of the vision.

Three figures are revealed: Joshua the high priest, the angel of the Lord and 'Satan'. Joshua was a key leader in the early post-exilic period. Here and in v. 8 he is called the 'high priest' (*hakkōhēn haggādôl*). While the usage of this title in the pre-exilic period is debated, the role is clearly established from the relevant texts as referring to the head of the priestly family (Duguid 1994: 59–61). Texts from the Pentateuch show that the high priest was responsible for ensuring the purity of the community through the temple cult, so removing the threat of Yahweh's judgment that fellowship may continue (e.g. Exod. 28:38; Lev. 16:1–17; 23:26–32). While some scholars argue that the 'high priest' had more of an administrative function at this time (collecting funds and instituting building projects rather than offering sacrifices), the context of the vision suggests it is Joshua's role in offering sacrifices that is chiefly in view. Cleansing was a massive theological problem for the returned community (O'Kennedy 2003; Tiemeyer 2003; C. J. Thomson 2013). Already Zechariah has shown that the exile was God's judgment on the nation's sin (1:1–6, 16). Not only did the high priest represent those who had returned from exile in their unclean state, but Joshua must be cleansed so that he can offer sacrifices that will cleanse the people.

The 'angel of the LORD' appears only in this and the first vision (see 'Comment' on 1:11). There it was noted that this is a mysterious figure in the OT, who often speaks for God and at other times is distinguished from God. Joshua is described as 'standing before' him, an expression used in legal contexts elsewhere to refer to coming before a judge (e.g Num. 27:2). Hence the 'angel of the LORD' is again closely associated with God.

'Satan' (*haśśāṭān*) is strictly not a proper name, but a descriptive title that means 'the accuser'. Interestingly, 'accuse' in this verse is the verb form of 'satan' (*lĕśiṭnô*). Many commentators seem keen to point out that this figure should not be understood as the devil but simply a functionary of the divine assembly. However, from a canonical perspective, the identification of this figure as the devil is certain (Rev. 12:9; 20:2). Furthermore, this is not something that is strange to this context. Here 'Satan' is said to be standing at Joshua's right hand (in the heavenly court) to accuse him. In this way 'Satan' is presented as opposed to the restoration of the priesthood and, by implication, Yahweh's return to the temple (Rudman 2008: 208).

2. Before 'Satan' can open his mouth, there is a repeated call for his rebuke. While 'the LORD' is said to speak, it may be that the angel of the Lord speaks on Yahweh's behalf, since the speech is addressed to 'the LORD' (see 'Comment' on v. 1). This rebuke of 'Satan' is also significant in establishing his character and identity. Elsewhere in the OT it is the forces of chaos that are the most common objects of Yahweh's rebuke, namely the nations and the chaos waters (e.g. Pss 9:5[6]; 106:7, 9; Isa. 17:3; 50:2; Nah. 1:4). 'Satan' is clearly an opponent of Yahweh.

God's choice of Jerusalem has been mentioned in 1:17 and 2:12[16]. The background of the 'choice' language is Deuteronomy, where Yahweh will 'choose' the place where he will 'put his Name there for his dwelling' (i.e. the temple in Jerusalem; e.g. Deut. 12:5). The phrase also emphasizes that God's sovereign purposes for Jerusalem will come to pass. Hence opponents like 'Satan' will be silenced.

Joshua is described as a 'brand plucked from a fire'. The 'brand' here is a firebrand (a smouldering stick) rather than a branding implement. The 'fire' is the fire of exile and brings to mind God's anger expressed in his judgment on sin (cf. 1:2). Love (1999: 196–205) traces the intertextual background and notes an almost identical phrase in Amos 4:11, where it refers to Yahweh's rescue of Israel, just as Lot and his family were snatched from the judgment of Sodom and Gomorrah (cf. Gen. 19). Similarly, in Zechariah it speaks of God's grace in saving Joshua from exile and bringing him to Jerusalem. Presumably, Joshua had heeded the call to 'return' (1:3). This is another instance of God's sovereignty and human responsibility working together.

3. The adj. 'foul' (*ṣô'îm*) occurs in the OT only here and in v. 4. The related noun (*ṣē'â* or *ṣô'â*) can mean 'excrement' (Deut. 23:13[14]; Ezek. 4:12; Isa. 36:12) or 'vomit' (Isa. 28:8). The strength of this term underlines the seriousness of the sins associated with Joshua and his helpless position, especially given the ritual cleanliness required by the priesthood (Rudman 2008: 194). Joshua is 'standing before the angel', which is most naturally taken as a further reference to the angel of the Lord who represents God as judge (see 'Comment' on v. 1). The description conveys Joshua's perilous position.

Therefore, the opening of this vision (vv. 1–3) conveys a massive problem. Given the high priest's representative role, it suggests that the people, even though they have returned from the fire of exile, still stand condemned. The problem is heightened by reference in the previous visions to Yahweh's return to Jerusalem (cf. 1:16; 2:5[9], 10[14], 13[17]). How can Yahweh dwell in the midst of a sinful and defiled people and bless them and the world? It is this problem that the vision moves to resolve.

4–5. 'He' could refer to Yahweh or the angel of the Lord speaking on his behalf. In either case, the command comes from Yahweh to remove Joshua's foul garments, and the declaration is made, 'See, I have taken your iniquity from you, and I will clothe you in clean garments.' The word 'iniquity' (*'āwōn*) refers to sin and its associated guilt (Koch 1999: 546), but no sin of Joshua is explicitly mentioned here. The imagery of vv. 1–3 suggests it is the sin associated with the exile that was the cause of guilt and defilement for both the priesthood and the people. In addition to this, the book of Haggai indicates that the people were also suffering the covenantal curses for their sin committed after they had returned to the land. The sin identified by Haggai is their ignoring of Yahweh by not rebuilding the temple. This not only defiled the people, but all they did and offered (Hag. 2:14).

The declaration of Yahweh that he has 'taken' (*he'ĕbartî*) Joshua's iniquity from him uses a verb that elsewhere always refers to forgiveness (e.g. 2 Sam. 12:13; 24:10; Job 7:21; 1 Chr. 21:8) (C. J. Thomson 2013: 72). The imagery of reclothing in 'clean garments' also suggests purification (see 'Notes on the text'), though neither washing nor anointing (cf. Exod. 40:12–15) nor sacrifice is explicit in the vision. A different word for 'clean' (*ṭāhôr*) is used to describe the 'turban' of v. 5, but the context suggests the same idea as the 'clean garments'. These are the new clean high-priestly garments required for Joshua's reinstatement as high priest. There is an interesting connection between these ideas in the Hebr., not clear in my translation: just as the foul garment is taken *mē'ālāyw* (lit. 'from upon him'), so also Joshua is told that his iniquity will be taken *mē'āleykā* (lit. 'from upon you'). This reinforces the symbolic link between sin and defilement.

Like the previous vision, Zechariah gets directly involved (cf. 2:2[6]) and requests that the clean turban be put on Joshua's head. This request is carried out along with the reclothing (requested by Yahweh in v. 4). Those who carry this out ('they') are not identified; possibly they are other angels in the heavenly court.

Many commentators note that the word for 'turban' here (*ṣānîp*) is not the usual word for the high priest's headwear as found in Exod. 28:39 (*miṣnepet*). Some argue that it is a royal turban indicating that the high priest is being given the role of the pre-exilic king; for example, Chary 1969: 77. While *ṣānîp* is associated with royalty in Isa. 62:3, this more likely indicates the dignity of the clothing than the office of the wearer, since the same term is also used to describe the headwear worn by rich women in Isa. 3:23, and by Job in Job 29:14, neither having royal associations. The argument that this is a coronation of Joshua goes beyond the evidence (Petterson 2009: 53–60).

Some commentators suggest it is an ordination of Joshua to the role of high priest since the reclothing of the chief priest was part of an ordination rite in Exod. 29 and Lev. 8 – 9; for example, Sweeney 2000b: 593. However, Petersen (1985: 199–200) rightly argues against this, noting there are no washing rites, no costume details and no sacrifices. Furthermore, Joshua is already called the high priest in 3:1. It seems better to speak of a 're-instatement' of Joshua to the role of high priest than ordination.

'And the angel of the LORD was standing by' refers again to the 'angel of the LORD' from v. 1, who has observed the cleansing and reclothing of Joshua. He is now reintroduced before he speaks again on Yahweh's behalf in v. 6.

6–7. The 'angel of the LORD' gives Joshua a charge. Commentators debate where the protasis ends (the 'if' clause) and the apodosis begins (the 'then' clause). The syntax is complex, but favours seeing the protasis as 'If you walk in my ways and if you keep my requirement' (see 'Notes on the text').

There are two conditions, both introduced by 'if' (*'im*). The first, 'walk in my ways', is a call to covenant fidelity in the language of Deuteronomy (cf. Deut. 10:12–22; 28:9). The second, 'keep my requirement', is a parallel phrase and some commentators argue that since it frequently refers to priestly duties, it has more of a ritual sense. However, the phrase is also used in non-priestly contexts to refer to the broader idea of covenant faithfulness (e.g. Gen. 26:5; Lev. 18:30; Num. 9:19, 23; Deut. 11:1; Josh. 22:3; 1 Kgs 2:3; Mal. 3:14). While priestly duties may be in the background, covenant faithfulness seems the uppermost idea.

Three privileges that flow from obedience to these conditions are given.

First, 'you shall rule my house', where the 'house' is the temple, rather than the community. The word 'rule' (*tādîn*) can also be translated 'judge', and many commentators take this as an extension of the powers of the high priest, where he is now being given privileges that formerly belonged to the king, such as the administration of justice and management of the temple; for example, Elliger 1982: 120–121. However, a number of passages give evidence of the Levitical priests and the high priest dispensing justice in the pre-exilic period (Deut. 17:9–12; 19:17; Ezek. 44:15; 2 Chr. 19:8–11). Whether 'rule my house' is limited to juridical activity or also includes the administration and management of the temple, there is no evidence that this privilege is anything more than a reinstatement to what was enjoyed by the high priest before the exile (Tollington 1993: 160–161; Petterson 2009: 55–58).

Secondly, 'guard my courts' refers to the courts of the temple where the priests were to serve and protect their sanctity (cf. Num. 3:7–8; 18:5). While later than Zechariah, 1 Chr. 23:28–32 lists a broad range of activities of the priesthood, summarized in v. 32: literally 'they shall keep the guard of the tent of meeting and the guard of the sanctuary and the guard of the sons of Aaron their brothers – to serve the house of the LORD'. These activities include 'to be in charge of the courtyards, the side rooms, the purification of all sacred things and the performance of other duties at the house of God' (v. 28). This strongly suggests that this also is no new function being given to Joshua, but the reinstatement of Joshua to the role the priesthood enjoyed before the exile. It was a role that had a juridical component, but its main focus was the maintenance of the temple cult. It is not a charter for the high priest to take over the role of the king.

A more literal translation of the final clause is, 'I will give you walkings among these standing here'. Debate over the meaning of this clause centres around the difficult word 'walkings' (*mahlĕkîm*). Butterworth (1992: 116) notes the symmetry in word usage in this verse. The words 'walk' and 'keep' in the conditions are repeated in the privileges ('keep' and 'guard' are the same word in Hebr.). Therefore, it seems to be a wordplay, where if Joshua 'walks' in the ways of Yahweh, he will be given 'walkings' among the standing ones. Who are the 'standing' ones? Joshua's associates can be eliminated, since they are described as '*sitting* before you' (v. 8). Others who are said to be 'standing' are Joshua and Satan in v. 1, and the angel of the Lord in v. 5. These ones are standing in the divine council in Yahweh's presence. Presumably, the anonymous ones who clothed Joshua in v. 5 are also standing there. Hence 'walkings among the standing ones' indicates 'admittance' to the divine presence. Sweeney (2000b: 599) captures what it means in earthly terms: 'it appears to refer to the exclusive right of the high priest to enter the holy of holies in the Jerusalem Temple to appear before YHWH as the representative of the Jewish community to make atonement for the people's sins on Yom Kippur or the Day of Atonement (see Leviticus 16)'.

8. The angel of the Lord continues to address Joshua and now also his associates. These persons have not been mentioned to this point in the vision. There are three descriptions of them. First, they are 'friends' or 'associates' (see BDB 946) of Joshua. Secondly, they are 'sitting before' him. These two descriptions suggest they are Joshua's fellow priests. Thirdly, they are a 'sign' (*môpēt*) that God 'will bring my servant – Shoot'. The word *môpēt* is used in other parts of the OT to mean 'portent' or 'sign' (e.g. Exod. 4:21; 1 Kgs 13:3; 2 Chr. 32:24; Isa. 8:18; Ezek. 12:6; 24:24). Before discussing the significance of Joshua and his associates functioning as a sign, I will trace the significance of the phrase 'my servant – Shoot'.

In the OT, the expression 'my servant' is used in many different ways: to refer to individuals such as Abraham, Isaac, Jacob, Moses, David and even Nebuchadnezzar; to refer to the nation of Israel; and to refer to a future suffering figure. In the prophets, it is used with Davidic overtones, not least because the designation 'my servant' is used thirty-one times of David, including twice in 2 Sam. 7. Its combination with the term 'Shoot' underscores the Davidic associations here. The background to the term 'Shoot' (*ṣemaḥ*) is to be found in the earlier prophets, particularly Isaiah, Jeremiah and Ezekiel (Petterson 2009: 87–92). Given Zechariah's reference to the 'earlier prophets' (1:4; 7:7, 12) it is entirely appropriate to read his reference to this figure against this background. While there is differing terminology, a common metaphor is used to depict the hope for a future Davidic king (the Messiah) beyond the exile, based on the covenant with David and the earlier expectation for a royal deliverer. The prophets Isaiah, Jeremiah and Ezekiel each liken the house of David to a tree cut down or severed in the judgment of the exile, and from which a new growth will come and grow into something vast (Isa. 11:1; Jer. 23:5–6; 33:14–18; Ezek. 17:3–6, 22–23). This 'new growth' or 'Shoot' is a Davidic king of humble origins, who is associated with the coming kingdom of God with all its blessings. The metaphor of a 'shoot' captures three important ideas: first, it expresses the idea of something new springing from what had been cut down (i.e. the removal of the king in exile); secondly, it expresses the idea of some measure of continuity between the old and the new (i.e. an ongoing concern for the line of David); and thirdly, it captures the idea of small or humble beginnings of the new growth, which at the same time will grow to produce something magnificent (i.e. the humble origins of the future king). Jeremiah uses the term 'Shoot' (*ṣemaḥ*) to capture these common ideas, and it is this term that is utilized by Zechariah here and in 6:12. The absence of the art. in the Hebr. suggests it is used as a name (cf. 6:12).

It is important to note that Joshua is not Shoot. Rather, he and his fellow priests function as a sign that God will bring 'my servant – Shoot'. As Joshua and his fellow priests carry out their priestly duties, they anticipate through their actions the coming Davidic king. This suggests that Shoot has a priestly function, something that becomes clearer in 6:13.

Miller-Naudé and van der Merwe (2011: 65–66) argue that 'For look' (*kî hinnî*) can indicate either the imminence of the accompanying promise or its irreversibility. The context suggests it is the irreversibility of God's promise to send Shoot (see 'Comment' on 2:9[13]).

9. As well as the priesthood's functioning as a sign of the coming Shoot, Zechariah is told to observe a stone placed before Joshua that Yahweh is engraving (in the vision). Commentators are divided over the nature of the stone. Some understand it to be a stone of the new temple; for example,

Petitjean 1966. This view arose partly from the supposition that 3:9 was originally joined to 4:6b–10a, which features temple-building. However, there is no evidence that the passages were ever linked in this way (VanderKam 1991: 566–567), but the wider context still gives weight to this interpretation. It explains the 'seven eyes' as the eyes of Yahweh, which are focused on the stone (cf. 4:10) (Jauhiainen 2009: 159). Van Groningen (1990: 881), on analogies with the building stone of Isaiah (8:13–15; 28:16), argues that the stone represents the Messiah. While the stone does represent the coming of Shoot, it is difficult to determine if Zechariah drew from Isaiah here. A second suggestion is that the stone is part of Joshua's high-priestly clothing; for example, VanderKam 1991. The ephod of the high priest had two onyx stones set on the shoulder pieces that were engraved with the names of the sons of Israel, six on each stone (Exod. 28:9–11a). Similarly, the breastpiece of the high priest had twelve precious stones, each with a name of the twelve tribes (28:21). VanderKam (1991: 568–569) proposes that this stone placed before Joshua is a gemstone with seven pairs of 'eyes' or 'facets' (pairs, since the noun for 'eyes' is dual), and this corresponds to the fourteen stones in Aaron's garments. However, C. J. Thomson (2012) has recently demonstrated that the dual form is pl. in meaning, so there are only seven 'eyes'. Still, since the high priest's clothing has been an item of focus in vv. 1–5, and a gemstone more readily explains the 'engraving', on balance the interpretation of the stone as a gemstone placed before Joshua best complements other features of the vision.

Some commentators who adopt this interpretation suggest that what is being inscribed on the stone is, 'I will remove the iniquity of that land in a single day'; for example, Webb 2003: 88. However, it is again impossible to be certain of this from the syntax. In any case, this stone with its inscription, placed before (and worn by?) the high priest, is connected to the single day in which Yahweh will remove the iniquity of 'that land'. Whereas Joshua and his fellow priests were a sign of Yahweh's bringing Shoot, it is possible that this stone, set before Joshua, functioned as a reminder to Yahweh (like the rainbow sign of Gen. 9:13–16) of his promise to remove the sin of the land in a single day (cf. Exod. 28:29). 'That land' is the 'holy land' of 2:12[16], but viewed from the heavenly setting of the vision (C. J. Thomson 2013: 66, 99). It may be the 'sin of that land' in the sense that it is the sin of the inhabitants of the land, or the sin may attach to the land itself (cf. Lev. 18:25).

The reference to 'a single day' brings to mind the Day of Atonement, especially given the removal of Joshua's iniquity in v. 4 and his reinstatement to serve as high priest in the new temple. However, the association of this day with Shoot and the eschatological time frame given in the next verse ('on that day') suggest that this is a day of greater magnitude than the Day of Atonement.

10. This is the second occurrence of 'on that day'. It was noted in relation to the first instance (in 2:11[15]) that all but two of the features of 'that day' from the earlier prophetic expectation were present. The two missing features were a Davidic king and a time of paradise in the land. Interestingly, these are the two elements present in this passage. The phrase 'to come under your vine and fig tree' is an image of prosperity drawn from the experience of Israel in the time of Solomon (1 Kgs 4:25[5:5]; cf. Mic. 4:4). Here it is expanded by the idea of inviting one's 'friend' or 'neighbour', emphasizing the communal aspect of this day.

Explanation

The first three visions picture Yahweh's acting to reverse the situation brought about by the exile. Jeremiah's seventy years of judgment were coming to an end. Yahweh had turned to his people with mercy, the temple would be rebuilt and he would return with glory to an uncontainable Jerusalem. The nations whom Yahweh had used to judge his people would themselves be judged, and those who joined themselves to Yahweh would be saved on that day.

Zechariah's fourth vision turns to address the underlying problem that led to the exile and persisted after it, namely the nation's sin (cf. 1:1–6). The problem they faced was that even though they had returned to Jerusalem, their sin defiled them. How could God truly return to bless them unless they were forgiven and cleansed? And how could there be forgiveness and cleansing without a cleansed priesthood? Under this dark shadow, this vision provides God's solution to the problem of sin and defilement. Zechariah's vision of the high priest Joshua having the accusations of Satan silenced, and then being forgiven, cleansed and clothed (vv. 1–5), offered great hope for the future. As the people's representative, Joshua's acceptance anticipated their own.

Furthermore, if Joshua walked in the way of Yahweh and kept his requirement (vv. 6–7), then once the new temple was constructed, he would have the privilege that the priesthood and high priest enjoyed before the exile, namely of exercising judicial responsibility, administering the sacrificial system and having the special privilege of access to Yahweh's presence in the holy of holies on the Day of Atonement. This was all-important for the returned community as it offered hope of cleansing once the temple had been reconstructed.

But this vision goes much further and anticipates a later day – an eschatological day. As Joshua and his associates conduct the various sacrifices and intercede on behalf of the people, Yahweh declares that they will function as a sign of his promise to send his servant Shoot (cf. Jer. 23:5; 33:15). In addition, an inscribed stone placed before Joshua seems to serve a similar purpose. The priesthood and the stone anticipate the coming of Shoot, in whose arrival the iniquity of the land will finally be removed in a single day, and who will usher in the age of prosperity and abundance. The fact that (1) the priesthood serves as a sign of the coming Shoot and (2) the close connection between the coming of Shoot and the removal of the iniquity of the land suggest that Shoot may have a priestly function when he comes (cf. 6:13).

Christians know the single day Zechariah foresaw – the day when the Messiah ('Shoot') Jesus was hung up on a cross outside Jerusalem, suffering the judgment of God and taking sin on himself. As the great high priest he offered the superior sacrifice, the once-for-all sacrifice of his own body. If the cleansing of Joshua fitted him for service, 'How much more, then, will the blood of Christ, who through the eternal Spirit offered himself unblemished to God, cleanse our consciences from acts that lead to death, so that we may serve the living God!' (Heb. 9:14).

There are a number of lines of application of this passage to Christians today. Joshua is cleansed by God and given a specific commission to serve as the high priest in the temple when it is built (vv. 6–7). It is very important to see the order in which this happens – Joshua is cleansed, clothed and then commissioned to serve God. Joshua does not have to obey in order to be cleansed and accepted – that is religion, not grace. There is nothing Joshua can do to be forgiven and cleansed. He cannot even offer sacrifices to be cleansed since his clothing marks him as unfit for priestly service. His cleansing is an act of God's grace. Joshua is commissioned to serve because he has been accepted by God. Religion says, 'If I just obey enough, then I will be accepted . . . If I just go to church, say my prayers, sing songs, do enough good works, God may be impressed and bless me.' The Bible says there is nothing people can do to be made worthy. Salvation is by God's grace alone, completely undeserved. Good works are to be done in response to his forgiveness and cleansing, in thankfulness. Indeed, what God does for Joshua is exactly what he did in the exodus. He saved his people from slavery by his grace so they might serve him. It is what God does today through Jesus, who cleanses and clothes his people with his righteousness to serve him.

Having been forgiven and cleansed, Joshua has a responsibility to serve, and this service involves obedience (v. 7). God does not request Joshua's service; he demands it. God's grace is not a licence to live as one pleases. It is a freedom to live as God pleases. It is as Paul says in Rom. 12:1, 'in view of God's mercy . . . offer your bodies as a living sacrifice'. Both in the OT and the NT, God saves people by his grace, not by their works, so that they might serve him. The movement seen in Joshua's life is the movement of the Christian life – Christians are forgiven and set free from the accusations of Satan to serve God.

There are two chief ways this can come undone. The first is pride, which is the antithesis of grace. Graceless Christians become proud and unwilling servants. Or if they serve, they do so begrudgingly, or with a martyr complex, or only for the recognition of others, or with feelings of insecurity. This is the curse of religion. The antidote is the gospel of grace.

Alternatively, Piper (2007: 73–76) observes how guilty consciences can paralyse Christian service. Zechariah would say to Christians who have ongoing feelings of guilt that stop them serving others that they are listening to the accusation of Satan rather than to the voice of God. God does not trivialize sin or say that sin does not matter. But as horrific as any sin may be, God has dealt with it in the death of Jesus. Indeed, the accusation of Satan is what often wastes Christian lives. The greatest weapon against Satan is the knowledge that the punishment for sin has been paid in Christ. Whatever accusation Satan can bring has been silenced for those whose trust is in Jesus.

The end of the vision must not be neglected. When the Messiah comes and removes the iniquity of the land, those who have experienced this cleansing will invite their friends to share in it with them. To come under your vine and fig tree is a Jewish way of picturing heaven. It is a picture of God's blessing. This is a chief reason why Christians tell others about Jesus – it is because of the desire for others to enjoy God and enter heaven. Those who know the forgiveness of sins and the blessings of God should be inviting others to share in it. This is the book of Zechariah's 'Great Commission'!

Zech. 3 is a wonderful vision of cleansing for God's people. It is a vision that has found its fulfilment in Jesus, the great high priest, and the forgiveness he offers through his death on the cross.

ZECHARIAH 4:1–14

Translation

4:1 The angel who was speaking with me returned, and he roused me as a man who
is roused from his sleep. 2 And he said to me, 'What do you see?' And I said, 'Look,
I see a menorah – all of it gold, and a bowl on top of it, and seven lamps on it,
and seven streams to each of the lamps which are on top of it, 3 and two olive
trees by it, one by the right of the bowl, and one by its left.' 4 And I said to the
angel who was talking with me, 'What are these, my lord?' 5 And the angel who
was speaking with me answered and said to me, 'Do you not know what these
are?' And I said, 'No, my lord.'

6 And he said to me, 'This is the word of the LORD to Zerubbabel: Not by might,
and not by power, but by my Spirit, says the LORD of hosts. 7 Who are you, great
mountain? Before Zerubbabel you shall become level ground. And he will bring
forth the top stone amid shouts of "Grace, grace to it!"'

8 The word of the LORD came to me, 9 'The hands of Zerubbabel have founded
this house, and his hands will finish it, and you shall know that the LORD of hosts
has sent me to you. 10 For who has despised a day of small things? These seven
shall rejoice when they see the chosen stone in the hand of Zerubbabel. These are
the eyes of the LORD that are roaming through the whole earth.' 11 And I answered

and I said to him, 'What are these two olive trees on the right of the menorah and on its left?' [12]And I answered a second [time] and I said to him, 'What are these two streams of the olive trees, which by means of two golden pipes are pouring out from them the golden oil?' [13]And he said to me, 'Do you not know what these are?' And I said, 'No, my Lord.' [14]And he said, 'These are the two sons of oil who are standing by the Lord of the whole earth.'

Notes on the text

4:2. 'and I said' follows Q (*wāʾōmar*), rather than K, 'and he said' (*wayōʾmer*). *BHQ* notes that Q is followed by LXX, Vg, Syr and Tg and is required by the context. K is followed by a single Greek witness.

'Look, I see': translates 'I saw and look!' (cf. 1:18[2:1]). *wĕhinnēh* here points to the presence of an entity in a speech situation (Miller-Naudé and van der Merwe 2011: 61).

'and a bowl': *wĕgullāh*. MT has a mappiq in the final he, which suggests a 3 f. sg. pr. suff. ('its'). Yet, the noun *gl* is otherwise unattested (with the suff. one would expect *gullāhāh*). Since in context it clearly refers to a bowl (cf. v. 3 where there is no mappiq), the mappiq either serves some unknown function or is a kind of dittography, where the mappiq from the preceding word has been mistakenly repeated by the scribe. LXX, Syr and some targums translate it as if there is no mappiq.

'seven lamps on it': translates 'and seven its lamps upon it seven'. LXX and Syr omit 'its'. LXX also omits the second 'seven'.

'streams': *mûṣāqôt* is difficult to translate as it appears only here in the OT (see 'Comment'). Archaeological discoveries of clay lamps have given rise to the translation 'lips' (e.g. NRSV, ESV), but this is mistaken since it is the temple menorah that is in view. *mûṣāqôt* is the hoph. f. pl. ptc. form of the verb *yāṣaq* (pour, pour out, cast [metal]), which is here functioning as a noun. The form of the Hebr. is seven 'pourings' to each of the lamps. Given the overall context of supplying the lamps with oil from the trees through the bowl, it must refer to the oil pouring from the bowl to the lamps. The traditional reading, 'pipes' (cf. 'channels' of the NIV), while problematic in some ways, supplies a mechanism by which the oil streams.

'seven . . . to each': *šibʿâ wĕšibʿâ* has a distrib. sense. Yet it is difficult to know if it is one stream to each of the lamps, or seven streams to each of the seven lamps (forty-nine in all). 2 Sam. 21:20, which uses the same syntax, seems to suggest the latter. LXX has only seven. I have maintained the ambiguity in my translation. See 'Explanation'.

3. 'by it': *ʿālêhā*. The reference to 'right' and 'left' indicates the olive trees are *by* the bowl, rather than over it. It is a horizontal relationship (Arnold and Choi 2003: 121). See also v. 11 (cf. Zech. 12:6).

4. 'And I said': translates 'And I answered and I said . . . saying' (cf. 3:4; 4:6).

6. 'And he said': translates 'And he answered and he said . . . saying' (cf. 3:4; 4:4).

'but by': *kî 'im* is an adversative, noting an alternative to a negative statement (Arnold and Choi 2003: 152).

7. 'Who': *mî* is usually personal (cf. *mâ*), but here refers to a great mountain, perhaps personifying the mountain. Otherwise, 'What are you' (e.g. NRSV).

'you shall become level ground': *lĕmîšōr*. Holladay (1988: 168) explains that *lĕ* can be used to express the material or object into which something is made and that *mîšōr* is often used metaphorically to refer to 'level ground' (193).

'the top stone': *'et-hā'eben hārō'šāh*. See 'Comment'. LXX translates 'top stone' as 'stone of inheritance'.

'amid shouts': *tĕšu'ôt*. The prep. has been supplied in translation.

8. 'The word of the LORD came to me': translates 'And it came, the word of the LORD to me, saying.'

9. 'you shall know': *wĕyāda'tā*. Some Cairo manuscripts along with the Syr, Tg(s), and Vg have a 2 m. pl. suff. This is probably to make it consistent with the pl. pr. suff. at the end of the verse (*'ălêkem*). MT can be understood as switching between Zechariah's reporting what God said to him (with a sg. 'you') to what Zechariah is saying to the community (with a pl. 'you').

10. 'has despised a day': after the verb *bûz*, the prep. *lĕ* denotes the object being despised. Stead (2009: 180, n. 169) argues the sense of the construction is 'contempt for'.

'the chosen stone': *hā'eben habbĕdîl* is difficult to translate. *habbĕdîl* also occurs in Num. 31:22, where it refers to 'tin', and many propose that the 'tin stone' is therefore a plumb line or plummet used in the construction of the temple. However, the context indicates that this is a stone linked with the completion of the temple (see 'Comment'), so this translation is unsatisfactory. Alternatively, it refers to some kind of completion stone, probably the same stone referred to in v. 7 (as *BHS* suggests). Baldwin (1972: 122) proposes that *habbĕdîl* derives from *bādal*, which means 'to separate, divide'. Hence the translation 'the chosen stone', as it has been separated from others.

11. 'these': *hā'ēleh*. *BHS* notes that many medieval MSS and editions of the HB have a dagesh in the lamed as expected, so *hā'ēlleh*.

12. 'I said to him': translates 'And I answered and I said to him' (cf. v. 11).

'streams of the olive trees': *šibbălê hazzêtîm*. BDB 987 supplies two alternative translations of *šibbălê*. The first is 'ears of grain' as they grow or are harvested (e.g. Gen. 41:5; Ruth 2:2; Job 24:24; Isa. 17:5). The second is 'flowing stream' (e.g. Ps. 69:3, 16; Isa. 27:12). In the context of the vision, it seems best to understand the phrase as clarifying the relationship between the two olive trees and the oil – the olive trees directly provide the streams of oil.

'which by means of': lit. 'which [are] in the hand of' (*'ăšer bĕyad*) has been translated in an instrumental sense. See Hag. 1:1; 2:1; Zech. 7:7, 12; cf. Meyers and Meyers (1987: 257).

'two golden pipes': *šĕnê ṣantĕrôt hazzāhāb* is difficult to translate since *ṣantĕrôt* is a hapax legomenon. Most scholars take it to be related to *ṣinnōr*, which is found in 2 Sam. 5:8 and Ps. 42:8 and refers to a 'pipe, spout, conduit'. Wolters (2012a: 5) rejects this and argues *ṣantĕrôt* are 'oil-pressers'. This seems no less speculative, so I have followed the traditional rendering.

'the golden oil': *hazzāhāb*. Lit. 'the gold'. 'Oil' is understood from the wider context, being referred to by its colour.

14. 'sons of oil': *bĕnê-hayyiṣhār*. 'Anointed Ones' is misleading. See 'Comment' and 'Explanation'.

Form and structure

Zech. 4 comprises a fifth vision that is structured around a question-and-answer dialogue between the interpreting angel and Zechariah, with both participants being introduced in 4:1. Some scholars have seen 4:6–10a as an addition to the original text, interrupting the flow of the vision and its explanation. From a literary point of view, if this text is read as it is written, namely as a dialogue, then it is perfectly natural to expect repetition, disruptions and asides, while at the same time detecting a coherent thread that runs through it all. Reading it in this way, the first word of Yahweh to Zerubbabel (vv. 6–7) is an integral part of the dialogue between the angel and Zechariah, forming an answer to Zechariah's question and providing the setting for the menorah vision (vv. 1–5). The second word (vv. 8–10) is a message that comes to Zechariah for the community based on what he has seen and heard from the angel (vv. 1–7). This second word interrupts the dialogue between the angel and Zechariah, but continues the main theme. The text then moves back to the dialogue between Zechariah and the angel to relate the overall explanation given in these two words of Yahweh (vv. 6–10) to the two olive trees (vv. 11–14). This reading makes sense of the repeated questions in vv. 11–12: the angel seems to be dismayed (v. 13) because for him the vision has already been explained in the two words of Yahweh (vv. 6–10).

The chapter can be structured as follows:

4:1–5	**The vision report**
4:1	Introduction
4:2–3	The vision of the menorah, bowl, lamps, pipes and olive trees
4:4	Question: Zechariah to the angel about the vision
4:5a	Counter-question: the angel to Zechariah
4:5b	Zechariah's reply

4:6–10	**Two words of Yahweh explaining the overall vision**
4:6–7	A word of Yahweh from the angel to Zechariah for Zerubbabel
4:8–10	A word of Yahweh to Zechariah for the community
4:11–14	**Further details of the vision identified**
4:11	Question: Zechariah to the angel about the olive trees
4:12	Question: Zechariah to the angel about the streams of the olive trees
4:13	Counter-question: the angel to Zechariah
4:14	Answer: the angel to Zechariah about the two sons of oil

Comment

4:1. The 'angel who was speaking with me' has not been mentioned explicitly since 2:3[7] (the 'he' of 3:1 is more likely Yahweh). There the angel was 'going out' (*yōṣē'*), hence the statement that he 'returned' to Zechariah is appropriate. On returning, 'he roused me, as a man who is roused from his sleep', which indicates that Zechariah is experiencing visions rather than dreams. It does not necessarily mean that Zechariah fell asleep after the previous vision; just that his visionary experience is more vivid than his normal state.

2–3. The details of this vision are complex. Five components are mentioned: a menorah (lampstand) all of gold, a bowl on top of it, seven lamps upon it, seven streams to each of the lamps on top of it, and two olive trees by it (see 'Notes on the text' for an explanation of these components). While the descriptions of the objects themselves are reasonably specific, their exact nature and relationship to one another is difficult to picture.

While many commentators suggest on the basis of archaeological discoveries that this is a clay lamp, this is mistaken. The menorah in the vision is to be associated with the gold menorah of the tabernacle and temple (e.g. Exod. 25:31–40; 37:17–24; Num. 8:2; cf. 1 Kgs 7:49). Stead (2009: 173) notes that earlier references to 'seven lamps' occur only in the context of the tabernacle. However, the bowl, the streams and the olive trees set this menorah apart. Keil (1949: 265) suggests that these three additional elements form a contrast with the menorah of the tabernacle and temple in that this menorah is continually supplied with oil without the intervention of humans (the priests). This contrast certainly fits with the tenor of the vision, as will be seen. (See 'Comment' on v. 10 for a discussion of what the menorah represents.)

4–5. Zechariah asks the interpreting angel for an explanation: 'What are these, my lord?' It is unclear whether 'these' (*'ēlleh*) refers to the olive trees, the seven lamps or the vision as a whole. The former is most likely since they are the items mentioned most recently and Zechariah mentions them explicitly when he repeats the question in v. 12.

The angel responds with a counter-question, 'Do you not know what these are?' This has the effect of delaying the response, heightening the tension, and thereby highlighting the explanation that is given in the form of two oracles (4:6–10). The question is asked again in v. 13. Zechariah's failure to understand gives later readers some encouragement!

6–7. These verses contain the first of two words of Yahweh concerning Zerubbabel that function as the overall explanation of the vision of vv. 1–5. Zerubbabel is an enigmatic figure whose Babylonian name means 'seed of Babylon'. He is also mentioned in Haggai, Ezra, Nehemiah and Chronicles. In Ezra and Nehemiah, Zerubbabel is listed among the returnees from Babylon who rebuilt the altar and relaid the foundation of the temple (Ezra 2:2; 3:2, 8; Neh. 12:1). Haggai refers to him as the 'governor' (*paḥat*) of Judah (cf. Hag. 1:1, 14; 2:2, 21). While it is difficult to know exactly what this role entailed, it seems that he would have had oversight of the returned exiles but also have been accountable to the Persian authorities (Meyers and Meyers 1987: 13–16). Haggai also refers to him as the 'son of Shealtiel', which speaks of his Davidic lineage and qualification to rebuild the temple (Hag. 1:1, 14; 2:2, 23; cf. 1 Chr. 3:17).

In this first 'word of the LORD to Zerubbabel', Zerubbabel is told first that the temple-building project will be accomplished 'Not by might, and not by power, but by my Spirit'. Eising (1980: 353) determines the word for 'might' (*ḥayil*) is commonly used to mean 'strength', 'wealth' or even 'military forces', and is often associated with God. The accompanying term 'power' (*kōaḥ*) refers to human strength or ability given by God (e.g. Deut. 8:17; Amos 2:14; Isa. 10:13). Ps. 33:16 also combines these terms to declare that it is not by a king's 'might' nor by a warrior's 'power' that they are saved, but by God. Similarly, Ps. 127:1 declares:

> Unless the LORD builds the house,
> the builders labour in vain.

This message is consistent with the vision of the menorah that is continually supplied with oil. Whereas the menorah in the temple needed constant attending from the priests to remain alight, in Zechariah's vision the menorah is continually supplied with oil without the need for human attendants, and is supplied directly from resources outside itself. In the same way, Zerubbabel will be supplied with resources outside himself to rebuild the temple – Yahweh of hosts (cf. 1:3) will provide his Spirit (cf. Hag. 2:5). While the oil is not directly equated with the Spirit in the vision, the similar role the oil and Spirit serve supports their identification (Story 2010: 43). The means by which God's Spirit will build the temple becomes more apparent as the vision is further explained (cf. 'Comment' on vv. 13–14).

Zechariah is further told that all opposition to this project will be overcome: 'Who are you, great mountain? Before Zerubbabel you shall become level ground.' The Hebr. *mî* (Who?) is usually personal, which has led some to understand the 'great mountain' as an individual such as Joshua, the Samaritan governor Tattenai or hostile political powers such as Persia or the Samaritan authorities. Others have suggested it refers to the mound of rubble that remained after the destruction of the first temple (Halpern 1978). More likely, the 'great mountain' is a personification of all the difficulties Zerubbabel faced in his building project, which would include many of the suggestions above as well as spiritual and economic difficulties (cf. Hag. 1). The 'mountain' becoming 'level ground' echoes Isa. 40:4.

All the difficulties Zerubbabel faced will be overcome and there will be shouts of joy when he brings forth the 'top stone' (*hā'eben hārō'šāh*). A number of scholars argue that this stone is one that would commence the building process, based on analogies with Mesopotamian building practices, where a 'former brick' was removed from the ruin of the earlier building to become a part of the new building (Petersen 1974: 366–372; Halpern 1978: 167–180; Laato 1994). While there are some similarities between the account of the laying of the temple foundation and Mesopotamian practice (see 'Comment' on Hag. 2:18), there are difficulties in the timing if the stone here is understood as a foundation stone. The laying of the foundation was a past event, probably occurring on two different occasions: once in the second year after the exiles returned (Ezra 3:8; 5:16), and a second time some two months earlier than Zechariah's vision (Hag. 2:15, 18; Zech. 4:9; 8:9). Stead (2009: 179) argues that the closest intertextual parallel to 'top stone' is Ps. 118:22, which is not a 'foundation stone' but a 'capstone'. This type of stone suits the context much better.

The shouts of 'Grace, grace to it!' can be understood as a cry for Yahweh to bless the stone or the building. Alternatively, it is an acclamation of Yahweh's 'grace' or 'kindness' in bringing about the temple's construction, acknowledging that it has not been built by Zerubbabel's might and power, but by God's Spirit. The cry acclaims Yahweh's covenant faithfulness in keeping his promises.

8–10. A second word follows, which is a direct word to Zechariah from God (unmediated by the angel). This second word unambiguously states that Zerubbabel will complete the temple rebuilding project. This will confirm the authenticity of Zechariah's message (cf. 1:16; 2:9, 11; 8:9).

The statement that Zerubbabel 'has founded this house' corresponds with the account in Ezra 3:8–13, which has the foundation for the temple being laid by Zerubbabel some twenty years earlier. The attribution of this work to Sheshbazzar in Ezra 5:16 probably means that Zerubbabel was initially working under the authority of Sheshbazzar, who was the one mentioned in the official Persian records (H. G. M. Williamson 1985: 79).

Alternatively, the founding of 'this house' could refer to a second occasion that marked the recent recommencement of the work (cf. Hag. 2:15, 18). Zech. 8:9 connects the laying of the foundation of the temple with the work of the prophets (presumably Haggai and Zechariah), which must refer to this second occasion.

The statement 'his hands will finish it' indicates that whatever is meant in v. 6 by the temple being built by the Spirit of God, it does not mean that Zerubbabel will be a passive observer. This is a temple that will be built by human hands (cf. 6:12–13), but the linking of its completion with a confirmation of the prophet Zechariah's authenticity underlines again that the rebuilding of the temple will ultimately be a work of Yahweh of hosts.

The syntax of v. 10 is difficult but I have tried to follow the pointing of the MT (see 'Notes on the text'). Those who have 'despised a day of small things' describes those who were pessimistic about the building project, or who thought the temple (and the associated sacrifice) was still only a pale reflection of its former glory (cf. Ezra 3:12; Hag. 2:3). The phrase 'day of small things' reflects the slow and painful progress of rebuilding the temple (and the city and the community). It probably also indicates that the events of Zechariah's day were 'small' in comparison to what lay in the future (Webb 2003: 96). The implication of this question is that those who have despised the day of small things will be proved wrong.

As well as giving assurance that Zerubbabel will complete the temple (vv. 7, 9), this verse speaks of Yahweh's joy in seeing 'the chosen stone in the hand of Zerubbabel'. This 'chosen stone' most likely refers to the same completion stone of v. 7 (see 'Notes on the text'). 'These seven' seems to connect back to the 'seven lamps' of v. 2 which are now identified as 'the eyes of the LORD that are roaming through the whole earth'. This phrase is also found in 2 Chr. 16:9, where it is a statement of the omniscience and omnipotence of Yahweh being exercised to strengthen his people. A similar usage is also found in Ezra 5:5. This meaning connects well with what immediately precedes by implying God's presence to strengthen his people to complete the temple. The prospect of God's joy upon its completion would act as a great incentive to get on with the work. This word also further explains the menorah vision.

Some scholars argue from this phrase (and v. 14) that the menorah is a symbol for Yahweh. Others believe it represents the worshipping community since this menorah is dependent on outside resources (unlike Yahweh). The wider associations in the OT suggest that the menorah represents the concept of God's presence in the temple and hence his presence among his people. The menorah described in Exodus has tree-like qualities with branches, blossoms, calyxes and flowers (Exod. 25:31–40; 37:17–24). Longman (2001: 21) notes the connection between trees and places of worship (e.g. Gen. 12:6; 13:18) and argues that the connection evokes the Garden of Eden. Eden represented the special presence of God on earth, which dwelt with humanity. After Gen. 3, this special presence was associated with the tabernacle, and then the temple and gold menorah served as a symbol of this presence.

Fire is also associated with the presence of Yahweh in the OT (e.g. Gen. 15:17; 19:18; 24:17; Ezek. 1:13), and the burning menorah tree of the tabernacle brings to mind the revelation of Yahweh to Moses at the bush that was on fire but did not burn (Exod. 3:2–6). These wider associations suggest that the vision of a burning menorah is another way of representing the return of Yahweh to the temple and to his people (cf. 1:16; 2:5[9], 10[14], 13[17]). It is easy to see how this vision of a constantly burning menorah as a representation of Yahweh's presence in the temple would spur on Zerubbabel and the people to rebuild it, yet there are still details of the vision that remain unclear.

11–12. The prophet Zechariah responds with further questions. He returns to the question of v. 4, asking more explicitly about the 'two olive trees on the right of the menorah and on its left' (v. 11) and then about the 'streams of the olive trees' (v. 12). There are several difficult translation issues in this verse that are discussed in the 'Notes on the text' above. While some of the details of v. 12 are hard to pin down because of rare vocabulary, the overall picture is clear: the two olive trees provide oil for the menorah via two golden pipes, presumably emptying into the bowl, and from there fuelling each of the lamps. Zechariah focuses on these two trees that are pouring out this oil.

13–14. To Zechariah's repeated question the angel replies, seemingly despairing (v. 13), 'Do you not know what these are?' The implication is that Zechariah should have understood by now the significance of the two olive trees in his vision. He has not, and admits this to the angel, who then replies somewhat cryptically, 'These are the two sons of oil who are standing by the Lord of the whole earth.'

The expression 'sons of oil' explains that the olive trees produce the oil, like the expression 'sons of a flame' in Job 5:7 refers to 'sparks' that produce a flame. The 'two sons of oil' have traditionally been identified as Joshua and Zerubbabel, the two leaders of the post-exilic community, and in many cases the expression is translated as 'two anointed ones'. The main argument for this identification is the fact that the overall literary context of chs. 3 and 4 deals with Joshua and Zerubbabel respectively, and that the context apparently makes it clear that anointing is being alluded to. On this reading, the message of ch. 4 is that amid all the difficulties of rebuilding the community and the temple in Jerusalem, Yahweh would sustain his people, by his Spirit, through his Spirit-appointed leaders Joshua and Zerubbabel.

This traditional interpretation has been challenged. Boda (2004: 275), building on the work of Rose (2000: 177–207), argues that the 'two sons of oil' are the prophets Haggai and Zechariah (though Rose argues they are not human figures at all, but heavenly beings, attendants of the heavenly court). They note that the term used for 'oil' (*yiṣhār*) in v. 14 refers to 'fresh oil', the raw material, freshly squeezed, before it is prepared, whereas *šemen* is the more general word for oil, including oil as a final product used for anointing. This distinction is valid, as other scholars have observed, yet it must be noted that while *yiṣhār* is never used in contexts dealing with oil for anointing, neither is it used in contexts dealing with oil for burning lamps (as it is here), so too much should not be made of this distinction. Nonetheless, in the vision the 'sons of oil' are oil providers rather than oil recipients (as anointing would require). Kline (2001: 164) notes the expression 'sons of oil' is also used in Isa. 5:1 to refer to a plentiful source of oil, and this meaning of abundance and fertility seems to be the association here as the 'sons of oil' pour out the oil.

The expression 'who are standing by the Lord of all the earth' suggests that the 'sons of oil' have been admitted to the divine council, and are standing in God's presence (contra NIV, 'serve the Lord'). The prep. 'by' (*'al*) is used elsewhere in the context of the heavenly court (cf. 1 Kgs 22:19; Isa. 6:2). Indeed, it was one of the key marks of prophetic authority for the prophet to be admitted to the divine council (cf. Jer. 23:18–22) (Routledge 2008: 212).

Perhaps the key factor in identifying the two sons of oil as Haggai and Zechariah is their prominence in this period and their crucial role in rebuilding the temple. These two prophets are linked in Ezra 5:1–2 and 6:14–15, and are connected with the successful rebuilding of the temple. Furthermore, Zech. 8:9 sees these prophets as instrumental in its construction: 'So says the LORD of hosts, "Let your hands be strong, you who have been hearing in these days these words from the mouth of the prophets who [were present] in the day the house of the LORD of hosts was founded in order that the temple might be built"' (my tr.).

Boda (2004: 281) also helpfully highlights the way that the Spirit is most often connected with the prophetic office in the HB. The great prophet Moses is empowered by the Spirit, and through this same Spirit, seventy elders are enabled to prophesy (Num. 11:24–29). Other prophets are also said to prophesy through the enabling of the Spirit (e.g. Num. 24:2; 2 Kgs 2:9, 15–16; 2 Chr. 15:1; Neh. 9:30; Ezek. 2:2; 11:5; Dan. 4:18; Joel 2:28–29; Mic. 3:8.), and Zech. 7:12 later makes the connection between the work of the prophet and the Spirit explicit: 'They made their hearts as hard as flint and would not listen to the law or to the words that the LORD Almighty had sent by his Spirit through the earlier prophets.' As noted in the comments on v. 6, the menorah vision does not directly equate the oil with the Spirit; however, it is natural enough to equate them given the way Yahweh's word and Spirit work together. Furthermore, priests and kings were generally those who were anointed with oil, while the prophets anointed and spoke God's word to the kings. Kline (1980: 87), who also identifies the two sons of oil as prophets (though not limited to Haggai and Zechariah), comments, 'The prophets, outstandingly the paradigm prophet Moses, were God's chief agents for anointing.' In the vision, the 'two sons of oil' are oil providers, which fits the office of prophet better than the office of priest or king. Importantly, when this passage is cited in Rev. 11, the two olive trees are prophetic figures (Rev. 11:3–4).

The connection between Yahweh's Spirit and prophecy throws light on several key elements of this vision. In the context of the chapter as a whole, the vision report of 4:1–5 suggests that, since the menorah is supplied with oil without human instrumentation, it is a picture for Zechariah of how the temple will be reconstructed. While there are clearly humans involved, the main driving force will not be Zerubbabel, but Yahweh by his Spirit through his word proclaimed by the prophets. Hence when Zerubbabel is told that he will build the temple 'Not by might, and not by power, but by my Spirit', given the link between Yahweh's Spirit and the role of the prophets, this word from Yahweh indicates also that his word will be the main driving force behind the construction of the temple (cf. 8:9). Further evidence for the key role of the prophets is seen in 4:9, where the completion of the temple will be evidence that Zechariah is a true prophet of Yahweh (cf. 6:15).

This also may explain the difficulty that Zechariah has in understanding the identity of the two olive trees. Just as Moses and Jeremiah were hesitant to see the important role they would play as prophets (Exod. 4:10; Jer. 1:6), in a similar way, Zechariah may underestimate the key role he will play. He has to ask three times about the two olive trees that pour out the oil and fails to see himself in the vision.

While it is impossible to be certain of the identification of the 'two sons of oil' since they are not explicitly identified, on balance, the interpretation that they are the prophets Haggai and Zechariah best suits the wider context of Zechariah and best explains the menorah vision itself.

Explanation

The returned exiles were living in 'a day of small things' (4:10). With their return to Jerusalem they were facing major challenges, challenges described metaphorically as a 'great mountain' (4:7). The books of Ezra and Haggai give us a picture of both internal and external challenges: financial difficulties (Hag. 1:6), challenges from outside enemies (Ezra 4:1–3) and challenges of low morale (Hag. 1:14). Amid these difficulties, God had given this post-exilic community the task of restoring the temple and reconstructing their community life (chs. 1–2). The fourth vision envisions Joshua's being reinstated as the high priest (ch. 3), which offers the hope of forgiveness and cleansing. Against this background, Zechariah promises that the day of the Lord is coming along with Shoot (ch. 3). In the meantime, what will sustain the community as they rebuild? The answer of this fifth vision (ch. 4) is that it is God himself who will sustain them, by his Spirit, though his prophets. Indeed, this explains the central significance of 4:6 in this vision, which on this reading is anything but a later insertion into the text. Not only will Zerubbabel complete his task by the Spirit of God, but the Spirit, symbolized by oil in this vision, is also God's empowering presence among his people, who will sustain them through these challenges.

Boda (2004: 285) helpfully draws out an implication of this connection between the Spirit and the prophetic word: 'As in the early church, so today the powerful combination of Spirit and Word is essential to advance the church's mission. One of our greatest needs is a return to Spirit-filled proclamation of God's Word in our churches.' A further biblical-theological connection that strengthens this link between word and Spirit is the temple imagery. Just as the temple in Zerubbabel's day would ultimately be built by God's Spirit through the prophetic word, so Jesus' temple, the church, is built. Eph. 2:19–22 speaks of the temple of God's people being built on the foundation of the apostles and prophets, with Christ as the cornerstone, being built by the Spirit. The building method God uses today is exactly the same as in Zechariah's day. The temple of Christ's church is built by God's Spirit through his proclaimed word. Furthermore, just as there were those in Zechariah's day who scoffed at the day of small things, there are those today who have a diminished view of the power of preaching God's Word. The message of the vision is that God's Word in the power of the Spirit will accomplish his purposes – it sustains and achieves his mission. Furthermore, the continuous supply of oil suggests God will continue to supply the needs of his people in this work.

A second implication relates to the nature of the hope for the house of David in the book of Zechariah. This passage is often used to support the view that Zechariah believed Zerubbabel (and/or Joshua) to be the promised Shoot of 3:8; 6:12 (cf. Jer. 23:5; 33:15). However, in Zechariah 4, the 'two sons of oil' are oil suppliers, and not recipients. Furthermore, the word for 'oil' is not the word usually associated with anointing. For these reasons, even if the 'two sons of oil' are to be identified as Joshua and Zerubbabel, it seems inappropriate to see them as anointed or 'messianic'. Translating 'two sons of oil' as 'two anointed ones' is misleading. On balance, the identity of the 'two sons of oil' is more likely to be the prophets Haggai and Zechariah anyway. Elsewhere I have argued that Zechariah exhibits a robust hope for a future king from the house of David who will restore the fortunes of the people of Yahweh (Petterson 2009). While the building of the temple raises the hopes for a king to be reinstated on David's throne, particularly because of the hope held out by the covenant with David in 2 Sam. 7, there is no support from ch. 4 for the view that Zechariah envisaged Zerubbabel as this king. Zechariah obviously holds a high view of Zerubbabel and sees a significant role for him in the restoration community, especially as the builder of the temple, but there is no suggestion here or elsewhere in Zechariah that he is the promised Shoot. That one is a Davidide beyond him.

ZECHARIAH 5:1–4

Translation

5:1And again I lifted my eyes, and look! A flying scroll! 2And he said to me, 'What do you see?' And I said, 'I see a flying scroll – its length is 20 cubits and its breadth is 10 cubits.' 3And he said to me, 'This is the curse that is going out over the face of all the land, because every one who steals has been [wrongly] acquitted from what is on one side and every one who swears falsely has been [wrongly] acquitted from what is on the other side. 4I have sent it out,' declares the LORD of hosts, 'and it will enter into the house of the thief and into the house of the one swearing falsely in my name, and it will remain in the midst of his house, and it will destroy it and its timbers and its stones.'

Notes on the text

5:1. 'And again': *wā'āšûb* (cf. 6:1) emphasizes a repeated action and connects the vision with the previous one (LeCureux 2012: 179–180); see GKC 120d.

'and look!' translates 'and I saw and look!' (cf. 1:18; 2:1[5]; 5:9; 6:1).

'scroll' is translated 'sickle' in LXX, possibly reflecting a *Vorlage* where the final *h* was lost or obscured (Gelston 2010: 138*).

2. 'cubits': lit. 'by the cubit' (*bā'ammâ*). See GKC 134n.

3. 'from what is on one side . . . from what is on the other side': *mizzeh kāmôhā . . . mizzeh kāmôhā*. For this construction, see BDB 262. There are many instances where *mizzeh . . . mizzeh* refers to two sides or ends of an object (e.g. Exod. 25:19; 32:15; 37:8; Num. 22:24; 1 Sam. 14:4; 17:3; 2 Sam. 2:13; Ezek. 47:7).

'every one who swears falsely': lit. 'every swearer' (*wĕkol hannišbā'*). See 'Comment'.

'has been [wrongly] acquitted': *niqqâ* (ni. pf.) occurs twice in this verse. Elsewhere in the OT, *nqh* in the ni. means 'to be free (from guilt), be blameless' (e.g. Num. 5:31; Judg. 15:3; Jer. 2:35; Ps. 19:13[14]); or 'to be free, exempt' from an obligation such as an oath (e.g. Gen. 24:8, 41) or from a curse (e.g. Num. 5:19, 28); or 'to be clear, be exempt from punishment, be acquitted' with respect to a crime (e.g. Jer. 25:29; 49:12; Prov. 6:29). In the pi. this verb means 'to leave unpunished' (e.g. Deut. 5:11; Exod. 34:7; Jer. 30:11) or 'to declare as innocent, acquit' (Job. 9:28; 10:14). The only instance of the qal form is Jer. 49:12, where it is an inf. abs. combined with a ni. yiqtol in the same stem to make it emphatic: 'to indeed be acquitted' (Arnold and Choi 2003: 74–75). Apart from the two instances in 5:3, translations along these lines account for forty-one of the forty-two other instances of *nqh* in the OT. Only in Isa. 3:26 does it refer to Jerusalem, which is 'cleared out' or 'emptied' (H. G. M. Williamson 2006: 297). Nowhere else does *nqh* have the sense of being 'banished' (NIV), 'cleaned out' (ESV), 'cut off' (NRSV, AV) or 'expelled' (NKJV). In addition, as noted in the comment on 1:16, the 'rhetorical perfect' is infrequent (if not absent) in Zech. 1 – 8. '[wrongly]' is inserted to clarify the meaning for the reader. See further, Petterson 2014a: 347–361.

4. 'I have sent it out': *hôṣêʼtîhā* (hiph. pf.) is rendered with a past tense, rather than as a 'rhetorical perfect' (contra NIV and ESV). The scroll has already been sent out according to v. 3.

'the one swearing falsely in my name': lit. 'the one swearing in my name to the lie'.

'it will remain': *wĕlāneh*. For this unusual form, see GKC 73d, 80i.

'it will destroy it': *wĕkillattû*. For this form, see GKC 75mm.

Form and structure

While some scholars have argued that ch. 5 forms one vision (e.g. Keil, Kline), this seems to be driven by the concern to total the visions at seven rather than eight (Leupold 1956: 97). Zech. 5 contains two distinct visions, yet they are closely connected by structure and themes. The expression 'And again' (*wāʼāšûb*) begins 5:1 and 6:1, but is absent from 5:5. Furthermore, Butterworth (1992: 128) notes that *yāṣāʼ* (going out) is a significant word in both visions (5:3, 5–6). This movement of 'going out' is explained well by Webb (2003: 106), who demonstrates that there is an overall pattern to the visions: visions 1–3 represent Yahweh's returning to Jerusalem to dwell among his people; visions 4–5 centre on Jerusalem, with the cleansing and restoration of the priesthood along with the rebuilding of the temple; visions 6–7 are the outworking of Yahweh's return, with those who have wrongly been acquitted of covenant violations being judged by God with the curse that is 'going out' (vision 6), and then wickedness is 'going out' from his presence and the community in Jerusalem (vision 7).

The sixth vision can be divided into two parts. Vv. 1–2 report what Zechariah sees, and vv. 3–4 explain the vision. The genre is again that of a 'prophetic vision report' (Floyd 2000: 390).

Comment

5:1–2. 'I lifted my eyes, and look!' (see 'Comment' on 1:18). Zechariah is twice said to see a 'flying scroll' (*megillāh ʻāpāh*). The word for 'scroll' appears elsewhere in the OT only in Jer. 36 (fourteen times); Ezek. 2 – 3 (four times) and Ps. 40:7[8]. In Jer. 36 the scroll contains the words of God spoken to Jeremiah. They were words of judgment 'against Israel and Judah and all the nations' (36:2 ESV). As three or four columns of the scroll were read to king Jehoiakim, he cut them off with a knife and burned them in the fire. Afterwards, God assures that he will bring disaster on the royal house along with the inhabitants of Jerusalem and Judah, and another scroll was written on, confirming the earlier word of judgment (36:30–32). In Ezekiel, the prophet was given a scroll to eat that had writing on the front and back, and contained 'words of lament and mourning and woe' (Ezek. 2:10). Ezekiel was literally to internalize the message; and surprisingly, when he ate it, it tasted as sweet as honey (Ezek. 3:3; cf. Jer. 15:16). While the scroll contained a message of judgment on the disobedient, for those who obey, God's Word is sweet like honey (cf. Ps. 19:10). In Ps. 40:7, King David compares his reign to what is written in 'the scroll of the book' (ESV). This seems to be a reference to a scroll of the 'book' (*sēper*) of the Torah (cf. Deut. 31:24, 26) and the passage he is thinking of may well be Deut. 17:14–20. These passages suggest that the scroll Zechariah sees is to be connected with God's written words (Stead 2009: 193), something that becomes clearer in v. 3.

The identity of the one who questions Zechariah in vv. 2–4 about what he sees is not explicit, but it is almost certainly the angel of 4:1 who questions Zechariah in the previous vision (4:2, 5–6), and who speaks on behalf of Yahweh (cf. 1:14).

While seeing a scroll connects readily with the world of Zechariah's normal experience, two other aspects of the vision are extraordinary: the scroll is 'flying' and its dimensions are huge. The fact that it is 'flying' is interpreted variously as conveying notions of swiftness, omnipresence or imminence. Merrill (1994: 166) suggests that the fact that it is flying diminishes human agency, and this is certainly consistent with the interpretation of the vision in vv. 3–4 (and is similar to the previous vision). No one is holding or reading (or burning or eating) this scroll – it does the work of God directly.

Regarding the scroll's size: 'its length is 20 cubits and its breadth is 10 cubits'; that is, about 33 by 16.5 ft (10 by 5 m). Normal scrolls could be around 20 cubits in length (the great Isaiah Scroll from Qumran is close to 25 ft [7.5 m] in length), but the width of 10 cubits indicates that if this scroll is in the same proportions as a normal scroll, then this giant scroll is only partly unfurled. Meyers and Meyers (1992: 281–283) discuss this at some length.

Many scholars note that the dimensions are the same as the vestibule in front of the temple (1 Kgs 6:3) and suggest that it was here that the law was read to the people. This connects the scroll with the temple. Similarly, scholars point out that the two cherubim on the ark would have occupied the same dimensional space, and suggest that the scroll has replaced the ark and its tablets of the law. However, these links seem to be coincidental rather than intentional. There is nothing else in the vision that directly connects the scroll with the temple. Willi-Plein (2007: 104) suggests the dimensions are those of an average house in Judah so that when the scroll later visits the houses of v. 4 in judgment, it extends to every part of the house and destroys it totally. However, this is only an inference.

The size of the scroll at least indicates that it is clear for all to see. The intertextual background of the scroll, traced above, points to the scroll's containing God's written words, and this suggests that this scroll also has an imposing nature. It also raises the question of what the scroll has to say.

3–4. The scroll is explained as 'the curse that is going out over the face of all the land'. In his study of 'curse' in the HB, Brichto (1963: 70) concludes that a 'curse' (*'ālâ*) is present explicitly or implicitly in every oath and every covenant, and when the word 'curse' appears on its own, it may represent either of these. An oath with a curse may be taken when a crime cannot be proven, in asking God to punish if there is guilt (e.g. Num. 5:21–22). Similarly, the curses of a covenant were to fall on those who disobeyed (e.g. Deut. 28:15). Here the curse of the scroll is associated with punishment for theft and false swearing, both covenant violations.

'all the land' is a phrase that can mean the whole earth, or the land of Judah (see 'Comment' on 1:10). The same phrase is used in v. 6 and is contrasted with the 'land of Shinar' in v. 11. In the immediate context, where the curse of the covenant is applied to the inhabitants of 'all the land', the 'land' is best understood as the land of the people of Yahweh rather than the whole earth.

The two crimes mentioned in vv. 3–4 are often understood to be representative crimes of the Decalogue, where swearing falsely is a crime against Yahweh (commandment 3) and stealing is a crime against one's neighbour (commandment 8). With this interpretation, the two sides of the scroll are similar to the two sides of the Mosaic tablets (Exod. 32:15). A problem with this interpretation is that false swearing more closely correlates to the ninth rather than the third commandment, and the vocabulary of this crime deviates from that of the Decalogue, whether it is the third or the ninth commandment. Furthermore, the scroll is said to represent 'the curse that is going out over the face of all the land'. While the Decalogue says that God will judge iniquity to the third and fourth generation (Exod. 20:5; Deut. 5:9) and will not acquit the one who lifts up his name for vanity (Exod. 20:7; Deut. 5:11), it does not contain any specific curses. Both these crimes are mentioned elsewhere in Exodus, Leviticus and Deuteronomy, with the only context in which they appear in close proximity being Lev. 19:11–12. If the crimes are to be understood as a reference to Lev. 19, the problem is that the two crimes are part of a list in Lev. 19 and do not even appear consecutively – one would expect consecutive appearance if a direct quotation or allusion was intended. Another suggestion is that the commands of the Decalogue have been refracted through Jer. 7:9, where they are mentioned together (Freedman 1990: 46). However, these two crimes are part of a list in which crimes more directly related to the Decalogue are mentioned (e.g. murder, adultery and idolatry). This raises the question why these other crimes were not mentioned if Zechariah simply intended a clear inner-biblical allusion to the Decalogue.

Hence it seems that the scroll contains much more than the Decalogue and represents the 'law of Moses' more broadly (cf. Dan. 9:11), especially since the scroll is identified as 'the curse' (v. 3). This description suggests the scroll includes the covenant curses stipulated elsewhere in the law (e.g. Lev. 26; Deut. 28 – 29). Furthermore, if the vision was intended to bring to mind the Decalogue only, one might wonder why Zechariah did not see a giant stone tablet or two (Petterson 2014a: 356–357). Perhaps the scroll represents a form of the scroll of Deuteronomy (cf. Deut. 28:61; 29:20; 30:10; 31:26; Josh. 1:8; 8:31, 34; 23:6; 24:26; 2 Kgs 24:6; 22:8, 11; 2 Chr. 17:9; 34:14–15; Neh. 8:1 – 9:3).

In any case, it is more likely that these crimes were mentioned in the first instance because they were the crimes that were actually impacting the post-exilic community. There is evidence in Hag. 1:6 of socioeconomic disadvantage, a circumstance in which these crimes might be prevalent (cf. Baldwin 1972: 126). Redditt (1995: 72) and Boda (2004: 295) suggest that the theft was in relation to real estate, particularly since the judgment involves the destruction of the perpetrator's house. They suggest this was a problem with those who had remained in Palestine during the exile, who had not relinquished control of the land to those who were returning from Babylon. In addition, the charge in 8:17 to 'not love a false oath' also suggests that swearing falsely was a problem in Zechariah's day, and the charge in 8:17 to render 'a judgment of peace' in 'your gates' also implies a failure of justice (cf. 7:8–12).

While it is common to translate the verb *nāqâ* along the lines of 'shall be cleaned out', this is unlikely in terms of both lexicography and grammar (see 'Notes on the text'). Furthermore, it obscures important inner-biblical connections. Throughout the Book of the Twelve, God's character as revealed in Exod. 34:6–7 is frequently referred to (e.g. Hos. 2:19[21]; Joel 2:13; 3:21[4:21]; Jon. 4:2; Mic. 7:18–19; Nah. 1:3). Whereas Zech. 3 portrays God's 'forgiving wickedness, rebellion and sin' (Exod. 34:7; cf. Zech. 3:4, 9), this vision declares that God 'does not leave the guilty unpunished' (lit. 'will by no means acquit') (Exod. 34:7; cf. Joel 3:21[4:21]; Nah. 1:3). The vocabulary of acquittal in Exod. 34:7 is exactly the same as here (twice in this verse). It is also found in the Decalogue in Exod. 20:7. The problem being addressed is that rather than being punished, the guilty have wrongly been acquitted. The statement implies a corruption of justice in the post-exilic community, where those who had committed these crimes had not yet received the penalty their crimes were due. The vision looks to God's coming to bring justice and set things right. He will not acquit the guilty.

In the vision, the Lord of hosts (see 'Comment' on 1:3) has sent out the scroll of his curse (v. 4). This gives assurance that his justice is coming. The word 'house' is used three times in v. 4. While the 'house' of 3:7 and 4:9 is the temple to which Yahweh will return and provide forgiveness, these houses of the guilty will be destroyed. While a house normally provides refuge, here the scroll of God's curse will enter it and remain in its midst and 'will destroy it and its timbers and its stones' (cf. Hab. 3:13; Dan. 2:5; 3:29; Ezra 6:11). While not explicit, the death of the inhabitants is implied by the imagery and by association with the curse on covenant breakers in the law (cf. Deut. 30:15).

Explanation

Chs. 1–4 portray Yahweh's turning with mercy to his people and promising to return to dwell once again in his house in Jerusalem. This vision and the next show how the return of Yahweh will bring about the destruction of the ungodly and their houses and cause iniquity, wickedness and idolatry to be driven far from the land.

This is all consistent with God's character as proclaimed to Moses on the mountain as God's glory passed by (Exod. 34:6–7). Zech. 2:8 has already connected God's glory with his departure from Jerusalem, as depicted by Ezekiel. With God's return, this sixth vision underlines the fact that God will by no means acquit the guilty (Exod. 34:7). The vision of a huge flying scroll represents the curse of the law of Moses going out over the land to bring destruction on all who have gone unpunished for their continued rebellion.

This vision has two implicit functions. First, it comforts those who have been sinned against and are troubled by those who seem to sin and get away with it. It provides assurance that God will be true to his word and that it will accomplish its purposes (cf. Isa. 55:11). Secondly, it provides a warning to those who continue to do these things to repent (cf. 1:3; 7:8–10). In the vision, the huge flying scroll has already gone out – God's judgment is imminent and there is no escaping it. Calvin (1986: 132) puts it clearly: 'by these words he [Zechariah] reminds us how terrible it is to fall into the hands of God, for he will punish the ungodly and the wicked until he reduces them to nothing'.

This passage reminds Christians of the curse that fell on Jesus (Gal. 3:13). The marvellous truth is that he redeemed his people from the curse of the law by becoming a curse for them. However, for all who reject the Lord Jesus and seem to get away with it in this life, this vision is a reminder of another scroll that is in the hands of the risen Lord Jesus, the Lamb who was slain (Rev. 5:9). A scroll whose seals he is breaking, bringing judgment that will culminate in the great day of God's wrath from which no one can hide (Rev. 6:12–17).

ZECHARIAH 5:5–11

Translation

5:5 And the angel who spoke with me went out and he said to me, 'Lift up your eyes and look. What is this that is going out?' 6 And I said, 'What is it?' And he said, 'This is an ephah going out.' And he said, 'This is their iniquity in all the land.' 7 And look, a talent of lead was being lifted up, and this was one woman who had been enthroned in the midst of the ephah. 8 And he said, 'This is wickedness.' And he thrust her into the midst of the ephah and thrust the lead stone on its opening.

9 And I lifted my eyes, and look! Two women were going out, and the wind was in their wings. And they had wings like the wings of the stork, and they lifted up the ephah between the earth and the heavens. 10 And I said to the angel who spoke with me, 'Where are they taking the ephah?' 11 And he said to me, 'To build for it a house in the land of Shinar. And it will be established and it will be set there upon its base.

Notes on the text

5:5. 'went out': *yāṣā'* is the same verb translated 'going out' at the end of this verse and in vv. 6 and 9. While most translations translate it as 'came forward' (e.g. NIV, NRSV), since the ephah is going out (*yāṣā'*) and the angel is later directly involved with the ephah (v. 8), the usual translation of *yāṣā'* has been followed (cf. 2:3[7]).

6. 'an ephah': *hā'êpâ* contains a generic use of the art., which is not translated (Waltke and O'Connor 1990: 246).

'their iniquity' follows the suggested emendation in *BHS* of 'their eye' (*'ênām*) to *'ăwōnām*. This supposes that MT contains a simple copying error (waw to yod), a supposition supported by LXX and Syr. See 'Comment'.

7. 'was being lifted up': *niśśē't* is a contracted f. ptc. form. See GKC 74i.

'and this was': *wĕzō't* is an anaphoric pr., referring to the talent of lead that has the form of 'one woman' (C. J. Thomson 2013: 130).

'who had been enthroned': *yôšebet* is an attrib. ptc., and its time and aspect are determined from context. It could also be translated, 'who had been sitting' (C. J. Thomson 2013: 130).

8. 'wickedness': *hāriš'â* contains a generic use of the art., which is not translated (Waltke and O'Connor 1990: 246).

9. 'and look!' translates 'and I saw and look!' (cf. 1:18; 2:1[5]; 5:1, 6:1).

'their wings': *bĕkanpêhem* has a m. pr. suff., when one would expect f. Yet this also happens in 5:10 and 3:9.

'And they had wings like': lit. 'And to them were wings like'.

10. 'they': *hēmmâ* is the m. pr., but here stands for the f. See GKC 32n.

'taking': *môlikôt* is the f. pl. hiph. ptc. of *hālak*.

11. 'Shinar': LXX, Syr and Tg all read 'Babel' instead of Shinar.

'it will be established and it will be set': *wĕhûkan wĕhunnîḥâ* are 3 m. sg. and 3 f. sg. respectively (hoph. pf.). J. C. L. Gibson (1994: 24) notes that when there are several predicates, one may be in agreement and the other left uninflected. More likely, the first refers to the 'house' (m.) and the second verb refers to the 'ephah' (f.). The syntax is unusual.

Form and structure

The two visions of ch. 5 are distinct, yet are closely connected by structure and themes. Together they portray the removal from the land of all that is opposed to Yahweh. In addition to the features noted under 'Form and structure' for 5:1–4, v. 6 closely connects the visions since the pr. 'their' most naturally refers back to the thief and the one who swears falsely in v. 4. An unusual feature of the seventh vision is the direct participation of the interpreting angel in the vision as he thrusts the woman back into the ephah (cf. 2:4[8] where the interpreting angel in the vision is told to speak to the man with the measuring line).

The seventh vision can be divided into two parts (vv. 5–8 and 9–11). In v. 5, Zechariah is told by the interpreting angel to 'lift up your eyes and look'. After Zechariah's question, the angel reports and explains what is seen. In v. 9, Zechariah says, 'I lifted my eyes, and look!', reports what he sees and asks a question, to which the angel replies. Thematically, each section provides a different view: vv. 5–8 picture an ephah with a woman sitting inside, and vv. 9–11 picture the ephah being transported to Shinar by two women with wings like those of a stork for it to be set up in a purpose-built house. The 'house' theme echoes that of the previous three visions (3:7; 4:9; 5:4).

Several scholars note direct allusions to the themes of Ezek. 1 – 11. For instance, Stead (2009: 197–199) observes that Yahweh departed from his house in Jerusalem on a throne chariot attended by winged creatures riding on the wind. The reason for his departure was iniquity (Ezek. 4:4), wickedness (Ezek. 3:18–19; 5:6) and idolatry (Ezek. 8). Now that Yahweh is returning to Jerusalem with his house being rebuilt, this vision portrays the forced departure of iniquity, wickedness and idolatry in a parody of Yahweh's earlier departure. Stead (2009: 197) argues, 'Zech 5:5–11 depicts an "anti-ark" borne by "anti-cherubs," to be put in an "anti-temple" in an "anti-Jerusalem."'

Comment

5:5–6. The 'angel who spoke with me' is the same angel of the previous visions who questions Zechariah, explains aspects of the visions and speaks on behalf of Yahweh (cf. 1:14; 4:6). While many scholars understand the angel to be moving towards Zechariah from the temple, the verb *yṣ'* is better translated as 'went out'. The angel moves away from Zechariah towards the ephah, which is also 'going out' (the same verb is used at the end of v. 5). The angel later thrusts the woman into the ephah (v. 8), so it seems natural to understand the angel as moving towards the ephah here. The movement is in the same direction as the flying scroll (5:3).

Meyers and Meyers (1987: 295) note the importance of the movement throughout the vision. The movement *away* mirrors the movement of Yahweh *towards* Jerusalem in the first five visions. As Yahweh returns to his people and a temple is built for him, all that opposes him is destroyed and driven from the land (5:3, 5–6).

As the angel goes out, he says to Zechariah, 'Lift up your eyes and look. What is this that is going out?' This phrase indicates that the sequence of visions continues. Yet, unlike the earlier visions, here Zechariah does not report anything that he sees; instead, he asks, 'What is it?'

The angel replies, 'This is an ephah going out.' The word 'ephah' occurs forty times in the OT. Elsewhere it is always a unit of measure for grain or flour and by extension refers to the measuring vessel itself. The material of the ephah is not stated in the vision, but it could have been ceramic or a basket of woven reeds (Hoglund and Walton 2009: 215). It is thought to be around 7 gal (36 l) (Powell 1992: 904). In half of its instances 'the ephah' is associated with priestly offerings at the tabernacle or temple (e.g. Lev. 5:11; 1 Sam. 1:24; Ezek. 45:13). On nine occasions, it is found in an injunction to use a 'just' or 'honest ephah' (e.g. Lev. 19:36; Deut. 25:14–15; Prov. 20:10; Ezek. 45:10; Amos 8:5; Mic. 6:10). The ephah therefore has associations with both worship and trade. Sweeney (2000b: 621) suggests that since Judah was a province of the Persian Empire, Judah would be expected to send back tribute to their Persian overlords, and this might have taken the form of grain in an ephah. In this vision something quite different is sent back.

After identifying the object in the vision, the angel explains, 'This is their eye' or 'This is their iniquity in all the land.' This raises a text-critical issue that is difficult to resolve (see 'Notes on the text'), but fortunately the decision does not significantly change the overall meaning of the vision.

The difficulty of understanding the MT ('their eye') is seen in the number of different proposals, such as this is 'the appearance' of the people, or what wickedness looks like (NIV footnote); this is what the wicked (or the nations) 'have their eye on' or are relying on (Ollenburger 1996: 780); that it is an idiom meaning 'what they see', namely everyone will see the removal of wickedness (Smith 1984: 209); that 'their eye' is a reference to the Persian authorities (Sweeney 2000b: 620) or the eye of the forces of evil who assert dominion (woefully) over all the earth (Merrill 1994: 173); or, taking the suff. as an objective gen., referring to the 'eye of God', who sees the evildoers (Calvin 1986: 134). While difficult, in favour of following the MT is the way 'eye' is used in the earlier visions, with similar challenges in understanding its meaning (2:8[12]; 4:10).

Alternatively, the MT contains a copying error and should read 'their iniquity'. This suits the context much better, but the fact that it fits the context well could also explain why a scribe copied 'eye' as 'iniquity'. On either reading, the referent of the 3 m. pl. pr. ending ('their') is not clear, but the previous pl. reference is the thief and the one who swears falsely in the prior vision (Floyd 2000: 393). If we follow the reading 'iniquity', then the ephah represents the iniquity of those who transgressed the covenant. 'Iniquity' refers to sin and its associated guilt, and can also extend to its punishment (Koch 1999: 546). In 3:4, it referred to the guilt of the high priest Joshua, which was taken away as he was reclothed. Here it is the iniquity 'in all the land' that is best understood as the land of the people of Yahweh rather than the whole earth (cf. 5:3 and 'Comment' on 1:10). It is later contrasted with the 'land of Shinar' (v. 11).

On this reading there is a clear connection between what is seen and what it represents: an ephah representing 'their iniquity in all the land' brings to mind an unjust ephah, noted earlier, and makes it an apt vessel to transport iniquity. This association and the intertextual connection with Ezek. 4:4 tip the balance in favour of following LXX and Syr in reading 'their iniquity'.

7–8. After identifying the 'ephah', the action in the vision continues: 'And look' (*wĕhinnēh*). Most translate 'talent of lead' as a 'cover of lead' or 'lead[en] cover' (e.g NIV, NRSV, ESV, NASB). Yet the word translated 'cover' (*kikkar*) is normally associated with silver or gold as a unit of currency (a 'talent'). Translating it 'cover' would be unique in sixty-eight instances of the word in the OT. Following the Hebr. more closely, C. J. Thomson (2013: 138–142) argues that it is a 'talent of lead' that is lifted out of the ephah and this is then identified as a woman, namely a statuette. Since a talent of lead (around 66 lb [30 kg]) would occupy only about 4 pt (2.5 l), there is no problem fitting it into the ephah (C. J. Thomson 2013: 137). Yet there would be no problem with its being a regular woman either, since this is a vision and real-life proportions are unnecessary in the visionary world (cf. the huge size of the scroll in the previous vision).

Stead (2009: 201) makes the intriguing suggestion that 'talent of lead' (*kikkar 'ōperet*) is a play on words with the 'mercy seat' (*kappōret*), which covered the ark of the covenant. Whereas Yahweh was enthroned on the mercy seat, this woman is 'enthroned' in the ephah. He argues that the ephah is an anti-ark. There are additional features of the vision that support this (below).

The reason for numbering her as 'one woman' is unclear. Meyers and Meyers (1987: 302) suggest the number 'one' (*'aḥat*) may simply anticipate the 'two' flying women in v. 9. Alternatively, it may be an echo of the Shema (Deut. 6:4; cf. Zech. 14:9), further indicating the woman is an anti-god figure. The interpreting angel identifies the woman as 'wickedness' (*hāriš'â*). Ringgren (2004: 3–5) notes that this term is strikingly infrequent in prophetic literature, but significantly it does occur in Ezek. 3:18–19 in the context of the throne-chariot vision. He believes that Mal. 3:18 almost provides a definition of this term with its assertion that the 'righteous' is one who serves God, while the 'wicked' (*rāšā'*) is one who does not.

There are several possibilities for why the woman is identified as 'wickedness'. The first is that the Hebr. word for wickedness is f. (Baldwin 1972: 129). However, there seems to be more going on than this. The second is to see a connection between the woman and the way that covenant unfaithfulness is portrayed as an unfaithful woman by other prophets (e.g. Hos. 1 – 3; Ezek. 16, 23). This covenant unfaithfulness also connects with the unjust ephah and passages such as Mic. 6:10 (Petersen 1985: 259). The third is to understand the woman as representing idolatry. Stead (2009: 202) notes that the best evidence for this is that the word for 'wickedness' (*hāriš'â*) is a near anagram for 'Asherah', with the foreign god being mocked by using a pun on her name. In Jer. 7:18, 'the Queen of Heaven' is another name for Asherah, and wickedness is associated with idolatry in Deut. 9:4–5; Ezek. 5:6–7; Mal. 1:4; 3:15, 19. While the worship of Asherah is not otherwise known in the post-exilic period, the word 'Asherah' would continue to be known and bring to mind idolatry. This suits the identification of the talent of lead as a woman, namely an idol statuette. Fourthly, some scholars suggest that the woman represents the foreign women brought into the Jewish community in the post-exilic period. While there is no direct evidence for this in Haggai and Zechariah, Meyers and Meyers (1992: 301) cite Ezra 10:18 as later evidence for this in Zechariah's day. However, this is less likely given the associations of idolatry in the vision.

With the woman identified, the angel 'thrust her into the midst of the ephah and thrust the lead stone on its opening'. The word for 'thrust' (hiph. of *šālak*), used twice here, suggests reasonable force was used (cf. Exod. 7:10; 32:19; Judg. 15:17; 2 Kgs 23:6; 2 Chr. 33:15; Jer. 26:23).

'The lead stone' (*'eben hā'ōperet*) uses a different phrase to the 'talent of lead' (*kikkar 'ōperet*) of the previous verse (further indicating they are different objects). The 'lead' may emphasize the weight of the cover that is forced over the mouth of the ephah. There may also be further trade associations since the term 'stone' (*'eben*) is also used as a measure of weight and is often found in injunctions for 'honest weights' (lit. 'righteous stones') (e.g. Lev. 19:36; cf. Deut. 25:13; 2 Sam. 14:26; Prov. 16:11; 20:10, 23; Mic. 6:11).

9. 'And I lifted my eyes, and look!' provides a transition into the next scene (cf. 1:18; 2:1; 6:1). Here Zechariah looks without being asked (cf. v. 5). It is not an entirely new scene, but new characters are introduced (*wĕhinnēh*). Two women are 'going out' (cf. comments on v. 5) with the wind in their wings. These are not regular women. Meyers and Meyers (1987: 305) contrast them with the two cherubs on the ark of the covenant with wings that spread out over the mercy seat. Stead (2009: 198) observes further connections with the winged cherubs of Ezekiel's vision, who are also animated by the wind (*rûaḥ*; cf. Ezek. 1:4–6, 20–24; 10:16–21) and who 'lift' the ephah 'between the earth and the heavens' (cf. Ezek. 8:3). The phrase 'I lifted my eyes' also echoes Ezek. 8:5.

Many scholars note that the stork is listed among the unclean animals in the law (Lev. 11:19; Deut. 14:18). However, eagles are also listed as unclean, yet they elsewhere have a positive function (e.g. Exod. 19:4; Isa. 40:31), so too much should not be made of this. Similarly, it is difficult to determine whether the similarity between the word for 'stork' (*ḥăsîdâ*) and 'faithful' (*ḥāsîd*) is significant, particularly since it is not the birds that are primarily in view, but women with stork's wings. The fact that storks are large birds with powerful wings, which migrate northwards from the land of Judah each year (cf. Jer. 8:7), make their wings appropriate for these women who lift up the woman in the ephah 'between the earth and the heavens', a phrase that simply indicates 'above the ground' (cf. 2 Sam. 18:9; Ezek. 8:3).

10–11. Zechariah, again responding with a question to the angel (cf. v. 6), asks, 'Where are they taking the ephah?' The angel's response clarifies the meaning of the vision and ties it into the wider visionary sequence of chs. 1–6.

The phrase 'to build for it a house' mirrors the earlier theme of Yahweh's 'house' being built in Jerusalem (1:16; 3:7; 4:9). Stead (2009: 200) calls this structure an anti-temple. The location 'Shinar' is the ancient name for Babylonia, which occurs in Gen. 11:2 with the tower builders. The use of the older name probably reflects the fact that Babylon as such no longer posed a threat to God's people (cf. 1:15, 18–21; 2:7), but what it represented did. Delkurt (2008: 247) argues that by using the older name 'sin is banished from the present history of Israel and brought to a far, lost realm from where it can never return and where it belongs'. The reference to a 'house' also echoes the end of the previous vision, where the curse of the flying scroll enters the house of the thief and the one who swears falsely to destroy it.

In the final phrase, each verb is inflected for a different gender (see 'Notes on the text'). The first most likely refers to the 'house' (m.) or temple: 'And it will be established' (*wĕhûkan*). Then the ephah (f.): 'and it will be set' (*wĕhunnîḥâ*) there. This latter idea also connects with the next vision, where God's Spirit is 'set at rest' in the land of the north (6:8).

The word translated 'base' (*mĕkunātâ*) occurs twenty-five times in the OT, and in every other instance refers to a stand on which some cultic object is set (e.g. 1 Kgs 7:27; 2 Kgs 25:23; Jer. 27:19; Ezra 3:3). Again, this portrays the ephah as an anti-ark. There seems to be a sense in which the woman in the ephah is set up as a giant idol, especially since idolatry was one of the key sins that drove Yahweh from the temple in Jerusalem in the first place (Ezek. 8). However, the woman in the ephah should not be understood as representing only idolatry, but covenant unfaithfulness more broadly.

Explanation

The background for this vision is found in the opening chapters of Ezekiel, where Yahweh departs from Jerusalem on a throne chariot because of iniquity (Ezek. 4:4), wickedness (Ezek. 3:18–19; 5:6) and idolatry (Ezek. 8). Each of these sins clearly violates Yahweh's covenant with Israel. Yahweh's departure was the death sentence for Jerusalem with the destruction of the temple and Babylonian exile. With the exile over, chs. 1–4 portray the return of Yahweh with mercy and his promise to return to dwell once again in his house in Jerusalem. The sixth and seventh visions of ch. 5 show how the return of Yahweh will be mirrored by the destruction of the ungodly and cause iniquity, wickedness and idolatry to be driven far from the land.

The vision itself evokes many associations that remain elusive until the whole picture is developed. The ephah, talent and stone of lead are words associated with trade and bring to mind issues of injustice. The ephah is also associated with worship and offerings in the temple. As mentioned above, in Hebr. 'wickedness' (*hāriš'â*) sounds like 'Asherah' and brings to mind idolatry. However, it is the second half of the vision, with its clear allusions to Ezek. 8, which makes it clear that the ephah is a parody of the ark of the covenant with anti-cherub attendants who raise up the ephah between the earth and heaven to carry it to Shinar where an anti-temple will be established for it. In doing this, wickedness will be sent back to where it belongs. This then clarifies some of the earlier ambiguous associations such as the 'talent of lead', which sounds like 'mercy seat', and the posture of the woman who is 'enthroned' in the basket under the lid. It is an ingenious presentation. There is also an echo of the Day of Atonement ritual in Lev. 16, which has two distinct phases: after the temple is cleansed, the scapegoat is sent far away. These two phases are mirrored in the wider visionary sequence with Joshua being cleansed and the temple being built (visions 4 and 5), and now wickedness itself is being sent far away. An important function of this vision and the previous one is 'to reassure God's people that he himself will deal with the sin that in the past has incurred his wrath and precluded his blessing' (C. J. Thomson 2013: 153).

For Christians, the message of the final eradication of idolatry and wickedness points towards the second coming of Jesus Christ. In his first coming, Jesus brought cleansing and bought redemption from wickedness through his death on the cross. This passage connects more readily with the way Jesus will deal with iniquity, wickedness and idolatry in his second coming, and that is by casting out of his presence all who reject him and thereby continue in wickedness (2 Thess. 1:7–10).

The house in 'Shinar' connects with the biblical portrayal of Babylon (cf. 'Explanation' of Zech. 2). Rev. 17 portrays Babylon as a prostitute because of its attractiveness that seduces people away from God. Babylon was marvellous in its technology and wealth. The hanging gardens of Babylon were one of the ancient wonders of the world and represented human ingenuity at its best. Today Babylon is anti-God Western society with its glamour, glitz, technology and entertainment that promises so much pleasure. Yet Revelation shows that Babylon turns out to be a hideous beast that seduces people for destruction. The danger for the people in Zechariah's day is the same for Christians today – the seductiveness of the wickedness and idols of Babylon. This vision portrays Babylon (Shinar) as the polar opposite of God's kingdom and shows that there is no place in God's kingdom for wickedness and idolatry.

More broadly, these chapters of Zechariah challenge God's people with two very different building projects with radically different outcomes. There is the building of God's temple to which God would return to dwell in their midst and bring blessing. The alternative is the building of houses of iniquity and wickedness, houses that will ultimately come under his judgment and be put out of his kingdom. Zechariah challenges God's people to be busy with building God's kingdom. For Christians that involves proclaiming Jesus and living by his Word. That is the building that will last.

Finally, some scholars are concerned about what this passage says about women. For instance, Ollenburger (1996: 781) says, 'The outright misogyny in this text cannot be ignored . . . There is no simple solution to the disturbing attitude toward women proclaimed in this text.' While the image of a woman constrained in a basket is disturbing, those who read this passage as misogynistic or promoting violence against women have not understood the intent of the imagery nor the logic of what is being said. The passage does not say that a 'woman' *equates* with 'wickedness'. It says that this visionary statuette of a woman in the ephah *represents* wickedness. To abstract this out as a statement about every woman is illegitimate. It would be the same as saying that because wisdom is represented as a woman in Proverbs, Proverbs presents all women as wise. Or because folly is represented as a woman, then Proverbs presents all women as foolish. The fallacy of such an argument is clear. In addition, this argument misrepresents the positive portrayal of women throughout the rest of the OT, beginning with their being made in the image of God (Gen. 1:27). Indeed, the people of God are often represented in f. terms (e.g. Zech. 2:10; 9:9). The image of a woman statuette in a basket is meant to shock to some degree. But as horrifying as the image may be, the horror of the wickedness the woman in the ephah represents is greater still. It is true that this passage shows that sometimes force must be used to restrain wickedness, but to read this passage as promoting violence against women is gravely mistaken.

ZECHARIAH 6:1–8

Translation

[6:1]And again I lifted my eyes, and look! Four chariots going out from between the two mountains and the mountains were mountains of bronze. [2]With the first chariot were chestnut horses and with the second chariot were black horses. [3]And with the third chariot were white horses and with the fourth chariot were piebald horses – they were valiant. [4]And I said to the angel who spoke with me, 'What are these, my lord?' [5]And the angel said to me, 'These are the four winds of the heavens going out on account of the taking of a stand against the Lord of the whole earth, [6]against which the black horses were going out to the land of the north and the white ones went out after them and the piebald ones went out to the land of the south. [7]The valiant ones went out and they sought to go to patrol in the earth.' And he said, 'Go, patrol in the earth.' So they patrolled in the earth. [8]And he summoned me and he spoke to me, 'See, the ones going out to the land of the north have set at rest my Spirit in the land of the north.'

Notes on the text

6:1. 'And again': *wā'āšub* (cf. 5:1) emphasizes a repeated action and connects the vision with the previous one (LeCureux 2012: 179–180); see GKC 120d.

'and look!' translates 'and I saw and look!' (cf. 1:18; 2:1[5]; 5:1, 9).

2. 'chestnut': see 'Notes on the text' for 1:8.

'black': *šĕḥōrîm* is an achromatic colour lexeme that references colours ranging from 'dark brown' to 'black' (Hartley 2010: 33). As a verb it describes the dark colour of a person's skin after a long illness (Job 30:30); as a noun it stands for 'soot' (Lam. 4:8); as an adj. (as here) it often modifies 'hair'; and in Song 5:11 it is compared to the colour of a raven.

3. 'white': see 'Notes on the text' for 1:8.

'piebald': *bĕruddîm* is a colour lexeme with restricted usage. It is also a description of the breeding he-goats of Jacob in Gen. 31:10, 12. Rather than being a solid colour, it more properly refers to 'speckles, spots, or patches', which are likely 'white' or 'light' in colour (Hartley 2010: 156).

Gelston (2010: 139*) and many translations (e.g. NIV, ESV) believe 'valiant' (*'ămuṣṣîm*) applies to all four groups of horses. Gelston argues that LXX and Tg mistakenly assume it is a further colour, and Syr has omitted it by accident or because it was felt to be unintelligible in context. The construction is unusual, but one might expect a waw before *'ămuṣṣîm* if it applied only to the piebald horses. The translation and interpretation of v. 7 are also significant here.

4. 'And I said to': lit. 'And I answered and I said to' (cf. 4:4).

5. 'And the angel said': lit. 'And the angel answered and he said' (cf. 4:14). LXX has 'The angel who was speaking to me'.

Tg reads, 'These are the four kingdoms which are like the four winds'. Gordon (1994: 197) believes 'it is influenced by Dan. 7:2ff.'

'on account of the taking of a stand': *mēhityaṣṣēb* is an inf. clause with a causal use of *min* (Rogland 2014: 121).

6. 'against which': *'ăšer bâ*. Lit. 'which against it'.

'after them': *'el- 'aḥărêhem*. Many translations emend the text (without textual support) to yield horses going in four different compass points, but this is unnecessary and obscures the overall meaning of the vision, which focuses on 'the land of the north' (v. 8). See 'Comment'.

7. LXX and Tg have only the fourth chariot here, as in v. 3. Syr has *pyrroi* for 'valiant ones'.

BHQ notes that MT^{L} contains an error in not having a raised silent shewa in the final kaph of *lĕhithallēk*. It is present in MT^{C}.

The verb 'to seek' (*bāqaš*) governs its verbal complement, in this case the inf. 'to go' (Waltke and O'Connor 1990: 602).

'So they patrolled': *wattithallaknâ* is f. and refers to the chariots (v. 1) rather than the horses.

8. 'And he summoned me': *wayyazʿēq 'ōtî* (hiph. with acc.). Clines (1996: 128) gives the meanings of *zʿq* as 'cry out to, call together, summon' (cf. 2 Sam. 20:4–5; Judg. 4:10, 13).

'have set at rest': *hēnîḥû* (hiph.). Gelston (2010: 139*) suggests that some LXX MSS and Syr may reflect an earlier text with a waw prefix, though it is more likely to have been added for stylistic reasons.

Form and structure

This is the final vision in the sequence of eight visions that began in 1:7. It rounds out the sequence nicely with a number of connections back to the opening visions and the resolution of themes raised there. In the first vision there was a single rider on a chestnut horse, with a group comprising multiple chestnut, sorrel and white horses that patrolled (hith. of *hālak*) the earth and returned with the lamentable news that the earth, rather than God's people (1:11), was 'at rest' (*šōqāṭet*). In this final vision there are four groups of coloured horses (chestnut, black, white and piebald), this time with chariots, that are sent out to patrol (hith. of *hālak*) the earth and in doing this 'set at rest' (*hēnîḥû*) God's Spirit in the land of the nations (6:8). The second and third visions envision the coming destruction of the nations, particularly Babylon, 'the land of the north' (2:6[10]). In this vision, 'the land of the north' is finally judged (6:8).

The vision can be divided simply into two sections. Vv. 1–3 report what Zechariah saw, and vv. 4–8 explain the vision. The comment of Keil (1949: 294) is apt: 'in all these visions the interpretations of the angel do not furnish a complete explanation of all the separate details of the vision, but simply hints and expositions of certain leading features, from which the meaning of the whole may be gathered'.

There is an increasing frequency of the verb 'going out' (*yāṣā'*) through the visions. It occurs seven times in this final vision (cf. twice in vision three, once in vision five, twice in vision six and four times in vision seven). In this final vision, God's chariots are sent out to patrol in the land and this completes the 'outwards' movement (Stead 2009: 208). Whereas God had driven wickedness to the land of Shinar in the previous vision, in this vision his Spirit is said to be set at rest in the same region.

Comment

6:1. 'And again I lifted my eyes, and look!' (see 'Comment' on 1:18). Compared to the other visions, this vision has quite an extended description of what is seen, before the interpreting angel is mentioned in v. 4. Zechariah sees 'four chariots'. The number 'four' has been used in several other visions. In the second vision, 'four' seems to represent the entirety of the world since the 'four horns' signify all the nations on earth that scattered God's people (1:19[2:2]). The 'four craftsmen' simply correspond to the horns who cast them down (1:20[2:3]). In the third vision, the Babylonian exile that scattered God's people in all directions is likened to the 'four winds' that blow in every direction (cf. 6:5). Hence the number 'four' seems to represent 'the four compass directions and thus the entire world' (Meyers and Meyers 1987: 317). It corresponds with the description 'the Lord of the whole earth' (v. 5).

'Chariots' were principally used as military vehicles, but could also be used for hunting, parade and travel (Littauer and Crouwel 1992: 890). In battle, they were especially useful in open country for rapid flanking movements or for pursuing the enemy. They often contained an archer and a shield bearer, were used by the Canaanites and the Philistines against the Israelites (Josh. 17:16; Judg. 1:19; 1 Sam. 13:5) and were adopted only later by the Israelites, possibly by David (2 Sam. 8:4), but definitely by Solomon (1 Kgs 10:26). Because of their association with war, chariots were a symbol of power and connected with kings and their courts (Gen. 41:43; 2 Sam. 15:1; 1 Kgs 1:5). Cantrell (2011: 59) notes that they were 'also assigned a key role in religious thought as an integral and useful component of the divine realm'.

The chariots Zechariah sees are said to be 'going out [*yōṣĕ'ôt*] from between the two mountains'. Since chariots were limited to smooth and level ground, their association with mountains suggests these are not normal chariots. Their identity will be discussed in relation to v. 5. The identity of the mountains is elusive. Some scholars argue that these mountains are actual mountains, such as Mount Zion and the Mount of

Olives. However, the presence of chariots on these mountains is difficult to conceive, even if they are not normal chariots. Further, there is nothing in the immediate context to indicate that it is these mountains.

Many scholars understand these mountains against the background of Akkadian mythology, where a number of cylinder seals depict the sun god (Shamash) appearing between two mountains (or mountain ranges or hills?). Pritchard (1969: 220, 331) reproduces two of these scenes and cautions that 'it must be emphasized that as yet there is a high degree of uncertainty in the interpretation of these scenes'. In both relevant examples, the 'mountains' do not appear to be made of bronze. Furthermore, Shamash is not riding a chariot in either scene. Caution is called for here, especially in the suggestion of some scholars that solar imagery is being applied to Yahweh as a polemic against this mythology; for example, Boda (2004: 319). This seems to be importing too much into Zechariah's vision. However, the connection between mountains and the presence of the gods is well established in the ANE (Clifford 1972). Interestingly, Deut. 33:2–3 pictures Yahweh's coming from Sinai, dawning from Seir and shining forth from Mount Paran, along with myriads of holy ones at his right, a host of his own who march at his heels. However, there are enough differences (e.g. Yahweh is not seen in Zechariah's vision) to hesitate in establishing a direct connection with this passage.

Alternatively, scholars pick up on the description of the mountains as 'bronze' and connect them with the two bronze pillars that stood at the entrance of Solomon's temple (1 Kgs 7:13–22). These pillars formed part of the entrance to the temple and had the names Jachin and Boaz. By analogy, the two bronze mountains of Zechariah's vision are understood to be the heavenly counterparts of these bronze pillars, forming the entrance to the heavens. This seems a more likely connection since the temple was an earthly representation of the cosmos (Clifford 1972: 177–181; Beale 2004: 29–59), and the pillars outside the holy place therefore represented the entrance to the visible heavens. In Heb. 8:5, the earthly sanctuary is said to represent the heavens in its layout.

Given this symbolism, the mountains are best understood as representing the entrance to the heavens. The phrase 'the two mountains' contains the art., which would normally specify something well known. However, the need for a further description of the mountains as 'bronze' suggests that this was not the case. Instead, the art. seems to indicate that the mountains were 'definite in the imagination', where the use of the art. is 'vividly portraying someone or something whose identity is not otherwise indicated' (Waltke and O'Connor 1990: 243). This seems appropriate here.

2–3. The four chariots are distinguished by the colours of their horses. The pl. for 'horses' (*sûsîm*) indicates that there are at least two horses on each chariot, possibly more since the pl. rather than the dual form is used.

Early chariots were drawn by two horses, but chariots of the Assyrian period had teams of three or four horses. Nicol (1979: 636) reproduces a picture of a model of a Persian chariot with three horses, but the number in Zechariah's vision is not stated.

The colours of the horses on the first three chariots are undisputed: chestnut, black and white (cf. the first vision in 1:8, which also had chestnut and white horses, along with sorrel). There are two adjectives connected to the horses of the fourth chariot (*bĕruddîm 'ămuṣṣîm*), which is an unusual construction, as reflected in the various renderings in the early versions (see 'Notes on the text'). While these adjectives are sometimes understood as a colour (e.g. NRSV has 'dappled grey'), the second adj. ('valiant') is better taken as applying to all the horses together, since in v. 7 the 'valiant ones' most naturally refers to all of the horses. The adj. 'piebald' is not so much a colour as a pattern of mixed colours (see 'Notes on the text'). Like the first vision, any significance of the colours must remain speculative since the interpretation makes nothing of them. They simply serve to distinguish the chariots.

4. Zechariah again responds to the vision by asking the interpreting angel, 'What are these, my lord?' Exactly the same form of words is used in the first and fifth visions (1:9; 4:4), which shows the interrelatedness of all the visions (Meyers and Meyers 1987: 322).

5. The angel identifies the four chariots as 'the four winds of the heavens' (cf. v. 1). The word translated 'winds' is the pl. of *rûaḥ*, which has been translated as 'Spirit' in 4:6 and 'wind' in 5:9. The same phrase was used in 2:6[10], where it referred to the winds of a storm that blow in all directions. There it was a metaphor of the Babylonian exile, which scattered God's people in all directions like the 'winds', and did the will of God in bringing judgment on his people. The same phrase is found in Dan. 8:8 and 11:4; and a slight variation is found in Jer. 49:36 ('the four winds from the four quarters of heaven'), where it speaks of the breadth of God's judgment across the world. The metaphor of 'winds' also characterizes the movement of the chariots. Psalm 104:4 likens the winds to God's messengers, and flames of fire to his servants.

It is common to understand the chariots as presenting themselves before the Lord in the heavenly court (e.g. NIV: 'from standing in the presence of the Lord'; ESV: 'after presenting themselves before the LORD'). This is done by comparing the expression with 4:14 ('who are standing by the Lord'), yet the Hebr. expression is different here. Rogland (2014) argues that the Hebr. is better translated 'on account of the taking of a stand' (i.e. opposition or rebellion) against the Lord, similar to Ps. 2:2. In this case, the angel is giving the reason for the chariots' 'going out', indicating it is in response to the rebellion of the nations.

All of this suggests that the chariots are to be understood as representing the hosts of heaven. They are the hosts of 'the LORD of hosts' (a title that has occurred eighteen times already in Zechariah); the armies of heaven (cf. 2 Kgs 6:17). This fits with the warfare connotations of the chariots noted in the comments on v. 1. These hosts go out to do Yahweh's bidding in the 'whole earth' (see 'Comment' on 1:10). They represent his kingship and go out on his behalf.

6. The chariots are now referred to by the colour of their horses. They are going out against those who have taken their stand against the Lord. The 'land of the north' was referred to in 2:6[10], from which the exiles were to flee. There it was noted as a typical Jeremianic expression for Babylon, the nation that had scattered God's people 'like the four winds of the heavens' (also 2:6[10]; cf. v. 5).

Many scholars suggest that the subsequent text is corrupt and should have all four groups of horses going in different compass directions to match the 'four winds of the heavens'. However, there is no textual support for this and there is an important logic to the text as it stands. Rather than postulating that the white horse go to the west (e.g. NIV, NRSV), it is better to follow the Hebr. and see a second chariot with white horses also going to the north (lit. 'to behind of them'; cf. 2 Sam. 5:23), since this reflects the significance of the north as the place of the captivity of God's people, as just noted (Stead 2009: 213). The exclusive focus on the horses that have gone to the north in v. 8 is consistent with seeing two chariots going to this location and underlines the significance of the north.

The chariot with the piebald horses went out to 'the land of the south'. Unlike 'the land of the north', this phrase is unique to Zechariah. There are three occasions where Edom is associated with the 'south' (*têmān*) or 'Teman' (Josh. 15:1; Jer. 49:20; Obad. 8–9), and given the significance of Edom elsewhere in the Book of the Twelve as an enemy of God's people (cf. Amos 9:12; Obad. 1:1; Mal. 1:4), this may be the intended reference. Alternatively, it may refer to Egypt, a long-time enemy and the place to which some in Judah fled after the destruction of Jerusalem (Jer. 44).

Perhaps more important than identifying the implied nations is to note that the north and south are the directions of travel into and out of the land, since the Mediterranean lay to the west and desert to the east. It was from the north and the south that the traditional enemies of Israel came into their land. It is these directions in which the horses and chariots go out.

There is no mention of the chestnut horses. Duguid (2010: 123) suggests that if the pattern follows the analogy of a military campaign, then their omission may suggest they are being held in reserve.

7. The 'valiant ones' is best understood as a description of all the horses, especially since the 'piebald' horses have just been described as going out to the land of the south (see 'Comment' on v. 3). The timing of their mission is a little difficult to understand if v. 7 is understood as consecutive to v. 6, since they go out in v. 6 and then are commanded to go in v. 7. It is best to understand v. 7 as occurring prior to the action of v. 6, hence as a retrospective that adds to the scene by noting the eagerness of the horses and also that they go at God's command, presumably given before they went out from between the two mountains.

The nature of their mission is to 'patrol in the earth', a phrase used of the horses in 1:10 (cf. Job 1:7; 2:2). Yet the additional presence of chariots in this vision suggests that whereas the horses in the first vision had been sent on a surveillance or reconnaissance mission, these horses go out as the 'host' or 'army' of 'Yahweh of hosts' to subdue the nations. Stead (2009: 209–210) notes how in the first vision the angel cried out, 'Yahweh of hosts, how long . . . ?' (1:12), in effect 'entreating Yahweh to send out his hosts to act for his people's sake . . . The final night-vision is an intra-textual response to the entreaty of the first.'

8. The identity of the 'he' who summoned and spoke to Zechariah could be either the interpreting angel or Yahweh. In favour of understanding 'he' as Yahweh is the fact that the previous 'he' in v. 7 refers to Yahweh, and the reference to 'my Spirit' in the direct speech of the second half of v. 8 is a reference to Yahweh (Meyers and Meyers 1987: 328). An argument against this is that it would require Zechariah to be taken into Yahweh's presence. However, this would not be unique, as Zechariah was in the heavenly court in the fourth vision of Zech. 3 (in his visionary experience). Furthermore, it suits the language of 'summon' (see 'Notes on the text') and is a fitting conclusion to the sequence of visions to have the prophet Zechariah being directly addressed by Yahweh in the heavenly court, the location from which he had just commissioned his hosts.

The content of the address is that 'the ones [chariots] going out to the land of the north have set at rest my Spirit in the land of the north'. While there is clearly a wordplay with the 'winds' (*rûḥôt*) of v. 5, the sg. *rûaḥ* here must be understood as the divine 'Spirit' since the 'winds' (chariots) setting at rest 'my wind' makes little sense.

'Rest' is an important biblical-theological idea. It is associated with the seventh day (e.g. Exod. 20:11; 23:12; Deut. 5:14), the Promised Land of Canaan (e.g. Exod. 33:14; Deut. 3:20; 12:10; 25:19; Josh. 1:13, 15), and the kingdoms of several kings, including David and Solomon (2 Sam. 7:1, 11; 1 Kgs 5:18; 1 Chr. 22:9; 23:25; 2 Chr. 14:6; 15:15; 20:30). In Solomon's prayer at the dedication of the temple, God's resting place, along with the ark, is said to be the temple (2 Chr. 6:41). The same Spirit that will rebuild the temple (4:6) has now been 'set at rest'. These associations lead some scholars, such as Floyd (2000: 397), to see a positive message here of God's creation influence being extended in the world. However, the 'rest' that most readily connects with this vision of the armies of Yahweh is when his wrath is said to 'rest' upon his people for their sins (e.g. Ezek. 16:42; 21:17[22]; 22:20; 24:13). Stead (2009: 210) notes that the connection between *rûaḥ* and anger is seen in Ezek. 13:13 (cf. Judg. 8:3; Prov. 16:32; 29:11; Job 15:13; Eccl. 10:4). Ezek. 21 contains an extended prophecy of judgment spoken of in militaristic terms that culminates in Yahweh's wrath resting (v. 17). Significantly, the next oracle in Ezekiel prepares the way for the king of Babylon and then announces judgment on Israel's wicked prince, a judgment that involves removing his crown, a theme that connects perfectly with the sign action in Zech. 6:9–15, where this situation is reversed. Here the judgment that had come on God's people at the hands of the nations is inverted as the nations, particularly the land of the north, experience his wrath.

Explanation

In this vision, the conditions of the first vision are reversed. Where the nations were at rest, and God was angry and jealous for his people, in this last vision God's Spirit is at rest because the land of the north has been defeated (cf. 1:18–21). Similar connections are found with the second and third visions. The second vision portrayed the nations who had been responsible for the scattering of God's people, as horns who were being terrified and cast down by craftsmen (1:20[2:3]). The third vision called on those who remained in exile in Babylon to flee 'the land of the north' in view of God's coming to vanquish his enemies (2:6–9[10–13]). In this final vision, the heavenly hosts, pictured as chariots with coloured horses, go out to bring this earlier hope to completion. The two chariots going to the land of the north perhaps reflects the greater culpability that the land of the north bore for Jerusalem's destruction (cf. 1:15).

There are also important connections with the seventh vision, where wickedness and idolatry were removed to 'Shinar' (Babylon) where a temple was established for it, a vision of the cleansing of the land. The implication from this final vision is that wickedness, having been sent to the land of the north, is finally destroyed, or at least is finally subjugated, by the hosts of Yahweh. The 'outward' movement of the visions is complete (see 'Form and structure').

The rhetorical effect of this vision is to assure the readers and hearers of the book that Yahweh is sovereign over the nations and his purposes will prevail. As noted earlier, the visions of Zechariah give content to the initial call to repent in 1:1–6. This repentance involves returning from exile (2:6–8), rebuilding the city (1:17; 2:4), rebuilding the temple (1:16; 4:7–10), singing and rejoicing (2:10), and covenant obedience (3:7; 5:4, 8). The vision of the hosts of Yahweh of hosts going out over the earth, to patrol and to set Yahweh's Spirit at rest over the nations that had troubled his people, underlines his sovereignty and so inspires confidence to act on the word he has spoken.

The book of Revelation draws on Zechariah's first and last visions to picture four different coloured horses: white, red, black and pale (Rev. 6:1–8). Each horse rides out in judgment when a seal of the scroll in the hand of the Lamb is opened. Unlike Zechariah, the colours of the horses seems to reflect their judgment tasks, with white representing conquest; red, bloodshed; black, famine; and pale (or 'chlorine'), death. These are not a sequence of judgments so much as a combination of judgments that have fallen on the world now that Christ has died and been raised (Rev. 5:8–14). They are evidence of God's present activity in the world and point to his final judgment, as Wilcock (1991: 76) notes, 'Seals 1 to 5 portray different aspects of the whole of history; Seal 6 describes the day which will end it.' The vision of John in Revelation is to comfort Christians that God has all things in hand, no matter how horrible. It is also a challenge not to grow complacent and get caught up in a world that is coming to judgment.

It is perhaps the rider on the white horse in Rev. 19:11–16 that has a greater affinity with Zechariah's last vision since it connects with the final judgment where the nations of the world will be subjected to his rule. This rider is called the Word of God, who is followed by the hosts of heaven, also on white horses, and who strikes down the rebellious nations with his sword. He is the 'KING OF KINGS AND LORD OF LORDS'. Like the victory of Yahweh's hosts in Zech. 6, Christ's assured victory is to give courage to God's people today and to inspire obedience to the word he has spoken.

Elsewhere in the NT, like Zechariah, the coming judgment of God is to motivate repentance (e.g. Luke 3:7–8; Acts 17:30–31). This repentance (in the context of the coming judgment of God) is to holiness of living (2 Cor. 5:9; 2 Thess. 2:15; 2 Peter 3:14), persuading others about Christ (2 Cor. 5:11), taking care how one 'builds' in ministry (1 Cor. 3:10–15), caring for those in need (Matt. 25:31–46), meeting together to spur on other Christians to love and good deeds (Heb. 10:24–25), perseverance (Heb. 10:30–39), and giving thanks and worshipping God in reverence and awe (Heb. 12:28–29).

ZECHARIAH 6:9–15

Translation

6:9 The word of the LORD came to me, 10 'Take from the exiles, from Heldai and from Tobijah and from Jedaiah, who have come from Babylon, and go on that day, go to the house of Josiah son of Zephaniah. 11 And take silver and gold and make a crown and set it upon the head of Joshua son of Jehozadak, the high priest.

12 'And say to him, "So says the LORD of hosts, 'Look, a man, Shoot is his name, and from beneath him he will shoot up and he will build the temple of the LORD. 13 He himself will build the temple of the LORD, and he will bear majesty, and he will sit and rule by his throne, and he will be a priest by his throne, and a counsel of peace will be between the two.'"'

14 And the crown will be to Helem, to Tobijah, to Jedaiah and to Hen son of Zephaniah for a memorial in the temple of the LORD. 15 And the ones who are far

off shall come and build in the temple of the LORD. And you will know that the LORD of hosts has sent me to you. And it will come to pass if you diligently obey the voice of the LORD your God.

Notes on the text

6:10. 'Take': *lāqôaḥ* is an inf. abs. that functions as a command (Waltke and O'Connor 1990: 593). It has no object and *BHS* suggests emending *mēʾēt* (from) to *maśʾōt* (offerings of) or *mattĕnōt* (gifts of). However, the MT makes sense in first specifying the group in v. 10 and then the object ('silver and gold') in v. 11.

LXX translates the names as appellatives; however, they are names attested elsewhere in the OT. See Klein 2008: 196–198.

'who have come from Babylon' is the last phrase in the Hebr. (it comes after 'Josiah son of Zephaniah'); 'who' is pl., which indicates it refers to the exiles, but its position in the sentence indicates it probably also includes Josiah.

'go': *ûbāʾtā* is repeated. While it is a 2 m. pf., with *û* it expresses action consequent to the command ('take') and is translated as an imper. (Waltke and O'Connor 1990: 529).

11. 'a crown': *ʿăṭārôt* is pl. in form, but Gelston (2010: 139*) notes it may be sg. in meaning. A few medieval Hebr. MSS, some versions of LXX, Syr and Tg have a single crown. Cf. v. 14. See 'Comment'.

'set it': *wĕśamtā*. Lit. 'set' – there is no pr. suff.

12. Lit. 'And say to him, saying [*lēʾmōr*], "So says the LORD of hosts, saying [*lēʾmōr*]"'. The second *lēʾmōr* is not translated in LXX or Syr.

'Shoot': *ṣemaḥ* is often translated 'Branch'. See 'Comment' on 3:8 for an explanation of this translation. Tg has 'Anointed' (cf. 3:8).

'from beneath him': *ûmittaḥtāyw*. See 'Comment'.

13. 'and he will be a priest by his throne': *wĕhāyâ kōhēn ʿal-kisʾô*. This phrase on its own can legitimately be read in two ways: (1) as a further description of Shoot (cf. the syntax of 9:7; e.g. NIV); (2) as a separate figure 'and there shall be a priest upon/by his throne' (e.g. ESV, NRSV; cf. LXX, 'and the priest shall be on his right hand', and Tg, 'there shall be a high priest beside his throne'). The prep. *ʿal* can be translated 'upon' or 'by' (Clines 2007: 388). See 'Comment'.

'and a counsel of peace': *waʿăṣat šālôm* is a gen. of effect. That is, the counsel between the two will bring peace (Rose 2000: 65).

14. 'And the crown': *wĕhāʿăṭārōt* is def. and pl. in form, but takes a sg. verb (*tîhyeh*). See the note on v. 11. LXX and Syr translate as a single crown. Tg does not mention the crown.

Note the different names from v. 10: Heldai is Helem and Josiah is 'kindness' (or 'Hen') from v. 10. For various explanations of why these names are different, see 'Comment'.

15. 'in the temple': *bĕhêkal*. BDB 88 notes the prep. *bĕ* is used with some verbs when the action refers only to part of the object. See 'Comment'.

'if you diligently obey': *'im-šāmôa' tišmĕ'ûn*. Waltke and O'Connor (1990: 584) argue that the inf. abs. '*usually* emphasizes not the meaning denoted by the verb's root but the force of the verb in context' (their italics).

'the voice': *bĕqôl*. BDB 90 notes the prep. *bĕ* is sometimes used with verbs of sense perception (e.g. *šāma'*) to denote the faculty concerned (here the voice).

Form and structure

Zech. 6:9–15 comprises an oracle instructing Zechariah to perform a sign action and speak a word to the high priest Joshua. It is the first of three sign actions that Zechariah is called to perform, the other two being in ch. 11. The introductory phrase 'The word of the LORD came' (v. 9) occurs elsewhere at key structural points in the book (i.e. 1:1, 7; 7:1). It indicates a new section, rather than a continuation of the final vision (contra Baldwin, Sweeney). However, this oracle is closely connected to the visions that precede it, bringing a number of the key themes of the visions together.

The interpretation of this passage is complex since a number of phrases can legitimately be understood in quite different ways. The wider context of Zechariah and the way earlier OT texts are used are therefore very significant factors in its interpretation. Many commentators read this sign action only in the context of chs. 1–8, which poses difficulties if Zerubbabel is identified as Shoot, but I will seek to interpret it in the light of the book as a whole (Petterson forthcoming). It is my contention that Shoot is a future figure (cf. ch. 3), and the action of crowning the high priest Joshua functions to transition from the present circumstances of the post-exilic community to the eschatological future when Shoot will come and establish the peace that the visions looked forward to. Chs. 7–8 also function to transition between the days of Zechariah and the eschatological future, and hence also between the two halves of the book.

Tidiman (1996: 150) observes the way that this passage pivots around 6:12–13 with the repetition of the statement that Shoot will build the temple of Yahweh. This is a key hope of this vision, and repeated for emphasis (Rudolph 1976: 129). This passage has a chiastic structure:

A The word of the Lord (v. 9)
  B Exiles come from Babylon (v. 10a, c)
    C Exiles named (v. 10b)
      D A crown to be made (v. 11a)
        E Joshua the high priest (v. 11b)
          F Shoot introduced (v. 12a)
            G Build the temple of the Lord (v. 12b)

G' Build the temple of the Lord (v. 13a)
F' Bear majesty, sit and rule (v. 13b)
E' A priest by his throne (v. 13c)
D' Crown in the temple (v. 14a, c)
C' Exiles named (v. 14b)
B' Far-off ones shall come (v. 15a)
A' The voice of the Lord (v. 15b)

Comment

6:9–10. 'The word of the LORD came to' occurs at key structural points in Zechariah (see 'Form and structure'. It is a standard message-reception formula that underlines Zechariah's status as a prophet. The pr. 'me' closely links this oracle with the preceding visions, where Zechariah also speaks in the first person.

Zechariah is told to 'take from the exiles'; however, no object of 'take' is supplied until v. 11. While most translations supply an object, it is not necessary, since in this verse the focus is on the exiles before the focus shifts to what was taken and what was done with it.

The 'exiles . . . who have come from Babylon' are named (see 'Notes on the text'). This probably indicates that they were well known in the community. Boda (2004: 336) cites evidence from Ezra that suggests they are priests (Ezra 2:36, 60; 8:24–34). Having come from Babylon, we can assume that these men have heeded God's call to 'Flee from the land of the north' (2:6[10]). Strictly, it is Heldai, Tobijah and Jedaiah from whom Zechariah is to 'take', and he is to go to the house of Josiah, son of Zephaniah. The phrase 'on that day' suggests there is urgency to these actions.

Meyers and Meyers (1987: 345) hypothesize that Josiah son of Zephaniah is a grandchild of Zephaniah, the priest next in rank to the high priest (cf. 2 Kgs 25:18; Jer. 29:25). In this case, the crowning of Joshua son of Jehozadak, son of Seraiah (the last pre-exilic high priest), would have taken place in the home of the grandson of Zephaniah (next in rank to the high priest).

11. What Zechariah is to take is now stated: 'silver and gold'. Ollenburger (1996: 787) notes that in the priestly legislation, 'take' can refer to the taking of an offering. Ezra 1:11 reports 5,400 articles of gold and silver that were brought from Babylon to Jerusalem, and Ezra 2:68–69 details a large freewill offering of gold and silver for the rebuilding of the temple. Like the Israelites despoiling the Egyptians (Exod. 12:35), this has second exodus connotations (Smith 1984: 218).

This silver and gold is to be made into a crown. While the form of 'crown' is pl. (*'ăṭārôt*), the context favours a single crown, especially since a sg. verb, 'will be' (*tihyeh*), is used in v. 14 with the same crown (cf. Job

31:36, where the same pl. form is used to refer to one crown). In addition, Zechariah normally numbers items when there is more than one present (e.g. 1:18, 20; 3:9; 4:2, 14; 5:9; 6:1), which also suggests a single crown since there is no number here. Smith (1984: 218) suggests the pl. form indicates a two-tiered or composite crown with gold and silver rings making the one crown. Alternatively, it is a superlative pl. of excellence (Baldwin 1972: 133).

This crown is to be set 'upon the head of Joshua, son of Jehozadak, the high priest' (cf. 'Comment' on v. 10). Joshua was the focus of the fourth vision in ch. 3, where he was cleansed, clothed and commissioned to serve in the reconstructed temple as high priest along with his fellow priests. Joshua and his associates were also to serve as a sign of the coming Shoot (3:8). This vision is crucial to bear in mind in the interpretation of this sign action.

12–13. After setting the crown on the head of Joshua, Zechariah is told to speak to him. This word helps to explain the significance of the crowning and comes from 'the LORD of hosts' (see 'Comment' on 1:3). Zechariah is to say to Joshua, 'Look, a man; Shoot is his name' (see 'Comment' on 3:8 for a discussion of the significance of the term 'Shoot'). While at first it seems that Zechariah is to identify Joshua as Shoot, several factors indicate otherwise. First, one would more naturally expect the Hebr. to say 'Look, you are the man; Shoot is your name' if Joshua were being identified with Shoot (Rose 2000: 125–126). When the phrase 'Look, a man' occurs in direct speech elsewhere in the OT, it refers to a third party (Boda 2001: §4.3.1). Secondly, Shoot was clearly a different figure to Joshua in Zech. 3 since Joshua and his associates served as a sign of the coming Shoot. Thirdly, Joshua's high-priestly ancestry, mentioned in v. 11, is incompatible with the hope for Shoot, who is of the line of David. Hence Joshua represents Shoot only for the purposes of the sign action.

Zechariah gives seven descriptions of Shoot to Joshua. First, Shoot is 'a man' (*'îš*). The fact that Joshua is to represent Shoot as 'a man' indicates that the 'shoot' (*ṣemaḥ*) of earlier prophetic hope (Isa. 11:1; Jer. 23:5–6; 33:14–18; Ezek. 17:3–6, 22–23) was a known and hoped for figure in Zechariah's day.

Secondly, Zechariah says, 'from beneath him he will shoot up'. There is a play on the name 'Shoot' (*ṣemaḥ*) with the verb 'shoot up' (*yiṣmāḥ*), but the exact meaning of this phrase is difficult to determine. The expression 'beneath him' occurs ninety-seven times in the OT, and well over eighty of these refer to a king's son taking his father's place as king (e.g. 2 Sam. 10:1; 2 Chr. 1:8). It may be that Shoot will replace Joshua ('him') as he takes the crown presently on Joshua's head. Similarly, it may indicate that Shoot will be a legitimate descendant of David (to be understood as 'him'), unlike Joshua, who simply represents Shoot (Mackay 2003: 138).

Thirdly, Shoot 'will build the temple of the LORD', an expression repeated in v. 13 to emphasize it (see 'Form and structure'). Since 4:9 says that Zerubbabel will build 'the house' (*habbayit*), many scholars conclude that Shoot is to be identified with Zerubbabel. However, there are several difficulties with this, including the fact that subsequent descriptions of Shoot were never realized for Zerubbabel (bearing majesty and sitting and ruling by/on a throne); the failure of Zerubbabel to usher in the day of peace and prosperity as anticipated in 3:8–10; and the problems this poses for the book of Zechariah's authenticity if a key prophecy failed to come to pass (cf. v. 15). As Floyd (2006: 269) puts it, 'How could unkept divine promises fan the flames of even more ardent faith in divine promises?' (See further, Petterson forthcoming.) Instead, Zechariah uses the term 'Shoot' to point away from current historical figures (who are elsewhere named) and towards a future Davidic king (Tollington 1993: 172). This indicates that Shoot is a Davidic king beyond Zerubbabel and beyond Zechariah's day. What then is the temple that Shoot will build? Davis (1920: 257) suggests it is a metaphor for the community of the Lord's people. However, there is nowhere else in Zechariah that would indicate that this is the primary reference. It is more likely that just as the 'earlier prophets' (cf. 1:4) spoke of an eschatological temple (e.g. Isa. 2:2–4; Jer. 3:16–18; Ezek. 40 – 42; Mic. 4:1–5; Hag. 2:7–9), so Zechariah here speaks of Shoot's building this temple, in contrast to the temple of Zerubbabel. An eschatological temple is also anticipated in ch. 14, and is developed in the intertestamental literature (e.g. Tob. 14.5; *Jub.* 1.29; 11Q19 XXIX, 8–10; 4Q174 1 I,2). It is the building of this temple that is attached to the future Shoot of David since temple-building is the task of a Davidide (cf. 2 Sam. 7).

The fourth description of Shoot is that 'he will bear majesty'. While the noun translated 'majesty' (*hôd*) can simply mean 'glory' or 'honour' (e.g. Ps. 8:2; Zech. 10:3), when it is used in connection with a king, including Yahweh, it is best translated 'majesty' (e.g. 1 Chr. 29:25; Pss 21:5[6]; 45:3[4]; 96:6; 104:1; 111:3). It refers to the majesty of king Jehoiakim in Jer. 22:18, and since this passage is in the background of 6:12–13 with its reference to Shoot, this meaning seems certain here.

Fifthly, 'he will sit and rule by [*'al*] his throne'. Boda (2004: 340) observes that the only place in the OT where the combination 'sit . . . rule . . . throne' appears is Jer. 22:30, the passage that denies these things to Jehoiachin just before the prophecy of the righteous Shoot (Jer. 23:5). This phrase indicates that Shoot is a royal figure, but the significance of the throne and Shoot's relationship to it is tied up with the next two descriptions.

The sixth and seventh descriptions pose several difficult issues for the interpreter. The sixth literally reads, 'He [*wĕhāyâ*] will be a priest upon/by [*'al*] his throne'. Given that Shoot is the subject of the previous five verbs, one would expect Shoot to be the subject of this phrase also (Jauhiainen 2008: 509). The problem with this is that the seventh description mentions two individuals (not roles): 'a counsel of peace will be between the two'. If Shoot is being designated a priest, who then is the second figure in the final description? Because of this, many scholars propose that the sixth description be rendered, 'And there shall be a priest on his throne' (e.g. ESV). In this case, Zechariah expresses the hope for a second figure: a priest, based on the promise of a Levitical priest in Jer. 33:17–22, who will accompany the Davidic Shoot, and will make offerings and sacrifices in God's presence for ever (Stead 2009: 137). The difficulties with this interpretation are that it seems unnatural, given the sequence of verbs noted above, to translate 'He will be' (*wĕhāyâ*) as 'there will be'. In addition, the priest of Jer. 33:18 is not said to sit (on a 'throne' or a 'seat'), as this interpretation demands.

Ancient scholars (e.g. Jerome) and several modern ones (e.g. Kline 2001: 223–224; Jauhiainen 2008: 509) offer another interpretation that overcomes these difficulties. They suggest that 'the two' of the seventh description refers to Shoot and Yahweh. Psalm 110 provides the conceptual background (evident in LXX and Tg, even though they seem to struggle with the idea of the king's being a priest; see 'Notes on the text'). In this psalm, the king is to sit (*yāšab*) at the right hand of Yahweh (v. 1); and later, Yahweh is said to be 'by' (*'al*) the right hand of the king (v. 5). This is not a contradiction, but is a metaphor that indicates the ideal relationship between the two: 'God is the real king. David rules not in his own right but as co-regent and representative, deriving his authority from his divine counterpart' (Allen 1983: 86). A similar idea is found in Ps. 2, where the joint rule of Yahweh and his anointed king results in blessing for his people. Significantly, the king of Ps. 110 is also designated as a priest (110:4). On this interpretation, the 'LORD', who is mentioned twice in relation to his temple in 6:12–13, is also the subject of 'his throne' (cf. 1 Chr. 29:23, where Solomon is said to sit on [*'al*] Yahweh's throne).

While it may seem strange, the sudden switch between the first-person address of Yahweh ('I'/'me') to the third person about Yahweh ('he'/'him') is also found in the visions (e.g. 2:10–13[14–17]), and many times in the oracles of 9–14 (e.g. 9:7, 13–14; 10:3–4, 5–8; 12:6–7, 8–9; 14:1–4). In this case, what is being said is that the coming of Shoot to sit and rule by (or 'on') Yahweh's throne (as his co-regent), and his priestly service in this capacity, will issue in peace for the community. Hence the implicit contrast is with the kings of the past (such as Jehoiachin in Jer. 22:24–30 and Zedekiah in Ezek. 21:30) who ruled without regard for God and brought about the exile. Instead, the counsel of Shoot and Yahweh shall bring peace (*šālôm*), or well-being, to the community of those who have returned from exile (cf. 8:16; 9:10). Just as the visions of chs. 1–6 anticipated a future day of prosperity for God's people, and the fourth vision tied this to the coming Shoot, this sign action restates this hope.

14. After being set upon the head of Joshua, the crown will become a memorial in the temple. The temple must be Zerubbabel's temple since the crown is placed in it and Shoot (who will build the eschatological temple) has not yet come. In terms of syntax, the crown could be either a memorial 'for' the named exiles or 'of' them (I have maintained the ambiguity with the translation 'to'). Given the way that other memorials function to remind Yahweh (e.g. Exod. 28:29), and its location in the temple, in the first place it is probably a memorial of the exiles. Either way, it suggests that the crown serves a similar purpose to the signs of ch. 3 (the priesthood and the stone) as a further portent of the coming Shoot. Love (1999: 111) notes a wordplay and inclusio between 1:1, 7 where the word of Yahweh comes to Zechariah (*zĕkaryâ*, which means 'Yah[weh] has remembered') and this 'memorial' (*zikkārôn*).

It is difficult to know why two of the names of the exiles are changed between vv. 10 and 14 (Heldai to Helem, and Josiah to Hen or 'kindness'). Some scholars think it reflects different textual traditions (Laato 1997: 205); however, it is unclear why a redactor would not simply have brought the two lists of names into line. Unger (1963: 117) and Petersen (1985: 278) suggest that the second two names are nicknames (like 'Jim' is a nickname for 'James'). Baldwin notes how elsewhere Heldai (1 Chr. 27:15) is also Heled (1 Chr. 11:30) and Heleb (2 Sam. 23:29), which supports the nickname theory. Love (1999: 110) thinks there may be a play on the names for stylistic effect and this seems more likely for Josiah, which has become *ḥen* (or 'grace') and so reflects the 'kindness' of Josiah the son of Zephaniah in this symbolic act (Baron 1918: 203). Nogalski (2011: 881) suggests that two may be different individuals (since Josiah in v. 10 and Hen are both sons 'of Zephaniah', they must be brothers).

15. The word finishes with the promise that 'the ones who are far off shall come and build in the temple of the LORD'. Who are these people and which temple do they build? The phrase 'the ones who are far off' refers to Jewish exiles in Esth. 9:20 and Dan. 9:7, and this is consistent with the returned exiles, just named, who have contributed their gold and silver. In this case, the temple is probably Zerubbabel's temple and this promise could be understood to have been fulfilled before the book of Zechariah took its final form. It may be significant that these far-off ones are not said to build the temple (as in vv. 12–13), but build 'in the temple' (*bĕhêkal*) (see 'Notes on the text'). The prep. 'in' may indicate that they are contributing to the furnishing of the temple and that it had substantially been built by the time of the sign action (since it housed the crown), but it is difficult to be certain about this. Alternatively, 'the ones who are far off' could refer to the nations. Elsewhere Zechariah envisages the nations sharing in the blessings of God's people (e.g. 2:11[15]; 8:20–23; 9:10; 14:16–19), as do the 'earlier prophets'. Isaiah foresees the nations coming to the temple (Isa. 56:4–7) and bringing their offerings (Isa. 60:6–10). Zechariah's contemporary Haggai also envisages the nations contributing their treasures to the temple (Hag. 2:6–9). In this case, the temple is most likely the eschatological temple of Shoot. It is difficult to decide between the two, but on balance the first option connects better with the sign action, with the named exiles a harbinger of more to come. It also sits better with the chiastic structure of the passage (see 'Form and structure').

Either way, 'the ones who are far off' coming to build is evidence of the prophet Zechariah's authenticity (cf. 1:16; 2:9[13], 11[15]). As with 4:9, this implies that the building is ultimately a work of Yahweh. Yet, paradoxically, it is also dependent on the obedience of those who hear God's voice through the prophet Zechariah. This blend of unconditionality and conditionality is similar to Deuteronomy and has an important rhetorical function (Millar 1998: 55–62). The referent of 'it' in 'it will come to pass' is ambiguous. It appears to refer to the temple construction in the first instance, but for readers and hearers after the temple construction it could also refer to the fulfilment of the entire passage, including the coming of Shoot. This challenges readers and hearers of the book of Zechariah after the temple reconstruction to continue to trust the promise of Yahweh, and to obey his voice diligently, being assured that he keeps his word.

Explanation

This sign action functions to shift the focus from the present historical reality to a future day and begins the transition between the visions of chs. 1–6 and the oracles of chs. 9–14. Its historical context is the near-completion of Zerubbabel's temple. From 8:10–11, there are indications that even with the temple reconstruction underway, circumstances are less than ideal. Ezra 3:12 also indicates that from the beginning Zerubbabel's temple did not compare with the expectations of the 'earlier prophets'. This sign action, which involved making a crown and crowning the high priest Joshua, and the word that accompanies it, reiterates the hope for the future king of prophetic expectation, the Davidic Shoot, or, to use later terminology, 'the Messiah' (cf. Tg Jonathan), who is associated with God's coming kingdom (Isa. 11:1; Jer. 23:5–6; 33:14–18; Ezek. 17:3–6, 22–23; 21:26–27). The word that accompanies this sign action establishes that he will build the eschatological temple hoped for by the prophets. He will bear majesty and rule as Yahweh's co-regent and priest, issuing in a reign of peace. In the meantime, the crown will remain in Zerubbabel's temple as a memorial of the exiles and the hope that they had for his coming. Hence the crowning of Joshua looks forward to the crowning of Shoot and therefore to the coming king of 9–14.

The crowning of the high priest Joshua and the temple focus make strong connections back to the visions. In 3:8, the coming of Shoot was associated with the removal of the iniquity of the land in a single day and the priesthood functioned as a sign of the coming Shoot. The fourth vision suggested that Shoot might have some priestly function in removing sin when he comes. This is confirmed in this sign action, where Shoot is identified as a priest. To many, this simply reads NT ideas back into the OT. However, there are several lines from the OT itself that converge to support this identification by Zechariah.

From a biblical-theological perspective, Adam was the first priest-king who served in the garden sanctuary (Dumbrell 1994: 25; Beale 2004: 81). This priestly kingship later devolved on the nation of Israel at Sinai in their appointment to serve as priest-kings (Exod. 19:6) in the sanctuary of the land of Canaan (Alexander 2012: 210). Yet, like Adam, the people of Israel sinned and were cast out of the 'sanctuary'. As noted above, Ps. 110 connects priestly prerogatives to the monarchy and looks to a kind of kingship that existed in Jerusalem at the time of Abraham, the father of Israel (Block 2003: 43). The 'crown' on the head of the future king in Ps. 132:18 is the same word used of the priest's mitre in Exod. 29:6, and it literally 'will blossom' (*yāṣîṣ*), the same verb used to describe Aaron's staff (Num. 17:8[23]). Jer. 30:21 also envisages a priestly dimension to the future Davidic king as he will 'draw near' and 'approach' God. Indeed, both David and Solomon acted as priests on several occasions (e.g. 2 Sam. 6; 1 Kgs 3:3–4, 15) and David's sons are called priests in 2 Sam. 8:18. Therefore, the association of kingship and priesthood has good precedent and the designation of the coming Shoot as a priest (6:13) suits the progress of this theme across the OT (Petterson 2009: 120–123). While Jer. 33:14–22 indicates that the throne of Shoot will be supported by a priest, Zechariah seems to bring these together with Shoot himself being identified as a priest. In ch. 3, the priesthood functioned as a sign of the coming Shoot who would usher in a day of prosperity and abundance. Similarly, in ch. 6 the crowning of the high priest anticipates the rule of Shoot, which will issue in peace – kingship and priesthood naturally converge in Shoot.

The significance of the symbolism of placing the crown on the head of the high priest Joshua is not explicit. However, the wider OT background suggests its meaning. Ezek. 21:26–27[31–32] speaks of the turban and crown of the prince of Israel being made a ruin on account of sin and guilt. Ps. 89:38–40[39–41] describes Yahweh's rejection of the king at the exile as a defiling of his crown in the dust. As the reinstated high priest, Joshua was in a position to cleanse and sanctify objects that had become defiled. Hence, against the background of the purification rituals of the Torah, it seems legitimate to hypothesize that the crown made by Zechariah from the offerings of the returned exiles is placed on the head of the high priest in order to sanctify it. Having been sanctified, the 'crown' that has been defiled by the exile is ready to be taken up again by the future righteous king when he comes, with the hope that he will be so holy as not to defile it as previous kings have done. Until that time, it is kept in the temple for safe-keeping, as well as functioning as a memorial to the exiles.

Christian readers understand the fulfilment of Zechariah's hope to be found in Jesus, for whom the seven descriptions of Shoot are true: he is the man of prophetic expectation (Matt. 11:3–6; Mark 8:27–30; John 19:5);

a descendant of David (Matt. 1:1; Rom. 1:3; Rev. 5:5); the one who is building the eschatological temple, the church (Matt. 16:18; 1 Cor. 3:16–17; 2 Cor. 6:16; Eph. 2:17–22; Heb. 3:3; 1 Peter 2:5); who bears majesty (Matt. 25:31; Acts 2:34–36; Heb. 1:3; 2:9; Rev. 19:12); who as king is seated at the right hand of God (Matt. 26:64; Acts 2:33; 5:31; Rom. 8:34; Col. 3:1); who as a priest has sat down at the right hand of God's throne (Heb. 1:3; 5:10; 8:1; 10:12; 12:2; 1 Peter 3:22); and whose rule with his Father has brought peace (Eph. 2:14–18).

All the synoptic Gospels record that after Jesus rode the donkey into Jerusalem (cf. Zech. 9:9), he went to the temple (Matt. 21:1–17; Mark 11:1–19; Luke 19:28–48). While it is not explicit in any of the Gospels, I wonder whether, against the backdrop of Zechariah, he went to the temple to receive Zechariah's crown? Instead of being crowned, he finds the temple defiled, so he cleanses it and the religious leaders look to kill him (Mark 11:18; Luke 11:47). The outcome is that instead of being given Zechariah's crown, he is given a crown of thorns and crucified as the king of the Jews. This connects with the 'humility' entailed in Shoot imagery (see 'Comment' on 3:8) and the description of the king of 9:9 as 'afflicted'. But his crucifixion was the priestly sacrifice that 'takes away the sin of the world' (John 1:29). As the risen King of kings and Lord of lords he now wears many crowns (Rev. 19:12). From humble beginnings, something magnificent has grown.

This passage also connects well with Eph. 2, which talks about the temple the Messiah Jesus is building (v. 21). Those who were far away (Gentiles) have been brought near through Jesus' blood (v. 13). His work on the cross now issues in peace (v. 17).

ZECHARIAH 7:1–14

Translation

7:1It came to pass in the fourth year of Darius the king, the word of the LORD came
to Zechariah on the fourth day of the ninth month, in Chislev. 2Bethel had
sent Sharezer and Regem-melek and his men to entreat the favour of the LORD,
3saying to the priests who belong to the house of the LORD of hosts and to the
prophets, 'Should I mourn in the fifth month, fasting, just as I have done this –
how many years?'

4And the word of the LORD of hosts came to me, 5'Say to all the people of the
land and to the priests, "When you fasted and lamented in the fifth and the seventh
months, even these seventy years, was it indeed for me that you fasted? 6And when
you eat and when you drink, do you not eat for yourselves and drink for yourselves?
7Were not these the words which the LORD proclaimed by the earlier prophets,
when Jerusalem was inhabited and prosperous, even her towns surrounding her,
and the Negev and the Shephelah were inhabited?"'

[8]And the word of the LORD came to Zechariah, [9]"So says the LORD of hosts, Judge true justice, and show kindness and mercies to each other. [10]Do not afflict a widow or an orphan, a foreigner or a poor one. And do not devise evil in your heart against one another.'

[11]But they refused to listen and they gave a stubborn shoulder and they stopped their ears from hearing, [12]and they set their heart as diamond against hearing the Torah and the words which the LORD of hosts sent by his Spirit through the earlier prophets. And great wrath came from the LORD of hosts. [13]And just as he called and they did not listen, so they would call and I would not listen, says the LORD of hosts, [14]and I scattered them over all the nations which they had not known. And the land was desolate after them, [with no] one crossing over or one returning, and they made a desirable land into a wasteland.

Notes on the text

7:1. With the date formula here, 'of the . . . month' is circumscribed by *laḥōdeš* and 'day' is omitted (J. C. L. Gibson 1994: 50). Months are always numbered by ordinals and days of the month with cardinals (Gesenius 2006: 435, §134p).

2. 'Bethel' is understood to be the subject, but this is not clear. LXX and Tg separate Bethel from Sharezer and understand it as the place to which the delegation was sent, understood either as 'Bethel' or 'the house of God' (Cathcart and Gordon 1989: 199). See 'Comment'.

'Regem-melek': LXX reads an art. with *melek* and understands it to be a title (the king).

'had sent': *wayyišlaḥ* is treated as a plupf. (J. C. L. Gibson 1994: 96).

'to entreat the favour of the LORD': lit. 'to make favourable the face of Yahweh' (cf. 8:21–22).

3. 'who belong to': *'ăšer lĕ* is a periphrastic gen. (Waltke and O'Connor 1990: 158).

'fasting': *hinnāzēr* is an adv. use of the inf. abs. to describe the manner of the mourning (J. C. L. Gibson 1994: 126). See 'Comment'.

'how many?': *kammeh* is an interr. (J. C. L. Gibson 1994: 185).

4. 'of hosts' is not present in the LXX, Syr and some Tgs.

5. 'and lamented': *wĕsāpôd* is an inf. abs. that continues the action of the preceding finite verb (Waltke and O'Connor 1990: 596).

'months' is supplied in translation.

'even these': *wĕzeh* (lit. 'even this'; cf. 1:12). Anarthrous *zeh* occurs with numerals in expressions of time apparently to emphasize the time (Waltke and O'Connor 1990: 311).

'was it indeed for me that you fasted': *hăṣôm ṣamtunî 'ānî* is an unusual phrase. The inf. abs. before the cognate verb emphasizes the strength of the question, hence 'indeed' (J. C. L. Gibson 1994: 124). Meyers and

Meyers (1987: 389) argue that the pr. suff. is a dat. suff. ('for me'). The personal pr. (*ānî*) adds emphasis to the verbal suff.

6. 'And when': *wĕkî* is used temporally (Arnold and Choi 2003: 151).

7. Following *BHS*, which suggests reading 'these' (*'ēlleh*) for the def. object marker (*'et*) as is done in LXX and the Syr. Waltke and O'Connor (1990: 178) note that Mishnaic Hebr. uses *'et* as a demons. Alternatively, Keil (1949: 308) suggests a verb has been omitted, such as 'know' or 'do': 'Do you not know the words?' or 'Should you not do the words?' Clark and Hatton (2002: 187) suggest it is the word 'proclaimed': 'Have I not proclaimed the words?'

'by the earlier prophets': lit. 'by the hand of the earlier prophets' (also v. 12; cf. Hag. 2:1).

9. 'So says the LORD of hosts': lit. 'thus says the LORD of hosts, saying'.

'to each other': *'îš 'et-'āḥîw*. Lit. 'a man with his brother'; cf. v. 10. *'îš* has a distrib. sense (J. C. L. Gibson 1994: 14).

10. 'against one another': *'îš 'āḥîw*. Lit. 'a man his brother'; cf. v. 9. *'îš* has a distrib. sense (J. C. L. Gibson 1994: 14).

11. 'they stopped their ears': lit. 'their ears they made heavy'.

12. 'diamond' (*šāmîr*) is probably not the stone mentioned here (also 'adamant'), but it best conveys the meaning.

'through the earlier prophets': lit. 'by the hand of the earlier prophets' (also v. 7; cf. Hag. 2:1).

13. 'And just as he called': lit. 'And it was just as he called'.

14. When *min* follows the verb 'was desolate' (*nāšammâ*), it indicates what the land has been deprived of (McComiskey 1998: 1135).

'[with no] one crossing over or one returning': *mē'ōbēr ûmiššāb* (cf. 9:8). Here *min* appears twice.

Form and structure

Zech. 7 – 8 forms a unit closely connected to chs. 1–6 and functions as a transition into the oracles of chs. 9–14. The dating formula indicates that it is a new section (cf. 1:1 where it introduces the book, and 1:7 where it introduces the night visions). Assis (2010b: 6–7) correctly observes that many of the oracles of ch. 8 summarize the content of chs. 1–7, and that there is an affinity between 7:1, 7, 9–12 and 1:1–6, but this is not enough to warrant treating ch. 8 as a separate unit to chs. 1–7 as he does. That chs. 7–8 function as a unit is evident from the observation that the question asked in 7:1–3 is not directly answered until 8:18–23 (Boda 2003c: 394–395). In addition, the delegation that goes to Jerusalem 'to entreat the favour of the LORD' (7:2) is matched at the end by the nations going to Jerusalem to do the same thing (8:21–23). While chs. 7–8 form a unit, I will treat each chapter separately to make the presentation more manageable.

Several commentators detect a chiastic structure through these chapters (e.g. Ollenburger 1996: 790; Scalise 2009: 246). While the outer elements fit this schema well (ABC), the inner elements of the chiasm are not mirrored as clearly (DE):

A Entreating the Lord in Jerusalem (7:1–3)
  B What the Lord says about fasting (7:4–7)
    C What the Lord wants (7:8–10)
      D Ancestors' refusal and punishment (7:11–14)
        E Future salvation (8:1–13)
      D' Ancestors' refusal and punishment (8:14–15)
    C' What the Lord wants (8:16–17)
  B' What the Lord says about fasting (8:18–19)
A' Entreating the Lord in Jerusalem (8:20–23)

The form of ch. 7 is of a dating formula (7:1) introducing a short narrative about a delegation sent to the priests and prophets of the house of the Lord (in Jerusalem) to enquire about the need to fast, presumably on account of the imminent completion of the temple rebuilding (7:2–3). This provides an occasion for Zechariah to challenge the people of the land about their true motivations by asking a series of questions (7:4–7). Zechariah rehearses key elements of the message of the 'earlier prophets' (7:8–10) and uses the example of their ancestors' refusal to listen in order to challenge his contemporaries (7:11–14). In the final form of the book, this section stands to challenge subsequent readers and hearers about their own response to the words of Yahweh of hosts and warns of the dangers of religious hypocrisy. The end of ch. 6 called for obedience to the voice of God in view of the soon to be completed temple, and these chapters further indicate what obedience to the word of God entails.

Comment

7:1. Like the two instances in chapter 1, the dating formula locates this episode in Zechariah's ministry in relation to the reign of the Persian king Darius (now titled 'king'; cf. 1:1, 7). It is a subtle reminder that even though the temple reconstruction is well under way, the people of God are still under a foreign power (Petersen 1985: 282). Like 1:7, the Babylonian name for the month is used (Chislev), a further indicator that things are not as they should be, with the people of God reckoning their history in the language of the nations. As noted in the 'Comment' on 1:1, Curtis (2006: 94–113) argues that the dating formula should bring to mind the seventy years of desolation for Judah that Jeremiah had prophesied (Jer. 25:11–12). The mention of the seventy years in 7:5 supports this (cf. 1:12). Hence, although Darius is king, there is hope that the seventy years of judgment of God's people and rule by the nations is near its end.

The 'fourth day of the ninth month' in the 'fourth year of Darius' (7 Dec. 518 BC) is almost two years after the night visions (cf. 1:7) and just over two years before the temple is completed, which according to Ezra 6:14–16 happened in the sixth year of Darius (early 515 BC). At this time, 'the word of the LORD came to Zechariah'. This phrase underlines again Zechariah's status as a prophet of Yahweh, especially since it does not directly introduce prophetic speech.

2–3. The nature of the delegation is variously understood. The beginning of v. 2 is lit. 'And sent Bethel Sharezer and Regem-melek and his men'. Baldwin (1972: 142) argues that 'Bethel Sharezer' should be understood as a personal name and refers to the sender, so 'Bethel-Sharezer sent Regem-melek'. The problem with this is that it requires the omission of the conj. 'and' before Regem-melek. Alternatively, most scholars argue that 'Bethel' is the subject of the verb 'sent' and refers to the people or leaders of the town who send a delegation of 'Sharezer and Regem-melek and his men'. While it seems a little unusual to refer to a town in this way, Floyd (2000: 421) observes that the wider emphasis on Jerusalem's 'towns surrounding her' (v. 7) and the way this section finishes with the inhabitants of 'many towns' coming to Jerusalem to do just what this delegation is doing (8:20–21) indicates that this delegation represents the town of Bethel.

Bethel was a town about 12 mi. (20 km) north of Jerusalem. Brodsky (1992: 711) notes that it was strategically located along the route to Jerusalem from the north (a road ran from Shechem to Hebron through Bethel and Jerusalem). While Bethel was allotted to Benjamin (Josh. 18:22), it was taken over by Ephraim (Judg. 1:22). After the division of the kingdom, Jeroboam I established a sanctuary in Bethel as an alternative to the temple in Jerusalem (1 Kgs 12:29–33). The prophets Hosea and Amos both decried the town (also called 'Beth Aven' by Hosea; see Hos. 4:15; 5:8; 10:5, 15; Amos 3:14), and Josiah later captured it and broke down and defiled its altar (2 Kgs 23:15–16). After the exile, it appears that Bethel was considered part of Judah, with returned exiles settling there (Ezra 2:28; Neh. 7:32).

This delegation from Bethel is sent 'to entreat the favour of the LORD'. Variations on this phrase occur twelve times in the OT and three times in Zech. 7 – 8 (also in 8:21–22). Stead (2009: 221) observes that elsewhere the phrase typically occurs in a judgment context, where Yahweh's face has been turned away in anger (e.g. Exod. 32:11; Jer. 26:19). Some scholars understand the phrase simply as seeking an answer to a question, which they ask in v. 3. Yet the background to the phrase suggests they are seeking more than simply an answer to their question: they are seeking an end to the oppression they experience as the judgment of God.

The delegation speaks 'to the priests who belong to the house of the LORD of hosts and to the prophets'. These leaders were responsible for guidance. The priests were responsible for determining God's will through the Urim and Thummim in the pre-exilic period (Exod. 28:30; Num. 27:21; Deut. 33:8) and through the instruction of the Torah (e.g. Deut. 31:9; Hag. 2:11; Mal. 2:6–7). Reference to 'the prophets' (pl.) implies at least Haggai's presence in Jerusalem along with Zechariah, although Haggai is not named here (cf. Ezra 6:14). The response to the delegation is given by the prophet Zechariah and continues to the end of ch. 8, where the question posed by the delegation is answered more directly.

Mention of 'the house of the LORD' does not mean it had been completed, since this would be inconsistent with the dating of Ezra, noted above (Ristau 2009: 205). Zech. 8:9 also suggests there is more work to be done before the temple is finished. Yet the question posed by the delegation indicates its completion is very close.

The question concerns the need to continue to 'mourn in the fifth month' (v. 3). The verb translated 'mourn' (*bākâ*) denotes weeping or crying, but is often associated with penitence and lamentation (e.g. 2 Sam. 12:21–22). As well as mourning, the questioner, speaking in the first person, says that he has been 'fasting' (*nāzar*). This word is not the usual word for fasting (as used in v. 5), but is from the same root as 'Nazirite' and has the idea of 'separating' or 'abstaining' from something. Zechariah's response in v. 4 makes it clear that it refers to abstaining from food, hence it is translated 'fasting' (Clines 2001: 651). The fast of the fifth month is one of four fasts mentioned in 8:19. While there is no direct biblical evidence, it is thought that this fast was instituted to recall the destruction of the Jerusalem temple in 586 BC by Nebuchadnezzar (2 Kgs 25:8–9; Jer. 52:12–13). The question 'how many years?' implies that they have kept this fast for a long period of time. It also functions to anticipate the explicit mention of seventy years in v. 5. Given the near completion of the temple, it seems appropriate to ask whether they need to continue this fast since what it symbolized (the temple's destruction) is nearly rectified.

4–6. While the mission of the delegation to this point seems entirely reasonable, the word of God that comes to Zechariah cuts to the heart of their motives. Zechariah poses a series of three questions he wants the delegation to ask 'all the people of the land', presumably the peoples of Bethel and other towns surrounding Jerusalem in Yehud (cf. 8:19–21) and 'to the priests' who were responsible for providing guidance to the people (see 'Comment' on v. 3).

The first question expands their question about the fast of the fifth month to include the fast of the seventh month (cf. 8:19), thought to commemorate the murder of Gedaliah, whom Nebuchadnezzar had appointed governor after capturing Jerusalem (2 Kgs 25:25; Jer. 41:1–3). The addition of 'even these seventy years' recalls Jeremiah's prophecy about the years of Babylonian service because of the people of Judah's refusal to listen to the word of God (Jer. 25:1–12; 29:10). While the Babylonians had been overthrown by the Persians some twenty years earlier, the seventy years seems to be tied here to the completion of the temple. Interestingly, if the temple was destroyed in 586 BC, its completion in 515 BC accounts for the seventy years. Alternatively, the seventy years may represent a lifetime and it may not be meant to be understood precisely (at the time of the question, they are still two years short of the 'seventy'). In any case, Zechariah wants them to ask themselves whether their seventy years of fasting and lamenting were done for Yahweh: 'was it indeed for me that you fasted?' Implicit in this is the alternative: that they fasted for themselves. Isa. 58:3–6 indicates that fasting for yourself is hypocritical – this includes fasting and yet oppressing workers, or quarrelling and fighting with one another: fasting without obedience to the word of God.

It is difficult to know exactly how to understand the second question, 'And when you eat and when you drink, do you not eat for yourselves and drink for yourselves?' If the eating and drinking is associated with festivals such as the Passover, Weeks and Booths (Redditt 1995: 82), then this would suggest that like their fasting, their feasts were also being celebrated hypocritically. Alternatively, if this refers simply to eating and drinking for one's own nourishment (Petersen 1985: 286–287), then the question clearly expects the answer 'yes', and it functions to imply that the answer to the first question is that their fasting, like their eating and drinking, had been done with self-interest, rather than in repentance.

7. The Hebr. text of the third question is unusual (see 'Notes on the text'). Reading it as 'Were not these the words which the LORD proclaimed by the earlier prophets?' scholars disagree on whether the question points backwards to vv. 5–6, or forwards to vv. 9–10, or to both (Wenzel 2011: 169). The phrase 'earlier prophets' is used in 1:4 and refers to the earlier prophets, such as Isaiah, Jeremiah and Ezekiel. Some argue that there is nothing in the earlier prophets like vv. 5–6, yet there are similarities to Isa. 58:3–6 (noted above). In addition, if these questions simply point to the incongruence of ritual action without concern for relationship with Yahweh and obedience to his word, then this idea runs all through the 'earlier prophets' (e.g. Isa. 1:10–11; Jer. 7; Joel 2:12–13; Amos 5; Mic. 6:6–8). The delegation has come with a question about fasting, and Zechariah's point is that God is more interested in relationship and obedience to his word (ethics). The words of the earlier prophets still apply.

To illustrate this, Zechariah again uses the example of the earlier pre-exilic generation (cf. the 'fathers' of 1:1–6) and the word that came to them in more prosperous days, 'when Jerusalem was inhabited and prosperous, even her towns surrounding her, and the Negev and the Shephelah were inhabited'. The 'Negev' is the region 50 mi. (80 km) to the south of Jerusalem that was used for grazing and agriculture, and was part of an important trade route. Under Solomon, Israelite control extended through the Negev to the port of Ezion-geber on the Gulf of Aqabah (1 Kgs 9:26). The 'Shephelah' refers to the tract of low hills between the high central ranges of Judea and the coastal plains. Zechariah implies that these regions are now not inhabited by God's people as they were before the exile, and the need for obedience to God's word is just as great as it was then. Importantly, Jeremiah refers to the restoration of both regions (Jer. 32:44; 33:13; cf. 17:26), and this may account for their mention here (Stead 2009: 231). The description of prosperity in v. 7 forms a frame with v. 14, where the situation is reversed.

8–10. While some scholars (e.g. Baldwin 1972: 145) argue that v. 8 is out of place (particularly if v. 7 is understood to refer in the first instance to vv. 9–10, rather than vv. 5–6), the sentence serves a dual function. As well as underlining again the divine status of Zechariah's words as he challenged his contemporaries, it has the effect of challenging the readers and hearers of the book with the ongoing relevance of Yahweh's word. Floyd (2000: 415) comments on this aspect of the passage's rhetoric:

> As the prophet speaks to his contemporaries, they are in effect hearing the words of the preexilic prophets; and as the narrator addresses the readers of the text, they are in effect hearing the words of Zechariah. The prophetic word formula, which occurs where this rhetorical ambiguity is most dense, thus fails to identify any particular recipient of the revelation.

Hence in the final form of the text the different audiences are effaced so as to continue to address subsequent readers and hearers. The ambiguity is seen in that where vv. 8–10 at first appear to be Zechariah's challenge to the delegation, v. 11 indicates that he is recounting the words of the earlier prophets to their generation ('they refused to listen'). This not only has the effect of recounting Zechariah's challenge to his own generation, but also challenges subsequent readers and hearers of his book.

Zechariah's word comes from the 'LORD of hosts' (see 'Comment' on 1:3), and is a summary of what the earlier prophets valued more than religious ritual. It comprises two positive commands and two negative ones. Stead (2009: 231–236) notes many parallels with Jer. 7, the famous 'temple sermon' that rebuked a false confidence in the temple as giving impunity from the consequences of unethical behaviour, which has clear relevance here. There are also 'overtones' from other passages.

'Judge true justice' (*mišpaṭ 'ĕmet šĕpōṭû*) involves more than simply making just rulings in legal cases, though it certainly includes this. 'Justice' (*mišpaṭ*) is first and foremost an attribute of Yahweh and indicates that all his ways are right (Deut. 32:4; Ps. 89:14). 'Justice' is often associated with 'righteousness', and together they comprise an ethical ideal for God's people that involves walking in his ways (e.g. Gen. 18:19). 'Justice' involves right relationships in the social sphere and is also often associated directly with 'kindness' and 'mercy' (Isa. 16:5; Jer. 9:24[23]; Hos. 2:19[21]; 12:6[7]; Mic. 6:8). Many commentators argue that 'true' is to be understood in the sense of 'faithful', and what is called for here is for the leaders to administer justice faithfully. Alternatively, if 'justice' is conceived more broadly, the call is to judge or determine what is 'true justice' (i.e. God's ways), rather than their own. In this sense, 'true justice' originates in God and is revealed by his word, namely the Torah and the prophets (cf. v. 12). 'True justice' is to be shown in the way God's people treat one another, particularly the needy. Weinfeld (1995: 43) comments, 'Zechariah here is not referring to the correct execution of justice in court, but rather to the establishment of social justice, and the restoration of equilibrium to the society by aiding the needy: the stranger, widow and orphan.' Weinfeld also notes the influence of Jer. 7:5–6 on Zechariah.

Parallel to 'Judge true justice' is 'show kindness and mercies to each other' (lit. 'and kindness and mercies do, each to his brother'). The word translated 'kindness' is *ḥesed*, which no English word does complete justice to. Again, it is usually associated with God (in two-thirds of its OT usage) and expresses his faithful covenant love to his people, despite their sin, and the means by which the relationship may continue (Routledge 2008: 109). Like 'justice', when it refers to human behaviour it refers to proper conduct within relationships, particularly a steadfast commitment to each other (cf. Hos. 12:6; Mic. 6:8). 'Mercies' (*raḥămîm*) is from the same root as 'compassion' (*raḥûm*) and expresses the love of a parent for a child (Isa. 49:15; Ps. 103:13). Likewise, it is a characteristic of God (Exod. 34:6; Jon. 4:2), again displayed in his persevering commitment to a stubborn and rebellious people (e.g. Neh. 9:17). This same mercy was to characterize the relationships of God's people with one another.

This is spelled out in concrete terms: 'Do not afflict a widow or an orphan, a foreigner or a poor one.' These were the vulnerable in society who were open to being exploited by others. The Torah made special provision for these people (e.g. Exod. 22:21–22; Lev. 19:15–18; Deut. 10:18–19), and the prophets, particularly Isaiah and Jeremiah, often reiterated this (e.g. Isa. 1:17; Jer. 7:6). Justice, kindness and mercies (v. 9) were seen chiefly in the way these vulnerable groups were treated. Finally, 'do not devise evil in your heart against one another' may refer to evil such as the violence of Isa. 58:4 or Jer. 7:6. It reveals God's concern not only with actions, but thoughts and motivations (in Hebr. thought, the 'heart' is the seat of the will).

11–12. The way God's people responded to the words of the pre-exilic prophets is made absolutely clear, with essentially the same thing being said in four different ways: 'they refused to listen' (Jer. 7:24; cf. Zech. 1:4); 'they gave a stubborn shoulder' uses the metaphor of an animal that refuses the yoke (Exod. 32:9; Deut. 9:6; Jer. 7:24; Neh. 9:29); 'they stopped their ears from hearing' denotes a wilful refusal (Isa. 6:10; cf. Zech. 1:4); and finally, 'they set their heart as diamond against hearing the Torah and the words which the LORD of hosts sent by his Spirit through the earlier prophets' (Jer. 6:28; 17:1; Ezek. 3:7–9; 11:19). This last description is of great theological interest in directly linking the words of the prophets with the agency of God's Spirit, something that was done indirectly in the menorah vision of ch. 4 (cf. Ezek. 11:5; Mic. 3:8). It also displays the dual authority of the Torah (cf. Deut. 31:9) and prophecy in the life of the nation (cf. Mal. 4:4–6[3:22–24]).

On account of this refusal, 'great wrath came from the LORD of hosts'. This explanation of the exile as being the outworking of God's anger was also seen in 1:2. It is God's response to those who refused him time and time again, and reinforces the importance of obedience to his word.

13–14. The correspondence between sin and punishment is demonstrated: 'And just as he called and they did not listen, so they would call and I would not listen, says the LORD of hosts'. Like other places in Zechariah (as noted in the 'Comment' on 6:12–13), here there is a switching in the same verse between third-person speech about Yahweh to first-person speech of Yahweh. Because they refused to listen to him, he shut his ears to their prayers and petitions (this is wonderfully reversed in 13:9).

The result is that God 'scattered them over all the nations'. The verb 'scatter' (*sʿr*) contains the idea of being blown by the wind in a storm, and Petersen (1985: 294) notes that it is used in Isa. 41:16 (cf. 40:24) in connection with seed and chaff. This would explain the use of the prep. 'over' (*ʿal*) here. While it uses a different verb, 'scattering' is one of the covenant curses (Lev. 26:33; Deut. 28:64) and refers to the judgment of exile and dispersion among the nations. The sense of 'they had not known' is that they were not in any relationship with the nations. It does not mean that the people of Judah did not know of them.

The idyllic situation of v. 7 is reversed. The people were scattered, and 'the land was desolate after them, [with no] one crossing over or returning', indicating no one travelling across the land and possibly indicating lack of security or trade. While some scholars (e.g. J. M. O'Brien 2004: 215) see 'empty land' ideology here (the notion that no one was left in the land after the exile), this probably overreads the imagery.

This verse expresses a double agency: it was God who scattered, but it was the people who 'made a desirable land into a wasteland' by refusing to listen to God's word. God is sovereign in judgment and the people are held responsible for their actions.

Explanation

With the imminent completion of the temple, a delegation from Bethel is sent to Jerusalem to entreat the favour of Yahweh and to enquire of the temple leadership whether fasting in repentance for the destroyed temple some seventy years earlier is still appropriate. The initial response is perhaps not what they expected. Before addressing the question directly (at the end of ch. 8), Zechariah uses the occasion to challenge the delegation about their motives and about their obedience to the word of God.

In a similar fashion to the opening of the book (1:1–6), Zechariah uses the example of the ancestors as a warning to his contemporaries about the dangers of religious hypocrisy and of refusing to listen to the words of the prophets. The ancestors' refusal to listen brought God's wrath and the judgment of exile. The rhetorical effect of this section is to challenge subsequent readers and hearers about their own motives and their obedience to God's word.

The key point of this section is that repentance and covenant obedience are more important than sacrificial ritual (and implicitly, having a rebuilt temple). This is a theme not only of the earlier prophets (as noted in the 'Comment'), but elsewhere in the OT, for instance in Samuel's rebuke of Saul (1 Sam. 15:22) and David's prayer of confession (Ps. 51:16–17). Christian readers well recognize the same theme in the teaching of Jesus. Indeed, some of his most stinging indictments were against religious leaders who performed their 'religious duties' but failed in the weightier matters of the law, namely justice, mercy, faith and the love of God (e.g. Matt. 23:23; Luke 11:32; John 7:24). In Luke 18:9–14, Jesus teaches that more important than fasting is confession of sin and humility (cf. Luke 20:45–47). In addition, Jesus teaches the ongoing authority of Moses and the prophets in his own day, particularly concerning care for the poor (Luke 16:20–21, 29). The wider NT also reiterates the teaching of the Torah and the prophets concerning love of the disadvantaged, particularly those in the Christian community (1 Cor. 11:17–34; Gal. 6:10; 1 Tim. 5:8–16; 1 John 3:17).

The vital difference between Zechariah's day and our own is the inauguration of the new covenant through Jesus' death, resurrection, ascension and giving of his Spirit. Not only does the word of God come by the Spirit of God today, as it came to the people in Zechariah's day (7:12; cf. Eph. 3:5; 1 Peter 1:10–12; Rev. 19:10), but the Spirit is at work within the believer to enable what is impossible apart from the Spirit (Ezek. 36:26–27; cf. Rom. 5:5; 8:9–16; 1 Cor. 12:3; 1 Thess. 4:8).

ZECHARIAH 8:1–23

Translation

8:1 And the word of the LORD of hosts came: 2 So says the LORD of hosts, 'I am jealous for Zion with a great jealousy, and with a great anger I am jealous for it.'

3 So says the LORD, 'I have turned to Zion and I will dwell in the midst of Jerusalem. And Jerusalem shall be called the city of truth, and the mountain of the LORD of hosts, the mountain of holiness.'

4 So says the LORD of hosts, 'Old men and old women shall again sit in the squares of Jerusalem, and each [with] his staff in his hand on account of many years. 5 And
the squares of the city shall be filled, with boys and girls playing in its squares.'

[6]So says the LORD of hosts, 'If in the eyes of the remnant of this people it will
be incredible in those days, will it also be incredible in my eyes?' declares the LORD
of hosts.

[7]So says the LORD of hosts, 'Look, I will save my people from the land where
the sun rises to the land where it sets. [8]I will bring them and they will dwell in the
midst of Jerusalem, and they will be my people and I will be their God, in truth
and in righteousness.

[9]So says the LORD of hosts, 'Let your hands be strong, you who have been hearing
in these days these words from the mouth of the prophets who [were present] in
the day the house of the LORD of hosts was founded in order that the temple might
be built. [10]For before those days there was no wage for human and there was no
wage for animal, and for the one going out and for the one coming in there was
no peace from the enemy. And I sent every person against his neighbour. [11]But now
I will not be as the former days towards the remnant of this people,' declares the
LORD of hosts. [12]'For there will be a sowing of peace: the vine will give its fruit
and the earth will give its produce and the heavens will give their dew. And I will
cause the remnant of this people to inherit all of these. [13]And it will be – just as
you have been a curse among the nations, house of Judah and house of Israel, so
I will save you and you will be a blessing. Do not fear! Let your hands be strong!'

[14]For so says the LORD of hosts, 'Just as I planned to bring disaster to you when
your fathers made me angry,' says the LORD of hosts, 'and I did not have com-
passion, [15]so I have turned. I plan in these days to do good to Jerusalem and to
the house of Judah. Do not fear! [16]These are the things that you shall do: Speak
truth with each other; truth and a judgment of peace render in your gates; [17]and
do not devise evil in your heart [against your] neighbour; and do not love a false
oath, for all these are what I hate,' declares the LORD.

[18]And the word of the LORD of hosts came to me: [19]So says the LORD of hosts,
'The fast of the fourth and the fast of the fifth and the fast of the seventh and the
fast of the tenth months shall become for the house of Judah rejoicing and
gladness and pleasing assemblies. So, love truth and peace!'

[20]So says the LORD of hosts, 'It will yet be that peoples will come, and inhabit-
ants of many towns. [21]The inhabitants of one [town] will go to another, saying,
"Come! Let us go to entreat the favour of the LORD and to seek the LORD of hosts
– I also am going." [22]And many peoples and mighty nations shall go to seek the
LORD of hosts in Jerusalem, and to entreat the favour of the LORD.'

[23]So says the LORD of hosts, 'In those days, it will be that ten men from every
tongue of the nations will seize – they will seize by the corner of a garment of each
– a Judahite, saying, "Let us go with you, for we have heard that God is with you."'

Notes on the text

8:2. 'I am jealous . . . with a great jealousy' (cf. 1:14) uses a cognate object to express a concrete instance of the verbal action (J. C. L. Gibson 1994: 115).

'with a great anger': *wĕḥēmâ gĕdôlâ* (see 'Comment'). Tg indicates the object of the anger: 'the nations which provoked her' (Cathcart and Gordon 1989: 201).

3. 'I have turned' is future in LXX.

4. 'on account of': *min* indicates the cause of the situation (Gesenius 2006: 383, §119z).

5. 'playing' agrees with the m., as being the prior gender (Gesenius 2006: 428, §132d).

6. 'If': *kî* is translated with a conditional sense (Arnold and Choi 2003: 151).

'will it also be incredible in my eyes?': Gesenius (2006: 473, §150a) argues that even though there is no special interr. pr. or adv., the natural emphasis of the words indicate an interr. 4Q80, LXX and Vg make the interr. explicit.

7. 'the land where the sun rises to the land where it sets': lit. 'the land of the rising and from the land of the setting of the sun'.

10. 'human', 'person' (both translate *hā'ādām*) and 'animal' are used generically (Arnold and Choi 2003: 31) and the art. (with each) is not translated.

'I sent every person against his neighbour': lit. 'I sent every man – each against his neighbour'; cf. v. 17.

11. 'But now': *wĕ'attâ* requires an adversative sense (Arnold and Choi 2003: 146).

'be' is understood from the context since there is no explicit verb. LXX and Vg have 'I will do'.

13. 'just as': *ka'ăšer* introduces the protasis, and 'so' (*kēn*) introduces the apodosis of a comparison (also vv. 14–15).

15. 'so I have turned': *kēn šabtî*. Many translate this 'so again' (e.g. ESV, NIV, NASB), but in context it more likely speaks of God's turning in mercy (cf. 1:16) (LeCureux 2012: 197). See 'Comment'.

16. 'with each other': lit. 'a man with his friend'.

17. 'do not devise evil in your heart [against your] neighbour': lit. 'a man his neighbour do not devise evil in your heart'.

19. 'months' is not present in the Hebr., but is understood from 7:3.

'shall become . . . rejoicing and gladness and pleasing assemblies': the verb *hāyāh* is followed by three lameds, which indicate the goal (Waltke and O'Connor 1990: 209).

'Love': *'ĕhābû* is a qal imp., where the guttural causes ḥireq to change to sĕgōl (Gesenius 2006: 167, §63l).

'truth and peace': *wĕhā'ĕmet wĕhaššālôm*. As abstract terms both have generic articles that are not translated (Waltke and O'Connor 1990: 246). Cf. Mal. 2:5, 17.

20. 'it will . . . be' is supplied to smooth the translation (also v. 23). The Hebr. is unusual.

21. 'Come! Let us go': *nēlkâ hālôk*. The inf. abs. following the finite form of *hālak* is emphatic (Arnold and Choi 2003: 75).

'to entreat the favour of the Lord': lit. 'to make favourable the face of Yahweh' (also v. 22; cf. 7:2; Mal. 1:9).

23. 'it will be' is supplied to smooth the translation (also v. 20).

'by the corner of a garment': *biknap*.

'for we have heard that God is with you': lit. 'for we heard God with you'. Gesenius (2006: 491, §157a) notes that a clause depending on a verb of perception (such as 'to hear') may be added as a noun or verb clause with no conj. Hence 'that' is supplied in translation.

Form and structure

Zech. 7 – 8 forms a unit that deals with a question from a delegation from Bethel to Jerusalem, and many of the comments under 'Form and structure' in the previous chapter are also relevant here. There is, however, a different tone in each chapter. Whereas ch. 7 called for covenant obedience in view of the sin and judgment of the ancestors, ch. 8 contains a series of prophetic oracles that call for the same obedience in view of future salvation and blessing. In addition, Boda (2003a: 400) observes how the judgment on people and land in 7:14 is reversed in ch. 8, with the city being filled (8:1–8) and the land being fruitful (8:9–13).

The form of ch. 8 is a series of oracles of salvation, with the oracles of vv. 9–19 including prophetic exhortations. The chapter also contains many allusions and references to themes of chs. 1–6 (Assis 2010b), and to the earlier prophets, particularly the eschatological blessing of Jerusalem and the pilgrimage of the nations to it. These themes are also prominent in chs. 9–14. Indeed, Webb (2003: 116) argues that chs. 7–8 encapsulate the movement of the entire second half of the book: from mourning and fasting to celebration and joyful festivals (cf. 14:16–21). Similarly, Sweeney (2000b: 636) believes chs. 9–14 provide a detailed scenario of the process by which the nations will ultimately recognize Yahweh in Jerusalem (cf. 8:18–23).

In terms of structure, ch. 8 can be divided into two broad sections, each introduced by the phrase 'And the word of the Lord of hosts came' (8:1–17, 18–23). The first section contains seven oracles, each introduced by 'So says the Lord of hosts' (vv. 2, 3, 4, 6, 7, 9, 14; there is minor variation with 'of hosts' absent from v. 3 and 'for' introducing v. 14). The second section contains three oracles, also introduced by 'So says the Lord of hosts' (vv. 19–20, 23).

Comment

8:1. 'And the word of the Lord of hosts came' marks a new section (cf. 7:4, 8:18 and 'the word of the Lord came' in 7:1, 8). There is a minor variation here with 'to me' absent, but the context demands that Zechariah be the recipient. The phrase highlights his status as a prophet and the divine authority of his word. The description 'LORD of hosts' occurs eighteen times in this chapter (see 'Comment' on 1:3). It speaks of God's might, especially relevant for a people facing hardship and oppression to be reminded of (cf. vv. 6, 10). It also underlines why the reader should pay attention to Zechariah.

2. In the first oracle (v. 2), God's great jealousy for Zion echoes the first night vision (cf. 1:14). God's jealousy refers to his concern for what is rightly his and his willingness to overthrow all opposition to defend it (e.g. Exod. 20:5; 34:13; Deut. 5:9).

The word translated 'anger' (*ḥēmâ*) is sometimes translated as 'burning' (NIV) or 'passion' since the wider context suggests a positive attitude towards Zion is being expressed. However, it is better to translate *ḥēmâ* as 'anger' now being directed towards the nations (cf. Ezek. 25:17; 36:6), as it was in 1:15 (though 'anger' there was *qeṣep*). The nations as the object of God's anger is made explicit in the Tgs (see 'Notes on the text').

3. The second oracle (v. 3) is closely connected to the first. Like 1:14–16, Yahweh's jealousy for Zion is the grounds for his having turned to his people with mercy, after they experienced his wrath (in exile). On the translation 'I have turned' (*šabtî*), see 'Comment' on 1:16 (the same phrase is found in 8:15). Though God has turned from anger towards his people to mercy, his dwelling in Jerusalem with his glory returning to the temple as Ezekiel prophesied (cf. Ezek. 43:4) is still in the future, after the completion of the temple (cf. 2:10–11[14–15]). According to Ezra 6:15, the completion of the temple was still almost two years beyond the time of this prophecy (cf. 7:1).

When Yahweh returns, Jerusalem will express his character. It will be called 'the city of truth', possibly echoing the description of Isa. 1:21, though it uses different vocabulary. The word 'truth' (*'emet*) means 'reliability, dependability, trustworthiness, faithfulness, constancy', and is usually an attribute of Yahweh (Clines 1993: 328). It occurs six times in Zechariah, with all occurrences in Zech. 7 – 8. In three instances it is clearly an ethical quality that God's people are to display: 'true justice' (7:9; 8:16) and 'true speech' (8:16). In two other instances (8:8, 19), as here, it is unclear whether it is distinctly an attribute of humans or of God. In this present verse it could represent God's faithfulness to his covenant promises, or the character of the refined and transformed inhabitants of the city, or both.

Yahweh's 'mountain' is a reference to Mount Zion, the temple mount (cf. Hag. 1:8). With his return to dwell in the midst of Jerusalem, it will be 'the mountain of holiness', a theme of the earlier prophets (e.g. Isa. 11:9; Jer. 31:23; Ezek. 20:40; Joel 2:1; Obad. 16; Zeph. 3:11). It will be holy because it will belong exclusively to God. This topic is developed at the end of Zechariah (14:20–21).

4–5. A third oracle (vv. 4–5) pictures the future prosperity of Jerusalem (cf. Isa. 65:20; Zech. 2:4[8]). The elderly and children were the first to perish when cities were besieged and had to work in times of adversity. Here the elderly are pictured at a ripe old age, 'each [with] his staff in his hand on account of many years', and having leisure time to sit. The boys and girls are pictured as numerous: they fill the squares, and are not working but playing. The picture encompasses men and women, boys and girls.

Meyers and Meyers (1987: 415–416) note that the 'squares' are not transport routes ('streets' in ESV, NASB, NIV), but 'open places' between houses. There is possibly also a contrast with the 'squares' described in Lamentations, which were associated with death after Jerusalem's destruction (e.g. 2:11–12).

6. This fourth oracle (v. 6) forms a transition between the picture of a renewed and prosperous Jerusalem in vv. 2–5 and what God promises to do to bring it about in vv. 7–8 (and the rest of the chapter). The word translated 'it will be incredible' (*yippālē'*) has the sense of wonder or miracle as well as impossibility (cf. Gen. 18:14; Job 42:2; Jer. 32:17, 27). The promised prosperity of Jerusalem may seem 'incredible' to the remnant in 'those days' (i.e. the future), but it is certainly not beyond God's power.

Sweeney (2000b: 648) notes that the concept of a 'remnant' who survive Yahweh's judgment to rebuild Jerusalem and Israel for the future underlies the messages of Isaiah (e.g. Isa. 7:3; 10:20–22), Micah (e.g. 7:18) and Zephaniah (e.g. 2:7). Reference to the 'remnant' is also found in Hag. 1:12, 14, 2:2 and Zech. 8:11–12.

7–8. The fifth oracle (vv. 7–8) reverses the judgment of scattering in Zech. 2:6[10] and 7:14 with an act of God's salvation (cf. 8:13; 9:9). The expression 'the land where the sun rises to the land where it sets' denotes poetically all lands to which the people had been scattered. God's salvation will be displayed as he brings them to 'dwell in the midst of Jerusalem' (cf. v. 3). Presumably, they are also saved from the coming judgment on the nations, implicit in v. 2 and explicit in Zech. 1:21 and 6:6–8.

Many of the ideas here are present in Jer. 31:7–8, where God promises to save the remnant of his people from the land of the north and the ends of the earth (cf. Jer. 30:10–11) (Stead 2009: 242). The phrase 'they will be my people and I will be their God' also echoes Jeremiah (24:7; 30:25; 31:1, 33; cf. Ezek. 11:20), and speaks of restored relationship and a new covenant (cf. 2:11[15]).

While 'in truth and in righteousness' could arguably refer to the character of the restored people (Clark and Hatton 2002: 204), in context it is better understood as the character of Yahweh that will be displayed in salvation and restoration. Yahweh's salvation will be an expression of his truth or 'faithfulness' (see 'Comment' on v. 3) and his righteousness. Elsewhere in the HB, 'righteousness' is often associated with salvation (cf. also 9:9), where salvation is 'the result of God's right action in accordance with his covenant relationship with his people' (Routledge 2008: 107).

9. The sixth oracle (vv. 9–13) is the longest. It contains echoes of Haggai, and behind that the blessings and curses of the covenant with Israel at Sinai. It begins and ends with a call to 'Let your hands be strong'. Elsewhere this phrase is a general command to take courage (e.g. Judg. 7:11; 2 Sam. 2:7; 16:21; Ezek. 22:14), but in the immediate context it also implies rebuilding the temple (Stead 2009: 228). The command is directed to those who have been hearing from 'the prophets who [were present] in the day the house of the Lord of hosts was founded'. This description creates a difficulty in that the founding of the temple occurred some twenty years before Haggai and Zechariah began their prophetic ministries (Ezra 3:8–13; cf. Hag. 1:1; Zech. 1:1). Furthermore, no other prophets are mentioned in connection with the building of the temple, and Ezra attributes the completion of the temple to them both (5:2; 6:14). The best solution seems to be to see the founding here not referring to the initial laying of the foundation by Zerubbabel under the patronage of Sheshbazzar (see 'Comment' on 4:9), but to some kind of ceremony on the twenty-fourth day of the ninth month in the second year of Darius, which marked the recommencement of the work in response to the prophesying of Haggai and Zechariah (see 'Comment' on Hag. 2:18; cf. Ezra 4:24 – 5:2). The role of the prophets in building the temple was the focus of the fifth night vision in ch. 4.

Meyers and Meyers (1987: 420) argue that the phrase 'from the mouth of the prophets' in other places refers to written words of an earlier prophet, and that here Zechariah is referring to the words of Haggai (cf. Hag. 2:18).

10. There are several echoes of Haggai (Stead 2009: 239): 'before those days' (cf. Hag. 2:15), which corresponds to the period before v. 9, namely the prophesying of Haggai and Zechariah and the recommencement of the temple. At this time 'there was no wage for human and there was no wage for animal' (cf. Hag. 1:11). McComiskey (1998: 1144) argues this phrase is not describing unemployment, but the failure to be remunerated for work (note the ni. form of *hāyâ*). The 'wage for animal' likely refers to a fee for hiring it out. There are two further descriptions of this time: 'for the one going out and for the one coming in there was no peace from the enemy', which describes insecurity and lack of safety for those who travel outside Jerusalem (cf. Ezra 4:1–5). Furthermore, there was conflict within the community with 'every person against his neighbour'. The reason for such conflict is not given. Webb (2003: 25) suggests there were tensions between those who had returned and those who had never gone into exile, with each having reasons to think they were superior. Some who returned from Babylon came with considerable wealth (Ezra 2:69; Zech. 6:10–11), and this may have caused conflict with those who remained. Land title may also have caused disputes. In any case, it was a sorry situation.

11–13. 'But now' is an adversative that introduces a contrast. God will no longer deal with the remnant as he had in 'former days', the same 'days' identified in v. 10, namely the days before the temple-building recommenced. The 'remnant' is mentioned twice in these verses (cf. 'Comment' on v. 6), and is a further echo of Haggai (1:12, 14; 2:2).

'For there will be a sowing of peace' indicates the positive results of God's turning towards his people with compassion. There will be agricultural plenty. The vine is used as a symbol of peace and prosperity in 3:10 (along with the fig tree). It took four to five years from planting before the vine would begin to produce a usable crop of fruit (MacDonald 2008: 22) and warfare often saw vineyards destroyed (e.g. Jer. 12:10; Ps. 80:16). Hence connecting the vine with 'a sowing of peace' is very appropriate. The promise of 'peace' (*šālôm*) is a contrast to the 'no peace' in 8:10, and 'peace' is later promoted in 8:16 and 8:19. 'Peace' is also one of the fruits of the coming Davidic king (6:13; 9:10).

The next clause, 'the earth will give its produce and the heavens will give their dew', contains a number of verbal parallels with Hag. 1:10 (Stead 2009: 239). The blessing of the land is one of the covenant blessings of Deut. 28 and Lev. 26 (e.g. Deut. 28:4, 11–12). Indeed, the curse involves the fruits of the field being given to Israel's enemies (Deut. 28:30–33). This connection also explains the use of 'inherit' at the end of v. 12, which is connected with the blessings of the Promised Land in the Pentateuch and Former Prophets, and that the Latter Prophets hold out as a future hope (e.g. Isa. 49:8; 57:13; Jer. 3:18; Ezek. 47:14).

The connection with the Mosaic covenant is also seen in v. 13, where God promises to remove the curse of being 'among the nations' by saving them so they 'shall be a blessing'. The 'be a blessing' language also echoes the promise to Abraham that through him all peoples on earth will be blessed (Gen. 12:3). This turning of God from cursing to bless and to save reiterates the themes of 8:3 and 8:7 and highlights the covenantal background of Zechariah's message. The reference to the 'house of Judah and house of Israel' shows a concern for the restoration and reunification of the nation, a theme of chs. 9–14 (e.g. 9:1, 10, 13; 10:6).

The final injunction of this oracle, 'Do not fear! Let your hands be strong' (cf. v. 9), is also an echo of Haggai (2:4–5). In both contexts, the challenge is to trust in God's promises and to work on the temple.

14–15. The seventh oracle (vv. 14–17) begins by reiterating themes from the first two oracles (vv. 2–3; cf. 1:2, 6, 12, 15–16). 'For' (*kî*) indicates a summation or conclusion to the previous six oracles (Sweeney 2000b: 652). In the past God was angry with the fathers and 'did not have compassion'. He brought disaster on his people in the judgment of exile. But now God says, 'I have turned' (*šabtî*). Many translations simply translate this phrase as 'again' (ESV, NIV, NRSV), but this obscures an important theme of the book: God's turning from anger to compassion (cf. 1:16; 8:3). God plans to 'do good', a concept associated with his keeping his promise to bless (cf. Josh. 24:20; Ezek. 36:11; Zech. 1:17). Assis (2011b: 7–8) detects an allusion to the restoration and new covenant promises of Jer. 32:37–42.

In Zechariah, Jerusalem and the house of Judah are at the centre of God's purposes, from which the nations will be included (vv. 20–23).

16–17. On account of God's gracious compassion, the people are not to fear (v. 15), but to obey. The words of the earlier prophets to the fathers continue to apply (cf. 7:9–10). There are four injunctions, two positive and two negative. The first positive and first negative injunctions deal with honesty in personal relationships: 'Speak truth with each other . . . do not devise evil in your heart' (see 'Comment' on 7:10). The second positive and the second negative injunctions concern the administration of justice in the community: 'truth and a judgment of peace render in your gates . . . do not love a false oath'. The 'gates' were the location where the city elders gathered to administer justice (Deut. 21:19; 25:7; Ruth 4:1, 11; Amos 5:15). The word translated 'render' is literally 'judge' (*šipṭû*). The 'false oath' refers to giving false testimony, or perjury, and connects with 'the one who swears falsely' in the sixth vision, who will be destroyed (5:3–4). The two negative injunctions involve actions God hates (cf. ch 5) and are contrary to what people are exhorted to love in v. 19 (truth and peace).

Stead (2009: 235) makes an important observation: 'While Zech. 1–6 is clearly very interested in the temple reconstruction, this is not to be taken as an end in itself . . . the ethical transformation of God's people is essential.' This is the challenge to readers and hearers of the final form of the book of Zechariah, for whom the temple is completed.

18–19. 'And the word of the LORD of hosts came to me' marks a new section within the chapter (see 'Comment' on v. 1). This section links back to the original question of the delegation from Bethel concerning fasting (7:2–3) and rounds out the unit (chs. 7–8). The three final oracles have an eschatological focus.

In the eighth oracle (v. 19), God declares that the fasts 'shall become for the house of Judah rejoicing and gladness and pleasing assemblies'. Two additional fasts are referred to (cf. the 'fifth' in 7:3 and the 'seventh' in 7:5). Again, these are not mentioned elsewhere in the OT, but scholars suggest that the fast of the fourth month commemorated the day on which the Babylonian army breached the walls of Jerusalem (2 Kgs 25:2–4; Jer. 39:2), and the fast of the tenth month recalled the beginning of the siege of Jerusalem (2 Kgs 25:1; Jer. 29:1).

The earlier prophets also associated joy and gladness with the restoration of Jerusalem (Isa. 35:10; 51:3, 11; Jer. 31:13; 33:10–11). The phrase 'and pleasing assemblies' (*ûlĕmō'ădîm ṭôbîm*) does not occur elsewhere in the OT, but most commentators associate it with feasting at Israel's festivals (implied in the pilgrimage in vv. 20–23 and explicit in 14:18; cf. Isa. 33:20), so that the answer to the question concerning the ongoing need for fasting is that it will be replaced with feasting.

Floyd (2000: 437) observes that the final imper., 'So, love truth and peace!', ties together key elements of 7:9 – 8:17 with God's affinity for 'truth' seen in 7:9, 8:3, 8, 16, and 'peace' in 8:10, 12, 16. They are a summary of the interpersonal or social dimensions of the law and are the opposite of the things God hates (v. 17). Hence the turning of God with compassion to Zion (8:3, 15) involves much more than changing one set of holidays for another; it is the basis for radical ethical transformation.

20–22. The ninth oracle (vv. 20–22) continues to look forward. The delegation from Bethel came to Jerusalem 'to entreat the favour of the LORD' (see 'Comment' on 7:2). This journey becomes a pattern for a greater pilgrimage to come – a pilgrimage of 'many towns' (v. 20) and 'many peoples and mighty nations' (v. 22). The 'many towns' of v. 20 probably refers to towns surrounding Jerusalem (such as Bethel; cf. 7:7), which are caught up in the excitement of what God has done in Jerusalem (cf. v. 19). The news will spread like wildfire as pilgrims invite others also to journey to Jerusalem (v. 21; cf. Isa. 2:2). The 'many peoples and mighty nations' refers to foreign nations who will come to Jerusalem to seek God's mercy. The inclusion of the nations in God's salvation purposes is a theme that goes back to the beginning of the OT. The promise to Abraham involved blessing to all peoples on earth (Gen. 12:3; 17:4–7). Indeed, the promise to Abraham is set in the context of world history, which claims that the God who made the promise to Abraham is the creator of the universe, whose purpose in creation was blessing for humanity (Gen. 1:28). This context also establishes Abraham's God as the God of all nations (Gen. 4 – 11). The pilgrimage of the nations to Jerusalem is a theme of the earlier prophets, especially Isaiah (e.g. Isa. 2:2–4; 42:1–7; 49:22–23; 60:14; 66:18–24), and has been foreshadowed earlier in 2:11[15]: 'And many nations shall join themselves to the LORD'. At the end of the night visions, the army of Yahweh went out to judge the nations (6:8). Now the nations come in pilgrimage to entreat the favour of Yahweh. The same elements of judgment and salvation of the nations will be seen in chs. 9 and 14:16–19.

23. The tenth oracle (v. 23) continues the eschatological focus. 'In those days' contrasts 'in these days' of 8:9, 15 and points to the future day of blessing (see 'Comment' on 'on that day' in 2:11[15] and 3:10). The 'men from every tongue of the nations' may be an echo of Gen. 10:4, 20, 31, in which case this is a reversal of the judgment at Babel where the nations were scattered over the face of the earth (Gen. 11:1–9). The proportion of ten to one conveys the vast number of the men of the nations who will be involved (cf. Isa. 4:1). Scalise (2009: 264) argues that the custom of seizing the corner of a garment lays claim to a desired relationship or outcome (cf. Ruth 3:9; 1 Sam. 15:27; Matt. 9:20–22). Presumably, the reference to 'ten men' would never have been understood to exclude women (the requirement in Deut. 16:16 of men to pilgrimage to the place God would choose did not preclude women, as Deut. 16:11, 14 show).

A 'Judahite' (*yĕhûdî*) refers to one from the tribe of Judah (cf. Jer. 34:9; 43:9; 52:28, 30; Esth. 2:5; 3:4). The importance of the tribe of Judah in God's future salvation is a feature of chs. 9–14. Judah has been mentioned three times in this chapter (vv. 13, 15, 19) and occurs fourteen times in chs. 9–14. It is the tribe of the house of David. The reason that the people of the nations want to go to Jerusalem with a Judahite is that they 'have heard God is with you' (cf. 'Immanuel' in Isa. 7:14; 8:8, 10). This summarizes the hope of Zechariah: God once again dwelling among his people will turn the nations from enemies to friends.

Explanation

The previous chapter noted the way this unit (chs. 7–8) begins with a question from a delegation from Bethel to the priests and prophets in Jerusalem about the appropriateness of continuing to fast in view of the near completion of the temple. Zechariah began his response to this question with a challenge to listen to the words of the earlier prophets and a warning not to repeat the religious hypocrisy of the ancestors who fell under God's judgment (ch. 7). The implication is that Zechariah's earlier call to be different from the ancestors (1:4) is not being heeded (Wenzel 2011: 167). Moving into ch. 8, there is a shift in tone. The call for covenant faithfulness remains, but now it is in view of future salvation and blessing, and the privilege and responsibility that the houses of Judah and Israel have in God's purposes for the salvation of the nations. In both chapters, Zechariah maintains that God's character as presented in the requirements of the Torah and the words of the earlier prophets is to be reflected in their lives together. Hence in the book of Zechariah this unit functions not only to explain further what 'repentance' looks like for God's people, but to call its readers and hearers to this repentance in view of God's return (cf. 1:1–6). Assis (2010b: 1–26) demonstrates these oracles reiterate many of the themes of chs. 1–7.

In Zech. 8, the first series of seven oracles (8:1–17) emphasizes again the fact that God has turned from judgment to compassion (esp. vv. 3, 11, 14–15; cf. 1:16). God's future return to dwell in Jerusalem will be an outworking of the covenant blessings (esp. vv. 4–5, 12; cf. Jer. 30 – 31). The sixth oracle in vv. 9–13 clearly echoes the message of Haggai, Zechariah's contemporary, whose message is explicitly set in the context of the Mosaic covenant (e.g. Hag. 2:5), with its consequent blessings and curses.

The first of the final three oracles (8:18–19) directly addresses the question asked by the Bethel delegation (7:3). The fasts will become occasions for joy, gladness and joyous assemblies. However, more important than fasting is the radical ethical transformation required of those who have experienced God's mercy, expressed succinctly in the imper. 'Love truth and peace' (8:19; cf. 7:10; 8:16–17). As was God's purpose for the nation from their beginning (cf. Gen. 12:3; Exod. 19:5–6), Israel is to reflect the character of God in their national life with a view to the salvation of the nations (8:20–23; cf. 14:16–21).

As noted in the 'Explanation' of 1:1–6, God's mercy and grace precede the call for obedience. The order is crucial (cf. the exodus salvation that precedes the giving of the law at Sinai). Both ethics and rebuilding the temple are predicated on God's prior action in turning in mercy to his people on account of his covenant. Hence ethics and cult are an outworking of restored relationship between God and his people now that the 'seventy years' of judgment are over (Stead 2009: 246–247). At the same time, obedience in response to God's mercy is a prerequisite of knowing the full blessings of the covenant (Wenham 1978: 6). It is here that the dislocation between their present experience and the earlier prophetic expectation for a glorified Jerusalem after the return from exile is to be understood. Zechariah understands that the failure to enter into the full experience of the covenant blessings promised by the earlier prophets is not because God's promises have failed. Rather, it is because the people seem to exhibit the same behaviour as their fathers. The many allusions in ch. 8 to the earlier prophetic hopes show that these prophecies remain in force. What is called for in order to experience them is covenant faithfulness (Wenzel 2011: 177).

Christians know that ultimately this obedience proved too difficult for the nation, but was achieved by God in his mercy through the faithful obedience of his Son, the Lord Jesus (Rom. 5:19). As the obedient Son, he won the blessings of the covenant not only for Israel, but for the nations. What seemed 'incredible' in human eyes has been achieved by the power of God. In Jesus Christ, the hope expressed in this chapter for the dwelling of God in the midst of Jerusalem (cf. 'God is with you' in v. 23) finds its fulfilment and expansion (cf. 'Immanuel' in Isa. 7:14; 8:10; Matt. 1:23). This theme will be elaborated upon in the treatment of chs. 9–14.

The related theme of the salvation of the nations, which is found at the end of this chapter (cf. 2:11[15]; 9:7; 14:16–19), finds its roots in the promise to Abraham (Gen. 12:3; 17:4–7), and is a major theme of Isaiah (Oswalt 2006). There are a number of echoes of ch. 8 in relation to this theme in the NT, where its fulfilment is again found in the Judahite Jesus Christ (e.g. Acts 15:17; 1 Cor. 14:25; Col. 1:26–27; Rev. 15:4). Jesus also fulfils and expands all that Jerusalem represents, namely the presence and rule of God (Gal. 4:25–26; Heb. 13:14).

Many of these themes are also reflected in Ephesians. The saints (Christians) have every spiritual blessing in Christ (Eph. 1:3). Ephesians explains how through Christ Jesus, Gentiles have also become members of the household of God (2:11–22). Those in Christ are called to new covenant obedience in view of God's mercy and grace (Eph. 2:10), and the consummation of all things (Eph. 1:10–12). In addition, Ephesians makes it clear that God's character is to be reflected in the lives of his people. Interestingly, in Eph. 4:25 Paul issues the same imper. as 8:16 to 'speak truthfully to your neighbour' and this is because it reflects God's own character (Eph. 4:24; cf. 5:1).

ZECHARIAH 9:1–17

Translation

[9:1]An oracle: the word of the LORD is against the land of Hadrach, and Damascus is its resting place, for to the LORD belongs the eye of humankind and all the tribes of Israel. [2]And Hamath also [which] borders upon it. Tyre and Sidon, for it is very wise. [3]Tyre has built a fortification for itself and has heaped up silver as dust and gold as mud of the streets. [4]Look, my Lord will dispossess it and strike down its army in the sea, and it will be consumed by fire.

[5]Ashkelon will see it and be afraid. Gaza too, and will tremble greatly. Ekron too, for its hope has been put to shame. A king from Gaza will perish, and Ashkelon will not be inhabited. [6]An outcast will dwell in Ashdod and I will cut down the pride of the Philistines. [7]I will remove its blood from its mouth and its abominations from between its teeth, and he will remain, even he, for our God. And he will be like a clan in Judah, and Ekron like a Jebusite.

[8]I will encamp at my house as a guard [against] one passing through and one returning, and an oppressor will not pass through them again. For now I am watching with my eyes.

[9]Rejoice greatly, daughter of Zion! Shout, daughter of Jerusalem! Look! Your king will come to you. He is righteous and saved, afflicted and riding upon a donkey, namely upon a purebred jackass. [10]I will cut off the chariot from Ephraim and the horse from Jerusalem, and the battle bow will be cut off, and he will speak peace to the nations. His rule will be from sea to sea, and from the river to the ends of the earth.

[11]You also, because of the blood of your covenant, I will set free your prisoners from a waterless pit. [12]Return to the stronghold, prisoners of hope. Moreover, today I declare that I will return to you double.

[13]For I will bend Judah to me; as a bow I will fill it with Ephraim, and I will incite your sons, Zion, against your sons, Greece. And I will make you as a warrior's sword. [14]And the LORD will appear over them, and his arrow will go forth as lightning, and my Lord, the LORD will sound the horn and will come in storms of the south. [15]The LORD of hosts will defend them, and they will devour and will subdue the sling stones and they will drink and will roar as with wine, and they will be full like the bowl, like corners of an altar.

[16]The LORD their God will save them on that day as a flock of his people. Surely they will be jewels of a crown sparkling upon his land. [17]For how good is it and how beautiful is it! Grain will make young men flourish and new wine young women.

Notes on the text

9:1. 'An oracle': *maśśāʾ* is omitted in Syr (perhaps seen as a tautology, but it is present in 12:1 and Mal. 1:1). See 'Comment'.

'against': *bĕ*. Some translate it 'upon' or 'in' (e.g. Meyers and Meyers 1993: 87) because of the later reference to 'its resting place', but the wider context suggests 'against'. See 'Comment'.

Tg translates 'Hadrach' as 'the south'. Cathcart and Gordon (1989: 203) explain that this occasionally occurs when the location is not known.

'to the LORD belongs': *layhwh*, where the prep. *lĕ* is understood as indicating possession by Yahweh (Arnold and Choi 2003: 112). See 'Comment'.

'the eye of humankind': *'ên 'ādām*. The article has been provided in translation. Some suggest emending to 'cities of Aram' (*'ārê 'ărām*), but there is no textual basis for this.

2. '[which] borders upon it': *tigbol-bāh*. The Hebr. is difficult to render here and the rel. pr. 'which' has been provided. There may be a wordplay on 'Gebal', which was a Phoenician city near Tyre and Sidon (cf. Ezek. 27:9).

'it is very wise' is unexpected. LXX and Vg translate with a pl. verb. Either the two cities are considered a single entity or the description applies only to Sidon. See 'Comment'.

4. 'Look': *hinnēh* modifies the previous proposition with further newsworthy information (Bartholomew and O'Dowd 2011: 77).

7. The sg. 'he' continues the personification of the Philistines. See 'Comment'.

'even he': *gam-hû'* adds emphasis (Arnold and Choi 2003: 133).

'like a clan': *kê'allup*. Sometimes translated 'as a leader'. See 'Comment' on 12:5–6.

9. 'Look!': *hinnēh* points to the arrival of a newsworthy entity (Bartholomew and O'Dowd 2011: 61).

'and saved': *wĕnôšā'*. The ni. ptc. connotes completed action (Arnold and Choi 2003: 78). LXX, Syr, Vg and Tgs all render in the active. See 'Comment'.

'namely, upon a purebred jackass': *wĕ'al-'ayir ben-'ătōnôt*. The waw functions in an explanatory way ('namely').

The translation 'upon a donkey, namely upon a purebred jackass' follows the suggestion of Way (2011: 163), who argues that here the general term for 'donkey' (*ḥămôr*) is being more closely defined as 'a purebred male donkey' (lit. 'a jackass, the son of a jenny', where a 'jackass' is a male donkey and a 'jenny' is a female). Hence it is not a mule (the cross of a jackass and a mare), nor a young 'foal' or 'colt' as it is usually translated, but a purebred.

10. LXX and Syr have 'and he will cut off'. MT has been followed as the more difficult reading.

'the chariot . . . the horse . . . the battle bow' lack the art. in Hebrew, but each is understood to be a class.

The second sentence is a verbless clause – 'will be' is supplied.

11. 'I will set free': *šillaḥtî* is understood as a rhetorical pf., presenting the future as if it had occurred (Arnold and Choi 2003: 55–56).

'a waterless pit': lit. 'a pit – there is no water in it'.

12. 'the stronghold' is a hapax legomenon. The article has been provided in translation. See 'Comment'.

'hope': *hattiqwâ* has a generic art. (Waltke and O'Connor 1990: 246).

13. 'I will bend . . . I will fill' are understood as rhetorical perfects (see note on v. 11).

The Hebr. of the first part of this verse is difficult to unravel. It is lit. 'For I will bend to me Judah a bow I will fill Ephraim'. Meyers and Meyers (1993: 145–146) are probably correct to suggest it is a technical expression. See 'Comment'.

14. Rather than 'will appear', LXX has 'will be', possibly to avoid the anthropomorphism.

15. 'and will roar': *hāmû* is an unusual construction as it contains no waw cons. Alternatively, a number of LXX codices read it as 'their blood' (cf. NRSV), which requires a minor emendation of MT to *dāmô*. The construction then flows more logically and it is understandable why a scribe would change this to avoid having Israelites drink blood (even metaphorically). However, I have followed MT as the more difficult reading. Meyers and Meyers (1993: 154) suggest the waw has dropped out through haplography.

16. 'their God' is absent from LXX.

'Surely': *kî* is taken as asseverative, emphasizing the clause it modifies (Arnold and Choi 2003: 153).

'they will be' is supplied in the second phrase.

'jewels of a crown': *'abnē-nēzer*. The context indicates they are gemstones.

'sparkling': *mitnôsĕsôt* occurs only here and in Ps. 60:4, where it refers to setting up a banner or flag. The hithpo. suggests 'causing to be displayed' and, since it refers to jewels, 'sparkling' seems an appropriate translation.

17. 'how . . . and how': *mah . . . ûmah* introduce exclamatory questions (Waltke and O'Connor 1990: 316).

Form and structure

Chs. 1–6 envisaged God's return to his people to fulfil his promises of a glorious new age. Chs. 7–8 highlighted the contrast between the circumstances of Zechariah's day and this incredible future 'in those days' (e.g. 8:6, 23) when God will dwell in the midst of his people to bless them and the nations. The two oracles of chs. 9–14 function to explain further the people's present circumstances, while dramatically picturing and holding out hope for God's return 'on that day'.

The first oracle, 9:1 – 11:17, portrays the future in terms drawn from Israel's history. In poetic language it presents God's subduing enemy nations and their kings, saving and restoring his own people under a

Davidic king and restoring covenant blessings in which a remnant from the nations will share. While many had returned from Babylon, the exodus imagery indicates that theologically they were still in exile and awaiting a 'second exodus'. The first oracle also contains two sign actions that explain Israel's past (11:4–14) and present (11:15–17) circumstances.

While there are thematic connections between chs. 9 and 10, 10:1 is the beginning of a new section, marked by the imper. 'Ask' (Butterworth 1992: 75). The focus of ch. 10 is on the 'shepherds' or leadership of God's people, a theme that continues into the sign actions of ch. 11.

Zech. 9 can be structured thematically:

9:1–8	The restored land
9:9–10	The restored king
9:11–17	The restored people

There are also several structural markers that support these divisions. These include paragraph markers at the end of 9:8 in the MT, sharp imperatives to 'rejoice' and 'shout' in 9:9 (cf. 10:1), and 'you also' in 9:11, which shifts the topic from the king to what the coming of the king will mean for his people. The paragraph markers indicate how Jewish rabbis of the Talmudic period (AD 135–500) understood the division of the text (Brotzman 1994: 47).

Commentators debate why these cities are mentioned in 9:1–8. Some suggest it correlates to a military campaign, as early as one of the Neo-Assyrian monarchs in the eighth century (Sweeney 2000b: 661). Others, that it refers to Alexander the Great in the fourth century (Stade 1881). However, efforts to correlate the material with any known military campaign have proven elusive. Curtis (2006: 167) demonstrates that it 'does not represent Alexander's itinerary, nor . . . the itinerary of any other Hellenistic conqueror'. A second view is that these cities mark out the ideal land of Israel (Hanson 1979: 317), or, more particularly, the boundaries of the old Davidic empire (Redditt 1995: 102). Under King David, many of these cities were incorporated into his empire, or paid him tribute. They existed during Zechariah's time, but did not threaten Judah. Zechariah thereby draws on Israel's past to portray God's future kingdom. Hanson (1979: 319–320) comments, 'Israel's traditional enemies and rivals alike would be absorbed into a kingdom surpassing even that of David.' A third view, which is compatible with the second, is that Zechariah is drawing on earlier prophetic oracles against the nations (e.g. Amos 1; Jer. 25; Ezek. 26 – 28) that promised the downfall of these cities before the kingdom would be restored to Israel (Wenzel 2011: 209). The movement from north to south mirrors earlier enemy campaigns, but here God comes to subdue the nations and return to his temple (v. 8). There is much to commend the second and third views.

Comment

9:1–2a. 'An oracle' (*maśśā'*) is taken as a heading that introduces chs. 9–11. The same word begins Zech. 12:1 and the book of Malachi. There has been much discussion of this term. In terms of etymology, a *maśśā'* has been understood as something weighty or burdensome to lift, hence a prophecy of doom; yet there is much hope in this section as well (e.g. 9:9; 10:6). Alternatively, it has been understood as being related to 'lifting up' one's voice, hence a 'pronouncement' or 'proclamation'. Floyd (2002: 422), building on the work of Weis (1986), argues that as a descriptor of a prophetic book, *maśśā'* indicates a prophecy concerned to reinterpret earlier 'prophecies that have over time become problematic in some way'. His expression here is unfortunate. It is certainly true to say that chs. 9–14 wrestle with the questions of when and how earlier prophecies will be fulfilled, but to say that earlier prophecies had 'become problematic' could imply that a *maśśā'* is some kind of prophetic corrective or cover up, which is unlikely. In a comprehensive study of this word, Boda (2006: 350) concludes that *maśśā'* is not a specific genre description since it can denote prophetic imaginative pictures, laments or poems. Instead, it is a general tag denoting 'prophetic revelation'. Contrary to Floyd and Weis, who consider that a *maśśā'* is concerned only with previous revelation by showing how it is coming to pass in human history, rather than giving any new revelation itself, Boda (2006: 356) contends that a *maśśā'* introduces the word of Yahweh that renews prophecy along the lines of earlier prophecy. As a heading, it bolsters the status of the ensuing prophecy.

'The word of the Lord is against' in context seems to mean that the oracles of the earlier prophets against the cities and regions mentioned in vv. 1–7 still stand. Zechariah reiterates that these places will be judged before God returns to his temple (v. 8). Earlier prophetic oracles against Damascus include Amos 1:3–5; Isa. 17:1–9; Jer. 49:23–27.

While some scholars connect the 'resting place' of God's word with 6:8, where God's Spirit is 'set at rest . . . in the land of the north' after the nations have been judged, the sense is different here. Here God's word rests on Damascus, awaiting its fulfilment in the judgment of the city. Alternatively, Petersen (1995: 40) proposes 'its resting place' refers to Damascus as the capital of the land of Hadrach. While Petersen thinks the author is 'mistaken geographically', administratively it did operate this way (see below). However, there is no other instance of 'its resting place' functioning in this way.

The phrase 'to the Lord belongs the eye of humankind and all the tribes of Israel' is quite ambiguous on account of the poetic nature of the Hebr. and has given rise to many different interpretations. The best, which requires no emendation of the text, is that there is an echo of Isa. 17:1–9 (Larkin 1994: 58–59). Isaiah's oracle against Damascus ends with the statement 'In that day people [*hā'ādām*] will look to their [lit. 'his'] Maker, and turn their [lit. 'his'] eyes to the Holy One of Israel' (v. 7). The 'people' here are the nations who will turn from their idols as their cities are overcome in judgment. This fits the context of Zechariah well, where judgment of the nations will result (*kî*) in the nations looking towards Yahweh, along with the tribes of Israel. The idea also connects well with chs. 1–8, where the nations will be judged, but also will entreat the favour of Yahweh along with the tribes of Israel, the very note on which ch. 8 finished. Ridding the nations of their idols and incorporating them into God's people anticipates 9:7. The phrase 'all the tribes of Israel' seems to envision a restoration of the united kingdom, such as it was at the time of David and Solomon (cf. 9:10–13; 10:6).

Turning to the place names, 'the land of Hadrach' is not mentioned elsewhere in the OT, but an Assyrian stele from the late eighth century mentions Hadrach (Hatarikka) as a city along with Hamath (mentioned in 9:2) (Meyers and Meyers 1993: 91). The phrase 'land of Hadrach' suggests a district named after this city. Curtis (2006: 167–169) proposes that its connection with Damascus is based on the earlier narrative of 2 Sam. 8, where King David put garrisons in Damascus and made it his administrative centre for several northern districts. Hamath is another city or district, which is thought to be located between Hadrach and Damascus (Meyers and Meyers 1993: 96). Hamath gave gifts to David (2 Sam. 8:9) and Solomon later controlled it (2 Chr. 8:4). Curtis (2006: 169) summarizes the significance of these places:

> Yahweh reasserts Davidic empire [*sic*] for the postexilic context. The boundaries of this empire are to conform to those in the tradition found in Gen. 15:18 [cf. v. 10; Ps. 72:8], demarcating the territory in rather aggrandized terms . . . By including Hamath and the land of Hadrach, the author of 9:1–8 asserts Davidic empire [*sic*] to the fullest northerly extent exhibited by the ancient traditions, and perhaps beyond [cf. Ezek. 47:16–17; 48:1].

2b–4. 'Tyre and Sidon, for it is very wise' seems rather abrupt, but continues to list those whom God's prophetic word is against (v. 1). These cities were sea ports on the Mediterranean coast in Phoenicia, Tyre being about 25 mi. (40 km) south of Sidon. The referent of the sg. verb ('it is very wise') could be Sidon, or both cities, which have a reputation for 'wisdom' (*ḥākĕmâ*: not a 'fear of the Lord' wisdom, but 'skill' or 'shrewdness'; cf. Ezek. 28:3–4). As a trade port, Tyre was a wealthy city, which is captured in the description of its having 'heaped up silver as dust and gold as mud of the streets' (v. 3). In Hebr., 'fortification' (*māṣôr*) is a wordplay on Tyre (*ṣōr*) and refers to the breakwater it had built to defend its island city.

Significantly, there are a number of earlier prophetic oracles against both these cities (Isa. 23; Jer. 25:22; Ezek. 26 – 28; Joel 3:4–8), and Zechariah reconfirms their judgment (cf. 6:1–8). The judgment will come from 'my Lord' (*'ădōnāy*), the first of only two instances of this reference to God in the book (cf. 'my Lord, the LORD' in v. 14). Larkin (1994: 56) suggests it is a pun on the name Adon, the god of Tyre.

God will 'dispossess' Tyre, presumably of its wealth, and 'strike down its army in the sea'. The word 'army' (*ḥayil*) can also mean 'strength' or 'wealth', and all these ideas may be present. I have translated 'army' since this is what is most likely to be violently struck down (the verb 'strike down' also occurs in 10:11; 12:4; 13:6–7). There may also be a parallel with the exodus and Pharaoh's army being struck down in the sea (Exod. 14:28; 15:21; Ps. 136:15). Destruction by fire may imply military conquest (Meyers and Meyers 1993: 103). Destruction by fire is also the culmination of the oracle against Tyre in Amos 1:9–10.

It is significant that during the monarchy, the king of Tyre built houses for David and Solomon (2 Sam. 5:11; 1 Kgs 9:11). While Tyre and Sidon were never incorporated into Israel, Curtis (2006: 169) notes that in Ezekiel's vision of the idealized land of Israel, Tyre falls into Manasseh's territory, and Sidon into Naphtali's.

5–7. The judgment of Tyre will sound a siren to the region of Philistia on the Palestinian seacoast. Four Philistine cities are mentioned: Ashkelon, Gaza, Ekron and Ashdod. Again, earlier prophets had prophesied judgment on these cities (Jer. 25:20; 47:1–7; Amos 1:6–8; Zeph. 2:4). Jer. 47:4 indicates that Tyre and Sidon were seen as supporting the Philistines, hence the Philistine fear at Tyre and Sidon's demise: 'Ashkelon will see it and be afraid. Gaza too, and will tremble greatly. Ekron too, for its hope has been put to shame.' Judgment will come on these cities too. Gaza's king will perish and Ashkelon will lose its inhabitants. The term 'outcast' (*mamzēr*) (v. 6) appears only here and Deut. 23:2[3]. McConville (2002a: 348) notes it can refer to the offspring of an incestuous or forbidden marriage, the offspring of an Israelite and a foreigner, or the offspring of ritual prostitution. In context it seems to refer to people born from a mixture of nations, along the lines of the second of McConville's examples. In Deut. 23:2[3] a *mamzēr* is to be excluded from the assembly of Yahweh to the tenth generation, a notion that seems to lie behind the next verse in Zechariah. Hence I have used the more general term 'outcast', which is also derogatory. In summary, God will 'cut down the pride of the Philistines', where 'pride' refers to their self-reliance and opposition to God. The change to first person from third-person address highlights divine agency and is common in Zechariah.

Along with Gath (not mentioned here), these Philistine cities comprised a pentapolis of power for the region in the twelfth and eleventh centuries (cf. Josh. 13:1–2). The Philistines had a reputation for being a strong military force, with iron weapons, chariots and formidable fighters (Bright 1981: 176, 185). Interestingly, there is no real evidence that these cities were threats to the people of Judah in the Persian period (Curtis 2006: 169). Rather, they defined the borders of the territory of Judah (Josh. 15:11,

45–46) and had been subdued in David's time (2 Sam. 5:17–25; 21:15–22). Here Zechariah seems to draw on the past to paint a picture of the future restoration of the Davidic empire (Petterson 2009: 134–135).

Not only will the Philistines be humbled, but a remnant will be cleansed and incorporated into God's people (the 'outcast' will be brought in). God had forbidden the eating of meat with its lifeblood still in it (Gen. 9:4; Lev. 17:10–14; Deut. 12:23), and this is presumably the Philistine practice God will put an end to among the survivors (who are personified as 'he'). An 'abomination' (*šiqqūṣ*) most often refers to an 'idol', but it seems incongruous to have an idol in the mouth, unless it is meant to be a grotesque image. Conrad (1999: 159) notes that a different form of the same Hebr. root is used for 'unclean food' (*šeqeṣ*) in Lev. 7:21; 11:10, 12–13, 20, 23, 41, and this meaning fits the context better here where it is removed 'from between its teeth'. In any case, idolatry was closely associated with food. The result is that after the blood and abominations have been removed, 'he will remain, even he, for our God'. Meyers and Meyers (1993: 115) note that the verb 'remain' is a derivative of the noun 'remnant', often associated with those from Israel who will emerge from judgment (cf. 8:6, 11–12). Their belonging to 'our God' is similar to 8:23.

A comparison is made with the Jebusites, who were the inhabitants of Jerusalem before it was captured by David (2 Sam. 5:6–9). While Jebusites were struck down in its capture, some were also incorporated into David's kingdom, indicated by the later reference to David's buying the threshing floor of Araunah the Jebusite (2 Sam. 24:18–24).

8. After God has swept around the borders of the land to judge the nations, the end point will be his return to his house to 'encamp' and to 'guard [against] one passing through and one returning', a reference to those from the nations who would aggressively come through the land, probably on some military exploit (cf. 7:14). God's protective presence in Jerusalem was also the theme of the third night vision (2:4–5[8–9]). The 'encamp' reference also brings David to mind as his reign was the only time when God encamped in the tabernacle (tent) in Jerusalem. The term 'house' (*bayit*) can refer to the temple (cf. 6:10) or tabernacle (e.g. 2 Sam. 12:2).

'For now I am watching with my eyes' forms an inclusio with 'the eye of humankind' in v. 1. This could be a further reference to God's watching over or guarding his people (Petersen 1995: 53). Alternatively, it could function in a similar way to the phrase in Exod. 2:25, where the 'seeing' of God invokes his memory of the covenant he had made with his people (cf. 9:11), which in view of the Egyptian oppressor (cf. 9:8) resulted in his raising up Moses as a saviour (cf. 9:9). This logic connects well with the king who comes in v. 9. It also assumes that the exile is an ongoing condition for Israel (Boda 2004: 414).

9. With the land reclaimed by Yahweh and his encamping at his house, Jerusalem's inhabitants are exhorted to rejoice and shout at the prospect of their coming king. The king is described as 'your king', that is Jerusalem's king, perhaps in contrast to the king of Gaza who perished (v. 5), but certainly bringing to mind the ideal king of earlier prophetic expectation (including Shoot of 3:8; 6:12). The call for 'daughter Zion' to 'rejoice greatly' and 'shout' recalls 2:10[14], where daughter Zion is exhorted to sing and rejoice because Yahweh is coming to dwell in her midst in the context of both judging the nations (2:9[13]) and incorporating them into his people (2:11[15]). Similar ideas are found in the context of Zeph. 3:14. Meyers and Meyers (1993: 121) argue that the personification of the city as a daughter indicates that the people must rely on God and the king for their future, just as an unmarried daughter cannot act independently of her parents, but is reliant on them.

Four descriptions are given of Jerusalem's coming king in v. 9. First, 'He is righteous' (*ṣaddîq*). While some understand 'righteous' in a military sense, translating 'triumphant' (NRSV), or 'victorious' (JPS), it is best understood in its usual sense. Not only is 'righteous' to be a key characteristic of the Davidic king; his essential role is to establish righteousness (and justice) (e.g. 1 Sam. 24:17; 2 Sam. 8:15; 23:3–5; Ps. 72:1–7; Isa. 9:7; 11:4–5; 32:1; Jer. 23:5).

Secondly, this king is 'saved' (*yāšaʿ*). The Hebr. has a pass. sense, so that with Yahweh's conquest of the nations the king has 'been saved' and is enabled to assume power (Meyers and Meyers 1993: 127). Many take it as a reflex., 'having salvation' (ESV), or extend the reflexive idea and that of the previous description to 'victorious' (NIV, NRSV) or 'triumphant' (JPS). Yet there are only two other instances of this verb form in the OT and both have a pass. sense (Deut. 33:29; Ps. 33:16). What it most naturally means is that the coming king has been saved, not by his own might, but by God's. In the context of Yahweh's conquest in 9:1–8, the salvation of the king implies the salvation of the people (cf. Isa. 49:6), but Zechariah here seems to be drawing on a suffering David tradition seen in the Psalms and developed in Isaiah's servant songs. Stead (2013) has demonstrated how descriptions of the 'suffering David' in the Psalms lie behind the portrait of the suffering servant in Isaiah, and these have been woven together in the portrait of the future king in Zech. 9 – 14. Righteousness and salvation are often paralleled in Isaiah.

There are two ways of translating the next description (*ʿānî*): 'humble' (e.g. Num. 12:3; Ps. 18:28; Isa. 66:2; Zeph. 3:12) or 'afflicted' (e.g. Ps. 22:24; Isa. 53:4, 7). The translation is closely connected with how 'riding upon a donkey' is understood. This latter description is often taken to be a contrast to the king who rides on a warhorse and trusts in his own might and despotism (cf. 9:10; Ps. 33:17). Zion's king trusts in Yahweh and rides on a donkey (Laato 1997: 209–210). In this case, 'humble' complements the picture and is a positive image of the one who trusts in God. Alternatively, some argue that the background for Zechariah's portrait is David's return to Jerusalem after putting down Absalom's revolt (Scalise

2009: 274). During this period of exile he rode on a donkey (cf. 2 Sam. 16:2). Furthermore, in this episode David was humiliated and nearly defeated by his enemies, before God saved him. The picture of David as he returns to Jerusalem is one of distress and suffering (e.g. 2 Sam. 16:12), and the translation 'afflicted' complements this negative picture. Given the wider connections in the book between the suffering David, the suffering servant of Isaiah and Zechariah's coming king, this second suggestion is compelling. Indeed, the contrasting ideologies of kingship in the first proposal also lie behind the second proposal.

Many scholars detect an echo of the promise of 'kingship' to Judah in Gen. 49:8–12, which is the only other instance of the phrase 'son of a jenny' in the OT (v. 9) (Steiner 2013: 51–53). The donkey reference more likely links with the suffering David in the first instance, though a composite allusion to 2 Samuel and Genesis cannot be dismissed. This future king stands apart from most kings of Israel and Judah, including David, who used their power so often in arrogance, defiance and self-service. Zion's future king trusts in Yahweh, who has delivered him.

Against the backdrop of chs. 1–8, the presentation of this chapter shows that central to the coming of Yahweh to his people is the coming Davidic king. This king also plays a key role in the second oracle of chs. 12–14, where he is pierced and struck as part of God's salvation purpose.

10. Yahweh will 'cut off the chariot from Ephraim and the horse from Jerusalem', where to 'cut off' means to destroy. The horse and chariot were key components of warfare for Israel and Judah during the ninth and eighth centuries (Cantrell 2011: 143). 1 Kgs 9:22 and 10:26–29 indicate that Solomon established substantial chariotry and cavalry, which was contrary to the instructions for kingship in the Torah (Deut. 17:16). Zechariah continues to draw on the past to paint a picture of the future: the coming of Zion's king will be a return to ideal kingship, one that trusts in God and issues in peace with the implements of war being removed (cf. Isa. 2:4).

Two further descriptions of the king are given in v. 10. First, 'he will speak peace to the nations'. Webb (2003: 132) comments, 'The king is a preacher,' and notes the connections with Isaiah (52:7; 40:9; cf. 9:6[5]). This peace (*šālôm*) is not just the absence of war, but the peace of salvation, the peace of God's kingdom being re-established with its entire covenant blessings (cf. vv. 16–17). This also closely connects with 6:13 and the rule of Shoot. Reference to 'Ephraim' (the northern kingdom of Israel) also signifies a reunified kingdom, as it had been under David (cf. 2 Sam. 2:10–11; 5:1–5). Secondly, 'His rule will be from sea to sea, and from the river to the ends of the earth.' This expression is also found in Ps. 72:8 as part of a prayer for the king's son, which in the final form of the psalter is to be understood as expressing the universal extent of the future Davidic king's dominion. The focus is not so much on the geography (as in 9:1–8), as that he will rule all nations. The universal rule of the future Davidic king is a common feature in the Psalms and Isaiah (e.g. Pss 2:7–8;

89:25–27[26–28]; 110:1–2; Isa. 9:1–6; 11:10; 42:2–4; 49:6–7; 52:15; 55:3–5; cf. Gen. 49:10–12). While some scholars suggest that the king is Yahweh himself (Hanson 1979: 320–321; Rose 2012: 226), or that the king is a personification of God's faithful people (Petersen 1995: 59), the background to the descriptions and the eschatological context indicate that this king is the Davidic king of prophetic expectation (i.e. the Messiah) (Petterson 2009: 135–142). Meyers and Meyers (1993: 169) capture the importance of this figure when they say, 'The restored royal figure is the lynchpin of the restored land [9:1–8] and people [9:11–17].'

11–12. Yahweh ('I') continues to address the people ('you' is f. sg., indicating 'daughter of Zion'). The benefits of the king's rule are specified. God promises to act 'because of the blood of your covenant', a phrase found only once elsewhere in Exod. 24:8, where it refers to the covenant with Israel at Sinai and the blood dashed on the people to ratify it. In this act the people committed themselves to obey Yahweh, and Yahweh bound himself to keep his words. It is the basis for God's setting his people free from a 'waterless pit' (or 'cistern' or 'well' with 'no water in it'). There may be an allusion here to Joseph (Gen. 27:24), Jeremiah (Jer. 38:6) or the psalmist (Pss 40:2[3]; 69:15). In any case, the waterless pit is clearly a metaphor for Israel's exile from which Yahweh 'will set free your prisoners', a further echo of the exodus (e.g. Exod. 5:1). Meyers and Meyers (1993: 140) note that prisons were not a means of formal punishment in ancient Israel. The connotation is more a lack of freedom at the hands of a foreign political power than punishment. Yet the exile was God's punishment on his people.

Having been set free, the prisoners are called to 'return' (m. pl. imp.) to 'the stronghold', a hapax legomenon that in the present context is best understood as Jerusalem (cf. v. 8; 2:6–7). They are 'prisoners of hope' on account of these promises of salvation from exile in which they trust (cf. Deut. 30:1–5). As the people 'return' (*šûb*), God promises to 'return' (hiph. of *šûb*) 'double'. It is difficult to know exactly what this promise involves. The idea is similar to Isa. 61:1–7, where prisoners are set free and given a double portion in the land (Isa. 61:7; cf. 40:2). Behind this may lie the experience of double blessing after the return from 'exile' of Joseph (Gen. 48:22) or Job (Job 42:10). In any case, the idea reflects the promise of 1:3: 'return to me and I will return to you', with restoration again centred on Jerusalem (LeCureux 2012: 201).

13. While the king will speak peace to the nations (v. 10), the means by which this peace will come about is war. Presumably, v. 10 expresses the outcome, and vv. 13–15 express the means to this end. God will use his people as weapons – using the metaphor of Judah as a bow, filled with Ephraim as an arrow, and later calling his people a 'warrior's sword'. Like v. 1, which speaks of 'all the tribes of Israel', mentioning Ephraim and Judah (cf. v. 10) points towards a reunited kingdom – the metaphor of a bow and arrow nicely has them working together.

The reference to 'Greece' (*yāwān*) has generated much discussion in the history of interpretation, with many arguing that it reflects the time of Alexander the Great, whose armies arrived in the area in 333 BC. However, 'Greece' can also be understood to be an authentic echo of Zechariah's time (Meyers and Meyers 1993: 148; Curtis 2006: 174–181; Wenzel 2011: 211). Indeed, Greece had proven to be quite troublesome to the Persians. In 498 BC an Athenian-led force revolted against Persia and burned Sardis, the satrapic capital, and in 490 BC the Persians were famously defeated by the Greeks at Marathon (Curtis 2006: 175–176). Hence a prophecy of the 'sons of Zion' defeating the 'sons of Greece' is a huge claim of God's power (reference to 'sons' balances the double use of 'daughter' in v. 9, and the change probably reflects the war context). An alternative or further explanation for referring to Greece is found in Joel 3:4–8, which indicates that Tyre, Sidon and Philistia sold people of Judah and Jerusalem to the Greeks, hence the concern for their release here (Scalise 2009: 278).

14–15. The warfare imagery continues, with Yahweh's appearing over his people to fight for and defend them. Yahweh is pictured as a warrior, shooting arrows like lightning and sounding the horn for war (the only time in the OT when Yahweh is said to sound the horn). It is reminiscent of Moses' song after the exodus (Exod. 15), and this may explain the expression 'storms of the south' as further drawing on exodus themes to portray the future salvation that God will win (cf. v. 11). Horbury (1998: 43–44) argues that many of the prophetic texts that speak of a coming saviour have in their background a corporate recollection of the exodus (e.g. Isa. 63:11–14), and it seems appropriate to see these ideas connected here.

In these verses, God is called 'my Lord, the LORD' (*'ădōnay yhwh*) and 'LORD of hosts' (*yhwh ṣĕbā'ôt*). The first title is unique in Zechariah (though common in Ezekiel) and the second title is the most common across the book of Zechariah and speaks of God's might as ruler of the heavenly armies (see 'Comment' on 1:3).

God's people will obliterate their enemies in war ('they will devour and will subdue the sling stones'). It is difficult to know whether the second half of the verse continues this idea of consuming enemies (metaphorically, of course) or switches to speak of a post-victory banquet celebration ('and they shall drink and shall roar as with wine'). The image of being 'full like the bowl, like corners of an altar' comes from the temple and an abundant flow of blood in the sacrifice (e.g. Exod. 29:12; Lev. 4:7). This could fit the war or banquet ideas as it could refer to the blood of enemies (cf. Isa. 63:1–6), or simply convey the abundance of wine at the banquet. Both ideas fit the context, but the idea found elsewhere of God's victory over his enemies being compared to a sacrifice (e.g. Isa. 34:6; Jer. 46:10; Ezek. 39:17–20; Zeph. 1:7) tilts the balance in favour of its referring to warfare (Wenzel 2011: 210). This also seems to be how the LXX interprets it with 'their blood' inserted after 'drink' (see 'Notes on the text'). The judgment seems to be that the nations will become what they worshipped: just as they consumed blood (v. 7), so their blood will be consumed.

16–17. 'The LORD their God will save them' is a summary of all that has gone before in this chapter. The description of Yahweh as 'their God' recalls the covenant relationship (cf. v. 11; 10:6; 13:9; Hag. 1:12, 14). The phrase 'on that day' picks up on 'those' days in 8:23. It is the eschatological day of salvation, pictured as a land that brings forth bountiful provision (grain and new wine; cf. Deut. 33:28) that will cause young men and young women to 'flourish', a verb that can also mean to 'bear fruit' (Ps. 92:14[15]) and may imply offspring. The description of God's people as a 'flock' is a common one in the Prophets and the Psalms (e.g. Ezek. 36:37; Jer. 23:1; Ps. 100:3), and prepares for the shepherd imagery so prominent in chs. 10–11. God's people on that day are also likened to 'jewels of a crown sparkling upon his land' (see 'Notes on the text'). Precious stones represented the people of Israel on the ephod and the breastplate of the high priest (Exod. 28:12, 21). Here they will adorn the land. The magnificence of this day is underlined with the exclamation 'For how good is it and how beautiful is it!' Just as Yahweh had saved his people in the past and brought them in to the Promised Land, eventually establishing them as a united people under David, so he will again save, establish and bless his people in his land under the heir of David's throne.

Explanation

Zech. 9 begins the first of two oracles that portray the return of God to overthrow his enemies and save and establish his people 'on that day' (chs. 9–11; 12–14). It continues to hold out the hopes of chs. 1–6 and the earlier prophets in a form more akin to the earlier prophets than chs. 1–6. Zech. 9:1–8 announces that the word of Yahweh is against various lands and cities that marked the boundaries of the old Davidic empire (in Syria, Phoenicia and Philistia). In other words, in Zechariah's day the words of judgment of the earlier prophets against these places still awaited fulfilment before God's kingdom would be established, and Zechariah reaffirms the earlier oracles of judgment.

While ch. 9 envisages God's return to his temple to protect and bless his people (vv. 1–8), the centre of the chapter focuses on a future human king (9:9) and in this way restates the earlier prophetic hope for a future ideal Davidic king, or 'Messiah', who is central to God's salvation purposes (e.g. Isa. 9:6–7; 11:1–10; 16:5; Jer. 23:3–6; 33:14–22; Ezek. 37:21–25; Hos. 3:5; Mic. 4:8 – 5:5[4:9 – 5:6]; Amos 9:11–15; cf. Zech. 3:8; 6:12). The portrait of this king draws particularly on the suffering David of 2 Samuel, the book of Psalms and Isaiah's servant. He is not a mighty warrior king who trusts in his own strength, but one who trusts in God. Some suggest that this king is almost passive, and the focus shifts to God, who is the true king who saves, but this is overstated, especially in the light of v. 10, where this human king preaches and rules over all the earth. If he is 'passive', it is only because he trusts in God in his work, much like the 'silent action' of Isaiah's servant (Isa. 42:1–4).

Zechariah's portrait of a suffering Messiah, of weakness and power, is clearly seen in Jesus' life, climaxing in his crucifixion and resurrection. All four Gospels record that Jesus acquired and rode a donkey into Jerusalem, claiming to be this king (Matt. 21:1–11; Mark 11:1–11; Luke 19:28–38; John 12:12–19). On Matthew's two donkeys, see Coppins 2012: 275–290. Jesus' righteousness and suffering to the point of death meant he was saved by God in his resurrection and now through his gospel proclaims peace to the nations (cf. Eph. 2:17; Phil. 2:6–11). The power of the gospel displayed in human weakness is the pattern for Christian ministry (cf. 1 Cor. 1 – 4).

Like chs. 1–8 (esp. the end of ch. 8), v. 7 promises that a remnant from the nations will also be incorporated into God's people (this theme was elaborated upon in the 'Explanation' of the previous chapter). Ch. 9 makes a number of further contributions to this theme. First, the eyes of the nations (along with Israel) belong to Yahweh and it is his judgment that will cause the nations to look to him (v. 1). Secondly, God will remove the unclean and idolatrous practices of a remnant of the nations, a process at work among the church today (1 Cor. 6:9–11). Thirdly, Mason (2003: 23) makes the encouraging point 'The Philistines, after all, were always "the uncircumcised" *par excellence*. If such can be cleansed by God for his own, then so can any.' Fourthly, there is a particularity as well as a universalism to God's salvation of the nations. While the Messiah will rule over all nations of the world (v. 10), only those who take up his offer of peace will experience it. Those of the nations who live in rebellion will be consumed (cf. 14:14–19).

The picture that is prominent in chs. 9–14 of a 'warrior God' is not a popular one today. At the same time, it is one that is often misunderstood. It is so much easier to project our own sentiments and preferences on to God than to deal with the God who reveals himself. The point of the portrayal is captured well by Achtemeier (1986: 149) when she says:

> the Bible is testifying to the fact that evil must be actively resisted and done away. It does not disappear by itself. Hitlers must be made to cease their holocausts; civil rights must be guaranteed with the force of law. Someone has got to break the swords and fashion the spears into pruning hooks. But by testifying that God is the Divine Warrior, the Bible is saying that the ultimate destruction of evil belongs to him.

This character of God is ultimately what gives hope in the midst of violence in our world: that God will one day set all things aright. The same portrayal runs through Revelation. Zech. 9:13–15 also gives God's people a role in this, as instruments of his warfare. Between Jesus' first and second comings, it is chiefly as God's people proclaim the word of the gospel and pray that the battle is engaged (e.g. 2 Cor. 10:3–6; Eph. 6:10–20).

This chapter also depicts the sheer abundance that will be found in God's kingdom: there is the joy of the redeemed (v. 9); there are the 'new exodus' themes that point to the blessed life in the land in which God's people will be secure and prosper (John 8:36). Interestingly, the Garden of Eden contained jewels (Gen. 2:12) and so will the new Eden, the jewels being God's own people (Zech. 9:16; cf. Rev. 21:18–21).

ZECHARIAH 10:1 – 11:3

Translation

[10:1]Ask for rain from the LORD in the season of spring rain – the LORD makes thunderbolts. And he will give a rain shower to them, [namely] to each plant in the field. [2]For the teraphim have spoken evil and the diviners have seen a lie. And the false dreams they will speak will give empty comfort. Therefore they have set out just like sheep – they will be afflicted for there is no shepherd.

[3]My anger has flared against the shepherds and I will visit [judgment] against the male goats, for the LORD of hosts has visited his flock, the house of Judah, and will establish them as his majestic horse in the battle. [4]From him a keystone, from him a peg, from him a battle bow, from him will go forth every oppressor together. [5]And they will be like warriors, trampling down in the mud of the streets in the battle, and they will do battle, for the LORD will be with them, and they will put to shame those who ride horses.

[6]I will strengthen the house of Judah and I will save the house of Joseph. I will bring them back, for I have mercy on them. And they will be as though I had not rejected them. For I am the LORD their God and I will answer them. [7]And Ephraim will become like a warrior – their hearts will rejoice as with wine. And their sons will see and they will rejoice – their hearts will delight in the LORD.

[8]I will whistle to them and I will gather them. For I have redeemed them and they will become numerous, just as they were numerous. [9]And I have sown them among the peoples, and in distant places they will remember me. And they will live, [along] with their sons, and they will return. [10]And I will bring them back from the land of Egypt and from Assyria I will gather them. And I will bring them to the land of Gilead and Lebanon, and not [enough room] will be found for them. [11]And he will pass through the sea of distress and he will smite with the sea waves and all the depths of the Nile will dry up. And the pride of Assyria will be brought down and the sceptre of Egypt will be taken away. [12]And I will strengthen them in the LORD, and in his name they will walk, declares the LORD.

[11:1]Open your doors, Lebanon, and let fire consume among your cedars. [2]Wail, cypress, for a cedar has fallen; because majestic ones have been ruined. Wail, oaks of Bashan, for the thick forest has been felled. [3]Listen to the shepherds wailing, for their majesty has been ruined. Listen to lions roaring, for the thicket of the Jordan has been ruined.

Notes on the text

10:1. 'the season of spring rain'. The def. art. has been supplied in translation. The art. seems to be dropped quite frequently in chs. 9–14.

'The LORD makes thunderbolts'. The use of the qal ptc. (*'ōśeh*) expresses a truth 'valuable for all time' (Arnold and Choi 2003: 80).

2. 'false': *haššāw'*. *BHQ* states that MT^{L} has been pointed incorrectly and that MT^{A} and MT^{C} have *haššāwĕ'* (Gelston 2010: 136).

'will give . . . comfort': *yĕnaḥēmûn* contains a paragogic nun (Waltke and O'Connor 1990: 516).

5. 'the mud of the streets'; cf. 9:3. The def. articles have been supplied in translation.

'those who ride horses': lit. 'riders of horses'.

6. 'I will bring them back': *wĕhôšbôtîm* is an unusual form, sometimes explained as a conflation of the verbs 'return' (*šûb*) and 'dwell' (*yāšab*) since one would expect *wahăšîbôtîm* (cf. v. 10; Vg, Syr) or *wĕhôšabtîm* (cf. LXX). The connection with 'mercy' supports the translation 'I will bring them back' since these ideas are connected earlier in the book. See 'Comment'.

7. In both instances, 'their hearts' (*libbām*) is sg. (heart) and takes a sg. verb, but the pr. suff. is pl. (lit. 'their heart').

'will rejoice': *yāgēl* is juss. in form, but translated as an ordinary impf.

8. 'and they will become numerous just like they were numerous': *wĕrābû kĕmô rābû*.

9. 'And I have sown them': *wĕ'ezrā'ēm*. The *wĕyiqtol* would normally be translated with a future tense, but the context demands a past tense. See LeCureux 2012: 202.

'And they will live': *wĕḥāyû* follows the vocalization of the MT (as does Vg and Tgs) and reads *'et* as the prep. 'with'. The LXX and Syr read it as a pi. (*wĕḥîyyû*), which means 'to keep alive, make live', and translates *'et* as the object marker.

11. LXX reads, 'they will pass through'. MT is to be preferred as the *lectio difficilior*.

With certain verbs of movement, *bĕ* denotes the route 'through' (Arnold and Choi 2003: 103). *bĕ* can also indicate the instrument used to perform the action 'with' (Arnold and Choi 2003: 104).

12. 'they will walk': *yithallākû*. The hith. seems to indicate repeated action (Arnold and Choi 2003: 48). Cf. Gen. 6:9. LXX and Syr translate 'they will walk' as 'they will glory', but this is unnecessary.

11:1. 'and let fire consume': translates *wĕtō'kal* as a juss. Smith (1984:

266) argues that the prep. *bĕ* prefixed to 'cedars' is a late substitute for the object marker *'et*.

2. 'thick': *habbāṣîr* follows Q.

'because majestic ones have been ruined' is a difficult phrase to translate. The rel. pr. *'ăšer* is taken as causal, in parallel to *kî* of the next clause (R. J. Williams 2007: 166). There are similar instances in 11:5 and 13:6.

3. 'Listen to': *qôl* is a nominal exclamation (Waltke and O'Connor 1990: 681).

'thicket': *gĕ'ôn* is best translated 'thicket' rather than 'pride' given the way it seems to function as a covert for the lions (cf. Jer. 49:19; 50:44). See further, Thompson 1992: 960–961.

Form and structure

Zech. 10:1 – 11:3 is a unit with its own integrity (Butterworth 1992: 190). It begins with a call to prayer (10:1–2), followed by a series of prophetic judgment and salvation speeches (10:3–12), and concludes with a call to lament in the form of a 'taunt song' directed at foreign kings (11:1–3). The main theme of the wider unit of chs. 10–11 is leadership and its consequences for the people of God (Webb 2003: 135). Through this wider unit the key leadership image is that of a shepherd.

In view of the bountiful crops of 9:17, ch. 10 begins by calling on God's people to ask him for rain, necessary for the growth of the crops, rather than looking to false mediums. Indeed, the people's previous dependence on teraphim and diviners is the reason for their affliction by the nations and their lack of a shepherd (10:1–2). God promises to punish their current foreign shepherds and raise up new leadership (10:3–4) who will save his people from their affliction (10:5). God also promises to gather his people who remain scattered among the nations (10:6–11), and have them walk in his ways (10:12). This is a massive work, pictured once again as a new exodus (cf. 9:11–17).

Zech. 11:1–3 functions as a transition. The geography and reference to shepherds connect it with ch. 10, but the three sharp imperatives mark it as a separate section (along with paragraph markers in the MT at the end of 10:12 and 11:3). It reveals that God's intention to raise up a new leadership and to reunite his people will have devastating consequences for those who are currently shepherds. It also prepares for the further use of the shepherd theme in the two sign-action reports of 11:4–17.

The unit can be structured thematically:

10:1 – 11:3	**The results of good and bad leadership**
10:1–2	Affliction for lack of a shepherd
10:3–12	The establishment and result of new leadership
11:1–3	Foreign shepherds judged

Comment

10:1–2. The unit opens with a call to ask Yahweh for rain 'in the season of spring rain', considered to be March/April (Smith 1984: 261). If the rain did not come at this time, it meant crop failure and famine, something experienced in Zechariah's day (cf. Hag. 1:10–11). The reason for asking God for rain is that he is the one who 'makes thunderbolts' and 'will give a rain shower' (cf. 14:17–18). He is the one who is sovereign over the weather (cf. Pss 65:9; 68:9; 104:13; 135:7; Job 38:24–28, 34–35; Jer. 14:13–22). God gives the rain 'to each plant in the field', an echo of Gen. 2:5. Times of drought increased the temptation to turn to other gods, as earlier generations of Israelites demonstrated (e.g. 1 Kgs 18). This passage seems to be either a direct reapplication of the Mosaic instruction in Deut. 11:10–18 or a refraction of this through Jer. 14:1 – 15:4 (Person 1993: 119–120).

Teraphim are small household gods or idols (e.g. Gen. 31:19, 34; 1 Sam. 19:13, 16). In Ezek. 21:21[26] teraphim are associated with determining the future. Similarly, diviners were those who sought to predict the future, presumably to determine the best time to plough, sow or harvest (Webb 2003: 138). 'Teraphim' and 'diviners' are often associated (e.g. Judg. 17:5; 18:14–20), and both practices are forbidden in the law (Deut. 5:8–9; 18:9–14; cf. 2 Kgs 23:24). Zechariah says that the words of the teraphim are 'evil' (*'āwen*) and the visions and dreams of the diviners are a 'lie' or 'deception' (*šeqer*) and are 'false' or 'delusional' (*šāwĕ'*). They give 'empty comfort', where the word for 'empty' is *hebel* (cf. Ecclesiastes) – any comfort soon vaporizes in the face of reality.

The result (*'al-kēn*) of consulting teraphim and diviners is that the people 'have set out just like sheep – they will be afflicted for there is no shepherd'. The idea of Yahweh's people being afflicted for lack of a shepherd is found in other parts of the OT (Num. 27:17; 1 Kgs 22:17; Ezek. 34:8; 2 Chr. 18:16). Shepherding was a central part of Israel's economy and hence the shepherd was a well-understood metaphor for leadership. In the first instance, Yahweh is the shepherd of his people, who are his flock (e.g. Gen. 49:24; Ps. 23:1). When this metaphor is explained, it is in terms of Yahweh's guiding (e.g. Pss 77:20; 80:1), protecting (Ps. 78:52; Isa. 40:11), saving (Ezek. 34:22), gathering (Isa. 40:11; Jer. 31:10) and nourishing (Jer. 50:19; Mic. 2:12–13) his people (Ryken et al. 1998: 784). Shepherd imagery is also applied to human leaders such as Moses and Cyrus as they act as agents of Yahweh (e.g. Isa. 44:28; 63:11). Significantly, King David was the human shepherd par excellence (Ps. 78:70–72). While David is said to shepherd Israel (e.g. 2 Sam. 5:2), there seems to be a reticence to use the term 'shepherd' for Israel's kings, perhaps because of the way it was used in other ANE contexts to describe foreign gods or to deify kings, associations the biblical writers wished to avoid (Wallis 2004: 550). However, there is no hesitation in using this title to denounce unworthy leaders of Israel or the nations. Ezekiel and Jeremiah both refer to unworthy kings of Judah and Israel as shepherds (e.g. Jer. 2:8; 10:21; 22:22; 23:1–2; 50:6–7; Ezek. 34:1–10). They were responsible for the scattering of the flock and the experience of exile (e.g. Jer. 10:21; Ezek. 34:5).

Shepherd imagery is used in a variety of ways in chs. 10–11. Zechariah claims the people have 'no shepherd' (v. 2). What does this mean? It is clear from chs. 1–8 that the post-exilic community did not lack priests or prophets. The exact status of the governor Zerubbabel is unclear. Some argue that he had been removed by this time, but this is speculative. What the people did lack was a king, and the shepherd metaphor most naturally refers to this (cf. Ezek. 34:23–24). In addition, Achtemeier (1986: 155) notes the way the OT frequently connects fertility in nature with the faithfulness of God's people, especially their kings (e.g. Ps. 72:1, 3, 16; Isa. 32:1, 12–18). Given idolatry was the chief sin in the pre-exilic community that culminated in the exile and removal of the Davidic king, Zechariah challenges the people to learn from the past and look to Yahweh for their provision in view of the future righteous king's coming (in 9:9), and in view of the great harvest that will accompany that day (9:17; cf. 14:17). Failure to heed this command will lead to affliction, as it has in the past. Interestingly, the king of 9:9 will emerge from affliction, and idolatry and false prophecy will finally be removed in the aftermath of the king's being pierced (13:2–6).

3. The shift from saying 'there is no shepherd' (v. 2) to announcing that Yahweh's 'anger has flared against the shepherds' (v. 3) has caused some to doubt the literary integrity of 10:1–2. This judgment must not be made too quickly. A closer examination of the text and its background suggests that most likely two different groups of shepherds are in view. In v. 3, Yahweh's anger is not only against the shepherds, but will fall on the 'male goats' (*hā'attûdîm*). The term is used on several occasions to refer to the leaders of foreign nations, in particular their kings (e.g. Isa. 14:9; Ezek. 39:18). It never clearly refers to Israel's kings. Furthermore, it becomes evident later in this unit that there are 'shepherds' who are foreign kings (cf. 11:3). In my view, the 'shepherds' and 'male goats' of v. 3 are best understood as parallel terms for the same group, namely foreign kings who rule and oppress Yahweh's people. Yahweh is about to visit his anger against these foreign kings, because he has visited his own flock, the house of Judah. Yahweh's 'visitation' will involve judgment and salvation.

This explains the shift between vv. 2 and 3. Yahweh's people had no shepherd (of their own) and his anger has flared against the shepherds (of the nations). While foreign kings ruled over Judah in the post-exilic period, Yahweh now promises to act against this group in the first instance by strengthening his own people – he will establish the house of Judah as 'his majestic horse in the battle'. Cantrell (2011: 11) explains this image:

> Addiction to speed is the single most salient quality of a war-horse. The battle horse shivers, trembles, leaps, stomps, snorts, tosses its head, and sometimes rears up and paws the air in anticipation of running all out, into the frenzy of battle . . . to reach bursts of speed over 40 miles per hour . . . In the ancient world, the awe-inspiring energy and power of the horse was most often witnessed in battle.

4–5. As well as strengthening his people, Yahweh will raise up an alternative leadership, which by implication will include their own shepherd. A number of leadership metaphors are piled up: a 'keystone', a 'peg', a 'battle bow'. Each is said to come 'from him' (*mimmennû*). It is uncertain whether the antecedent of this is the house of Judah or Yahweh himself. The syntax that earlier refers to the house of Judah as 'them' (v. 3) and the context that stresses Yahweh's activity suggest Yahweh is the antecedent of 'from him' (Mason 1976: 236–237). However, the wider theology of the OT indicates that it is from Judah that the nation's leadership would arise (cf. Gen. 49:10). Furthermore, the fact that these leaders are from Judah forms a contrast with the foreign kings of v. 3, who rule in their own interests.

Unpacking the metaphors, a 'keystone' (lit. 'corner' or *pinnâ*) often refers to the corner of a structure (Matties and Walton 1997: 640). When it denotes a part of a building, it can refer either to a capstone that completes the building (e.g. Ps. 118:22) or to the cornerstone of the foundation (e.g. Isa. 28:16). In both cases it designates a crucial stone in the structure from which the building finds its stability (hence it is translated 'keystone' here). It is used as a metaphor for leadership in Judg. 20:2, 1 Sam. 14:38 and Isa. 19:13. Similarly, in 10:4 it refers to a leader, who, given the way the metaphor works, should be understood as a key figure for strengthening the house of Judah and saving the house of Joseph (cf. 10:6). Given the importance of the keystone for a 'house', the metaphor may also function at another level with an association between the keystone and the support it will provide for the 'house' of Judah and the 'house' of Joseph.

A 'peg' (*yātēd*) elsewhere refers to one of the pegs that secured the tabernacle (e.g. Exod. 27:10; Num. 3:37), but can also refer to a peg for hanging items from (e.g. Ezek. 15:3). A peg provides support for the object it holds, and as a metaphor conveys a very similar meaning to the keystone. It is used as a metaphor for leadership in Isa. 22:22–25. Here in v. 4, the peg is a leader who strengthens the house of Judah and saves the house of Joseph (cf. 10:6). Kitchen (1982: 1175) notes that 'tent' in ordinary speech came to be used of any kind of dwelling, and so again there may be another level of association between the 'peg' and the 'house' of Judah and the 'house' of Joseph (elsewhere called the 'tents of Judah' in 12:7, and the 'tents of Joseph' in Ps. 78:67).

A 'battle bow' (*qešet milḥāmâ*) is not used as a metaphor for leadership anywhere else in the OT, though Mason (2003: 82) notes Egyptian literature where a 'bow' represents royal military leadership. A 'battle bow' readily connects to the ideas in the previous two metaphors. A strong bow leads to victory in battle, a weak or broken bow to defeat. In 9:13, Judah is described as Yahweh's 'bow' with associations of warfare and conquest. In Gen. 49:22–25, the 'bow' of Joseph is said to be unmoved against the attacks of his enemies. It is clear that as a metaphor for leadership, the 'bow' pertains to a leader's military strength. This image connects with the warfare that will secure the salvation of the house of Judah and the house of Joseph from their enemies (cf. 10:5, 7).

These leaders are described collectively as 'every oppressor' (*kol-nôgēś*) who 'will go forth' (*yāṣā'*). This is surprising, and many translate 'oppressor' less negatively as 'ruler', yet all other instances in the OT describe an oppressor or tyrant (e.g. Exod. 3:7; Job 3:18; Dan. 11:20; Zech. 9:8). Mason (2003: 83) plausibly suggests that what is in view here is a reversal of roles. Those who had persecuted Israel will be oppressed by a new group of 'oppressors' raised up by Yahweh (cf. the craftsmen who 'terrify' in 1:21[2:4]).

While these leadership metaphors are sometimes understood as each referring to the future Davidic king (cf. 9:9), the plurality mitigates against their referring to one figure (Petterson 2009: 162–167). However, the king of 9:9 is probably to be understood as included within this group, especially since he is the ruler of rulers. Jer. 23:3–6 also speaks of shepherds (pl.) being raised up, among whom 'a righteous Branch, a [Davidic] King' is one.

While the referent of 'they' who 'will be like warriors' (v. 5) at first seems to be the rulers of v. 4, the description of their 'trampling' is best understood as an action of the 'majestic horse' of v. 3. The horse is frequently associated with military activities, particularly in the Persian period when preferences had moved from chariots to mounted horses in warfare. Cantrell (2011: 29; cf. 136–141) argues that in battle 'as many warriors were killed by the crushing blows of horses' hooves landing on vital body parts as by the random wounds of arrows and spears piercing the flesh'. Hence 'they' is best taken as a reference to the house of Judah (cf. v. 3), and the metaphors used to picture their future activity are combined in v. 5: the 'majestic horse in the battle . . . trampling down' and the 'warriors . . . will do battle'. This is paralleled in v. 7 with Ephraim, who will also become 'like a warrior'. The activities of these warriors 'will put to shame those who ride horses', which effectively means that the enemies of the house of Judah, including the shepherds and male goats of v. 3, will be defeated. Significantly, this victory comes about since 'the LORD will be with them'.

6–7. Yahweh will save his people and gather them from among the nations. The house of Judah has a special role in this salvation (cf. vv. 3–4). Yahweh will 'strengthen' them (a word that has the same root as 'warrior') and save the 'house of Joseph'. The 'house of Joseph' is another name for the northern tribes, also called 'Ephraim' (v. 7; cf. 9:10, 13), who had been judged by God at the hand of the Assyrians in the late eighth century BC (cf. 2 Kgs 17). Yahweh's salvation is of a larger scope than just the people of Judah: his commitment is to save and reunite all his people (cf. 9:13). The nation that had been divided in judgment will be united again. Similarly, Ps. 78 notes that King David was the shepherd of 'Jacob' and 'Israel' (v. 71), and in its final canonical form this psalm anticipates a future David who will do the same.

Yahweh's gathering his people from the nations was a major theme of chs. 1–8 (e.g. 2:7[11]; 6:15; 8:7) and also runs through these verses (10:6, 8–10). Like chs. 1–8, the exile is understood as Yahweh's judgment of his people (cf. 1:2; 7:12–13) and the time when he 'rejected them'. Zech. 1:12 explains the exile as Yahweh's withholding mercy, but now he has turned in mercy to save all his people (north and south), bringing them back from exile and restoring them as they had been in former times (cf. Deut. 30:1–10, esp. v. 3). God's acting in mercy reverberates across the Twelve Minor Prophets (e.g. Hos. 1:6–7; 2:1[3], 4[6], 23[25]; 14:3[4]; Mic. 7:19; Hab. 3:2). His salvation is more than simply a return to the land, but is restored covenant relationship: 'I am the LORD their God' echoes 8:8 and 'I will answer them' speaks of prayers being heard once again (cf. 7:13; 13:9; Jer. 29:12).

Ephraim is also likened to a warrior (*kĕgibbôr*), whose 'hearts will rejoice as with wine' as a result of God's actions. Reference to 'sons' (cf. v. 9) indicates the wider benefits of this salvation for family and heritage. The fact that the sons' 'hearts will delight in the LORD' shows that they recognize that the victory has been won through God's presence with them (cf. vv. 3, 5).

8–10. The idea of Yahweh's bringing his people back from exile (v. 6) is developed in vv. 8–12, and echoes many of the themes of Deut. 30:1–10. Yahweh will 'whistle to them' and Judg. 5:16 indicates that whistling is the sound made to call sheep. Hence, he will 'gather' his scattered flock (cf. v. 2). The grounds for the gathering here is his redemption (cf. Deut. 7:8). This introduces a series of statements that portray Yahweh's future salvation in terms of the exodus. While not explicit in v. 8, the wider context indicates that the redemption will be won through the work of the future righteous Davidic king (cf. 9:9), a theme developed in chs. 12–14. The exile had devastated the population in Judah, and Yahweh promises that they will 'become numerous', which echoes the promises in Genesis (Gen. 1:22, 28; 9:1, 7; 35:11), the hopes of Moses (Deut. 30:5), and the earlier prophets (Jer. 23:3; Ezek. 36:11).

Whereas elsewhere the metaphor of 'scattering' is used for exile (e.g. 2:6[10]; 7:14), here it is 'sowing': 'I have sown them'. Boda (2004: 445) comments, 'This is an appropriate word for the experience of the northern tribes, whose long exile resulted in deep roots in their respective locales.'

Among the foreign peoples and distant places to which they had been exiled, identified as Egypt and Assyria in v. 10, 'they will remember me' (v. 9). Remembrance is a key idea in Deuteronomy, of which Craigie (1976: 185) comments:

> The act of remembering prompts obedience to the covenant law, for it brings to the forefront of the mind the reality and faithfulness of God; forgetfulness is tantamount to disobedience, for the self and human concerns have pushed into the background of the mind the reality and claims of God.

The phrase 'they will live, [along] with their sons' is difficult to translate (see 'Notes on the text'). Meyers and Meyers (1987: 179) follow the LXX and Syr in translating it, 'they will give life to their children and they will return'. That is, their children have no future in exile, so by returning they give them life. Alternatively, if the MT is followed, which seems preferable, it may be understood as a statement that the exiles have survived while living among the nations, along with their children (cf. v. 7), and will return from there.

They will return from Egypt in the south and from Assyria in the north (cf. 6:6). The pairing of Egypt with Assyria (cf. v. 11) reflects past events. The Egyptians had enslaved the Israelites and continued to threaten them throughout their history. Reference to Egypt also brings to mind exodus and deliverance themes. In addition, in the Babylonian captivity many from the land of Judah had fled to Egypt (Jer. 24:8). The Assyrians destroyed Damascus and conquered the northern tribes in 722 BC. These countries are also linked in Isa. 7:18 as threats to Israel's freedom in the eighth century BC.

Yahweh will bring the exiles back to 'the land of Gilead and Lebanon'. The geography here is not arbitrary. 'Gilead' refers to the region of Transjordanian land that was occupied by the tribes of Reuben, Gad and the half-tribe of Manasseh, including Bashan in the north (e.g. Deut. 23:6; 34:1; Judg. 10 – 12; 20:1; 1 Kgs 4:13; 2 Kgs 15:29). It was the territory through which Israel first approached the Promised Land under Moses (Deut. 1:4; 3:1–11), and probably refers to the route of the exiles returning from Egypt (Zech. 10:10). 'Lebanon' is used to define the northernmost extent of the Promised Land (e.g. Deut. 11:24; Josh. 1:4). While separate from Israel for most of Israel's history, 1 Kgs 9:19 says that Lebanon was part of Solomon's dominion. In a similar way to Gilead, Lebanon was the region through which those from Assyria would return (10:10). The Jordan (11:3) was also very significant in the entry of the Israelites into the Promised Land under Joshua (Josh. 1 – 4). In addition, Meyers and Meyers (1987: 222) believe that Gilead, along with Lebanon, represented relatively empty territory that belonged to the northern kingdom. It would be filled by Israelites only when they were exceedingly numerous, exactly the condition specified in v. 8, and the end of v. 10, which goes even beyond this in its expression of abundance.

11–12. Exodus imagery continues to be prominent here, indicating that this future restoration to the land is a new exodus. Already Yahweh's people are said to be 'redeemed' (v. 8), they will be brought back 'from Egypt' (v. 10), and the imagery of v. 11 recalls the journey through the Re(e)d Sea, although in this instance it is the Nile. The subject ('he') is best understood as Yahweh (rather than Ephraim), who will lead his people through the waters (cf. Isa. 43:2) and 'smite with the sea waves' (cf. 9:3), as he did to the Egyptian army (Exod. 14:27–28). The new exodus will be of the same order as the first, and yet it will not be exactly the same. Like 9:1–8, Zechariah draws on the past to paint a picture of the future. Yahweh's control of the waters complements his control of the rain in 10:1 (Floyd 2000: 478).

Those who are proud and powerful (Assyria and Egypt) will be humbled (cf. Deut. 30:7). There is a wordplay here, with Assyria (*'aššûr*) sounding like 'take away' (*yāsûr*). The removal of the scepter indicates a removal of their power. Conversely, Yahweh will strengthen his people (cf. v. 6) and 'in his name they will walk'. This expression is unique in the OT. Elsewhere Yahweh's name is associated with his character and his people (e.g. Exod. 20:7; Mal. 1:11). The idea here seems to be that in living as the people of God and reflecting his character in their lives, they will make Yahweh known to the nations (cf. 9:16).

11:1–3. In preparation for the return of his people to fill the Promised Land (10:6–12), Yahweh will clear the way by felling as trees and destroying with fire those who are in the way (cf. Ps. 29:5–9). Prophetic literature frequently appropriates arboreal imagery to speak of the majesty and power of rulers that often precedes their fall. Like a 'shepherd', the image of a tree is frequently used in relation to kingship, as has already been noted with the related term 'Shoot' (cf. 3:8; 6:12). Zech. 11:1–3 speaks of the destruction that is coming on proud nations, particularly their kings. Lebanon had a reputation for its cedars and cypresses, which, as 1 Kings records, were even used in the construction of the Jerusalem temple and Solomon's palace (1 Kgs 5:6; 7:2). Bashan was known for its mighty oaks (e.g. Isa. 2:13; Ezek. 27:6). While Lebanon and Bashan had been in Israelite hands for a time, Israel is not mentioned as being in Lebanon after Solomon, and the Israelites were removed from Bashan by Tiglath Pileser III of Assyria in the eighth century BC (Slayton 1992: 624). For the pre-exilic and exilic prophets, Lebanon and Bashan epitomized all that was proud (e.g. Isa. 2:13). Bashan was an idolatrous place (Amos 4:1). Both were the objects of God's wrath (Hanson 1979: 336).

In many ways, 11:1–3 is a return to the theme of 9:1–8, which pictured Yahweh's coming to re-establish the kingdom of David. Just as 9:1–8 chose cities that represented the extent of the land during David's reign, here Gilead, Lebanon and the Jordan represent the borders of the land promised to Abraham, through which the returning exiles will pass (cf. Deut. 1:7–8; 2:36). As these nations and their leadership are destroyed, it results in the wailing of shepherds and the roaring of lions (v. 3). The juxtaposition of the shepherds and lions suggests they refer to the same group. Floyd (2000: 286) states, 'This identification suggests that the shepherds have been more like predators than protectors, and that they are more upset by their own loss of a resource to exploit than by any damage done to the flock's own well-being.'

Commentators disagree about whom this group of shepherds/lions represents. Some argue that they are Israel's own worthless leaders. However, the immediate context suggests they are the leaders of foreign nations, namely the cedars of Lebanon and oaks of Bashan (note how both speak of 'majestic ones' or 'majesty' being 'ruined'). J. G. S. S. Thomson (1955: 410–411) identifies several passages that speak of the leaders of foreign nations as shepherds (Isa. 44:28; Jer. 6:3; 12:10; Mic. 5:5–6; Nah. 3:18). In particular, Jer. 12 speaks of the desolation of the exile that is the direct result of Yahweh's abandoning his heritage, Israel. The shepherds who have brought about this desolation (Jer. 12:10) are identified as being of the nations (cf. Jer. 12:14–17). Significantly, these shepherds are also likened to wild beasts that devour God's people (Jer. 12:9). In addition, in Jer. 50:17 the kings of Assyria and Babylon are both called lions. These passages give further grounds for understanding Zech. 11:3 as simply switching metaphors to speak of the same group, namely foreign kings who have ruled over and afflicted God's people, who will be humbled (Larkin 1994: 190).

Explanation

In view of Yahweh's future coming (ch. 9), this unit provides another perspective on the battle of ch. 9 with the focus now on the leadership (shepherds) of Yahweh's presently oppressed people (vv. 1–2). Yahweh promises to judge the foreign leaders and raise up a new leadership who will overthrow their enemies in the battle (vv. 3–5). He promises to strengthen, save and reunite Judah and Ephraim, and restore them in a new exodus to the Promised Land, where they will live in a way that reflects God's character (vv. 8–12). A transitional passage taunts the nations with the announcement of the fall of their leaders and their dominion (11:1–3).

The comments above note how these themes tie into the wider hopes for restoration in the earlier prophets and echo Moses' speech in Deut. 30:1–10. As part of this restoration programme, a question raised is whether the metaphors used in v. 4 to depict the new leadership convey the hope for a Messiah. The keystone or 'cornerstone' clearly becomes an image of the Messiah in later times (e.g. *Tg. Zech*. 10.1; Acts 4:11; 1 Peter 2:6–7), but it is not clear whether Zechariah drew on earlier biblical material with Davidic associations for this metaphor. While there are a number of texts that open up the possibility, particularly with the keystone and peg (e.g. Isa. 28:14–16; Ps. 118:22; Isa. 22:22–25), it seems more likely that these metaphors came to mind simply because of their associations with the 'house' of Judah and the 'house' of Joseph, the keystone and peg providing support and strength for these houses.

Many have noted the similarities between chs. 9 and 10. Both have a positive tone, they envisage a battle victory, are concerned for Judah and Ephraim, and both promote the theme of return from exile (Boda 2003b: 289). Since the king was the linchpin of the restoration of land and people in ch. 9, it seems appropriate to understand the king's continuing this role in ch. 10. This is especially the case since ch. 10 begins by identifying the people's need for their own shepherd, a metaphor mostly associated with kingship. The other factor that supports seeing the king of ch. 9 in view is that the king was the leader of leaders, and if the phrase 'every oppressor together' (v. 4) is taken on face value, then we should expect it to include the already identified future Davidic king. Moreover, this is also consistent with Jer. 23:3–6, which speaks of shepherds (pl.) being raised up, of which the 'righteous Shoot' for David is one. Hence the picture of the coming king, albeit among other leaders, can be understood to run along the same lines as ch. 9. The king will be involved in a victory whereby the enemies of God will be judged and his kingdom will be re-established, reuniting Judah and Ephraim (9:1, 10; 10:6). As in ch. 9, exodus imagery is used to describe the ultimate end of Israel's exile that this will bring (10:8–11), accompanied by blessing (10:7) and the joy of the redeemed (9:9; 10:7) (Schellenberg 2001: 101–115).

The metaphor of a shepherd is developed in the NT. In Matt. 9:36, Jesus says that the people in his day are 'like sheep without a shepherd' (cf. 10:2). It is this situation that is the occasion for his 'compassion' (cf. 10:6), where he sends out the twelve disciples with authority to drive out evil spirits and to heal every sickness and disease in anticipation of the coming kingdom (cf. Matt. 10). The battle that the disciples wage is not against flesh and blood, but against powers and principalities (cf. Eph. 6:12). Hence, interpreting this passage from a canonical point of view, the battle imagery of this chapter must be understood as a spiritual battle, coming to its climax in Jesus' death and resurrection. Indeed, Jesus calls himself the 'good shepherd' in John 10:11, 14 (cf. Heb. 13:20; 1 Peter 5:4; Rev. 7:17). In contrast to the hired hand, who cares nothing for the sheep and runs away when the wolf comes, Jesus promises to lay down his life for the sheep (John 10:10, 15).

The restoration of the nation of Israel, north and south, is something envisaged in Acts as being fulfilled by Jesus. Acts 1:8 establishes the programme for the restoration of the kingdom to Israel, which begins in Jerusalem and then goes to 'all Judea and Samaria', Samaria being the old capital of the northern kingdom (cf. Acts 8). It only then goes 'to the ends of the earth'. Hence Israel is envisaged as being reconstituted before the gospel goes to the nations (cf. Acts 26:7). This reunification of the nation in Jesus is also reflected in Jas 1:1, which is addressed to 'the twelve tribes scattered among the nations', those who have come to believe in Jesus as Lord and Christ. Similarly, John's vision in Rev. 7 is first of 144,000 from the twelve tribes of Israel (vv. 4–8), and then of a great multitude that no one could count from every nation, tribe, people and language (v. 9).

In addition to these themes, the call to 'Ask for rain from the LORD' is theologically significant, particularly since it is 'in the season of spring rain' when one would expect rain to come. This contradicts the deistic world view, where a significant distinction is made between the natural and supernatural. Deists see the hand of God only in supernatural events, whereas the Bible sees the hand of God in all events. It is only because God superintends all things in the world that the call to pray in the season of spring rain makes sense. There is no clockwork universe here – people are dependent on God in all things. Furthermore, divination and ancestor worship continue to hold many people in bondage today. They are superstitions that can bring great affliction (from fear to poverty). Christians likewise are to keep themselves from idols (1 Cor. 10:14; 1 John 5:21; cf. 2:15–17) and have nothing to do with these things, including the idolatry of greed (Col. 3:5).

ZECHARIAH 11:4–17

Translation

[11:4]Thus said the LORD my God, 'Shepherd the flock for the slaughter. [5]Because
those buying them will slaughter them and will not be condemned, and those
selling them will say, "Blessed be the LORD! I have become rich!" And their
shepherds will not have compassion on them. [6]For I will no longer have com-
passion on the inhabitants of the land,' declares the LORD. 'But rather, I am
delivering each person into the hand of his neighbour, and into the hand of his
king, and they will devastate the land, and I will not rescue from their hand.'

[7]So I shepherded the flock for the slaughter, indeed the afflicted of the flock. And
I took to myself two staffs, one I named 'favour', and one I named 'union', and I
shepherded the flock. [8]I caused the three shepherds to perish in one month. And
my soul became short with them and, moreover, their soul abhorred me. [9]And I
said, 'I will not shepherd you. Let the dying one die, and let the perishing one
perish, and let the remaining ones each eat the flesh of their neighbour.'

[10]I took my staff 'favour' and I cut it in two to break my covenant that I had
made with all the peoples. [11]And it was broken on that day, and so the afflicted of
the flock, the ones watching me, knew that it was the word of the LORD. [12]And I
said to them, 'If it seems good in your eyes, pay my wage, but if not, cease.' And
they weighed out my wage – thirty pieces of silver. [13]And the LORD said to me,

'Throw them to the moulder – the handsomeness of the price at which I was priced by them.' And I took the thirty pieces of silver and I threw them into the house of the LORD – to the moulder. 14And I cut into two my second staff, 'union', to break the brotherhood between Judah and Israel.

15The LORD said to me, 'Take once more the equipment of a foolish shepherd. 16For look, I am raising up a shepherd in the land. The perishing he will not care for. The young he will not seek, and the maimed he will not heal. The standing he will not support, and he will consume the flesh of the fat ones, and tear off their hoofs.

17'Woe to my worthless shepherd that forsakes the flock! A sword against his arm and against his right eye! May his arm be completely withered and his right eye totally blinded!'

Notes on the text

11:4. 'for the slaughter' is a gen. of purpose, indicating intended use (Arnold and Choi 2003: 11).

5. 'Because': *'ăšer* is unusual here. It seems to link with the previous sentence to introduce the reason for the sign action (a causal clause) (R. J. Williams 2007: 166). There are similar instances in 11:2 and 13:6.

While 'those selling' is pl., the verb 'say' (*yō'mar*) is sg., consistent with the speech reported in the first person. The LXX, Vg, Syr and Tg render it as pl. The sg. in MT is best understood in a distrib. sense (Gelston 2010: 144).

'I have become rich': *wa''ēšir* is one of forty-eight words in the HB with a medial aleph, which is not read. LXX, Vg and Tg again harmonize to pl. (Gelston 2010: 144). Its form is 1 sg. waw cons. hiph. with an ingressive stative sense (i.e. entry into a state) (Arnold and Choi 2003: 51).

6. 'For': *kî* introduces the reason for the sign action in v. 4 (cf. *kî* in v. 15) (Clark and Hatton 2002: 283).

'But rather': *wĕhinnēh* functions as an adversative here (Arnold and Choi 2003: 161).

'each person': *'et-hā'ādām 'îš*. Lit. 'the man, a man', where *'îš* is used distrib.

7. 'indeed the afflicted of the flock': many propose that the consonantal text should be divided differently by combining *lkn* with *'nii* and repointing it to give the translation 'on behalf of the sheep merchants' (cf. NRSV). They believe this lies behind the LXX (*eis tēn chanaanitin*). Nevertheless, Finley (1982: 60) notes, 'The MT is supported by all the other ancient versions and is represented in a fragment of a Qumran commentary on Isaiah (4Q163 21).' Yet Finley prefers the LXX on the basis that the more difficult textual variant is to be preferred. He also notes that the LXX omits any translation of 'the flock' (*haṣṣô'n*). Yet it seems more likely that the LXX translator has struggled with the two Hebr. phrases, and rendered them inaccurately as *eis tēn chanaanitin* (11:7) and *hoi chananaioi* (11:11). Finley concludes that the LXX reading makes better sense within the context, but this is disputed (Larkin 1994: 111; Wenzel 2011: 231). Larkin notes the use of the adj. in a const. state is unusual, but when it does occur it is strongly emphatic. She translates it 'yes indeed, of the poor of the flock'. Like her, I have followed MT (see 'Comment').

8. 'abhorred': *bāḥălâ* is found only elsewhere in Prov. 20:21 as a pual ptc.

9. The three imperfect forms are translated as jussives: 'let . . . let . . . let . . .'

'each': *'iššâ* is used distrib. (cf. v. 6). It is f. because of the subject.

'their neighbour' is literally 'her neighbour'. I have translated it as pl. to agree with the subject.

12. 'thirty pieces of silver': lit. 'thirty of silver' (also v. 13).

13. 'the moulder': *hayyôṣēr*. Often translated 'the potter', but this is too restrictive in limiting it to one who works with clay. More literally it is 'the former'. Syr has 'the treasury' (*hā'ôṣār*) and LXX has 'the furnace' (*to chōneutērion*). See 'Comment'.

'Throw them . . . threw them'. The Hebr. pr. is sg. in both instances, but I have translated as pl. to agree with the subject ('thirty pieces of silver').

'into the house of the LORD': 'into' is supplied. The prep. *bĕ* is sometimes omitted before a word beginning with *b*.

14. 'brotherhood': *'aḥăwâ* is a hapax legomenon, but it 'is clearly an abstraction based on the kinship term *'āḥ*, "brother"' (Meyers and Meyers 1993: 280).

'between': *bên . . . ûbên.*

16. 'The young': *hanna'ar* follows MT (lit. 'the young man'). It is unusual in that elsewhere it never refers to animals. Some suggest emending the text to 'the wandering [one]', which is reflected in LXX and Syr.

'the fat ones': *habbĕrî'â* is sg. in Hebr.

17. 'that forsakes': *'ōzbî* contains a 'suffix of connection' (*î*), which is an unexplained ending found in a noun in const. (Waltke and O'Connor 1990: 127–128).

'completely . . . totally': the inf. abs. adds emphasis (Waltke and O'Connor 1990: 584).

Form and structure

Zech. 11 comprises two sign actions involving shepherds (11:4–14, 15–17), given to Zechariah as instructions from Yahweh (11:4, 13, 15). Elsewhere, sign actions are visible representations of the prophetic message that seem designed to elevate the affective element in communication (e.g. Isa. 20:1–4; Jer. 13:1–11; Ezek. 4 – 5; Hos. 1:2–9; 3:1–5; Zech. 6:9–15). However, it is not clear how the sign actions in this chapter could be enacted. It is difficult to envisage how the disposal of three shepherds in one month (v. 8) and the response of the flock (vv. 8, 12) were acted out. Because of this, it is more likely that the sign actions of this chapter are a literary device than actual prophetic acts, and it may be more precise to designate the genre as 'report(s) of symbolic action' (Petersen 1995: 89). By adopting the literary form of the sign action, the prophet is portrayed as intimately involved in the message, even if it is not played out in space and time. Yet Floyd (2000: 490–491) contends that 'this narrative at least purports to describe something that actually happened', and this possibility cannot finally be dismissed. Nevertheless, whether they are enacted or not, the effect on the reader is the same. The reader (and hearer) of the report is called to identify the situation or event(s) the sign actions represent and unpack the meaning. In this way the report functions in an allegorical way. Since many of the elements are not explicitly identified within the report, there is a vast array of interpretations of this chapter.

It is possible to identify broadly three interpretative approaches to ch. 11, which I have outlined in detail elsewhere (Petterson 2009: 168–194). The most common approach understands the sign actions as representing the future. However, there is little agreement as to what this future is, whether the events of the Greek period, those surrounding Judas Maccabaeus or events of the Roman period, with the shepherd being Jesus Christ. The details of ch. 11 do not fit precisely with any of these situations. For instance, if it is a future prophecy of the events of Jesus' ministry, it is not clear who the three shepherds that Jesus destroyed were, how he deserted the flock of his people to judgment, or how he annulled the brotherhood between Judah and Israel. This is not to say that ch. 11 does not anticipate the ministry of Jesus in some way, and how it does will be explored later. Nevertheless, interpretations of this passage as future prophecy lack coherence with the rest of the book of Zechariah. Elsewhere Zechariah promises a future reunion of Judah and Israel (8:13; 9:10, 13; 10:6–7; 12:12), yet here this brotherhood is annulled (11:14). While the wider context of the book of Zechariah certainly speaks of difficult days ahead for the people of God (esp. ch. 12–14), elsewhere suffering always ends with salvation, but here suffering ends in decimation. This interpretation is difficult to reconcile with the rest of the book.

A second interpretative approach seemingly thrives on the discord in the passage and understands it as characterizing contemporary tensions in the community (Hanson 1979: 241–242; Redditt 1993: 676–686; Foster 2007: 735–753). While the details of their interpretations differ, most argue that the passage is a critique of contemporary leadership, either the Davidic governor(s) and/or temple leaders or Persian monarchs. Most scholars taking this approach believe this passage functions to contradict earlier prophetic hope. This is made explicit by Redditt (1995: 127–128): 'Thus, the allegory contradicted the hope for the reunion of north and south . . . Zechariah 11:4–17 reversed the hopes of the post-exilic community for reunion under a Davidic king.' This interpretative approach faces the same difficulty as the first, namely lack of coherence with the book of Zechariah and the Book of the Twelve (Petterson 2010: 231). More fundamentally, those who propose such a significant reversal of prophecy never face the obvious questions this raises: Why would a redactor clearly contradict earlier prophets such as Ezekiel and Isaiah who had an authoritative role in the community (as seen in the later use of their works)? Why were the earlier prophets preserved if their prophecies 'failed' and needed to be 'corrected'? This is especially pertinent given the way Zechariah elsewhere testifies to the importance of the prophetic word coming true (e.g. Zech. 4:9; 6:15; 13:2–6). Since these scholars propose radical redactional changes elsewhere, why would the redactor not also have reworked earlier material in Zechariah to reflect the later changed expectations?

Some have responded to the difficulties in this passage by arguing that it can no longer be understood (Conrad 1999: 172). Others seek to draw a more general message from the passage (Petersen 1992b: 91). However, there is another approach to this text that makes sense of most of its details and is coherent with Zechariah and the Book of the Twelve. This third approach understands this passage to be portraying the past (Meyer 1977; Meyers and Meyers 1993; Merrill 1994; Webb 2003; Stead 2011). That is, the prophet in the first sign action plays the role of Yahweh as shepherd to enact a dramatic representation of Israel's history to the time of the exile to explain the people's present circumstances, particularly why they are currently ruled by foreign shepherds who oppress them. This interpretation best explains the breaking of the two staffs 'union' and 'favour', which represent the division of the kingdom and the exile respectively. The shepherd in the second sign action (vv. 15–17) represents contemporary abusive leadership (cf. 11:3). This is the approach taken in this commentary as I believe it best accounts for the data.

Many of the elements of the sign action report are like puzzle pieces. The frame of the puzzle has been constructed (the wider context of the chapter in the book), and several key pieces have been set in place (the breaking of the shepherd's staffs representing the division of the kingdom and the exile), but there is no picture on the box apart from a very general description (a dramatic representation of Israel's history to the time of the exile). Clues to the puzzle construction can be found in the way this passage interacts with earlier shepherd passages in the prophets such as Jeremiah and Ezekiel (Curtis 2006: 197; Stead 2011). However, the placement of the pieces in these verses is tricky and the reader must finally determine whether my construction is the best fit.

In terms of structure, Butterworth (1992: 77) comments, 'Despite the acute problems of interpretation, there is no dispute about the fact that vv. 4–17 belong together, and that the section falls into two unequal parts: vv. 4–14, 15–17).' The thematic structure below is supported by paragraph markers in the MT at the end of ch. 11, vv. 3, 14, 16 and 17. These indicate how Jewish rabbis of the Talmudic period (AD 135–500) understood the division of the text (Brotzman 1994: 47).

11:4	Command to perform the first sign action
11:5	Further descriptions of the flock
11:6	Reason for the sign action
11:7–14	Enactment
11:15	Command to perform the second sign action
11:16	Reason for the sign action
11:17	Announcement of woe

Comment

11:4. Zechariah is commanded to perform a sign action, playing the role of a shepherd. The metaphor of a shepherd as a leader is introduced in 10:2–3 (see 'Comment' on these verses for the background). Elsewhere Yahweh is the shepherd of his people, who are his flock (e.g. Gen. 49:24; Ps. 23:1). It is also a title used of both Israelite and non-Israelite kings. The most significant human shepherd in Israel was David, who was taken from shepherding sheep to shepherd God's people (e.g. 2 Sam. 5:2; 7:8–16; Jer. 23:4–5; Ezek. 34:23–24; 37:24; Mic. 5:1–3; Ps. 78:70–72), but David was only ever an under-shepherd of Yahweh. In the context of the first sign action, Zechariah is to represent Yahweh as Shepherd and characterize Yahweh's relationship to his people ('the inhabitants of the land' in v. 6). The expression 'my God' indicates the close relationship between the prophet and God (cf. Deut. 4:5).

The description of the people of Israel as 'the flock for the slaughter' (*'et-ṣō'n hahărēgâ*) strikes an ominous note. When used as a verb, *hārag* can refer to murder (e.g. Gen. 4:8), capital punishment (e.g. Deut. 13:9), killing in warfare (e.g. Josh. 8:24) or the killing of animals (e.g. Isa. 22:13). Here it describes a flock on the way to slaughter (cf. Jer. 12:3). While sheep were bred for food, normally only some were killed, with ewes spared to bear young and conserve the flock. Applied to the flock, this is a much more destructive slaughter. Nevertheless, the description does not necessarily mean that the entire flock will die – 'devastation rather than annihilation fits the metaphoric thrust of the verses to follow' (Meyers and Meyers 1993: 253).

5. The connective 'because' (*'ăšer*) is unusual. It seems to introduce the reason for the sign action in which the circumstances of the flock are described. The sheep of the flock are traded and will suffer 'the slaughter' of v. 4. Three groups are mentioned: 'those buying', 'those selling' and 'their shepherds'. While it is difficult to be certain about the identities of these groups, there are clues from the text and the wider context.

The ones 'buying them' will slaughter them and not incur guilt. The verb *'āšam* can be translated 'incur guilt', 'be guilty' or 'be condemned' (e.g. Jer. 2:3; Ps. 34:22–23; 2 Chr. 19:10). The identity of these buyers is not explicit, but the wider context opens up the possibility that they are foreign shepherds who have not been held accountable for their slaughter of the flock (cf. 10:3; 11:3, 6). The idea that the nations are yet to be judged for their evil is also present throughout the night visions (1:15, 18–21; 2:6[10]; 6:8).

The sellers say, 'Blessed be the Lord! I have become rich!' Their words indicate a perverse religious hypocrisy, where pious words mask greed. Their praise of Yahweh indicates that the sellers are Israelite. Their ability to sell the flock indicates that they are leaders, most likely kings who not only failed to feed and protect the flock, but often used the flock for their own gain and entered into political alliances with foreign shepherds that were costly and detrimental to the flock (e.g. Hoshea in 2 Kgs 17:3 and Ahaz in 2 Kgs 16:8). The selling was not a one-time event, but a pattern exhibited through Israel's history.

The final group, 'their shepherds', is probably a combined reference to the buyers and sellers, to the kings of Israel and Judah and to the foreign kings into whose hands the flock is sold (cf. 10:2–3). In this case, the phrase sums up the situation of the flock: 'their shepherds will not have compassion on them'. The verb translated 'have compassion' (*ḥāmal*) has the idea of 'sparing' or 'taking pity' (cf. Mal. 3:17). The background for much of this scenario is found in Jeremiah and Ezekiel, prophets who condemned the shepherd leaders of their day and announced the judgment of exile (e.g. Jer. 23:1–2; Ezek. 34).

While many aspects of the first sign action are set in future time (e.g. 'will slaughter . . . will not be condemned . . . will say . . . will not have compassion'), this does not mean that the reality it depicts is future. Stead (2011: 155–156) notes there is a difference between 'acted time' and 'actual time'. While the symbolic actions of this chapter are acted out in sequence and the imperfect form of many of the verbs look to future prophetic acts, the events depicted (such as the exile and division of the kingdom) are clearly past. This phenomenon is seen also in Ezek. 4:4–5, where Ezekiel is commanded to lie upon his side (future) to depict a period of 390 years that has been running for centuries.

6. 'For' (*kî*) introduces the reason the flock will be slaughtered (v. 4). It is not the reason for the leaders' actions in v. 5, for logically the reverse is the case (i.e. the leaders' actions are the reason for God's judgment). Yahweh announces that he will 'no longer have compassion on the inhabitants of the land' (the word 'compassion' is repeated from v. 5). The expression 'no longer' (*lō' . . . 'ôd*) can also be translated 'not again' and implies that Yahweh has spared his people in the past, but now his patience has run out (cf. v. 8). Hence v. 6 anticipates the end point of the sign action, where Yahweh's patience finally runs out and he delivers the inhabitants of the land to their enemies, described as 'his neighbour, and . . . his king'. While 'neighbour' (*rēa'*) most often refers to a fellow Israelite in the OT (as it does in v. 9), it is difficult to conceive a time in either the pre- or post-exilic periods when the land was 'devastated' by the people of Israel and their king. However, there are instances in the OT where 'neighbour' (*rēa'*) refers to a foreigner or adversary (e.g. Exod. 11:2; 1 Sam. 28:17; Prov. 6:1). The word may have been used in this verse to form a wordplay with 'shepherd' (*rō'eh*). In this case, 'his king' refers to the king of the neighbour. Hence a neighbouring nation and their king will devastate the land. The verb 'devastate' (*kātat*) means to grind, crush or beat something to pieces (e.g. Deut. 9:21; 2 Kgs 18:4). Here this meaning is extended to describe the destruction of battle, hence 'devastate' (e.g. Num. 14:45; Deut. 1:44). The verb 'rescue' at the end of this verse is used elsewhere with reference to God's saving Israel from Egypt (e.g. Exod. 3:8). Hence it ironically heralds a reversal of the exodus (Meyers and Meyers 1993: 261). The 'land' (*hā'āreṣ*) in this context refers to the Promised Land.

Historically, the judgment of v. 6 came upon the northern kingdom of Israel by the Assyrians and their king Shalmaneser in 722 BC, and upon the southern kingdom of Judah by the Babylonians and their king Nebuchadnezzar in 586 BC, ultimately at Yahweh's hand (note the phrases 'I am delivering . . . I will not rescue'). As powerful as Shalmaneser and Nebuchadnezzar were, they are portrayed here as agents of Yahweh. Yahweh's judgment of his people through the agency of Nebuchadnezzar is expressed many times in Jeremiah (Jer. 21:7; 22:25; 25:9; 27:6; 32:28).

7–9. Zechariah is reported as enacting the sign action by shepherding the flock of the slaughter. The phrase 'the afflicted of the flock' may be a further description of the flock (appropriate given the report of vv. 5–6), or may refer to a part of the flock. Many translators emend the MT and translate this phrase, 'on behalf of the sheep merchants'. However, this reconstructed translation lacks support from all the ancient versions apart from the LXX (see 'Notes on the text'). Sense can be made of the MT, so it is followed as the more difficult reading. Those 'afflicted' are mentioned again in v. 11, and their identity will be discussed in that context.

Zechariah takes up two staffs. Some suggest two different implements on the basis of the 'rod and staff' of Ps. 23:4, though the implements of Ps. 23 use different vocabulary to the 'staffs' here. The number 'two' is more important for the purpose of the sign action. Nevertheless, a 'staff' (*maqqēl*) is the equipment of a shepherd, used for disciplining sheep (e.g. Ezek. 20:37; cf. Num. 22:27) and as a weapon against wild animals (such as dogs) that might attack the flock (1 Sam. 17:43). It probably also provides stability for the shepherd as he walks (cf. Exod. 12:11). These staffs are given the names 'favour' (*nō'am*) and 'union' (*ḥōblîm*), which represent important aspects of the sign action. The significance of their names will be explored in relation to vv. 10 and 14 respectively.

Zechariah's first reported action as shepherd is, 'I caused the three shepherds to perish'. The verb 'caused . . . to perish' (*kāḥad*) is used elsewhere to speak of the destruction of an enemy (e.g. Exod. 23:23; 1 Kgs 13:34; Ps. 83:5[4]; 2 Chr. 32:21) and appears twice in v. 9 and once in v. 16. There is a myriad of proposals regarding the identity of the three shepherds and any identification must remain speculative. Merrill (1994: 293–294) and Webb (2003: 149) suggest that they are the last three kings of Judah (Jehoiakim, Jehoiachin and Zedekiah), removed in rapid succession ('one month'). A recent proposal from Stead (2011) takes its cue from the numerous echoes of Jeremiah, which he argues is the key intertext that unlocks the enigmas of Zechariah's imagery. As well as the general allusion to the shepherds of Jeremiah's day, Stead (2011: 150) notes how v. 4 echoes Jer. 4:3; v. 9 echoes Jer. 19:9; and vv. 16–17 echo Jer. 23:2. In the account of the fall of Jerusalem in Jer. 52, on the ninth day of the fourth month (v. 6), the city wall is breached and the army scattered. Significantly, king Zedekiah is captured and his sons perish. Jer. 52 notes that one month later, on the tenth day of the fifth month (v. 12), Nebuchadnezzar's commander Nebuzaradan arrived and burned the temple, palace and houses of the city, broke down the city wall and carried many into exile. In this 'month' in which Jerusalem fell, its leadership is exiled or killed. Against this background, Stead proposes that 'the three shepherds' are the three types of leadership that 'perish' when Jerusalem fell: the king, the prophets and the priests (vv. 10–11; 15, 24–27). While only the king and the priests are explicitly identified in Jer. 52, the prophets can be assumed to be eliminated on the basis that elsewhere in Jeremiah these leadership roles are grouped together (e.g. Jer. 2:26; 4:9; 8:1; 13:13). Stead's hypothesis is coherent and attractive, but probably in the end too subtle. The identity of the three shepherds remains an enigma.

The remaining elements of vv. 8–9 are consistent with the Babylonian exile. Representing Yahweh as shepherd (cf. v. 4), Zechariah's actions reflect the way that Yahweh's longsuffering patience with his people ran thin (lit. 'my soul became short with them'; cf. Num. 21:4; Mic. 2:7; Job 21:4) and the people's soul abhorred or detested him ('soul' does not refer to one's eternal spirit, but to the inner self – the desires and feelings). Historically, the people had detested Yahweh by refusing the prophets who called them to repentance, so Yahweh ceased to be their shepherd (v. 9). Rather than saving the dying and perishing flock, he handed them over to the nations, resulting in the destruction of Jerusalem and exile. In other words, Yahweh judged his people by handing them over to the full consequences of their rejection of him as Shepherd.

Three phrases depict the horror of Yahweh's judgment. The first two contain a present ptc. and impf. of the same verb (translated as a juss.): 'Let the dying one die, and let the perishing one perish'. The third phrase contains different verbs: 'let the remaining ones each eat the flesh of their neighbour'. This horrible image refers to consuming dead corpses during a siege, when hunger was fierce. Indeed, during the siege of Jerusalem the book of Lamentations attests women consuming their dead offspring (Lam. 2:20; 4:10; cf. Jer. 19:9).

While much later, the Jewish Targum provides support for this overall interpretation as it identifies the exiles of Israel and Judah as corresponding to the breaking of this staff:

> And I brought the king of Assyria against the king of Israel and I drove him into exile because they changed the covenant which was made with them, that they should not serve idols; therefore they went into exile among the nations. And because they changed the covenant they went into exile at that time . . .
>
> And I brought Nebuchadnezzar the king of Babylon against Zedekiah king of the tribe of the house of Judah, and I drove him into exile because the people of the house of Judah also changed the covenant, like their brethren of the house of Israel. (*Tg. Zech.* 11.10–11a, 14) (Cathcart and Gordon 1989: 214–215)

10–11. Zechariah breaks the first staff called 'favour', 'grace' or 'kindness' (*nōʿam*). It is a word associated with Yahweh in Pss 27:4 and 90:17, and is sometimes also translated 'beauty'. This word is also associated with wisdom, knowledge and words in Proverbs (2:10; 3:17; 15:26; 16:24). The breaking of this staff represents the breaking of God's covenant 'with all the peoples'. What is this covenant? The covenants with Noah or Abraham are often suggested since they have a universal aspect ('all the peoples'), yet it is difficult to see how either of these connect with Zechariah's sign action. Alternatively, Meyers and Meyers (1993: 270–271) argue that there are precedents for referring to the component tribe and people groups of Israel as 'peoples' (e.g. Gen. 27:29; 48:4; 49:10; 1 Kgs 22:28; Isa. 3:13; Mic. 1:2). Similarly, Redditt (1993: 683) cites 1 Kgs 22:28 and Job 36:20 as examples of how 'the nations' (pl.) can refer to a single, specific nation. In this case, the covenant is the covenant made with the 'peoples' of Israel and Judah, namely the national covenant mediated by Moses at Sinai.

Breaking this staff makes a unique claim in the OT – the Mosaic covenant is broken from God's side. Elsewhere this covenant is said to be broken from the people's side (e.g. Jer. 31:32; Ezek. 44:7; although it is contemplated as being broken by God in Ezek. 14:21). The difficulty is that Yahweh himself promised never to break this covenant (cf. Lev. 26:44; Judg. 2:1). How can this be reconciled? While the Mosaic covenant is said to be broken by God, the people still suffer its curses, including destruction of the cities of the land and scattering of the survivors among the nations (cf. Deut. 28:45–68), so in this sense the Mosaic covenant, though broken, is still active in some sense. Furthermore, the Mosaic covenant itself anticipates restoration after exile upon repentance and a new work of Yahweh where he will circumcise the hearts of his people (Deut. 30:1–10, esp. v. 6). Indeed, this hope for restoration upon repentance is fundamental to the book of Zechariah (cf. 1:1–6). The best way to resolve this dilemma of Yahweh's breaking the covenant is to see elements of both continuity and discontinuity between the Mosaic covenant and the new covenant. The continuity is found in Yahweh's commitment to his people. This is essentially what it means when Yahweh earlier promises never to break the Mosaic covenant. While the people prove unable to live under its terms to the extent that it is finally broken, not only from the people's side, but from Yahweh's side, he remains firmly committed to his people and will establish the aims of the Mosaic covenant, namely a relationship where they will be his people and he will be their God. However, this relationship will be established on different grounds. Meyers and Meyers (1993: 269) capture it well: 'The new covenant will be the same as the old one but will be constructed in such a way that the people will no longer be able to violate its terms. It will be written on the hearts of the people.' That is, Yahweh will enable his people to do what they could not do for themselves – to obey its stipulations (cf. Jer. 31:31–34; Ezek. 16:60; 36:26–27).

With the breaking of the staff 'favour', the afflicted of the flock who have been carefully watching the prophet know that this is the word of Yahweh. That is, they recognize the covenant curses of Leviticus and Deuteronomy have been enacted. There is irony in the use of the word 'watching' (*šāmar*) since it is usually a shepherd's task to 'watch', 'guard' or 'tend' the sheep, but here it is the flock that does this – the roles have been reversed. The 'afflicted of the flock' is a phrase found also in v. 7, and there it was noted that it could be a further description of the flock or refer to a subgroup within the flock. If it is a subgroup, then it could correspond to the righteous remnant who recognize God's word being fulfilled and yet still undergo the affliction of exile (e.g. Isa. 4:2–4; 46:3). Yet the way this group acts in v. 12 by paying off the prophet is contrary to what is expected of a righteous remnant. Therefore it seems best to understand 'the afflicted of the flock' to be a further description of 'the flock for the slaughter'.

12–13. Zechariah gives the flock an ultimatum: pay and relieve him of his shepherding duties, or 'cease' from loathing him. The imper. 'cease' (*ḥădālû*) is sometimes translated 'keep it' (NIV) or 'keep them' (NRSV, ESV) and understood to be referring to the wages (the pr. is added in translation). Nevertheless, in other contexts *ḥădālû* simply means 'cease' or 'stop' (e.g. Isa. 1:16; 2:22), and here is better understood as a call to stop abhorring the prophet (cf. v. 8).

Without discussion or hesitation, the flock weighs out Zechariah's wage, 'thirty pieces of silver'. This is the amount stipulated as compensation for the death of a slave in Exod. 21:22 and could be considered a substantial sum (cf. Neh. 5:15). Yet, any amount is an insult to Yahweh, as paying Zechariah out is effectively rejecting Yahweh as their Shepherd. The phrase 'the handsomeness of the price' is therefore ironic. This response to the prophet proves the attitude of the sheep is no different from that of the shepherds (Wenzel 2011: 232). The flock abhorred the prophet in v. 8; now they are happy to get rid of him. This act shows that the people are the problem, just as much as the leaders.

Zechariah is commanded by Yahweh to throw the money to 'the moulder' (often translated 'the potter'; see 'Notes on the text') who is in 'the house of the LORD' (cf. 2 Chr. 24:10). Some scholars suggest that the idea of a 'potter' being present in the temple is what created problems for ancient translators, who rendered 'potter' (*yôṣēr*) as 'treasury' (*'ôṣār*). Torrey (1936: 256–257) argues that this conjecture is ill-founded and posits, on the basis of Persian practice elsewhere (citing Herodotus), that a foundry was present in the temple to melt down gifts of gold and silver to be stored in earthen jars. Elsewhere it is evident that a 'potter' not only works with clay, but also works metal (Exod. 32:4; 44:9, 12; Hab. 2:28), hence I favour the translation 'the moulder'. Schaper (1995) takes Torrey's proposal further and suggests that the *yôṣēr* had an important administrative role in the Persian administration and was responsible for sending the gold and silver back to Persia as taxes. It may be on this basis that ancient versions translated 'moulder' as 'treasury' since the two functioned together. In effectively giving over the money to the Persian administration, Zechariah is anticipating the second sign action, where the flock is given over to foreign leadership. Furthermore, this action shows that Zechariah, unlike the sellers, does not profit from his prophetic activity, even though he asked for payment (cf. Amos 7:12).

14. The second staff called 'union' is broken. 'Union' (*ḥōblîm*) is a ptc. of *ḥbl*, which means 'to bind' or 'to take on pledge' (Meyers and Meyers 1993: 264). As a noun, *ḥebel* denotes a band or cord used for measuring. The idea that seems to lie behind the name is the binding of two parties together in relationship, possibly as with rope, hence 'union'. This staff is broken 'to break the brotherhood between Judah and Israel'. Elsewhere Zechariah promises reunion of these two groups (e.g. 10:6–7; 12:1, 12–14). A major problem for those who see this sign action relating to events in the post-exilic period is that during this time any 'brotherhood' had well and truly been broken. The book of Nehemiah reveals antagonism between Judah and the leadership of Samaria concerning the rebuilding of the city walls of Jerusalem. In addition, the staffs bring to mind Ezekiel's sign action in Ezek. 37:15–23, where he joined two sticks into one to represent the reunification of Judah and Ephraim and the restoration of covenant relationship (Ezek. 37:27). The people in Zechariah's day had never seen this promised restoration (Stead 2011: 158), and if Zechariah is here 'reversing' this hope, as some suppose, it surely poses problems for the authenticity of either Ezekiel or Zechariah. Hence the breaking of this staff is best understood to represent the division of the kingdom into Judah and Israel under Jeroboam and Rehoboam (cf. 1 Kgs 12). Again, the

Targum explains the staff in these terms and demonstrates a very early interpretation of this passage along these lines:

> And I appointed rulers over the people and they ruled over them as if they were a flock for the slaughter; they impoverished and drove my people astray, and they were divided before me into two parts, the house of Israel seceded from the people of the house of Judah – they loathed the kingdom of the house of David with whom I was well pleased that they should be rulers over my people. (*Tg. Zech.* 11.7) (Cathcart and Gordon 1989: 212–213)

Hence the first sign action explains why the division of the kingdom and the exile came about, namely because the people rejected Yahweh as their Shepherd. While historically the division of the kingdom (the breaking of 'union') happened before the destruction of the northern and southern kingdoms by the nations (the breaking of 'favour'), it seems that Zechariah's sign actions convey these momentous moments in the history of the nation in a more general way.

15–17. The second sign action explains how the people received the leadership they deserved for their rejection of Yahweh as shepherd (Webb 2003: 152). In this second sign action (note 'once more'), the prophet takes up the 'equipment' (*kĕlî*) of a 'foolish shepherd'. The 'equipment' is not specified, but could refer to 'clothing' (cf. Deut. 22:5), or an 'article' such as a 'weapon' (Gen. 49:5), possibly another staff. The adj. 'foolish' refers to one who rejects God and engages in evil behaviour, in stark contrast to the wise one who fears God and shuns evil (e.g. Prov. 1:7; Job 28:28). Rather than caring for and prospering the flock, this foolish shepherd devours the flesh of the flock and tears off their hoofs like a lion (v. 16; contrast Ezek. 34:16). The image of a 'lion' connects with the 'lions' of 11:3, namely foreign rulers who presently ravage the flock by oppressing and feeding on them.

'For' (*kî*) introduces the reason for this second sign action (cf. v. 6). The future timing ('I am raising up') is best understood as 'acted time' rather than 'actual time' (see 'Comment' on v. 5). In this case, the 'foolish shepherd' is a reference (perhaps intentionally veiled) to the present foreign rulers whom Yahweh had raised up to rule his people in judgment for his people's rejection of him. The possessive pr. '*my* worthless shepherd' (v. 17) indicates that this shepherd functions as an agent of Yahweh. It was true of Nebuchadnezzar, of Cyrus and of the Persian king in Zechariah's day. Furthermore, this foolish shepherd would continue to represent whoever ruled over the people until the true shepherd of the people came (the king anticipated elsewhere in Zechariah; e.g. 3:10; 6:12; 9:9; cf. Ezek. 34:23).

The final word announces judgment on this worthless shepherd. 'Woe' (*hôy*) is an interjection used by the prophets to introduce a judgment oracle (cf. 1 Kgs 13:30; Isa. 5:8; Jer. 23:1; Amos 5:18). This note of woe also connects back to the short oracle at the beginning of this chapter (11:1–3; cf. 10:3), which also looks forward to the destruction of foreign shepherds. 'May his arm be completely withered and his right eye totally blinded!' would render the shepherd unable to continue in his role. He would be not only morally but also functionally worthless (Merrill 1994: 305).

Explanation

While there are several different interpretative approaches to this difficult chapter, the approach that sees the first sign action as representing Israel's history to the time of the destruction of Jerusalem best coheres with the rest of the book. As Meyers and Meyers (1993: 293) note, it answers the question 'Why, after the resoundingly hopeful mood of chapters 9 and 10, does this horrifying picture of strife and destruction present itself?' The answer is that the prophet is explaining why things are as they are in his own day, so as to make his vision of the future compelling. The overall message of the two sign actions complements the message of chs. 9–10, which reveals that Yahweh is coming to save his people, to re-establish them in the land, and in doing so will remove all foreign kings and their agents, just as he had removed false shepherds in the past.

The first sign action reminds the reader and hearer of the judgment that came on the false shepherds of Israel and the people themselves, namely the division of the kingdom and the judgment of the flock in the experience of the destruction of the land and exile. The ultimate reason for these judgments is their rejection of Yahweh as shepherd. The second sign action portrays the nature of the present destructive leadership and speaks of the judgment that is coming on these foreign shepherds, a judgment that Zechariah has already established will usher in the day of Yahweh (10:2–12). On this day, Yahweh will deliver his people, save them from the nations and install his shepherd-king as ruler over all, as is depicted in the wider context of the book.

The images in this chapter are not rated 'G' or 'Universal', especially those of survivors eating their dead neighbours. These horrible sign actions graphically portray what happens when people reject God. In many ways it is the flip side to ch. 1, where God calls to the people, 'Return to me and I will return to you.' These sign actions say, 'Reject God and he will reject you.' This is the ultimate horror scenario – but it is the choice people make for foolishly rejecting God's shepherding care. The same reality is found in the opening chapters of Romans, where those who reject God are given over to the terrible consequences of that choice – consequences can be experienced as judgment in this life (Rom. 1:18–32), or, if not in this life, certainly in the life to come (Rom. 2:5–11). God is a good Shepherd who wants what is best for his sheep, but there is certain peril for those who reject his care. These sign actions drive home the horror of sin and judgment and paint the black backdrop against which God's salvation shines all the more brilliantly. Indeed, the wider context of the book looks forward to God's salvation, and central to this is a shepherd-king who will save the flock.

Jesus claimed to be the king promised by Zechariah when he rode into Jerusalem on a donkey (9:9). Jesus also claimed, 'I am the good shepherd' (John 10:11), a claim made against the backdrop of oppressive shepherds such as those portrayed in this chapter. But what happened when the good shepherd came? Staggeringly, God's people still had not learnt the lessons of history. This prophetic drama of Zechariah is acted out on a larger stage when it finds its fulfilment in the betrayal and rejection of Jesus Christ.

Matthew 27:1–10 (cf. 26:14–16) connects the betrayal of Jesus by Judas for thirty pieces of silver with Zechariah's sign action, but intriguingly attributes this to the prophet Jeremiah. It is not entirely clear why Matthew does this. The most common theories are that, named as the first book, 'Jeremiah' is a general reference to the prophets (like calling the Writings 'the Psalms' in Luke 24:44); or that the rabbis often linked texts via common words and created composite quotations of Scripture but referred only to one of the sources by name, either the more obscure (as here) or the more notable one. For more suggestions, see Knowles 1995: 60–67. The purchase of the potter's field may connect with Jer. 32, where Jeremiah buys a field near Jerusalem as a sign action that indicates the people of Israel will be restored to the land after exile. Alternatively, Blomberg (2007: 95–96) believes that Jer. 19 fits better with Matthew's emphasis, with reference to 'the blood of the innocent' (19:4), the 'potter' (19:1, 11; cf. 18:2–3), the renaming of a place in the Valley of Hinnom, which is the traditional location of the Potter's Field (19:6), and coming violent judgment on the city and nation (19:11–15). In any case, 'the thirty pieces of silver, the price set on him by the people of Israel' (Matt. 27:9) is drawn from Zech. 11. Matthew's use is not a promise fulfilment or fulfilment of predictive prophecy, but a typological fulfilment. That is, the same pattern whereby God's people despised and rejected God as their shepherd is repeated when the good shepherd Jesus is betrayed and rejected for thirty pieces of silver. Jesus came to bring forgiveness and grace, to bring favour and unity, and yet he was rejected and betrayed – sold off for silver. The next oracle of Zechariah (chs. 12–14) will reveal that a different shepherd to the shepherds of Zech. 11 will be struck and killed, not because he deserves it, but to bring forgiveness for the sins of his people. This readily connects with Jesus.

How does Jesus shepherd his people today? He is in heaven; we are on earth – how does he do it? Jesus says, 'My sheep listen to my voice; I know them, and they follow me' (John 10:27). Later in John's Gospel, Jesus promises the disciples that when has gone into heaven he will reveal his truth to them by the Holy Spirit, and these same disciples will recall the words of Jesus, which they did and had them written down (John 14:26). Jesus shepherds his people today when they hear the words of the Bible and follow them in the power of the Holy Spirit. This is why the Bible is to be at the heart of church life, in families, small groups and individually. Not just studying the Bible, but obeying it. Especially when it is costly to do so, or goes against what society thinks is 'normal', trusting that what Jesus teaches in all matters is for the good of his people.

The NT uses the shepherd image for church leaders, the 'pastor' (e.g. 1 Peter 5:2–3) (Jobes 2009: 144–145). Pastors are literally 'under-shepherds' – they shepherd under the Good Shepherd, Jesus Christ. Hence central to the pastoral task is teaching the Word of God. This is what guides, protects and feeds God's people. Pastors are not to serve themselves, but the flock. Christians can stagnate and suffer when they choose pastors who will not nourish them by teaching them the Scriptures. To pastors, Peter says they are to

> be shepherds of God's flock that is under your care, watching over them – not because you must, but because you are willing, as God wants you to be; not pursuing dishonest gain, but eager to serve; not lording it over those entrusted to you, but being examples to the flock. And when the Chief Shepherd appears, you will receive the crown of glory that will never fade away. (1 Peter 5:2–4)

ZECHARIAH 12:1–14

Translation

12:1An oracle: the word of the LORD concerning Israel. A declaration of the LORD,
who stretched out the heavens, and founded the earth, and formed the spirit of
man within him: 2'Look, I will make Jerusalem a cup of staggering to all the
surrounding peoples, and it will be against Judah also, in the siege against
Jerusalem. 3And it will be on that day that I will make Jerusalem a burdensome
stone to all the peoples. All who carry it will severely cut themselves, when all
the nations of the earth will be gathered against it [Jerusalem]. 4On that day',
declares the LORD, 'I will strike every horse with confusion, and its rider with
madness. And I will open my eyes upon the house of Judah, and I will strike
every horse of the peoples with blindness. 5And the clans of Judah will say in
their heart, "The inhabitants of Jerusalem are a strength to me, because of the
LORD of hosts, their God." 6On that day I will make the clans of Judah as a pot
of fire in wood, and as a torch of fire in sheaves. And they will consume to the

right and to the left all the surrounding peoples. And Jerusalem will dwell again in its place, in Jerusalem.'

[7]And the Lord will save the tents of Judah first, so that the splendour of the house of David and the splendour of the inhabitants of Jerusalem will not be promoted over Judah. [8]On that day the Lord will defend on behalf of the inhabitants of Jerusalem. And it will be that the one who stumbles among them on that day [will be] like David, and the house of David like God, like the angel of the Lord [going] before them. [9]And it will be on that day that I will seek to destroy all the nations that come against Jerusalem.

[10]And I will pour out upon the house of David and upon the inhabitants of Jerusalem a spirit of grace and supplication, and they will look to me whom they pierced, and they will wail for him, as wailing for the only child and grieve for him as grieving for the firstborn.

[11]On that day the wailing in Jerusalem will become great, as the wailing of Hadad-Rimmon in the plain of Megiddo. [12]And the land will wail, each clan by itself: the clan of the house of David by itself, and their wives by themselves, and the clan of the house of Nathan by itself, and their wives by themselves, [13]the clan of the house of Levi by itself, and their wives by themselves; the clan of the Shimeites by itself, and their wives by themselves. [14]All the remaining clans, each clan by itself, and their wives by themselves.

Notes on the text

12:1. 'An oracle': see 'Comment' on 9:1.

'who': the attrib. ptc. frequently requires a rel. clause in translation (Arnold and Choi 2003: 78–79).

'stretched . . . founded . . . formed': the time/aspect of these participles is determined from context.

'the heavens' and 'the earth' are indefinite in the MT, but must be translated as def. The same phenomenon occurs in Hag. 1:10.

'spirit of man within him' could be translated in a gender inclusive way (e.g. NRSV: 'the human spirit within'), yet this obscures the probable reference to Gen. 2:7, which refers to the first 'man' (*'ādām*), Adam.

2. 'I will make': *'ānōkî*. Following 'Look', the ptc. usually expresses future action (cf. 3:8). It does not necessarily imply imminent future (e.g. 2 Kgs 21:12; Isa. 13:13; Jer. 30:10; 31:8; 32:37; 33:6; 46:27; 50:18; Zeph. 3:19) (C. J. Thomson 2013: 158).

'and it will be against Judah also' is a fairly literal rendering of an ambiguous phrase. LXX and Syr have 'and also against Judah will be a siege'. Tg and Vg have 'and also Judah will be in a siege [against Jerusalem]'. See 'Comment'.

3. 'And it will be . . . that': *wĕhāyâ* (cf. 12:9; 13:2–4, 8).

'carry it': *'ōmsêhā* has the same root as 'burdensome' (*ma'ămāsâ*).

'will severely cut themselves': *śārôṭ yiśśārēṭû*, where the inf. abs. with the impf. is emphatic. The ni. is reflex.

4. 'confusion' and 'madness' have the generic art. (Waltke and O'Connor 1990: 246).

5. 'clans of Judah' (also v. 6). There is some uncertainty whether the phrase *'allupê yĕhûdâ* should be translated 'chiefs', 'rulers' or 'leaders of Judah' (so NIV1984), or whether *'allupê* should be pointed differently and read as 'clans of Judah' (*'alpê*) (so NIV2011, ESV, *BHS* critical apparatus). Several arguments are advanced for translating it as 'leaders'. First, this seems to be how it is understood in other contexts (namely Gen. 36:15; Exod. 15:15; 1 Chr. 1:51) where it refers to the tribal chiefs of Edom (Baron 1918: 296–297, 432). Secondly, LXX and Vg translate it as 'leaders of a thousand' (Meyers and Meyers 1993: 116, 322). Furthermore, some argue from the wider context that these are the leaders 'from him' (understood as Judah) promised in 10:4 (Conrad 1999: 181). There is a possible parallel between the situation in Zech. 12 and that in 10:5 where the leaders trample their foe and shame the riders on horses. Yet there are a number of problems with this. While the translation of *'allupê* in 9:7 is also difficult, the context favours 'clan' (note how the NIV1984 is forced to translate the sg. form into a pl. in 9:7). Furthermore, *'alpê* or *'alpî* elsewhere refers to the clans into which the tribes were subdivided (e.g. Judg. 6:15; 1 Sam. 10:19; 23:23; cf. Isa. 60:22). This meaning makes best sense of the immediate context of Zech. 12, where the people of Judah are numbered for battle. It refers to the same group described as the 'house of Judah' in v. 4, but now with military overtones (cf. Num. 31:4–6; 1 Sam. 2:2). Either *'allupê* can also have this meaning of 'clan' or the consonantal text has been wrongly pointed.

A medieval MS of the HB and Tg have repointed *lî yōšĕbê* (to me inhabitants of) as *lĕyōšĕbê* (to the inhabitants of). MT is followed as the more difficult reading.

'because of': a causal use of the prefixed prep. *bĕ*.

6. 'in its place': *taḥtêhā* (cf. 14:10).

LXX deletes the final phrase 'in Jerusalem'.

7. 'first': lit. 'in the first'.

'inhabitants': *yōšēb* is sg. (also 4Q80). LXX, Tg, Vg, Syr and many medieval Hebr. MSS have 'dwellers' (*yōšĕbê*), as do v. 5 and 13:1. MT is treated as a sg. of class and has been translated pl. This recurs in vv. 8, 10.

'will not be promoted': *lō'-tigdal*. Lit. 'it has not increased' or 'grown' (cf. v. 11).

8. 'inhabitants': see note on v. 7.

10. 'inhabitants': see note on v. 7.

'and supplication': *wĕtaḥănûnîm* is pl. but translated sg. LXX, Tg and Syr translate as 'mercy'.

'the only child': *hayyāḥîd* is more formally 'the only one'. 'Child' is understood from the immediate context and comparative use in Gen. 22:2 and Jer. 6:26.

'and grieve': *wĕhāmēr*. Waltke and O'Connor (1990: 596–597) note that the inf. abs. with waw introduces a separate situation to that of the preceding finite verb, but the verb specifies the person and aspect of the inf.

'for': *'al* in each instance specifies the sphere in which the verb applies or the extent to which the verb occurs (R. J. Williams 2007: 113).

12. 'each clan': *mišpāḥōt mišpāḥōt* is a distrib. construction (Waltke and O'Connor 1990: 116).

'by itself' and 'by themselves' translate *lĕbād*, which occurs only in the sg. (also vv. 13–14).

13. Two medieval Hebr. MSS, Syr and Tg have 'house of Shimei'.

14. 'each clan by itself': see note on v. 12.

Form and structure

Zech. 12 returns to the theme of the final victory Yahweh will win for his people, resulting in the re-establishment of his kingdom and all of its blessings. This unit begins the second oracular section (chs. 12–14), also entitled 'An oracle' (*maśśā'*; cf. 9:1). This second oracle reveals that God's kingdom will not come without great cost. There will be another exile-like experience for Jerusalem, but its outcome will be glorious. The phrase 'on that day' runs through this section. It occurs seven times in ch. 12 (only translated six times in NIV), three times in ch. 13 and seven times in ch. 14. While it does not appear to be a structural marker, it does serve to accelerate the cycle of events and to underline the importance of this future day of battle.

It has been difficult to decide where to break the material for this commentary so that it is manageable, since there is a flow of ideas through chs. 12 and 13. Zech. 12:2–9 depicts a battle where the nations will come against Jerusalem, but God will act to defend and save his people. Zech. 12:10–14 concerns the aftermath of this battle where attention shifts to one who has been pierced, leading to an outpouring of mourning and grief. This then gives way in 13:1 to the cleansing from sin and impurity that will issue for God's people, and then in 13:2–6 to the removal of impurity from the land. Finally, a short but very significant oracle in 13:7–9 speaks of judgment that lies ahead for God's people with his shepherd struck, but it is a judgment that will refine and renew those who emerge. While Butterworth (1992: 216) is probably right to see 13:1 connecting more closely with chapter 12 than chapter 13:2–6, I will break at the end of ch. 12 so that the themes can be readily picked up in the next chapter of this commentary.

Zech. 12:1 is best taken as an introduction to the wider oracle of chs. 12–14. The chapter can be structured thematically as follows:

12:1	**Introduction**
12:2–9	**A siege and salvation**
12:2–4	The assault against Jerusalem repelled by Yahweh
12:5–6	Yahweh acts for Jerusalem through Judah
12:7–8	Yahweh saves and protects
12:9	Summary
12:10–14	**Mourning for the pierced one**

There are many points of contact in the themes of ch. 12 with what has gone before, and what comes after, summarized in the table below.

	Zech. 9	*Zech. 10*	*Zech. 12*	*Zech. 14*
Battle against the nations	9:4–7, 13	10:5	12:2–9	14:1–2, 12–15
Yahweh fights for his people	9:4–7, 14	10:11–12	12:3–4, 6, 9	14:3–5, 12–15
Yahweh protects Jerusalem	9:8		12:3, 8	14:10–11
Future king	9:9–10	10:2, 4	12:10	14:9, 16–17
Yahweh saves his people	9:9, 16	10:6	12:7	14:5, 11
Exiles will return/be gathered	9:11–12	10:8–11		14:11, 16–19

These recurring themes strongly suggest that chs. 9–14 are neither a collection of disparate prophecies nor a chronology of separate events, but are the same broad event (the coming kingdom of God), viewed from different perspectives. In each cycle there is a focus on a different aspect of this final-day battle that will usher in Yahweh's kingdom, but all the time building on and developing what has gone before, rather than negating or modifying it. The oracles of chs. 9 and 12 give the 'big picture' of what will happen on that day, each from a different perspective, with chs. 10–11 focusing on what this day means for the leadership of Yahweh's people, and chs. 13–14 on the cleansing that will come on that day. Therefore, what is envisaged in 12:1–9 is not a further battle to that of chs. 9–11, but another perspective on the ultimate battle that will bring salvation and abundance to Jerusalem and the world. There is also a thematic connection between the ends of chs. 8 and 14, where the nations come to recognize Yahweh as king and seek to worship him.

Comment

12:1. Like 9:1, this section is titled 'An oracle' (*maśśā'*) (cf. 'Comment' on 9:1). This term is best understood as a structural device that introduces 'The word of the LORD' that renews prophecy along the lines of earlier prophecy (Boda 2006: 356). Whereas the oracle in ch. 9 began by indicting cities that circumscribed the Davidic kingdom, this oracle is said to be 'concerning Israel', and begins with Jerusalem (12:2). The use of 'Israel' to refer to God's people (rather than Jerusalem or Judah as in v. 2), gives the oracle an eschatological thrust (Mason 1977: 114–115). Since 'Israel' was historically past, it looks forward to the time when the exiled and scattered people will return to become the people of God once more (cf. 10:6). The ensuing oracle displays the centrality of Judah and Jerusalem to this restoration (Meyers and Meyers 1993: 310). Indeed, 'Jerusalem' is mentioned eleven times in 12:1 – 13:1. It is from Jerusalem that salvation will spread to all the nations and families of the earth (cf. 2:11; 8:23; 9:7; 14:16–19). This pre-empts Zech. 14, where it is from Jerusalem that the entire cosmos will be reshaped. Like the earlier prophets, Zechariah draws on the promises of God that were associated particularly with Jerusalem and the house of David (cf. 2 Sam. 7) to give hope for the future.

The power that guarantees the prophetic word ('A declaration of the LORD') will come to pass is seen in the threefold description of Yahweh as the one 'who stretched out the heavens, and founded the earth, and formed the spirit of man within him' (cf. Gen. 1 – 2; Isa. 42:5; 44:24; 51:13). The 'spirit of man' (*rûaḥ-'ādām*) alludes to the 'spirit' or 'breath' Yahweh breathed into Adam (*'ādām*) at creation (Gen. 2:7). It anticipates a further work of God and 'spirit' (*rûaḥ*) in v. 10. This description of God's creative work implies that the salvation of Jerusalem with the establishment of the kingdom promised to David (cf. ch. 9) is equivalent to a new act of creation. It also contests that Yahweh is the Creator, perhaps over against the Persian god Ahuramazda of whom similar claims are made in Achaemenid royal inscriptions (C. Mitchell 2014).

Yet before Jerusalem is finally vindicated, this chapter also specifies the suffering and sorrow it will have to undergo. Yahweh's creative work is also seen in that he 'will make' Jerusalem a cup of staggering (v. 2), he 'will make' Jerusalem a burdensome stone (v. 3) and 'will make' the clans of Judah as a pot of fire in wood and a torch of fire in sheaves (v. 6). Yahweh's work as Creator demonstrates his power and dominion over all nations of the earth (cf. 14:6–9).

2. 'Look' (*hinnēh*; cf. 14:1) indicates the introduction of information that is new or unexpected (Miller-Naudé and van der Merwe 2011). The one who made the heavens and earth 'will make Jerusalem a cup of staggering to all the surrounding peoples', that is, to those who have laid siege to Jerusalem (12:2b). The 'cup of staggering' does not use the usual word for 'cup' (*kôs*), but the word *sap* that elsewhere means 'bowl', 'basin' (e.g. 1 Kgs 7:50; Jer. 52:19) or 'threshold' (but this does not readily suit the context). In Isaiah 51:17, 22, the 'cup that made you stagger' is used in parallel with 'cup of his [God's] wrath' (using *kôs* in both instances) and refers to the destruction of Jerusalem by the Babylonians in 586 BC. The 'staggering' indicates that people who drink from the vessel will be put off balance or stagger as if drunk (cf. Jer. 25:15–31). Whereas in Isaiah Jerusalem drank the cup of staggering and the cup of God's wrath, now

Jerusalem itself will be the agent of God's judgment against those who come against it, causing them to stagger.

The phrase 'and it will be against Judah also, in the siege against Jerusalem' is difficult. Some scholars (and translations) believe that the reference to Judah simply specifies a little more broadly whom the siege is against (e.g. NIV, ESV), or that Judah is caught up in the siege against Jerusalem, but does not oppose it. For instance, Nogalski (2011: 946) argues that in the larger context of the book, Judah and Jerusalem are not in conflict, and so it is inappropriate to interpret Zech. 12:2 otherwise. An alternative interpretation is that Judah is initially caught up with the nations in the siege against Jerusalem and opposes it, but then turns to support it (Baldwin 1972: 189). In this case, the verse says, 'it [the cup of staggering] will be against Judah also [i.e. Judah will also be knocked off balance because, like the nations, Judah has opposed Jerusalem]'. There are a number of reasons to prefer this interpretation. First, it explains why v. 4, where Yahweh strikes those who come against Jerusalem, says he will discriminate in favour of Judah. Secondly, it explains what seems to be a change of heart on the part of the clans of Judah in v. 5, when they see Yahweh protecting Jerusalem and then turn against the surrounding peoples. Thirdly, it is difficult to envision a 'siege' against the region of Judah since it is normally cities that are besieged. Note also the reference to Judah's fighting at Jerusalem in Zech. 14:14.

3–4. The phrase 'on that day' recurs throughout this section (see 'Form and structure'). It refers to the day when God will establish his kingdom on earth in glory. On this day, when all the nations of the earth gather against Jerusalem, Yahweh will ensure her victory. Jerusalem has already been pictured as a 'cup of staggering'. To this further repulsive measures are added. First, Jerusalem will be a 'burdensome stone'. The exact nature of this stone is elusive – it is simply described as 'burdensome' or 'heavy' (*ma'ămāsâ*; cf. 'oracle' [*maśśā'*] in v. 1). One thinks of a stone that might be dropped over the side of a city wall on an invading army, yet the effect of this stone is that 'All who carry it will severely cut themselves'. Elsewhere 'cut' refers to the incisions of pagan worship (Lev. 21:5; 1 Kgs 18:28), but it does not seem to have any worship connotations here, though it may indicate self-inflicted injury. The summary statement 'all the nations of the earth will be gathered against it' reiterates the situation introduced in v. 2. This is a tumultuous day for Jerusalem.

God will continue to defend Jerusalem with the horses that come against it being struck with confusion and blindness, and their riders with madness (v. 4). Cantrell (2011: 27) notes that horses were pivotal in battle, and ancient battle strategies often included plans to try to panic the enemies' horses. There is an interesting reuse of Deut. 28:28 in this description, where a covenant curse against Israel is turned against their enemies (Person 1993: 130). Yahweh will create chaos and mayhem among all who come against Jerusalem. However, for the sake of the house of Judah,

Yahweh promises to keep his eyes open, presumably so that the house of Judah, which was initially caught up with the nations in their attack on Jerusalem, will not be harmed as God acts to deliver Jerusalem.

5–6. The 'clans of Judah' (see 'Notes on the text'), situated outside Jerusalem, recognize the hand of Yahweh in the ensuing disarray (cf. v. 4) and say in their hearts, 'The inhabitants of Jerusalem are a strength to me, because of the LORD of hosts, their God.' In effect, when they see God defending Jerusalem and protecting them, they have a change of heart.

The 'clan' refers to a unit smaller than a 'tribe' and larger than a 'family'. A 'family' could comprise up to three generations of a living ancestor. The 'clan' would be a larger group defined by kinship and territory with obligations to assist one another. The usual word translated 'clan' is *mišpāḥâ* (as is used in vv. 12–14 and 14:17–18). The term *'alpê* seems to refer to the same unit, but with military connotations (cf. Mic. 5:2[1]).

The initiative of Yahweh in the battle continues with the clans of Judah becoming his agents in the destruction of all the surrounding people, in spectacular fashion, with twin analogies that speak of a spreading destructive presence: 'a pot of fire in wood' and 'a torch of fire in sheaves'. The clans of Judah will destroy the nations that surround them who have come against Jerusalem (cf. 9:15). The statement that 'Jerusalem will dwell again in its place, in Jerusalem' (cf. 14:10) implies that the inhabitants were cut off from the city in this battle. This is rather cryptic at this point, especially given the victory Yahweh has just assured his people. However, chs. 13–14 will reveal that victory will not come without a heavy toll on the inhabitants of Jerusalem, and this expression gives a glimpse of that (cf. 14:2, 11).

7–9. The outcome of God's actions is spoken of in terms of salvation. There is a clear parallel with earlier material where Yahweh's salvation also flows directly from the military victory he is said to give to his people (9:9, 16; 10:6, 8). There is not a strict battle chronology in vv. 7–8, but different perspectives on the activities and outcomes of 'that day': v. 7 speaks of the salvation that will be granted first to Judah; v. 8 speaks of the protection that will be given the inhabitants of Jerusalem (cf. 12:3, 5); and v. 9 is a summary of vv. 2–8, forming an inclusio with vv. 2–3 with the reference to the nations.

With this salvation, God is concerned that the tents of Judah should not miss out on the splendour (or 'fame') that the house of David and the inhabitants of Jerusalem will experience. The 'tents of Judah' is probably a reference to the dwellings of soldiers in the field (cf. 1 Sam. 17:54; 2 Sam. 20:22) since this suits the battle context here. The 'house of David' is mentioned five times in 12:7 – 13:1. While there was no Davidic king in the post-exilic period, the hope of the earlier prophets and in Zechariah was for a king from the line of David who would be central to Yahweh's restoration purposes (e.g. Isa. 9:6–7; 11:1–10; 16:5; Jer. 23:3–6; 33:14–22; Ezek. 37:21–25; Hos. 3:5; Mic. 4:8 – 5:5[4:9 – 5:6]; Amos 9:11–15; cf. Zech. 3:8; 6:12). This verse presupposes that the descendants of David were a viable political force (Nogalski 2011: 949). It also 'assumes that Davidic rule will be part of the eschatological scheme' (Meyers and Meyers 1993: 331).

This day of salvation will be a splendid one for the house of David and the inhabitants of Jerusalem, and, in order that the tents of Judah are not neglected in what will be a famous day for Jerusalem, they are given salvation first. The statement of v. 7 is probably on account of the earlier participation of Judah in the siege against Jerusalem (v. 2). Not only will all the people of Yahweh be caught up in the splendour of this salvation, but all will be of equal standing before God (Merrill 1994: 316).

Another perspective is provided on 'that day' in v. 8, where Yahweh promises to defend the inhabitants of Jerusalem, with the result that 'the one who stumbles among them on that day [will be] like David'. This most naturally alludes to the might of David, who on many occasions saved Israel by defeating its enemies, not least the mighty Goliath, by which he began his career with renown (cf. 1 Sam. 17). Yet David's deliverance was given to him by Yahweh (cf. 1 Sam. 17:33–37), and the weak of the inhabitants of Jerusalem will also be saved like David, namely through Yahweh's power (cf. the 'salvation' of the king in 9:9 and 'Not by might, and not by power, but by my Spirit' in 4:6).

Even greater is the promise that 'the house of David' will be 'like God, like the angel of the Lord [going] before them'. This is best understood in functional terms, particularly given the complementary description 'like the angel of the Lord'. While some suggest that this complementary description is an insertion by a later scribe who sought to protect the sanctity of Yahweh in this text, there is much in the background of this description that makes sense in this context. First, it was the 'angel of the Lord' who was responsible for leading Yahweh's people on many occasions and providing protection, particularly in the exodus (e.g. 13:21; 14:19; 33:2). Secondly, David himself was likened to the 'angel of God', which enabled him to judge for his people between what was good and evil (e.g. 2 Sam. 14:17, 20; 19:27; cf. 1 Sam. 29:9). Therefore, the addition of 'like the angel of the Lord' more closely defines the way in which the house of David will be like Yahweh – the house of David will once again lead and protect Yahweh's people like Yahweh himself (Webb 2003: 159). This verse continues to hold out high hope for the house of David (contra Rose 2012).

V. 9 serves as a summary of vv. 2–8. The future destruction of nations hostile to Jerusalem is a theme that runs through the book of Zechariah (1:15; 2:6[10]; 6:8; 9:1–8, 13–15; 10:5, 7, 11; 11:1–3; 14:1–3, 12–15, 17–19).

10. There is a continued focus on David and the house of David in 12:10–14. Since the house of David and the inhabitants of Jerusalem are still in view, and because the reference to someone being 'pierced' suggests the aftermath of a battle, this section should be read in close connection with 12:1–9. Victory now gives way to bitter mourning as the house of David and the inhabitants of Jerusalem look to one they have pierced, presumably in the battle itself. They will look and mourn ('wail' and 'grieve') as the result of Yahweh's pouring out 'a spirit of grace and supplication'. The reference to 'a spirit' (*rûaḥ*) could simply refer to a disposition Yahweh gives his people. Yet given the background of Isaiah, Ezekiel and Joel, who all associate the sending of Yahweh's Spirit on the day his kingdom comes (e.g. Isa. 32:15; Ezek. 39:29; Joel 2:28–32), it is attractive to see God's Spirit at work here. In this case, 'grace and supplication' are produced in the people of God by the work of his Spirit (Meyer 1972: 80–82). Mason (2003: 159–160) recalls that in ch. 4, the completion of the temple by Zerubbabel was a mark of Yahweh's power at work by his Spirit (v. 6), and similarly resulted in cries of 'grace' (v. 7).

In either case, it is a work of God that changes the disposition of the people so that they look upon the one they pierced and mourn for him as one mourns for an only child, and grieve as one grieves the death of a firstborn, expressions that convey the depth of anguish and sorrow on this occasion (cf. Jer. 6:26; Amos 8:10). While not explicit, the implication is that those who have pierced this figure have offended Yahweh, and that they are deserving of his judgment. Yet Yahweh in his grace has restored relationship and moved them to grieve because of their sin and to supplicate him (i.e. 'pray for mercy').

A key question concerns the identity of the one who has been pierced. Meyers and Meyers (1993: 337) comment that this is 'surely one of the major interpretative cruxes in Second Zechariah, if not all of prophecy'. Before directly addressing this question, there are a couple of further exegetical points to deal with. The first is the expression 'look to me'. Since Yahweh is the speaker, the suff. identifies him as the one who is pierced. Because it seems incongruous to speak of Yahweh's being pierced, many scholars doubt the integrity of the MT and emend it to fit with the third-person reference concerning the one for whom they mourn, mentioned in the next phrase ('and they will wail for him'). The resulting translations are represented by the NRSV: 'when they look upon the one whom they have pierced, they shall mourn for him'. However, there is overwhelming support in the versions for the MT (see 'Notes on the text') (Meyers and Meyers 1993: 337).

Meyers and Meyers (1993: 338) establish that the root *dqr* means 'to stab, pierce, wound' with a thrusting weapon (e.g. Lam. 4:9; Isa. 13:15; 1 Sam. 31:4 = 1 Chr. 10:4). They point out that this does not necessarily mean that the one stabbed died (e.g. Jer. 37:10; 51:4), but this would usually be expected. In the case of the one pierced here, it is almost certain that death ensued, given the subsequent reference to mourning and cleansing. Yet if it refers only to the piercing of God, this seems inappropriate – how can God be killed? Delcor (1951: 193–195) cites two instances where being pierced by the sword is used in a metaphorical way (Lam. 4:9; Prov. 12:18), but there seems to be more going on here.

Who then is the one who is pierced? If this passage is read in isolation, it is not clear who is meant and a myriad of suggestions have been made

(Petterson 2009: 227–231). Yet if this passage is read in the light of the unfolding themes of the book, not just chs. 9–14 as Redditt (2012: 108–109) does, then the interplay of the themes of the coming Shoot, king and shepherd strongly suggest that the one who is pierced is to be associated with the coming Davidic king, especially given the focus on the house of David in the immediate context. Ch. 3 established that with the coming of Shoot, the iniquity of the land would be removed in a single day (3:8–9). The same cleansing from sin is envisaged here in connection with the one pierced (13:1). Ch. 6 identified Shoot as a priest who would rebuild the temple and thereby re-establish Yahweh's rule in Jerusalem (6:13). Here the salvation and restoration of Jerusalem along with the people's forgiveness are key parallel themes that connect with the pierced one. In 9:9 and 10:4, the future Davidic king is central to the salvation of Jerusalem, Judah and Ephraim. Similarly, the salvation of Judah, Jerusalem and Israel is connected with the pierced one in ch. 12. Perhaps the strongest line of identification comes from 13:7, where the shepherd, who will be shown to be the coming Davidic king, is struck by the sword. This naturally connects back with the pierced one in this passage. The death of the royal figure in 13:7 has tragic consequences for the flock, and this seems an appropriate cause for the intense mourning of 12:10–14, particularly if the description is patterned on the death of the Davidic king Josiah (see below). The great irony is that the death of the king comes at the hands of his own people ('whom they pierced'). But this in itself is not surprising given the history of the people in rejecting Yahweh as their shepherd, as enacted in 11:4–14.

Furthermore, the association of the pierced one with the future Davidic king provides a reasonable explanation for the abrupt shift in v. 10 from the first to third person in reference to the pierced one. Kingship in Israel, rightly understood, saw the king as Yahweh's agent on earth (e.g. Ps. 72). Given this representative function, to pierce the king is also to pierce Yahweh (Bruce 1969: 112). Identifying the pierced one as the future Davidic king allows the Hebr. text to be explained without emendation (Keil 1949: 388). The absence of an explicit reference to the Davidic king can be explained if, in the bringing of this salvation, the king was pierced and killed by his own countrymen, even members of his own house. This is such an unspeakable act that it is described in the way it is, namely as piercing Yahweh. The question remains, why is the king pierced? This becomes clearer in ch. 13.

11. The mourning that the piercing occasions is likened to the mourning of Hadad-Rimmon in the plain of Megiddo. Hadad was the Syrian storm god, otherwise called Baal, and Rimmon was also a deity (cf. 2 Kgs 5:18). Many scholars argue that this therefore refers to a pagan mourning ritual (Maier 1992: 13). However, others consider that the reference here is geographical and that Hadad-Rimmon refers to a place on the plain of Megiddo (Meyers and Meyers 1993: 343–344). One of the difficulties is that there is no place otherwise known as Hadad-Rimmon. However, there are greater problems with its referring to a cult-mourning ritual. Merrill (1994: 324) rightly says, 'the fact that deep sorrow for sin in Judah should be compared to the lament of pagans over a catastrophe that had befallen one of their mystic deities seems most unlikely'. Petersen (1995: 122) believes that the connection with Josiah 'seems more consistent within the overall unit – namely an important lamentation that lasts a long time after the event it commemorates'.

Furthermore, the Hebr. construction is not wailing 'for' (*lĕ*) Hadad-Rimmon, but wailing 'of' Hadad-Rimmon (a gen. construction). Additional support for the view that Hadad-Rimmon is a place is the fact that Rimmon is a place name in various passages and is associated with different regions (e.g. Josh. 15:32; 19:7; 19:13; Judg. 20:45, 47; 21:13; 1 Chr. 4:32). Zech. 14:10 refers to a Rimmon south of Jerusalem. It seems likely that since there was more than one Rimmon, 'Hadad' functions to identify it further. Hence the statement could be a way of saying that on this day the whole of the land will mourn, not only Jerusalem, but also the outlying regions such as Hadad-Rimmon. Just as the tents of Judah have been saved along with the inhabitants of Jerusalem (v. 7), so the mourning in the regions such as Hadad-Rimmon in the plain of Megiddo will be as great as in Jerusalem.

It is also likely that this location is intended to bring to mind the death of Josiah. 2 Kgs 23:29 states that King Josiah was killed at Megiddo by Pharaoh Neco. The mourning on that day is described in 2 Chr. 35:24–25 (cf. *Tg. Zech.* 12.11). In this case, v. 10 provides a description of the death of the future Davidic king patterned on the death of Josiah at Megiddo. Both were pierced and the people mourn both (Laato 1992: 293).

12–14. The mourning in the land is described in some detail with a pattern repeated for the house of David, the house of Nathan, the house of Levi, the Shimeites and all who are left. Who or what is meant by 'the land' (*hā'āreṣ*)? In the rest of the book of Zechariah, 'the land' refers either to the whole earth (e.g. 1:10–11; 4:14; 6:5; 12:1, 3; 14:9) or perhaps to the land of Judah (e.g. 7:14; 11:6; 13:2, 8; 14:10), but is never limited to Jerusalem. Given that it is the 'clans' (*mišpāḥôt*) of Israel that are in view (see 'Comment' on v. 5), the claim seems to be that not only Jerusalem but the whole nation will mourn (v. 12). Ollenburger (1996: 828) contends that the extent of the mourning in vv. 12–14 also supports the suggestion that the victim is of royal status.

The names that are mentioned (David, Nathan, Levi and Shimei) seem significant, yet their significance remains elusive. Larkin (1994: 277) argues that David, Nathan, Levi and Shimei represent the offices of king, prophet, priest and sage respectively. Yet it is difficult to see how Shimei could be understood as a sage (cf. 2 Sam. 16:5–14).

Ulrich (2010) proposes that these figures represent the sordid events surrounding David's death and Solomon's accession to the throne – a time when everyone sought their own interests. In this case, Nathan is David's prophet and Shimei is the descendant of Saul who cursed David, and is eventually struck dead by one of Solomon's officers at his command (1 Kgs 2:46). Ulrich takes these names to represent a period of division in the nation as a result of failed leadership: 'Zechariah traces the root of the current problem back to Solomon's accession' (259). As attractive as this proposal is, it does not explain the presence of 'Levi'.

The most popular interpretation takes David and Levi to be the heads of the royal and priestly families respectively (Meyers and Meyers 1993: 348). Nathan is taken to be David's son (2 Sam. 5:14; 1 Chr. 3:4) and Shimei is Levi's grandson (Exod. 6:17; Num. 3:21; 1 Chr. 6:17), thereby representing subsidiary members of these respective families. The difficulty with this interpretation, which Ulrich (2010: 253) identifies, is knowing why Nathan and Shimei are mentioned, since they are otherwise obscure members of these families and not at all readily identified. Why not mention Solomon and Aaron, particularly given their sins? Yet they may be significant from a genealogical point of view. There is evidence from the NT with Luke's genealogy (Luke 3:31) that after the exile, royal descent was traced through Nathan, rather than through Solomon (Chary 1969: 205). The same may have been true for Shimei and the promise associated with the Levites (cf. Jer. 33:20–22; Mal. 2:8), though admittedly there is no evidence elsewhere for this. The mourning of the royal and priestly lines connects temple and throne and is consistent with the royal ideology.

Baldwin (1972: 194) argues that the repetition of 'each clan by itself . . . and their wives by themselves' stresses that the repentance is genuine: 'None is merely being influenced by the tears of others, nor acting hypocritically, as the professional mourners did.' J. M. O'Brien (2004: 266) helpfully observes a literary connection with Jer. 44:9, which speaks of the sins of the kings of Judah and their wives, and the people of Judah and Jerusalem and their wives. If this verse is in the background, it indicates that the women were 'equally responsible for the need for mourning'. Alternatively, Meyers and Meyers (1993: 346) suggest mentioning the wives may simply be a way of further emphasizing the extent of the mourning, as women were often associated with mourning rituals in the ANE (e.g. Jer. 9:17–26[9:16–25]; Ezek. 32:16; 2 Chr. 35:25).

Explanation

After the sign actions of ch. 11, which portray God's rejection of his people for their rejection of him, chs. 12–14 reveal again that God's ultimate purpose for his people is salvation, forgiveness, cleansing and worship. Yet the path to this outcome is not without cost to God's people, God's representative and God himself. Ch. 12 pictures a future 'day' when the nations will lay siege to Jerusalem, a siege in which those from the surrounding territory of Judah will also be caught up (v. 2). Yet, unlike the Babylonian siege in 586 BC, God will act to repel the nations and restore Jerusalem to its rightful place. He will cause those who come against Jerusalem to stagger (v. 2) and cut themselves (v. 3), and he will confuse their cavalry (v. 4). When the clans of Judah see God defending Jerusalem, they will turn against the invading people and destroy them as fire (vv. 5–6). In this way, God will save the people of Judah and the inhabitants of Jerusalem and give them the same status (v. 7), and the house of David will resume its position of leadership (v. 8). Nations who come against Jerusalem will be destroyed (v. 9).

When is the 'day' Zechariah looks forward to? When is the day when Jerusalem will go through another exile-like experience and be delivered? Many, particularly those of a dispensational tradition, have understood chs. 12–14 to be all about the events at the end of this age. My problem with this is that it neglects the primary way in which the NT understands this day, for the NT first and foremost identifies this 'day' with the crucifixion of the Messiah Jesus, and secondarily with his return. Conceptually, the OT prophets looked forward to a 'day' when God's kingdom would come. The NT expands this 'day' to encompass both the first and second comings of Jesus – in some ways the 'day' also becomes the period of time in between. Over the coming chapters I will attempt to trace the way in which the NT applies the imagery of chs. 12–14 to both 'comings' of the Messiah.

The clearest point of NT application of this passage is also the most controversial among OT scholars. As noted in the 'Comment', the identity of the pierced one in v. 10 is debated, with options including Zerubbabel, the prophet Jeremiah, Onias III or 'the true prophets of Yahweh' (see further Petterson 2009: 225–231). However, if this passage is read in the light of the unfolding themes of the book, and the elements in the immediate context that highlight the house of David are given weight (i.e. mentioning the 'house of David' or 'David' five times; the Hebr. pronouns closely connect Yahweh with the pierced one; the comparison with the mourning for King Josiah in Megiddo), then it is natural to identify the pierced one as the future Davidic king of prophetic expectation (the 'Messiah') (Duguid 1995: 276). The NT makes this identity in John 19:37 when one of the soldiers pierced the crucified Jesus' side with a spear, and in Rev. 1:7, where Jesus is referred to as having been pierced. Some argue that this messianic identity has been read back into Zechariah (Sweeney 2000b: 689). It is my contention that John has read it out of Zechariah and this will become even clearer in Zech. 13:7–9. It is surely significant that a number of Jewish rabbis also interpret this verse in terms of a pierced Messiah, though it is a second Messiah, ben Joseph/Ephraim, who is killed, rather than the triumphant Messiah ben David (Gordon 2003: 184–195). This indicates that there is an interpretative tradition outside the NT that identifies the pierced one as a future king (even if this king is not identified as Jesus). The great irony is that the death of the hoped for Davidic king comes at the hands of his own people. Yet this should not be surprising given the history of the people in rejecting Yahweh as their shepherd (as enacted in 11:4–17). The reason for the king's death is not explicit, and I will return to this in the next chapter.

What of the future battle at Jerusalem depicted here and in ch. 14? In the 'Explanation' of 2:1–13[5–17], I argue that the promises concerning Jerusalem and the temple are greatly expanded in Jesus' first coming. All that the temple and city represent (God's presence, rule, protection and blessing) are fulfilled in him. What of an attack on Jerusalem? My argument here is a little speculative, but I think it is also important to connect this battle in the first instance with Jesus' death. There are several points of connection between ch. 12 and the believers' account of Jesus' crucifixion in Acts 4. In Luke's account, the believers quote Ps. 2, which mentions the raging of the Gentiles and the 'peoples' (Jews?) against the Lord and his Messiah. This is seen to be fulfilled with the plotting of Herod and Pontius Pilate along with the Gentiles and the people of Israel 'against your holy servant Jesus, whom you anointed' (Acts 4:27). While Zech. 12 is not quoted in Acts 4, there are clear thematic parallels with the nations and God's people gathering against God and his anointed 'in this city', namely Jerusalem (Acts 4:27), which is also prominent in Ps. 2. This gathering against the Messiah in Jerusalem proved to be the day of salvation for God's people, even though it involved the Messiah's death. A further parallel with 12:10 can be seen in Acts, where, after Jesus' death, God's Spirit is poured out on the around 120 believers in Jerusalem, and God-fearing Jews are then 'cut to the heart' and repent (Acts 2:32–37). Hence the NT connects this 'day' with Jesus' death. Jesus ends up drinking the cup of God's wrath (Luke 22:42), so that God's people from Israel and the nations do not have to. Boda (2004: 500) rightly comments, 'God's rescue of Jerusalem and defeat of the nations was already accomplished prior to AD 70. Although unknown to the Jews and Gentiles at the time, Christ's death on the cross was God's means of delivering Jerusalem.' Yet, the NT also connects the 'day' with Jesus' return, when all the nations will mourn the one who was pierced (e.g. Rev. 1:7). Indeed, the nations continue to rage against God and his Messiah to the present, and so the 'day' to some extent encompasses the period between Jesus' two comings also.

The events of ch. 12 are also alluded to in Matt. 24:30, 'Then will appear the sign of the Son of Man in heaven. And then all the peoples [lit. 'tribes'] of the earth will mourn', and Luke 21:20, 'When you see Jerusalem being surrounded by armies, you will know that its desolation is near.' While it is common to interpret these solely in relation to Jesus' second coming, I think Jesus is drawing on the 'apocalyptic' imagery of the OT surrounding the coming 'day' and applying it in the first place to his death. Note for instance, how Matthew reports many of the apocalyptic signs as taking place at the crucifixion (Matt. 27:45, 51–55). This also offers the most straightforward explanation of Jesus' statement that 'this generation will certainly not pass away until all these things have happened' (Matt. 24:34; Luke 21:32).

In Rev. 16, there is a battle at 'Armageddon', which in Hebr. means 'Mount of Megiddo', where Megiddo is the location mentioned in Zech. 12:11 (cf. 2 Kgs 23; Judg. 5:19). Yet no armies are mentioned in Revelation. It is not nation battling against nation – it is kings coming to do battle against God. In Rev. 16:17, the cry goes up, 'It is done!' (cf. John 19:30), and there is thunder, lightning and a severe earthquake. This brings to mind the earthquake that split the curtain of the temple in two at Jesus' death. If this is connected with the end of Rev. 15, it means that the judgment that fell on Jesus in his death on the cross opens the temple so that people can enter God's presence. From this perspective, Armageddon has already taken place.

The battle at 'Armageddon' is first and foremost the death of Jesus – but it is not limited to Jesus' death. It is a battle that continues. 'Armageddon' is every conquest of the gospel as it shines into a darkened world. And Armageddon is the final putting down of Satan at Jesus' return – but they are minor skirmishes compared to the battle that has been won at the cross.

In terms of Zechariah's themes, this passage returns to the earlier theme of repentance. Repentance is portrayed as a work of God by his Spirit as he graciously moves his people (individually and corporately) to pray for mercy and to grieve the death of the Messiah and (implicitly) their sins that led to it (12:10–14). The repentance that the first half of the book calls for (1:3–6; 7:3) is shown to be ultimately a work of God by his Spirit, poured out as a result of the Messiah's death. Similarly, in the NT the gospel is a call to repentance (e.g. Acts 2:38; 3:19) and true repentance can come only from the rebirth and regeneration of God's Spirit (cf. Titus 3:4–7). Repentance not only marks the beginning of the Christian life, but the continued daily experience of turning to the Lord and being transformed from one degree of glory to another (2 Cor. 3:18), while waiting for Jesus' return and the full consummation of his kingdom.

ZECHARIAH 13:1–9

Translation

13:1On that day there will be a fountain opened for the house of David and for the inhabitants of Jerusalem for sin and for impurity. 2'And it will be on that day', declares the LORD of hosts, 'that I will cut off the names of the idols from the land, and they will not be remembered again. Furthermore, the prophets and the unclean spirit I will remove from the land. 3And it will be that if a man ever prophesies, his father and his mother who bore him shall say to him, "You shall not live, for you have spoken a lie in the name of the LORD." And his father and his mother who bore him shall pierce him through when he prophesies. [4]And it will be on that day that the prophets will be ashamed, each one because of his vision when he prophesies. And they will not put on a hairy cloak in order to deceive. [5]And he will say, "I am not a prophet. I am a man working the land, for a man owned me from my youth." [6]And he will say to him, "What are these wounds between your hands?" He will say, "Because I was struck in the house of the ones who love me."

[7]'Awake, sword, against my shepherd, namely against the man [who is] my associate,' declares the LORD of hosts. 'Strike the shepherd and let the sheep scatter. I will turn my hand against the little ones. [8]And it will be that in all the land', declares the LORD, 'two parts in it will be cut off and perish, but the third [part] will remain in it. [9]And I will put the third [part] into the fire, and I will refine them as refining the silver, and prove them as proving the gold. They will call on my name, and I will answer them. I will say, "They are my people," and they will say, "The LORD is our God."'

Notes on the text

13:1. 'for sin and for impurity': *lĕ* functions as a dat. of advantage (Holladay 1988: 168). This phrase is absent from LXX.

2. 'And it will be . . . that': *wĕhāyâ* (cf. 12:3, 9; 13:3–4, 8).

'declares the LORD' translates the noun phrase *nĕ'um yhwh* ('oracle' or 'utterance' of the LORD').

'Furthermore': *wĕgam*. Lit. 'and also'.

'the prophets': LXX is 'the false prophets' (*tous pseudoprophētas*). So too, Tg and Syr.

3. 'ever': *'ôd*.

'when he prophesies': *bĕhinnāb'ô*. The prep. *bĕ* with the inf. connotes action that is simultaneous with the finite verb (Arnold and Choi 2003: 69).

4. 'when he prophesies': *bĕhinnāb'ōtô* has an unexpected suff. One would expect the same form as v. 3, as indicated in *BHS*.

5. 'a man owned me':*'ādām hiqnanî* has a suggested emendation in *BHS* to *'ădāmāh qinānî*, which has been followed by many translations (e.g. NRSV: 'the land has been my possession'). I have tried to follow MT, reading *hiqnanî* as a hiph. qatal of *qānâ* (to buy [as a slave]) (Clines 2010c: 267).

6. 'Because': *'ăšer* is unusual here. It seems to introduce a reason for the wounds (a causal clause) (R. J. Williams 2007: 166). There is a similar instance in 11:5. Alternatively, it could be the rel. pr. referring to the wounds, but the Hebr. and resulting translation is awkward ('[the wounds] I was struck').

'in the house of the ones who love me': *bêt mĕ'ahăbāy*. Lit. 'a house of my lovers' or 'my loving house'. The prep. 'in' (*bĕ*) seems to have dropped out through haplography. See 'Comment'.

7. Some LXX MSS have *patazō* (I will strike), which is followed in Matt. 26:31. *BHS* suggests reading *hakēh 'akeh* (I will surely strike). MT is followed as the more difficult reading.

'namely': waw is explicative or epexegetical since there is only one figure in view (R. J. Williams 2007: 154).

'and let the sheep scatter': *ûtĕpûṣênā haṣṣō'n* contains a juss. with an irregular 3 f. pl. ending (*nā* instead of *nâ*).

8. The first 'in it' is omitted in the LXX.

'and perish' is in apposition in MT and Tg. The conj. is present in LXX, Vg and Syr. Gelston (2010: 147) comments that it is difficult to decide whether the *Vorlage* contained a waw, which was lost in the MT by haplography after the previous word.

9. 'I will say': *'āmartî*. The context suggests that a waw has been lost by haplography, which, if present, would convert the pf. Furthermore, LXX and Syr translate with a future tense (Gelston 2010: 147).

The 3 pl. pronouns in the second sentence ('they'/'them') are m. sg. ('he'/'it') in the MT. They refer to the group as a singular entity (cf. 'sheep' or 'remnant'). The final 'our God' (lit. 'my God') has been adjusted accordingly.

Form and structure

There is a flow of ideas through chs. 12 and 13. In ch. 12, there is an eschatological battle where the nations come against Jerusalem, but God acts to defend and save his people (12:1–9). In the aftermath of this battle (12:10–14), attention shifts to one who has been pierced, leading to an outpouring of mourning and grief. This then gives way in 13:1 to cleansing from sin and impurity that will issue for the house of David and the inhabitants of Jerusalem, and then to an oracle concerning the removal of idolatry, false prophecy and the unclean spirit from the land, particularly focusing on the removal of false prophets (vv. 2–6).

The short poetic oracle of 13:7–9 is of far greater significance than its size would suggest. It is marked as a new discourse unit by the vocative noun and imper. verb with which it begins ('Awake, sword') (Clark and Hatton 2002: 334), yet it draws together a number of earlier themes, and attempts to relocate it to the end of ch. 11 (e.g. NEB) are misguided. It contains the final 'shepherd' reference in Zechariah, and brings together the various strands concerning leadership that have been woven through the book of Zechariah to this point. It continues from ch. 13 the theme of the cleansing of the land and also speaks about adversity that lies ahead for Yahweh's people with another exile-like experience. With Yahweh's shepherd struck, there is a judgment of the people that results in great loss, but it is a judgment that will refine and renew those who survive. This oracle effectively captures key themes in what precedes, and functions as a transition into ch. 14 by bringing into clearer perspective another feature of the eschatological battle, namely that it will be won at great cost to God's people.

Many ideas from Ezekiel's vision of the future (Ezek. 36:16–38) are echoed throughout 12:10 – 13:9 (Larkin 1994: 169; Mason 2003: 163), in particular cleansing with water from uncleanness and idolatry (Ezek. 36:18, 25; cf. Zech. 13:1–2); being given Yahweh's Spirit (vv. 26–27; cf. Zech. 12:10); having covenant relationship restored so that 'you will be my people, and I will be your God' (Ezek. 36:28; cf. Zech. 13:9); loathing past sin (Ezek. 36:31–32; cf. Zech. 12:10–14); restoring the 'flock' of God's people (Ezek. 36:37–38; Zech. 13:7–9); and restoring the holiness of God's 'name' (Ezek. 36:20–23; Zech. 13:2, 9). Significantly, in Ezek. 37:24, 26–28, a future king is central to this restoration:

> My servant David will be king over them, and they will all have one shepherd . . . I will make a covenant of peace with them; it will be an everlasting covenant. I will establish them and increase their numbers, and I will put my sanctuary among them for ever. My dwelling-place will be with them; I will be their God, and they will be my people. Then the nations will know that I the LORD make Israel holy, when my sanctuary is among them for ever.

The unit can be structured thematically as follows:

13:1–6	**Forgiveness and cleansing**
13:1	A fountain opened
13:2–6	The removal of idolatry, false prophets and the spirit of impurity from the land
13:7–9	**The shepherd and restored relationship**
13:7	Strike the shepherd
13:8–9a	The people refined
13:9b	Covenant relationship restored

Comment

13:1. The phrase 'On that day' connects this unit with ch. 12 (see 'Comment' on 12:3). The scene at the end of ch. 12 of the whole community's mourning for the pierced one dramatically shifts in 13:1 to one of hope, with a fountain opened, presumably in Jerusalem, for the cleansing of those who pierced him. A 'fountain' or 'spring' suggests an abundant supply of water (cf. Ps. 36:9[10]; Jer. 2:13). It anticipates the 'living water' that will flow out from Jerusalem in 14:8 (cf. Ezek. 47). The Hebr. construction of the verb 'there will be' (*yihyê*) with the ni. 'opened' indicates not a single act of opening, but that the fountain will remain continuously open

(Clark and Hatton 2002: 326). The fountain is said to be 'for the house of David and for the inhabitants of Jerusalem for sin and for impurity' (cf. 12:10). The two words 'sin' (*ḥaṭṭāʾt*) and 'impurity' (*niddâ*) are closely related but different concepts in the priestly system. 'Sin' is moral wrong-doing against another person or Yahweh. It can be unintentional (e.g. manslaughter) or intentional (e.g. murder). 'Impurity' is a state that often results from amoral causes (e.g. childbirth or bodily emissions), but can also be caused by unintentional sins (e.g. Lev. 5:2–3) and intentional sins (e.g. Lev. 20:2–5). 'Impurity' can be graded according to the extent of the pollution (whether or not it defiles the sanctuary), whether it is communicable and the means of cleansing (sacrifice is required only for major impurity). Sklar (2005: 157) observes that while 'sin' and 'impurity' may have different starting points, the end point is the same for major impurity and unintentional sin as both require 'atonement' (*kipper*) (i.e. ransoming and purging), through sacrifice. Intriguingly, there is no direct reference to sacrifice here (see 'Explanation'). Furthermore, in the priestly system water is never used for purification from 'sin', only purification from 'impurity' arising from amoral causes. D. P. Wright (1992: 738) notes, however, that washing occurs as a literary figure of repentance and purification elsewhere in the prophets (e.g. Isa. 1:16; 4:4; Jer. 2:22; 4:14; Ezek. 16:9; 36:25; Mal. 3:2). This seems to be in the background here and fits with the images of repentance in 12:10–14, particularly the cleansing water of the new covenant in Ezek. 36:25, which is also associated with the gift of God's Spirit (vv. 26–27).

2–3. Idolatry and false prophecy are closely associated in pre-exilic times (e.g. 1 Kgs 22; Ps. 106; Jer. 6:13–14; 8:10–11; Ezek. 14). While idolatry is not condemned by the post-exilic prophets nearly as frequently as it was by the pre-exilic and exilic prophets, this does not mean that it 'need not be taken literally' (Curtis 2006: 215). Foreign marriages as in Ezra 9:1–2 and Neh. 13:23 would certainly pose the issue of idolatry. In Zechariah, the vision of the woman in an ephah being removed to Babylon (5:5–11) had several associations that suggested the removal of idolatry from the community when God returns to Jerusalem. There is also a combination of idolatry and false prophecy in 10:2 that strongly suggests these were an issue for the post-exilic community as well.

To 'cut off the names of the idols' is a unique idea in the OT. Elsewhere the penalty 'to cut off the name' of a person meant premature death with the possibility of the family line (hence 'name') being extinguished from the people of Israel (e.g. Ruth 4:10; 1 Sam. 24:21[22]). In Deuteronomy, Yahweh's 'name' is given as an avenue of relationship and worship (e.g. Deut. 12:5–7). Extrapolating from this data, to 'cut off the names of the idols' is not only to eliminate the idols themselves, but also any avenue of relationship and worship (cf. Hos. 2:17[19]). Hence there will be no enduring memory of the idols among Yahweh's people, who will call on Yahweh's name (v. 9). The removal of the false prophets is elaborated upon in vv. 3–6, and the removal of both of these serves as a picture of the way all defiling practices will be removed and not be tolerated by those who have been cleansed. Since it was these practices that lead to the exile (e.g. Ezek. 22:3–15; 24:13; 39:24), their removal is naturally a necessary part of the cleansing of the land (cf. 3:9; 5:1–4; 5:5–11).

The phrase 'the unclean spirit' (*wĕ'et-rûaḥ haṭṭum'â*) is not found elsewhere in the OT either. The immediate context connects it with false prophecy, which provides an interesting contrast. Whereas God's Spirit is associated explicitly with true prophecy in 7:12 and implicitly in the night vision of Zech. 4 (cf. 4:6), here false prophecy is associated with 'the unclean spirit'. It also forms a contrast with the 'spirit' God pours out in 12:10.

Many scholars argue that it is not simply false prophecy, but all prophecy that is in view and that this passage is challenging the very possibility of prophetic activity in the contemporary and future age (e.g. Hanson 1979: 367; Conrad 1999: 185–188; Floyd 2000: 532–537). While it is true that 'the prophets' are not explicitly described as 'false', it is clear from the context that false prophets are in view (the term 'false prophet' is not found in the OT; it is determined only from context that the prophet is 'false'). First, their activity is associated with 'the unclean spirit' (v. 2). Secondly, the prophets are described by their own parents as having 'spoken a lie in the name of the LORD' (v. 3), which readily identifies them as false. Thirdly, while their attire is that of the true prophet (e.g. 2 Kgs 1:8; 2:8, 13), it is worn specifically 'in order to deceive' (v. 4). Fourthly, the wounds of v. 6 suggest self-inflicted wounds as the result of activities such as those of the false prophets on Mount Carmel in Elijah's day (1 Kgs 18:28; cf. Deut. 14:1; Jer. 16:6). Fifthly, the judgment in v. 3 reflects the judgment of the law on false prophets found in Deut. 13:6–11. One difference between the two passages is the nature of the judgment: stoning in the law, and piercing in Zechariah. In both cases, however, the emphasis falls upon the penalty of execution rather than the means, and it may be that Zechariah has drawn upon the piercing language of 12:10 (using the same verb *dāqar*) to make a comparison between the sinful piercing of God and his king that results in cleansing, and then the cleansing that will come through the sinful (prophets) being pierced. Another possibility is that there is an echo of Phinehas's action in Num. 25:7–8, when he pierces (same verb *dāqar*) the Israelite and Midianite woman who blatantly sleep with one another in the camp. While the penalty sounds severe, the force of the promise in v. 3 that the parents of the false prophet will pierce him through when he prophesies is well captured by McComiskey (1998: 1220): 'Nothing will stand in the way of the complete elimination of false prophecy – not even an emotion as strong as parental love.' Three further points that indicate false prophecy and not prophecy in general is in view is that Zechariah himself is described as a prophet (1:1, 7), and it would be incongruous, to say the least, if he saw his ministry being removed along with idols and the unclean spirit so as to cleanse the land. Secondly, those who argue that it is talking about the demise of prophecy in the fifth century BC fail to recognize that it is not speaking about contemporary events, but what will happen 'on that day'. Finally, the translators of the LXX understood it to refer to false prophets (see 'Notes on the text').

4–6. The theme of the elimination of false prophets continues: those who were false prophets will be ashamed and eschew their past. They will be ashamed of their visions (the mode in which the prophecy came; cf. Zech. 1:7–8; Jer. 14:14; 23:16). They shall no longer dress as a prophet with 'a hairy cloak' (cf. Elijah in 1 Kgs 19:13; 2 Kgs 1:8). The deception may relate to their words, or to pretending to be true prophets. Nor will they desire ever to have been known as a prophet, but claim to have been working the land from their youth, probably as an indentured slave ('a man owned me' in v. 5; see 'Notes on the text'). If there is an allusion to Amos 7:14, it may also be a way of denying that they earned any money by prophesying, claiming rather that it came from farming (Nogalski 2011: 962–963).

Some have argued that the 'wounds between your hands' (v. 6) are a reference to the suffering Messiah (Pusey 1907: 325; Samaan 1989: 118). However, the idiom 'between the hands' elsewhere seems to refer to the upper torso (i.e. the part of the body that joins the hands or 'arms'). In 2 Kgs 9:24, an arrow is shot into this part of the body and pierces the heart. Merrill (1994: 332) also cites a parallel in the Ugaritic Ba'al epic that supports this. Calvin (1986: 393) states in characteristic style, 'Some apply this to Christ, because Zechariah has mentioned wounds on the hands; but this is very puerile; for it is quite evident that he speaks here of false teachers, who had for a time falsely pretended God's name.'

The wounds their body bore as a result of false prophetic activity (cf. Deut. 14:1; 1 Kgs 18:28; Jer. 16:6) is explained in another way: 'I was struck in the house of the ones who love me' (v. 6). The exact meaning of this statement is difficult to determine. It has been understood as the discipline of parents (Keil 1949: 395), the result of drunken brawling or as an accident with friends (Ackroyd 1963: 654). Any of these are possible explanations. Another suggestion is that the 'lovers' are illicit (cf. Hos. 2:5, 7, 10, 12–13; Ezek. 16:33, 36–37; 23:5, 9, 22), and that it refers to pursuing foreign gods or idols as lovers (Conrad 1999: 188). Yet it is difficult to understand how this would function as an excuse. As Meyers and Meyers (1993: 383) state, 'it would make no sense to have a person disclaiming the role of false prophet to be admitting to another unacceptable activity'.

Whatever the case, the fact that vv. 4–6 depict the false prophets engaging in deception about their past raises the problem of how, if these defiling practices are to be removed 'on that day', those who lie and deceive will remain in the land to continue their deception (even if it is only to cover their tracks). Baron (1918: 469) cites Hengstenberg's attempt to resolve this problem by arguing that the prophet in vv. 4–6 is repentant, and, when confronted, humbly confesses to his guilt of being involved in idolatrous rites (v. 6). While this would resolve the problem, it is difficult to read

v. 5 as an honest confession of sin, and v. 6 seems to be a concealing of the truth. The problem dissolves if these verses are not read in a strictly chronological manner, but are seen simply to picture different aspects of the situation 'on that day'. This is consistent with what happens elsewhere in chs. 9–14. On the 'day' that Yahweh cleanses the land, the false prophet will be ashamed and want to hide, but the implication of the wider context is that this will be to no avail. The false prophet will be unmasked and removed from the land. A further perspective that vv. 3–6 provide is that on that day God's people will no longer tolerate sin and uncleanness in their midst – it will be rooted out, by parents and the community.

7. The imper. ('Awake, sword') dramatically begins a new oracle, but is thematically connected to what precedes (see 'Form and structure'). The expression 'awake . . . against' is used on four other occasions in the OT, and in three of these it refers to Yahweh's raising up some agent of judgment against the nations (Isa. 10:26; 13:17; Jer. 51:1). Only in Job 8:6 is it used in a positive sense, where Yahweh rouses himself to restore Job. A similar command to a sword is found in Jer. 47:6–7, where the sword of Yahweh is ordered 'to attack Ashkelon'. In this Jeremiah passage, the question is posed to the sword of Yahweh, 'how long till you rest?' It is also charged to 'Return to your sheath; / cease and be still.' Hence, a sword that is at rest is still in its sheath or scabbard, and the charge to 'awake' is probably best understood as a charge by the Lord for a sword to be 'drawn', ready to strike the shepherd in judgment.

There have been many suggestions for the identity of the shepherd, including the high priest (Plöger 1968: 88), Cyrus (representing the contemporary Persian king) (Sweeney 2000b: 695–697), one of the prophets to be struck in 13:2–6 (Conrad 1999: 188–189) or the worthless shepherd of 11:17 (Redditt 1995: 136). While the shepherd is not explicitly identified, there are several descriptors that limit the possibilities. First, the shepherd is 'my shepherd', that is, the shepherd of the 'LORD of hosts'. Secondly, the shepherd is 'the man [who is] my associate'. The word 'associate' (*'āmît*) occurs elsewhere eleven times, all in Leviticus, where it means 'neighbour' or 'friend'. It suggests one who dwells with Yahweh as his equal, hence 'associate' (Baldwin 1972: 198), or one 'with an intimate connection to God' (Meyers and Meyers 1993: 387). This is in keeping with the promise in Jer. 30:21 (Stead 2013: 72):

> their ruler will arise from among them.
> I will bring him near and he will come close to me . . .

These descriptions naturally exclude identifying the shepherd as the worthless shepherd of 11:15–17, who deserts the flock and is cursed by Yahweh. In addition, the term 'man' (*geber*) is not the usual word for man, but has the nuance of 'strength, or courage, or uprightness' (Kosmala 1969: 160), appropriate for someone who has been to battle (cf. Isa. 22:17;

Jer. 17:5). It can also indicate a man 'who stands in a special, close relationship with God' (Kosmala 1969: 162). It is used of David in 2 Sam. 23:1 and the future Davidic king in Isa. 9:6[5].

If this verse is approached in isolation, it is not clear who the shepherd might be. However, if this verse is read as an integral part of the book of Zechariah, then the referent should be found in what has gone before. Given the expectation of a future Davidic king to this point in Zechariah (including Shoot in 3:8 and 6:12, the coming king of 9:9, the rulers of 10:4 and the one who is pierced in 12:10) it is entirely fitting to identify the shepherd as this future king (S. A. Cook 1993: 462). This also accords well with the descriptions 'my shepherd . . . the man [who is] my associate', which, as noted, suggests a close relationship between the figure and Yahweh, appropriate for the king who is Yahweh's agent (seen also in 12:10). It also readily suits the wider expectations in the OT such as Jeremiah and Ezekiel, who both depict the future king of the house of David as a faithful shepherd, unlike the unworthy shepherds who betrayed the flock (Jer. 23:1–6; Ezek. 34:23–24; 37:24; cf. Mic. 5:4). The reason behind the shepherd's being struck is discussed in the 'Explanation'.

The verb 'strike' (*nākâ*) is different from that used in 13:3 of the false prophet who is pierced (*dāqar*) by his parents, and the one who is pierced (*dāqar*) in 12:10. It is used in 9:4; 10:11; 12:4; 13:6. Striking on its own does not necessarily imply death (e.g. 13:6), but when one is struck with a sword it does, especially when it is an individual who is struck (e.g. 2 Sam. 12:9; Isa. 37:38). Intriguingly, the subject of the imper. verb 'strike' is m., which does not agree with the sword (f.). Hence some unnamed person or party is responsible for striking the shepherd, yet Yahweh stands behind it as its instigator.

The purpose of striking the shepherd is to 'scatter' (*pûṣ*) the sheep, language often associated with exile and judgment (e.g. Gen. 11:8–9; Deut. 28:64; 30:3; Neh. 1:8; Jer. 9:16; Ezek. 34:5). While not exactly the same, the idea of sheep without a shepherd (cf. 10:2) occurs throughout the OT as representing a state of disarray for Yahweh's people that comes from a lack of leadership (e.g. Num. 27:17; Ezek. 34:5). In 1 Kgs 22:17, it refers to the scattered state that Israel will become without a king. Significantly, the only king ever said to have been killed with the sword was Zedekiah (Jer. 21:7), a death that coincided with exile (Gregory 2010: 197). Just as Zechariah drew on the death of Josiah in his portrayal of the future piercing of the king in 12:10, so he may be drawing on this episode here to portray the future.

The expression 'turn my hand against' occurs on four other occasions in the OT, where it always means to destroy in judgment (Ps. 81:14; Isa. 1:24–26; Ezek. 38:12; Amos 1:8). In Isa. 1:24–26 it is used, as here, in conjunction with the idea of refining a remnant, hence it is a judgment that will purify God's people. The term 'little ones' is unusual and most naturally refers to the sheep that are scattered. If there is a similarity with the expression 'the young [lit. 'little ones'] of the flock' in Jer. 49:20 and 50:45, which seems likely, then it refers particularly to the lambs of the flock, highlighting the severity of the coming judgment, where even the lambs will not escape.

8–9. In context, 'the land' (*hā'āreṣ*) is best conceived as the region in which God's people dwell, rather than the whole earth (cf. 12:12). Yet what begins in Jerusalem and its immediate surrounds spreads to all the earth in ch. 14. The idea of refining a remnant is a common theme among the pre-exilic prophets (e.g. Isa. 1:8–9; Amos 3:21; Mic. 5:7–8; 7:18). The division of the people of Yahweh into thirds is reminiscent of Ezekiel's sign action in Ezek. 5, which represents a third of the people burned with fire, a third struck by the sword and a third scattered to the wind with the sword unsheathed after them (Ezek. 5:2). From this final third, a small number are preserved, but even they are further refined (Ezek. 5:3–4). In Zechariah 'two parts in it shall be cut off and perish', and the third that remains is put into the fire where God will 'refine' and 'prove' them. These concepts differ slightly from one another: to 'refine' (*ṣārap*) is to subject the metal to high temperature in a furnace to burn off impurities; to 'prove' (*bāḥan*) is to test or judge the quality of the metal after it has been refined (Meyers and Meyers 1993: 395). For all the prophets just mentioned, the refining process was the exile from which a purified remnant would emerge. For Isaiah, it is the refinement of God's people that will lead to the elevation of Jerusalem and the pilgrimage of the nations, which is also the pattern for Zechariah (Isa. 2:1–4; cf. Zech. 14:10, 16).

The language used ('I will say, "They are my people," and they will say, "The LORD is our God"') is classic covenant language, also seen earlier in Zechariah (2:11[15]; 8:8; 9:16; cf. Exod. 3:10; 5:1; 19:5–6; Lev. 26:12; Deut. 26:17–18; Jer. 7:23; 24:7; 30:22; 32:38; Ezek. 11:20; 14:11; 36:28; 37:23, 27; Hos. 2:23). It indicates that those who emerge will enter into a restored covenant relationship with Yahweh. Jer. 31:33 uses this language to speak of the 'new covenant' and it is natural to associate Zechariah's hope with this. One of the great privileges of this restored relationship is answered prayer: 'They will call on my name, and I will answer them.' This situation is also reflected in the promise of 10:6: 'they will be as though I had not rejected them. For I am the LORD their God and I will answer them' (cf. 2:11; 8:8; 9:16; Jer. 31:33). This verse (and the wider unit) indicates that in Zechariah's day the exile was not envisioned as over. The nation will have to endure another exile-like experience in which a remnant is refined before the blessings of 'that day' come.

Explanation

Zech. 9:16 promises that 'The LORD their God will save them on that day as a flock of his people', and chs. 12–13 unfold the way in which this salvation of the flock will happen, underlining that it will not be without cost. Ch. 12 looks to a time ('on that day') when the nations will come against Jerusalem, and God will act to destroy them (12:1–9). After this battle, Yahweh will pour out a spirit of grace and supplication upon the house of David and the inhabitants of Jerusalem so it becomes apparent to them that they have pierced Yahweh in the person of his king, with the result that mourning and grief spread throughout the whole community (12:10–14).

Keeping ch. 12 in view, the main theme of ch. 13 is the purification of God's people and the land that comes in the aftermath of the battle victory. It is not a strictly chronological presentation, but telescopes different aspects of cleansing and refinement that will come 'on that day'.

First, there is a fountain that opens for the house of David and inhabitants of Jerusalem (cf. 12:10) to cleanse from sin and impurity. In the priestly system, there is normally some kind of sacrifice that brings cleansing from sin. Water is only ever used for cleansing from impurity from amoral causes. Even though there is washing in the ordination of Aaron's sons in Lev. 8:6, there is also sacrifice in 8:18–29. Yet in 13:1 the fountain brings cleansing from sin as well as impurity. *Tg. Zech.* 13.1 suggests this was perceived by ancient Jewish scholars as an anomaly since it adds, '*and by the ashes of a cow* for a sin-offering' (Cathcart and Gordon 1989: 220; emphasis theirs). Another way of resolving this is by inferring that the piercing of Yahweh and the king served as a type of sacrifice. Admittedly, this is only implicit in Zechariah, but the case for deducing this is strengthened if Zechariah is read against the backdrop of Isaiah's suffering servant, where the servant is made an offering for sin (e.g. Isa. 53:10; see 'Excursus'). In any case, the NT makes this connection explicit when it identifies the one they have 'pierced' as Jesus Christ, whose death was a once-for-all sacrifice for sin (Heb. 9:22–28; see 'Explanation' of Zech. 12). Through Jesus, 'rivers of living water' flow to believers (John 7:38; cf. Zech. 14:8), and John explains this metaphor as referring to the Spirit who is given after Jesus is glorified (v. 39). In addition, forgiveness of sin and cleansing from impurity are two key fruits of Jesus' atoning sacrifice (e.g. Matt. 26:28; Acts 26:18; Eph. 1:7; 5:26; Col. 1:14).

The removal of idolatry and false prophecy portrayed in 13:2–6 is also a key concern for the church in view of Jesus' death. Worshipping idols is one of the characteristics of 'pagan' living (1 Peter 4:3) and is associated with the acts of the 'flesh' (Gal. 5:20; Eph. 5:6; Col. 3:5). Followers of Christ are to 'flee from idolatry' (1 Cor. 10:14; 1 John 5:21). Similarly, false prophets and teachers pose a grave danger to God's people (2 Peter 2:1; 1 John 4:1). While the judgment of the law on false prophets in the community is no longer directly applicable (i.e. their being put to death), Christians are to be intolerant of false teaching (2 Tim. 3:5; Rev. 2:20). In Revelation, the 'false prophet' does the work of the antichrist (16:13; 19:20; cf. 1 John 4:3; 2 John 1:7), which emphasizes the powerfully destructive influence of false prophecy for God's people. The 'false prophet' is ultimately destroyed at Jesus' return when he is thrown into the lake of burning sulphur along with the devil and the beast (Rev. 20:10). Until that time, false prophecy (including any ideology that denies the gospel) remains a threat to God's people and is to be combatted with the sword of the Spirit, which is the word of God (Eph. 6:17; Rev. 2:14–16).

Zech. 13:7–9 offers a further perspective on the coming day of Yahweh by indicating that the death of God's king will be by his own purpose and design: God commands a sword to strike the shepherd. Like the pierced one, the identity of the shepherd is contested by scholars. If this verse is read as an integral part of the book of Zechariah, then it is entirely fitting to identify the shepherd as the future Shoot (3:8; 6:12), 'king' (9:9) and pierced one (12:10). Indeed, Jesus quotes 13:7 and connects it with his own imminent death (Matt. 26:31; Mark 14:27). Obviously, Jesus understands striking with the sword to be a metaphor for the passion, since the means of death in his case is crucifixion (this may account for the shortened quotations in the Gospels, which do not mention the sword). This connection explains the enigma of why, if there is such a close relationship between the shepherd and Yahweh, God commands his death – the shepherd suffers not for his own sins, but for the sins of others (see 'Excursus'). He is the good shepherd who lays down his life for the sheep (John 10:11).

The quotation in Matthew and Mark emphasizes two things. First, that it is God who strikes the shepherd ('I will strike the shepherd') – the death of the future king is God's design. Secondly, the result is that 'the sheep of the flock will be scattered', which the gospel writers see fulfilled in the desertion of the disciples at Jesus' arrest (Matt. 26:31, 56; Mark 14:27, 49–50). The timing of the quote is also significant as it comes just after the Last Supper, where Jesus explains that his death will be for the forgiveness of sins and the establishment of the new covenant (Matt. 26:28; Mark 14:24; cf. Luke 22:20). Jesus' designation of his followers as 'little ones' (Matt. 10:42; 18:6, 10, 14; Mark 9:42) may also be against the backdrop of 13:7. R. E. Watts (2007: 233) says of the disciples in Mark, 'for all their self-confident grasping for greatness . . . and desire to "shepherd" others . . . the Twelve will finally be forced to admit that they too are only "little ones" (Zech. 13:7b; cf. Mark 9:42–48) who themselves will stumble (14:31, 50)'. In the end, it is only the Messiah Jesus who proves faithful unto death and emerges from the fires of God's judgment as the nucleus around which a purified remnant will grow, not only from the house of David and the inhabitants of Jerusalem, but from those in every place who call on the 'name' of the Lord Jesus Christ (1 Cor. 1:2; Zech. 14:16).

Excursus: the pierced one, the stricken shepherd and the suffering servant of Isaiah

Many scholars conclude that the differences between Isaiah's suffering servant and Zechariah's pierced one and stricken shepherd are greater than the similarities, and that any comparison is of little use. For instance, Petersen (1995: 121) states:

> The differences remain important. In Isaiah 53, the suffering of an individual results from Yahweh's intent. Moreover, the suffering and death have some sort of vicarious effect on the people. In Zechariah, the people have killed the individual, and the effect is one of lamentation – which is not present in Isaiah 53 – and then, there is an outpouring of divine spirit.

Yet the similarities between these figures must not be understated, especially if the pierced one and stricken shepherd are also connected with the future king of 9:9. The figures in Zechariah and Isaiah are presented as humble and gentle (Zech. 9:9; Isa. 42:2). They bring blessing to the nations (Zech. 9:10; Isa. 42:1, 4, 6; 49:6). They release captives from the pit or dungeon (Zech. 9:11–12; Isa. 42:7; 61:1). They gather those who have been scattered from Israel (Zech. 9:12; Isa. 49:5–6). Significantly, they are 'struck' (*nākâ*) (Zech. 13:7; Isa. 53:4) and 'pierced' (Zech. 12:10 [*dāqar*]; Isa. 53:5 [*ḥālal*]). They are associated with shepherd imagery (Zech. 13:7–9; Isa. 53:6–7), though the servant is likened to a sheep rather than a shepherd. The figures in Zechariah and Isaiah are rejected by the people (Zech. 12:10; 13:7; Isa. 53:3). They are connected with the pouring out of a 'spirit' upon people (Zech. 12:10; Isa. 44:3–5). Contrary to Petersen's assessment, they are said to suffer by Yahweh's intent (Zech. 13:7; Isa. 53:6, 10), and their deaths result in forgiveness for the sins of the people (Zech. 13:1; Isa. 53:5–6). In addition, the people later mourn over them, though the mourning in Isaiah is implicit (Zech. 12:10; Isa. 53:4–12). There is also an echo of Isa. 53:12 in Zech. 14:14 with the spoil that is divided as a result of the servant's death. These similarities seem too numerous to be coincidental. Lamarche (1961: 147) devotes a whole chapter of his monograph to comparing Zech. 9 – 14 with Isa. 40 – 55, and his conclusion is valid:

> Whatever the differences between our two authors, whatever the obscurities that still surround the suffering servant, through and perhaps beyond the part played by contemporary communities or persons, it is finally the same prophetic current, heralding a humble and suffering Messiah, which traverses these two books. (My tr.)

As Lamarche acknowledges, identifying the servant of Isa. 40 – 55 as the future Davidic king is hotly contested by scholars, but recent studies have demonstrated the dependence of Isaiah's portrait of the servant on the 'suffering David' in the Psalms and 2 Samuel (Dempster 2007; Stead 2013). Stead convincingly shows how the servant songs resound with echoes of the 'suffering David' psalms (22; 31; 34; 38; 39; 41; 69; 118). Furthermore, he argues that the stricken shepherd of Zechariah is 'a clear fusion of the suffering David of the Psalms and the historical narratives with the suffering servant of Isaiah 40–55' (Stead 2013: 74).

That the suffering David is in the background of Zechariah is made clear from Zech. 9:9, where the future king is said to be 'saved' and 'afflicted'. David had been 'afflicted' (cf. Ps. 22:24) and, humiliated by Absalom, driven from Jerusalem. It was also a time when he rode a donkey (2 Sam. 15 – 16), before he was 'saved' by God (cf. Ps. 118:14) and returned to Jerusalem (see 'Comment' on 9:9). Hence from the outset of Zech. 9 – 14, the way God will save his people is through another suffering David. Zechariah is drawing on the past to paint a picture of the future. In 12:10 – 13:7, the suffering David is also fused with the suffering servant in the portraits of the one who is pierced and the stricken shepherd. In addition, the past sufferings of Davidic kings (Josiah and Zedekiah) also contribute to these portraits.

The significance of this for reading Zechariah is that if this connection with the suffering servant is admitted, then this indicates that the pierced one and stricken shepherd are an essential part of Yahweh's project to bring forgiveness to the people (Crotty 1982: 47). Hengel (2004: 85–90) argues for the influence of the suffering servant song of Isa. 53 on Zech. 12:10–14 and 13:7–9, and states, 'we must assume that the unknown authors of these prophetic oracles, which were already apocalyptically colored, knew the older prophetic literature – here once again supremely Isaiah – extremely well'. Citing Rudolph (1976: 213–214), he explains:

> This offensive 'pessimism of the prophet, that even the Messiah would suffer such a terrible fiasco with Yahweh's approval in 13:7,' is best explained by the fact that 'the prophet had before him the figure of the Servant in Deutero-Isaiah.' . . . Just as the prophet Second Isaiah learned that the Messiah's demise at human hands could not alter God's saving plan (Isa 53:10), so our prophet in Zechariah received the divine message that Yahweh would take this human guilt into his saving plan.

While some argue that this is simply a 'retrofitting of 13.7–9 with the hermeneutic of the New Testament Gospel writers' (Nogalski 2003: 297), there is some evidence that this is not the case. Horbury (1998: 31–35) argues that, along with the suffering Moses of the Pentateuch, the suffering David in Psalms and 2 Samuel, the suffering servant of Isaiah and the cutting off of a rightful ruler called Messiah in Dan. 9:26 (cf. *2 Esdras* 7.29), Zechariah contributes to the notion of a slain Messiah, likely to have been current in the Second Temple period. Similarly, D. C. Mitchell (1997: 202, 331–332) notes several apocalyptic midrashim dating from the early to late first millennium AD that cite 13:9 and 14:2 in connection with the death of Messiah ben Joseph. This is not the victorious Messiah ben David, but a second Messiah figure who dies in a battle against Gog and Magog. When and how this second Messiah figure developed within Judaism is unclear. It may have been an attempt by Jewish scholars to reconcile the expectations concerning the victorious Messiah ben David, who would live for ever, with 13:7 and other texts, which they understood to be referring to a Messiah who is killed. At the least, this demonstrates that ancient Jewish scholars understood the concept of a future king who suffers as existing in Zechariah, and this is not a case of Christian eisegesis.

When Zech. 12:10 and 13:7 are read in this way against the rest of the book of Zechariah, it makes sense of the way in which the coming Davidic king will be instrumental in dealing with sin. Zech. 3:9 connects the coming of Shoot with the removal of the iniquity of the land in a single day, and 6:12–13 says that Shoot will build the eschatological temple, re-establish the rule of Yahweh in Jerusalem and rule as 'a priest on his throne' (6:13). In 12:10 – 13:9, the case for seeing a sacral function for the future Davidic king is strengthened further: it is through the death of the king (12:10; 13:7) that purification and cleansing will come to the people of Yahweh and to the land (13:1–6). In the priestly system, cleansing from sin comes from priestly sacrifice rather than washing with water alone. This suggests that the death of the future king in Zechariah is to be understood as this sacrifice, a concept explicit with Isaiah's suffering servant (Isa. 53:4–10). Through the king's death as representative and substitute for the people a new covenant relationship will be established (13:9). In this way the coming king will function as both priest and sacrifice for Yahweh's people. This brings the earlier themes of the book into resolution. While not drawing out the priestly associations, the conclusion of Larkin (1994: 170) on this matter is apt:

> Zechariah has applied his study to the problem of how to remove human guilt, something promised by [Zech. 1 – 8] (3:9), but not accounted for. His solution is to portray a figure strongly identified with God, perhaps a kingly/divine figure, who seeks no attention at all but focuses both the hostility and the repentance of the people. In this way, the fact of human guilt is taken up into the promise of the outpouring of the spirit of grace and supplication. The writer has done more than either Ezekiel or Second Isaiah to illuminate those who stand around the kingly figure, widening the circle imperceptibly from the house of David and the inhabitants of Jerusalem (12:10) to 'all the families that are left' (12:14) and perhaps beyond (13:8).

Hence it seems that Zechariah is announcing to those in his day that the judgment and purification Isaiah prophesied along with the suffering of Yahweh's servant still lie in the future for Yahweh's people with the work of a coming Davidic king. This king will suffer death, and the people will be judged, but the outcome of the judgment of Yahweh on his shepherd and sheep will be glorious. Those who emerge will enter into a restored covenant, or even a new covenant relationship with Yahweh (cf. 13:9). The same pattern of suffering, refinement and restoration is seen in 12:1 – 13:6 and 13:7–9 and prepares for the presentation in Zech. 14.

ZECHARIAH 14:1–21

Translation

14:1Look, a day is coming for the LORD when your plunder will be divided in your
midst. 2And I will gather all the nations against Jerusalem for the battle. And the
city will be captured and the houses looted and the women raped. And half of
the city will go out into the exile, but the remainder of the people will not be cut
off from the city. 3And the LORD will go out and battle against those nations, just
as he battles on a day of war. 4And his feet will stand on that day upon the Mount
of Olives which faces Jerusalem from [the] east, and the Mount of Olives will
split in half, eastward and westward, [forming] a very great valley. And half of
the mountain will recede northward and half of it southward. 5And you will flee
[by] the valley of my mountains, for the valley of the mountains will extend to
Azal. And you will flee just as you fled from the earthquake in the days of Uzziah,
king of Judah. Then the LORD my God will come, all the holy ones with you.

6And it will be on that day there will not be light – splendid ones will congeal.
7And it will be one day – it is known to the LORD – not day and not night. And
when the time of evening comes, it will be light. 8And it will be on that day living
waters will go out from Jerusalem, half of them to the eastern sea and half of
them to the western sea, in the summer and in the winter it will be. 9And the LORD
will become king over all the earth. On that day the LORD will be one, and his
name one. 10He will surround all the land like the Arabah, from Geba to Rimmon,
south of Jerusalem. And it [Jerusalem] will rise and it will dwell in its place, from
the Gate of Benjamin to the place of the First Gate, to the Gate of the Corners,
and from the Tower of Chananel to the winepresses of the king. 11And they will
dwell in it and it will not be a devotion to destruction again; and Jerusalem
will dwell securely.

12And this will be the plague with which the LORD will strike all the peoples who
waged war against Jerusalem: their flesh will rot while still standing on their feet,
their eyes will rot in their sockets, and their tongue will rot in their mouths. 13And
it will be on that day – a great panic of the LORD will come on them. And each
one will seize the hand of his neighbour – and his hand will rise up against the
hand of his neighbour. 14And even Judah will fight at Jerusalem. And the wealth
of all the surrounding nations will be collected: gold, silver and garments in great
abundance. 15And so a plague will be [on] the horse, the mule, the camel and the
donkey, and all the cattle which will be in those camps – just like this plague.

[16]And it will be that all the survivors of all the nations that had come against Jerusalem will go up year by year to worship the King, the LORD of hosts, and to keep the Feast of Sukkoth.

[17]And it will be that if any of the clans of the land do not go up to Jerusalem to worship the King, the LORD of hosts, the rain will not come on them. [18]And if the clan of Egypt will not go up and will not come, then [the rain will] not [come] on them. The plague will come with which the LORD will strike the nations that will not go up to keep the Feast of Sukkoth. [19]This will be the punishment of Egypt and the punishment of all the nations that will not go up to keep the Feast of Sukkoth.

[20]On that day 'Holy to the LORD' will be on the bells of the horses, and the pots in the house of the LORD will be like the bowls in front of the altar. [21]And every pot in Jerusalem and in Judah will be holy to the LORD of hosts. And all who sacrifice will come and take from them and they will cook in them. And there will not be a trader again in the house of the LORD of hosts on that day.

Notes on the text

14:1. 'a day is coming': LXX and Vg have 'days are coming'.

'when . . . will be divided': *wĕḥullaq* uses the pual to denote indirect implicit action (Waltke and O'Connor 1990: 421).

2. 'against': *'el* expresses disadvantage (Arnold and Choi 2003: 98).

'raped': *tiššāgalnâ* translates K (as do LXX and Vg). Tg follows Q, which is euphemistic ('lain with': *tiššākabnâ*).

3. 'just as he battles': *kĕyôm hillāḥămô*. Lit. 'just as a day of his battling'.

4. 'on that day' is absent from Syr and Tg.

'which faces': *'ăšer 'al-pĕnê*. Lit. 'which [is] upon the face of'.

'split in half': lit. 'split from its half'.

'eastward and westward': *mizrāḥâ wāyāmmâ*. Lit. 'towards sunrise and towards sea', where both have a directional (or locative) he suff., indicating the goal of a movement (Miller-Naudé et al. 1999: 227). Similarly, 'northward' and 'southward' later in the verse also have the he suff. 'southward': *negbâ* is lit. 'towards the Negev'.

'will recede': *ûmāš* normally means 'to remove, depart'. This translation follows Meyers and Meyers (1993: 423).

5. 'you will flee': Many suggest repointing *nastem* to *nistam* (will be blocked), which seems to lie behind the LXX, Tg and a few Hebr. MSS. The MT is followed by Vg and Syr, and since it makes better sense, it is followed. See further, Meyers and Meyers 1993: 424; Schaefer 1993a: 183–184.

Some suggest emending 'valley of my mountains' (*gê'-hāray*) to 'valley of Hinnom' (*gê'-hinnōm*), but there is no ancient textual witness to this and Hinnom lies to the west of Jerusalem, not to the east as Zechariah's vision requires (Merrill 1994: 353).

'Azal' is translated as a place name (otherwise unknown). LXX interprets it as a different place name. Hanson (1979: 369–371) and others emend it to 'its side', presumably the eastern side of Jerusalem. I have followed MT. See further, Meyers and Meyers 1993: 426.

'with you': *'immāk* contains a 2 sg. suff. after a third-person reference to God. Gelston (2010: 147) notes this is not unique (cf. Deut. 33:3; Mic. 6:9; 7:17). Tg, LXX, Syr and Vg have 'with him'.

6. 'splendid ones': *yĕqārôt* is translated as a noun (a subst. adj.). The three other instances of this form in the OT are adjectives describing the foundation stones of the temple (1 Kgs 5:31; 7:10–11). As an adj., *yāqār* describes the moon in Job 31:26. All the versions read a waw cons. and all the versions except Tg translate it as 'and cold' (Gelston 2010: 147).

'shall congeal': *yĕqippā'ôn* translates K, which is a qal imperf. of *qāpā'*. Q (*wĕqippā'ôn*) changes the yod to a waw and reads it as a second noun, and all the versions follow this and translate it 'and ice'.

7. 'And when the time of evening comes': *wĕhāyâ lĕ* means 'become' (cf. v. 9).

10. 'will surround': *yissôb*. Tg and a single witness to LXX have 'will become'.

'in its place': *taḥtêhā* (cf. 12:6).

11. 'a devotion to destruction': *ḥērem*. See 'Comment'.

'securely': *lābeṭaḥ* uses the prep. *lĕ* to denote manner. It is best rendered adverbially (Waltke and O'Connor 1990: 206).

12. 'the plague' (*hammaggēpâ*) and '[he] will strike' (*yiggōp*) have the same root.

Lit. 'rotting of his flesh while still standing on his feet, his eyes will rot in their sockets, and his tongue will rot in their mouth'. Gelston (2010: 148) notes, 'Hebrew can easily move between sg. and pl. in dealing with collectives.'

13. 'each one will seize the hand of his neighbour': lit. 'they will seize – a man the hand of his neighbour '.

14. 'at Jerusalem': *bîrûšālāim*. The LXX and Syr translate it 'at Jerusalem'; Tg and Vg translate it 'against Jerusalem'. See 'Comment'.

'wealth': *ḥêl* can also be translated 'might' or 'army' (cf. 4:6; 9:4).

15. 'the horse, the mule, the camel and the donkey': the LXX translates with plurals. The Hebr. is sg., but has a collective sense (Gesenius 2006: 406, §126m).

16. 'the survivors': *hannôtār* is sg. in Hebr. but expresses a collective idea.

'year by year': *middê šānâ bĕšānâ*.

'to worship': *lĕhištaḥăwōt* is the hish. of *ḥwh* (Barker 2008: 832).

'the King, the LORD of hosts' is more formally, 'King Yahweh of hosts'. The shewa instead of a pataḥ under the lamed of *lĕmelek* means that it is a title (Meyers and Meyers 1993: 466).

'to keep the Feast': *lāḥōg 'et-ḥag* contain the same Hebr. root (also vv. 18–19).

18. The apodosis is difficult to construe and as it stands the Hebr. contradicts what has gone before, but if the same phrase from v. 17 is understood ('the rain will not come'; inserted in translation), it makes sense (McComiskey 1998: 1242).

19. 'punishment': *ḥaṭṭa't*. Sklar (2005: 21) notes that terms for sin are often used as a metonymy for the punishment that results from them (cf. Gen. 19:15; 1 Sam. 28:10).

20. 'the bells': *mĕṣillôt* is a hapax legomenon.

'the horses': *hassûs* is sg., but understood as a collective noun.

21. 'trader': *kĕna'ănî*. Tg and Vg translate as 'trader'. LXX understands 'Canaanite'.

Form and structure

As the final chapter, ch. 14 brings the themes of the book to their climax. It offers a further perspective on the great battle 'on that day' in which Yahweh's enemies are subjugated and his people are saved and blessed. It shows that the coming of God's kingdom comes at great cost to his people, a theme anticipated in the battle of 12:2 and in 13:7–9, where a remnant of God's people is refined. It also reveals the end point of Yahweh's purposes: his people (which include the nations) worship him as king in a new creation with all that is unholy removed.

Meyers and Meyers (1993: 409) note that, as elsewhere in the second half of Zechariah, ch. 14 speaks of the future in terms of events in Israel's history. There are also many similarities with the battle against Gog of Magog in Ezek. 38 – 39 (Schaefer 1993a: 172; 1995: 74). Gog will come with a coalition of nations to 'invade a land that has recovered from war' (Ezek. 38:8), a description that fits Israel in the post-exilic period. Gog will come to plunder and loot (38:13; 39:10). Gog will come with many nations, riding on horses, a mighty army (38:15). This battle will also be God's initiative: 'against my people Israel . . . I will bring you against my land' (38:16). On the day when Gog attacks, Yahweh's anger will be aroused against him and the nations. As in ch. 14, there will be a great earthquake and mountains will be overturned (Ezek. 38:19–20; cf. Zech. 14:4–5), soldiers will fight one another (Ezek. 38:21; cf. Zech. 14:13), there will be plunder (Ezek. 38:13; cf. Zech. 14:1, 14) and there will be plague against the nations who make war (Ezek. 38:22; cf. Zech. 14:12). In Ezekiel, the purpose of this battle is that God's holy name will be known among Israel and the nations (38:16, 23; 39:7). While it is expressed differently, in Zech. 14 the nations also come to acknowledge the holiness of Yahweh.

The form and genre of this chapter are debated by scholars. Its radical eschatology, where God visits the earth and transforms the heavens and the earth 'on that day', leads some to classify the chapter as apocalyptic or proto-apocalyptic (Hanson 1979). Yet the chapter also lacks many of the requisite features of apocalypse. For instance, there is no other-worldly journey, there is no angelic mediation and in its final form it is not pseudonymous. As noted in the 'Introduction', the book of Zechariah often frustrates attempts to classify it neatly. Floyd (2000: 557) classifies it as a prophecy of salvation. This is certainly correct, but is a rather broad category.

In terms of structure, Sweeney (2000b: 697) notes the disjunctive clause that begins v. 12, and also the way vv. 1–11 and 12–21 conclude with sections that portray the secure or holy status of Jerusalem as a result of Yahweh's sovereignty over the city (vv. 9b–11 and vv. 20–21). Zech. 14:1–11 divides further into two parts on the basis of its themes: vv. 1–5 describe the disaster that will overtake Jerusalem before God's ultimate triumph; and vv. 6–11 present a series of five statements (each introduced by *wĕhāyâ* [and it will be]) that together describe the transformation of the heavens and the earth as Yahweh's sovereignty is recognized.

Zech. 14:12–21 divides thematically into vv. 12–15, which explain the way in which God will defeat the peoples who came against Jerusalem in v. 2, and vv. 16–19, which portray the survivors of the nations recognizing Yahweh's sovereignty over the world at Jerusalem at the Feast of Sukkoth, and the punishment on those who do not come. Finally, vv. 20–21 picture the holiness of the temple spreading to encompass the city of Jerusalem and Judah.

This structure is represented as follows:

14:1–11	**Battle, victory and transformation of Jerusalem**
14:1–5	Battle at Jerusalem and Yahweh's deliverance
14:6–11	Transformation of the heavens and the earth
14:12–21	**Yahweh as king over the nations**
14:12–19	Punishment on all who do not worship Yahweh
14:20–21	Holiness for Jerusalem and Judah

The history of interpretation of this chapter is skillfully traced by Wolters (2002: 39–56; 2004: 261–285). He urges exegetical and hermeneutical humility, noting Luther's frank admission in his 1527 commentary: 'Here, in this chapter, I give up. For I am not sure what the prophet is talking about'! Wolters's conclusion (2004: 284) is that many interpreters have made the mistake of seeking 'to correlate these predictions too exclusively with a narrowly defined set of events in history'. My own approach in the 'Explanation' is to trace the various ways that the NT authors reuse and echo this chapter. I will demonstrate that the NT applies the language, images and themes of this chapter to both the first and second comings of Jesus. There is a 'now and not yet' perspective on its fulfilment: the 'day' has come with the Messiah Jesus' death and resurrection and will come at his return.

Comment

14:1. 'Look' (*hinnê*; cf. 12:2) marks a new unit and calls attention to a newsworthy or unexpected entity (Miller-Naudé and van der Merwe 2011: 61). While 13:9 anticipates that God's people will be tested by fire, the extent and graphic portrayal of Jerusalem's suffering is certainly unexpected. This 'day' recalls the 'day' mentioned seven times in ch. 12 and three times in ch. 13. The phrase 'on that day' occurs seven times in ch. 14 (vv. 4, 6, 8, 9, 13, 20, 21). It is the day when God will intervene in human history to establish his kingdom fully by overcoming his enemies, saving his people and reshaping the cosmos to fulfil his divine purpose. The battle of this day is not one in addition to the earlier battle, but a further perspective on the one battle that will bring in Yahweh's rule, hence this day is 'for the LORD'. The perspective of this chapter is cosmic, but the epicentre remains in Jerusalem.

While Webb (2003: 178) understands this verse to anticipate the final victory when God's people who survive the battle will divide up the plunder they have taken (cf. v. 14), the immediate context suggests that it is the inhabitants of Jerusalem who will be plundered (Schaefer 1993a: 171). The narrative is not chronological, which has a jarring effect on the reader, suiting the content (note also the abrupt change of person in vv. 1–3). The 'plunder' (*šālāl*) refers to property taken forcibly by military action (Meyers and Meyers 1993: 410). It includes prisoners (usually women and children), precious metals, food, livestock, textiles and garments (e.g. Deut. 20:13; Judg. 5:30; 8:24; 1 Sam. 30:20; 2 Chr. 28:15; Ezek. 38:13). At the outset, it looks like the judgment of Jerusalem in 586 BC all over again, but this time God will intervene for his people (v. 3).

2. There are similarities with Zech. 12 where the nations come against Jerusalem (12:3, 9) and Yahweh fights for his people (12:2–9). But this verse gives more explicit details and makes it clear that the day of battle is Yahweh's initiative. As sovereign over all the earth (cf. v. 9), he 'will gather all the nations against Jerusalem'. The same initiative is seen in Gog's battle 'against my people Israel', when Yahweh says to Gog, 'I will bring you against my land' (Ezek. 38:16) (see 'Form and structure'). Gog will also come to plunder and loot (38:13; 39:10), echoed here.

These images of the future destruction of Jerusalem are also drawn from what happened in 586 BC when the Babylonian army 'captured' (*lākad*) Jerusalem (e.g. Jer. 32:3, 24, 28; 34:22; 37:8; 38:3, 28), 'looted' (*šāsas*) it (e.g. Ps. 89:41[42]; Jer. 30:16) and took 'into the exile' (*baggôlâ*) half of the city (e.g. 2 Kgs 24:15–16; Jer. 29:1, 4, 16, 20; Ezek. 12:11; 25:3). The rape of women is a common feature of warfare and depicts its horror (cf. Isa. 13:16). Although not mentioned directly in connection with the events of 586 BC, it is one of the covenant curses in Deut. 28:30 associated with exile. The Masoretes found Zechariah's reference to 'rape' so offensive that they softened the language (see 'Notes on the text').

Like elsewhere in chs. 9–14, Zechariah recalls the past to picture the future. Yet Redditt (1995: 139) rightly makes the point that these images of destruction are images and not precise predictions, so the details should not be pressed. For instance, it would be wrong to read the percentages here and in 13:7–9 as contradictory.

The 'remainder' (*yeter*) uses the same root as the verb 'remain' (*yātar*) in 13:8. This suggests that the 'remainder' are somehow refined in the battle, but this is only implied by the context.

3. Like elsewhere in chs. 9–14, Yahweh will fight ('battle') for his people against the nations, but where in earlier passages he uses his people as instruments of judgment (e.g. 9:13–15; 10:5, 7; 12:2–3, 6), here he fights directly. The place God 'will go out' from is not stated, but given that elsewhere in Zechariah God's return to Jerusalem is depicted as a future event (1:3; 2:5[9], 10–11[14–15]; 4:9–10; 8:3; 9:8, 14), it is best to understand that he 'will go out' from heaven. This is his abode in 6:5, the final night vision that parallels the themes of this chapter where God sends out his heavenly army to bring judgment on the nations.

This future fight of God is likened to other battles (not 'the day of war' but 'a day of war') where God fought against the nations on behalf of his people (e.g. Exod. 15:1–21; Josh. 10:14, 42; 23:3; Judg. 4:15; 1 Sam. 7:10; 2 Chr. 20:15). His victories in the past assure readers and hearers that he will be victorious on the coming day.

4–5. The return of Yahweh to Jerusalem has been anticipated throughout Zechariah (see 'Comment' on v. 3 for verses). When Yahweh comes, he will shatter the earth. It will be a day of earth-shaking significance (cf. Exod. 19:18; Judg. 5:5; Ps. 68:8; Ezek. 38:20; Mic. 1:3–4; Nah. 1:5; Hag. 2:21–22). With grand anthropomorphism, God's 'feet will stand . . . upon the Mount of Olives'. This mountain is a ridge to the east of Jerusalem, about 2.5 mi. (4 km) long, which runs in a north and south direction. When Yahweh departed from the temple and Jerusalem in Ezekiel, his glory 'stopped above the mountain east of it' (Ezek. 11:23). His return is by the same path (cf. Ezek. 43:2). The location of the mountain ('which faces Jerusalem from [the] east') is significant since the sanctuaries of Eden, the tabernacle and the temple were all entered from the east (see 'Comment' on v. 8).

His feet will cause the mountain to be split in half. All four directions are mentioned, but 'eastward' and 'westward' are more formally (and poetically) 'towards sunrise and towards sea' (see 'Notes on the text'). The idea is that half the mountain will move northward and half southward with 'a very great valley' forming that runs from east to west. The verb 'split' (*bāqa'*) also describes the parting of the waters in Exod. 14:21, which seems significant since in v. 5 God's people will 'flee' (see 'Notes on the text') from Jerusalem through this valley – like the path through the sea in the exodus, it forms a way of escape and salvation.

As already mentioned, the location of 'Azal' is otherwise unknown, but must lie to the east of Jerusalem. The people will flee from Jerusalem just as they 'fled from the earthquake in the days of Uzziah, king of Judah'. This earthquake occurred over 200 years earlier and left a lasting impression (Amos 1:1–2; cf. 2 Kgs 14:22).

After saving his people in the battle, 'the LORD my God will come; all the holy ones with you'. Referring to Yahweh as 'my God' emphasizes the prophet's personal relationship with God (cf. 11:4) (Meyers and Meyers 1993: 429). Yahweh's coming envisages his return to Jerusalem after defeating his enemies rather than his leaving Jerusalem in defeat as Floyd (2000: 548) contends. The means of Yahweh's victory is later explained in vv. 12–15.

The identity of the 'holy ones' is ambiguous, as is the referent of 'you' (which is 'him' in the versions and most English translations – see 'Notes on the text'). The 'holy ones' could refer to the heavenly host of angels (cf. 6:1–8; Deut. 33:2; Job 5:1; Ps. 89:5, 7; Isa. 13:31; Dan. 4:13; 7:9–10; 8:13) (Keil 1949: 404–405; Petersen 1995: 143). This is most likely if the MT is followed, as 'you' must refer to the people since 'you' is used only once of Yahweh (in 1:12), but this is in direct speech. Yet all the versions understand 'you' as Yahweh and translate it as 'him'. Switching between the pronouns 'him', and 'I'/'me' to refer to Yahweh is frequent in chs. 9–14 (cf. 9:7, 13–14; 10:3, 5–8; 12:6–7, 8–9; 14:1–3). This opens up the possibility, which suits the context better, that the 'holy ones' is a reference to the people who had gone out from the city, either by exile (v. 2) or by fleeing (v. 5), who now return as the 'holy ones' along with Yahweh (cf. Lev. 21:7–8; Num. 16:5, 7; 2 Chr. 35:3) (Webb 2003: 179; Boda 2004: 525). These are probably the ones referred to in v. 11 as 'they' who dwell in Jerusalem. The 'holy ones' return to inhabit the city that is 'holy to the LORD' (vv. 20–21).

6–7. The Hebr. of v. 6 is difficult and the ancient versions struggled to translate it (see 'Notes on the text'). I have tried to follow the MT (K) as closely as possible in my translation, 'splendid ones will congeal', and understand this as the heavenly bodies (stars, sun, moon) becoming stationary (cf. the use of *qāpā'* in Exod. 15:8; Job 10:10; Zeph. 1:12). Alternatively, most of the ancient versions translate it 'cold and frost' (cf. ESV, NIV). The MT makes better sense in view of v. 7, which speaks of a change in the distinction between day and night, a logical outcome of the suspension of the heavenly bodies. What is clear is that the effects of God's return are not only felt in Jerusalem and its surrounds, but disrupt the present created order. Zechariah may be drawing on the episode at Gibeon in Josh. 10:12–14, when the sun stood still and the moon stopped and God fought for his people.

The absence of light (v. 6) precedes a new creation (v. 7) marked by 'one day' (*yôm-'eḥād*), an echo of Gen. 1:5 (*yôm 'eḥād*). This new day is 'known to the LORD', indicating the radical changes seem beyond human understanding. With the heavenly bodies congealing, the sequence of day and night is suspended: 'not day and not night' (a further echo of Gen. 1). Yet this is not a day of darkness: it is a day of continual light that continues to shine in the evening, and presumably through what would have been the night. A similar idea is presented in Isa. 60:19–20 (cf. Rev. 21:23).

8. The phrase 'living waters' has the dual connotations of waters that are fresh (not old or contaminated) and waters that give life (Meyers and Meyers 1993: 434–435). The picture of 'living waters' flowing out from Jerusalem reflects several OT passages. In Gen. 2:10–14, life-giving water flows out of Eden, the first earthly sanctuary, to water the garden and then divide into four rivers to take water to the earth. Joel 3:18[4:18] speaks of a fountain flowing out of the temple to water the valley of acacias. Ps. 36:8–9[9–10] depicts a 'fountain of life' flowing as a river from the temple. In Ezek. 47, a river that trickles from the temple (v. 2) grows to a river that no one can cross (v. 5), revivifying the Dead Sea and all else that it supplies (vv. 8–12). Like Ezekiel, Zechariah's 'living waters' flow to the Dead Sea ('the eastern sea'), but they also flow in the opposite direction to the Mediterranean Sea ('the western sea') – the supply is doubled. In contrast to Jerusalem's usual water supply, which often dried up in summer, in the new created order the water supply will be continual: 'in the summer and in the winter'. For a city that often experienced water-supply difficulties (e.g. Isa. 7:3; 22:11), this picture of the future offers great hope.

The major difference between Zechariah's picture and the other OT passages is that in Zechariah the water is said to flow from Jerusalem itself, rather than the sanctuary/temple. This suggests that in the new created order, Jerusalem will take the role of the temple. This is consistent with v. 4, where God approaches Jerusalem as a sanctuary ('from [the] east'), and the end of this chapter, where the holiness that once belonged to the priesthood and the temple spreads to all Jerusalem and Judah (cf. vv. 20–21).

9. The high point of Zechariah's vision of the future is Yahweh's kingship over 'all the earth' (*kol-hā'āreṣ*). Wenzel (2011: 243) identifies this as the theological centre of the chapter, where Yahweh's intervention on behalf of Jerusalem will prove his reign, and Zechariah's previous prophecies will be fulfilled. The kingship of God is basic to the establishment of his kingdom.

The expression 'the LORD will be one' cites the Shema of Deut. 6:4 (Moberly 1990: 214). Scholars debate its meaning in that context, whether it expresses God's uniqueness (the only god who is truly God), unity (ontological indivisibility) or integrity (not being two-faced or inconsistent). The first idea is a key one in Deuteronomy (e.g. 3:24; 4:35, 39; cf. Exod. 15:11), and is the way later scribes understood it (cf. Mark 12:29–32). The other ideas are certainly true and may overlap somewhat, but the addition of 'his name one' in Zechariah supports seeing it primarily as an expression of Yahweh's uniqueness. Ch. 13 spoke of the banishment of the names of the idols (v. 2), and the refined and tested people calling on Yahweh's name (v. 9). Here this acknowledgment is made by the whole earth.

10. The transformation of the earth continues with the elevation of Jerusalem from its surrounds. My translation 'He will surround all the land like the Arabah' differs from most English translations, but follows the Hebr. more closely. Meyers and Meyers (1993: 441) note 'will surround' (*yissôb*) 'never means "turn" in the sense of change or transformation into something else', yet this is the translation in all the major English Bible translations. The Arabah extends from the Dead Sea in the north, to the Gulf of Aqaba in the south. It is a dry rift that forms the Jordan River Valley. Given the Arabah is largely desert, it seems strange to talk about the land of the new creation being transformed in this way. A more significant geographical feature of the Arabah is that it is surrounded by steep escarpments. Hence just as the Arabah is surrounded, so God will surround the land. The prep. attached to Arabah (*kĕ*) is comparative. The idea seems to recall the third night vision, where Jerusalem will be 'a city without walls' and God will be 'a wall of fire all around' (2:4–5[8–9]). That there is a similar idea here is supported by the reference to Jerusalem's security in v. 11. While 'all the land' (*kol-hā'āreṣ*) is the same expression as 'all the earth' in the previous verse, the context indicates it is a more limited area, 'from Geba to Rimmon, south of Jerusalem'. These cities represent the northern and southern boundaries of the territory of Judah, respectively, either at the time of Zechariah (cf. Neh. 11:25–36) or idealized from the time of Josiah (Schaefer 1993a: 206). Like v. 8, where what was earlier said about the temple expands to Jerusalem, here what was earlier said about the city expands to the region of Judah (cf. vv. 20–21).

With Yahweh's return to dwell in the city along with his holy people (cf. v. 5), and the implied promise of protection, Jerusalem will rise to 'dwell in its place', a phrase found also in 12:6. In both instances it seems to mean 'its rightful place' or 'where it should be'. The elevation of Jerusalem is in keeping with its functioning as a temple/sanctuary and the living waters flowing from it (cf. v. 7). It is also consistent with earlier prophetic hope (e.g. Isa. 2:1–4; Ezek. 40:1–2; Mic. 4:1–5).

Zechariah again draws on the past to paint a picture of the future by defining the borders of Jerusalem in pre-exilic terms (Meyers and Meyers 1993: 445). The precise location of these landmarks is not possible to determine. Sweeney (2000b: 702–703) makes the following suggestions. The 'Benjamin Gate' was situated on the northern side of the city to give access to the territory of Benjamin. It is also mentioned in Jer. 37:13 and 38:7. The 'First Gate' or 'Former Gate' is not elsewhere mentioned, but possibly refers to the main gate on the east side of the city. The 'Gate of the Corners' or 'Corner Gate' is also mentioned in 2 Kgs 14:13; Jer. 31:38; 2 Chr. 26:9. Its location is thought to be on the west side of the city. The 'Tower of Chananel' (often transliterated 'Hananel') is also mentioned in Jer. 31:38; Neh. 31:1; 12:39. Its location is unknown, but thought to be west of the Benjamin Gate, at the north-west corner of the Temple Mount. The 'winepresses of the king' are not otherwise mentioned in the OT, but are probably to be located to the south of the city, near the 'King's Pool' and the 'King's Garden' (cf. Neh. 2:14; 3:15). This final landmark with its reference to 'the king' is clearly a pre-exilic term and seems strange to use if Zechariah was seeking to mute any messianism in this chapter, as many scholars contend (see 'Explanation'), particularly since Zechariah draws on the past to depict the future.

Jer. 31:38 also talks about the rebuilding of the city 'from the Tower of Hananel to the Corner Gate'. In both visions, the city is 'holy to the LORD' (Jer. 31:40; cf. Zech. 14:20) (Gregory 2010: 209).

11. This verse is a summary of vv. 1–10 (Nogalski 2011: 977). It seems to link particularly to v. 5 with the referent of 'they' in v. 11 being 'the holy ones' who return with Yahweh to Jerusalem. Floyd (2000: 550) also notes that the threefold repetition of 'dwell' in vv. 10–11 matches the threefold use of 'flee' and 'fled' in v. 5. Those who have returned will dwell in a city that 'will not be a devotion to destruction again', where 'a devotion to destruction' translates the Hebr. *ḥērem*, a term that elsewhere denotes either consecration or destruction. Schaefer (1993a: 211) explains, 'The object of the *ḥrm* is devoted to God either because it belongs to him (involving consecration) or it is harmful to religious interests and therefore is an affront to God (involving utter destruction).' This implies that God's action against Jerusalem in vv. 1–2 is for the purpose of cleansing it from contamination as a result of sin, particularly idolatry (cf. Exod. 22:19; Deut. 7:25–26; 20:17–18). Idolatry was mentioned in 13:2 and implied in 14:21. Cleansing is also associated with Yahweh's return in Mal. 3:2–5; 4:1–3[3:22–24].

The end result is that Jerusalem 'will dwell securely' (see 'Notes on the text'). This idea can describe either military protection (cf. Jer. 49:31) or agricultural abundance (cf. Ezek. 28:26), both of which are features of vv. 1–10 (Nogalski 2011: 977). It is also one of the promised covenant blessings of Lev. 26:5 (cf. Lev. 25:18–19). As noted in the comments on v. 10, in the wider context of the book it connects with the protection of Jerusalem envisaged in the third night vision.

12–13. A new section begins that explains the means by which Yahweh will 'battle against those nations' (v. 3). Those who 'waged war against [*'al*] Jerusalem' will be struck with plague. This recalls the plagues that came on the Egyptians in the exodus (Exod. 7 – 12). Baldwin (1972: 205) suggests an allusion to the defeat of the Assyrian army under Sennacherib during king Hezekiah's reign (2 Kgs 19:8–37; Isa. 10:5–34; 37:8–38), but 'plague' is not explicitly mentioned as the means of death for those in the Assyrian army, and there is no mention of death in 14:12. The horrific plague will strike the people's flesh, eyes and tongues, presumably debilitating them to some extent and causing them to fall into a great panic (v. 13). Meyers and Meyers (1993: 450) highlight the destructiveness of plague by noting dysentery in the Crimean War claimed the lives of ten times more British soldiers than battle wounds.

Like the plague in v. 12, the 'great panic' in v. 13 is 'of the LORD', expressing Yahweh's sovereignty in judgment. The nations will then turn to fight one another, where raising one's hand against another denotes military activity (Meyers and Meyers 1993: 457). There are a number of similar episodes in Israel's history (e.g. Judg. 7:22; 1 Sam. 5:9; 14:15–20). Plague from God and infighting are also pictured in the battle against Gog and his troops in Ezek. 38:21–22.

14. The phrase 'even Judah will fight at Jerusalem' recalls the circumstances of 12:2–5. The prep. *bĕ* can be translated as Judah's fighting 'at Jerusalem' or 'against Jerusalem'. The LXX, Syr and most of the English translations adopt the former idea (ESV, NASB, NIV, NRSV). Clark and Hatton (2002: 361) suggest that 'even' (*gam*) prepares the reader for a statement that is contrary to expectation and favour 'against Jerusalem' (supported by the Tgs and Vg). Judah is initially opposed to Jerusalem in 12:2, but the clans of Judah turn to fight for Jerusalem against the nations when they see God's hand at work. The translation 'at Jerusalem' best captures this overall situation.

Like Israel's plundering the Egyptians in the exodus (cf. Exod. 12:35–36), the defeat of the nations will result in the collection of their wealth 'in great abundance'. This contrasts the situation portrayed in v. 1. What had happened to God's people will happen to their enemies. Collecting the wealth of the nations into Jerusalem is an idea found also in Isa. 60:4–14; Ezek. 38:12–13; 39:10; Hag. 2:7–8.

15. Not only will a plague 'strike all the peoples that waged war against Jerusalem' (v. 12), but non-human instruments of war will also be struck with a similar plague. The 'horse' was used in combat, either mounted or with chariots, and was a formidable weapon (see 'Comment' on 1:8; 6:1; 9:10; 10:3, 5). The next three animals ('the mule, the camel and the donkey') were used for transportation (cf. 9:9). Finally, 'the cattle' (*habbĕhēmâ*) can refer to all domestic animals, but in this context it probably refers to livestock taken along by an army as a food resource (cf. 2 Kgs 3:9) (Meyers and Meyers 1993: 462). The phrase 'in those camps' makes it clear that they were animals used by an army.

16. The topic changes to address the aftermath of the battle and the dual prospects for 'the survivors of all the nations' (vv. 16–19). First is a picture of those who have survived going up to Jerusalem 'year by year' (annually) to worship Yahweh and keep the Feast of Sukkoth (v. 16). The nations are changed from warring enemies to become friends who share in the blessings of God's people. The word 'worship' is literally 'to bow down' and is 'the ancient and traditional sign of obeisance or paying homage' (Meyers and Meyers 1993: 466). The nations will worship the 'King', a title used of Yahweh in v. 9 (see 'Notes on the text'). The title 'LORD of hosts' speaks of Yahweh's might and sovereign rule (see 'Comment' on 1:3; it occurs also in 14:17 and 14:21 [twice]). Since Yahweh is one (v. 9), the assumption is that these survivors of all the nations now worship and recognize him alone. This is an important theme across the book (cf. 2:11; 8:20–23).

Associated with their worship of Yahweh is their annual pilgrimage 'to keep the Feast of Sukkoth'. Held in the seventh month, Sukkoth is a seven-day festival of joy and thanksgiving for the harvest and God's goodness. The Hebr. word 'Sukkoth' can be translated 'tabernacles' or 'booths' and refers to the tents the Israelites lived in when they came out of Egypt (cf. Exod. 23:14–17; Lev. 23:33–43; Deut. 16:13–15; 31:9–13). Why is this 'feast' or 'festival' chosen to represent the future? There are certainly new-exodus connections in this chapter. Additionally, this feast is closely associated with the temple and includes the foreigner (cf. Deut. 16:13–15). The people celebrated the dedication of Solomon's temple at Sukkoth (1 Kgs 8:2, 65). The people also celebrated Sukkoth after Joshua and Zerubbabel set up the altar at the old temple site (Ezra 3:1–4). Rubenstein (1996: 190) argues Sukkoth was the leading temple festival, where God's kingship was experienced and acknowledged. By referring to Sukkoth, Zechariah presupposes the full restoration of the temple as part of the future Jerusalem (J. M. O'Brien 2004: 280). Furthermore, the fact that the nations keep the feast implies the centrality of the temple for all creation (Sweeney 2000b: 705).

17–19. The alternative for those who do not 'worship the King' is portrayed in a way that expands out from Jerusalem, throughout Judah, to Egypt, and then to 'all the nations' (v. 19). It includes lack of rain and plague as punishment, as people are cut off from blessing. The use of 'clans' (*mišpěḥôt*) is unusual. Most English translations translate this 'families of the earth' and see it as an equivalent phrase to 'all the nations' in vv. 16 and 19. However, 'clans' is used in ch. 12 in reference to the houses of David, Nathan, Levi and Shimei (vv. 12–14; cf. *'allupê* in vv. 5–6). (See 'Comment' on 12:5.) Although *'ereṣ* can be translated 'earth' or 'land', Pakula (2003: 73–74) suggests 'clans of the land' is best understood to be those living in the Promised Land (primarily Jews, but also Samaritans and those from other nations). The consequence for not going to Jerusalem to worship Yahweh is 'the rain will not come on them' (v. 17). A lack of rain would devastate the harvest and potentially shatter an agriculturally based subsistence economy. It is a classic covenant curse (e.g. Deut. 28:22–24).

The boundary then widens to include the survivors of Egypt (v. 18), also designated a 'clan' (sg.). Describing the survivors of Egypt as a 'clan' could be a demotion of their status, since they would otherwise normally be called a 'nation' (*gôy*; cf. vv. 2–3, 16, 18–19) or 'people' (*'am*). However, if the 'clans' of v. 17 are understood primarily as Jewish people, it is instead an elevation of the status of these survivors of Egypt since they are described in the same terms as those living in the Promised Land. The Egyptian people are singled out in vv. 18–19, possibly because they were not so dependent on rain on account of the Nile, which flooded annually (Baldwin 1972: 207). Alternatively or additionally, the focus on Egypt may draw on the exodus traditions, where Egypt has come to represent the enemy. The Hebr. text is unclear about the punishment on Egypt (see 'Notes on the text'). It seems that the lack of rain in v. 17 is also the punishment on Egypt: 'then [the rain will] not [come] on them' (v. 18). In addition, they will be struck with plague, along with other nations, as the circle widens to include 'all the nations' (v. 19). This is a different plague to the one that struck 'all the peoples that waged war against Jerusalem' (v. 12) and their animals (v. 15). Unlike the earlier plague, the effects are not spelled out, but it again recalls the plagues that fell on Egypt in the exodus as a demonstration of God's incomparable power (cf. Exod. 9:14). The lack of rain and plague are together described as God's 'punishment' (*ḥaṭṭa't*; see 'Notes on the text').

20–21. Zechariah finishes with a picture of the holiness that will result from God's presence among his holy people (cf. v. 6). The inscription 'Holy to the LORD' was engraved on the gold plate attached to the turban of the high priest (Exod. 28:36–38). It is located in the place of supreme holiness in the priestly system (cf. 3:1–5). In the future age, the holiness that once belonged to the high priest will spread to the 'bells of the horses'. Cantrell (2011: 21–22) notes that bells were attached to the horse's harness as part of its battle regalia and had a number of functions: to ward off biting insects; to govern cadence in a particular gait (esp. important if yoked together); to create a white noise to block out the heinous sounds of the battlefield; to alert others to a horse's arrival on a roadway; and if inscribed, the bell would act as an identifier to facilitate its return. Zechariah seems to have a fondness for the horse (mentioned ten times throughout the book, particularly in the context of warfare), and God's holiness extending to its bells is a fitting image at the book's conclusion. Meyers and Meyers (1993: 481) suggest that it is appropriate since the priest also has bells on his regalia (cf. Exod. 28:33; 39:25). J. M. O'Brien (2004: 277) notes that from a literary point of view, referring to horses brings the book full circle (cf. 1:7–17).

The holiness associated with 'the bowls in front of the altar' (cf. Exod. 27:3; Num. 4:14; Zech. 9:15) will also spread to the 'pots' in the temple and to 'every pot in Jerusalem and in Judah' (v. 21). These 'pots' were used for 'sacrifice', presumably by those who have come to share in the Feast of Sukkoth (vv. 16–19). Again, it speaks of holiness spreading from the temple, through Jerusalem and throughout the land of Judah (cf. the 'holy land' in 2:12[16]).

Finally, the removal of the 'trader' from the temple can have two senses. The vision of the 'ephah' in ch. 5 exposed trade as an area in which wickedness impacted the post-exilic community. The removal of the 'trader' from the temple conveys the cleansing and holiness of the community (cf. 13:2–6). In addition, the word 'trader' (*kĕna'ănî*) can also be translated 'Canaanite' (see 'Notes on the text'). Webb (2003: 182) argues that from a post-exilic standpoint, the Canaanites were the archetypal idolaters. Hence Zechariah looks forward to the time when everything impure, including the idolatrous 'Canaanite', will be removed from God's presence (cf. 13:2).

Explanation

I have argued that chs. 9–14 are not a collection of disparate prophecies, nor a chronology of separate events, but the same broad event (the coming kingdom of God), viewed from different perspectives. In each cycle there is a focus on a different aspect of this final-day battle that will usher in Yahweh's kingdom, but all the time building on and developing what has gone before. The oracles of chs. 9 and 12 give the 'big picture' of what will happen 'on that day', each from a different perspective, with chs. 10–11 focusing on what that day will mean for the leadership of Yahweh's people, and chs. 13–14 on the cleansing that will come on that day.

Chs. 9–14 also reveal that the kingdom will not come without cost to God's people. Achtemeier (1986: 165) observes how the themes of ch. 14 are anticipated in 13:7–9, with the refinement of God's people through trial. In ch. 14, Yahweh will gather the nations to Jerusalem, which will involve another attack like that in 586 BC. Yet this time Yahweh will go out and fight against the nations directly and provide a supernatural means of escape before returning to Jerusalem with those who have been made holy (vv. 1–5). This is no ordinary day, and this chapter reveals it will transform the heavens and the earth before Jerusalem fulfils its destiny (vv. 6–11). The chapter shifts back to provide a retrospective view on how Yahweh will defeat the nations – by striking the people who waged war and their animals with plague and panic (vv. 12–15). Whereas elsewhere in chs. 9–13, God used his people as instruments of his warfare, here he fights directly. The outcome is that Yahweh of hosts will be worshipped as king in Jerusalem both by his people and by survivors of the nations (vv. 16–19). The holiness that had been associated with the priesthood and the temple will spread throughout Jerusalem and Judah (vv. 20–21).

Ch. 14 continues and completes many of the themes found in the rest of the book. These themes include the battle against the nations (14:1–2, 12; cf. 9:4–7, 13; 10:5; 12:2–9), God's fighting for his people (14:3–5, 12; cf. 9:4–7; 10:11–12; 12:3–4, 6, 9), saving them (14:5, 13–15; cf. 9:9, 16; 10:6; 12:7), gathering them (14:5, 11, 16–22; cf. 9:11–12; 10:8–11; 12:6), blessing them (14:8, 14, 20–21; cf. 1:17; 3:10; 8:4–6, 12–13; 9:17), protecting Jerusalem (14:11; cf. 2:5; 9:8, 15; 12:3, 8) and excluding all other rivals (14:9; cf. 5:1–11; 13:2–6). Similarly, the idea of the nations joining with Yahweh's people and acknowledging his sovereignty over their lives (14:16) was seen in 2:11[15] and 8:20–23.

This chapter also makes an important contribution to several key OT theological themes. First, Yahweh's kingship or sovereignty. He is called 'King' (v. 16) and will be 'king over all the earth' (v. 9). Another four times he is called 'the LORD of hosts' (vv. 16–17, 21 [twice]; see 'Comment' on 1:3). He is unique and will be seen to be so (v. 9). Just as he raised up the Assyrians and the Babylonians in the past, so he will 'gather all the nations against Jerusalem' (v. 2) and then defeat them (v. 3). He works judgment on his enemies as punishment (vv. 13, 19). He also works salvation for his people (vv. 4–5) and protection (vv. 10–11). This chapter speaks not only of his control of the weather (v. 17), but also of the cosmos (vv. 7–8). As difficult as it may be to come to terms with, the Bible does not shrink back from expressing God's use of force (e.g. fighting, striking with plague) to overthrow evil. Yet in this he orders all things ultimately for his name and reputation (v. 9), and the good of his people (vv. 11, 20–21).

Another theme is Yahweh's return to Jerusalem (14:4, 9, 16–17). This is also a key theme of the book (1:3; 2:5[9], 10–11[14–15]; 4:9–10; 8:3; 9:8, 14). Throughout chs. 1–13 the coming of Yahweh is placed alongside the coming Davidic king (e.g. 3:8; 6:12; 9:9). Indeed, the coming of the Davidic king is tied to cleansing of the land from sin. By functioning as a priest for Yahweh's people he ushers them into his presence (3:8–9; 6:12–13; 12:10 – 13:9).

Some argue that the earlier Davidic hope is eclipsed in ch. 14 by the hope for Yahweh to be king (Schaefer 1993b: 372; Leske 2000: 677; Rose 2012: 229). However, this claims too much. Given the prominence of the Davidic hope throughout the book, there is nothing to suggest that ch. 14 is negating this in any way. Indeed, the focus on Jerusalem in this chapter is consistent with it, since Jerusalem is the royal Davidic city. Furthermore, the focus on the temple draws together previous themes of the book. Since it was the coming Davidic king who would build this eschatological temple (6:12), it is surely appropriate to see the temple of ch. 14 as the fruit of his work. This is fully consistent with the promise to David in 2 Sam. 7 that closely connects the temple with an eternal throne of David (J. M. O'Brien 2004: 284). Meyers and Meyers (1995: 221) acknowledge, 'Certainly the eschatological vision of chap. 14 focuses on Yahweh's universal sovereignty, not on that of a restored Davidide. But the difference between the two chapters [chs. 9, 14] may be one of emphasis rather than contradiction.' Yet this does not go far enough. Ch. 14 finishes on a note of cleansing, with the holiness that will spread throughout Judah and Jerusalem (14:20–21). Ending in this way highlights a key aspect of the coming Davidic king's work that has been anticipated throughout the book – the death of the king (cf. 12:10 and 13:7) resulting in the cleansing of the land, which enables God's return to dwell among his people. Ch. 14 therefore continues the hopes associated with a future king from the house of David right to the end of the book.

The NT applies the language and images in ch. 14 to both the first and second comings of the Messiah Jesus. Hence there is a 'now and not yet' perspective on the fulfilment of this chapter. The kingdom has come with Jesus' death and resurrection, and will come at his return. In the synoptic

Gospels, Jesus begins his ministry by proclaiming the nearness of God's kingdom (e.g. Matt. 4:17; Mark 1:15; Luke 4:43). In John 7, Jesus' work is connected with the Feast of Sukkoth (Tabernacles). Jesus' offer of 'living water' (John 4:10, 14; 7:38; cf. Zech. 14:8) and his claim to be the 'light of the world' (John 8:12; 9:5; cf. Zech. 14:7) are to be understood in part against the background of the expectations created by ch. 14 (Köstenberger 2007: 453). Rubenstein (1996: 191) argues that in John, Jesus replaces the temple and its institutions as the source of fertility and life and so the pre-eminent temple festival is no longer necessary (John 7:1 – 8:59; cf. Matt. 12:6; 26:61; Mark 14:58; 15:29; John 1:14; 2:19–21; 4:20–24). Jesus' cleansing of the temple (Matt. 21:12; Mark 11:15–16; Luke 19:45; John 2:16) involved driving out the traders, an allusion to Zech. 14:21 (Menken 2009: 92–93). Jesus is said to have gone to the Mount of Olives several times, especially just before his death (Matt. 21:1; 24:3; 26:30; Luke 19:29, 37; 21:37; John 8:1; Acts 1:12). In language borrowed from Zech. 14 he taught his disciples about the coming kingdom (Luke 21:20–28). According to Matt. 27:45, when Jesus died on the cross, 'darkness came over all the land' (cf. Zech. 14:6) and 'the earth shook, the rocks split' in an earthquake (v. 51; Zech. 14:5) and 'many holy people . . . were raised to life . . . and went into the holy city' (Jerusalem) (vv. 52–53; cf. Zech. 14:5). The Gospel of Matthew connects these prophetic signs from Zech. 14 with the salvation that came in Jesus' death. The Gospels also anticipate the ingathering of the Gentiles (e.g. Luke 24:47; John 11:52).

The epistles also contain ideas from this chapter. In Jesus' death (exile), God's people have been made holy or 'sanctified' and are called to be holy (e.g. 1 Thess. 4:3). 1 Thess. 3:13 connects this call to be holy with the return of the Lord Jesus 'with all his holy ones'. Similarly, Jude 14 speaks of the coming of the Lord 'with thousands upon thousands of his holy ones'. In these and other passages, the epistles associate ideas attributed to Yahweh in Zechariah with Jesus; so exhibiting a high Christology. In 1 Thessalonians, the 'day of the Lord' (cf. 5:2) is the day when Jesus will return (cf. 4:16). It is at Jesus' return that he will hand over the kingdom to God the Father and be made subject to him, 'so that God may be all in all' (1 Cor. 15:24, 28). Similar ideas are expressed in the statements of God's kingship in Zech. 14:9, 16.

The book of Revelation draws on many aspects of this chapter, and applies them to the kingdom to come, particularly in its visions of the true temple. At the end of Rev. 7, the nations that have come through the tribulation will serve God in the heavenly temple and God will 'spread a tabernacle over them' (v. 15). With echoes of Zech. 14, the nations are not troubled by the sun (v. 16) and are given 'springs of living water' (v. 17). The new Jerusalem in Rev. 21 also has 'gates' (vv. 12–13), and is the source of the 'water of life' (21:6; 22:1, 17). As in the book of Zechariah, there are cosmic changes that accompany the new Jerusalem, with no need for the sun or moon (21:23; 22:5) and 'no night' (21:25; 22:5). It is 'holy' (21:2,

10), with everything impure excluded (21:8; 22:11, 15). It also has a place for 'the nations' (21:24; 22:2; cf. 7:9), with the tribute or 'glory and honour of the nations' brought into it (21:26). Finally, the new Jerusalem is an expression of God's and the Lamb's kingship (22:1, 3).

MALACHI

INTRODUCTION

1. SETTING

Unlike the books of Haggai and Zechariah with their prominent dates, the book of Malachi is undated and lacks any features that enable a precise setting to be confidently determined. Evidence from the book indicates that it is set some time in the Persian period after the completion of the temple, which was in 515 BC (Mal. 1:10; 3:1, 10). Malachi's relationship with the books of Ezra and Nehemiah is discussed in the next section.

Regardless of the lack of precise historical setting, the canonical setting of Malachi is as the final book in the Old Testament and the last of the post-exilic prophets. In the HB Malachi is the final book of the Prophets and the final book of the Book of the Twelve (see 'General introduction', 'The "Book of the Twelve"'). The focus of Haggai and Zechariah is the restoration of the temple and kingship in Jerusalem, and through this the transformation of the world. Haggai speaks about the shaking of the heavens and the earth that will overthrow the enemies of God and bring glory and peace (Hag. 2:6–9, 21–23). Zechariah looks to the coming of Yahweh to transform Jerusalem and establish his kingship over all the earth (Zech. 14:4–9). This glorious hope is in line with the earlier prophets, but it seemed far from the experience of the people of God in Malachi's day, who remained under Persian rule (see 'General introduction', 'Historical context'). The difficult economic circumstances of Haggai's day remain (cf. 3:11), and the people appear cynical and complacent about Yahweh's promises and purposes.

Throughout the book, Malachi quotes the people and responds to their poor attitudes and behaviours in a series of six 'prophetic disputations' (see 'Genre and structure'). He addresses their failure to appreciate God's love for them (1:2–5). He challenges the priests about their lack of respect towards God – they were simply going through the motions and failing to appreciate their high calling. Malachi charges them with turning a blind eye to the second-rate offerings of the people (1:7–14) and failing to live out and teach faithfully the ways of the Lord (2:1–9). Malachi rebukes the people for their covenant unfaithfulness, particularly in their marriages (2:10–16), but also their immorality and social injustices (3:5), and their failure to support the priests by paying their tithes and offerings (3:8). The people's cynicism towards God's ways and their arrogance is seen in their accusation that God delights in evil and fails to judge the wicked, an accusation Malachi mentions twice (2:17; 3:14–15).

Like Haggai and Zechariah, Malachi continues the call for repentance and covenant obedience in view of God's love and faithfulness. He restates Yahweh's intention to come and to save his 'treasured possession' (3:17) and to judge the wicked on 'the great and dreadful [day]' (4:5[3:23]). The book continues to challenge readers today about our attitude to God and his ways, and our sincerity in worship and obedience.

2. AUTHOR AND DATE

The designation 'Malachi' (lit. 'my messenger' or 'my angel') has long been disputed, with the LXX translating it 'his messenger' and one Tg reading it as 'my angel whose name is Ezra the scribe'. The Jewish Talmud, Jerome and Calvin follow the view that Malachi is a pseudonym for Ezra (Hill 2012a: 277). Alternatively, some scholars argue that the book was originally anonymous and when the superscription was added to the book, 'my messenger' (*mal'ākî*) from 3:1 was introduced as the author (Torrey 1898: 1; Mason 1977: 134; J. J. Collins 2012: 121). Beth Glazier-McDonald (1987: 29) notes the logical problem this suggestion creates, since the messenger in 3:1 is a future figure (cf. Childs [1979: 493]). Others contend that 'my messenger' (as a contraction of 'messenger of Yahweh' [*malākîyâ*]) cannot be a proper name since no Jewish father would give his son that name: it would be presumptuous (Rudolph 1976: 247). Yet the prophet could have assumed this name upon his call by God (Glazier-McDonald 1987: 29).

While there is no prophet 'Malachi' spoken of outside this book in the OT (probably due to the lateness of the book compared to the other prophets whose names appear elsewhere), on balance it seems best to treat 'Malachi' as an actual name. There are two main reasons for this. First, it would be unique to have a prophetic book of the OT linked to an anonymous person or title (Johnston 2000: 261). Secondly, 'If the purpose of the prophetic superscriptions is to "inscripturate" the prophetic books as authoritative writ for the Hebrew religious community, it seems little is gained in advancing the idea of authority by appealing to an ambiguous and unnamed prophet of Yahweh' (Hill 1998: 144).

Assuming that the prophet is largely responsible for the book, the difficulty of locating a precise 'setting' (noted above) also relates to the date of composition. It is universally agreed that the book comes from the Persian period since it assumes a functioning temple. The word 'governor' (*peḥâ*) (1:8) refers to a Persian official in other post-exilic literature (cf. Ezra 8:36; Neh. 2:7, 9; Esth. 3:12; Hag. 1:1, 14). While this term was in use as early as the Old Babylonian period (Baker 2006: 208), Judah was not administered by a 'governor' before the exile (Verhoef 1987: 157). Attempts to date the book with reference to the fortunes of Edom (cf. 1:3–4) prove frustrating on account of the scarcity of historical sources concerning Edom following the Assyrian period (Drinkard 1987: 388; Bienkowski 2001: 199).

Many note that Malachi deals with similar issues that faced Nehemiah: a corrupt priesthood (1:6 – 2:9; cf. Neh. 13:28–31), marriages outside the covenant faith and divorce (2:11–16; cf. Ezra 9:1–15; Neh. 13:23–28), immorality and social injustice (3:5; 4:4; cf. Neh. 5:1–13; 13:15–22), and neglect of the tithes and offerings (3:8–10; cf. Neh. 13:10–12). While these circumstances correlate well, it seems unlikely that Malachi and Nehemiah were exact contemporaries since Nehemiah as 'governor' refused offerings from the people (Neh. 5:14, 18; cf. Mal. 1:8). Furthermore, the ideal situation 'in the days . . . of Nehemiah' reported in Neh. 12:47, seems incompatible with Malachi.

If Malachi precedes Nehemiah, it is perhaps unusual that Malachi is not referred to (cf. the prophets Haggai and Zechariah in Ezra 5:1; 6:14), but an argument from silence is weak. Some argue that Malachi must be located beforehand, since Nehemiah reformed the people (Mackay 2003: 274). However, the book of Nehemiah itself testifies that the reforms were short-lived (cf. Neh. 13). If Malachi is located after Nehemiah, then it is further evidence that the religious reforms of these leaders did not last (McConville 2002b: 259).

Some argue from the general disillusionment in the community that Malachi is a long time after Haggai and Zechariah (Verhoef 1987: 157), but there is already a measure of covenant failure present in Zechariah even with the imminent completion of the temple (cf. Zech. 7 – 8). David Baker (2006: 209) rightly comments, 'dating by categories of sin is not very productive, since specific sins are also not restricted to certain times, and sin is not known to stay eradicated, even if preached against'.

Thankfully it is not necessary to pinpoint a precise date for the setting or composition of the book in order to appreciate and appropriate its message. It is fruitfully read against the historical backdrop of any time between the completion of the temple (515 BC) and the end of the Persian Empire (*c*.332 BC). Indeed, the lack of specific dates in Malachi may suggest hermeneutically that God's Word is not bound to a specific context, but continues to confront new generations of God's people with questions about covenant faithfulness.

There are a couple of other compositional issues worth commenting on. Some have argued that the book of Malachi is the third 'oracle' in a series of 'deuteroprophetic collections', the other two being Zech. 9 – 11 and Zech. 12 – 14 (Petersen 1995: 163, 165; Curtis 2012). Apart from there being no external textual evidence for this hypothesis (all extant texts connect the oracles in Zech. 9 – 14 to chs. 1–8), it also assumes a greater affinity between these three units than is warranted. The two oracles in Zech. 9 – 14 are clearly related thematically to Zech. 1 – 8, and bear a distinct style compared to the book of Malachi (Childs 1979: 491–492; Glazier-McDonald 1987: 27; Mariottini 1998: 151; Floyd 2000: 563; Sweeney 2000b: 719–720). Moreover, nothing seems to be gained for the interpretation of Malachi in viewing these three oracles as an earlier collection. Yet there is certainly value in interpreting Malachi in view of the book of Zechariah and the Book of the Twelve (see 'General introduction', 'Canonical context').

There is considerable debate about the conclusion of Malachi (4:4–6[3:22–24]) as to whether it is original to the book (Glazier-McDonald 1987: 245; Verhoef 1987: 337–338; Floyd 2000: 571; Sweeney 2000b: 714), or was a later addition to round out the collection of the prophets (Rudolph 1976: 7; Redditt 1995: 185; Hill 1998: 363–366). Andrew Hill (1998: 27) maintains that there is a 'complete two-line blank space separating' 4:3[3:21] and 4:4[3:22] in the MT, which indicates that the Masoretes considered the last three verses to be an appendix. Yet this simply is not the case (Freedman 1998: 663). The argument that these verses are secondary because of unique terminology and phraseology is refuted by comparison with other prophetic books, where such stylistic variation is also present. Glazier-McDonald (1987: 251) notes, 'Variety of expression is a characteristic of Israel's literature.' Furthermore, J. M. Gibson (2014a: 294) demonstrates that around 80% of the forty-one words in these verses are used elsewhere in Malachi and are found in each of the main pericopes of the book. Where there are 'syntactical dissimilarities', these can be accounted for as allusions to other texts. For instance, while there is a predicative use of the adjectives 'great' and 'fearful' in 1:14, the attributive use in 4:5[3:23] can be explained as being an allusion to Joel 2:31[3:4], where they are also used attributively. Perhaps the strongest argument for treating these verses as a late addition is the Deuteronomic language and the references to Moses and Elijah. This suggests that 'postexilic editors and/or compilers deliberately selected vocabulary from Deuteronomy (and the Primary History) to cement the literary and theological relationship of the Latter Prophets with the Primary History by means of this appendix' (Hill 1998: 369). Yet Marvin Sweeney (2000b: 714) contends that the statements in the conclusion are integral to the argument of the wider speech. Moreover, Michael Floyd (2000: 571) demonstrates that 'they can hardly be appendices. They are rather an essential part of what Malachi has to say.' My own view, which I discuss further in the commentary, is that they were originally composed as an ending to the book of Malachi, but in doing so there was also a certain canonical consciousness given Malachi's use of the Torah and other biblical material. In the providence of God the conclusion took on a greater canonical significance as the books were collected and further canonical associations were realized.

3. GENRE AND STRUCTURE

The form of the book of Malachi is a series of six disputation speeches with a superscription (1:1) and a concluding exhortation (4:4–6[3:22–24]). The heading 'An oracle' (*maśśā'*) is not a specific genre tag, but introduces the word of Yahweh that renews prophecy along the lines of earlier prophecy and reinforces the status of the book as prophetic (see 'Comment' on 1:1). Joyce Baldwin (1972: 216) notes that out of fifty-five verses, forty-seven record the first-person address of Yahweh to Israel. She comments, 'This use of the first person presents a vivid encounter between God and the people, unsurpassed in the prophetic books.' Malachi also exhibits significant use of earlier biblical texts, which will be explored in this commentary. The study of how these texts are used goes by various names: 'inner-biblical exegesis', 'inner-biblical interpretation' or 'intertextuality'. Studies specifically on Malachi's use of earlier biblical material include Karl Weyde (2000) and Jonathan Gibson (2014a).

The disputation speeches are mostly readily demarcated by theme and structure and do not always follow the chapter divisions, especially in the fourth and sixth speeches. The only exception to ready demarcation is the fourth and fifth speeches, where there are clearly two different topics, but a transitional section between the two speeches makes it difficult to divide them. Most commentators divide at the end of 3:5; however, I divide after 3:7a and give reasons in the commentary. The speeches are 1:2–5; 1:6 – 2:9; 2:10–16; 2:17 – 3:7a; 3:7b–12; and 3:13 – 4:3[3:21].

Egon Pfeiffer (1959) identifies three basic elements in each disputation speech: a statement of the people's belief or attitude, a counter-statement by the prophet, and an argument supporting the counter-statement designed to persuade the audience to change its beliefs or behaviour (as an oracle of threat, admonition or salvation). While this reflects the overall structure of the speeches in general terms, and 'disputation speech' is a helpful genre classification if it is understood broadly, there is some variation within individual speeches. Most speeches begin with a statement (1:2; 2:17;

3:6, 13), but sometimes they begin with rhetorical questions (1:6; 2:10). Sometimes Yahweh presents a counter-statement to the people's belief (e.g. 1:2–5), and sometimes the people present a counter-statement to Yahweh's statement, which is then countered by the prophet (e.g. 1:6). Sometimes the speech has a second statement or question of the people to advance the speech (e.g. 2:14). I discuss this variation further in the 'Form and structure' section of each unit. I also consider 4:4–6[3:22–24] more closely connected to the final speech than Pfeiffer does, for whom it is a secondary appendix.

Looking at the content as well as the form, Elie Assis (2012: 217–218) notes that three speeches (the second, third and fifth) are accusations directed by God against the people for their sins ('prophetic rebuke'). The other three speeches (the first, fourth and sixth) are God's response to the complaints of his people against him. In this way, the speeches are 'mutual accusations' and reflect a central issue of the book – the breach in the covenantal relationship between God and his people.

In terms of audience, the first speech (1:2–5) is directed towards the people as a whole ('Israel'). The second speech (1:6 – 2:9) is directed towards the priests serving in Zerubbabel's temple (1:6; 2:1), but the people are also indirectly addressed. The final four speeches (2:10 – 4:6[3:22]) are all directed towards the people as a whole ('Judah' in 2:10; 'descendants of Jacob' in 3:6).

The rhetorical effect of the speeches has three aspects (Scalise 2009: 318). First, in identifying and voicing the issue that has contributed to the people's cynicism, the audience is drawn in and is perhaps more ready to listen to the answer. Secondly, the meta-communication of voicing the people's complaints is that God knows what they are thinking and is seriously concerned about their attitudes and behaviours. Thirdly, the broad initial accusation is often narrowed to a specific example, which demonstrates that the specific issue relates to a much larger concern. For instance, the priests offering defiled food on the altar is symptomatic of the broader and more serious concern that they are showing contempt for Yahweh (1:6–7).

4. OUTLINE

Superscription: the word of Yahweh to Israel	1:1
First prophetic disputation: Yahweh's love for Israel	1:2–5
Second prophetic disputation: priests despise Yahweh's name	1:6 – 2:9
Third prophetic disputation: unfaithfulness in marriage	2:10–16
Fourth prophetic disputation: Yahweh's justice	2:17 – 3:7a

Fifth prophetic disputation: bring the full tithe	3:7b–12
Sixth prophetic disputation: the day of Yahweh and his justice	3:13 – 4:3[3:13–21]
Concluding exhortation: Moses, Elijah and the coming day	4:4–6[3:22–24]

5. TEXT

This commentary is based on the Hebr. text of *Biblia Hebraica Quinta*, prepared by Anthony Gelston (2010). This reproduces the MT of the Leningrad Codex and collates it with the Aleppo and Cairo codices, noting differences in the apparatus beneath the text.

Only a few pre-Masoretic texts of Malachi survive. Qumran texts that include parts of Malachi are 4Q76 (portions of 2:10 – 4:6[3:24]), 4Q78 (small portions of 3:6–7) and 4Q253a (small portions of 3:16–18). These are well set out in *Biblia Qumranica*, edited by Ego et al. (2005: 190–195).

BHQ also notes variant readings in the LXX, Tg Jonathan, Syr and Vg. In almost all instances, divergences from MT can be explained as a misreading, translational adaptation or stylistic variation (Gelston 2010: 7*–9*). These are noted where relevant in the commentary under 'Notes on the text' for each passage.

6. KEY THEMES

6.1. Covenant

The covenant concept is fundamental to Malachi (McKenzie and Wallace 1983: 549–563; Klein 1987: 35; Verhoef 1987: 180; Berry 1996: 287; Hill 1998: 37; J. M. Gibson 2014a: 2). The word 'covenant' (*bĕrît*) appears six times in Malachi, identifying the 'covenant with Levi' (2:4–5, 8), the 'covenant of our fathers' (2:10), the 'covenant' of marriage (2:14) and 'the messenger of the covenant' (3:1). A covenant is essentially the formalizing of an existing relationship involving promises and obligations that are sealed with an oath (P. R. Williamson 2007). It is often accompanied by a symbolic ceremony such as a sacrifice. A covenant is not simply a legal, contractual matter, but one that is intensely personal, one in which the relationship is primary, often expressed in terms of kinship. This is seen in Malachi, where as well as being a 'great king' (1:14), God is also called 'father' (1:6; 2:10; 3:17). His relationship with his people is expressed in terms of love (1:2; 2:11), hate (1:3; 2:13, 16), anger (1:4), weariness (2:17) and pleasure and displeasure (1:10; 3:4). He is a God who blesses (3:10–12) and curses (2:2, 9, 12; 3:9). The other covenants in Malachi, particularly the covenant of marriage, are modelled on Yahweh's covenant relationship with Israel.

It is essential to understand Malachi's prophecy in the framework of the Mosaic covenant, or else his exhortations may simply appear legalistic. Deuteronomy makes it clear that God saved his people on account of his love and his faithfulness to the covenant with the patriarchs (Deut. 7:7–9). Indeed, in Deuteronomy the saving acts of God are reiterated before the stipulations of the covenant are imposed (e.g. Deut. 5:6). Hence Israel is to keep the covenant requirements because of who Yahweh is and what he has done. Chris Wright (2004: 53–54; italics original) explains this well:

> Israel has had a *unique experience* of God's revelation and redemption. As a result of this, secondly, they now have a *unique knowledge* of the identity of the Lord as God. That in turn means, thirdly, that they now have a *unique responsibility* to live in the midst of the nations in a manner that reflects in their own behaviour the ethical character of the Lord as expressed in the commands he has given them for their own good.

It is no accident that the focus of the first prophetic speech is Israel's failure to understand Yahweh's love for them (1:2–5). Each of the issues Malachi addresses relates to the people's failure to honour and fear Yahweh in response to his love, and to live out their unique covenant responsibility in the midst of the nations. Yahweh's covenant faithfulness contrasts with the priests' unfaithfulness in violating the covenant with Levi (1:6 – 2:9), and the people's unfaithfulness in violating the covenant of the fathers (2:10–19; 3:5, 8–12), including unfaithfulness in their marriage covenants (2:14–16) (McKenzie and Wallace 1983: 558; Klein 1987: 33–34).

Mark Boda (2009: 349) notes with respect to the post-exilic prophets that although there are signs of hope in Haggai and Zech. 1 – 6, Malachi shows that covenant unfaithfulness remains an enduring problem even within this remnant who have returned from the experience of exile. While there was repentance and obedience to the words of Haggai and Zechariah and the temple was rebuilt (e.g. Hag. 1:12–14; Ezra 6:14), Malachi as a whole finishes the collection of the prophets on a note of disappointment and pessimism about human ability to remain faithful to God. Yet, like the end of the Pentateuch (Deut. 30:6), and prophets such as Jeremiah (Jer. 31:31–34) who prophesy a new covenant, the end of Malachi looks towards God to change the hearts of his people (Mal. 4:6[3:24]). This anticipates the work of the Lord Jesus and the new covenant inaugurated by him. In addition, the brief narrative in Mal. 3:16 describes how a part of Malachi's audience ('the fearers of the LORD') respond appropriately to God's call to repent. In doing so, they become a model for subsequent readers and hearers of the book.

6.2. Priesthood and leadership

In Malachi, the priests have a key leadership role in the community and bear a large measure of responsibility for Israel's unfaithfulness in this period. Their responsibility to live out the ways of the Lord before the people and to give regular instruction is clearly identified in 2:5–9 (cf. Zech. 7:3). Malachi calls on the priests to recognize this responsibility and to live up to it. See further Tiemeyer (2006) and Boda (2011).

Julius Wellhausen advanced an evolutionary view of the development of the priesthood that was quite influential (see Pohlig 1998: 6–10). He argued that originally the heads of families in Israel served as priests. Over time those who took on the function of the priests assumed the title of 'Levites' and claimed descent from Levi to gain legitimacy. When David established Jerusalem as the capital in the tenth century, he also established a hereditary priesthood with Zadok in Jerusalem. At this time the Levites were relegated to rural shrines. In the seventh century, when Josiah did away with the rural shrines, the Levites were elevated to the same status as the Zadokite priests, but the reality was that the Zadokites held sway over the Levitical priests, who became unemployed. Wellhausen believed that Ezekiel condoned this situation, saying it was the judgment of God for the unfaithfulness of the Levitical priests. In the post-exilic period, the priesthood was further restricted to a Zadokite priesthood, who were legitimized by calling them 'the sons of Aaron'. For Wellhausen, these distinctions were written back into the Pentateuch in the post-exilic period.

In her study of the priesthood in Malachi, Julia O'Brien (1990) demonstrates that Malachi cannot bear the weight of this proposal. For instance, in 2:5–9 the Levitical priests are praised, but in 3:3 they are said to need purification. Malachi does not distinguish between the sons of Aaron and the Levites. The only division is between the contemporary priests and the ideal priests of the past, who proved faithful in their service (represented by 'Levi' and the 'covenant with Levi').

6.3. The day of Yahweh

The 'day of the LORD' is a uniting theme across the Twelve (cf. Hos. 1:5; 2:18; Joel 1:15; 4:18; Amos 5:18; 9:11) (J. D. W. Watts 1987: 379; Rendtorff 2000). David Petersen (1992a: 579) summarizes the features of the prophetic expectation 'on that day': the coming of Yahweh (often pictured in military terms); Yahweh's enemies receiving their just deserts; those who fear Yahweh (including the nations) being incorporated into his kingdom; his kingdom bringing a time of paradise in the land; the mediation of Yahweh's rule through a righteous Davidic king; and a new covenant. These features of the day of Yahweh accumulate through the Twelve.

In Malachi, the coming day of Yahweh is a prominent theme in the fourth and sixth disputation speeches (3:2, 17; 4:1 [twice], 3, 5[3:19] [twice], 21, 23]). It is a day that the people whom Malachi addresses seem to deny will come (cf. 2:17; 3:14–15), but Malachi assures them that it surely will. It will be a day that refines God's people and transforms their worship (3:2–4), a day where the righteous will be spared and shown compassion (3:17), when they will be healed, blessed and vindicated (4:2[3:20]). Yet it will also be a day when the arrogant and evildoers will be consumed with fire (4:1[3:19]) and destroyed (4:6[3:24]). Malachi (and hence the OT) ends looking to the future, with the exhortation to keep the requirements of the Mosaic covenant, lest the people suffer Yahweh's curse (Hill 2012b: 531).

Unlike the books of Haggai and Zechariah, God's coming is not portrayed by Malachi in military terms (overthrowing the nations). Instead, Malachi's concern is for the cleansing and refining of the priesthood and the people (there is some overlap with Zechariah here; e.g. 3:4–6, 9; 13:1). This focus may account for the absence of explicit reference to a future Davidic king, a prominent feature of Haggai and Zechariah. Yet Malachi's silence is not to be interpreted as a rejection of this hope. Instead, Malachi's hope for the day of Yahweh would also inflame messianic hopes expressed elsewhere in Israel's Scriptures.

A significant development in Malachi with respect to the coming day of Yahweh is the sending of a 'messenger' to prepare the way for Yahweh's coming (3:1) (Snyman 1988: 65). This messenger later seems to be equated with the prophet Elijah, who will restore covenant fidelity or else the land will be totally destroyed (Mal 4:5–6[3:23–24]). In the NT, the 'messenger of the covenant' is John the Baptist (Matt. 11:7–15; Luke 7:18–35) and Jesus is the coming 'Lord' of Mal. 3:1, who brings in the day of Yahweh. The NT also uses the OT imagery of the day of Yahweh with reference to the second coming of Jesus (e.g. 2 Peter 3:10–13). I will explore the 'now and not yet' dimensions of the day of Yahweh in the relevant 'Explanation' sections of the commentary.

TEXT AND COMMENTARY

MALACHI 1:1–5

Translation

1:1 An oracle: the word of the LORD to Israel through Malachi.
2 'I have loved you,' says the LORD. 'But you say, "How have you loved us?" Was
not Esau Jacob's brother?' declares the LORD. 'And I loved Jacob; 3 but Esau I
hated, and I made his mountains a wasteland and his inheritance for jackals of
[the] desert. 4 If Edom says, "We have been demolished, but we will return and we
will rebuild the ruins," so says the LORD of hosts, "They may rebuild, but I will
destroy, and they will call them a territory of wickedness, and the people whom
Yahweh cursed for ever." 5 And your eyes will see [it] and you will say, "The LORD
is great beyond the territory of Israel."'

Notes on the text

1:1. 'to': *'el*. Syr and Tg read 'concerning' (*'al*); but there is some equivalence between *'el* and *'al*, which means that Syr and Tg probably reflect the same *Vorlage* as MT (Gelston 2010: 148*).

'through': *bĕyad*. Lit. 'by the hand of' (cf. Hag. 1:1; see 'Comment').

LXX translates 'Malachi' as 'his angel' and adds, 'Lay it, I pray you, to heart.' Gelston (2010: 148*) suggests this is a gloss from Hag. 2:15, 18.

Tg follows MT in understanding 'Malachi' as a proper name, but one version (Codex Reuchlinianus) adds, 'whose name is Ezra the scribe' (Cathcart and Gordon 1989: 229).

2. 'How': *bammâ*. Lit. 'in what'.

'declares the LORD': *nĕʾum-yhwh* is strictly a noun phrase ('oracle' or 'utterance of the LORD'). Cf. Hag. 1:13; Zech. 1:3.

3. 'for jackals of [the] desert': LXX has *domata*, which seems to be a corruption of *dōmata*, found in Syr and one Tg MS: 'dwellings in a wilderness'. Vg translates as 'serpents of a wilderness'. MT makes sense and I have followed it.

4. 'If': *kî* is translated with a conditional sense. It could also be concessive: 'though' (Arnold and Choi 2003: 151–152).

'We have been demolished': *ruššašnû*. The verb *rāšaš* is used elsewhere in the HB only in Jer. 5:17, and is associated with the destruction of cities (so LXX and Vg). Syr and Tg incorrectly translate, 'we are poor'.

'but we will return': *wĕnāšûb*. Many translate this as 'again' (e.g. Hill 1998: xl; Eddinger 2012:14) or omit and take it to express repetition with the next verb 'rebuild' (e.g. NIV, ESV). Yet there are important thematic reasons for translating it this way (see 'Comment').

'They may rebuild': *hēmmâ yibnû*. The yiqtol is translated with a contingent sense (Arnold and Choi 2003: 59).

'they will call them': *wĕqārʾû lāhem*. The verb *qārāʾ* is often followed by the prep. *lĕ*, which is not translated (cf. Gen. 1:5).

5. 'beyond': *mēʿal*. This translation is supported by Syr and Tg (see 'Comment'). Alternatively, most other occurrences of *mēʿal* in the HB demand the translation 'above' or 'over', which is how it is translated in LXX, though LXX can also have the sense 'above and beyond'. Vg (*super*) can mean 'beyond' as well as 'above' (Stuart 1987: 1292).

Form and structure

This unit contains a superscription for the book of Malachi (v. 1) and the first speech (vv. 2–5). The superscription functions as a preface that identifies and catalogues the literature (Hill 1998: 136). Since the study of Pfeiffer (1959), a majority of scholars have seen the book of Malachi dividing into six disputation speeches, each beginning with a question and answer arrangement. Assis (2010a: 358–359) observes that form-critical study of Malachi has tended to treat the individual speeches of the book in isolation from each other and pursued questions of genre and *Sitz im Leben* rather than explore how the speeches connect with each other in the final form of the book. Yet the theme of Yahweh's love for Israel and implicitly his covenant faithfulness, which is defended in the first disputation speech, undergirds the rhetoric of the whole book, establishing the foundation for later exhortations (Keil 1949: 430; Stuart 1998: 1249;

Clendenen 2004: 245; Anderson 2011: 215). Yahweh's covenant faithfulness contrasts the priests' unfaithfulness in violating the covenant with Levi (2:1–9), and the people's unfaithfulness in violating the covenant of the fathers (2:10–19; 3:5, 8–12), including unfaithfulness in their marriage covenants (2:14–16) (McKenzie and Wallace 1983: 558).

The first disputation speech begins with a declaration by the prophet of Yahweh's point of view (v. 2a–b). This is quickly followed by a counter-question that indicates a contradictory attitude of the people (v. 2c). The body of the speech then disputes the people's attitude and demonstrates Yahweh's point of view (vv. 2d–5). This is slightly different from the typical prophetic dispute, where the prophet first states the popular view and then takes issue with it (Floyd 2000: 584).

Nogalski (2011: 1011) demonstrates a pattern of three pairings in an A/B B/A parallelism as follows:

(A) I have loved you	(B) says the LORD
(B) But you say	(A) How have you loved us?
Was not Esau Jacob's brother?	
(A') And I loved	(B') Jacob
(B') but Esau	(A') I hated
I made his mountains a wasteland . . .	
(A") We have been demolished	(B") we will rebuild the ruins
(B") They may build	(A") but I will destroy
Your eyes will see . . .	

This structure demonstrates the coherence of the unit, with each pairing developing from the previous one. The final line answers the question posed in A.

Comment

1:1. 'An oracle' (*maśśāʼ*) is a heading for the book. The same word begins the books of Nahum and Habakkuk, as well as introducing units within prophetic books (e.g. Zech. 9:1; 12:1). It also appears throughout prophetic literature (e.g. Isa. 13:1; 14:28; 15:1; 17:1; 19:1; 21:1, 11, 13; 22:1; 23:1; 30:6; Jer. 23:33–38; Ezek. 12:10). A precise definition is elusive. Some scholars seek its meaning from the word's etymology; others by its usage. In terms of etymology, a *maśśāʼ* (possibly related to *nāśāʼ*) is understood as something weighty or burdensome to lift (cf. Exod. 23:5; Num. 11:11), hence it describes a burdensome prophecy or one of doom (Smith 1984: 302). Yet there is often much hope in prophecies titled 'an oracle' as well (e.g. the statement of Yahweh's love for Israel in this first speech). Alternatively, a *maśśāʼ* has been understood as being related to 'lifting up' one's voice, hence a 'pronouncement' or 'proclamation' (Sweeney 2000b: 423). In a comprehensive study, Boda (2006: 350) concludes that *maśśā'* is not a specific genre description since it can denote prophetic imaginative pictures, laments or poems. Rather, it is a general tag denoting 'prophetic revelation'. Some argue that a *maśśā'* interprets previous revelation only and shows how it is coming to pass in human history, rather than giving any new prophetic revelation itself (Weis 1986; Floyd 2002). However, Boda (2006: 356) shows that a *maśśā'* introduces the word of Yahweh that renews prophecy along the lines of earlier prophecy. As a heading, it bolsters the status of the prophetic book.

The noun phrase 'The word of the LORD' is best understood as being in apposition to 'An oracle' (so NIV) rather than being an extended const., which is awkward (e.g. ESV: 'The oracle of the word of the LORD'). This is the only time this phrase occurs in the book of Malachi, though it occurs five times in Haggai and thirteen times throughout Zechariah. Like 'An oracle', it also functions to legitimize the book as divine revelation from 'Yahweh', the covenant name of God revealed to Israel (cf. Exod. 3:14–15).

That this word comes 'to Israel' is striking given the nation's history (cf. 1:5; 2:16; 4:4[3:22]). As a name, 'Israel' had most recently been attached to the northern tribes in contrast to the southern kingdom of 'Judah' (e.g. Hos. 1:1; Amos 1:1). The kingdom split after Solomon's reign, under Jeroboam and Rehoboam (cf. 1 Kgs 12). The kingdom of 'Israel' was judged by Yahweh through the Assyrians in 722 BC, and Judah was later judged by Yahweh through the Babylonians, culminating in the destruction of Jerusalem and the temple in 586 BC. Yet the prophets foresaw a time when the exiled and scattered people would return and reunite to become again the one people of God (e.g. Ezek. 37:15–28; Zech. 9:9–13; 10:6–10). This hope seems to lie behind the use of 'Israel' in Zech. 12:1, where the prophet looks forward to its fulfilment. This reunion had certainly not taken place in Malachi's day since hostilities with the people of Samaria (the old capital of 'Israel') are evident in Ezra and Nehemiah. Its use in this verse, especially given the focus on Jacob and Esau in the first speech (vv. 2–5), seems to look way back to God's dealings with the patriarchs to indicate that the people to whom this book was addressed were heirs of the promises concerning 'Israel'.

The translation 'through' is literally 'by the hand of' (*bĕyad*). This expression is used in relation to the prophets generally (e.g. Ezek. 38:17; Dan. 9:10; Zech. 7:7, 12), once of Isaiah (20:2), twice of Jeremiah (37:2; 50:1) and three times of Haggai (1:1, 3; 2:1). It indicates that they are agents of Yahweh and mediate his word. It is used almost thirty times of Moses' words (e.g. Exod. 9:35; Lev. 8:36; Josh. 14:2; 1 Kgs 8:53; Neh. 8:14); and if this allusion is picked up by the reader, it suggests Malachi's prophetic authority is like that of Moses.

Concerning the designation 'Malachi' (lit. 'my messenger'), see 'Author and date' in the 'Introduction to Malachi' above. For the reasons given there, I consider it an actual name.

2–3. The first prophetic disputation speech begins with Yahweh's statement 'I have loved you.' The Hebr. indicates that it is not only God's love in the past, but also his love in the present that is in view since the qatal expresses anterior action that leads to a state relevant to the moment of speaking (Joosten 2012: 194). The Hebr. word for 'love' here is not *ḥesed* (also translated 'grace', 'kindness', 'loyalty') but *'āhab*, which is the basis for Yahweh's choice of Israel in the first place (cf. Deut. 4:37; 10:15; 1 Kgs 10:9; Jer. 31:3). God's love for his people is fundamental to the relationship, a relationship that is to be understood in covenantal terms (McKenzie and Wallace 1983). Importantly, a covenant is not simply a political arrangement, but a familial experience of belonging (Hafemann 2007: 34). At the beginning of the Book of the Twelve, Hosea compares God's 'love' (*'āhab*) to the bond of a husband and wife (Hos. 3:1), and a father and child (Hos. 11:1–4). In Deuteronomy, Yahweh's election of Israel is linked with his love (4:37; 7:7; 10:15). In response to God's love, Israel is called to love God with all their heart, soul and strength (Deut. 6:5). Just as mutual love is what holds members of a family together, so it holds the relationship between Yahweh and his people together. Yet tragically, in Hosea's day Israel loved almost everything apart from God (cf. Hos. 2:5, 7, 10, 12–13; 3:1; 4:18; 9:1, 10; 12:7).

To this statement Malachi represents the people's response 'How have you loved us?' Or, more literally, 'In what way have you loved us?' This question can be seen in two very different ways: as an insolent question expressing doubt (Clendenen 2004: 244), or as a painful cry from the midst of suffering, similar to Job or the laments of the psalms (Achtemeier 1986: 173). These are not necessarily mutually exclusive options and both attitudes were probably present among the people. The book of Malachi reveals economic circumstances similar to the time of Haggai that would have proven troubling (e.g. 3:9–12) and one can imagine a crisis of confidence since many of the promises of the earlier prophets had not yet been realized. Perhaps people felt that God had rejected them (Assis 2009: 112). At the same time, the tone of other disputations indicates that people's attitude towards Yahweh was far from what it should have been (in 1:6, the priests despise his name; in 2:17 the people have wearied him with their words; in 3:13 they have spoken harshly against him). Whether the people are insolent or distressed, Yahweh responds with grace. In this first disputation he reminds them of their chosen status and how this is evident in their present circumstances. Referring back to the outworking of the patriarchal covenant, Yahweh argues that his choice of Jacob over Esau and hence his love for Israel is being played out before their eyes.

The intriguing story of the twins Jacob and Esau points to God's grace in choosing Israel. From the time the boys were womb-mates, they jostled each other. Indeed, sibling rivalry is a theme of Genesis: from Cain and Abel through to Joseph and his brothers. The twins' mother, Rebekah, is told after enquiring of Yahweh:

Two nations are in your womb,
  and two peoples from within you will be separated;
one people will be stronger than the other,
  and the older will serve the younger.
(Gen. 25:23)

Significantly, this oracle refers to 'nations' and looks to its fulfilment beyond the brothers in their descendants, as is the focus of Malachi, with 'Edom' (v. 4) referring to the descendants of Esau, and 'Israel' (vv. 1, 5) to the descendants of Jacob. The motif 'the older will serve the younger' is found elsewhere in Genesis, where God often chooses and approves of the younger sibling, through whom he will accomplish his purpose and bring blessing. For instance, the offering of the younger brother Abel is chosen over Cain's, and then the line of promise goes through Seth rather than the older Cain (Gen. 4:26 – 5:8), Rachel is chosen over her older sister Leah (29:18), Joseph, the youngest son of Jacob, is chosen over the rest (37:3), and then Judah is chosen over his older brothers (49:8). Sailhamer (1992: 186) comments:

> Behind each of these 'reversals' was the recurring theme of God's sovereign plan of grace. The blessing was not a natural right, as a right of the firstborn son would be. Rather, God's blessing was extended to those who had no other claim to it. They all received what they did not deserve.

God does not always act according to human expectations.

Yahweh's statement in Malachi 'And I loved Jacob; but Esau I hated' is not a direct quote from Genesis. The closest echo is the narrator's statement 'Isaac, who had a taste for wild game, loved Esau, but Rebekah loved Jacob' (Gen. 25:28). In this context, 'loved' indicates favour and the divided affections of the parents towards their boys. There is nothing to indicate that the parent 'hated' or felt animosity towards the other offspring (Mathews 2005: 391). Yahweh's statement 'And I loved Jacob; but Esau I hated' in so far as it reflects the Genesis account refers to God's choice of Jacob over Esau and how it plays out in their lives with Esau despising his birthright (25:36) and being tricked out of Isaac's blessing (27:35). These are human actions that reflect God's prior choice (see 'Explanation').

Some commentators argue that 'hated' is only a relative term: that Yahweh loved Esau less than he loved Jacob (Laetsch 1956: 512; Elliger 1982: 190), or that 'hate' is covenant language and the English translation 'hate' 'is too strong here' (Smith 1984: 305), or that it is only 'an expression of Judah's feelings' (Redditt 1995: 162). It is true that there are instances where 'loved' and 'hated' or 'not loved' are used with a relative sense (e.g. Gen. 29:30–33; Deut. 21:15; cf. Matt. 6:24; Luke 14:26; John 12:25), and in so far as the Genesis narrative is concerned it seems appropriate to understand 'hated' with the relative sense. Genesis does not indicate that Esau is absolutely 'hated' by God. Esau is later reconciled with Jacob, who bows down seven times before him (Gen. 33:3), and the end of the account tells of the way Esau has been blessed (though it does not use this word) during his time in Canaan. His possessions have become too numerous for him to remain in the land; so he moves to what Malachi calls his 'inheritance', the hill country of Seir (the region directly to the south-east of the Dead Sea) as the father of the Edomites (Gen. 36:6–8). It has even been said that Esau leaves the stage as 'a noble man' (Krause 2008: 484).

However, the deft switching from Esau to Esau's descendants in Mal. 1:3–4, and the descriptions of what Yahweh has done to Edom and why, indicate that in Malachi Yahweh's hatred of Esau should be understood as his anger, expressed in his righteous judgment of Edom. 'Love' and 'hate' are not used as relative terms, but as 'stark language of choice' (Anderson 2011: 218). God's hatred of Esau is explained: 'I made his mountains a wasteland and his inheritance for jackals of [the] desert' (v. 3). The 'mountains' refers to the home of the Edomites (cf. Jer. 49:10, 16; Ezek. 35:2–3, 7–8, 15; Obad. 3–4), and 'wasteland' (*šĕmāmâ*) can also be translated 'desolation' (cf. Ezek. 35:12, 15; Joel 3:19[4:19]). The 'jackals' are wilderness animals associated with death and disorder (cf. Isa. 34:13). The language of this phrase is designed to evoke the depth of God's wrath (Eggleston 2012: 844).

The reason for Yahweh's judgment is Edom's wickedness (v. 4). Edom had a reputation for anger and violence, particularly against Israel (cf. Amos 1:11–12). In several passages, Edom is indicted for the way it supported the Babylonians against its brother Jacob on the day Jerusalem fell (e.g. Ps. 137:7; Ezek. 25:12–14; 35:1–15; Obad. 10–14). Hill (1998: 152) explains, 'The Edomites were guilty of false worship, violence, of rejecting God and hating his people Israel – all things Yahweh hates . . . Because Yahweh is a God who hates, he also judges and destroys in his wrath all those who oppose and hate him (cf. Exod. 20:5; Deut. 7:15; 30:7; 32:41).'

'I made' (*wā'āśîm*) indicates a judgment of God prior to Malachi's day. However, not a lot is known about Edom in this period due to 'a dearth of historical sources following the Assyrian period' (Bienkowski 2001: 199). Several scholars argue that the Neo-Babylonian king Nabonidus (555–539 BC) brought an end to the independence of Edom during the military campaigns of his third year in 553 BC (Lindsay 1976: 32; Bartlett 1989: 159–161). While there was destruction, it seems Nabonidus' intention was not to annihilate the Edomites, but to subjugate them, and presumably some level of exile took place given the Babylonian practice elsewhere. A destructive campaign against Edom by Nabonidus is consistent with the picture in Malachi, which also envisages survivors. But there could have been another campaign against Edom that is not recorded elsewhere.

4. The Edomites, like the Israelites, had suffered great loss to their 'inheritance' prior to Malachi's day (v. 3). The parallel with Israel's situation is clear, for the people of Judah had already returned from exile to rebuild their inheritance in the land after Cyrus' decree (*c.*538 BC). Indeed, LeCureux (2012: 212) suggests Judah's restoration could be behind Edom's statement of hope that 'we will return and we will build the ruins'. Many translations neglect the theological significance of the word 'return' (*šûb*) and translate it 'again' (or omit it), but this word conveys the hope of renewal throughout the Book of the Twelve.

The main point of difference is that whereas Yahweh has enabled the people of Judah to return and to rebuild, here he states his intention to destroy again anything the Edomites might rebuild. They will be known as 'a territory of wickedness', a country without a name (J. M. Gibson 2014a: 93) – 'the people whom Yahweh cursed for ever'. While it is common to translate *zā'am* with the sense of '[he is] angry' (e.g. NIV, ESV, NASB; cf. Zech. 1:12), Glazier-McDonald (1987: 34) favours '[he has] cursed' since one of the features of the curse is 'its unqualified and irrevocable execution'. This suits the context here as the curses on the inheritance of Edom correspond to the covenant theme of the passage (McKenzie and Wallace 1983: 556). The curse also reflects the promise to Abram: 'whoever curses you I will curse' (Gen. 12:3). As well as being judged in the past (like Israel), Israel's traditional enemy and brother Edom will continue to come under God's curse in the future (unlike Israel). In this, Yahweh's love for Israel will be seen.

The description of Yahweh as 'LORD of hosts' (or 'Yahweh of armies', or 'Yahweh, the Almighty') occurs 24 times in Malachi (14 times in Haggai and 53 times in Zechariah). See 'Comment' on Hag. 1:2 for its background. It is a phrase that speaks of the might of Yahweh as king and here underlines the certainty of his word coming to pass.

V. 4 also echoes the judgment announced in Jer. 49:13 for the Edomite capital Bozrah (aka Busayra). Like v. 3, it is difficult to pinpoint when this destruction might have taken place. J. M. O'Brien (2004: 292–293) notes that the Greek writer Diodorus Siculus indicates that Edom was inhabited by Nabateans by 312 BC, but it is not known when this Nabatean control began – they may not have conquered Edom so much as settled there over a period of time as Edom declined.

Significantly, Ezekiel also prophesies the demise of Edom as a prelude to the restoration of Israel (Ezek. 35 – 36; cf. Obadiah), and J. M. Gibson (2014a: 84) demonstrates that Malachi is drawing on this passage to show how Yahweh has kept his word against Edom spoken through the prophet Ezekiel, proving his covenant faithfulness.

5. Hill (1998: 160) rightly notes there is no explicit object of 'will see' and suggests that Israel will 'perceive' or 'understand' God's love (v. 2). Yet the phrase 'your eyes will see' recalls Deuteronomy, where Israel is reminded of specific instances of Yahweh's deliverance rather than his character (e.g. Deut. 3:21; 4:3, 9; 7:19; 10:21; 11:7; 29:2). Yahweh's people will see Edom's demise.

There are two competing interpretations of the final phrase depending on whether *mēʿal* is translated 'beyond' or 'over' (see 'Notes on the text'). The usual interpretation is that when God finally destroys Edom, the people of Israel will acknowledge that 'The LORD is great *beyond* the territory of Israel' (cf. ESV, NIV, NASB). The acclamation that 'The LORD is great' is elsewhere found on the lips of the psalmist to praise God's righteousness (Ps. 35:27) and his salvation (Pss 40:16[17]; 70:4[5]). Goswell (2013: 627–628) suggests that if v. 5 is analogous with Israel's prayers in the psalter, which move from lament to thanksgiving, this indicates that the expression 'The LORD is great' is Israel's future response to Yahweh's action in their favour against the enemy nation of Edom. The final phrase is therefore an expression of joy by God's people for his judgment of Edom (which is *beyond* the territory of Israel). It celebrates God's sovereignty over the nations and his love for Israel in destroying their traditional enemy (and brother).

The alternative interpretation is that when Yahweh's people see the demise of Edom, they will declare a hymn of praise that 'The LORD is great *over* the territory of Israel' (Verhoef 1987: 221; Hill 1998: 160; Baker 2006: 221). Those who offer this interpretation contend that the first interpretation does not directly address Judah's question 'How have you loved us?' (v. 2). In addition, they argue that the spreading fame of God does not fit the context. In response to these objections, note that the acclamation is not made by the nations; instead, it is Israel's recognition that God is at work beyond their own borders to bring about his purposes for his people. Furthermore, the wider context of the book expresses an international focus (1:11, 14). Therefore the usual interpretation is preferable (*beyond* the territory of Israel), but both interpretations make it clear that Yahweh has worked out his purposes in the history of the nation of Edom, and so demonstrated his love for his people with the result that his people will one day be moved from insolence and doubt to praise.

Explanation

The book of Malachi is introduced in v. 1 as the word of Yahweh to Israel and comes with all of his authority. Being addressed to 'Israel' in the post-exilic period, it looks behind the disaster of exile and the history of the divided nation to God's covenant with Israel mediated through Moses, and behind that to the promises to the patriarchs, of which the Jewish community in Malachi's day are the heirs. God's promise to Abraham included land, a great nation, a great name and blessing for his descendants (Gen. 12:1–2). Furthermore, just as God's purpose in creation was to bless all people, so his promise to Abraham was to extend blessing to the nations who bless him (Gen. 12:3; cf. Exod. 19:6; Deut. 28:10; Pss 72:17; 86:9; Isa. 19:24–25; 25:6–8; 48:18–19; Jer. 4:1–2; Zech. 8:13; Rom. 10:12–13;

Rev. 5:9–10). God also promises a curse on those who curse Abram and his people (Gen. 12:3), and this is played out in the history of Edom in this passage. In the wider story of the Bible, God chose Abraham and Israel for the benefit of the nations and it seems that Israel in Malachi's day had forgotten this. They saw themselves as being no different from the nations, and this is reflected later in the book in their assimilation of the practices of the nations.

In many ways, this first dispute cuts to the heart of the problem that will show itself in the other matters Malachi raises. A failure to appreciate God's love cannot but show itself in a failure to love him and to live as his chosen people. Indeed, Clendenen (2004: 245) argues that understanding God's sovereign covenant love functions as motivation for all of Malachi's exhortations: giving him the worship he deserves (1:6 – 2:9), being faithful in relationships (2:10 – 3:6) and living in dependence on him (3:7 – 4:6). God's love is the indicative that undergirds the later imperatives.

With Israel's failure to appreciate God's love, one might expect the prophet to rehearse the history of God's dealings with his people. Yet that history was already on the public record and presumably well known. Instead, Malachi points to God's dealings with Israel's brother-nation Edom to show how 'Israel had experienced the covenant love of Yahweh but sadly did not recognize it in the fall of Edom nor appreciate it as the handiwork of God' (Hill 1998: 169). In other words, Malachi argues that evidence of God's love lies before their very eyes.

Nogalski (2011: 1001) usefully outlines how this passage resolves, from a literary point of view, the fate of Edom in the Book of the Twelve. Earlier judgment oracles against Edom always project this judgment into the future (Joel 3:19; Amos 1:11–12; 9:12; Obad. 1–21). The logic of Mal. 1:2–5 is that Edom has been punished and will remain under God's curse. When read against the backdrop of Obadiah, this opening passage of Malachi also raises the expectation that the day of Yahweh is near and this day becomes the focus of the second half of the book of Malachi.

The opening disputation speech of Malachi challenges contemporary readers with some profound and difficult theological issues. God's election of individuals and nations is a topic that has aroused controversy and debate among Christians from NT times. In addition, the 'love of God' sounds straightforward enough until one attempts to articulate it in a postmodern, sentimental, syncretistic and often pluralistic Western culture (Carson 2000: 9–17). The challenge is not to speak more than the Bible speaks, nor to speak less.

Some commentators find the idea of election problematic. For instance, Nogalski (2011: 1015) states, 'theological paradigms with a strong emphasis on election tend to justify the status quo as part of God's plan more often than they change behavior to fit God's expectations'. While emphasizing election certainly can lead to complacency, down-playing election can have just as serious spiritual implications such as pride and insecurity.

The challenge is to hold together the scriptural teaching on the sovereignty of God in election (including the inscrutability of his ways) and the responsibility the Bible lays on all people for their decisions and actions in life. Tipping the balance too far in one direction or the other is when problems arise. The balance is captured simply in Phil. 2:12–13: 'continue to work out your salvation with fear and trembling [human responsibility], for it is God who works in you to will and to act in order to fulfil his good purpose [God's sovereignty over human wills and actions]'. The balance is also seen in Genesis where God's sovereign choice of Jacob over Esau in the womb is not worked out in a way that is contrary to the desires of either of the brothers. While Esau was the firstborn, he sold his birthright to Jacob for a pot of lentil stew, and the narrator concludes, 'So Esau despised his birthright' (Gen. 25:34). Later, with the help of his mother, Jacob tricks his father Isaac by impersonating his brother Esau, and receives the blessing of the firstborn, which includes being lord over his brothers (Gen. 27:29). These are portrayed as real human decisions that bring about the foreordained purposes of God. This is part of a much wider pattern in Genesis that can be traced through the Abraham stories where God achieves his purpose through the faithful and unfaithful actions of Abraham, through to the Joseph stories, which culminate in Gen. 50:20–21 with Joseph's statement about his brothers' evil actions: 'You intended to harm me, but God intended it for good to accomplish what is now being done, the saving of many lives. So then, don't be afraid' (cf. Gen. 45:5–8).

Similarly, in Malachi, God's statement 'Esau I hated' is worked out in the judgment on Edom for its wickedness and there is no sense in which this is undeserved (even though it fulfils the word of God; cf. Ezek. 35). God's love for Israel is what is undeserved and seemingly unappreciated by the people in Malachi's day.

That God elects some and rejects others is a scriptural fact (cf. John 10:26; Rom. 9:18; 11:7–8; 1 Peter 2:6–8; Jude 3–4). Why God chooses some and not others is a mystery (Rom. 11:33–36), but in the end will demonstrate his glory. Paul quotes Mal. 1:2 in Rom. 9:13, a passage where he explores why so many of his Jewish brothers and sisters have rejected Jesus as the Christ. One of the pegs that Paul stakes in the ground early on in his argument is God's election, of which his choice of Jacob over Esau is an illustration. For Paul, election is a corollary of God's sovereign power (Rom. 9:17, 22), and grace is only grace if there is election, otherwise people would be saved by their good works (Rom. 9:11, 16). The doctrine of election, rightly understood, leads not to disobedient complacency, but to faith and obedience in thankful response to God's love and grace. The reality is that neither Jacob nor Esau nor any human being deserves God's love. All have sinned and fall short of the glory of God. That he elects any for his good purposes in history, or for eternal salvation, is the wonder of it all.

MALACHI 1:6 – 2:9

Translation

1:6'A son honours a father and a servant his master. But if I am a father, where is my honour? And if I am a master, where is my fear?' says the LORD of hosts to you, O priests, who are despising my name. 'But you say, "How have we despised your name?" 7Offering upon my altar defiled food. But you say, "How have we defiled you?" When you say, "The table of the LORD – it is despised." 8And when you offer blind ones for sacrifice [and say], "There is no evil!" And when you offer lame and sick [and say], "There is no evil!" Indeed, offer it to your governor – will he accept you or show you favour?' says the LORD of hosts.

9'And now, entreat the favour of God, so that he will be gracious to us. This was from your hand. Will he show you favour?' says the LORD of hosts. 10'Who is [there] even among you [who] will shut [the temple] doors – so you may not light my altar for nothing. I take no pleasure in you,' says the LORD of hosts. 'And I will not accept an offering from your hand. 11For from [the] rising of [the] sun even to its setting, my name will be great among the nations, and in every place a burnt sacrifice will be offered in my name and a pure offering. For my name will be great among the nations,' says the LORD of hosts. 12'But you are profaning it when you say, "The table of my Lord: it is defiled; and its fruit – its food – is despised." 13And you say, "Look, what a burden!" And you snort [at] it,' says the LORD of hosts. 'And you bring injured and the lame and the sick – and you bring [them as] the offering! Should I accept it from your hand?' says the LORD. 14'So cursed be the deceiver when there is a male [animal] in his flock and he vows [to give it] but sacrifices a blemished [animal] to the Lord. For I am a great king,' says the LORD of hosts, 'and my name will be feared among the nations.

2:1'And now, this command is for you, O priests. 2If you will not listen and if you will not take it to heart to give glory to my name,' says the LORD of hosts, 'then I will send the curse against you and I will curse your blessings and indeed I have cursed them because you are not taking it to heart. 3Look, I will rebuke your offspring, and I will splatter crap on your faces – the crap of your festivals. Then he will carry you to it. 4And you will know that I sent you this command so that my covenant with Levi might continue,' says the LORD of hosts. 5'My covenant with him was life and peace – and I gave them to him. Respect – and he respected me. And before my name he was awestruck. 6True instruction was in his mouth, and wrong was not found on his lips. He walked with me in peace and in uprightness, and he turned many from sin. 7For [the] lips of a priest should guard knowledge and they should seek instruction from his mouth, for he is the messenger of the LORD of hosts. 8But you have turned from the way. You have caused many to fall by [your] instruction. You have violated the covenant of Levi,' says the LORD of hosts. 9'And so I made you despised and humiliated before all the people, because you are not keeping my ways and are showing partiality in [your] instruction.'

Notes on the text

1:6. 'his master': *'ădōnāyw* is pl. in form, but clearly sg. in meaning; possibly a pl. of majesty (Eddinger 2012: 20) or indicating the abstract (Stuart 1998: 1294).

7. 'defiled': *měgō'āl* may be a byform of *gā'al*, which means 'defiled' (Averbeck 1997).

'food': *leḥem* is more usually translated 'bread', but the word can have a wider connotation (e.g. Neh. 5:14), and the sacrifices mentioned in v. 8, if they are the same, are animal sacrifices. The many parallels in this verse with v. 12, which uses *'ōkel*, also suggests 'food' is appropriate.

'When you say': *be'ĕmorkem*. When *bĕ* is used with the inf. const., it frequently connotes 'when' or 'whenever' (Arnold and Choi 2003: 104). The pr. suff. functions as the subject.

LXX changes 'How have we defiled you?' to 'How have we defiled them?' to remove the claim of defiling God.

LXX adds to the end of the verse, 'and the food set upon it is despised', which Gelston (2010: 149*) believes is derived from v. 12.

8. 'And when': *wĕkî* continues the temporal sense from v. 7.

'you offer': *taggišûn* has a paragogic nun in the first instance.

'[and say]' is understood from the previous verse. It introduces a verbless clause that some translations follow LXX in rendering as a question (e.g. NIV, ESV, NRSV), or as a statement of the prophet. See 'Comment'.

'Indeed': *nā'* seems to indicate the imper. is a logical consequence of the previous statements (Waltke and O'Connor 1990: 578).

'accept you': some LXX MSS have 'accept it'.

'show you favour': lit. 'lift up your faces', an idiom (Eddinger 2012: 25).

9. 'entreat the favour of God': lit. 'make favourable the face of God' (cf. Zech. 7:2; 8:21–22; Mal. 1:9).

'so that': The sequence imp. + waw + prefix conjugation expresses purpose or result (Hill 1998: 182).

'show you favour': lit. 'lift up from you faces', an idiom (cf. v. 8). LXX and Syr render in the first person in view of the subsequent oracle formula 'shall I accept you?

10. 'Who is [there] even among you [who] will shut [the temple] doors?': *mî gam-bākem wĕyisgōr dĕlātayim* is a difficult phrase to translate on account of its idiomatic language. Compare the versions: LXX: 'because [reading *kî*?] even among you the doors shall be shut'; Syr: 'who is there among you who would guard my doors' (Hill 1998: 184); Tg adds, 'doors *of my Sanctuary*' (Cathcart and Gordon 1989: 230). The form of 'doors' is dual.

'for nothing': *ḥinnām* is an adv. phrase. LXX and Vg translate as 'freely'.

'I take no pleasure in you': lit. 'There is not to me pleasure in you.'

11. 'a burnt sacrifice': *mūqṭār* is a hophal ptc. taken as a subst. Glazier-McDonald (1987: 57) argues it 'can easily be understood as a general term for that which is sacrificed since verbs derived from the stem *QṬR* indicate the rising of the smoke of sacrifice (Lev 1:9f; 2:11; 6:15; 8:21; 9:13f, 17, 20; Num 5:26)'.

12. 'its fruit': *nîbô* occurs elsewhere only in Isa. 57:19. Gelston (2010: 150*) believes LXX guessed at its meaning and was followed by Vg. It is omitted in Syr and Tgs, but MT makes sense and is followed as the more difficult reading. See Glazier-McDonald 1987: 62.

13. 'what a burden!': *mattĕlā'â* comprises the interr. particle *mâ* and the noun *tĕlā'â*. Eddinger (2012: 32) argues it is best translated as an expression of exasperation. The versions all interpret the *m* as the prep. *min* (Gelston 2010: 150*).

'And you snort [at] it': *wĕhippaḥtem 'ôtô*. Lit. 'and you blow it'. This is taken by most commentators to be a colloquial expression of contempt or exasperation (Pohlig 1998: 58).

'injured': *gāzûl* derives from the verb 'to steal' (Lev. 19:3; Judg. 9:25; Job 24:2). Since the other animals are 'lame' and 'sick', many scholars suggest that these animals have been violently stolen by wild animals and recovered in an 'injured' condition and then offered to the priests (Pohlig 1998: 58–59). See 'Comment'. Syr and Vg introduce a partitive sense. LXX and Vg render as a pl. (Gelston 2010: 150*).

14. 'the deceiver': lacks the art. in Hebr., but refers to a class, so is added (Hill 1998: 194).

2:2. 'take it to heart': lit. 'you will set upon a heart' (cf. Hag. 1:5). See 'Comment'.

'taking it to heart': lit. 'setting upon a heart' (see above).

'then I will send': *wĕšillaḥtî*. The waw represents the beginning of the apodosis, hence 'then'. The context demands that the qatal be translated in the future (an irrealis qatal) (J. A. Cook 2012: 249–256). The same holds for 'and I will curse' (*wĕ'ārôtî*).

'I have cursed them': lit. 'I have cursed it'. The referent of 'it' (f. sg.) is 'blessings' (f. pl.), but they are understood in a comprehensive manner (Hill 1998: 199).

'committing': lit. 'setting upon heart' (see above).

3. 'I will rebuke your offspring': LXX and Vg read, 'I will cut off the shoulder'. The word 'offspring' (*zera'*) can be given different vowels and read as 'arm' (*zeroa'*), which may account for this difference. In this instance it seems to be understood as God's rendering the priests powerless to act (Verhoef 1987: 241), or being deprived of the choice portions of the sacrifice (J. J. Collins 2012: 131).

'then he will carry': *wĕnāśā'*. The waw expresses consequent action, hence 'then'. The context demands that the qatal be translated in the future (an irrealis qatal) (J. A. Cook 2012: 249–256).

4. 'so that . . . might continue': *lihyôt* (from the verb 'to be'). The prep. *lĕ* with the inf. const. expresses purpose (Arnold and Choi 2003: 111).

5. 'life and peace': *haḥayyîm wĕhaššālôm* both have the def. art. since they refer to abstract states, but the articles are not translated (Waltke and O'Connor 1990: 246). Cf. Zech. 8:19; Mal. 2:17.

6. 'True instruction': lit. 'It was instruction of truth'.

7. 'should guard': *yišmĕrû*. The context suggests yiqtol indicates obligation (Arnold and Choi 2003: 59).

9. 'And so': *wĕgam* (lit. 'and also') here seems to mark the climax of the exposition (Waltke and O'Connor 1990: 663; Clendenen 2004: 317).

'before all': *lĕkol*, where *lĕ* is used to specify the object of the prep.; that is, 'with regard to all' (Arnold and Choi 2003: 113).

'the people': *hā'ām*. LXX and Vg have 'the nations', a 'misinterpretation' (Gelston 2010: 150*).

'because': *kĕpî 'ăšer*. This is an idiomatic expression that occurs only here in the OT (Eddinger 2012: 52).

'and are showing partiality': *wĕnōś'îm pānîm*. Lit. 'lifting up faces'. See 'Comment'.

Form and structure

This passage forms the longest disputation speech in the book. It is a stinging rebuke directed at the priests (1:6; 2:1) for the way they fail to honour Yahweh. While directed at the priests, the people are also implicated for their defiled and blemished offerings and for turning from the way (Boda 2011: 16). The passage serves to challenge all readers and hearers about their attitudes in serving and obeying God and graphically portrays the offensiveness of not giving him the glory he deserves.

The speech can be divided thematically into two main sections that reflect the different responsibilities in which the priests failed: in their sacrificial duties (1:6–14); and in their instruction and behaviour (2:1–9). Glazier-McDonald (1987: 47) argues that 1:6–14 is a speech of condemnation, followed by a speech of punishment in 2:1–9, but there is punishment in 1:14 and condemnation in 2:8. Floyd (2000: 589) argues that 1:6–14 is a 'prophecy of punishment' and 2:1–9 is a 'call to repentance', with 1:6 – 2:16 as a whole being a 'prophetic exhortation'. Yet the call to repent is only implicit, and 2:2 and 2:9 indicate that the punishment has already begun. J. M. O'Brien (1990: 64–66) argues that the speech is a covenant lawsuit, yet covenant violation does not form the heart of the accusation. Like the other speeches in Malachi, it begins as a 'disputation speech', particularly to the end of ch. 1. The disputation is between Yahweh and the priests, but the dialogue of the priests is reported indirectly, with the phrase 'you say' being used four times (vv. 6, 7, 12, 13; it is possibly implicit twice more in v. 8). The speech formula 'says the LORD of hosts' is used seven times in 1:6–14, and three times in 2:1–9, with an additional 'says the LORD' in 1:13. In the second part of the speech (2:1–9), the dialogue drops out. The speech formula 'says the LORD of hosts' is used three times with no reported speech of the priests. Schuller (1996: 859) comments, 'no questions or comments are allowed to interrupt what is the most extended word from the Lord in the whole book'. Malachi condemns the priests directly for their failure to live up to the Levitical ideal. This second part of the passage is better understood as a 'reproof speech'. While Floyd does not categorize it in this way, he explains the 'reproof speech' as containing a description of the positive consequences of good behaviour while implicating the addressees as being in violation of this behaviour (Floyd 2000: 648). The two parts of the disputation speech hold together with repeated words and ideas. Particularly noteworthy is the way that the priests who are initially charged with 'despising my name' (1:6) are themselves 'despised' in judgment in the end (2:9).

The passage reveals that even with a functioning temple after the judgment of exile, the problems that led to the experience of exile have not been resolved. It lays the ground for the revelation that when Yahweh comes, he will purify the sons of Levi (3:2) and judge the immoral in the community (3:5).

Comment

1:6. Malachi begins with a principle that would be generally accepted without argument: 'A son honours a father and a servant his master.' The verb translated 'honour' (*yĕkabbēd*) is from the same root as the noun 'glory' or 'weight' (*kābôd*) (cf. 2:2). Hence to 'honour' someone is to recognize their weight or significance. The fifth commandment requires children to 'honour' their father and mother (Exod. 20:12; Deut. 5:16), which includes obedience in childhood through to care for parents into old age (McConville 2002a: 128–129). It goes without saying that servants should honour their masters by obeying them, but the law also envisages servants being so well treated by their masters that they love them and voluntarily indenture themselves for life, a supreme honour (e.g. Deut. 15:16–17). Having stated the principle, Malachi turns the focus to the one from whom all earthly authority derives its source, the Lord of hosts (cf. 1:4). The fatherhood of God is taught in Deut. 32:6, Isa. 63:16 and 64:8, and is implied in the description of Israel as 'son' (Exod. 4:22; Hos. 1:11). Similarly, God as 'master' is taught in Exod. 23:17, Deut. 10:17, Isa. 26:13 and Mic. 4:13, and is implied in the description of Israel as Yahweh's 'servants' or 'slaves' (Lev. 25:55).

Two pointed questions imply the failure of the priests both to honour Yahweh as a father and to fear him as a master, where 'fear' means to 'revere' or 'stand in awe' of God so as to obey his requirements (e.g. Lev. 19:14; 25:17; Deut. 17:19). The argument is from the lesser to the greater, where what is accepted as normal in the human realm is expected all the more in relation to Yahweh. With this theme, the Book of the Twelve closes as it opened, with Yahweh as a spurned father (cf. Hos. 11:1).

In failing to honour and fear Yahweh, the priests are 'despising my name'. The 'name' of God refers to his character and reputation and is a recurring theme of this passage (1:6 [twice], 11 [twice], 14; 2:2, 5). When Yahweh proclaimed his 'name' to Moses on the mountain in response to Moses' request to see Yahweh's glory, he proclaimed:

> The LORD, the LORD, the compassionate and gracious God, slow to anger, abounding in love and faithfulness, maintaining love to thousands, and forgiving wickedness, rebellion and sin. Yet he does not leave the guilty unpunished; he punishes the children and their children for the sin of the parents to the third and fourth generation. (Exod. 34:6–7)

In Deut. 12, God commands his people that when they enter the land, they are 'to seek the place the LORD your God will choose from among all your tribes to put his Name there for his dwelling' (v. 5). God's name is closely associated with his presence in the tabernacle and temple.

The Levites are charged to minister 'in the name of the LORD' (Deut. 18:5, 7; 21:5), which means as well as being his representatives, they are to reflect his holy character in their lives (Lev. 21:6). They are also to put Yahweh's name on the people by speaking a blessing (Num. 6:22–27). As a kingdom of priests, the Israelites are to bear Yahweh's name and so reflect his character in their lives that Yahweh's name will be known among the nations (e.g. Deut. 28:10; Josh. 7:9; 1 Kgs 8:41, 43; cf. Deut. 4:6–8; 26:19). The acclamation of Yahweh's name among the nations is an important theme of this passage (1:11, 14). In Malachi's day the priests are accused of failing in their calling. They are despising Yahweh's name, which equates to despising him. It is the opposite of honouring and fearing Yahweh (cf. 3:16; 4:2[3:20]): it is to treat him as insignificant or weightless, which is profoundly offensive. What is worse is that the priests appear blind to their sins and unrepentant. They are reported as responding, 'How have we despised your name?' While the tone of their response is not given, the harsh rebuke in 2:3 suggests it is said more with cynicism and insolence than genuine surprise (Hill 2012a: 298).

7–8. The first evidence mounted for the charge of despising Yahweh's name (v. 6) is the priests' actions and words associated with their sacrificial duties. They offer 'defiled food' upon Yahweh's altar (see 'Notes on the text'). There are essentially three major categories in the priestly world view: the holy, the pure/clean and the impure/unclean (Sklar 2005: 105). In the Levitical system, sin and physical impurity lead to the defilement of the holy and pollution of the pure/clean. A defiled object or person is unfit for God's presence. A crucial role of the priests is to offer sacrifices that can cleanse and sanctify by making atonement. By offering defiled food rather than pure/clean food, the priests rendered the system ineffective. Their actions not only despise God's name (v. 6), but defile Yahweh, a strong statement that is altered in the LXX (see 'Notes on the text'). It is not that Yahweh is actually defiled (an impossibility), but the actions of the priests are a direct affront to him (Glazier-McDonald 1987: 51).

Not only are the priests' actions defective, but so are their reported words: 'The table of the LORD – it is despised.' If these are the actual words of the priests, then they demonstrate a supreme insolence. It is more likely, as most commentators suggest, that Malachi has translated their actions into language for rhetorical impact (e.g. Petersen 1995: 180). Malachi reports what they are effectively saying by their actions. They are not honouring Yahweh's table – they give it no weight or significance. What is 'the table of the LORD'? The tabernacle had a 'table' for the 'bread of the Presence' (Exod. 25:23–30). Bread was to be baked each week and placed on it as a food offering for Yahweh, and for Aaron and his sons, as a lasting covenant (Lev. 24:5–9). This 'table' was also present in Solomon's temple (1 Kgs 7:48). The tabernacle also had a bronze altar for burnt sacrifice (Exod. 35:16; 38:1–7, 30) and an altar for incense (Exod. 30:1–10; 37:25–29). The bronze altar is also present in Solomon's temple (1 Kgs 8:64). In Malachi, the 'table of the LORD' seems to be used synonymously in v. 7 with 'my altar'. Significantly, Ezekiel's temple has an 'altar' that is also called a 'table' (Ezek. 41:22). Ezekiel's 'table' is later associated with animal sacrifice (44:16). There are also other 'tables' in Ezekiel on which the animals were prepared for sacrifice (40:39–43). Since v. 8 refers to defective animal sacrifices, which would not have been associated with the table for the bread of the Presence, it is best to understand the 'table' in v. 7 as the altar. Clendenen (2004: 268) suggests that a 'table' is a symbol of hospitality and relationship, where Yahweh is the host, the offerings are the food and the priests are the servants who bring the food to the table so that the people might enjoy fellowship with Yahweh. Yahweh's ownership of the table and altar is underlined in each instance ('my altar' and 'The table of the LORD'), which makes the priests' treatment of it all the more heinous.

The priests offer blind, lame and sick animals (v. 8), an activity expressly forbidden in the law (22:18–25; Deut. 15:21). Indeed, the law stipulated that sacrificial animals were to be 'without defect' (Lev. 1:3, 10; 22:19, 21). While the people brought these defective animals to the priests, the repeated statement 'There is no evil!' is the declaration of the priests, who condone the bringing of these second-rate animals, which are then sacrificed. In other words, rather than saying that the sacrifices themselves are 'not bad' (cf. Lev. 27:11–12) (Glazier-McDonald 1987: 53), the priests claim (contrary to the law) there is nothing wrong with what the people are doing (Petersen 1995: 180).

Like v. 6, Malachi makes a comparison with their treatment of the human 'governor', who was a Persian official and presumably received regular gifts of agricultural produce and livestock (cf. Hag. 1:1). The implication is that if the human governor would not accept the people or show them favour for this kind of offering, how much more does Yahweh find such an offering offensive.

9. 'And now' (*wĕʿattâ*) has a logical rather than a temporal force (cf. 2:1) (Waltke and O'Connor 1990: 667). Malachi urges the priests to 'entreat the favour of God' (cf. Zech. 7:2; 8:21–22). This entreaty typically occurs in a judgment context when God's face has been turned away in anger (Stead 2009: 221), and the suppliant is seeking God's grace and favour (e.g. Exod. 32:11). While this would be a very appropriate action, the immediate and wider contexts indicate that Malachi is continuing to be ironic (Baldwin 1972: 226; Verhoef 1987: 220; Hill 1998: 182). The question 'Will he show you favour?' repeats the question from the end of v. 8 and again expects the answer 'no' because there is no indication in what has gone before or what follows that the priests are repentant. Indeed, 'This was from your hand' directly lays the blame with the priests for Yahweh's turning away his face in anger.

10. Malachi continues to rebuke the priests and effectively tells them it would be better to shut down the temple than let them continue their offensive behaviour – the priests need to be protected from themselves. Not enough is known about the design of Zerubbabel's temple to be certain which doors were meant (cf. 1 Chr. 9:17–27; 26:1–19), but the intention is clear – God wants the despicable sacrifices of the priests to cease. As Scalise (2009: 333) rightly notes, the loss threatened is devastating. In the unfolding narrative of the Pentateuch, the sacrificial system is given after the apostasy of the golden calf, where the relationship between Yahweh and Israel was violently fractured. The sacrificial system set forth in the book of Leviticus is a gift of God's grace so that the mutual relationship can continue despite Israel's sin. In shutting up the temple, the means of grace is removed; the cleansing of atonement and access to God's presence is cut off. But the implication of the next three statements in the verse is that sacrifice has already become ineffective: 'So you might not light my altar for nothing' indicates there already was no benefit in their sacrifices. 'I take no pleasure in you' is also shattering. It brings to mind 1 Sam. 15:22:

> Does the Lord delight in burnt offerings and sacrifices
> as much as in obeying the Lord?
> To obey is better than sacrifice,
> and to heed is better than the fat of rams.

Finally, because their sacrifices are second rate and defiled, and offered in a way that despises God's name, he rightly says, 'I will not accept an offering from your hand.'

11. The corrupt worship of God's chosen people is contrasted with the worship of the nations. Whereas the priests are despising Yahweh's name

(v. 6) and profaning it (v. 12), Yahweh twice asserts that his name 'will be great among the nations' (cf. 1:5, 14). While the priests are offering 'defiled food' (v. 7), the nations will offer a 'pure offering', one that is ceremonially clean. The key questions that have divided commentators are who are these worshippers 'among the nations'? And where or when does this happen? Goswell (2013: 629–633) helpfully outlines and evaluates the main scholarly views. The first view is that it refers to secret believers in Yahweh among the pagan nations, possibly referring to the pure monotheistic worship of the Persians (Mason 1977: 144–145; J. J. Collins 2012: 129). However, this view falters at a number of points. The worship among the nations is done 'in my name', which excludes pagan worship unconsciously directed at Yahweh. More problematic is that acceptance of pagan worship is radically at odds with the rest of the Bible.

A second view is that it refers to Jewish believers who are living among the nations, such as in the Elephantine community in Egypt, in Babylonia, in Samaria or at the Jewish temple in Leontopolis (Petersen 1995: 184). The word 'place' (*māqôm*) can have a technical sense of 'sanctuary' (e.g. Deut. 12:5). Yet the phrase 'from [the] rising of [the] sun even to its setting' seems more expansive than just these few temple sites. The phrase is a merism, a literary device that encompasses everything between two points (cf. Pss 50:1; 113:3; Isa. 45:6; 59:19) and seems to refer to the whole known world, not just diaspora communities. Supporting this is the parallel phrase 'in every place'. Furthermore, the phrase 'among the nations' more naturally refers to Gentile peoples who recognize Yahweh (cf. 3:12) than to the Jewish Diaspora.

A third view believes that Malachi's irony continues and he is using 'prophetic hyperbole' to say that even the sacrifices offered by pagans are purer and more preferable to those offered by the Judean priests (Tiemeyer 2006: 262–263). Not that Malachi actually believed this, but the comparison is made for rhetorical effect. However, v. 14 continues the idea from v. 11 and the nations are said to fear God's name in a way that seems entirely positive rather than ironic. Furthermore, given Israel's strict monotheism, it is likely this rhetoric would be readily dismissed by the priests (and later readers). Since the offerings are made in Yahweh's name, the number of people who actually do this is clearly a null set.

A fourth view understands this verse to refer to future worship of Yahweh by the nations. One of the difficulties with the verse is that the first and last clauses are verbless (lit. 'great my name among the nations') and the second clause contains a pass. ptc. (lit. 'being offered'), which takes its tense from the context (Glazier-McDonald 1987: 61). Several scholars argue that since the immediate context focuses on the present inadequate sacrifices of the priests, the sacrifice of the nations must also be a present activity (Petersen 1995: 184). However, the last clause of v. 10 is future ('I will not accept an offering from your hand'). Goswell (2013: 633) rightly argues that if this verse is interpreted in the light of 1:5 and

1:14, which have a future reference to the worship of the nations, then the verse contrasts the present priestly abuses with the future plan of God for the nations. This future plan for the nations to worship Yahweh is a key theme of Zechariah (8:20–23; 14:16–21) and elsewhere in the OT (e.g. Isa. 2:2–4; 11:10; 24:14–16; 42:6; 45:22–24; 55:3–5; 66:18–21; Ezek. 36:23; 37:28; 38:23; 39:7; Mic. 4:1–3; Zeph. 3:8–9; Hag. 2:7). It is entirely fitting to see it here too. While Malachi's presentation of the worship of the nations is not focused on Jerusalem here (cf. Zeph. 2:11), 3:4 envisages a restoration of worship in Jerusalem (Goswell 2013: 636–637).

12–13. 'But you' contrasts the priests with the nations (v. 11). In these verses the language against the priests continues to ratchet up, as well as reiterating earlier points. Not only are the priests despising Yahweh's name (v. 6), but they are now said to be 'profaning it'. To 'profane' (*ḥālal*) something is to make it unholy, and to profane God's name means doing something he disapproves of (Wenham 1979: 259). In Leviticus, God's name is profaned by the worship of Molech and child sacrifice (e.g. 18:21; 20:3), which underlines its seriousness. The use of the ptc. here in Malachi suggests it is a settled disposition rather than a one-time act. Hence there is a complete inversion of Israel's calling – as noted in the comment on v. 6, God's people were called to make his name known among the nations. Here God's name will be great among the nations (v. 11), but is profaned among his people.

As in v. 7, it seems that Malachi is translating the priests' actions into language for rhetorical impact: 'you say, "The table of my Lord: it is defiled; and its fruit – its food – is despised."' Interestingly, the same objects are referred to as in v. 7, but the adjectives are reversed. In v. 7 the 'table' is 'despised', and it is 'defiled food' (a different word for 'food' is used). Also, the 'table of the LORD' (Yahweh) in v. 7 is now the 'table of my Lord' (master), possibly to link back to the fundamental problem in v. 6: a lack of fear for Yahweh as lord/master (Duguid 2010: 204). Their worship in words and deeds displays their poor attitude towards God.

The priests are further reported as saying, 'Look, what a burden!' (v. 13). They perversely express their disdain at performing duties that were an expression of God's grace. In addition, Yahweh accuses, 'And you snort [at] it,' which is more likely to be a colloquial expression describing their contempt for the altar or for their sacrificial duties, than continuing to ignite the altar fire, as Petersen (1995: 185) suggests. In contemporary English one might say, 'you turn up your noses at [it]' (NLT).

Like the people in v. 8, the priests are accused of offering second-rate sacrifices (v. 13). In addition to the 'lame and sick' (cf. v. 8), they offer 'injured' animals (cf. NIV, NEB), which could refer to animals recovered after being injured by predators, or animals that had been 'stolen' or 'taken by violence' (NRSV, ESV) and cost the worshipper nothing (see 'Notes on the text'). If the latter, it is difficult to know how the priests could detect this (Rudolph 1976: 264). The further rhetorical question 'Should I accept it from your hand?' expects the answer 'no', especially in the light of the explicit statement that Yahweh 'will not accept an offering from your hand' at the end of v. 10.

14. The focus does not seem to be so much on the priests in this verse as on any Israelite who substitutes a blemished animal to fulfil a vow. Tiemeyer (2006: 214) notes that the word 'blemished' (*mošḥāt*) is usually m., but is here a rare f. form. Whereas the law required an unblemished *male* animal (Lev. 22:18–19), the person has consciously substituted a blemished female. In accepting the animal, the priests are ultimately culpable for not following the prescribed regulations for sacrificial animals (cf. Lev. 27:11–12).

A vow is a way of promising something to Yahweh in the hope of deliverance in a time of need; it is a way of pleading before Yahweh. A classic example is Hannah's vow, in the midst of her affliction, to dedicate her son to Yahweh should she be given a child (1 Sam. 1:10). 'Vow offerings' and 'gifts' are mentioned in many places in the Pentateuch and often involved animal sacrifice (e.g. Lev. 7:16; Num. 15:3, 8; Deut. 12:17). Lev. 22:18–23 is clear that such animals were to be 'without defect or blemish'. What seems to be happening in Malachi's day is that when a prayer has been answered by God and the pressure is off, people substitute lesser animals supposedly to fulfil the vow. This is expressly forbidden in Lev. 27:9–11 (cf. Deut. 23:21[22]). Such people are deceivers and Yahweh pronounces a curse (*'ārar*) on them. They will be punished for violating the requirements of the covenant (cf. Deut. 27:26; Mal. 2:2; 3:9).

'For' (*kî*) introduces the reason for such a severe judgment: '"I am a great king," says the LORD of hosts.' Goswell (2013: 634) notes that this description is never used of an Israelite king, but Sennacherib is called 'the great king' in 2 Kgs 18:19, 28 (cf. Isa. 36:4, 13), and non-Mesopotamian kings are called 'great' (*gādôl*) in Ps. 136:17 and Eccl. 9:14 ('powerful' in NIV). The phrase 'great king' refers only to Yahweh here, and in Pss 47:2[3] and 95:3. In the Psalms it offers a reason (*kî*) for praising Yahweh. Importantly, in Ps. 47:2[3], Yahweh is 'to be feared' (*nôrā'*) (ESV, NASB), which uses the same ni. ptc. as this verse. Furthermore, Ps. 47 speaks of Yahweh's universal rule over the nations (cf. Pss 96:4; 99:3), which, given some of the details of the psalm and its setting in the book of Psalms, is clearly a future prospect (D. C. Mitchell 1997: 250). Goswell (2013: 635) concludes that 'Malachi is obviously drawing on this psalmic tradition, and 1:14b must be interpreted against this background.' Hence the ptc. is best understood with a future tense: 'my name will be feared among the nations' (cf. 1:5, 11). God is judging his people for the sake of his international reputation (cf. Ezek. 36:22–23).

2:1–2. The second half of Malachi's second speech (2:1–9) is again directed towards the priests (cf. 1:6) and condemns them for their behaviour and teaching. Like 1:9, 'And now' (*wĕ'attâ*) has a logical rather than a temporal force (Waltke and O'Connor 1990: 667).

The referent of 'this command' (*hammiṣwâ hazzō't*) is debated by commentators. Floyd (2000: 598) contends that there is no command as such, but only a tacit directive implied by the threat of punishment if the priests do not turn away from the offences of 1:6–14. Similarly, Clendenen (2004: 289) argues that it does not refer to a 'command' at all; rather, it is a warning of judgment and better translated 'admonition' (cf. NIV: 'warning'). However, this would be a unique meaning of 'command'. More typically, this idea would be expressed with 'reproach' (*ḥerpâ*) or 'warning' (*mûsār*).

'This command' occurs also in 2:4 in connection with the covenant with Levi, which leads to the suggestion that it refers to all the requirements for the priests under the covenant with Levi (Verhoef 1987: 238; Hill 1998: 204; Baker 2006: 241), or, more particularly, the requirement of the priests to teach the people (Redditt 1995: 167). Deuteronomy uses 'command' in the sg. to refer to the whole teaching of Moses (e.g. 5:31; 27:1; NIV translates as a plural 'commands'; cf. ESV, 'commandment'). Yet the demons. 'this' (*hazzō't*) expects something in the more immediate context and 'this command', while related to the covenant with Levi in v. 4, still seems to be something distinct from it.

Glazier-McDonald (1987: 64) argues that 'this command' refers both to a command to give honour to Yahweh (2:2) and to the sentence of a curse if they refuse. However, looking more closely at the syntax, the 'command' is best understood as what immediately follows in v. 2 and is presented as part of a conditional sentence. The two conditions in the protasis are each introduced by the particle 'if' (*'im*) and correspond to the 'command'. Essentially, the 'command' is to 'listen' to Yahweh's word through Malachi as well as committing to give glory to Yahweh's name. The command is twofold, but ends up boiling down to the same thing – give God glory by doing what he says. Sweeney (2000b: 728) argues that 'this command' refers back to the requirements in 1:6–14, to present proper offerings to Yahweh at the temple altar and to show Yahweh proper respect or reverence. This amounts to the same thing since the command to 'commit to give glory to my name' addresses the core of the problem in 1:6–14 (cf. 'Comment' on 'honour' in 1:6).

The idiom 'take/taking it to heart' appears twice in this verse. In Hebr. thought, the 'heart' is the seat of the will, whereas in Western thought the 'heart' implies more of an emotional response. Hence NIV captures the sense more accurately by translating the phrase as 'resolve' and supplies extra words to fill out the meaning at the end of the verse ('to honour me' is not present in the Hebr.). (Intriguingly, the similar phrase in Hag. 1:5, 7, 2:15, 18 is rightly translated 'consider' in most English translations.)

The apodosis of the conditional sentence is introduced by the simple conditional waw and contains the consequences of not listening and not committing to give glory to Yahweh's name, but continuing to despise and profane it (cf. 1:6, 12). Yahweh promises that he will send 'the curse' (*'et-hammĕ'ērâ*) if there is disobedience to this command. The use of the def. art. suggests this refers to the covenant curses of the Mosaic covenant. The only other instance of the expression 'the curse' (lit.) in the OT is Deut. 28:20 ('curses' in NIV). Significantly, this comes just after Yahweh has spelled out the blessings that will come for obedience to his word (28:1–14). This is standard covenant language.

There are two main interpretations of 'I will curse your blessings'. It could be saying that the material blessings that flowed to the priests as a consequence of serving as priests (e.g. tithes and offerings) will be struck (Glazier-McDonald 1987: 67). More likely, Malachi is referring to one of the important roles of the priests to pronounce blessing on the people (Num. 6:24–26; Deut. 10:8; 21:5). Fishbane (1985: 332–333) detects a number of allusions to the Aaronic blessing of Num. 6:24–26 in this passage. He argues, 'The prophet has taken the contents of the Priestly Blessing – delivered by the priests, and with its emphasis on blessing, the sanctity of the divine Name, and such benefactions as protection, favourable countenance, and peace – *and inverted them*' (italics original). In this case, the priestly blessings will turn out as curses. Hence if the priests do not change, not only will they experience the curse, but they will mediate the curse to others. In fact, they have already begun to experience the curse ('indeed I have cursed') because they have not yet resolved to give glory to Yahweh's name (cf. 3:9). This is an implicit call to repent, with the warning that time is short.

3. The rhetoric against the priests ratchets up another notch with further warnings of judgment. First, Yahweh threatens to 'rebuke your offspring' (lit. 'seed' [*zera'*]). This phrase has been variously understood from ancient times (see 'Notes on the text'). Following MT, commentators understand 'seed' to refer either to the priests' 'offspring' (cf. NIV 'descendants') (Verhoef 1987: 240; Petersen 1995: 189) or to their share of agricultural produce (cf. NIV footnote: 'corn') (Glazier-McDonald 1987: 66–68; Sweeney 2000b: 729). Significantly, 'the rebuke' (lit.) accompanies 'the curse' (lit.) in Deut. 28:20, where they bring destruction and ruin on both 'the fruit of your womb . . . and the crops of your land' (Deut. 28:18). The idea of 'rebuke' seems to be to restrain something so that it does not have its usual effect (Glazier-McDonald 1987: 66–67). For instance in Nah. 1:4 when the sea is rebuked, it dries up. When Satan is rebuked in Zech. 3:2, his accusation is held back. In Mal. 3:11 when the devourer is rebuked, he is restrained. If the rebuke is directed towards the priests' offspring, then it refers to the ending of the priestly line and the covenant. If it is their agricultural produce, it refers to famine. Since 'seed' clearly refers to 'offspring' in Mal. 2:15, and it more usually refers to what is planted than what is harvested, on balance it seems best to understand 'seed' as the priests' descendants (Tiemeyer 2006: 244–245). Since the priesthood is hereditary, it poses a dreadful threat (Harrison 1987: 67).

The second warning expresses graphic disgust: 'I will splatter crap on your faces – the crap of your festivals.' The language and imagery is designed to offend and 'I will splatter' (*wĕzērîtî*) is a play on 'offspring' (*'et-hazzera'*). 'Crap' (*pereš*) is variously translated 'dung' (ESV, JPS, NIV) or 'refuse' (NASB) and there is a fine line to tread here as a translator. One must not domesticate the sharpness of God's Word simply to cater for contemporary cultural sensitivities. At the same time, using language that is uncouth may be just as unhelpful if it distracts from hearing the intent of God's Word. Different cultures will draw the line at different points, but in my Australian culture, 'crap' seems to capture the offensiveness without tipping too far into vulgarity. Elsewhere *pereš* refers to animal intestines and their contents, which were removed by the priests and later taken outside the camp and burned (Exod. 29:14; Lev. 4:11–12; 8:17; 16:27). The reference to 'festivals' suggests a higher volume of the stuff (Stuart 1998: 1314). Splattering 'crap' on the priests' faces would not only be highly humiliating, but presumably render them defiled, profaned and unfit for temple service (Redditt 1995: 168). All the priests become fit for is to be carried outside the camp, just like the 'crap' of their sacrifices – this seems the most likely meaning of 'he will carry you to it'. How God might do this is not stated – the intent seems rhetorical at this point of the warning.

Fishbane (1985: 333) notes that whereas the priestly blessing in Num. 6:24–26 requests Yahweh to raise his countenance (lit. 'face') for the good of the people, because the priests have spurned the divine gift, what will be 'raised' for them or against their 'faces' will be the polluted refuse of their offerings.

4. The purpose (*lihyôt*) of the command to listen and to commit to give glory to Yahweh's name (v. 1) is 'so that my covenant with Levi might continue'. There is no account in the OT of Yahweh's formalizing a covenant with Levi, though it does record the making of a covenant with the Levite Phinehas (Num. 25). The covenant with Levi is also mentioned in Jer. 33:21, and Neh. 13:29 refers to 'the covenant of the priesthood and of the Levites'. Even though the term 'covenant with Levi' does not appear in the Pentateuch, the special role established for the priests therein can be understood in covenantal terms (i.e. in terms of a special relationship of responsibility and privilege).

Verhoef (1987: 244) notes that references to Levi himself in Genesis are not very complementary (Gen. 29:34; 34:25–26; 49:5–7). The 'covenant with Levi' must therefore refer to the role and responsibilities given to Levi's descendants in places such as Exod. 28 – 29; 32:25–29; Lev. 8 – 10; Num. 1:47–53; 3 – 4; 8; 15 – 20; 25; Deut. 10:8–9; 17:8–13; 18:1–8; 21:5; 33:8–11. These passages set out responsibilities for the priests and penalties for disobedience. The key elements of this covenant are identified in Mal. 2:5–7, and they can be traced back to the Pentateuchal traditions.

Num. 25:12–13 speaks of a 'covenant of peace' and 'a covenant of a lasting priesthood' that is made with Phinehas (Aaron's grandson) and his descendants for his role in averting Yahweh's judgment after the blatant immorality of the Israelite Zimri with the Midianite woman Kozbi in the camp at Shittim. Many argue this relates more to the office of high priest (Routledge 2008: 181). Yet the fact that Phinehas is also a Levite, and the way the word 'peace' connects with 2:5 suggests that the covenant with Phinehas could also be the 'covenant with Levi' (Merrill 1994: 407). Furthermore, the book of Malachi does not distinguish between the sons of Aaron and the Levites. 1 Sam. 2:30 seems to assume an earlier covenant with Levi when Yahweh says to Eli the priest, 'I promised that members of your family would minister before me for ever.' Despite the lack of earlier explicit reference to a 'covenant with Levi', Mal. 2:4–7 gives the main elements of it needed for interpretation.

5. Like the covenant with Israel mediated through Moses at Sinai, the goal of the covenant with Levi was 'life and peace'. 'Life' is a key theme of the Torah, which climaxes with Moses' plea to 'choose life' (Deut. 30:19). It speaks of the blessing of life in the land as a consequence of obedience, in contrast to 'death' and curses (e.g. Lev. 18:5; 25:18–29; 26:3–5; Deut. 5:33; 6:2; 11:8–9; 1 Kgs 3:14; Neh. 9:29; Pss 16:11; 91; 119; Prov. 6:23; Isa. 1:19; Ezek. 3:21; 18:5–9; 20:11; Amos 5:4–6). The idea of 'peace' is wholeness, well-being, prosperity and right relationships. These are typical blessings of a covenant relationship (Petersen 1995: 190).

The Hebr. is fairly abrupt, but the next phrase ('Respect – and he respected me') is best understood as the predicate of the earlier phrase 'My covenant with him was'. That is, the covenant with Levi called for 'respect' or reverence of Yahweh. It is a key obligation of the priesthood, which is said to have been observed by earlier Levites, in contrast to the priests in Malachi's day. Again, the episode in Num. 25 comes to mind where Phinehas was zealous for God's honour (25:11, 13). Rather than despising and profaning Yahweh's name, 'Levi' was 'awestruck' (*niḥat*). This is a verb that elsewhere in the ni. means 'be shattered' (e.g. 1 Sam. 2:10; Isa. 7:8) or 'be terrified' (e.g. Job 7:14; Isa. 31:4).

6–7. In these verses Malachi elaborates the Levitical ideal in terms that prepare for his final critique of the priests in vv. 8–9. The language shifts from description (v. 6) to prescription (v. 7) to admonition (vv. 8–9).

The 'covenant with Levi' required the Levites to teach God's law to Israel (cf. Lev. 10:11; Deut. 17:8–13; 31:9; 33:9–13; 2 Chr. 35:3; Neh. 8:7–9; Jer. 18:18; Ezek. 7:26; Hag. 2:11). The 'true instruction' (*tôrat 'ĕmet*) is what accords with God's ways, revealed to Israel through Moses and mediated through the priests (cf. Zech. 7:9). In doing this, the priests also exercised a judicial role by providing rulings at the temple for those who sought justice (e.g. Deut. 17:8–12; 19:17; 2 Chr. 19:8–11). In this way righteousness would be preserved in the community. The inverse statement clarifies this: 'wrong was not found on his lips', where 'wrong' (*'awlâ*) has the sense of 'unrighteousness', 'wickedness', 'injustice' or 'falseness'.

Echoing the language of Deuteronomy, the Levites 'walked with me' (Deut. 5:33; 8:6; 11:22; 13:4; 26:17; 28:9; 30:16), which denotes an obedient lifestyle that was displayed in 'peace' and 'uprightness'. It also indicates a close relationship with God. Furthermore, the Levites 'turned many from sin'. This again brings the episode with Phinehas to mind where his actions in dealing decisively with sin in the community served as a deterrent.

One of the key roles of the priests was to 'guard' (*šāmar*) the sanctity of the tabernacle and temple (cf. Num. 3:7–8; 8:26; 18:3–7). Here they are also required to 'guard knowledge' so that the people 'should seek instruction [*tôrâ*] from his mouth' (cf. v. 6). Hill (1998: 211) summarizes, 'the translation "guard" catches both nuances of obeying and preserving'.

The role of a 'messenger' is elsewhere one that describes prophets (e.g. Isa. 44:26; Hag. 1:13; 2 Chr. 36:15), or angels (e.g. Gen. 28:12; Isa. 63:9; Hos. 12:5). This is the only instance in the OT where it refers to priests. Malachi is not suggesting that the priest is taking the place of the prophet or that there is a diminution of the prophetic role in Malachi's day. Indeed, this is a title that the priests share with the prophet (1:1). Priests are 'the messenger' not only because of their role in teaching the law of Moses (cf. Deut. 31:9–13), but also because they consulted Yahweh to know his will in specific circumstances by means of the enigmatic Urim and Thummim (Exod. 28:30; Num. 27:21; Deut. 33:8; 1 Sam. 14:36, 41–42; 28:6).

8–9. After reviewing the covenant with Levi (vv. 4–6) and prescribing the ideal (v. 7), Malachi evaluates the contemporary priests (v. 8) and summarizes their present circumstances – they are under the judgment of God for their actions (v. 9). Rather than walking in the ways of the Lord, they have 'turned from the way'. Instead of turning many from sin, they 'have caused many to fall' by their 'instruction' (*tôrâ*). In straightforward terms, they have 'violated the covenant of Levi'. They have not received the blessings of life and peace for covenant faithfulness (v. 5); instead, God says he has made them 'despised and humiliated before all the people' (v. 9). This rounds out Malachi's second disputation speech – Yahweh's accusation at the beginning was that the priests were despising his name and not fearing him (1:6). The judgment is that Yahweh has now despised and humiliated them. They are under the covenant curse (cf. v. 2). They are not 'keeping' (lit. 'guarding') Yahweh's ways, that is, living in obedience to him. They are also accused of 'showing partiality' (lit. 'lifting up faces') in their instruction (Gruber 1983: 258–259). This means they are favouring some people over others in their Torah rulings, contrary to Deut. 16:18–20 (cf. 10:17; 17:9, 12; 19:17).

Explanation

Malachi's first disputation speech reveals that the people had forgotten God's love. A consequence of this is seen in the second disputation speech – the leadership of the nation, the priests, are not living in the light of God's reality. They are bringing Yahweh's glorious name into disrepute by failing in their priestly responsibilities. Their words and their actions show little regard for the sacrifices they offer (1:6–14). They are also failing to instruct the people in the Torah and to live it out in their own lives (2:1–9). A failure of leadership has consequences not only for the leaders, but for the people they lead. These consequences are already being felt (2:2, 9).

The priests were to be a microcosm of the nation of Israel, who themselves are designated 'a kingdom of priests' (Exod. 19:6). As leaders in the community, the priests were to exemplify the holiness that the Israelite nation was called to, in order to make Yahweh's name known to the nations (e.g. Isa. 45:5–6). There is a lot at stake. In Mal. 2:4–7, it is the Levites of old who displayed this priestly ideal and so received life and peace, the blessings of covenant relationship with God. Yet the priests in Malachi's day treated God as inconsequential or weightless (God was given no 'glory'). They carried on the sacrifices, but in a manner contrary to God's word. Their offerings were second-rate, unfit even for a human master (vv. 7–8, 13–14). Their attitude expressed utter contempt for God's gracious provision of the sacrificial system (vv. 12–13).

The offering of sacrifices was to be an expression of Israel's 'worship' and Malachi makes it clear that the underlying motivation and accompanying lifestyle is of primary importance (cf. Deut. 6:4; Hos. 6:6; Amos 4:4–5; Mic. 6:6–8). This is not new. Isaiah similarly rebuked the people of Judah for their failure to honour Yahweh as father and master (Isa. 1:2–3) and commanded them to 'stop bringing meaningless offerings!' (Isa. 1:13). If there are differences with the earlier prophets, it is in the lesser quality and quantity of the sacrifices being offered in Malachi's day (cf. Isa. 1:11) and the more concerted critique of social injustices by the earlier prophets (but condemnation of injustice is still present in the post-exilic prophets, such as the accusation against the priests of partiality in their Torah judgments here and condemnation of the people in 3:5).

Earlier prophets looked forward to a time when God's people would be given new hearts and moved to obey (e.g. Jer. 31:31–34; Ezek. 36:24–27). The book of Malachi reveals that the exile did not bring this about – the problem of the sinful human heart remained. Nevertheless, Malachi is convinced that Yahweh's purposes will prevail. God will turn things on their heads. Despite the sin of the priests, God's 'name will be great among the nations' (v. 11) and his 'name will be feared among the nations' (v. 14). Malachi will have more to say about how the priests will be purified (3:3) and how hearts will be changed (4:6[3:24]).

The priestly sacrificial system was a gift of God's grace to maintain a pre-existing relationship, never to earn it. In his study on worship, Peterson (1992: 49) comments:

> Within this covenant framework, the sacrificial system was the means by which God made it possible for a sinful people to draw

> near to him, to receive his grace and blessing, without desecrating his holiness and so incurring his wrath against them. By God's provision through the cult the covenant could be maintained.

The fulfilment of the OT sacrificial system is found in the one true worshipper – Jesus Christ. Through his sinless obedience to death, he made the complete and perfect sacrifice for sin, never to be repeated, as the letter to the Hebrews puts it, 'But when this priest had offered for all time one sacrifice for sins, he sat down at the right hand of God . . . For by one sacrifice he has made perfect for ever those who are being made holy' (Heb. 10:12, 14; cf. Rom. 3:21–26; 5:6–21; Eph. 5:2). Interestingly, the early church understood the 'pure offering' of the nations in 1:11 as fulfilled in Christ and represented among the Gentiles in the bread and cup of the Eucharist (Ferreiro 2003: 288–293). However, the worship of the nations is much broader than this.

In the NT, the 'worship' language of the OT is used first and foremost in relation to the worship of Jesus. As the great high priest, his death was the one perfect sacrifice for sin that has fulfilled the requirements of the old covenant for his people. At the same time, the NT also uses the language of sacrifice or 'worship' metaphorically to speak of the Christlike actions Christians should do in response to all that God has done in Christ. Significantly, Jesus opens this up for Jew and Gentile (1 Cor. 1:2), fulfilling the hopes of Malachi (1:5, 11, 14). Worship begins at conversion, when people turn to 'serve' the living and true God (1 Thess. 1:9). Christian worship is the logical response to the gospel: 'in view of God's mercy . . . offer your bodies as a living sacrifice, holy and pleasing to God – this is your true and proper worship' (Rom. 12:1–2). Such worship is made possible by the Spirit of God (Phil. 3:3). Whereas animal and grain offerings were made under the old covenant, Christians are to 'offer' themselves to God (Rom. 6:13, 16). Indeed, Christian living is said to be a 'sacrifice and service' of faith (Phil. 2:17). Paul speaks of his gospel ministry as service to God (Rom. 1:9), and that he ministers in this regard as a 'priestly duty' (Rom. 15:16; cf. Phil. 2:17). The terminology of 'sacrifice' (or 'service') is also used of meeting the needs of others (Rom. 15:17; 2 Cor. 9:12–13; Phil. 4:18). Christian sacrifices that are pleasing to God include prayer (1 Tim. 2:3), caring for widows (1 Tim. 5:4), caring for brothers and sisters in Christ (Rom. 14:13–18) and suffering for doing good (1 Peter 2:20). Peter describes these acts as 'spiritual sacrifices' (1 Peter 2:5). Sacrificial language is also used of financial gifts (Phil. 4:18). Hence Christian 'worship' or 'service' is much broader than simply what happens in church, although it certainly includes this (Acts 13:2). Moule (1977: 77) rightly comments, 'all work done and all life lived for God's sake is in essence, worship'. See further, Peterson 1992; Carson 2002; Block 2014.

The NT teaches that all believers in Christ are priests (e.g. 1 Peter 2:9) and the first part of the passage, although it is directed towards the priests in Malachi's day, has a ready application since it is easy to be a cultural Christian, that is, to claim the name 'Christian' and even do acts of Christian 'service' and still effectively treat God as weightless by not obeying his Word. The weightlessness of God in both broader culture and Christian theology is explored by David Wells (1994). Christians can too easily forget the glory or 'weight' of God, and 'worship' or 'service' becomes self-centred and offensive to him.

The second part of the passage, which addresses the teaching and lifestyle of the priests as leaders in the community, finds its parallel in the requirements for leadership in the church. These include the ability to teach and refute error (e.g. Titus 1:9; 1 Tim. 3:2; 2 Tim. 2:2) and setting a godly example of the Christian life (e.g. 1 Tim. 3:2; 4:12). False teaching and immoral conduct have the potential to cause many to fall (e.g. Matt. 5:29–30; 1 Tim. 4:1; 6:3–5; 2 Tim. 2:16–18; 3:6–9; 2 Peter 2:1–3; 2 John 7–11; Rev. 2:14, 20), just as true instruction and upright conduct can turn many from sin (e.g. 1 Tim. 4:16; Jas 5:19–20).

MALACHI 2:10–16

Translation

2:10 Is there not one Father for all of us? Has not one God created us? Why do we act faithlessly against one another to profane [the] covenant of our fathers? 11 Judah has acted faithlessly and an abomination has been committed in Israel and in Jerusalem, for Judah has profaned the holiness of the LORD, for he has loved and he has married the daughter of a foreign god. 12 May the LORD (rousing himself and answering) cut off the man who does it from the tents of Jacob, though he brings an offering to the LORD of hosts.

13 And this is a second [thing] you do: you cover the altar of the LORD [with] tears – [with] weeping and crying, because there is still no turning to the offering or accepting favour from your hand. 14 Yet you say, 'Why?' Because the LORD has testified between you and the wife of your youth that you have acted faithlessly against her, yet she is your companion and the wife of your covenant.

15 Did he not make [them] one? And a remnant of the Spirit for it [the oneness]. And why one? [Because he was] seeking godly offspring. So guard yourselves in your spirit and do not act faithlessly against the wife of your youth. 16 'If he hated [his wife] to divorce [her],' says the LORD, the God of Israel, 'then violence will have covered over his garment,' says the LORD of hosts. So guard yourselves in your spirit and you shall not act faithlessly.

Notes on the text

2:10. 'Is there not . . . ? Has not . . . ?': *hălôʼ* . . . *hălôʼ*. These mark rhetorical questions that cannot easily be contested by the person being addressed (Miller-Naudé et al. 1999: 322).

LXX puts the first two questions in the second person and inverts them, but Syr, Tg, Vg follow MT.

'against one another': lit. 'a man against his brother'.

11. 'for he has loved': takes *'ăšer* as introducing a reason (cf. Hag. 1:9; Zech. 11:2, 5; 13:6) (R. J. Williams 2007: 166). See 'Comment'.

'and he has married the daughter of a foreign god'. LXX: 'and he has been married to a foreign god.' Tg: '*and they have chosen to marry wives from the daughters of the nations*' (Cathcart and Gordon 1989: 233; their italics). The final phrase is lit. 'a daughter of a god of a foreigner'. 4Q76 reads *byt* (house) instead of *bt* (daughter), which should probably be considered a scribal error (Fuller 1991: 51).

12. 'May the LORD . . . cut off': *yakrēt yhwh*. The yiqtol is a juss., expressing a curse (Joosten 2012: 339).

'rousing himself and answering': *'ēr wĕ'ōneh* is a very difficult phrase to translate, evident in the versions. I have relocated the phrase in translation so that it clearly refers to Yahweh, but this is not necessarily the case. 4Q76 reads *'r* (one who rouses himself) as *'d* (witness). Gelston (2010: 150) believes this is a copying error. Syr and Tg take it to refer to the 'son and grandson' of the man who are cut off. Vg translates it as the 'master and disciple' of the man. See also Fuller 1991: 51.

13. 'you cover': *kassôt* is an inf. const. (lit. 'covering') and is used in place of a finite verb for emphasis (Waltke and O'Connor 1990: 595). Person and aspect are determined from the context.

'because . . . there is still no': *mē'ên 'ôd*. The prep. *min* is causal (Arnold and Choi 2003: 117).

14. 'Why': *'al-mâ*. Lit. 'concerning what?'

'that you have acted faithlessly against her' is omitted in 4Q76 (Fuller 1991: 52). It is present in all the versions (LXX, Syr, Tg, Vg).

15. Tg, Syr and Vg read *wĕlō'* as the interr. *hălō'*.

'And why one?' follows the Masoretic cantillation. The 'one' is definite and is understood as 'an article of previous reference' (Clendenen 2004: 355). Alternatively, 'the One' could be taken as a reference to God, as most of the English translations do.

'act faithlessly': *yibgōd*. 4Q76, LXX, Tg, Vg all read 'you act faithlessly', possibly to agree with v. 16.

16. 4Q76 reads, 'except he hates her, to divorce' (*ky 'm snth slḥ*), which is conditional (Ko 2014: 39). Some MSS, LXX and Tg translate it as a command to divorce one's wife: 'If having hated, divorce!' (Fuller 1991: 54–55). This takes 'divorce' as the apodosis of the conditional sentence. See also Elwolde 2011.

'then . . . will have covered': *wĕkissâ* is a weqatal in the apodosis of a conditional sentence. In this construction it has a 'past-in-the-future' meaning (J. A. Cook 2012: 253).

Form and structure

Malachi's third disputation speech accuses the people of Judah of being unfaithful to the Mosaic covenant by their marriage practices. Specifically, they are marrying foreign women who worship pagan gods (vv. 11–12), and/or divorcing the wives of their youth without adequate grounds (vv. 13–16). Some scholars argue that the two practices are related, with older Israelite men divorcing their Israelite wives in order to marry foreign women (Keil 1949: 447; Zehnder 2003: 230–231; Assis 2009: 114). While this is certainly possible, this connection is not explicit and raises other questions about motives for such marriages and contemporary beliefs and practices surrounding polygyny, but these issues are not directly addressed in Malachi and answers remain speculative. What is clear from Malachi is that the two issues are both contemporary marriage practices that threaten the unity of the post-exilic community and profane the national covenant.

Some scholars argue that 'he has married the daughter of a foreign god' should be understood figuratively as idolatry (Ogden 1988; Petersen 1995), but this view does not fit the textual data and is sometimes based on spurious emendations. Zehnder (2003: 228) identifies the difficulties with the 'figurative interpretation' and concludes, 'all these aspects can be explained in a much easier and natural way if the verses are understood literally, referring to mixed marriages, than with the assumption of a figurative view'. Hill (1998: 223) rightly concludes, 'Those who read Mal 2:10–16 figuratively as a series of metaphors for the priesthood fail to appreciate the hortatory nature and confrontational posture of the disputation speech form.'

Most commentators classify the speech as a further 'prophetic disputation' (e.g. Smith [1984: 320]; Hill [1998: 220]). In contrast, Floyd (2000: 605) contends that there is nothing particularly disputational about this speech. However, the element of dispute is found in v. 14 where the people question why their offerings have not been favourably accepted by God (Tate 1987: 401). This is an expression of the popular view (Yahweh should accept our offerings), which Malachi takes issue with. This also provides a link with the previous speech where Yahweh rejects the people's offerings (1:9–13).

Key words occur throughout this passage and highlight important themes: 'to act faithlessly' (*bāgad*) occurs five times (2:10, 11, 14, 15, 16); 'one' (*'eḥād*) occurs four times (2:10 [twice]; 15, 16); 'covenant' (*bĕrît*) occurs twice (2:10, 14; cf. 2:4, 5, 8). Malachi twice exhorts the people to 'guard yourselves in your spirit' and 'do not act faithlessly' (cf. 'you shall not act faithlessly') (vv. 15, 16).

The passage can be divided thematically as follows. This division is supported by the MT paragraph markers at the end of 2:9, 12, 16, which indicate how Jewish rabbis of the Talmudic period (AD 135–500) understood the division of the text (Brotzman 1994: 47).

2:10	Introduction: faithless actions profane the covenant
2:11–12	Marrying women who worship pagan gods
2:13–16	Divorce without adequate grounds

Comment

2:10. The third disputation speech begins with two rhetorical questions whose answers cannot easily be contested: 'Is there not one Father for all of us? Has not one God created us?' (See 'Notes on the text'.) These questions function to draw in the audience and to introduce a new topic – the breakdown of community and covenant relationship with Yahweh due to unfaithfulness in marriage. Some argue that the rhetorical questions in v. 10 quote the people as part of a disputation, since the pr. 'us' is used (Tate 1987: 401; Assis 2010a: 360; Assis 2012: 215). This is possible, but the content of the questions suggests that the prophet is setting up the subsequent accusations, and the third question seems more accusatory than ironic: 'Why do we act faithlessly against one another to profane [the] covenant of our fathers?'

The repetition of 'one' in the rhetorical questions underlines the unity and distinctiveness the covenant people of Yahweh were to display in their national life that flowed from the uniqueness of God and the unity of his purposes (see 'Comment' on Zech. 14:9). Some commentators understand the 'Father' to be Abraham, and the 'covenant of our fathers' as the Abrahamic or patriarchal covenant (McKenzie and Wallace 1983: 552; Calvin 1986: 539). However, if Abraham was intended, this would not mark out the distinctiveness of the nation since the Edomites (cf. 1:2–5) were also descended from Abraham (Keil 1949: 448). Furthermore, the 'covenant of our fathers' refers to the covenant with Israel at Sinai in Jer. 31:32 and 34:13 (cf. 1 Kgs 8:21; 2 Kgs 17:15) (Stuart 1998: 1328). Since the first two rhetorical questions are parallel, the 'Father' is best understood as Yahweh (Mason 1977: 149; Hill 1998: 225). Yahweh describes himself as 'a father' in 1:6 (cf. Exod. 4:22–23; Deut. 32:6, 18; Isa. 63:16; 64:8[7]; Jer. 3:4, 19; 31:9; Hos. 11:1). These two questions highlight the special relationship Yahweh has with his people: the national covenant is understood in terms of a kinship relationship with Yahweh and with one another. If these associations are recognized, then the creation is more likely a reference to the creation of the nation in the exodus (cf. Exod. 15:16; Deut. 32:6; Isa. 43:21) than to human creation (Berry 1996: 280).

A third question functions as a general accusation of covenantal unfaithfulness: 'Why do we act faithlessly against one another to profane [the] covenant of our fathers?' To 'act faithlessly' is to fail to keep covenant obligations. To 'profane the covenant' is to render it defiled or polluted; it is to break it (cf. Pss 55:20[21]; 89:31[32], 34[35]). This is a consequence of acting faithlessly or disobeying God's Word (see 'comment' on 1:12).

This general accusation is made more specific in what follows – the men of Judah have acted faithlessly by marrying women who worship pagan gods (vv. 11–12) and by divorcing the wives of their youth (vv. 13–16). In the light of the opening two questions, the implication is that these acts of unfaithfulness have undermined the community's unity – what happens 'in the privacy of the bedroom', so to speak, has impacted their national life. The prophet includes himself in the accusation ('we . . . our'), which underlines this sense of national solidarity, rather than confessing any personal sin.

11. The first way in which the people of Judah have acted faithlessly is by having 'married [lit. 'Baal-ed'] the daughter of a foreign god'. This has been understood in two main ways: as a reference to national idolatry, or as men in Judah marrying women who worship gods other than Yahweh. The first is often called 'figurative' or 'metaphorical', but in reality both interpretations are figurative or metaphorical in different ways. Those who argue that it refers to idolatry contend that the word 'abomination' is associated elsewhere in the OT with idolatry, especially in Deuteronomy (J. M. O'Brien 1990: 67–69; J. M. O'Brien 1996: 246); that the parallel expression 'sons of God' does not typically refer to humans, but to angels (Nogalski 2011: 1033); and that the weeping in v. 13 is a pagan ritual (J. M. O'Brien 2004). Petersen (1995: 194) argues that 'whom he loved' (*'ăšer 'āhēb*) can be emended to 'he loves Asherah' (*'ăšērāh 'āhēb*), but this is not generally accepted, even by those who argue for the first view.

In favour of reading it as a reference to men in Judah marrying women who worship gods other than Yahweh is the fact that this was a major problem in Ezra 9:1 – 10:17 and Neh. 13:23–30. Deuteronomy forbids the people of Israel from intermarrying with the people of the land because 'they will turn your children away from following me to serve other gods, and the Lord's anger will burn against you and will quickly destroy you' (Deut. 7:4; cf. Exod. 34:16; Lev. 21:14; Num. 36:6; Deut. 13:6–9). While strictly the foreign nations referred to in these passages were Canaanites, the principle readily transfers to other nations (cf. 1 Kgs 11:1–2). Neh. 13:24 says that the children of these marriages did not know how to speak the language of Judah, which would have serious implications for knowing Yahweh and his ways. It is a religious concern rather than a racial one since elsewhere foreigners who worship Yahweh are readily accepted into the covenant community (e.g. Moses' wife Zipporah, Rahab, Ruth, Abigail).

Carson (2012) has demonstrated that the expression 'son of' (or 'daughter of') often indicates identity and function rather than biology. In this case, 'daughter of a foreign god' simply indicates that these women have their identity in a foreign god – they are not worshippers of Yahweh. It could also describe Jewish women who had abandoned Yahweh (Scalise 2009: 341). There is a parallel with the expressions 'sons of Belial' (*bĕnê-bĕliyya'al*) (e.g. niv translates 'troublemakers' in Deut. 13:13 [HB 13:14];

'wicked men' in Judg. 19:22; and 'scoundrels' in 1 Kgs 21:10) and 'daughter of Belial' (*bat-bĕliyya'al*) (e.g. NIV translates 'wicked woman' in 1 Sam. 1:16). Each instance refers to wicked humans (rather than angels). The practice of marrying 'the daughter of a foreign god' is condemned because of the threat idolatry poses to the community. This is consistent with the charge of acting faithlessly against one another in v. 10, and explains why it is appropriately called 'an abomination'.

This behaviour is also said to have 'profaned the holiness of the LORD' (cf. 1:12). The word 'holiness' (*qōdeš*) is translated 'sanctuary' in many English versions (e.g. ESV, NASB, NIV). Other suggestions for what 'holiness' refers to include the people of Judah (Keil 1949: 449; Verhoef 1987: 268), or the covenant (Merrill 1994: 418), but these seem less likely. If the close connection between God's name and his holy character is recognized (e.g. Exod. 34:5–7), then the idea that God's holiness has been profaned by his people's exposure to idolatry readily suits the context. Hill (1998: 231) suggests that the term may have a dual reference to the temple and the character ('name') of Yahweh. This combination is seen for example in Lev. 20:3, in the context of idolatry.

The following phrase 'for he has loved' is translated as a rel. clause in most English translations: 'which he [the LORD] loves' (ESV, NASB) or 'the sanctuary the LORD loves' (NIV). Elsewhere Yahweh is said to love Zion (cf. Ps. 78:68; 87:2), but there is nowhere else that expresses the idea of his loving the temple. Alternatively, I have translated it as introducing a reason: 'for he [Judah] has loved and he has married the daughter of a foreign god'. This keeps the same referent for the final two pronouns and better suits the context and syntax (Baker 2006: 253). Rather than loving Yahweh (cf. Deut. 6:5), the men of Judah have diverted their love to others (cf. the book of Hosea, where the people are said to love almost everything except Yahweh).

12. The Hebr. of this verse is difficult to translate since a phrase in the middle appears to be idiomatic: 'rousing himself and answering' (*'ēr wĕ'ōneh*). J. M. Gibson (2014b) surveys ten interpretations (ancient and modern), which include (1) emending the MT *'ēr* (rousing himself) to *'ed* (witness), as is found in 4Q76 and reflected in LXX (see 'Notes on the text'). The phrase then has a legal connotation and refers to cutting off legal representation to the man who does this (so NRSV: 'May the LORD cut off from the tents of Jacob anyone who does this – any to witness or answer') (Fuller 1991: 51; Floyd 2000: 605), or cutting off those who are party to such marriages (NIV footnote: 'May the LORD remove from the tents of Jacob anyone who gives testimony on behalf of the man who does this') (Hill 1998: 235); (2) Vg translates it as 'master and disciple', but this does not readily fit the marriage context; (3) the phrase is a merism that expresses the idea of totality (Merrill 1994: 419). This is reflected in the NIV, 'whoever he may be', but this is very conjectural; (4) Glazier-McDonald (1987: 95–98) argues that the phrase has sexual connotations: 'the aroused one and the lover', but the sexual connotations are unlikely in Malachi (J. M. Gibson 2014b: 529); (5) an inner-biblical allusion to Er and Onan in Gen. 38 (Sweeney 2000b: 736–737; Weyde 2000: 246). Yet 'Onan' is not mentioned and there is little contextual congruence between the passages on closer analysis (J. M. Gibson 2014b: 535–536).

J. M. Gibson (2014b: 530–534) notes that the Hebr. construction (*krt* + *l* + two coordinated participles/nouns often displaying either alliteration and/or assonance) is elsewhere used as a punishment formula that speaks of the destruction of offspring as Yahweh's punishment (e.g. 1 Kgs 14:10; 21:21; 2 Kgs 9:8; Isa. 14:22; Jer. 44:7; 47:4). He contends that the phrase refers to the person's descendants, their 'kith and kin'. Therefore, for those who have married outside the national covenant, 'Malachi utters a solemn warning: "May YHWH cut off for the man who does this 'kith and kin' from the tents of Jacob."' Interestingly, this is consistent with Syr and Tg, which translate it 'son and grandson', and this interpretation is reflected in the ESV: 'May the LORD cut off from the tents of Jacob any descendant'. A problem with this (which Gibson acknowledges) is that it is not possible to connect this meaning philologically with the words themselves. Furthermore, the resulting translation has the curse of death falling on the offspring rather than directly on the man himself. None of the comparative passages Gibson cites uses the construction to refer to judgment on an ordinary Israelite; rather, it is a king or a nation or a broader group. For the normal Israelite, it is the individual who sins who is 'cut off' from the community, rather than his or her offspring (cf. Exod. 12:15, 19; 31:14; Lev. 7:20–21, 25, 27; 19:8; 20:18; 22:3; Num. 9:13; 15:31; 19:13, 20).

Given these problems, my own suggestion is that 'rousing himself and answering' refers to the hoped for response of Yahweh to Malachi's petition, interjected as part of the petition itself: 'May the LORD (rousing himself and answering) cut off the man who does it from the tents of Jacob.' *TWOT* (1587) observes that the most significant use of 'rousing' is causative, with God as subject. It is also used, as here, as a personal appeal to God to rouse himself (e.g. Pss 7:6[7]; 44:23[24]; 59:4[5]; 80:2[3]; Isa. 51:9). Similarly, 'answering' is commonly used of God's responding favourably to the petitions of his people (e.g. Pss 3:4[5]; 4:1[6]; 20:1[2]; 55:2[3]).

In this case, the prefixed prep. (*lě*) on 'the man' indicates the direct object of the verb ('to cut off'). He will be cut off from 'the tents of Jacob', a reference to the community of the families of Israel, perhaps in an idealized sense (cf. Jer. 30:18). As noted above, this punishment typically has the idea of 'blotting out or destroying the evildoer and his descendants' (Hill 1998: 233). The last phrase 'though he brings an offering to the LORD of hosts' is concessive. That is, even if the man brings a sacrifice, Malachi prays this will not avert the punishment due. This readily links to the condemnation of unworthy sacrifices in the previous speech, and the refusal of offerings in 2:13.

While the translation is difficult, the meaning across the various translations is reasonably clear. Malachi calls on Yahweh to judge those who have married women who worship foreign gods. There is a wordplay since the Hebr. construction 'cut off' (*krt* + *l*) is also used of making ('cutting') a covenant (e.g. Exod. 23:32; Deut. 7:2): 'those who are "cut into" a covenant are now in danger of being "cut off" from the covenant' (J. M. Gibson 2014b: 537). Because they have acted faithlessly against other members of the covenant community (v. 10), Malachi calls on Yahweh to cut them off from the benefits of belonging to the community.

13. A second act of faithlessness is identified in vv. 13–16, and it is introduced by means of one of the consequences: 'you cover the altar of the LORD [with] tears – [with] weeping and crying, because there is still no turning to the offering or accepting favour from your hand'. Some argue these are the tears of the divorced wives in v. 16 (Keil 1949: 451; Zehnder 2003: 233). But these women have not yet been mentioned and were unlikely to gain access to the temple altar. Others argue that the mourning is a pagan religious practice, like mourning for Tammuz in Ezek. 8:14 (Isaksson 1965: 31–33; Petersen 1995: 201), but the context indicates that they are seeking Yahweh's favour and 'tears . . . weeping and crying' are not necessarily pagan practices (see e.g. 1 Sam. 1:10; 2 Kgs 20:5 = Isa. 38:5; Ps. 6:6–9[7–10]; 12:5). The people mourn because Yahweh has not accepted their offerings. Malachi does not say how they know this, but Verhoef (1987: 273) is probably correct to suggest it was on account of their failed crops (3:10–12; cf. Hag. 1:10–11; 2:17).

14. The reason Yahweh has refused their offerings is introduced with a mini disputational statement: 'Yet you say, "Why?"' (cf. 1:2, 7–8, 12–13). The people appear oblivious to the reason for God's displeasure, which Malachi elucidates: 'Because the LORD has testified between you and the wife of your youth that you have acted faithlessly against her, yet she is your companion and the wife of your covenant.' This is the second act of faithlessness in marriage that Malachi identifies in this speech. Exactly what this 'acting faithlessly' involves is not spelled out until v. 16, namely 'If he hated [his wife] to divorce [her]'. Acting faithlessly towards one's covenant wife goes hand in hand with acting faithlessly towards Yahweh. Hence Yahweh refuses their offerings (Garland 1987: 420).

Thankfully, the translation of this verse is more straightforward than the surrounding verses and yields important information about marriage. Particularly, that marriage is a covenantal relationship witnessed by Yahweh. Some scholars argue that the covenant is not a marriage covenant, but the national covenant of 2:10 (Isaksson 1965: 31; Glazier-McDonald 1987: 101). Furthermore, if the 'daughter of a foreign god' in v. 11 is a goddess, the 'wife of your youth' refers to Yahweh (Petersen 1995: 203; J. M. O'Brien 1996: 249). However, a thorough study by Hugenberger (1984 [1994: 27–47]) convincingly demonstrates this refers to a marriage covenant and that arguments for the 'daughter of a foreign god' being a goddess are unpersuasive. There is nowhere else in the OT where Yahweh is Israel's wife – everywhere else Yahweh is father or husband (Dumbrell 1976: 47). Given how unlikely it is that Yahweh would be called Israel's wife in a patricentric culture, this surely finally rules out the view that the 'daughter of a foreign god' is a goddess. Hugenberger (1984 [1994: 312]) also identifies other OT passages that identify marriage as a covenantal relationship (e.g. Hos. 2:16–20[18–22]; Prov. 2:17; Ezek. 16:8, 59–60, 62; 1 Sam. 18 – 20). The violation of marriage covenants is an example of the wider issue in the book – the profaning of the covenant of the fathers (McKenzie and Wallace 1983: 558).

Hill (1998: 242) notes that the word 'companion' (*ḥăberet*) in the f. is unique in the HB. He observes that in the pi., the verbal root (*ḥbr*) is used in architectural contexts to designate a 'seam' or 'joint' in a building (e.g. Exod. 26:6, 9, 11) and suggests the connotation is one of 'permanent bonding' within marriage (cf. Gen. 2:24). The m. equivalent (*ḥăber*) occurs a dozen times, often referring to a 'friend, companion' (e.g. Song. 1:7; 8:13), or to business partners (e.g. Prov. 28:24; Isa. 1:23; 44:11). The wife is certainly not viewed in ancient Israel as a chattel or possession to be disposed of at will (Garland 1987: 420; Clendenen 2004: 347). She is an equal companion to her husband, even if she exercises different roles.

The word 'testified' (*hēʿîd*) is the same verb root as 'witnessed' and indicates that Yahweh is a witness to the covenant and has testified and now testifies (the sense of the verb in the qatal) to the faithless action of the husband. This is why faithlessness in marriage is a sin not only against the marriage companion, but against God (cf. Gen. 31:50). V. 10 also indicates that faithlessness in marriage is a sin against others in the covenant community.

15. Calvin (1986: 554) said in 1559, 'There is in this verse some obscurity, and hence it has been that no interpreter has come to the meaning of the Prophet.' Unfortunately, over four-and-a-half centuries later it is still difficult to make sense of the Hebr., but hopefully the meaning is now less obscure. Clendenen (2004: 350) offers a literal rendering of the first half of the verse: 'And not one [he] did/made, and a remnant of spirit [is/was?] to him. And what [is/was] the one? Seeking seed of God.' The suggestions for how to make sense of this are too numerous to evaluate fully here. See further, Zehnder 2003: 236–251. Ultimately, any interpretation must remain tentative, but it is partly a case of trying to fit the words into a framework that suits the immediate argument of Malachi and the wider context of OT theology.

The words 'one' and 'offspring' (lit. 'seed') bring to mind the early chapters of Genesis and its teaching about the nature and purpose of marriage, particularly Gen. 2:24. If this is the case, then the subject of 'make' must be God. The 'one' could refer to God (cf. 2:10), so NIV: 'Has not the one God made you?' Alternatively, 'one' could refer to the 'one flesh' relationship resulting from marriage (Gen. 2:24), so ESV: 'Did he not make them one . . . ?'. Both statements are true, but the second better suits the context of marriage. Some interpret the 'one' as Abraham, with the passage being a rebuttal of those who might justify their divorces by appealing to Abraham's conduct towards Hagar in sending her away (Keil 1949: 452; Merrill 1994: 421–422). But this does not fit the data as readily as reading it against the background of the early chapters of Genesis. For instance, Abraham remained with the wife of his youth, Sarah (Zehnder 2003: 238).

The phrase 'remnant of the Spirit' (lit. 'a remnant of spirit') is difficult to conceive since normally a 'remnant' refers to survivors of a larger group. For this reason some scholars suggest emending 'remnant' (*šĕ'ār*) to 'flesh' (*šĕ'ēr*), which involves repointing a single vowel and adding the conj. ('and') before 'spirit' (Baldwin 1972: 240; Rudolph 1976: 270; 1981; Scalise 2009: 346). This is followed by NIV: 'You belong to him in body and spirit,' and NRSV: 'Both flesh and spirit are his.' On this interpretation, the 'spirit' refers to the 'life force' or 'breath' that animates otherwise lifeless flesh and may indicate that since God made them one, their lives and hence their marriage belong to him. However, the word for 'flesh' (*šĕ'ēr*) is a different one from Gen. 2:24 (*bāśār*). Furthermore, all the ancient versions read it as 'remnant' rather than 'flesh', and so an interpretation that explains the MT is preferable.

Some suggest that 'the Spirit/spirit' refers to 'intelligence, sound judgment' (Verhoef 1987: 276), 'reproductive potential' (Glazier-McDonald 1987: 107–108) or 'sexual appetite' (Sweeney 2000b: 738), but these all seem forced. Clendenen (2004: 355) offers the most satisfying solution, that 'for it' (*lô*) refers to the 'one' in the first question, namely the unity ('one-ness') that God created in marriage. Despite the faithlessness of the men towards their wives (v. 14), these marriages retain a remnant of the divine Spirit, who created the unity or 'oneness' at its establishment. While the Spirit is not directly referenced in the first marriage in Gen. 2, God breathes his Spirit/breath into the nostrils of Adam in v. 7, and there could be a sense in which God's creative work by his Spirit continues through the chapter. This is reflected in ESV: 'with a portion of the Spirit in their union'.

The rhetorical question 'And why one?' follows the Masoretic pointing, which pauses before 'seeking', whereas most English translations interpret 'the One' as Yahweh and link it with 'seeking'. Either way, God's purpose in marriage unity is 'seeking godly offspring' (lit. 'seeking seed of God'). These are offspring who display God's character, walking in his ways. The language reflects Genesis, where the godly line of seed is fundamental and links to the promise of Gen. 3:15 (cf. Alexander 1993). It also serves to indicate why marrying the daughter of a foreign god (v. 11) undermines God's purposes, since it threatens the godliness of the offspring.

Yahweh's purposes of unity in marriage and godly offspring provide the basis for the exhortation 'So guard yourselves in your spirit and do not act faithlessly against the wife of your youth.' A similar urging is found at the end of v. 16. The word 'guard' is used in 2:7 of the priests' responsibility to preserve knowledge and instruction (*tôrâ*) given by God, and in 2:9 of their failure to obey God's ways. Reference to 'your spirit' probably is a wordplay with 'Spirit' in the previous verse, but here refers to 'the impulse that governs a person's life and controls his or her behaviour' (Routledge 2008: 144). Hence the exhortation is to be very careful to obey God in this matter and not to act in a way that separates what God has brought together (cf. Mark 10:9). The verse gives grounds for fostering and preserving marriage relationships.

16. The Hebr. of the first half of this verse also poses translation difficulties. A literal translation of MT is, '"For he hates divorce," says the LORD, the God of Israel, "and violence will have covered over his garment," says the LORD of hosts.' As it stands, God says that the man who hates divorce is guilty of violence, which clearly does not suit the context. A common translation, 'I hate divorce' (NASB, NIV1984, NRSV), involves adding consonants and repointing the MT, which is unsatisfactory (C. J. Collins 1994: 36). It is possible that the text was changed by scribes to soften its teaching about divorce, but this is only speculative. Alternatively, the third-person speech can be understood to be about Yahweh: 'he hates divorce'. While it is possible for a statement of Yahweh to be in the third person along with the two speech formulas ('says the LORD'; see Mal. 3:1 and 'Comment'), the second statement is clearly not about Yahweh: 'violence will have covered over his garment'.

Another way to render the MT is to take *kî* (if) as introducing the protasis of a conditional statement (Arnold and Choi 2003: 151), and to make explicit the idea of the wife as the object of the verbs: '"If he hated [his wife] to divorce [her]," says the LORD, the God of Israel, "then violence will have covered over his garment," says the LORD of hosts.' This is reflected in LXX: 'But if, since you hate her, you should send her away . . .'. This seems to be the best solution and is seen in ESV and NIV. A similar solution is offered by Ko (2014: 39–40): '"If he hates [her enough] to divorce," says Yahweh God of Israel, "he covers a violence on his garment."'

The verb 'to divorce' (*šallaḥ*) is lit. 'to send away', but has the legal meaning of divorce in Deut. 22:19, 29; 24:1, 3–4; and possibly Gen. 21:14; Ezra 10:44; Isa. 50:1; Jer. 3:1, 8 (Hugenberger 1984 [1994: 72]). The verse is sometimes seen to be in tension with the permission to divorce in Deut. 24:1, or with Ezra's command to those who had married foreign women to divorce them in Ezra 10:1–17, yet any tension is more apparent than real. The permission to divorce in Deut. 24:1 is on the grounds of 'something indecent', which is more literally 'a thing of nakedness' or 'a cause of sexual immorality', which some ancient Jewish interpreters understood as adultery (Instone-Brewer 2003: 23). On the other hand, Malachi states that hating one's wife is not grounds for divorce. Indeed, Hugenberger (1984 [1994: 71–72]), citing Westbrook's work on parallel

ANE texts (1986: 398), argues that the combination 'hate' and 'divorce' means 'he divorces without justification'. Hence Malachi's statement is that if divorce proceeds without adequate grounds, then violence is done to the wife. Malachi is not an absolute prohibition of divorce. Indeed, elsewhere Yahweh himself is said to have divorced his bride, Israel, for adultery (e.g. Jer. 3:8; Hos. 2:2[4]).

In Ezra's situation, where men had married women who worshipped foreign gods (cf. Mal. 2:11), the seriousness of breaking up marriages and families should not be understated. Yet at the same time, the sin of idolatry is what led to the exile and threatened the very existence of the nation. The people were in a bind and whatever they did would be displeasing to God (as this passage in Malachi attests). After consultation, Ezra and the leaders agreed that divorce was a lesser evil than living with idolaters whose children in all likelihood could not even speak Hebrew (cf. Neh. 13:23–27).

Intriguingly, a 'garment' is involved in marriage rituals in Ruth 3:9 and Ezek. 16:8, but it is difficult to know if there is an intentional allusion here, or if it is merely coincidental. The figure is best taken as a metaphor indicating that the man who divorces his wife without justification commits a violent act, the effects of which will be on public display as if the perpetrator were wearing a garment splattered in blood. Yahweh detests violence (it was the reason that he sent the flood in Gen. 6:13). Malachi's rhetoric seems designed to serve as a deterrent to divorce through the prospect of public shame. The same exhortation given at the end of v. 15 to foster and preserve one's marriage proactively is repeated: 'So guard yourselves in your spirit and do not act faithlessly . . .'.

Explanation

In Malachi's third disputation speech, the failure of the post-exilic community of Judah to understand God's love (cf. 1:1–5) shows itself in their failure to love God by being faithful to the national covenant, and their failure to love one another, especially in their marriages. This is seen in two ways: men from Judah are marrying women who worship gods other than Yahweh (vv. 11–12), and men are divorcing their wives without adequate grounds (vv. 13–16). While some commentators have proposed a relationship between these issues, with older Jewish men divorcing their wives of many years in order to marry foreign (younger?) women, this relationship is not explicit in the passage and must remain hypothetical in the absence of further evidence. In any case, the practices are both condemned in their own terms.

The first issue of marrying women who worship foreign gods raises the issue of allegiance to Yahweh. Solomon is the classic example of how such marriages end in compromise: 'As Solomon grew old, his wives turned his heart after other gods, and his heart was not fully devoted to the LORD his God, as the heart of David his father had been' (1 Kgs 11:4). The Mosaic covenant prohibited such marriages and the practice is also condemned by Ezra and Nehemiah (Ezra 9 – 10; Neh. 13:23–28). The NT makes similar demands of Christians, who are to marry other believers only (1 Cor. 7:39; cf. 2 Cor. 6:14). Yet if Christians find themselves married to an unbeliever (because they have been converted after marriage, or they were disobedient, or their spouse has given up the faith), then they must not initiate a divorce (1 Cor. 7:12–16). They are not defiled by such a union; in fact, they have the potential to save their spouse and their children by living out the gospel (cf. 1 Peter 3:1).

The second issue of divorce is a painful one for many – relationships that offer the most potential for joy and blessing can also bring the greatest hurt and sorrow. God's Word is designed to protect those who marry. The ANE was a cruel place for many women (Instone-Brewer 2003: 15–16). The Babylonian king Hammurabi's laws (eighteenth century BC) allowed men to walk out on their wives and children and then to come back at any time (law 36). This situation was devastating for women with no means of support and no ability to remarry. In contrast, an Israelite man had to write a certificate of divorce (Deut. 24:1), which meant she could remarry and be provided for. Furthermore, in OT times, the only legitimate grounds for divorce were adultery (Deut. 24:1), or a failure to provide food, clothing and conjugal love (Exod. 21:10–11) (abuse would be included in this). Malachi's teaching is to be understood in this context. It does not forbid divorce in general, but divorce where there are no legitimate grounds – where divorce itself is being used to break the marriage covenant. Simply falling out of love, so to speak, is not grounds for divorce.

Divorce is a recognition that we live in a fallen world. The grounds for divorce were debated in Jesus' day. Around AD 30, Rabbi Hillel devised the causeless divorce. Since Deut. 24:1 says literally that a man may divorce his wife for 'a cause of sexual immorality', Hillel said that this in effect was two reasons: 'sexual immorality' and 'any cause'. Sexual immorality had to be proven in court, but a certificate was all that was needed for 'any cause', which could include being a bad cook! Hillel was opposed by Rabbi Shammai who had a harder line. Jesus was asked to adjudicate on this debate by the Pharisees in Matt. 19:3: 'Is it lawful for a man to divorce his wife for any and every reason [any cause]?' This is not a question about the legality of divorce (after all, the law provided for it); it is a question about legitimate grounds for divorce. Jesus sides with neither Shammai nor Hillel and says that divorce and remarriage for 'any cause' is adultery, which shocks his disciples. They exclaim, 'it is better not to marry' (Matt. 19:10). For Jesus, marriage between a man and a woman is grounded in creation and he quotes Gen. 2:24: 'what God has joined together, let no one separate' (Matt. 19:6). Genesis reveals the divine purposes in marriage: for the birth and nurture of godly children (Gen. 1:28; cf. Mal. 2:15), for a different and complementary companion in fulfilling the divine mandate to subdue the earth (Gen. 1:28; 2:23), and for the expression of natural instincts and affections (Gen. 2:25; Exod. 21:11). God protects those who marry by prohibiting divorce without cause, as Malachi restates. At the same time, God protects those who are in marriages that have effectively stopped being marriages through repeated and unrepentant breaking of marriage vows by allowing victims to initiate divorce (cf. Matt. 19:8–9). In Christian marriages, where there are no grounds for divorce but the relationship has broken down, 1 Cor. 7:11 allows for separation, but prohibits divorce and remarriage to a third party, only reconciliation to one's spouse. The gospel of Jesus and the power of the Holy Spirit provide the means for repentance, forgiveness, reconciliation and change. If there are grounds for divorce, divorce is certainly not mandated; rather, it is permitted. In this case the victim can remarry someone who belongs to the Lord (1 Cor. 7:15, 39). Whether the guilty party can remarry is a controversial issue on which Christians disagree, and there are more issues involved than I can adequately survey in this commentary. For two different views see Cornes (2002) and Instone-Brewer (2003).

Malachi makes clear that marriage is a covenant relationship, witnessed by God. Covenants involve commitments or promises that the parties bind themselves to. For covenants to work, both faith and faithfulness are required – faith is required to trust the promises made, and faithfulness is needed to keep the promised commitments. When promises are not kept, then faith is damaged and relationships fall apart. This was the problem in Malachi's day – the word 'faithlessly' occurs five times in this passage. The people of Judah have been unfaithful in the national covenant and in their marriage covenants. The two are related in the sense that if one cannot remain faithful in the most intimate of human relationships, why would one expect the same person to keep their word in other relationships? This passage also brings to mind the earlier portrayal of Israel as an unfaithful wife in Hosea, at the beginning of the Twelve (J. D. W. Watts 2000). It indicates that by the end of the Twelve, Israel (cf. 1:1) is still to learn this faithfulness.

Contemporary debates in Western societies about marriage almost always misunderstand the character of marriage in the Bible. The biblical ideal is a lifelong, monogamous, procreative union of a man and a woman with faithfulness at the heart of the union. The introduction of no-fault divorce across Western societies over the last forty or so years reflects a view of marriage as impermanent and readily dissolved, similar to the situation Malachi is addressing. Across the Bible, marriage requires faithfulness and society abandons this emphasis to its peril. A report by Patrick Parkinson (2011: 112) of Sydney University on the state of children's well-being confirms the wisdom of God's ways:

> two parents tend to provide better outcomes for children than one, and . . . the most stable, safe and nurturing environment for

> children is when their parents are, and remain, married to one another. The difference marriage seems to make is in the commitment that it involves, providing a greater degree of stability and resilience, especially when times are difficult. Marriage involves a decision to commit, to dedicate oneself to the other and to the partnership.

Faithfulness in marriage is good for all of society, particularly the vulnerable.

MALACHI 2:17 – 3:7A

Translation

2:17'You have wearied the LORD with your words. But you say, "How have we
wearied [him]?" When you say, "Everyone doing evil is good in the eyes of the
LORD and he delights in them," or "Where is the God of justice?"

3:1'Look, I will send my messenger and he will clear a way before me. Then
suddenly he will enter into his temple – the Lord whom you are seeking and the
messenger of the covenant whom you are delighting in, look he will come,' says
the LORD of hosts.

2'But who will endure the day of his coming? And who will stand when he
appears? For he will be as a refiner's fire and as launderers' soap.
3Then he will sit
refining and purifying silver and he will purify the sons of Levi and he will refine
them as gold and as silver. Then they will be for the LORD ones who bring an
offering in righteousness.
4Then the offering of Judah and Jerusalem will be
pleasing to the LORD as [in] days of old and as [in] former years.

5'So I will draw near to you for judgment and I will be a swift witness against the
sorcerers, and against the adulterers, and against those swearing falsely, and against
oppressors of a labourer's wages, widow and orphan, and those turning away a
stranger – and they do not fear me,' says the LORD of hosts.
6'For I am the LORD
– I have not changed, so you, sons of Jacob, have not perished.
7aFrom the days of
your fathers you turned away from my statutes and you have not kept [them].'

Notes on the text

2:17. 'him' is not present in MT, but is added in LXX.

'justice': *hammišpāṭ* has a generic art. that is not translated. Cf. Zech. 8:19; Mal. 2:5.

3:1. 'I will send': *šōlēaḥ*. Following 'Look' (*hinnî*), the ptc. usually expresses future action. It does not necessarily imply imminent future (e.g. 2 Kgs 21:12; Isa. 13:13; Jer. 30:10; 31:8; 32:37; 33:6; 46:27; 50:18; Zeph. 3:19) (C. J. Thomson 2013: 56).

'he will come': *bā'*. This ptc. has the same syntax as 'I will send' (above).

5. 'swift': *mĕmahēr* is translated as an attrib. ptc. modifying 'witness' (*'ēd*).

'those swearing falsely': lit. 'those swearing to the lie/deception' (cf. Zech. 5:4).

'oppressors' is translated three times in LXX, repeating the idea for 'widow' and 'orphan'.

'a labourer's wages': *śĕkar-śākîr* is a const. gen. phrase (Chary 1969: 282).

'and those turning away': *ûmaṭṭê* is translated as a subst. ptc.

6. LXX amplifies 'LORD' to 'the Lord your God'.

'have not perished': *kĕlîtem* is rendered differently in the versions. LXX seems to combine with v. 7 and reads, 'have not abstained from the sins of your fathers'. Syr has 'have not departed from your injury' (Smith 1984: 331). MT seems to be followed by Tg and is reflected in 4Q78, but the latter is fragmentary.

7a. 'From the days of': *lĕmîmê* combines the preposition *lĕ*, which indicates a location in time, and *min*, which indicates a beginning point in time. The combination 'marks time that began at a point in the past (the days of [. . .]) and continues into the present' (Eddinger 2012: 89). It occurs elsewhere only in 2 Kgs 19:25. The difficulty of rendering this expression is seen in the versions. The prep. *lĕ* is *k* in 4Q78 (which agrees with Tg), and Vg appears to translate *kî*. Gelston (2010: 151*) believes these 'are respectively stylistic and exegetical renderings'. Syr leaves *lĕ* untranslated.

Form and structure

Malachi's fourth disputation speech begins with 2:17 (the MT has a paragraph marker at the end of 2:16). The chapter division at 3:1 is clearly misplaced, as the questions in 2:17 are addressed in the speech. While a majority of commentators (and English translations) understand 3:6 to be introducing the fifth disputation speech, a significant minority take it as the conclusion to this speech (Keil 1949: 455; Achtemeier 1986: 186; Floyd 2000: 612; Clark and Hatton 2002: 427; Clendenen 2004: 399; Assis 2010a: 357). McKenzie and Wallace (1983: 553) argue v. 6 is a transition and Sweeney (2000b: 742) believes the speech concludes with v. 7. A decision is difficult but not insignificant since the interpretation of 3:6 in some measure depends on whether it looks backwards or forwards.

Rudolph (1976: 277) argues that the section ends with 3:5 since 3:6–12 is not as eschatological as 2:17 – 3:5. Yet vv. 6–7a could also be explaining why the eschatological judgment of vv. 1–5 has not yet come on God's people, before the shift in v. 7b, where a call to 'return' is issued. Furthermore, Glazier-McDonald (1987: 174) demonstrates the future orientation of 3:6–12. Tiemeyer (2006: 25–26) argues that v. 6 introduces a new audience (the 'sons of Jacob'), where 2:17 – 3:5 addresses the priests. Yet the nation as a whole is in view in 3:4 and it seems more likely that the crimes of v. 5 are not restricted to the priesthood, but include the 'sons of Jacob'. On the other hand, Floyd (2000) argues that the conj. 'For' (*kî*) at the beginning of v. 6 (not translated in NIV) indicates a close link to what precedes. Yet *kî* can also be understood as asseverative, emphasizing the clause that follows (Verhoef 1987: 299; Arnold and Choi 2003: 153): 'Indeed, I am the LORD – I have not changed.' I have included vv. 6–7a as the conclusion of the fourth disputation speech, as I believe it contributes to the explanation of the question of God's justice in 2:17 and contributes a note of grace. Snyman (2011) also contends that the unit finishes with 7a. At the same time, vv. 6–7a also clearly connect with the call to 'return to me' in v. 7b, which precedes the people's dispute in the next speech. Mal. 3:6–7a is best understood as transitional, and a strict demarcation between the fourth and fifth speeches seems forced (cf. Willi-Plein 2007: 268). Assis (2010a: 357) comments that 'despite the clear division between the oracles, the author or redactor wished to make them a continuous sequence', and this is clearly the case here. After 2:16, the next paragraph marker in the MT is after 3:12.

This fourth prophetic disputation speech can be structured according to its content. It begins with a statement of how the people's words have wearied Yahweh. The people claim that Yahweh approves of evildoers and is not present to judge (2:17). Assis (2012: 217) classifies the speech not as a 'rebuke' but as a 'response of the prophet, speaking for God, to the people's claims against God'. Malachi declares that Yahweh is coming and his messenger will prepare the way (3:1). The day of Yahweh's coming will refine and purify the priests (3:2–3) and restore offerings by the people of Judah and Jerusalem that are pleasing to God (3:4). Yahweh's coming will also put the evildoers on trial and bring swift judgment (3:5). The reason Yahweh's day has not yet come is because he continues to hold out mercy to a rebellious people – he has not changed (3:6–7a). This links directly with the next speech.

Comment

2:17. The audience of Malachi's fourth disputation speech ('you') is best identified as the post-exilic community of Israel as a whole (cf. 1:1; 2:16; 3:6), rather than just the priests, since the priests are spoken of in the third person (v. 3). Malachi accuses the people, 'You have wearied the LORD with your words.' Elsewhere 'to weary' (*yāga'*) indicates fatigue from physical toil (e.g. Isa. 62:8), warfare (e.g. Josh. 7:3; 2 Sam. 23:10; Lam. 5:5) and grief (e.g. Pss 6:7; 69:4). Since Yahweh does not grow weary in these ways (Isa. 40:28), this expression describes figuratively his displeasure with the people (a similar form of the verb describes Yahweh's weariness with his people's iniquity in Isa. 43:24). The expression also suggests that his patience is running out. The words that have wearied Yahweh are reported in the second half of the verse, yet there is a sense that the words of the people reported in previous speeches have also contributed to his weariness (cf. 1:2, 6–7, 12–14; 2:8, 14).

Like the other speeches (cf. 1:2, 6; 2:14; 3:7–8, 13), the people's response to Malachi's accusation is reported: 'How have we wearied [him]?' The people are oblivious to the way their behaviour has impacted on their relationship with Yahweh.

Malachi answers by quoting a statement and a question of the people. The statement 'Everyone doing evil is good in the eyes of the LORD and he delights in them' pushes beyond the observation that the evil are prospering (cf. Job 21:7–15; Ps. 73:3–12; Jer. 12:1; Hab. 1:13) and draws the false deduction that Yahweh delights in evildoers. The question 'Where is the God of justice?' to some extent echoes the cries of the faithful for Yahweh to come and deliver them found in other parts of the OT (e.g. Pss 22:1; 89:46[47]; Hab. 1:2–4). J. J. Collins (2012: 137) contends that there is no reason to regard the question as cynical. However, the context of the preceding statement about Yahweh's delighting in evildoers and the overall charge that these words have wearied him provide two reasons to interpret the question as cynical. In this case, the question reflects a belief that Yahweh is unjust or that he does not exist. There are similar statements in Mal. 3:14–15 where it is clear that their words have been directed to other members of the community, rather than to Yahweh in prayer. Furthermore, the fact that God is referred to in the third person also indicates that the people are 'complaining' or 'grumbling' towards one another about Yahweh rather than directing their 'complaints' towards him. The direction of speech makes all the difference.

In response to the charge against Yahweh that he is unjust and absent, Yahweh promises in this speech to refine and purify the Levites so that the worship of his people might be pleasing once again.

3:1. There is no settled consensus about the identity of the figures present in this verse. Four titles are used. First, 'my messenger' (*mal'ākî*), which is the same Hebr. word as the prophet's name in 1:1. This figure is sent by the speaker ('I'), identified at the end of the verse as 'Yahweh of hosts' (the fourth title). The second title is 'the Lord' (*hā'ādôn*, not *yhwh*: 'the LORD'), who will enter into his temple. Third is 'the messenger of the covenant' (*mal'ak habbĕrit*), who will come.

In a study of this verse, Malone (2006: 218–219) notes with respect to the second title that elsewhere the indefinite 'Lord' more often has a human than a divine referent and is also translated 'master'. Yet the definite non-suffixed form which occurs here ('the Lord') occurs seven times elsewhere and is always linked with Yahweh (Exod. 23:17; 34:23; Isa. 1:24; 3:1; 10:16, 33; 19:4). Identifying 'the Lord' as Yahweh suits the context since the phrase 'suddenly he will enter into his temple' is difficult to attribute to anyone else. Furthermore, 'whom you are seeking' answers with irony the search for Yahweh in 2:17 (i.e. 'Where is the God of justice?').

Turning to the two messengers, Mal. 4:5–6 must also be considered since there God promises 'to send to you Elijah the prophet before the coming of the day of the LORD – the great and the dreadful [day]'. Malone (2006: 223) notes that 'consensus is near universal that the term ['messenger'] refers to a human, likely prophetic messenger'. Use of the term 'messenger' elsewhere in the post-exilic literature supports a reference to a prophetic figure (e.g. 2 Chr. 36:15–16). The first messenger ('my messenger') 'will clear a way before me', which echoes both Exod. 23:20 and Isa. 40:3. In Exodus, the 'messenger' or 'angel' goes ahead of the people to bring them into the land and defeat enemy nations. Here in Malachi, 'my messenger' goes ahead of Yahweh, but now faithless Israelites have become like the nations and are under threat (McKenzie and Wallace 1983: 554; Glazier-McDonald 1987: 130–133). The connection with Isa. 40:3 suggests Yahweh's coming is the delayed realization of the new exodus. In Isa. 40, the coming of Yahweh will bring redemption to God's people (cf. Isa. 35:1–10), but, in the wider context of the book of Isaiah, his coming will also bring judgment and refining (Isa. 1:25; 48:10), which are themes in this speech of Malachi.

Among the figures in this verse, it is the identity of 'the messenger of the covenant' that is most disputed by scholars. Traditionally, 'the Lord' is identified as the Messiah, who is also 'the messenger of the covenant' (Calvin 1986: 569). This connection is made because the NT clearly identifies John the Baptist as 'my messenger' and implies that 'the Lord' is Jesus (Matt. 11:10; Mark 1:2; Luke 7:27). However, Malone (2006: 228) rejects 'the Lord' as a messianic designation. While I agree that 'the Lord' refers in the first instance to Yahweh, I am not convinced that hopes for Yahweh's coming can be so neatly dissected from any accompanying messianic hope (see further, 'Explanation'). Likewise, Malone's (2006: 220) claim that 'the Lord' is also 'the messenger of the covenant' is not as clear as he contends, especially since the Hebr. most naturally distinguishes the two, and elsewhere a 'messenger' is always the delegate of a superior.

What is more likely is that Malachi is responding to the people's two complaints in 2:17 with great irony and 'the messenger of the covenant' is a further reference to 'my messenger'. The order of the presentation is not chronological but rhetorical. There are only two figures in view: a messenger ('my messenger'; 'the messenger of the covenant') who will prepare the way for Yahweh ('I'; 'me'; 'the Lord'). I have already noted how 'the Lord whom you are seeking' responds ironically to their charge 'Where is the God of justice?' Similarly, just as the people say Yahweh 'delights' in the evildoer (2:17), so Malachi responds with irony when he says that the people are 'delighting in' the messenger of the covenant, or the covenant itself. Lundbom (2010: 196) notes how the prophets use irony to say with subtlety or ambiguity the opposite of what is meant, perhaps to provoke a response. That is, the people want justice, but probably not in the way that Yahweh will bring it. Later, in 4:6, this messenger 'will turn hearts of fathers to sons and hearts of sons to their fathers, lest I come and I strike the land [with] complete destruction'. Hence the messenger will call for repentance and covenant faithfulness, or else people will be destroyed when Yahweh comes – the people are not really 'delighting in' this kind of messenger, nor the covenant he will prosecute. Malachi effectively turns the people's complaint about God's justice in 2:17 back on to themselves. Given this interpretation, the 'covenant' that the messenger will call the people to is the national covenant with Israel at Sinai.

Several scholars argue that 'the messenger of the covenant' is the angel of Yahweh (e.g. Baldwin 1972: 243; Smith 1984: 327; Glazier-McDonald 1987: 130–131). While there may be an allusion to Exod. 23:20, and 'the angel of the LORD' is present in that chapter, other connections are not so strong. Moses later explains that the law was given by Yahweh accompanied by 'myriads of holy ones' (Deut. 33:2; cf. Acts. 7:53; Gal. 3:19; Heb. 2:2). The plurality of angels associated with Yahweh's covenant with Israel at Sinai militates against identifying the angel of Yahweh in Mal. 3:1.

The identity of 'he' in the final phrase 'look, he will come' is ambiguous. The most immediate referent is 'the messenger of the covenant'. However, it is better understood as Yahweh speaking of himself in the third person, a feature not uncommon in the prophets (e.g. Isa. 22:19; Hos. 1:9; Amos 4:11; Zech. 1:17; 2:9; 3:2; 14:2–3). This is because the activities of vv. 2–4 are much more readily associated with Yahweh than with a prophet.

2. Yahweh's coming is linked with 'the day' for the first time in Malachi. This is a prominent theme through this speech and the sixth (3:17[19]; 4:1 [twice], 3[3:21], 5[3:23]). Reference to a coming 'day' occurs only once in Haggai (in the last verse, 2:23), and appears some twenty times across the book of Zechariah. It is also used by earlier prophets to refer to the time when Yahweh will establish his kingdom on earth in glory (e.g. Hos. 1:5; 2:18; Joel 1:15; 4:18; Amos 5:18; 9:11). Petersen (1992a: 579) summarizes the features of the prophetic expectation 'on that day': the coming of Yahweh (often pictured in military terms); Yahweh's enemies receiving their just deserts; those who fear Yahweh (including the nations) being incorporated into his kingdom; his kingdom bringing a time of paradise in the land; the mediation of Yahweh's rule through a righteous Davidic king; and a new covenant. Many of these themes are present in this and the remaining speeches of Malachi.

The questions 'who will endure' and 'who will stand' imply that none will be able to escape Yahweh's judgment when he comes. This language may initially imply a military battle (cf. Amos 2:15). Yet, rather than being a judgment that destroys, Yahweh's coming is further described as one that will refine and purify the Levites – his appearance is likened to 'a refiner's fire' and 'launderers' soap'. To 'refine' (*ṣārap*) is to subject metal to high temperatures in a furnace to burn off impurities. The image of

God's refining his people as metal is found throughout earlier prophets, though more often than not it has destructive consequences (e.g. Isa. 1:25; 48:10; Jer. 6:29–30; 9:7; Ezek. 22:17–22). Significantly, Zech. 13:7 uses the same imagery to refer to the purification of God's people resulting from the death of God's own king ('strike the shepherd'). In the wider context of Zechariah, this is also set 'on that day' where the result for those who emerge is a restored or new covenant relationship with Yahweh. The 'soap' (*bōrît*) is a term found only elsewhere in the OT in Jer. 2:22. It is thought to be some kind of alkaline salt or soda derived from the ice plant or the 'soda' plant and used as detergent in the ancient world (Hill 1998: 274). While some argue it may be a further reference to refining metal since this product was also used in the smelting process (Glazier-McDonald 1987: 147–148), the accompanying ptc. 'launderers' uses a root (*kābas*) that most commonly refers to washing clothes.

3–4. The imagery is further developed. Specifically, Yahweh will purify and refine 'the sons of Levi', a term equivalent to 'the priests' in Malachi (J. M. O'Brien 1990: 47). The Levites were charged to minister 'in the name of the LORD' (Deut. 18:5, 7; 21:5), which means that as well as being Yahweh's representatives, they were to reflect his holy character in their lives (Lev. 21:6). In the second disputation speech, the priests are condemned for failing in their sacrificial duties (1:6–14) and in their instruction and behaviour (2:1–9). Yahweh explains how he has judged the priests for not following his ways. Undoubtedly, the failure of the priests to teach is connected with the attitudes of the people reported in 2:17. The people have wearied Yahweh by complaining about his apparent injustice and absence. God says that he is coming and will begin his judgment by purifying the Levites and refining them like gold and silver. This also implies that the priests are at the core of the problem.

The result of Yahweh's visitation is that the priests' ministry 'will be for the LORD' as they serve as his representatives before the people. Their offerings will be brought 'in righteousness', which has the sense of the priests being restored to right relationship with God and hence their service will be as God intended (a right order of things). That is, the priests will no longer bring sacrifices that show contempt for Yahweh's name (cf. 1:6, 8) – the Levitical ideal reflected in 2:4–6 will be restored.

Since the priests mediated the sacrifices of the people, their purification and refining means that 'the offering of Judah and Jerusalem will be pleasing to the LORD'. Again this forms a contrast to what the sacrifices of the people of Judah and Jerusalem had become on account of their unfaithfulness (cf. 1:9–10; 2:13). It also implies that God's visitation will change his people, a point that becomes explicit in v. 5. It is difficult to know exactly to what '[in] days of old and as [in] former years' refers. Other prophets also look back to an ideal age of obedience (cf. Isa. 1:26). For Hosea, it is the exodus (Hos. 2:15; 11:1), yet Jeremiah sees only disobedience from the time of the exodus (Jer. 7:21–26; cf. Mal. 1:7), but this is probably rhetorical.

While some scholars suggest it is the patriarchal period, the reference to 'Jerusalem' suggests a period in the monarchy – probably a general reference to any time when the people offered sacrifices in faith and obedience. Hill (1998: 279) notes that in the post-exilic period, reference to 'Judah and Jerusalem' is especially associated with Davidic kingship and brings to mind the promises associated with the Davidic covenant (cf. 2 Chr. 2:7[6]; 24:9; 29:8; 32:9; 34:3; Ezra 10:7).

5. The people had effectively complained against Yahweh in v. 17 that he had failed to judge. Yahweh responds that he will 'draw near to you for judgment'. He is not only judge, but 'a swift witness', which indicates any trial will be speedy when he comes (cf. Ps. 50:6–7). Yahweh may have seemed absent to the people in Malachi's day, but he had in fact witnessed the crimes he will judge and there will be no need to hear any other witness statements. He will judge those who have violated the national covenant (cf. 4:4[3:22]). Many of these crimes were condemned by Zechariah (cf. Zech. 5:3–4; 7:10; 8:17), and mentioning them here suggests that they continued to be a problem later in the post-exilic period.

The 'sorcerers' refers to those who sought to control events by supernatural means (McConville 2002a: 301). Sorcery, described as one of the 'detestable ways of the nations' in Deut. 18:9–13, is condemned on account of the threat it posed to the people's loyalty to Yahweh alone. In Exod. 22:18[17], the sorceress is not to be allowed to live.

The 'adulterers' are those who have sexual relations with married women. McConville (2002a: 129) notes that in Deuteronomy, its orientation is m. It is primarily an offence committed by a man with another man's wife (22:22), yet both parties are held responsible, unless the woman is raped (22:23–27). Presumably, the m. orientation in Deuteronomy also meant that polygamy was not regarded as adulterous. Furthermore, the man is the one with the legal divorce options, which the woman did not have (cf. 24:1–4).

The phrase 'swearing falsely' is lit. 'those swearing to the lie/deception' (cf. Zech. 5:4) and refers to dishonesty in speech. Elsewhere the phrase is found in the context of making oaths (Lev. 19:12) and false prophecy (Jer. 27:15). It can also refer more specifically to false testimony or perjury (cf. Zech. 8:17). In any case it is a sin against others in the community and against Yahweh, who loves truth (cf. Zech. 8:16, 19).

Yahweh will also act as a swift witness and judge those who oppress the vulnerable and turn away the stranger. The law of Moses made special provision for the weak and defenceless (e.g. Exod. 21:21–22; Lev. 19:13–18; Deut. 10:18–19; 24:14–15). Ruth is an illustration – as a widow and a stranger she was provided for by Israel's law. This teaching is reiterated by the prophets (e.g. Isa. 1:17; Jer. 7:6; Zech. 7:10).

All of these sins are only symptoms of a deeper underlying disease – Yahweh says these people do not fear him, where 'fear' refers to the obedience of covenant faithfulness (cf. Deut. 6:13; Ps. 128:1; Hag. 1:12).

Earlier, the priests are said not to fear Yahweh (1:6), and to profane his name (1:12). However, Yahweh promises that his name will be 'feared among the nations' (1:14; cf. 3:16; 4:2[3:20]).

6–7a. While many scholars and translations believe this verse introduces the fifth disputation speech, there is a strong connection with the fourth. V. 6 begins with *kî* (For), which indicates a reason for the fact that Yahweh has not yet acted in judgment and responds to the basis of the people's complaint in 2:17 (see 'Form and structure'). The implied reason that God has not 'come' to judge finally on the 'day of the LORD' is that he is showing mercy and giving time to repent. If he judged as the people deserved, they would be destroyed (v. 7a; cf. Edom in 1:3–4). Yahweh's delay in judging those who do evil is not a new thing ('I have not changed'), but he has preserved his people 'from the days of your fathers', even though 'you turned away from my statutes and you have not kept [them]' (v. 7a). This is obviously not to say that there were not times when Yahweh judged his people for their disobedience to the covenant requirements ('statutes'), but it never resulted in the destruction of the nation ('so you, sons of Jacob, have not perished'). A classic instance of this is the golden calf incident, where Yahweh first decrees destruction (Exod. 32:10), but relents after Moses' intercession as a priest (32:14). Moses makes no attempt to excuse the people's behaviour, but pleads for them on the basis of Yahweh's character. The fact that Yahweh relents does not mean that his original threat was an idle one, or that he succumbed to the intensity of Moses' intercession. What it demonstrates is the way Yahweh remembers his promises to the fathers (32:13) and that he is 'the compassionate and gracious God . . . Yet he does not leave the guilty unpunished' (Exod. 34:6–7). In Exod. 32:27–35 the people do not go unpunished, but they are not destroyed as they deserve. This explains how 'I have not changed' answers the original complaint in 2:17 – Yahweh's delay in bringing the disobedient to judgment is a demonstration of his mercy, giving people time to repent. Baldwin (1972: 245) captures the idea: 'Israel has the opportunity to question His justice only because He is unchanging in His patient provision of opportunity for repentance.' In context, this is not so much a statement about God's character (immutability) so much as a statement about the way Yahweh has operated within his covenant relationship with Israel (Baker 2006: 288). The immediate context implies that the day will come when God will no longer hold out mercy and instead come in final judgment, but even then he will preserve a faithful remnant. For a study on God's immutability in the OT, see Moberly 2013: 107–143.

Explanation

The fourth disputation speech reveals that the post-exilic community had used the presence of injustice as an excuse to reject Yahweh. Yahweh responds through the prophet with biting irony that he will come to a people who claim to be 'seeking' him and 'delighting' in justice. He will come and judge. The way for Yahweh's coming will be prepared by a messenger, a prophetic figure who will enforce and prosecute the national covenant with Israel at Sinai.

Earlier prophets had laid the expectation for Yahweh's return after his departure from the temple in Jerusalem in the Babylonian exile (e.g. Ezek. 43:4–5; Zech. 2:10[14]; 9:8). Often associated with his return is peace, prosperity and protection (e.g. Zech. 2:4–5[9–10]). Yet even though the people in Malachi's day have returned from exile, the problem of sin that led to exile in the first place is clearly not solved and hardship remains (cf. 2:2; 3:9–11). For Malachi, Yahweh's return to his temple will refine and purify the priests and so transform the offerings of the people that they will once again be pleasing to Yahweh.

Yahweh may have appeared distant to the post-exilic community, but this speech assures them that the day of Yahweh will come when he will judge. The people are assured that Yahweh has not changed and this is why they have not perished (presumably they deserved to). Yahweh's delay is his patience, allowing his people time to repent.

The NT connects the coming of Yahweh to judge in the first instance with the coming of Jesus. All the Gospels quote or allude to Mal. 3:1 and claim that John the Baptist is 'the messenger' and that Jesus is both God and the Messiah. So Matt. 11:10 quotes Mal. 3:1 and identifies 'my messenger' as John the Baptist, who is both a prophet and 'more than a prophet' (v. 9). Interestingly, in the quote of Mal. 3:1 on Jesus' lips, the 'way before me' becomes 'ahead of you . . . your way before you'. The implication is that Jesus understands his own coming to be the coming of 'the Lord' promised in Malachi. Earlier in Matt. 3:11, the one who comes after John 'will baptize . . . with the Holy Spirit and fire'. The reference to fire connects with the refining work of God in Mal. 3:2–3 (cf. Luke 12:49).

In Mark 1:2–3, Mark explicitly combines Mal. 3:1 with Isa. 40:3 and then identifies John the Baptist as 'my messenger' and 'the Lord' as Jesus. Later in the Gospel (11:27–33), Jesus walks in the temple courts (cf. 'he will enter into his temple' in Mal. 3:1) and is questioned by the priests, teachers of the law and elders about his authority, to which Jesus asks them about John the Baptist. The connection between John the Baptist and Jesus' presence in the temple as 'Lord' also brings to mind Mal. 3:1.

Luke 1:16–17 combines allusions to Mal. 3:1 and 4:5–6[3:23–24] with reference to the ministry of John the Baptist, who 'will go on before the Lord, in the spirit and power of Elijah, to turn the hearts of the parents to their children and the disobedient to the wisdom of the righteous – to make ready a people prepared for the Lord'. In Luke 1:76, John

> will be called a prophet of the Most High;
>   for you will go on before the Lord to prepare the way for him.

In terms of Luke's presentation, the 'Lord' who comes and for whom John prepares the way is Jesus (Green 1997: 118).

Some scholars claim that since 'the Lord' (*hā'ādôn*) is Yahweh alone, the book of Malachi does not support hope for a future Davidic king. For instance, Goswell (2013: 636) argues in relation to Mal. 3:1 that 'nothing suggests any messianic agency in the forecast reformation of the Jerusalemite cult.' While I agree that 'the Lord' in Mal. 3:1 refers in the first instance to Yahweh, this does not mean that earlier messianic hopes have necessarily reduced or transferred to Yahweh. The adage 'Absence of evidence is not evidence of absence' is pertinent here. Goswell reads Malachi in the light of Zech. 14, but if Malachi is read in the light of the book of Zechạriah as a whole and the book of Haggai (and the Twelve), then the robust hope for a future king that is expressed in these other books must also infuse Malachi's hope for the coming of Yahweh and his 'day' since elsewhere these hopes are inseparably linked with the coming of a future Davidic king (Petterson 2010). In addition, the teaching of Isaiah, Jeremiah and Ezekiel all arguably exhibit hope for a future Davidic king. There is no evidence that the community in Malachi's day suddenly discarded the teachings of the earlier prophets or earlier books of the Twelve. On the contrary, the evidence is that they read and carefully preserved them. Furthermore, the psalter and Chronicles, both compiled in the post-exilic period, arguably contain a strong hope for a future Davidic king (Kelly 1995; Starling 1999; Grogan 2008: 348–359). Hence it is reasonable to suppose that the hope expressed for the coming of 'the Lord' in Malachi would also inflame messianic hopes expressed elsewhere in Israel's Scriptures. The Gospel of John is significant in this regard. In John 3:28, John the Baptist says, 'I am not the Messiah but am sent ahead of him.' The language alludes to Mal. 3:1 and John explicitly connects the 'Lord' with Israel's hopes for a Messiah (Köstenberger 2007: 437). This theme is further developed by John the Baptist when he depicts Jesus as the bridegroom: 'Rather obliquely John is therefore also saying that the Jesus he has introduced to the faithful remnant in Israel is none other than Israel's king and Messiah' (Carson 1991: 211). Therefore, connecting the hopes of Mal. 3:1 with messianic expectations seems justified.

In addition, Jesus is the one who through his death on the cross makes a kingdom of priests who offer sacrifices in righteousness (cf. 1 Peter 2:5, 9; Rev. 1:6; 5:10; 20:6) and are enabled to please the Lord (cf. Rom. 14:18; 2 Cor. 5:9; Eph. 5:10; 1 Thess. 3:4; 4:1; 1 Tim. 2:3; 5:4). Jesus also refines the faith of his people by the fire of 'all kinds of trials' (cf. 1 Peter 1:6).

The wider themes of this speech are very similar to those found in 2 Peter 3 and also connect with the second coming of Jesus. Peter says, 'in the last days scoffers will come, scoffing and following their own evil desires. They will say, "Where is this 'coming' he promised? Ever since our ancestors died, everything goes on as it has since the beginning of the creation"' (vv. 3–4). Peter responds by saying that the judgment day is coming and that 'The Lord is not slow in keeping his promise, as some understand slowness. Instead he is patient with you, not wanting anyone to perish, but everyone to come to repentance' (v. 9). Just as Yahweh had 'not changed' in Malachi's day and, rather than destroy the nation completely, gave people time to repent, so he continues to hold out mercy today. But Peter assures his readers that the final judgment day will come.

Pointedly, after Malachi announces judgment on those who continue to violate the covenant (3:5), he issues a call to repent: 'Return to me' (3:7b). In view of the coming final judgment, Malachi's charge remains the same for readers today. Proof of the final judgment is Jesus' resurrection as Lord and judge (Acts 17:31).

MALACHI 3:7B–12

Translation

[3:7b]'Return to me and I will return to you,' says the Lord of hosts. 'But you say,
"How will we return?" [8]Will a human rob God? For you are robbing me!
But you say, "How have we robbed you?" The tithe and the offering! [9]With the
curse you are being cursed, but you are robbing me – the whole nation! [10]Bring
the whole tithe into the storehouse, and let there be food in my house. So test
me in this,' says the Lord of hosts, 'if I will not open the windows of heaven
for you and pour out for you a blessing in abundance. [11]And I will rebuke the
devourer for you, and it will not ruin the fruit of the ground for you, and
the vine in the field will not fail to bear for you,' says the Lord of hosts. [12]'And
all the nations will call you blessed, for you will be a land of delight,' says the
Lord of hosts.

Notes on the text

3:7b. 'How?': *bammê*. Lit. 'in what?' (Also v. 8.)

8. 'The tithe and the offering!': the versions attempt 'to fill out the abrupt sense' of MT (Gelston 2010: 152*).

9. 'the whole nation': lit. 'the nation, all (of) it'.

10. 'So test me': *ûbĕḥānûnî nāʾ*. LXX ('do observe') and Tg ('and make trial') soften the abruptness, probably for theological reasons.

'in abundance': *ʿad-bĕlî-dāy*. Lit. 'until without sufficiency/need'.

11. 'the devourer': *bāʾōkēl*. The prep. *bĕ* often accompanies the verb *gāʿar* and identifies the recipient of the rebuke. It has an adversative sense ('against'), but is left untranslated (Eddinger 2012: 97).

Form and structure

Malachi's fifth disputation speech flows directly from the fourth and an exact demarcation between the speeches is difficult to determine (see 'Form and structure' for 2:17 – 3:7a). There is clearly a separate disputation and change of topic in vv. 8–12, but the segue between the two in vv. 6–7 is smooth (there is no paragraph marker in MT). Towards the end of the fourth speech, Yahweh explains that he has not destroyed his people in judgment (3:6; cf. 2:17) even though they have not kept his statutes from the time of the fathers (3:7a). The report of the people turning away naturally issues in a call to repent with a promise of Yahweh's return (v. 7b). The delay of Yahweh's judgment is effectively his patience (implicit in vv. 6–7a) and he continues to offer mercy to his people through Malachi. The genre is a 'reproof speech' (cf. 1:6 – 2:9) where the prophet describes the positive consequences of good behaviour while implicating the addressees as being in violation of this behaviour (Floyd 2000: 648).

Like the second speech, there is a double questioning on the part of the people in response to Yahweh's offer through the prophet (vv. 7b–8; cf. 1:6–7). In order to answer the first question 'How will we return?' Malachi exposes the people's covenant unfaithfulness with reference to their failure concerning tithes and offerings (v. 8). Malachi explains how their disobedience in this regard has brought them under the curse of God (v. 9). If they return to God (cf. v. 7b) by paying the 'whole tithe', then God will return to them (cf. v. 7b) and bless them with prosperity (vv. 10–11) such that their blessed state in the land will be reported by the nations (v. 12). The promise is so firm that Yahweh issues the call to test him in this (v. 10).

An implication of this disputation speech is that even though the people have returned to the land, rebuilt the temple and have a functioning priesthood, they have not fully returned to Yahweh in repentance and obedience. Whereas the previous speech threatens judgment on evildoers, this one promises blessing to those who repent.

Comment

3:7b. Malachi issues the same call that Zechariah had made to an earlier generation (Zech. 1:3). 'Return' or 'turn' (*šûb*) generally means 'motion to point of departure', but in the context of a covenant relationship the prophets use it to mean 'change of loyalty', 'return [to God]' or 'turn back [from evil]' (Holladay 1988: 362). With the accompanying prepositional phrase 'to me', God's call is to return to covenant obedience ('to repent'). The call to return is a key thematic thread through the Book of the Twelve, particularly in the opening writings (Hosea–Joel [cf. Hos. 6:1; 14:1[2]; Joel 2:12–13]) and the end (Zechariah–Malachi) (LeCureux 2012).

If the people return, Yahweh promises, 'I will return to you.' This expresses the restoration of covenant relationship after the judgment of the exilic experience and indicates that the return of Yahweh to his people and the ensuing blessings that the earlier prophets looked forward to have not yet taken place (cf. Zech. 1:16; 8:3, 15; 9:8–9; 14:16–21). These blessings are a feature of this speech.

The reported response of the people 'How will we return?' may have been asked in ignorance or in defiance (or a mixture of both), but in any case it portrays the people as unaware that their lives are out of step with the covenant requirements of Yahweh.

8–9. As if the previously identified covenant breaches in the book are not enough, Malachi identifies another with a stark accusation: 'Will a human rob God? For you are robbing me!' The verb 'rob' or 'despoil' (*qāba'*) is rare and some scholars suggest it is a miswriting of 'deceive' (*'qb*), being a play on words with 'Jacob' in 3:6 and reflected in the LXX (Mason 1977: 155). Yet 'rob' is attested elsewhere in the OT (Prov. 22:23) and Talmudic literature, and the reasons given for emending the Hebr. text are weak (Glazier-McDonald 1987: 187–188). The question is first asked in general terms, 'Will a human rob God?', which clearly expects the answer 'no', but then the accusation against the people is made in very personal terms: 'you are robbing me'. The people's second response ('How have we robbed you?') is perhaps to be expected given the prophet's blunt accusation and their lack of perception of their sin.

The prophet's answer is terse: 'The tithe and the offering!' The use of the def. articles suggests these refer to the specific tithes and offerings prescribed by the law of Moses (Verhoef 1987: 303). The 'tithe' (*ma'ăśēr*) was a tenth of the produce of the land that was given to support the Levites 'as their inheritance in return for the work they do while serving at the tent of meeting' (Num. 18:21; cf. Deut. 12:6, 11; 14:22–29). It included grain, fruit and animals from the herd and flock (Lev. 27:30–33; cf. Deut. 14:23). Deuteronomy distinguishes a yearly tithe that was eaten by the worshipper's family at the central sanctuary in the presence of Yahweh along with the Levites (Deut. 14:22–27) and a three-yearly tithe that was for the Levites along with foreigners, the fatherless and the widows (Deut. 14:28–29). The neglect of the tithe clearly had wider social and religious implications. Not only would it contribute to the neglect of the temple, but it also demonstrated a failure to reflect the character of Yahweh as one who is concerned for the weak and vulnerable in society.

The 'offering' or 'contribution' (*tĕrûmâ*) may refer to the tenth of the tithe that the Levites were to present to Yahweh (Num. 18:26–29), or more likely it refers generally to other offerings that the Israelites presented to Yahweh in which the priests shared, such as animal sacrifices (e.g. Lev. 22:12; Num. 5:9; 6:20; 18:8, 11, 19, 24; Neh. 12:44) or loaves of bread (e.g. Lev. 7:14). The book of Nehemiah gives further evidence of the people's failure concerning tithes and offerings in the post-exilic period (Neh. 13:4–13).

Like Haggai, in v. 9 Malachi explains the people's present adverse circumstances as a result of the curse for disobedience found in the national covenant. Moses warned that turning from Yahweh and failing to obey his commands and decrees would bring, among other things, devastation on crops and cattle (Deut. 28:18, 22–24, 38–40, 42). The promise of reversal in vv. 10–11 indicates that they are suffering these things. Back in 2:2 Yahweh threatens to send 'the curse' against the priests and at the same time says, 'I have cursed them'. Sweeney (2000b: 743) notes the irony: 'The people are already under the curse, and do not enjoy the benefit of fecundity, they nevertheless continue to rob God and thereby ensure the continuance of the curse.' They should have understood the curse as God's warning to repent.

The accusation is repeated for emphasis: 'but you are robbing me'. Yahweh makes it clear all (not just the priests) are responsible: 'the whole nation!' Elsewhere in Malachi 'nation' (*gôy*) refers to the surrounding pagan nations (*gôyîm*; 1:11 [twice], 14; 3:12). This use may indicate that in failing to keep the terms of the national covenant, the people of Judah are indistinguishable from the foreign nations (cf. Deut. 32:28; Judg. 2:20; Isa. 1:4; Ezek. 2:3).

10–11. The injunction to 'Bring the whole tithe into the storehouse' suggests that the problem is not one of completely neglecting 'the tithe and the offering' but of only partially giving and of responding only half-heartedly (Baker 2006: 285). The 'storehouse' (*'ôṣār*) is associated with the temple in Nehemiah and in the sg. is often translated 'treasury' since it houses silver and gold (Neh. 7:70–71[69–70]). In Nehemiah, the pl. form (*'ôṣārôt*) is translated 'storehouses' or 'storerooms' since they house grain, new wine and olive oil (Neh. 10:39; 12:44; 13:12–13). Some storage facility located in the temple complex ('my house') and administered by the Levites is in view. The word translated 'food' (*ṭerep*) is unusual in that it normally refers to animals' prey (e.g. Gen. 49:9; Amos 3:4). Yet there are a couple of instances where it is used poetically of food for human consumption (Ps. 111:5; Prov. 31:15) (Glazier-McDonald 1987: 194).

Giving in obedience to this command is a concrete way in which the people will demonstrate a 'return' to Yahweh. Hence the remainder of the speech explains what Yahweh's 'return' to the people as he promised in v. 7b will look like. So certain is Yahweh's promise that he invites the people to 'test me in this'. Another instance of a 'test' in the OT is where Yahweh asks king Ahaz to request a sign, but Ahaz refuses, saying, 'I will not ask; I will not put the LORD to the test' (Isa. 7:11–12). While it may appear pious, Ahaz's refusal to ask is in fact a refusal to trust Yahweh, for which Ahaz is judged (Petterson 2008). Likewise here, Yahweh's invitation to test him is a call to repentance and faith.

Yahweh's return will result in remarkable blessing. He speaks metaphorically of opening 'the windows of heaven' and pouring out a blessing. The language is phenomenological – when it rains it appears that the heavens are opened (cf. Gen. 7:11–12; 8:2; Deut. 11:17). In this instance, what is poured out is 'a blessing in abundance' (the opposite of 'the curse' in v. 9). The metaphor probably intentionally brings to mind actual rain that would water crops as part of the 'blessing'. J. M. Gibson (2014a: 251–253) sees an intentional reworking of the flood narrative on account of the rarity of the phrase 'windows of heaven' (Gen. 7:11), where 'the agent of curse will be turned into an agent of blessing'.

Yahweh promises to 'rebuke the devourer for you' (v. 11). The 'devourer' (*'ōkēl*) is as general in Hebr. as it is in English (ESV; cf. NIV, 'pests'). NRSV translates it 'locust' (cf. Deut. 28:38; Joel 2:5), yet it could also refer to other creatures, such as flies (Ps. 78:45) or worms (Deut. 28:39), that could devastate crops and vines (Petersen 1995: 218).

Hag. 1:11 suggests that 'the fruit of the ground' includes grain, new wine and new oil. The image of a productive vine is a common image of prosperity and elsewhere has eschatological overtones (e.g. Mic. 4:4; Zech. 3:10) (Stuart 1998: 1371).The similarities to the blessings and curses of the national covenant (e.g. Lev. 26:20; Deut. 28:11–12, 18, 38–40, 42) further indicate that 'the curse' will be turned to blessing if the people return to Yahweh and obey him (cf. Deut. 4:29–31; 11:13–15; 28:9–11; 30:9–10) (McKenzie and Wallace 1983: 555). The covenant background is essential for correctly interpreting the promises here (see 'Explanation').

12. The people of Israel (cf. 1:1) will fulfil their calling and be set apart from the nations (cf. v. 9). Being blessed by the nations echoes God's promise to Abram in Gen. 12:2–3 (cf. Deut. 28:9–10; Isa. 61:9; Zech. 8:13), though the word for 'bless' here is *'šr* rather than *brk* (Berry 1996: 284). Glazier-McDonald (1987: 203) helpfully notes the sacral character of the land that has become defiled (cf. Isa. 24:5; Jer. 2:7; 16:18). Disobedience is what brought the land under a curse (cf. Gen. 3:17–19; Jer. 12:11; Ezek. 12:19; Zech. 7:14). When the people return to Yahweh and the covenant relationship is repaired, the land will be restored to its blessed state and Yahweh will once again take delight in it (cf. Deut. 6:10–11; 8:7–10). Scalise (1987: 415) comments that fame among the nations and the fertility of the land are both important features of the prophetic hope (e.g. Isa. 62:1–5; Amos 9:13–15). The repetition of the messenger formula ('says the LORD of hosts'; vv. 10–12) underscores the certainty of this.

Explanation

The people of God in Malachi's day had grown cynical and complacent. They failed to appreciate God's love for them (1:1–5); the priests offered defiled and defective sacrifices (1:6–14) and failed in their teachings and obedience to the Torah (2:1–9); the people were breaking their marriage covenants (2:10–16) and they had become critical of Yahweh – complaining that he was unjust and slow in judging wickedness (2:17 – 3:7a). Through the prophet Malachi, Yahweh calls on them to change their ways: 'Return to me and I will return to you' (v. 7b) (on 'repentance', see further,

'Explanation' for Zech. 1:1–6). LeCureaux (2012: 220) comments, 'For those reading the Twelve as a whole, the fact that this [call to return] is the call that opened the book (Hos. 6:1; 14:2–3) implies that nothing has changed in the eleven writings since . . . the only reason they have not been destroyed is because of Yhwh's faithfulness.' The book of Malachi effectively asks readers to look towards Yahweh's doing a new work among his people that will deal finally with the problem of sin and change people's hearts. In this, the book of Malachi points towards the new covenant and the coming of Jesus Christ (cf. Jer. 31:31–36; Ezek. 11:19–20).

A further instance of the people's disobedience is identified in this fifth disputation speech – their failure to pay the tithe and the offering, effectively robbing Yahweh. Rather than threatening judgment as the previous speech had done, this speech states that the people are already under Yahweh's curse (v. 9) and that if the people repent by paying the 'whole tithe', God will restore the people to abundant blessing.

Like the book of Haggai, it is essential to interpret this passage against the background of the national covenant established with Israel at Sinai to avoid twisting the message into a 'prosperity gospel', where the message becomes 'Tithe so that God will make you rich' (see 'Introduction to Haggai', 'Key themes', 'Covenant'). Malachi here calls the people back to covenant obedience so that they may enjoy the blessings of covenant relationship. If they will just give what they are supposed to, Yahweh will pour out the blessings of the covenant that he has withheld from them for their disobedience, just as he promised.

In deriving the Christian application of this passage, it is crucial to understand how Jesus fulfils the hopes, practices and institutions of Israel in the OT. The tithe was a means of supporting the Levites as they maintained the temple system – effectively a form of national taxation. The coming of Jesus has brought huge changes. For a start, there is no temple in Jerusalem and no Levites to support. Indeed, Christians are not directly under the law of Moses (Rom. 7:1–6; 13:10; Gal. 2:19; 3:23–25; 5:1; Heb. 7:18–19) and there is no commandment in the NT for followers of Jesus to tithe. In addition, in the NT material wealth is never promised as a guaranteed reward for either obedience to God or simple hard work (Blomberg 1999: 242). This fact shows the lie of prosperity teaching that guarantees wealth through obedience. While the Bible views wealth as a good thing and there is no virtue in poverty, making wealth an end in itself poses great spiritual dangers, as indeed Moses warned the people of Israel (Deut. 8:10–18; cf. Eccl. 5:10; 6:2). It is certainly not sinful for a Christian to be wealthy, but the pursuit of wealth rather than God is (cf. Matt. 6:19–21; Mark 8:34, 36). The apostle Paul teaches that 'greed . . . is idolatry' (Col. 3:5). While many Christians experience material blessings in this age (cf. Mark 10:29–31), the OT promises concerning material blessings find their ultimate fulfilment for the Christian in the age to come (e.g. 2 Cor. 4:7 – 5:10; cf. 9:6–11) (Blomberg 1999: 242).

While there is no command to tithe in the NT, plenty is said about how Christians are to use their finances, which reapply the principles of the OT. For instance, the apostle Paul commends contentment with what God has given (1 Tim. 6:6–8; cf. Prov. 30:8), and generosity towards others in view of God's grace (1 Tim. 6:18; cf. Deut. 15:7). In the terms of Malachi, discontent and tightfisted Christians 'rob God' and this is where this passage of Malachi challenges readers today.

Rather than supporting the Levites, the NT lays other financial responsibilities on Christians. These include providing for family, particularly widows (1 Tim. 5:8). One of the primary motivations for work in 2 Thess. 3:6–12 is so that workers can provide food for themselves (and presumably their family). Another financial responsibility is paying taxes (Matt. 22:21; Rom. 13:6–7). The governing authorities are God's servants who are giving their time to govern. Taxes support them in their work of ensuring justice prevails in society, and taxes also support social infrastructure and those in need (much more a feature of modern Western societies than ancient Rome). Christians should be counter-culturally enthusiastic about the opportunity to pay tax. While some in society abuse the system and become 'welfare dependent' (cf. Matt. 26:11), there are also a great many people who are helped. Paying tax should be part of an attitude of generosity – of doing good to others.

In addition, Christians are obligated to support church gospel workers (1 Cor. 9:14; 1 Tim. 5:18) and those involved in missions (Rom. 15:24; 2 Cor. 11:8–9; Phil. 4:15). Finally, Christians have a responsibility to help other Christians in financial need as they have opportunity (Acts 11:29; 24:17; Rom. 15:25–27; 1 Cor. 16:1–4; Gal. 2:10).

Freedom from the laws concerning 'the tithe and the offering' raises the question of how much a Christian should give. There is no amount or percentage prescribed in the NT. However, 1 Cor. 16:2 and 2 Cor. 8:13–15 suggest giving in proportion to income. Different life circumstances will allow for greater or lesser amounts. Ten per cent of income can be considered a measure of the beginning of generosity under the new covenant and Christians should not feel restricted to 10% – for many it will be possible to give much more than this. One of the chief impediments to generosity is worry and fear about the future, something Jesus calls his followers to repent of (Matt. 6:25–34).

MALACHI 3:13 – 4:6[HB 3:13–24]

Translation

3:13'Your words are harsh against me,' says the Lord. 'But you say, "How have we spoken against you?" 14You have said, "[It is] futile to serve God, and what did it profit [us] that we kept his requirement and that we walked mournfully before

the LORD of hosts. 15But now we call the arrogant blessed. Not only have evildoers
been built up, but they also tested God and they escaped!"'
16Then the fearers of the LORD spoke, each with his neighbour. And the LORD
paid attention and he listened and a scroll of remembrance was written before
him for the fearers of the LORD and for those esteeming his name. 17'So they
will be mine', says the LORD of hosts, 'on the day when I will make a treasured
possession. And I will have compassion on them just as a man has compassion
on his son who serves him.' 18And you will return and distinguish between the
righteous and the wicked, between one serving God and the one who has not
served him.
4:1[3:19]'For look! The day is coming, burning like the furnace, when all the
arrogant and every evildoer will become chaff and the coming day will set them
ablaze,' says the LORD of hosts, '[the day] that will not leave for them root or
branch. 2[3:20]But for you – fearers of my name – a sun of righteousness will rise
and healing [will be] in its wings. And you will go out and you will leap like
calves from a stall. 3[3:21]And you will trample down the wicked, for they will
be ashes beneath the soles of your feet on the day when I act,' says the LORD
of hosts.
4[3:22]'Remember the law of Moses, my servant, which I commanded him at
Horeb for all Israel – [the] statutes and judgments. 5[3:23]Look, I will send to
you Elijah the prophet before the coming of the day of the LORD – the great and
the dreadful [day]. 6[3:24]And he will turn hearts of fathers to sons and hearts
of sons to their fathers, lest I come and I strike the land [with] complete
destruction.'

Notes on the text

3:13. 'harsh': *ḥāzqû*. Lit. '[they are] strong'.

16. 'then': *'āz* is translated as a temporal marker.

'spoke': *nidbĕrû*. The ni. form is reflex. and could be translated 'spoke with one another', but this idea is explicit in the next phrase, so I have not conveyed it twice.

17. 'who serves': *hā'ōbēd*. The def. attrib. ptc. indicates a rel. clause with the noun it modifies (Arnold and Choi 2003: 78).

18. 'you will return': *wešabtem*. Cf. 'again' (NIV, NASB) or 'once more' (ESV, NRSV). See 'Comment' and LeCureux 2012: 222–224.

'between . . . and' (twice): *bên . . . lĕ*. This construction expresses distinction (Waltke and O'Connor 1990: 200).

4:2[3:20]. 'calves from a stall': lit. 'calves of a stall'.

5.[3:23]. 'I will send': for the use of the ptc. following *hinnēh*, see 'Notes on the text' for 3:1.

6.[3:24]. 'hearts' (twice) is sg. in Hebr. LXX reads, 'who will restore the heart of the father to the son and the heart of a person to his neighbour'.

Form and structure

This unit contains the final disputation speech (3:13 – 4:3[3:13–21]) plus an exhortation that concludes the book (4:4–6[3:22–24]). The final speech continues many of the themes of the previous two, particularly the coming day of Yahweh and the subject of reward and punishment (Assis 2010a: 359). The issue (3:13–15) is similar to that of 2:17, where the justice of God is questioned since evildoers prosper and escape his judgment. Back in the fourth disputation speech (2:17 – 3:7a), the day of Yahweh is said to bring purification for the Levites so that the people of Judah and Jerusalem will bring acceptable sacrifices (3:2–4) and evildoers will be judged (3:5). The final speech is unique in containing a report of some who heed Yahweh's rebuke and are said to fear him and honour his name (v. 16). Yahweh continues to speak in v. 17, where he promises that on the judgment day they will be his 'treasured possession' and he will have compassion on them since they are righteous and serve him (vv. 17–18). At the same time, the wicked will be destroyed (4:1–3[3:19–21]). Hence, while the people may have objected that there is no distinction between the righteous and the wicked in their experience, Yahweh declares that the day is coming when a distinction will be seen – the wicked will be judged and the righteous vindicated.

In view of this coming day, a final exhortation is given to remember the law of Moses (4:4[3:22]) and a promise is given concerning the prophet Elijah (4:5–6[3:23–24]; cf. 3:1). Elijah will bring repentance among the people or else the land will be destroyed. Scholars debate whether these final verses were originally part of the book of Malachi or were a later addition to round out the collection of the prophets (see 'Introduction to Malachi', 'Author and date', for a discussion of the issues). My own view is that they were originally composed as an ending to the book of Malachi and in this there was a canon consciousness, but not in the way this is generally conceived. The book of Malachi is clearly composed in view of some form of the Pentateuch (Coggins 1987: 79; Stuart 1998: 1257–1262; R. Kessler 2012: 232). Malachi alludes to or exegetes passages from each book within the Pentateuch and calls on people to live in the light of it. As the books of the Twelve were collected, in the providence of God this ending of the book of Malachi came to serve a wider function in closing the Book of the Twelve, and eventually the Prophets in the HB, explicitly connecting these wider collections with the 'law of Moses'. In any case, the final three verses are presented as part of the book of Malachi and this is how they must be interpreted in the first instance.

Sometimes it is claimed that Malachi was placed last in the OT since it looks forward to the coming of Elijah, which the NT identifies early on with John the Baptist. For instance, LaSor et al. (1996: 421–422). Dumbrell (2002: 241) claims that in doing this, the English OT follows the Greek canon. However, these claims are inaccurate. In two major

Greek codices (Vaticanus from the early fourth century AD and Alexandrinus from the early fifth century AD), the Book of the Twelve is located *before* the Major Prophets. In Codex Sinaiticus (early fourth century AD), the Book of the Twelve is located after the Major Prophets (as in MT), but the books of Ezra-Nehemiah and the poetic books of Psalms, Proverbs, Ecclesiastes, Songs of Solomon, Wisdom, Sirach and Job come after the prophets and before the NT (Goswell 2009). Early copies of Vg also have the prophets before the writings. The order of the prophetic books in the English Bible reflects the order in MT, which clearly was not formulated with the NT in view (and is followed by the Writings). The first complete English Bible (Coverdale) included the apocryphal books in their own section between Malachi and the NT. It was only when these were later removed from Protestant Bibles that Malachi came to directly precede the NT. Hence the placement of Malachi in the OT seems completely unintentional in relation to the NT, but it is providential!

The chapter division at the end of Mal. 3:18 in the English Bible follows LXX (there is no ch. 4 in MT; ch. 3 continues). Those who made the division seem mistakenly to have understood 'For look!' at the beginning of 4:1[3:19] as disjunctive (Hill 1998: 327). Yet 4:1–3[3:19–21] clearly continues the argument of 3:13–18 and the chapter division is inappropriate.

The LXX places 4:4[3:22] after 4:5–6[3:23–24]), and the Masorah of the MT instructs that 4:5[3:23] be reread after 4:6[3:24]. Both of these suggest that the LXX translators and the Masoretes did not want to end the book on the note of curse (*ḥērem*). However, Hebr. textual witnesses (4Q76, MT^A, MT^C, MT^L) are all in agreement.

Comment

3:13. Yahweh directly accuses the people, 'Your words are harsh [*ḥāzqû*] against me.' This pushes further than 2:17, where the accusation by Malachi was, 'You have wearied the LORD with your words.' The people repeat Yahweh's charge in their own words: 'How have we spoken against you?' (the prep. 'against' [*'al*] is repeated). This indicates that the words of the people have been spoken against Yahweh, probably in discontent and with a measure of rebellion (cf. Jer. 29:32), hence their words 'have been harsh' (NRSV) or 'arrogant' (NASB; cf. NIV). It is evident in vv. 14–15 that the people have spoken these words as a complaint to each other (this is also suggested by the middle use of ni. for 'spoken' in v. 13), rather than being directed towards Yahweh in prayer (see 'Comment' on Mal. 2:17). Like the other disputation speeches, the people's response indicates that they are oblivious to the way their behaviour has impacted their relationship with Yahweh (cf. 1:2, 6; 2:14, 17; 3:7–8).

14–15. The 'harsh' words are reported and are similar in intent to 2:17 (esp. 3:15). The people have said, '[It is] futile to serve God, and what did it profit [us]?' The word 'futile' (*šāw'*) also means 'vanity, emptiness, ineffectiveness' (Clines 2011: 272). The word 'profit' (*beṣa'*) more often than not speaks of unjust or immoral gain (e.g. Gen. 37:26; Isa. 33:15; Mic. 4:13), but it can have a neutral meaning, as it does here (cf. Job 22:3; Ps. 30:10). The people's complaint is that service of God has not resulted in any benefit or reward. Furthermore, they believe that they deserve some gain for two reasons. First, 'we kept his requirement', a phrase that refers to covenant faithfulness (e.g. Gen. 26:5; Lev. 18:30; Num. 9:19, 23; Deut. 11:1; Josh. 22:3; 1 Kgs 2:3; Zech. 3:7). The meaning of the next reason is less certain. It is lit. 'we walked blackly before the LORD of hosts'. This is the only use of the adv. 'blackly' in the OT. Elsewhere the verbal form (*qādar*) means 'be dark, be black' (Joel 2:10; 3:15) and by extension connotes 'be in mourning, i.e. in dark clothes' (cf. Job 30:28; Jer. 8:21; 14:2) (Clines 2010b: 189). Hence the translation 'we walked mournfully', which most likely indicates penitence for sin. The LXX translates it, 'we went as suppliants into the presence of the Lord Almighty'. Some commentators argue that these actions were insincere and this is why they went unrewarded (Clendenen 2004: 437), yet this is not necessarily the case since elsewhere righteous actions may seem to be unacknowledged by Yahweh (e.g. Job; Ps. 73:1–16).

While the people's complaint in v. 14 is that righteous actions have brought no reward, in v. 15 they complain that the wicked are rewarded by God and not judged for their sin (cf. 2:17). This is conveyed in three sharp statements. First, the people complain that God blesses 'the arrogant' (*zēdîm*) – those who consider themselves above God's requirements. For instance, in Ps. 119 'the arrogant' stray from Yahweh's commands and spurn his law (vv. 21, 85). Secondly, the people complain that even 'evildoers' have been 'built up'. The 'evildoers' (*'ōśê riš'â*) are those who reject Yahweh's decrees (cf. Ezek. 33:14–20). The verb 'build up' (*bānâ*) is mostly used of building a structure such as a house or temple, but here it has a metaphorical sense of 'being established' (cf. Job 22:23; Jer. 12:16). Thirdly, they complain that those who have tested God have escaped his judgment. While God occasionally asks his people to test him to prove his faithfulness (as he does in 3:10; see 'Comment'), when people test him on their own initiative it demonstrates a lack of faith that is tantamount to rebellion, which one would expect him to judge (Exod. 17:7; Deut. 6:16). These three statements along with those of the previous verse are 'harsh' words (v. 13) because they essentially accuse Yahweh of injustice in his administration of the affairs of his people.

16. Malachi reports that a group described as 'fearers of the LORD' speak with each other. This is remarkable and it piques the curiosity to know exactly what they said. The fact that they are twice said to be 'fearers of the LORD' and those 'esteeming his name' contrasts with the priests who earlier are said not to fear Yahweh and despise and profane his name rather than give glory to it (1:6, 12; 2:2). It also contrasts with the people who break the requirements of the national covenant and 'do not fear me' (3:5). The best understanding of this group is that they are those who were earlier numbered among these people but have now repented at Yahweh's rebuke through the prophet (Mason 1977: 157; Scalise 1998: 573; Floyd 2000: 623). They have responded to Yahweh's call to 'return to me' (3:7) and now give him the honour due to him as father and master (1:6). They stand as an example to later readers and hearers of the book (cf. Hag. 1:12).

Yahweh hears their words and a 'scroll of remembrance' is written. Most scholars interpret this scroll against the background of the practice of Persian kings recording the events of their reigns as a 'royal memorandum' (e.g. Esth. 6:1). Yahweh's kingship is understood to be portrayed here in an analogous way (Deuel 1996). Yet rather than being a record of God's acts, this scroll contains the names of the God fearers and an ongoing account of their words and deeds, which in v. 18 will serve as the basis for Yahweh's judgment between the righteous and the wicked (Hill 1998: 340). Hence while it may appear that Yahweh is not paying attention, in fact he is keeping a scroll.

While it is true that elsewhere Yahweh is said to have a heavenly scroll he will consult on the judgment day (Exod. 32:32; Ps. 69:28; Neh. 13:14; Dan. 7:20; cf. Rev. 20:12, 15; 21:27), Nogalski (1993b: 206–210) and Scalise (1998: 577–579) rightly note that there are elements of the passage that indicate it is unlikely to be this kind of scroll in view here; rather, it is more likely to be some form of prophetic writing, probably some form of the scroll or 'book' of Malachi. First, the prep. *lĕ* more often means 'for' rather than 'concerning' – the scroll is 'for' the God fearers rather than 'concerning' them (e.g. in Deut. 24:3, the husband who divorces his wife writes a certificate of divorce 'for' [*lĕ*] her, which she then takes with her). Secondly, on analogy with the practice of Persian kings, it more likely contains a record of Yahweh's actions and words as king than those of the people. Thirdly, while the author of the scroll is not identified (assumed to be Malachi?), it is written 'before him', that is, in Yahweh's presence. This is consistent with the prophetic writing of Yahweh's words (cf. Isa. 8:1, 16; Jer. 30:2; 36:2, 28; 51:60; Hab. 2:2). Fourthly, Yahweh's heavenly scroll is never elsewhere called a 'scroll of remembrance'. Articles of 'remembrance' in the OT are always earthly objects or activities designed to sustain the relationship between Yahweh and Israel (Exod. 12:14; 13:9; 28:19; 30:16; Lev. 23:24; Num. 10:10; 31:54; Josh. 4:7; Zech. 6:14). The closest parallel to Malachi's expression is the scroll of remembrance written by Moses for Joshua as a reminder of God's promise of victory over the Amalekites (Exod. 17:14). As a prophetic writing, Malachi's 'scroll of remembrance' would have the function of renewing and maintaining the covenant relationship between Yahweh and faithful Israel by exposing sinful attitudes and practices, calling on people to return to Yahweh, and holding out Yahweh's promises of salvation and blessing to successive generations of readers who fear God and keep his commands (Scalise 1998: 579).

17–18. In reply to the objection that it is futile to serve God (v. 14), Yahweh promises that on the coming day there will be a distinction between those who serve God and those who do not serve him (the verb 'serve' occurs three times in vv. 17–18; cf. 'servant' in 1:6; 4:4 [3:22]). Those who fear and honour Yahweh's name 'will be mine', language that further reflects the covenant relationship between Yahweh and his people (cf. Zech. 13:9 and 'Comment'). The term 'treasured possession' (*sĕgūllâ*) also has covenant significance. It occurs eight times in the OT. Twice it refers to an immense amount of gold and silver (1 Chr. 29:3; Eccl. 2:8; cf. 1 Kgs 9:28; 10:10, 14, 21) and on five other occasions to Israel (Exod. 19:5; Deut. 7:6; 14:2; 26:18; Ps. 135:3). In particular, it highlights Israel's uniqueness and the special affection Yahweh has for them along with their call to holy obedience (Kaminsky 2007: 85). Here in Malachi 'treasured possession' does not refer to the whole nation, but to the faithful remnant in Israel who fulfil their calling by fearing, honouring and serving Yahweh. Towards those who return to Yahweh, he will 'have compassion' (*ḥāmal*), or spare them from his judgment, 'just as a man has compassion on his son who serves him' (cf. Zech. 11:5). This latter phrase reflects the kinship associations of the national covenant where Israel is Yahweh's son and he is their father (1:6; cf. Exod. 4:22–23). Describing the son as one who 'serves' alludes back to the objection that it is 'futile to serve God' (v. 14).

Most English translations render the verb *šûb* in the phrase 'And you will return' (v. 18) as an auxiliary – 'again' (cf. Zech. 5:1; 6:1). However, LeCureux (2012: 222) suggests that the verb could also look back to the imper. in 3:7 to 'return to me'. In this case, the implication is that only those who return to Yahweh (i.e. 'repent') will distinguish between the righteous and the wicked. In this verse, 'the righteous' is the one who is 'serving God' (the ptc. has a present continuous sense) and hence is in a right relationship with him – living in covenant faithfulness. On the other hand, 'the wicked' is the one who 'has not served him'. The contrast between the righteous and the wicked in their lives and destinies is portrayed poetically in Ps. 1.

4:1[**3:19**]. 'For look!' (*kî-hinnēh*) announces a future irreversible act of Yahweh that builds from the preceding argument (cf. Zech. 2:9[13] and 'Comment'). Essentially, the wicked will not stand in the judgment (cf. Ps. 1:5). Whereas the day of Yahweh's coming is portrayed in 3:2 as 'a refiner's fire' that will purify the Levites, now the day is depicted as bringing destructive fire that will consume the 'arrogant' and 'every evildoer', descriptions of the wicked in v. 15. Yahweh's presence is often associated with fire in the OT (e.g. Exod. 3:2; 19:18). Fire is also often connected with Yahweh's wrath (e.g. Isa. 30:27, 33; 42:25; Jer. 4:4; 7:20). The word 'furnace' (*tannûr*) can also be translated 'oven' (ESV), but the context suggests something more destructive than a domestic kitchen appliance (cf. Ps. 21:9). The wicked will become 'chaff' (*qas*]), which can refer either to the stems or stalks of grain crops cut into short lengths to feed cattle, or 'stubble', which refers to the lower parts of the stalks left standing in the field (Clines 2010b: 332). In Joel 2:25, the burning of 'chaff' is part of the description of what is left in the wake of Yahweh's coming. Elsewhere in the Twelve it is an image applied to the judgment of the nations (Obad. 18; Nah. 1:10). Here it refers to the destruction of the wicked among God's people.

Switching metaphors (since grain crops do not have branches), the wicked are said to be left without 'root or branch'. Since roots and branches play vital roles in sustaining a plant, their removal speaks of the complete destruction of the wicked (Sweeney 2000b: 748). There is no remnant and no hope of shooting up again to life (J. M. Gibson 2014a: 273).

2–3[3:20–21]. In contrast to the fate of the wicked, for the righteous (cf. v. 18), who are 'fearers of my name' (cf. v. 16), 'a sun of righteousness will rise and healing [will be] in its wings'. Most scholars interpret this image against the background of ANE iconography, where in both Egypt and Mesopotamia deities are represented as a winged sun (Keel 1997: 27–28). Some argue that 'Canaanite conceptions influenced the description of Yahweh' (Glazier-McDonald 1987: 237). Yet great caution is called for here, especially given Israel's strict aniconism enshrined in the Decalogue (Exod. 20:4–6; Deut. 5:8–10), which was to set them apart from other nations (e.g. Deut. 7:5–6, 25–26; Ezek. 8:16). Furthermore, Yahweh is careful to reveal himself in his own terms, rather than be subject to human invention, which is idolatry (cf. Isa. 44:6–11). While elsewhere Yahweh is likened to the sun (Deut. 33:2; Pss 50:2; 80:2; 84:12; Isa. 60:1–3; Hab. 3:4), it is quite another thing to say that Malachi is 'attributing to Yahweh the attributes of Shamash' (J. M. O'Brien 2004: 313). This is most unlikely. In any case, Yahweh is not directly likened to the sun. Here it is 'a sun of righteousness', that is, righteousness is likened to a sun that will rise, transforming night to day. The people complained that they saw no distinction between the righteous and the wicked (3:14) – they were effectively in the dark of night, to which Yahweh says they will see this distinction on the coming day (3:18). Just as the day dawns with the rising of the sun, so the coming day of Yahweh will restore righteousness, that is, it will set things right in the world and restore everything to its right order. Implicitly, it is saying that those who fear Yahweh's name will be vindicated. Explicitly, the sun will have 'healing . . . in its wings'. While the sun is often pictured with wings in ANE iconography, it may be that Malachi is simply mixing metaphors, like he did in the previous verse that switched between grain ('chaff') and a tree with root and branch. Here the metaphor of the sun shifts to the wings of a bird, which elsewhere are associated with salvation, shelter and protection (e.g. Exod. 19:4; Deut. 32:11; Ruth 2:12; Pss 17:8; 36:7[8]; 57:1[2]; 61:4[5]; 63:7[8]; 91:4). Interestingly, Ps. 139:9 speaks of the 'wings of the dawn', which seems to be a reference to the east, where the sun rises from the earth like a bird and brings light. Hence Malachi poetically combines images from creation to portray the difference the coming day will make – when the day dawns it will bring righteousness and healing to those who fear Yahweh's name. In this eschatological context, 'healing' encompasses spiritual and physical restoration (cf. Isa. 19:22; 53:5). It also comprises the restoration of life, blessing and wholeness in the land (cf. Jer. 33:6).

Two further images of restoration and vindication are given. On that day, 'you will go out and you will leap like calves from a stall'. The 'calves from a stall' (lit. 'calves of a stall') are well-fed calves that have been released from their confines and leap about in their new-found freedom. If the calves have been fattened for slaughter, then there may also be the sense that they have escaped death (cf. Jer. 46:21) (Scalise 1987: 416). The image of 4:3[3:21] is one of vindication. While the God fearers are not said to be involved in the destruction of the wicked (cf. 4:1[3:19]), in a great reversal they ultimately will triumph over them on that day. While in the present the arrogant seem blessed and the evildoers appear to be built up and to have escaped Yahweh's judgment (3:15), on the day when Yahweh acts the righteous will trample down the wicked as 'ashes beneath the soles of your feet'. The phrase 'under the feet' indicates subjugation of enemies and is elsewhere associated with kingship (1 Kgs 5:3[5:17]; cf. Gen. 3:15; Ps. 110:1). Calling God 'the LORD of hosts' underlines the certainty of his words coming to pass (see 'Comment' on 1:4).

4:4[3:22]. The final verses of Malachi function to draw the book to a close by bringing together the many exhortations in the book and urging preparation for the coming day of Yahweh. It is unlikely the book ever finished with 4:3[3:21], since ending then would be rather abrupt. In a recent study, J. M. Gibson (2014a: 275–327) has refuted many of the arguments made to date about Mal. 4:4–6[3:22–24] being a late addition to the book (see 'Introduction to Malachi'). Yet this is not to say the verses were composed without any canon consciousness. The final exhortation to 'Remember the law of Moses, my servant' captures the various exhortations throughout the book, most of which are reiterations of Pentateuchal laws. For instance: Mal. 1:6–14 contains allusions to the sacrificial laws of Lev. 22:17–25 and Deut. 15:21; Mal. 2:1–9 contains reference to the curse of Deut. 28:20 and reverses the priestly blessing of Num. 6:24–26; the teaching about marriage in Mal. 2:14–16 is in line with Gen. 2:23–25, Exod. 20:12 and Deut. 5:16, 7:3 and 24:1–4; the crimes listed in Mal. 3:5 violate Exod. 20:14, 16, Lev. 19:13 and Deut. 5:18, 20, 18:10 and 24:17; reference to the 'statutes' of Mal. 3:7 is an allusion to the law of Moses; and Mal. 3:7–12 assumes the tithe laws in Lev. 27:30–32, Num. 18:21–32 and Deut. 12:5–12, 14:22–29 (J. M. Gibson 2014a: 307). The phrase 'statutes and judgments' elsewhere refers to the body of the law, the stipulations of the covenant with Israel at Sinai mediated by Moses (e.g. Deut. 4:1–2, 5, 8, 14; Ezra 7:10; Neh. 10:29[30]). Because of the range of Malachi's allusions, the 'law of Moses' most likely refers to the books of the Pentateuch (Torah) rather than just Deuteronomy or the covenant code of Exod. 20 – 23. This conclusion connects the book of Malachi with the Torah. As the books of the Twelve and then the Prophets were collected, this conclusion functions to connect the wider collection of prophetic books with the Torah as well.

Normally the exhortation is to 'obey' (*šmʿ*) or to 'keep' (*šmr*) the Torah, and it is God's redemptive actions that Israel is exhorted to 'remember' (*zkr*). Assis (2011a: 209–210) seems right to argue that here 'remember' has a qualitative aspect to it. In 1:6 – 2:9 the priests and people are making sacrifices, but with blemished animals. In 3:7–12 the people bring tithes, but not the full tithe. Hence the emphasis is not so much on the observance (which they are doing), but the quality of their observance. The use of 'remember' focuses on *how* the people perform the commandments of the law of Moses. Calling Moses 'my servant' (cf. Num. 12:7–8; Josh. 1:2, 7; 2 Kgs 21:8; 1 Chr. 17:4, 7) indicates Moses' special relationship with Yahweh and the task he was given to do for Yahweh (Dempster 2007: 132–133). It also connects with the theme of 'service' of Yahweh in the previous speech (3:14, 17–18).

Horeb is an alternative name for Sinai. Moses was called at Mount Horeb (Exod. 3:1), and later returned with the Israelites after the exodus to receive the law (Exod. 18:5; 19:1; 33:6). The law was 'for all Israel', a phrase that denotes the entire nation that was present at Horeb/Sinai when Yahweh entered into covenant with them (cf. Exod. 19 – 24). See 'Comment' on 'Israel' in 1:1 (cf. 1:5; 2:11, 16).

4:5–6[3:23–24]. The phraseology 'Look, I will send to you Elijah the prophet' is almost identical to 3:1: 'Look, I will send my messenger'. In both instances, the figure is sent by and precedes Yahweh. Therefore Mal. 4:5[3:23] now clarifies the identity of the figure designated 'my messenger' and 'the messenger of the covenant' in 3:1 as 'Elijah the prophet'. Malachi's phraseology replicates exactly the phrase 'the great and the dreadful [day]' from Joel 2:31[3:4]. The switch from first-person speech of Yahweh ('I will send') to third-person speech about Yahweh ('the LORD') marks out the allusion (J. M. Gibson 2014a: 304). This 'day' was introduced in 3:2 (see 'Comment') and developed in 3:17 – 4:3[3:21]. But the new feature Malachi adds to the traditional understanding of the coming 'day of the LORD' is that it will be preceded by 'Elijah the prophet'.

There are many suggestions for why Elijah is chosen as the forerunner to the day of Yahweh. Since Elijah was taken to heaven in a whirlwind and did not die (2 Kgs 2:11), he is available for Yahweh to send him back in a way that neither Moses nor any of the other prophets were (Petersen 1995: 230). Childs (1979: 495–496) notes the following parallels between Elijah and the situation in Malachi's day: Elijah addressed 'all Israel' (1 Kgs 18:20; cf. Mal. 1:1; 4:4[3:22]); the Israelites were severely fragmented by indecision of faith (1 Kgs 18:21); the curse of drought had fallen on the land (1 Kgs 18:1–2; cf. Mal. 4:6[3:24]); Elijah pressed Israel to a choice between right and wrong (1 Kgs 18:21; cf. Mal. 3:16, 18). He made the right offering (cf. Mal. 3:3) and fire fell from heaven (cf. Mal. 3:3; 4:1[3:19]). While some of these connections are stronger than others, J. M. Gibson (2014a: 313–319) contends that Elijah's experience at Mount Horeb provides a more likely backdrop to Malachi than his activities at Mount Carmel. He notes that under Moses, the national covenant was ratified, broken by the idolatry of the golden calf incident, but then renewed at Horeb. Gibson (2014a: 313–319) suggests that Elijah returned to Mount Horeb after the idolatry of Israel, hoping, like Moses, to renew the covenant. Elijah's journey to Horeb recalls Moses' journey with the Israelites: 'a journey through the wilderness; miraculous provision of food; complaining on the way and wanting to die in the desert' (1 Kgs 19:4–6; cf. Exod. 16 – 19). Elijah's journey to Horeb of forty days and forty nights (1 Kgs 19:8) recalls both Moses' ratification of the covenant and the first covenant renewal (Exod. 24:18; 34:28). Yet at Horeb Yahweh has nothing to say to Elijah about covenant renewal; instead, he commissions Elijah to appoint men who will act as agents of his covenant judgment (1 Kgs 19:15–17). But Yahweh does promise to preserve a faithful remnant within Israel (19:18; cf. Mal. 3:16–18). J. M. Gibson (2014a: 319; italics original) concludes:

> Elijah and Moses are the prophets par excellence who stand for covenant faithfulness, and who are united by Horeb. Since the problem in post-exilic Israel is covenant infidelity, as demonstrated thus far in the book, it makes good sense for Elijah *redivivus* to be assigned the task of restoring covenant fidelity in the community. This . . . is why *Elijah* will return: to enact what he was not able to ensure when he travelled to Horeb.

The task of Elijah will be to 'turn hearts of fathers to sons and hearts of sons to their fathers'. The main interpretations of this unique OT phrase are first, it is an analogy that refers to Yahweh as father and Israel as children (Assis 2011a: 212–213). Yet the pl. 'fathers' makes this analogy unlikely (Reeder 2007: 703). Secondly, it is simply an example of reconciliation among the whole network of human relationships that Elijah will bring (Merrill 1994: 453). This is certainly possible, but there may be more going on in terms of the different generations of Israelites. Along these lines, a third interpretation is that it refers to reconciliation between generations of Israelites in conflict, probably on account of the younger people being influenced by the invasion of a thought world of a different culture. Some see this happening in the Persian period (Glazier-McDonald 1987: 254–255); others, in the Greek period (Rudolph 1976: 293) or perhaps the Hasmonean period (Fuller 2010: 108). Yet this interpretation assumes that one generation is faithful and the next generation is not, whereas Malachi sees unfaithfulness in the present generation (and every generation). Moreover, the threat of 'complete destruction' seems incommensurate with the problem of social discord (J. M. Gibson 2014a: 322).

A fourth interpretation also understands the 'fathers' and 'sons' to refer to different generations of Israelites – the 'sons' are the present (and subsequent) generations and the 'fathers' are the generation whom God entered into covenant with at Horeb (Verhoef 1987: 342; Hill 1998: 388; Reeder 2007: 703). Yet this suffers a similar shortcoming to the third interpretation, since the generation of the 'fathers' was just as unfaithful (cf. 3:7). A variation of this fourth proposal that avoids these problems picks up on the way Malachi sees fathers having their descendants cut off on account of sin (e.g. 2:3). J. M. Gibson (2014a: 323–326) suggests that the phrase refers to a future reconciliation of the generations. It is significant that the second mention of 'fathers' has the 3 pr. suff.: 'the hearts of sons to *their* fathers'. This indicates that the current generation are not the sons; otherwise it would be 'our fathers' (cf. 2:10). Instead, it is a future generation of 'sons'. This suits the wider context, which looks to the future day of Yahweh that Elijah precedes. Elijah will seek to restore covenant faithfulness across the generations with fathers honouring the law of Moses in a way that benefits their sons, and sons honouring the law of Moses in a way that honours their fathers. If not, Yahweh will bring 'complete destruction' (*ḥērem*; see 'Comment' on Zech. 14:11) on 'the land' (cf. Deut. 7:2, 26; Josh. 6:17; 10:1). In Deuteronomy, the land is the place where Israel was to live out and enjoy their relationship with Yahweh, and loss of the land is threatened for disobedience (Millar 1998: 62). The land also has a sacral character and must not be contaminated by covenant unfaithfulness. A key aspect of obedience in Deuteronomy is maintenance and restoration of human relationships, since a breakdown in human relationships will disrupt Israel's relationship with Yahweh (cf. Deut. 6:1–9). Against the background of Deuteronomy, Malachi's logic is clear – if there is no reconciliation between fathers and sons in covenant faithfulness, the land will be cleansed again by 'complete destruction' of its unfaithful inhabitants (cf. Isa. 66:24).

Explanation

Like the complaint in 2:17, the people believed that Yahweh was failing in his governing of the affairs of his people – he did not reward the righteous and judge the wicked (3:13–15). The people seem to be operating with the false notion that serving Yahweh puts God in their debt, that he owes them special treatment. After Yahweh identifies and airs their complaint, a group of 'fearers of the LORD' is identified (3:16). It appears that this group has heeded the earlier call to 'return to me' and Yahweh now effectively promises, 'I will return to you' (3:7). Yahweh is attentive to his people and a scroll of remembrance is written for those who fear and honour his name. While many interpret this as a heavenly scroll that Yahweh will consult on judgment day (when the righteous will be vindicated), it is better understood as a prophetic writing written *for* the 'fearers of the LORD' that will presumably serve as Scripture to teach, rebuke, correct and train in righteousness until the day comes (cf. 2 Tim. 3:16). The book of Malachi continues to serve this function for those who fear Yahweh.

Yahweh promises that on the day when he comes (3:17–18; cf. 3:2, 5), those who have returned to Yahweh will distinguish between the righteous and the wicked. The faithful remnant of Israel will be God's 'treasured possession' (cf. Exod. 19:5) and will be spared his judgment. In contrast, the wicked will be burned like chaff and destroyed with no hope of revival (4:1[3:19]). On the coming day, Yahweh will bring righteousness, healing, freedom and vindication to those who fear his name (4:2–3[3:20–21]). The coming day will bring about the restoration that the people complained had not taken place.

The final exhortation (4:4–6[3:22–24]) summarizes the themes of the book with the call to remember the law of Moses and the concern with the coming day of Yahweh. It functions as a mini-peroration, looking backwards and forwards. This conclusion to the book of Malachi also connects it and the wider canonical collection of the Prophets with the Torah and implies that the Prophets are to be read with reference to it. Childs (1979: 497) says, 'The canonical form of Malachi bears witness to Israel's conviction that the law and the prophets were not in opposition to each other, but constituted an essential unity within the divine purpose.' Looking forwards, before the great and the fearful 'day of the LORD' comes, Yahweh promises to send Elijah the prophet, who will restore covenant fidelity or else Yahweh will judge by striking the land with complete destruction. In this way, covenant faithfulness continues as a key theme of Malachi right to the end of the book.

In the NT, John the Baptist is portrayed as the eschatological Elijah who prepares the way for the Lord Jesus (see 'Explanation' for Mal. 2:17 – 3:7a). John is not literally Elijah (cf. John 1:21), but one who comes 'in the spirit and power of Elijah' (Luke 1:17; cf. Matt. 17:10–11). He wears the clothing of Elijah (Matt. 3:4; Mark 1:6; cf. 2 Kgs 1:8) and preaches a message calling on people to repent in view of God's coming judgment, a judgment portrayed in similar terms to Malachi: 'he will clear his threshing-floor, gathering his wheat into the barn and burning up the chaff with unquenchable fire' (Matt. 3:12; cf. 3:10). Luke explains the mission of John: 'He will bring back many of the people of Israel to the Lord their God. And he will go on before the Lord . . . to turn the hearts of the parents to their children and the disobedient to the wisdom of the righteous – to make ready a people prepared for the Lord' (Luke 1:16–17). At John's birth, his father, Zechariah, develops the themes of this passage in Malachi in a prophecy:

> And you, my child, will be called a prophet of the Most High;
> for you will go on before the Lord to prepare the way for him,

to give his people the knowledge of salvation
through the forgiveness of their sins, because of
the tender mercy of our God,
by which the rising sun will come to us from heaven
to shine on those living in darkness
and in the shadow of death,
to guide our feet into the path of peace.
(Luke 1:76–79)

Early Christian interpretation understood the 'rising sun' in Luke 1:78 (cf. Mal. 4:2[3:20]) as a reference to Christ (Lewis 1999: 95–100; Ferreiro 2003: 308–311). This may have been encouraged by two things: first, the LXX translation of 'Branch' in Jer. 23:5, Zech. 3:8, 6:12 as *anatolē* ('rising sun' in Luke 1:78), which has Davidic associations; secondly, the illumination in Luke 1:79 that elsewhere accompanies the coming of the Messiah (e.g. Isa. 9:1–7). While this identification draws some clever connections, it is not the intent of Mal. 4:3[3:20] (Lewis 1999).

When Jesus is transfigured on the mountain, he is in the company of Moses and Elijah (Matt. 17:1–13; Mark 9:2–8; Luke 9:28–36). Both of these prophets testify to Jesus (cf. Acts 10:43), and it may be that Moses represents the Torah and Elijah represents the Prophets. Yet each of them is associated with both law and prophecy. Their appearance is more likely in view of their prophetic roles – Moses preparing for the final Prophet to come (Deut. 18:15, 18), and Elijah preparing for the coming day of the Lord (Mal. 4:5–6[3:23–24]).

This final disputation speech of Malachi also confronts the reader today with the reality of God's judgment day – when the distinction between the righteous (the one serving God) and the wicked (the one who has not served him) will be seen. Ironically, while the people in Malachi's day were effectively complaining that God had not come to judge, many today ignore or totally reject the idea that God will judge – it is an 'inconvenient truth'. Yet the NT is just as clear about the judgment day, when Jesus will return and the dead will be raised and everyone 'will have to give account to him who is ready to judge the living and the dead' (1 Peter 4:5; cf. 2 Tim. 4:1). This is the 'day of the Lord' (1 Thess. 5:2; 2 Peter 3:10), the 'day of God' (2 Peter 3:12), the 'day of Christ' (Phil. 2:16) or 'that day' (1 Thess. 5:4). It will be a dreadful day for the enemies of God. It is also 'the day of God's wrath, when his righteous judgment will be revealed. God "will repay each person according to what they have done." . . . There will be trouble and distress for every human being who does evil' (Rom. 2:5, 6, 9). Like Malachi, in the NT the destiny of the wicked is also depicted as fire (e.g. Matt. 5:22; 13:40; 18:8–9; Mark 9:43, 48; Heb. 10:27; Jude 7; Rev. 20:15).

For the Christian, this 'day of the LORD' is not only future, but is also past. In the NT, there is a sense in which the expectations surrounding the

OT 'day of the LORD' are fulfilled first and foremost in the death and resurrection of the Lord Jesus (Matt. 26:56; Luke 24:19–27). It is because Jesus did what no other human could do and fully kept the requirements of the law of Moses that he could be both a true representative and a substitute for unfaithful Israel and sinful humanity. On the cross, Jesus became 'a curse for us' (Gal. 3:13; cf. Mal. 4:6[3:24]), he bore the judgment 'for our sins' (Rom. 8:3; 1 Cor. 15:3; Gal. 1:4). In his great love, God took on to himself the judgment humanity deserved so that that those who are in Christ need no longer fear condemnation (Rom. 8:1–4), but live in hope of resurrection life (Rom. 8:9–11; 1 Peter 1:3). In the terms of Mal. 3:17, Christians are children who have been spared by their Father and are now his 'treasured possession' (1 Peter 1:17–21; 2:9), and hence are not to give up or lose heart when struggling with opposition. Similarly, following the metaphors in Mal. 4:2–3[3:20–21], Jesus brings righteousness (Rom. 5:19; 2 Cor. 5:21), healing (Matt. 4:23–24; Acts 4:30; 9:34; 28:27; 1 Peter 2:24), freedom (John 8:32–36; Rom. 8:2, 21; Gal. 5:1; 1 Peter 2:16) and vindication (Rom. 16:20; Rev. 12:1–17). The judgment and compassion Malachi speaks of are displayed most clearly in the cross of Christ. Praise and glory and wisdom and thanks and honour and power and strength be to his name, for ever and ever. Amen!

BIBLIOGRAPHY

COMMENTARIES ON HAGGAI, ZECHARIAH AND MALACHI

Achtemeier, E. (1986), *Nahum–Malachi*, Atlanta: John Knox.

Ackroyd, P. R. (1963), 'Zechariah', in M. Black and H. H. Rowley (eds.), *Peake's Commentary on the Bible*, London: Nelson, 646–655.

Adam, P. (2013), *The Message of Malachi*, Nottingham: Inter-Varsity Press; Downers Grove: InterVarsity Press.

Amsler, S. (1988), 'Aggée, Zacharie 1–8', in S. Amsler, A. Lacocque and R. Vuilleumier (eds.), *Aggée, Zacharie, Malachie*, 2nd ed., Geneva: Labor et Fides, 11–126.

Baker, D. W. (2006), *Joel, Obadiah, Malachi*, NIVAC, Grand Rapids: Zondervan.

Baldwin, J. G. (1972), *Haggai, Zechariah, Malachi: An Introduction and Commentary*, TOTC, Leicester: Inter-Varsity Press.

Barker, K. L. (2008), 'Zechariah', in *EBC* 8:721–833.

Baron, D. (1918), *The Visions & Prophecies of Zechariah: An Exposition*, London: Morgan & Scott.

Boda, M. J. (2004), *Haggai, Zechariah*, NIVAC, Grand Rapids: Zondervan.

Calvin, J. (1986), 'Zechariah & Malachi', *A Commentary on the Twelve Minor Prophets*, vol. 5, Edinburgh: Banner of Truth Trust.

Chary, T. (1969), *Aggée–Zacharie, Malachie*, Sources Bibliques, Paris: Librairie Lecoffre.

Clendenen, E. R. (2004), 'Malachi', *Haggai, Malachi*, NAC 21A, Nashville: B. & H., 202–464.

Collins, J. J. (2012), *Joel, Obadiah, Haggai, Zechariah, Malachi*, NCBC 17, Minnesota: Liturgical Press.

Conrad, E. W. (1999), *Zechariah*, Readings: A New Biblical Commentary, Sheffield: Sheffield Academic Press.

Duguid, I. M. (2010), *A Study Commentary on Haggai, Zechariah and Malachi*, Darlington: Evangelical Press.

Floyd, M. H. (2000), *Minor Prophets: Part 2*, FOTL 22, Grand Rapids: Eerdmans.

Goldingay, J. (2009), 'Haggai', in *Minor Prophets II*, Peabody: Hendrickson, 137–175.

Gregory, B. R. (2010), *Longing for God in an Age of Discouragement: The Gospel According to Zechariah*, Phillipsburg: P. & R.

Hill, A. E. (1998), *Malachi: A New Translation with Introduction and Commentary*, *ABD* 25D, New Haven: Yale University Press.

——— (2012a), *Haggai, Zechariah and Malachi*, TOTC 28, Nottingham: Inter-Varsity Press; Downers Grove: InterVarsity Press.

Hoglund, K. G., and J. H. Walton (2009), 'Zechariah', in J. H. Walton (ed.), *Zondervan Illustrated Bible Backgrounds Commentary*, vol. 5, Grand Rapids: Zondervan, 202–231.

Keil, C. F. (1949), *The Twelve Minor Prophets*, vol. 2, tr. J. Martin, BCOT, Grand Rapids: Eerdmans.

Klein, G. L. (2008), *Zechariah*, NAC 21B, Nashville: B. & H.

Leupold, H. C. (1956), *Exposition of Zechariah*, London: Evangelical Press.

Mackay, J. L. (2003), *Haggai, Zechariah & Malachi*, FOB, Fearn: Christian Focus.

Mason, R. A. (1977), *The Books of Haggai, Zechariah, and Malachi*, CBC, Cambridge: Cambridge University Press.

McComiskey, T. E. (1998), 'Zechariah', in T. E. McComiskey (ed.), *The Minor Prophets: An Exegetical and Expository Commentary*, vol. 3, Grand Rapids: Baker, 1003–1244.

Meadowcroft, T. (2006), *Haggai*, Readings: A New Biblical Commentary, Sheffield: Sheffield Phoenix.

Merrill, E. H. (1994), *An Exegetical Commentary: Haggai, Zechariah, Malachi*, Chicago: Moody.

Meyers, C. L., and E. M. Meyers (1987), *Haggai, Zechariah 1–8: A New Translation with Introduction and Commentary*, New York: Doubleday.

——— (1993), *Zechariah 9–14: A New Translation with Introduction and Commentary*, New York: Doubleday.

Mitchell, H. G. (1912), 'A Commentary on Haggai and Zechariah', in S. R. Driver, A. Plummer and C. A. Briggs (eds.), *A Critical and Exegetical Commentary on Haggai, Zechariah, Malachi and Jonah*, The International Critical Commentary on the Holy Scriptures of the Old and New Testaments, Edinburgh: T. & T. Clark, 1–357.

Motyer, J. A. (1998), 'Haggai', in T. E. McComiskey (ed.), *The Minor Prophets: An Exegetical and Expository Commentary*, vol. 3, Grand Rapids: Baker, 963–1002.

Nogalski, J. D. (2011), *The Book of the Twelve: Micah–Malachi*, SHBC, Georgia: Smyth & Helwys.

O'Brien, J. M. (2004), *Nahum, Habakkuk, Zephaniah, Haggai, Zechariah, Malachi*, Abingdon OT Commentary, Nashville: Abingdon.

Ollenburger, B. C. (1996), 'The Book of Zechariah', in L. E. Keck, T. G. Long, B. C. Birch, K. P. Darr, W. L. Lane, G. R. O'Day, D. L. Petersen, J. J. Collins, J. A. Keller Jr., J. E. Massey and M. L. Soards (eds.), *The New Interpreter's Bible*, vol. 7, Nashville: Abingdon, 733–840.

Petersen, D. L. (1985), *Haggai and Zechariah 1–8: A Commentary*, OTL, London: SCM.

——— (1995), *Zechariah 9–14 and Malachi: A Commentary*, OTL, London: SCM.

Phillips, R. D. (2007), *Zechariah*, Phillipsburg: P. & R.
Pusey, E. B. (1907), *Zechariah*, The Minor Prophets 8, London: James Nisbet.
Redditt, P. L. (1995), *Haggai, Zechariah and Malachi*, NCBC, London: Marshall Pickering.
——— (2012), *Zechariah 9–14*, IECOT, Stuttgart: Kohlhammer.
Rudolph, W. (1976), *Haggai – Sacharja 1–8 – Sacharja 9–14 – Maleachi*, KZAT, Gütersloh: Mohn.
Scalise, P. J. (2009), 'Zechariah, Malachi', *Minor Prophets II*, Peabody: Hendrickson, 177–366.
Schuller, E. M. (1996), 'The Book of Malachi', in L. E. Keck, T. G. Long, B. C. Birch, K. P. Darr, W. L. Lane, G. R. O'Day, D. L. Petersen, J. J. Collins, J. A. Keller Jr., J. E. Massey and M. L. Soards (eds.), *The New Interpreter's Bible*, vol. 7, Nashville: Abingdon, 841–877.
Smith, R. L. (1984), *Micah–Malachi*, WBC 32, Waco: Word.
Stuart, D. (1998), 'Malachi', in T. E. McComiskey (ed.), *The Minor Prophets: An Exegetical and Expository Commentary*, vol. 3, Grand Rapids: Baker, 1245–1396.
Sweeney, M. A. (2000b), *The Twelve Prophets*, vol. 2: *Micah, Nahum, Habakkuk, Zephaniah, Haggai, Zechariah, Malachi*, Berit Olam: Studies in Hebrew Narrative & Poetry; Collegeville: Liturgical Press.
Taylor, R. A. (2004), 'Haggai', *Haggai, Malachi*, NAC 21A, Nashville: B. & H., 21–201.
Tidiman, B. (1996), *Le Livre de Zacharie*, Vaux-sur-Seine: Édifac.
Unger, M. F. (1963), *Unger's Bible Commentary: Zechariah*, Amsterdam: Drukkerij Holland.
Verhoef, P. A. (1987), *The Books of Haggai and Malachi*, NICOT, Grand Rapids: Eerdmans; Downers Grove: InterVarsity Press.
Webb, B. G. (2003), *The Message of Zechariah: Your Kingdom Come*, BST, Leicester: Inter-Varsity Press; Downers Grove: InterVarsity Press.
Willi-Plein, I. (2007), *Haggai, Sacharja, Maleachi*, Zürcher Bibelkommentare Altes Testament 24.4, Zürich: Theologischer Verlag.
Wolff, H. W. (1988), *Haggai: A Commentary*, Minneapolis: Augsburg.

OTHER WORKS

Ackroyd, P. R. (1968), *Exile and Restoration: A Study of Hebrew Thought of the Sixth Century B.C.*, London: SCM.
——— (1991), *The Chronicler in His Age*, JSOTSup 101, Sheffield: JSOT Press.
Albertz, R. (2003), *Israel in Exile: The History and Literature of the Sixth Century B.C.E.*, Studies in Biblical Literature 3, Atlanta: SBL.
Alexander, T. D. (1993), 'Genealogies, Seed and the Compositional Unity of Genesis', *TynB* 44:255–270.

——— (2012), *From Paradise to the Promised Land: An Introduction to the Pentateuch*, 3rd ed., Grand Rapids: Baker.
Allen, L. C. (1983), *Psalms 101–150*, WBC 21, Waco: Word.
Anderson, B. A. (2011), *Brotherhood and Inheritance: A Canonical Reading of the Esau and Edom Traditions*, LHBOTS 556, London: T. & T. Clark.
Arnold, B. T., and J. H. Choi (2003), *A Guide to Biblical Hebrew Syntax*, Cambridge: Cambridge University Press.
Assis, E. (2006), 'Haggai: Structure and Meaning', *Bib* 87:531–541.
——— (2007a), 'Composition, Rhetoric and Theology in Haggai 1:1–11', *JHS* 7:1–14.
——— (2007b), 'To Build or Not to Build: A Dispute Between Haggai and His People (Hag 1)', *ZAW* 119:514–527.
——— (2008a), 'A Disputed Temple (Haggai 2,1–9)', *ZAW* 120:582–596.
——— (2008b), 'The Temple in the Book of Haggai', *JHS* 8:1–10.
——— (2009), 'Love, Hate and Self-Identity in Malachi: A New Perspective to Mal 1:1–5 and 2:10–16', *JNSL* 35:109–120.
——— (2010a), 'Structure and Meaning in the Book of Malachi', in J. Day (ed.), *Prophecy and the Prophets in Ancient Israel: Proceedings of the Oxford Old Testament Seminar*, New York: T. & T. Clark, 354–369.
——— (2010b), 'Zechariah 8 as a Revision and Digest of Zechariah 1–7', *JHS* 10:1–26.
——— (2011a), 'Moses, Elijah and the Messianic Hope: A New Reading of Malachi 3,22–24', *ZAW* 123:207–220.
——— (2011b), 'Zechariah 8 and Its Allusions to Jeremiah 30–33 and Deutero-Isaiah', *JHS* 11:1–21.
——— (2012), 'Mutual Recriminations: God and Israel in the Book of Malachi', *SJOT* 26:212–219.
Averbeck, R. E. (1997), '*g'l*', in *NIDOTTE* 1:794–795.
Bartholomew, C. G., and M. W. Goheen (2004), *The Drama of Scripture: Finding Our Place in the Biblical Story*, Grand Rapids: Baker.
Bartholomew, C. G., and R. P. O'Dowd (2011), *Old Testament Wisdom Literature: A Theological Introduction*, Downers Grove: InterVarsity Press; Nottingham: Apollos.
Bartlett, J. R. (1989), *Edom and the Edomites*, JSOTSup 77, Sheffield: JSOT Press.
Beale, G. K. (2004), *The Temple and the Church's Mission: A Biblical Theology of the Dwelling Place of God*, NSBT 17, Leicester: Apollos.
Beaulieu, P.-A. (2007), 'Nabonidus the Mad King: A Reconsideration of His Steles from Harran and Babylon', in M. Heinz and M. H. Feldman (eds.), *Case Histories from Times of Change and Dissolving Order in the Ancient Near East*, Winona Lake: Eisenbrauns, 137–166.
Ben Zvi (2005), E., *Hosea*, FOTL 21A, Grand Rapids: Eerdmans.
Ben Zvi, E., J. D. Nogalski and T. Römer (2009), *Two Sides of a Coin: Juxtaposing Views on Interpreting the Book of the Twelve / the Twelve Prophetic Books*, Analecta Gorgiana 201, Piscataway: Gorgias.

Berquist, J. L. (1995), *Judaism in Persia's Shadow: A Social and Historical Approach*, Minneapolis: Fortress.

Berry, D. K. (1996), 'Malachi's Dual Design: The Close of the Canon and What Comes Afterward', in J. W. Watts and P. R. House (eds.), *Forming Prophetic Literature: Essays on Isaiah and the Twelve in Honour of John D. W. Watts*, Sheffield: Sheffield Academic Press, 269–302.

Beuken, W. (1967), *Haggai-Sacharja 1–8: Studien zur Überlieferungsgeschichte der frühnachexilischen Prophetie*, SSN 10, Assen: Van Gorcum.

Bienkowski, P. (2001), 'New Evidence on Edom in the Neo-Babylonian and Persian Periods', in J. A. Dearman and M. P. Graham (eds.), *The Land That I Will Show You: Essays in Honor of J. Maxwell Miller*, JSOTSup 343, Sheffield: Sheffield Academic Press, 198–213.

Block, D. I. (2003), 'My Servant David: Ancient Israel's Vision of the Messiah', in R. S. Hess and M. D. Carroll R. (eds.), *Israel's Messiah in the Bible and the Dead Sea Scrolls*, Grand Rapids: Baker Academic, 17–56.

——— (2014), *For the Glory of God: Recovering a Biblical Theology of Worship*, Grand Rapids: Baker Academic.

Blomberg, C. L. (1999), *Neither Poverty Nor Riches: A Biblical Theology of Material Possessions*, NSBT 7, Leicester: Apollos.

——— (2007), 'Matthew', in *CNTUOT*, 1–109.

Boda, M. J. (2000), 'Haggai: Master Rhetorician', *TynB* 51:295–304.

——— (2001), 'Oil, Crowns and Thrones: Prophet, Priest and King in Zechariah 1:7–6:15', *JHS* 3: article 10.

——— (2003a), 'From Fasts to Feasts: The Literary Function of Zechariah 7–8', *CBQ* 65:390–407.

——— (2003b), 'Reading Between the Lines: Zechariah 11.4–16 in Its Literary Contexts', in M. J. Boda and M. H. Floyd (eds.), *Bringing out the Treasure: Inner Biblical Allusion in Zechariah 9–14*, JSOTSup 370, London: Sheffield Academic Press, 277–291.

——— (2003c), 'Zechariah: Master Mason or Penitential Prophet', in R. Albertz and B. Becking (eds.), *Yahwism After the Exile: Perspectives on Israelite Religion in the Persian Era*, Assen: Royal Van Gorcum, 49–69.

——— (2005), 'Terrifying the Horns: Persia and Babylon in Zechariah 1:7–6:15', *CBQ* 67:22–41.

——— (2006), 'Freeing the Burden of Prophecy: *Maśśā'* and the Legitimacy of Prophecy in Zech 9–14', *Bib* 87:338–357.

——— (2007), 'Figuring the Future: The Prophets and the Messiah', in S. E. Porter (ed.), *The Messiah in the Old and New Testaments*, Grand Rapids: Eerdmans, 35–74.

——— (2008), 'Hoy, Hoy: The Prophetic Origins of the Babylonian Tradition in Zechariah 2:10–17', in M. J. Boda and M. H. Floyd (eds.), *Tradition in Transition: Haggai and Zechariah 1–8 in the Trajectory of Hebrew Theology*, LHBOTS 475, New York: T. & T. Clark, 171–190.

——— (2009), *A Severe Mercy: Sin and Its Remedy in the Old Testament*, Winona Lake: Eisenbrauns.

——— (2011), 'Perspectives on Priests in Haggai-Malachi', in J. Penner, K. M. Penner and C. Wassen (eds.), *Prayer and Poetry in the Dead Sea Scrolls and Related Literature: Essays in Honor of Eileen Schuller on the Occasion of Her 65th Birthday*, STDJ 98, Leiden: Brill, 13–33.

Bosshard, E., and R. G. Kratz (1990), 'Maleachi im Zwölfprophetenbuch', *BN* 52:27–46.

Brichto, H. C. (1963), *The Problem of 'Curse' in the Hebrew Bible*, SBLMS 13, Philadelphia: SBL.

Bright, J. (1981), *A History of Israel*, 3rd ed., London: SCM.

Brodsky, H. (1992), 'Bethel, Place', in *ABD* 1:710–712.

Brotzman, E. R. (1994), *Old Testament Textual Criticism: A Practical Introduction*, Grand Rapids: Baker.

Brown, F., S. R. Driver and C. A. Briggs (1979), *The New Brown-Driver-Briggs-Gesenius Hebrew and English Lexicon*, Peabody: Hendrickson.

Bruce, F. F. (1969), *New Testament Development of Old Testament Themes*, Grand Rapids: Eerdmans.

——— (1988), *The Canon of Scripture*, Glasgow: Chapter House.

Butterworth, M. (1992), *Structure and the Book of Zechariah*, Sheffield: JSOT Press.

Cantrell, D. O. D. (2011), *The Horsemen of Israel: Horses and Chariotry in Monarchic Israel, Ninth–Eighth Centuries B.C.E.*, HACL 1, Winona Lake: Eisenbrauns.

Carroll, R. P. (1979), *When Prophecy Failed: Reactions and Responses to Failure in the Old Testament Prophetic Traditions*, London: SCM.

Carson, D. A. (1991), *The Gospel According to John*, Leicester: Inter-Varsity Press.

——— (2000), *The Difficult Doctrine of the Love of God*, Wheaton: Crossway; Leicester: Inter-Varsity Press.

——— (ed.) (2002), *Worship by the Book*, Grand Rapids: Zondervan.

——— (2012), *Jesus the Son of God: A Christological Title Often Overlooked, Sometimes Misunderstood, and Currently Disputed*, Wheaton: Crossway; Nottingham: Inter-Varsity Press.

Cathcart, K. J., and R. P. Gordon (1989), *The Targum of the Minor Prophets*, ArBib 14, Edinburgh: T. & T. Clark.

Childs, B. S. (1979), *Introduction to the Old Testament as Scripture*, London: SCM.

Christensen, D. L. (1992), 'Impulse and Design in the Book of Haggai', *JETS* 35:445–456.

Clark, D. J., and H. A. Hatton (2002), *A Handbook on Haggai, Zechariah, and Malachi*, UBS Handbook Series, New York: United Bible Societies.

Clifford, R. J. (1972), *The Cosmic Mountain in Canaan and the Old Testament*, Cambridge, Mass.: Harvard University Press.

Clines, D. J. A. (1993), '*'emet*', in *DCH* 1:328–332.

——— (1994), 'Haggai's Temple, Constructed, Deconstruced and Reconstructed', in T. C. Eskenazi and K. H. Richards (eds.), *Second*

Temple Studies 2: Temple and Community in the Persian Period, JSOTSup 175, Sheffield: Sheffield Academic Press, 60–87.
——— (1996), '*z'q*', in *DCH* 3:127–128.
——— (2001), '*nzr*', in *DCH* 5:651.
——— (2007), ''*al*', in *DCH* 6:385–398.
——— (2010a), '*qaš*'', in *DCH* 7:332.
——— (2010b), '*qdr*', in *DCH* 7:189.
——— (2010c), '*qnh*', in *DCH* 7:266–268.
——— (2011), '*šāw*'', in *DCH* 8:271–272.
Clowney, E. P. (2003), *Preaching Christ in All of Scripture*, Wheaton: Crossway.
Coggins, R. J. (1987), *Haggai, Zechariah, Malachi*, OTG, Sheffield: JSOT Press.
Collins, C. J. (1994), 'The (Intelligible) Masoretic Text of Malachi 2:16', *Presb* 20:36–40.
Cook, J. A. (2012), *Time and the Biblical Hebrew Verb: The Expression of Tense, Aspect, and Modality in Biblical Hebrew*, Linguistic Studies in Ancient West Semitic 7, Winona Lake: Eisenbrauns.
Cook, S. A. (1993), 'The Metamorphosis of a Shepherd: The Tradition History of Zechariah 11.17 + 13.7–9', *CBQ* 55:453–466.
Coppins, W. (2012), 'Sitting on Two Asses? Second Thoughts on the Two-Animal Interpretation of Matthew 21:7', *TynB* 63:275–290.
Cornes, A. (2002), *Divorce and Remarriage: Biblical Principles and Pastoral Practice*, Fearn: Mentor.
Craig, K. M. (1996), 'Interrogatives in Haggai–Zechariah: A Literary Thread?', in J. W. Watts and P. R. House (eds.), *Forming Prophetic Literature: Essays on Isaiah and the Twelve in Honor of John D. W. Watts*, Sheffield: Sheffield Academic Press, 224–244.
Craigie, P. C. (1976), *The Book of Deuteronomy*, NICOT, Grand Rapids: Eerdmans.
Crotty, R. B. (1982), 'The Suffering Moses of Deutero-Zechariah', *Colloquium* 14:43–50.
Curtis, B. G. (2006), *Up the Steep and Stony Road: The Book of Zechariah in Social Location Trajectory Analysis*, AcBib 25, Atlanta: SBL.
——— (2012), 'The *Mas'ot* Triptych and the Date of Zechariah 9–14: Issues in the Latter Formation of the Book of the Twelve', in R. Albertz, J. D. Nogalski and J. Wöhrle (eds.), *Perspectives on the Formation of the Book of the Twelve: Methodological Foundations – Redactional Processes – Historical Insights*, Berlin: de Gruyter, 191–206.
Davis, J. D. (1920), 'The Reclothing and Coronation of Joshua; Zechariah iii and vi', *PTR* 18:256–268.
Delcor, M. (1951), 'Un Problème de Critique Textuelle et d'Exégèse', *RB* 58:189–199.
Delkurt, H. (2008), 'Sin and Atonement in Zechariah's Night Visions', in M. J. Boda and M. H. Floyd (eds.), *Tradition in Transition: Haggai and Zechariah 1–8 in the Trajectory of Hebrew Theology*, LHBOTS 475, New York: T. & T. Clark, 235–251.

Dempster, S. G. (2006), 'The Prophets, the Canon and a Canonical Approach: No Empty Word', in C. G. Bartholomew, S. Hahn, R. Parry, C. R. Seitz and A. Wolters (eds.), *Canon and Biblical Interpretation*, SHS 7, Grand Rapids: Zondervan, 293–329.
——— (2007), 'The Servant of the Lord', in S. J. Hafemann and P. R. House (eds.), *Central Themes in Biblical Theology: Mapping Unity in Diversity*, Nottingham: Apollos, 128–178.
Deuel, D. C. (1996), 'Malachi 3:16: "Book of Remembrance" or Royal Memorandum? An Exegetical Note', *MSJ* 7:107–111.
De Vries, S. J. (1962), 'Chronology of the OT', in *IDB* 1:580–599.
Drinkard Jr., J. F. (1987), 'The Socio-Historical Setting of Malachi', *RevExp* 84:383–390.
Duguid, I. M. (1994), *Ezekiel and the Leaders of Israel*, VTSup 56, Leiden: Brill.
——— (1995), 'Messianic Themes in Zechariah 9–14', in P. E. Satterthwaite, R. S. Hess and G. J. Wenham (eds.), *The Lord's Anointed: Interpretation of Old Testament Messianic Texts*, Carlisle: Paternoster, 265–280.
Dumbrell, W. J., (1976), 'Malachi and the Ezra-Nehemiah Reforms', *RTR* 35:42–52.
——— (1978), 'Kingship and Temple in the Post-exilic Period', *RTR* 37:33–42.
——— (1994), *The Search for Order: Biblical Eschatology in Focus*, Grand Rapids: Baker.
——— (2002), *The Faith of Israel*, 2nd ed., Grand Rapids: Baker Academic.
Eddinger, T. W. (2012), *Malachi: A Handbook on the Hebrew Text*, Baylor Handbook on the Hebrew Bible, Waco: Baylor University Press.
Edelman, D. (2005), *The Origins of the 'Second' Temple: Persian Imperial Policy and the Rebuilding of Jerusalem*, London: Equinox.
Eggleston, C. L. (2012), 'Wilderness, Desert', in M. J. Boda and J. G. McConville (eds.), *Dictionary of the Old Testament Prophets*, Downers Grove: InterVarsity Press, 843–847.
Eichrodt, W. (1961), *Theology of the Old Testament*, tr. J. Baker, vol. 1, London: SCM.
——— (1967), *Theology of the Old Testament*, tr. J. Baker, vol. 2, London: SCM.
Eising, H. (1980), '*ḥayil*', in *TDOT* 4:348–355.
Elliger, K. (1982), *Das Buch der zwölf kleinen Propheten*, ATD 25, Göttingen: Vanderhoeck & Ruprecht.
Ellis, R. (1968), *Foundation Deposits in Ancient Mesopotamia*, YNER 2, New Haven: Yale University Press.
Elwolde, J. (2011), 'Mal 2:16a, Hebrew *kî*, and the Proper Condemnation of Divorce', *JNSL* 37:91–107.
Ferreiro, A. (2003), *The Twelve Prophets*, ACCS 14, Downers Grove: InterVarsity Press.
Finitsis, A. (2011), *Visions and Eschatology: A Socio-Historical Analysis of Zechariah 1–6*, LSTS 79, London: T. & T. Clark.

Finley, T. J. (1982), 'The Sheep Merchants of Zechariah 11', *GTJ* 3:51–65.
Fishbane, M. (1985), *Biblical Interpretation in Ancient Israel*, Oxford: Clarendon.
Floyd, M. H. (1995), 'The Nature of the Narrative and the Evidence of Redaction in Haggai', *VT* 45:470–490.
——— (1999), 'Zechariah and Changing Views of Second Temple Judaism in Recent Commentaries', *Religious Studies Review* 25:257–263.
——— (2002), 'The *MAŚŚĀ*' as a Type of Prophetic Book', *JBL* 121:401–422.
——— (2006), 'Was Prophetic Hope Born of Disappointment? The Case of Zechariah', in E. Ben Zvi (ed.), *Utopia and Dystopia in Prophetic Literature*, PFES 92, Göttingen: Vanderhoeck & Ruprecht, 268–296.
Foster, R. L. (2007), 'Shepherds, Sticks, and Social Destabilization: A Fresh Look at Zechariah 11:4–17', *JBL* 126:735–753.
Freedman, D. N. (1990), 'The Flying Scroll in Zechariah 5:1–4', in J. A. Bellamy (ed.), *Studies in Near Eastern Culture and History*, Ann Arbor: University of Michigan Press.
Freedman, D. N. (ed.) (1998), *The Leningrad Codex: A Facsimile Edition*, Grand Rapids: Eerdmans.
Fried, L. S. (2004), *The Priest and the Great King: Temple–Palace Relations in the Persian Empire*, Winona Lake: Eisenbrauns.
Frolov, S. (2005), 'Is the Narrator Also Among the Prophets? Reading Zechariah Without Presuppositions', *BibInt* 13:13–40.
Fuller, R. (1991), 'Text-Critical Problems in Malachi 2:10–16', *JBL* 110:47–57.
Fuller, R. E. (2010), 'Hebrew and Greek Biblical Manuscripts: Their Intepretations and Their Interpreters', in A. Lange, E. Tov and M. Weigold (eds.), *The Dead Sea Scrolls in Context: Integrating the Dead Sea Scrolls in the Study of Ancient Texts, Languages, and Cultures*, vol. 1, Leiden: Brill, 101–110.
Garland, D. E. (1987), 'A Biblical View of Divorce', *RevExp* 84:419–432.
Gelston, A. (2010), *The Twelve Minor Prophets*, *BHQ*, Stuttgart: Deutsche Bibelgesellschaft.
Gentry, P. J., and S. J. Wellum (2012), *Kingdom Through Covenant: A Biblical-Theological Understanding of the Covenants*, Wheaton: Crossway.
Gesenius, W. (2006), *Gesenius' Hebrew Grammar*, ed. E. Kautzsch, tr. A. E. Cowley, Mineola: Dover.
Gibson, J. C. L. (1994), *Davidson's Introductory Hebrew Grammar*, 4th ed, Edinburgh: T. & T. Clark.
Gibson, J. M. (2014a), 'Covenant Continuity and Fidelity: A Study of Inner-Biblical Allusion and Exegesis in Malachi', PhD diss., University of Cambridge.
——— (2014b), 'Cutting Off "Kith and Kin," "Er and Onan"? Interpreting an Obscure Phrase in Malachi 2:12', *JBL* 133:519–537.
Glazier-McDonald, B. (1987), *Malachi: The Divine Messenger*, SBLDS 98, Atlanta: Scholars Press.

Goldsworthy, G. (1981), *Gospel and Kingdom: A Christian Interpretation of the Old Testament*, Exeter: Paternoster.
——— (2000), 'Kingdom of God', in *NDBT*, 615–620.
Gordon, R. P. (1994), *Studies in the Targum to the Twelve Prophets: From Nahum to Malachi*, Leiden: Brill.
——— (1995), 'A Story of Two Paradigm Shifts', in R. P. Gordon (ed.), *"The Place Is too Small for Us": The Israelite Prophets in Recent Scholarship*, Winona Lake: Eisenbrauns, 3–26.
——— (2003), 'The Ephraimite Messiah and the Targum(s) to Zechariah 12.10', in J. C. Exum and H. G. M. Williamson (eds.), *Reading from Right to Left: Essays on the Hebrew Bible in Honour of David J. A. Clines*, London: Sheffield Academic Press, 184–195.
Goswell, G. (2008), 'The Order of the Books in the Hebrew Bible', *JETS* 51:673–688.
——— (2009), 'The Order of the Books in the Greek Old Testament', *JETS* 52:449–466.
——— (2010), 'The Fate and Future of Zerubbabel in the Prophecy of Haggai', *Bib* 9:77–90.
——— (2013), 'The Eschatology of Malachi After Zechariah 14', *JBL* 132:625–638.
Green, J. B. (1997), *The Gospel of Luke*, NICNT, Grand Rapids: Eerdmans.
Grogan, G. W. (2008), *Psalms*, Grand Rapids: Eerdmans.
Groningen, G. van (1990), *Messianic Revelation in the Old Testament*, Grand Rapids: Baker.
Gruber, M. I. (1983), 'The Many Faces of Hebrew *nś' pnym* "Lift up the Face"', *ZAW* 95:252–260.
Hafemann, S. J. (2007), 'The Covenant Relationship', in S. J. Hafemann and P. R. House (eds.), *Central Themes in Biblical Theology: Mapping Unity in Diversity*, Nottingham: Apollos, 20–65.
Hallaschka, M. (2011), *Haggai und Sacharja 1–8: Eine redaktionsgeschichtliche Untersuchung*, BZAW 411, Berlin: de Gruyter.
——— (2012), 'From Cores to Corpus: Considering the Formation of Haggai and Zechariah 1–8', in R. Albertz, J. D. Nogalski and J. Wöhrle (eds.), *Perspectives on the Formation of the Book of the Twelve: Methodological Foundations – Redactional Processes – Historical Insights*, Berlin: de Gruyter, 171–189.
Halpern, B. (1978), 'The Ritual Background of Zechariah's Temple Song', *CBQ* 40:167–180.
Hanson, P. D. (1979), *The Dawn of Apocalyptic: The Historical and Sociological Roots of Jewish Apocalyptic Eschatology*, rev. ed., Philadelphia: Fortress.
Harrison, G. W. (1987), 'Covenant Unfaithfulness in Malachi 2:1–16', *CTR* 2:63–72.
Hartle, A. (1992), 'The Literary Unity of Zechariah', *JETS* 35:145–157.
Hartley, J. E. (2010), *The Semantics of Ancient Hebrew Colour Lexemes*, ANESSS 33, Louvain: Peeters.

Hengel, M. (2004), 'The Effective History of Isaiah 53 in the Pre-Christian Period', in B. Janowski and P. Stuhlmacher (eds.), *The Suffering Servant: Isaiah 53 in Jewish and Christian Sources*, Grand Rapids: Eerdmans, 75–146.

Hildebrand, D. R. (1989), 'Temple Ritual: A Paradigm for Moral Holiness in Haggai II 10–19', *VT* 39:154–168.

Hill, A. E. (1982), 'Dating Second Zechariah: A Linguistic Reexamination', *HAR* 6:105–134.

——— (2012b), 'Malachi, Book of', in M. J. Boda and J. G. McConville (eds.), *Dictionary of the Old Testament Prophets*, Downers Grove: InterVarsity Press, 525–533.

Holladay, W. L. (1988), *A Concise Hebrew and Aramaic Lexicon of the Old Testament: Based upon the Lexical Work of Ludwig Koehler and Walter Baumgartner*, Leiden: Brill.

Horbury, W. (1998), *Jewish Messianism and the Cult of Christ*, London: SCM.

House, P. R. (1990), *The Unity of the Twelve*, Bible and Literature Series 27, Sheffield: Almond.

——— (1998), *Old Testament Theology*, Downers Grove: InterVarsity Press.

——— (2002), 'Biblical Theology and the Wholeness of Scripture', in S. J. Hafemann (ed.), *Biblical Theology: Retrospect and Prospect*, Downers Grove: InterVarsity Press; Leicester: Apollos, 267–279.

Hugenberger, G. P. (1994), *Marriage as a Covenant: Biblical Law and Ethics as Developed from Malachi*, VTSup 52, Leiden: Brill (publ. ed., Grand Rapids: Baker, 1984).

Im, Y., and P. M. Venter (2013), 'The Function of Zechariah 7–8 Within the Book of Zechariah', *HTS* 69:1–10.

Instone-Brewer, D. (2003), *Divorce and Remarriage in the Church: Biblical Solutions for Pastoral Realities*, Carlisle: Paternoster.

Isaksson, A. (1965), *Marriage and Ministry in the New Temple*, Lund: C. W. K. Gleerup.

Jauhiainen, V. M. (2003), *'Behold, I Am Coming': The Use of Zechariah in Revelation*, Cambridge: University of Cambridge.

——— (2008), 'Turban and Crown Lost and Regained: Ezekiel 21:29–32 and Zechariah's Zemah', *JBL* 127:501–511.

——— (2009), 'The Minor Prophets in Revelation', in M. J. J. Menken and S. Moyise (eds.), *The Minor Prophets in the New Testament*, LNTS 377, London: T. & T. Clark, 155–171.

Jigoulov, V. (2009), 'Administration of Achaemenid Phoenicia: A Case for Managed Autonomy', in G. N. Knoppers, L. L. Grabbe and D. N. Fulton (eds.), *Exile and Restoration Revisited: Essays on the Babylonian and Persian Periods in Memory of Peter R. Ackroyd*, New York: T. & T. Clark, 138–151.

Jobes, K. H. (2009), 'The Minor Prophets in James, 1 & 2 Peter and Jude', in M. J. J. Menken and S. Moyise (eds.), *The Minor Prophets in the New Testament*, LNTS 377, London: T. & T. Clark, 135–153.

Johnston, P. S. (2000), 'Malachi', in *NDBT*, 260–262.
Joosten, J. (2012), *The Verbal System of Biblical Hebrew: A New Synthesis Elaborated on the Basis of Classical Prose*, Jerusalem Biblical Studies 10, Jerusalem: Simor.
Kaiser Jr., W. C. (1978), *Toward an Old Testament Theology*, Grand Rapids: Zondervan.
Kaminsky, J. S. (2007), *Yet I Loved Jacob: Reclaiming the Biblical Concept of Election*, Nashville: Abingdon.
Kashow, R. C. (2013), 'Zechariah 1–8 as a Theological Explanation for the Failure of Prophecy in Haggai 2:20–23', *JTS* 64:385–403.
Keel, O. (1997), *The Symbolism of the Biblical World: Ancient Near Eastern Iconography and the Book of Psalms*, tr. T. J. Hallett, Indiana: Eisenbrauns.
Kelle, B. E. (2012), 'Israelite History', in M. J. Boda and J. G. McConville (eds.), *Dictionary of the Old Testament Prophets*, Downers Grove: InterVarsity Press, 397–422.
Kelly, B. E. (1995), 'Messianic Elements in the Chronicler's Work', in P. E. Satterthwaite, R. S. Hess and G. J. Wenham (eds.), *The Lord's Anointed: Interpretation of Old Testament Messianic Texts*, Carlisle: Paternoster, 249–264.
Kessler, J. (2002), *The Book of Haggai: Prophecy and Society in Early Persian Yehud*, VTSup 91, Leiden: Brill.
——— (2006), 'Persia's Loyal Yahwists: Power Identity and Ethnicity in Achaemenid Yehud', in O. Lipschits and M. Oeming (eds.), *Judah and the Judeans in the Persian Period*, Winona Lake: Eisenbrauns, 91–121.
——— (2008), 'Tradition, Continuity and Covenant in the Book of Haggai: An Alternative Voice from Early Persian Yehud', in M. J. Boda and M. H. Floyd (eds.), *Tradition in Transition: Haggai and Zechariah 1–8 in the Trajectory of Hebrew Theology*, LHBOTS 475, New York: T. & T. Clark, 1–39.
——— (2012), 'Haggai, Book of', in M. J. Boda and J. G. McConville (eds.), *Dictionary of the Old Testament Prophets*, Downers Grove: InterVarsity Press, 301–307.
Kessler, J. A. (1987), 'The Shaking of the Nations: An Eschatological View', *JETS* 30:159–166.
Kessler, R. (2012), 'The Unity of Malachi and Its Relation to the Book of the Twelve', in R. Albertz, J. D. Nogalski and J. Wöhrle (eds.), *Perspectives on the Formation of the Book of the Twelve: Methodological Foundations – Redactional Processes – Historical Insights*, Berlin: de Gruyter, 223–236.
Kitchen, K. A. (1982), 'Tent', in *NBD*, 1175.
Klein, G. L. (1987), 'An Introduction to Malachi', *CTR* 2:19–37.
Kline, M. G. (1980), *Images of the Spirit*, Grand Rapids: Baker.
——— (2001), *Glory in Our Midst: A Biblical-Theological Reading of Zechariah's Night Visions*, Eugene: Wipf & Stock.

Knowles, M. (1995), *Jeremiah in Matthew's Gospel: The Rejected-Prophet Motif in Matthaean Redaction*, JSNTSup 68, Sheffield: Sheffield Academic Press.

Ko, M. H. (2014), 'Be Faithful to the Covenant: A Technical Translation of and Commentary on Malachi 2.10–16', *BT* 65:34–48.

Koch, K. (1999), '*ʿāwōn*', in *TDOT* 10:542–562.

Koops, R. (2012), *Each According to Its Kind: Plants and Trees in the Bible*, UBS Technical Helps, Reading: United Bible Societies.

Kosmala, H. (1969), 'The Term *geber* in the Old Testament and in the Scrolls', in G. W. Anderson, P. A. H. De Boer, G. R. Castellino, H. Cazelles, E. Hammershaimb, H. G. May and W. Zimmerli (eds.), *Congress Volume, Rome 1968*, VTSup 17, Leiden: Brill, 159–169.

Köstenberger, A. J. (2007), 'John', in *CNTUOT*, 415–512.

Krause, J. J. (2008), 'Tradition, History, and Our Story: Some Observations on Jacob and Esau in the Books of Obadiah and Malachi', *JSOT* 32:475–486.

Laato, A. (1992), *Josiah and David Redivivus: The Historical Josiah and the Messianic Expectations of Exilic and Postexilic Times*, ConBOT 33, Stockholm: Almqvist & Wiksell.

——— (1994), 'Zechariah 4:6b–10a and the Akkadian Royal Building Inscriptions', *ZAW* 106:53–69.

——— (1997), *A Star Is Rising: The Historical Development of the Old Testament Royal Ideology and the Rise of the Jewish Messianic Expectations*, Atlanta: Scholars Press.

Laetsch, T. (1956), *The Minor Prophets*, Bible Commentary, St. Louis: Concordia.

Lamarche, P. (1961), *Zacharie IX–XIV: Structure Littéraire et Messianisme*, ÉBib, Paris: Librairie Lecoffre.

Larkin, K. J. A. (1994), *The Eschatology of Second Zechariah: A Study of the Formation of a Mantological Wisdom Anthology*, CBET 6, Kampen: Kok Pharos.

LaSor, W. S., D. A. Hubbard and F. W. Bush (1996), *Old Testament Survey: The Message, Form and Background of the Old Testament*, 2nd ed., Grand Rapids: Eerdmans.

LeCureux, J. T. (2012), *The Thematic Unity of the Book of the Twelve*, HBM 41, Sheffield: Sheffield Phoenix.

Leith, M. J. W. (1998), 'Israel Among the Nations: The Persian Period', in M. D. Coogan (ed.), *The Oxford History of the Biblical World*, Oxford: Oxford University Press, 367–419.

Leske, A. M. (2000), 'Context and Meaning of Zechariah 9:9', *CBQ* 62:663–678.

Lewis, J. P. (1999), '"Sun of Righteousness" (Malachi 4:2): A History of Interpretation', *SCJ* 2:90–110.

Lindsay, J. (1976), 'The Babylonian Kings and Edom', *PEQ* 108:23–39.

Littauer, M. A., and J. H. Crouwel (1992), 'Chariots', in *ABD* 1:888–892.

Long, V. P. (1999), 'Historiography of the Old Testament', in D. W. Baker and B. T. Arnold (eds.), *The Face of Old Testament Studies: A Survey of Comtemporary Approaches*, Grand Rapids: Baker, 145–175.

Longman III, T. (2001), *Immanuel in Our Place*, Phillipsburg: P. & R.

Longman III, T., and R. B. Dillard (2006), *An Introduction to the Old Testament*, 2nd ed., Grand Rapids: Zondervan.

Love, M. C. (1999), *The Evasive Text: Zechariah 1–8 and the Frustrated Reader*, JSOTSup 296, Sheffield: Sheffield Academic Press.

Lundbom, J. R. (2010), *The Hebrew Prophets: An Introduction*, Minneapolis: Fortress.

McConville, J. G. (2002a), *Deuteronomy*, AOTC 5, Leicester: Apollos.

——— (2002b), *The Prophets*, Exploring the Old Testament 4, London: SPCK.

MacDonald, N. (2008), *What Did the Ancient Israelites Eat? Diet in Biblical Times*, Grand Rapids: Eerdmans.

McKenzie, S. L., and H. N. Wallace (1983), 'Covenant Themes in Malachi', *CBQ* 45:549–563.

Maier III, W. A. (1992), 'Hadadrimmon', in *ABD* 3:13.

Malone, A. S. (2006), 'Is the Messiah Announced in Malachi 3:1', *TynB* 57:215–228.

Mariottini, C. F. (1998), 'Malachi: A Prophet for His Time', *JBQ* 26:149–157.

Mason, R. A. (1976), 'The Relation of Zech 9–14 to Proto-Zechariah', *ZAW* 88:227–239.

——— (2003), 'The Use of Earlier Biblical Material in Zechariah 9–14: A Study in Inner Biblical Exegesis', in M. J. Boda and M. H. Floyd (eds.), *Bringing out the Treasure: Inner Biblical Allusion in Zechariah 9–14*, JSOTSup 370, Sheffield: Sheffield Academic Press, 1–208.

Mathews, K. A. (2005), *Genesis 11:27–50:26*, NAC 1B, Nashville: B. & H.

Matties, G. H., and J. Walton (1997), '*pinnā*', in *NIDOTTE* 3:640.

Menken, M. J. J. (2009), 'The Minor Prophets in John's Gospel', in M. J. J. Menken and S. Moyise (eds.), *The Minor Prophets in the New Testament*, LNTS 377, London: T. & T. Clark, 79–96.

Meyer, L. V. (1972), *The Messianic Metaphors in Deutero-Zechariah*, Chicago: University of Chicago.

——— (1977), 'An Allegory Concerning the Monarchy: Zech 11:4–17; 13:7–9', in A. L. Merrill and T. W. Overholt (eds.), *Scripture in History & Theology*, Pennsylvania: Pickwick, 225–240.

Meyers, C. L., and E. M. Meyers (1992), 'Zechariah, Book of (Zechariah 1–8)', in *ABD* 6:1061–1065.

——— (1995), 'The Future Fortunes of the House of David: The Evidence of Second Zechariah', in A. B. Beck, A. H. Bartelt, P. R. Raabe and C. A. Franke (eds.), *Fortunate the Eyes That See*, Grand Rapids: Eerdmans, 207–222.

Meyers, E. M. (1983), 'The Use of *tôrâ* in Haggai 2:11 and the Role of the Prophet in the Restoration Community', in C. L. Meyers and M. O'Connor (eds.), *The Word of the Lord Shall Go Forth: Essays in

Honor of David Noel Freedman in Celebration of his Sixtieth Birthday, Winona Lake: Eisenbrauns, 69–76.
Milgrom, J. (1991), *Leviticus 1–16*, AB 3, New York: Doubleday.
Millar, J. G. (1998), *Now Choose Life: Theology and Ethics in Deuteronomy*, NSBT 6, Leicester: Inter-Varsity Press.
Miller-Naudé, C. L., and C. H. J. van der Merwe (2011), '*Hinnēh* and Mirativity in Biblical Hebrew', *HS* 52:53–81.
Miller-Naudé, C. L., C. H. J. van der Merwe and J. H. Kroeze (1999), *A Biblical Hebrew Reference Grammar*, Biblical Languages: Hebrew 3, Sheffield: Sheffield Academic Press.
Mitchell, C. (2014), 'A Note on the Creation Formula in Zechariah 12:1–8; Isaiah 42:5–6; and Old Persian Inscriptions', *JBL* 133:305–308.
Mitchell, D. C. (1997), *The Message of the Psalter: An Eschatological Programme in the Book of Psalms*, JSOTSup 252, Sheffield: Sheffield Academic Press.
Moberly, R. W. L. (1990), 'Yahweh Is One: The Translation of the Shema', in J. A. Emerton (ed.), *Studies in the Pentateuch*, Leiden: Brill, 209–215.
——— (2013), *Old Testament Theology: Reading the Hebrew Bible as Christian Scripture*, Grand Rapids: Baker Academic.
Moule, C. F. D. (1977), *Worship in the New Testament*, Nottingham: Grove.
Newcome, W. (1785), *An Attempt Towards an Improved Version, a Metrical Arrangement, and an Explanation of the Twelve Minor Prophets*, Dublin: Robert Marchbank.
Nicol, T. (1979), 'Chariot', in *ISBE* 1:635–636.
Nogalski, J. D. (1993a), *Literary Precursors to the Book of the Twelve*, Berlin: de Gruyter.
——— (1993b), *Redactional Processes in the Book of the Twelve*, Berlin: de Gruyter.
——— (2003), 'Zechariah 13.7–9 as a Transitional Text: An Appreciation and Re-evaluation of the Work of Rex Mason', in M. J. Boda and M. H. Floyd (eds.), *Bringing out the Treasure: Inner Biblical Allusion in Zechariah 9–14*, Sheffield: Sheffield Academic Press, 292–304.
O'Brien, J. M. (1990), *Priest and Levite in Malachi*, SBLDS 121, Atlanta: Scholars Press.
——— (1996), 'Judah as Wife and Husband: Deconstructing Gender in Malachi', *JBL* 115:241–250.
O'Brien, P. T. (2010), *The Letter to the Hebrews*, PNTC, Grand Rapids: Eerdmans; Nottingham: Apollos.
O'Kennedy, D. F. (2003), 'The Theological Portrayal of Forgiveness in Zechariah 1–8', *Scriptura* 84:410–422.
Ogden, G. S. (1988), 'The Use of Figurative Language in Mal 2:10–16', *BT* 39:223–230.
Oswalt, J. N. (2006), 'The Nations in Isaiah: Friend or Foe, Servant or Partner', *BBR* 16:41–51.
Otzen, B. (1964), *Studien über Deutero-Sacharja*, Copenhagen: Munksgaard.

Pakula, M. B. (2003), 'The Literary Development of the Feast of Tabernacles in the Old Testament and Its Fulfilment in the New Testament', MTh thesis, Australian College of Theology.

Parkinson, P. (2011), *For Kids' Sake: Repairing the Social Environment for Australian Children and Young People*, Vos Foundation, Sydney: University of Sydney.

Patrick, F. Y. (2008), 'Time and Tradition in the Book of Haggai', in M. J. Boda and M. H. Floyd (eds.), *Tradition in Transition: Haggai and Zechariah 1–8 in the Trajectory of Hebrew Theology*, LHBOTS 475, New York: T. & T. Clark, 40–55.

Patton, M. H. (2013), 'Hope for a Tender Sprig: Jehoiachin in Biblical Theology', PhD diss., Wheaton College.

Person, R. F. (1993), *Second Zechariah and the Deuteronomic School*, Sheffield: JSOT Press.

Petersen, D. L. (1974), 'Zerubbabel and Jerusalem Temple Reconstruction', *CBQ* 36:366–372.

——— (1992a), 'Eschatology', in *ABD* 2:575–579.

——— (1992b), 'Zechariah, Book of (Zechariah 9–14)', in *ABD* 6:1065–1068.

Peterson, D. (1992), *Engaging with God: A Biblical Theology of Worship*, Leicester: Apollos; Downers Grove: InterVarsity Press.

Petitjean, A. (1966), 'La Mission de Zorobabel et la Reconstruction du Temple; Zach., III:8–10', *ETL* 42:40–71.

Petterson, A. R. (2008), 'Towards a Theology of the Virgin Birth', in P. G. Bolt and M. D. Thompson (eds.), *Donald Robinson Selected Works: Appreciation*, Camperdown: Australian Church Record, 65–71.

——— (2009), *Behold Your King: The Hope for the House of David in the Book of Zechariah*, LHBOTS 513, New York: T. & T. Clark.

——— (2010), 'The Shape of the Davidic Hope Across the Book of the Twelve', *JSOT* 35:225–246.

——— (2014a), 'The Flying Scroll That Will Not Acquit the Guilty: Exodus 34.7 in Zechariah 5.3', *JSOT* 38:347–361.

——— (2014b), 'The Eschatology of Zechariah's Night Visions', in L.-S. Tiemeyer and E. R. Hayes (eds.), *'I Lifted My Eyes and Saw': Reading Dream and Vision Reports in the Hebrew Bible*, LHBOTS 584, London: T. & T. Clark, 119–134.

——— (forthcoming), 'A New Form-Critical Approach to Zechariah's Crowning of the High Priest Joshua and the Identity of "Shoot" (Zechariah 6:9-15)', in M. J. Boda, M. H. Floyd and C. M. Toffelmire (eds.), *Form Criticism and the Twelve*, Atlanta: SBL.

Pfeiffer, E. (1959), 'Die Disputationsworte im Buche Maleachi: Ein Beitrag zur formgeschichtlichen Strukter', *ET* 19:546–568.

Pierce, R. W. (1984a), 'Literary Connectors and a Haggai/Zechariah/Malachi Corpus', *JETS* 27:277–289.

——— (1984b), 'A Thematic Development of the Haggai/Zechariah/Malachi Corpus', *JETS* 27:401–11.

Piper, J. (2007), 'Gutsy Guilt', *Christianity Today*, Oct., 73–76.
Plöger, O. (1968), *Theocracy and Eschatology*, tr. S. Rudman, Oxford: Basil Blackwell.
Pohlig, J. N. (1998), *An Exegetical Summary of Malachi*, Dallas: Summer Institute of Linguistics.
Portnoy, S. L., and D. L. Petersen (1984), 'Biblical Texts and Statistical Analysis: Zechariah and Beyond', *JBL* 103:11–21.
Powell, M. A. (1992), 'Weights and Measures', in *ABD* 6:897–908.
Pritchard, J. B. (1969), *Ancient Near Eastern Texts*, 3rd ed., Princeton: Princeton University.
Radday, Y. T., and D. Wickmann (1975), 'The Unity of Zechariah Examined in the Light of Statistical Linguistics', *ZAW* 87:30–55.
Redditt, P. L. (1993), 'The Two Shepherds in Zechariah 11:4–17', *CBQ* 55:676–686.
——— (1994), 'The Book of Malachi in Its Social Setting', *CBQ* 56:240–255.
Reeder, C. A. (2007), 'Malachi 3:24 and the Eschatological Restoration of the "Family"', *CBQ* 69:695–709.
Rendtorff, R. (2000), 'How to Read the Book of the Twelve as a Theological Unity', in J. D. Nogalski and M. A. Sweeney (eds.), *Reading and Hearing the Book of the Twelve*, SBLSS 15, Atlanta: SBL, 75–87.
Ringgren, H. (2004), '*rāsʿ*', in *TDOT* 14:1–9.
Ristau, K. A. (2009), 'Rebuilding Jerusalem: Zechariah's Vision Within Visions', in G. N. Knoppers, L. L. Grabbe and D. N. Fulton (eds.), *Exile and Restoration Revisited: Essays on the Babylonian and Persian Periods in Memory of Peter R. Ackroyd*, London: T. & T. Clark, 195–213.
Rogland, M. (2013), 'Two Philological Notes on Haggai 2:15–19', *HS* 54:69–77.
——— (2014), 'Heavenly Chariots and Earthly Rebellion in Zechariah 6', *Bib* 85:117–123.
Rose, W. H. (2000), *Zemah and Zerubbabel: Messianic Expectations in the Early Postexilic Period*, JSOTSup 304, Sheffield: Sheffield Academic Press.
——— (2012), 'Zechariah and the Ambiguity of Kingship in Postexilic Israel', in I. Provan and M. J. Boda (eds.), *Let Us Go up to Zion: Essays in Honour of H. G. M. Williamson on the Occasion of His Sixty-Fifth Birthday*, VTSup 153, Leiden: Brill, 219–231.
Routledge, R. (2008), *Old Testament Theology: A Thematic Approach*, Nottingham: Apollos; Downers Grove: InterVarsity Press.
Rubenstein, J. L. (1996), 'Sukkot, Eschatology and Zechariah 14', *RB* 103:161–195.
Rudman, D. (2008), 'Zechariah and the Satan Tradition in the Hebrew Bible', in M. J. Boda and M. H. Floyd (eds.), *Tradition in Transition: Haggai and Zechariah 1–8 in the Trajectory of Hebrew Theology*, LHBOTS 475, New York: T. & T. Clark, 191–209.
Rudolph, W. (1981), 'Zu Malachi 2:10–16', *ZAW* 93:85–90.

Rydelnik, M. (2010), *The Messianic Hope: Is the Hebrew Bible Really Messianic?*, Nashville: B. & H.

Ryken, L., J. C. Wilhoit and T. Longman III (1998), 'Sheep, Shepherd', *Dictionary of Biblical Imagery*, Downers Grove: InterVarsity Press; Leicester: Inter-Varsity Press, 782–785.

Sailhamer, J. H. (1992), *The Pentateuch as Narrative: A Biblical-Theological Commentary*, Grand Rapids: Zondervan.

Samaan, P. G. (1989), *Portraits of the Messiah in Zechariah*, Washington: Review & Herald.

Scalise, P. J. (1987), 'To Fear or Not to Fear: Questions of Reward and Punishment in Malachi 2:17–4:3', *RevExp* 84:409–418.

——— (1998), 'Malachi 3:13–4:3 – A Book of Remembrance for God-fearers', *RevExp* 95:571–581.

Schaefer, K. R. (1993a), 'The Ending of the Book of Zechariah: A Commentary', *RB* 100:165–238.

——— (1993b), 'Zechariah 14 and the Composition of the Book of Zechariah', *RB* 100:368–398.

——— (1995), 'Zechariah 14: A Study in Allusion', *CBQ* 57:66–91.

Schaper, J. (1995), 'The Jerusalem Temple as an Instrument of the Achaemenid Fiscal Administration', *VT* 45:528–539.

Schart, A. (2000), 'Reconstructing the Redaction History of the Twelve Prophets: Problems and Models', in J. D. Nogalski and M. A. Sweeney (eds.), *Reading and Hearing the Book of the Twelve*, SBLSS 15, Atlanta: SBL, 34–48.

——— (2012), 'Twelve, Book of the: History of Interpretation', in M. J. Boda and J. G. McConville (eds.), *Dictionary of the Old Testament Prophets*, Downers Grove: InterVarsity Press, 806–817.

Schellenberg, A. F. (2001), 'One in the Bond of War: The Unity of Deutero-Zechariah', *Did* 12:101–115.

Schöttler, H.-G. (1987), *Gott inmitten seines Volkes: Die Neuordnung des Gottesvolkes nach Sacharja 1–6*, TTS 43, Trier: Paulinus.

Schreiner, T. R. (2013), *The King in His Beauty: A Biblical Theology of the Old and New Testaments*, Grand Rapids: Baker Academic.

Seitz, C. R. (2007), *Prophecy and Hermeneutics: Toward a New Introduction to the Prophets*, Grand Rapids: Baker Academic.

Sizer, S. (2004), *Christian Zionism: Road-map to Armageddon?*, Leicester: Inter-Varsity Press.

Sklar, J. (2005), *Sin, Impurity, Sacrifice, Atonement: The Priestly Conceptions*, Sheffield: Sheffield Phoenix.

Slayton, J. C. (1992), 'Bashan', in *ABD* 1:623–624.

Snyman, S. D. (1988), 'Eschatology in the Book of Malachi', *OTE* 1:63–77.

——— (2011), 'Rethinking the Demarcation of Malachi 2:17–3:5', *Acta Theologica: Die Woord Verwoord* 31:156–168.

Stade, B. (1881, 1882), 'Deuterosacharja: Eine kritische Studie', *ZAW* 1:1–96; 2:151–172, 275–309.

Starling, D. I. (1999), 'The Messianic Hope in the Psalms', *RTR* 58:121–134.
Stead, M. R. (2009), *The Intertextuality of Zechariah 1–8*, LHBOTS 506, New York: T. & T. Clark.
——— (2011), 'The Three Shepherds: Reading Zechariah 11 in the Light of Jeremiah', in J. A. Grant, A. Lo and G. J. Wenham (eds.), *A God of Faithfulness: Essays in Honour of J. Gordon McConville on His 60th Birthday*, LHBOTS 538, New York: T. & T. Clark, 149–165.
——— (2012), 'Intertextuality and Innerbiblical Interpretation', in M. J. Boda and J. G. McConville (eds.), *Dictionary of the Old Testament Prophets*, Downers Grove: InterVarsity Press, 355–364.
——— (2013), 'Suffering Servant, Suffering David, and Stricken Shepherd', in M. R. Stead (ed.), *Christ Died for Our Sins: Essays on the Atonement*, Canberra: Barton, 62–83.
——— (2014), 'The Interrelationship Between Vision and Oracle in Zechariah 1–6', in L.-S. Tiemeyer and E. Hayes (eds.), *I Lifted My Eyes and Saw: Vision and Dream Reports in the Hebrew Bible*, LHBOTS 584, New York: Bloomsbury, 149–168.
Steiner, R. C. (2013), 'Genesis 49:10: On the Lexical and Syntactic Ambiguities of עַד as Reflected in the Prophecies of Nathan, Ahijah, Ezekiel, and Zechariah', *JBL* 132:33–60.
Story, L. (2010), 'Zechariah's Two Sons of Oil: Zechariah 4', *JBPR* 2:31–56.
Stuart, D. (1987), *Hosea–Jonah*, WBC 31, Waco: Word.
Sweeney, M. A. (1996), *Isaiah 1–39 with an Introduction to Prophetic Literature*, FOTL 16, Grand Rapids: Eerdmans.
——— (2000a), 'Sequence and Interpretation in the Book of the Twelve', in J. D. Nogalski and M. A. Sweeney (eds.), *Reading and Hearing the Book of the Twelve*, SBLSS 15, Atlanta: SBL, 49–64.
——— (2012a), *Tanak: A Theological and Critical Introduction to the Jewish Bible*, Minneapolis: Fortress.
——— (2012b), 'Twelve, Book of the', in M. J. Boda and J. G. McConville (eds.), *Dictionary of the Old Testament Prophets*, Downers Grove: InterVarsity Press, 788–806.
Tate, M. E. (1987), 'Questions for Priests and People in Malachi 1:2–2:16', *RevExp* 84:391–407.
Thompson, H. O. (1992), 'Jordan, Jungle of', in *ABD* 3:960–961.
Thomson, C. J. (2012), 'The "Seven Eyes" of Zech 3:9 and the Meaning of the Dual Form', *VT* 62:115–128.
——— (2013), 'The Removal of Sin in the Book of Zechariah', PhD diss., University of Cambridge.
Thomson, J. G. S. S. (1955), 'The Shepherd-Ruler Concept in the OT and Its Application in the NT', *SJT* 8:406–418.
Tiemeyer, L.-S. (2003), 'The Guilty Priesthood (Zech 3)', in C. Tuckett (ed.), *The Book of Zechariah and Its Influence*, Aldershot: Ashgate, 1–19.
——— (2004), 'Compelled by Honour – A New Interpretation of Zechariah II 12A (8A)', *VT* 54:352–372.

——— (2006), *Priestly Rites and Prophetic Rage: Post-Exilic Prophetic Critique of the Priesthood*, Tübingen: Mohr Siebeck.
Toffelmire, C. M. (2012), 'Form Criticism', in M. J. Boda and J. G. McConville (eds.), *Dictionary of the Old Testament Prophets*, Downers Grove: InterVarsity Press, 257–271.
Tollington, J. E. (1993), *Tradition and Innovation in Haggai and Zechariah 1–8*, JSOTSup 150, Sheffield: JSOT Press.
Torrey, C. C. (1898), 'The Prophet Malachi', *JBL* 17:1–15.
——— (1936), 'The Foundry of the Second Temple', *JBL* 65: 247–260.
Ulrich, D. R. (2010), 'Two Offices, Four Officers, or One Sordid Event in Zechariah 12:10–14?', *WTJ* 72:251–265.
Van der Woude, A. S. (1997), '*ṣābā'*, army', in E. Jenni and C. Westermann (eds.), *Theological Lexicon of the Old Testament*, vol. 2, Peabody: Hendrickson, 1039–1046.
Van Leeuwen, R. C. (1993), 'Scribal Wisdom and Theodicy in the Book of the Twelve', in L. G. Perdue, B. B. Scott and W. J. Wiseman (eds.), *In Search of Wisdom: Essays in Memory of John G. Gammie*, Lousville: Westminster, 31–49.
VanderKam, J. C. (1991), 'Joshua the High Priest and the Interpretation of Zechariah 3', *CBQ* 53:553–570.
Wallis, G. (2004), '*rā'â* ; *rō'eh*', in *TDOT* 13:544–553.
Walsh, J. T. (2009), *Old Testament Narrative: A Guide to Interpretation*, Louisville: Westminster John Knox.
Waltke, B. K. (2007), *An Old Testament Theology: An Exegetical, Canonical and Thematic Approach*, Grand Rapids: Zondervan.
Waltke, B. K., and M. O'Connor (1990), *An Introduction to Biblical Hebrew Syntax*, Winona Lake: Eisenbrauns.
Watts, J. D. W. (1987), 'Introduction to the Book of Malachi', *RevExp* 84:373–382.
——— (2000), 'A Frame for the Book of the Twelve: Hosea 1–3 and Malachi', in J. D. Nogalski and M. A. Sweeney (eds.), *Reading and Hearing the Book of the Twelve*, SBLSS 15, Atlanta: SBL, 209–217.
Watts, R. E. (2007), 'Mark', in *CNTUOT*, 111–249.
Way, K. C. (2011), *Donkeys in the Biblical World: Ceremony and Symbol*, Winona Lake: Eisenbrauns.
Weinfeld, M. (1995), *Social Justice in Ancient Israel and in the Ancient Near East*, Jerusalem: Magnes.
Weis, R. D. (1986), 'A Definition of the Genre *Maśśā'* in the Hebrew Bible', PhD diss., Claremont Graduate School.
Wellhausen, J. (1903), 'Zechariah, Book of', in T. K. Cheyne and J. Sutherland Black (eds.), *Encyclopaedia Biblica*, vol. 4, London: Adam & Charles Black, 5390–5395.
Wells, D. F. (1994), *God in the Wasteland: The Reality of Truth in a World of Fading Dreams*, Grand Rapids: Eerdmans.

Wenham, G. J. (1978), 'Grace and Law in the Old Testament', in B. Kaye and G. J. Wenham (eds.), *Law, Morality and the Bible*, Leicester: Inter-Varsity Press, 3–23.

——— (1979), *The Book of Leviticus*, Grand Rapids: Eerdmans.

——— (1994), 'Sanctuary Symbolism in the Garden of Eden Story', in R. S. Hess and D. T. Tsumura (eds.), *'I Studied Inscriptions from Before the Flood': Ancient Near Eastern, Literary, and Linguistic Approaches to Genesis 1–11*, Winona Lake: Eisenbrauns, 399–404.

Wenzel, H. (2011), *Reading Zechariah with Zechariah 1:1–6 as the Introduction to the Entire Book*, CBET 59, Leuven: Peeters.

Westbrook, R. (1986), 'The Prohibition on Restoration of Marriage in Deuteronomy 24:1–4', in S. Japhet (ed.), *Studies in Bible 1986*, ScrHier 31, Jerusalem: Magnes, 387–405.

Westermann, C. (1982), *Elements of Old Testament Theology*, tr. D. W. Scott, Atlanta: John Knox.

Weyde, K. W. (2000), *Prophecy and Teaching: Prophetic Authority, Form Problems, and the Use of Traditions in the Book of Malachi*, BZAW 288, Berlin: de Gruyter.

Wilcock, M. (1991), *The Message of Revelation: I Saw Heaven Opened*, BST, 2nd ed., Leicester: Inter-Varsity Press.

Williams, M. J. (2003), *The Prophet and His Message: Reading Old Testament Prophecy Today*, Phillipsburg: P. & R.

Williams, R. J. (2007), *Williams' Hebrew Syntax*, rev. and expanded J. C. Beckman, 3rd ed., Toronto: University of Toronto Press.

Williamson, H. G. M. (1985), *Ezra, Nehemiah*, WBC 16, Waco: Word.

——— (2006), *A Critical and Exegetical Commentary on Isaiah 1–27*, vol. 1, London: T. & T. Clark International.

Williamson, P. R. (2007), *Sealed with an Oath: Covenant in God's Unfolding Purpose*, NSBT 23, Nottingham: Apollos.

Winkle, R. E. (1987), 'Jeremiah's Seventy Years for Babylon: A Reassessment', *AUSS* 25:201–214, 289–299.

Winton Thomas, D. (1932), 'A Note on *mḥlṣwt* in Zechariah 3.4', *JTS* 33:279–280.

Wöhrle, J. (2006), 'The Formation and Intention of the Haggai-Zechariah Corpus', *JHS* 6:1–14.

——— (2008), *Der Abschluss des Zwölfprophetenbuches: Buchübergreifende Redaktionsprozesse in den späten Sammlungen*, BZAW 389, Berlin: de Gruyter.

Wolters, A. (2000), 'Confessional Criticism and the Night Visions of Zechariah', in C. Bartholomew, C. Greene and K. Möller (eds.), *Renewing Biblical Interpretation*, Grand Rapids: Zondervan; Carlisle: Paternoster, 90–117.

——— (2002), 'Zechariah 14: A Dialogue with the History of Interpretation', *Mid-America Journal of Theology* 13:39–56.

——— (2004), 'Zechariah 14 and Biblical Theology', in C. G. Bartholomew (ed.), *Out of Egypt: Biblical Theology and Biblical Interpretation*, Bletchley: Paternoster, 261–285.

——— (2008), '"The Whole Earth Remains at Peace" (Zechariah 1:11): The Problem and an Intertextual Clue', in M. J. Boda and M. H. Floyd (eds.), *Tradition in Transition: Haggai and Zechariah 1–8 in the Trajectory of Hebrew Theology*, LHBOTS 475, New York: T. & T. Clark, 128–143.

——— (2012a), 'The Meaning of *Ṣantĕrôt* (Zech 4:12)', *JHS* 12:1–15.

——— (2012b), 'Review: Martin Hallaschka, *Haggai und Sacharja 1–8: Eine redaktionsgeschichtliche Untersuchung*', *CBQ* 74:348–350.

——— (2012c), 'Zechariah, Book of', in M. J. Boda and J. G. McConville (eds.), *Dictionary of the Old Testament Prophets*, Downers Grove: InterVarsity Press, 889–899.

Wright, C. J. H. (2004), *Old Testament Ethics for the People of God*, Leicester: Inter-Varsity Press.

Wright, D. P. (1992), 'Unclean and Clean, Old Testament', in *ABD* 6:729–742.

Wright, N. T. (1992), *The New Testament and the People of God*, Minneapolis: Fortress.

Yamauchi, E. M. (1990), *Persia and the Bible*, Grand Rapids: Baker.

Zehnder, M. (2003), 'A Fresh Look at Malachi II 13–16', *VT* 53:224–259.

Zohary, M. (1982), *Plants of the Bible*, Cambridge: Cambridge University Press.

INDEX OF SCRIPTURE REFERENCES

INDEX OF AUTHORS

INDEX OF SUBJECTS